W9-ABY-567

WORD
BIBLICAL
COMMENTARY

General Editors
David A. Hubbard
Glenn W. Barker †

Old Testament Editor
John D. W. Watts

New Testament Editor
Ralph P. Martin

WORD
BIBLICAL
COMMENTARY

Volume 33A

Matthew 1–13

DONALD A. HAGNER

WORD BOOKS, PUBLISHER • DALLAS, TEXAS

Word Biblical Commentary
Matthew 1–13
Copyright © 1993 by Word, Incorporated

Library of Congress Cataloging-in-Publication Data
Main entry under title:

Word biblical commentary.

    Includes bibliographies.
    1. Bible—Commentaries—Collected works.
BS491.2.W67   220.7'7   81–71768
ISBN 0–8499–0232–0 (v. 33A) AACR2

Printed in the United States of America

The author's own translation of the Scripture text appears in italic type under the heading *Translation*.

3 4 5 9   AGF   9 8 7 6 5 4 3 2 1

To Beverly

Contents

Editorial Preface   x
Author's Preface   xi
Abbreviations   xiv
Commentary Bibliography   xxx
General Bibliography   xxxii

INTRODUCTION   xxxix
  About the Present Commentary   xxxix
  The Papias Tradition concerning Matthew   xliii
  Matthew's Sources   xlvi
  Oral Tradition in the Gospel of Matthew   xlviii
  The Structure of Matthew   l
  Matthew's Use of the Old Testament   liii
  The Genre and Purpose of Matthew   lvii
  Matthew's Theology   lix
  The Original Readers of Matthew   lxiv
  The *Sitz im Leben* ("Life Setting") of Matthew's Community   lxv
  On Matthew's "Anti-Judaism"   lxxi
  Date and Provenance   lxxiii
  Authorship   lxxv

TEXT AND COMMENTARY
THE BIRTH AND INFANCY NARRATIVES (1:1–2:23)   1
  The Ancestry of Jesus (1:1–17)   2
  The Birth and Naming of Jesus (1:18–25)   13
  The Magi Worship the Newborn King (2:1–12)   22
  The Massacre of the Innocents and the Flight to Egypt (2:13–23)   32
THE PREPARATION FOR THE MINISTRY (3:1–4:11)   43
  John the Baptist (3:1–12)   43
  The Baptism of Jesus (3:13–17)   53
  The Temptation of Jesus (4:1–11)   60
GALILEAN MINISTRY (4:12–25)   71
  Jesus Begins His Ministry in Galilee (4:12–17)   71
  The Calling of the Disciples (4:18–22)   74
  The Ministry of Jesus Encapsulated (4:23–25)   78
THE FIRST DISCOURSE: THE SERMON ON THE MOUNT (5:1–7:29)   82
  The Setting of the Sermon (5:1–2)   84
  Introduction (5:3–16)   87
    The Foundation of Righteous Living: The Beatitudes (5:3–12) 87
    The Essence of Discipleship: Salt and Light (5:13–16)   97
  The Main Body of the Sermon (5:17–7:12)   102
    The Relation between the Old and the New Righteousness (5:17–48) 102
    Continuity with the Old (5:17–20)   102

The Surpassing of the Old: The Six Antitheses (5:21–48)   **110**
    On Murder (5:21–26)   **113**
    On Adultery (5:27–30)   **118**
    On Divorce (5:31–32)   **121**
    On Oaths (5:33–37)   **126**
    On Retaliation (5:38–42)   **129**
    On Loving One's Enemies (5:43–48)   **132**
Outward vs. Inward Righteousness (6:1–18)   **136**
    Almsgiving (6:1–4)   **136**
    Prayer and the Lord's Prayer (6:5–15)   **141**
        The Setting of Prayer (6:5–6)   **141**
        On the Right Way to Pray: "The Lord's Prayer" (6:7–15) **143**
    Fasting (6:16–18)   **153**
    Dependence upon God (6:19–34)   **155**
        Serving God Rather Than Wealth (6:19–24)   **155**
        The Disciple and Anxiety (6:25–34)   **160**
Various Teachings and the Golden Rule (7:1–12)   **167**
    On Not Judging Others (7:1–5)   **167**
    Discernment in Proclaiming the Gospel (7:6)   **170**
    The Answering Father (7:7–11)   **172**
    The Golden Rule (7:12)   **175**
Conclusion (7:13–27)   **177**
    The Two Ways (7:13–14)   **177**
    The False and the Genuine (7:15–23)   **180**
        Warning concerning False Prophets (7:15–20)   **180**
        The Insufficiency of the Charismata (7:21–23)   **184**
    The Parable of the Two Builders (7:24–27)   **189**
    The Astonishment of the Crowds (7:28–29)   **192**
THE AUTHORITATIVE DEEDS OF THE MESSIAH (8:1–9:38)   **195**
    The Healing of a Leper (8:1–4)   **196**
    The Curing of the Centurion's Son (8:5–13)   **200**
    The Healing of Peter's Mother-in-Law and Others (8:14–17) **207**
    Two Comments on Discipleship (8:18–22)   **211**
    Excursus: Son of Man   **213**
    The Stilling of the Sea (8:23–27)   **219**
    Exorcism of the Gadarene Demoniacs (8:28–34)   **223**
    The Healing of a Paralytic (9:1–8)   **229**
    The Call of Matthew and a Dinner Party with Tax Collectors
        and Sinners (9:9–13)   **235**
    Combining New and Old (9:14–17)   **240**
    The Healing of the Hemorrhaging Woman and the Raising of
        the Ruler's Daughter (9:18–26)   **245**
    The Healing of Two Blind Men (9:27–31)   **251**
    The Healing of the Mute Demoniac (9:32–34)   **255**
    A Summary and the Call for Workers (9:35–38)   **258**
THE SECOND DISCOURSE: THE MISSIONARY DISCOURSE (10:1–11:1)   **262**
    The Empowering of the Twelve Apostles (10:1–4)   **263**
    Mission Instructions (10:5–15)   **267**

The Experience of Persecution (10:16–23) 274
The Maligning of Both Teacher and Disciples (10:24–25) 281
Have No Fear of Your Persecutors (10:26–31) 283
Confession and Denial (10:32–33) 287
Division and Discipleship (10:34–39) 289
A Concluding Note on Receiving the Servants of Christ (10:40–11:1) 294
THE NEGATIVE RESPONSE TO JESUS (11:2–12:50) 298
Jesus' Answer to the Baptist's Question (11:2–6) 298
Jesus' Estimate of John the Baptist (11:7–15) 302
The Dissatisfaction of Israel (11:16–19) 309
Oracles of Judgment (11:20–24) 311
The Mystery of Election and the Central Significance of
the Son (11:25–27) 315
A Renewed Invitation (11:28–30) 322
Plucking Grain on the Sabbath (12:1–8) 326
Healing a Withered Hand on the Sabbath (12:9–14) 331
The Gentle, Healing Servant (12:15–21) 335
Can Beelzebul Be against Himself? (12:22–30) 339
The Question of Unforgivable Sin (12:31–32) 345
Speaking Good and Evil (12:33–37) 348
The Sign of Jonah (12:38–42) 351
The Parable of the Returning Demons (12:43–45) 355
The True Family of Jesus (12:46–50) 358
THE THIRD DISCOURSE: TEACHING IN PARABLES (13:1–58) 361
The Parable of the Soils (13:1–9) 365
The Purpose of Parables (13:10–17) 369
The Explanation of the Parable of the Soils (13:18–23) 376
The Parable of the Wheat and the Weeds (13:24–30) 381
The Parable of the Mustard Seed (13:31–32) 384
The Parable of the Leavened Loaves and a Further
Comment on the Reason for the Parables (13:33–35) 387
The Explanation of the Parable of the Wheat and the Weeds (13:36–43) 391
The Parables of the Treasure and the Pearl (13:44–46) 395
The Parable of the Dragnet (13:47–50) 398
The Scribe Trained for the Kingdom: The End of
the Discourse (13:51–52) 400
The Unbelief of the People of Nazareth (13:53–58) 403

Editorial Preface

The launching of the *Word Biblical Commentary* brings to fulfillment an enterprise of several years' planning. The publishers and the members of the editorial board met in 1977 to explore the possibility of a new commentary on the books of the Bible that would incorporate several distinctive features. Prospective readers of these volumes are entitled to know what such features were intended to be; whether the aims of the commentary have been fully achieved time alone will tell.

First, we have tried to cast a wide net to include as contributors a number of scholars from around the world who not only share our aims, but are in the main engaged in the ministry of teaching in university, college, and seminary. They represent a rich diversity of denominational allegiance. The broad stance of our contributors can rightly be called evangelical, and this term is to be understood in its positive, historic sense of a commitment to Scripture as divine revelation, and to the truth and power of the Christian gospel.

Then, the commentaries in our series are all commissioned and written for the purpose of inclusion in the *Word Biblical Commentary.* Unlike several of our distinguished counterparts in the field of commentary writing, there are no translated works, originally written in a non-English language. Also, our commentators were asked to prepare their own rendering of the original biblical text and to use those languages as the basis of their own comments and exegesis. What may be claimed as distinctive with this series is that it is based on the biblical languages, yet it seeks to make the technical and scholarly approach to the theological understanding of Scripture understandable by—and useful to—the fledgling student, the working minister, and colleagues in the guild of professional scholars and teachers as well.

Finally, a word must be said about the format of the series. The layout, in clearly defined sections, has been consciously devised to assist readers at different levels. Those wishing to learn about the textual witnesses on which the translation is offered are invited to consult the section headed *Notes.* If the readers' concern is with the state of modern scholarship on any given portion of Scripture, they should turn to the sections on *Bibliography* and *Form/Structure/Setting.* For a clear exposition of the passage's meaning and its relevance to the ongoing biblical revelation, the *Comment* and concluding *Explanation* are designed expressly to meet that need. There is therefore something for everyone who may pick up and use these volumes.

If these aims come anywhere near realization, the intention of the editors will have been met, and the labor of our team of contributors rewarded.

General Editors: *David A. Hubbard*
Glenn W. Barker†
Old Testament: *John D. W. Watts*
New Testament: *Ralph P. Martin*

Author's Preface

Commentators are generally tempted to sing the praises of the book on which they comment. They do so because they have the privilege of studying the book in great detail, often over a long period of time, and hence are able to come to a special appreciation of it. The present writer is no exception. It is no surprise to me that the Gospel of Matthew was as popular as it was in the early Church. Each Gospel, of course, has its own beauty, and it would be invidious to make comparisons. Furthermore, it is impossible in just a few lines to do justice to this wonderful document. Matthew's story of Jesus, however, *is* a masterpiece. The drama of the gospel of the kingdom, as it is seen in the alternating accounts of the deeds and the words of Jesus, is exceptionally powerful. From the wonder of the infancy narrative to the glory of the resurrected Christ commissioning his disciples, the sweep of Matthew's salvation-historical perspective is breathtaking. Matthew's formula OT quotations, with their stress on promise and fulfillment, show the magnificent unity of God's purposes and the continuing importance of Israel's Scriptures to the Church. Matthew's distinctive compilations of the teaching of Jesus in the five discourses have understandably been treasured by Christians down through the ages. The Sermon on the Mount is itself an incomparable digest of the ethical teaching of Jesus. More often than not we know the teaching of Jesus in the striking and balanced cadences of Matthew's formulations. And if Matthew was the most quoted Gospel in the early Church, it may well be true that it is the most quoted today, certainly of the Synoptics at least.

Commentators who have come to appreciate a work will often feel inadequate to the challenge of conveying its meaning to others. Again the present writer is no exception. The problem lies not merely in attempting to explicate the difficult passages—a challenge not to be minimized—but also in doing justice to the "ordinary" passages. But in Matthew, even the "ordinary" has often an extraordinary character. The commentator knows that a monograph could be written on every pericope, which he or she must treat in only a few pages. What commentator, after finishing comments on any particular passage, has ever felt really satisfied? She or he must only hope that the reader has been given a glimpse of the meaning and significance of the material in view and has been pointed in the right direction for future study.

Those who buy commentaries will have noticed the trend toward ever larger commentaries. Two- and three-volume commentaries are becoming common. One reason for this is the constantly growing amount of secondary literature. If one is going to take account of all (most) of it and interact with some of it, one will need a great amount of space indeed. There are commentaries on Matthew underway that provide virtually encyclopedic coverage. I see no reason for every commentary to do this, however, and I have thus made a concerted attempt to resist the trend, keeping more to the original conception of the Word Biblical Commentary. I have tried above all to give a fresh reading of the Gospel of Matthew as I see it, exegeting the text using mainly the primary tools of research, interacting with the most important secondary literature only at selected points, and through the bibliographies pointing readers to much more that they can pursue in their study. Given the length of Matthew, however, even the present commentary has nevertheless been forced into a two-volume format.

Commentators usually find it hard to say good-bye to their manuscripts—much to the chagrin of their publishers—especially after they have worked on them for a number of years. Again, the present commentator is no exception. If not always on the front burner, Matthew has at least been simmering on a back burner for more than fifteen years. To change the metaphor, I know I will experience post-partum depression. And, then, the commentator worries, How will my offspring fare in this cold world? One must after all always let go of the manuscript in an imperfect state. On the other hand, there does finally come a time when one can no longer endure the perennial question about when the commentary will be published. Some people really are interested in seeing it. So too is the commentator!

Finally, commentators, including the present one, always have lots of people to thank. One is naturally always indebted to the many who have already written on the subject. I have learned much about Matthew from members of the Matthew seminar of the Society of New Testament Studies as well as the Matthew group of the Society of Biblical Literature. I am grateful to Fuller Theological Seminary for the generous sabbatical program that has allowed me the privilege of escaping to wonderful places like Lund, Cambridge, and Tübingen, where much of this commentary was written. I owe very much to discussions over the years with the premier Matthean scholar, Professor Birger Gerhardsson of the University of Lund in Sweden, who upon reading this commentary will recognize many of his own perspectives. I am thankful for the consistently warm hospitality of the Gerhardssons. I am also grateful to Professor and Mrs. Peter Stuhlmacher of the University of Tübingen, Germany, for wonderful hospitality and stimulating conversation during the better part of an academic year that I was privileged to spend there.

I am grateful to my brother-in-law, the Reverend David A. Smith, who did his best to keep my feet on the ground by constantly urging that I write a commentary useful to pastors. I only hope I have succeeded in doing so.

Also to be warmly thanked are the cheerful and cooperative editors of the manuscript for Word, including Ms. Melanie McQuere, Dr. Lynn Losie, and, of course, my former colleague, Professor Ralph P. Martin. And speaking of Word, Incorporated, I am also grateful to David Pigg, who, I am happy to say, knows the art of *gentle* exhortation.

I thank Dr. Michael Wilkins for reading a portion of the commentary and for making encouraging comments. Several students deserve thanks for their help at various stages of the project. I am especially grateful for the wonderful lift that was given to me by Carl Hofmann, now a Presbyterian pastor, who as a recent, talented M.Div. graduate walked into my office one day, said he had some time on his hands, and asked if there was anything I might like help on! What a kindness! He, together with Ph.D. student Darryl White, did general work on different parts of the manuscript. Two other Ph.D. students who have been generous with their time, and to whom I owe thanks, are Dwight Sheets for help with bibliography and Jon Huntzinger for expert help in proofreading.

I thank warmly the excellent staff of the word-processing office at Fuller Seminary, especially to David Sielaff and Anne White, who have the ability to decipher anything that is given to them, no matter how illegible to ordinary mortals.

I am grateful to the Wm. B. Eerdmans Publishing Company for permission to use material from my article on "Matthew" in the revised edition of the *International Standard Bible Encyclopedia* and to Scholars Press for permission to borrow paragraphs from my article "The *Sitz im Leben* of the Gospel of Matthew," which appeared in the 1985 Seminar Papers of the Society of Biblical Literature.

I want also to add a word of gratitude to my faculty colleagues at Fuller for the stimulating and supportive context they have always provided. It is a pleasure to work in their midst, and I do not take for granted the generous giving of themselves in friendship and collegiality.

Finally, there is no way that I can offer adequate thanks to the one to whom these volumes are dedicated. As a professional psychologist, my wife, Bev, knows well the art of empathic listening, and I have often been the privileged beneficiary of that listening. She has consistently encouraged me and has never complained—when well she might have—that Matthew was stealing time from her. It is astounding to me that I have been working on Matthew for half of our married life together! Though a busy career woman herself, Bev has never failed in her enthusiastic support and her loving interest in my work. I am deeply grateful to her.

Donald A. Hagner

September 1993
Fuller Theological Seminary
Pasadena, California

Abbreviations

A. General Abbreviations

A	Codex Alexandrinus	impf.	imperfect
ad	comment on	infra	below
Akkad.	Akkadian	Jos.	Josephus
א	Codex Sinaiticus	lat	Latin
Ap. Lit.	Apocalyptic Literature	lit.	literally
Apoc.	Apocrypha	LXX	Septuagint
Aq.	Aquila's Greek Translation	masc.	masculine
	of the OT	mg.	margin
Arab.	Arabic	MS(S)	manuscript(s)
Aram.	Aramaic	MT	Masoretic text (of the Old
B	Codex Vaticanus		Testament)
C	Codex Ephraemi Syri	n.	note
c.	*circa,* about	N.B.	*nota bene,* note well
cent.	century	n.d.	no date
cf.	*confer,* compare	Nestle	Nestle (ed.), *Novum*
chap(s).	chapter(s)		*Testamentum Graece*[26],
cod., codd.	codex, codices		rev. K. and B. Aland
contra	in contrast to	no.	number
D	Codex Bezae	n.s.	new series
dat.	dative	NT	New Testament
DSS	Dead Sea Scrolls	obs.	obsolete
ed.	edited by, editor(s)	o.s.	old series
e.g.	*exempli gratia,* for example	OT	Old Testament
et al.	*et alii,* and others	p., pp.	page, pages
ET	English translation	*pace*	with due respect to, but
EV	English Versions of the		differing from
	Bible	//, par(s).	parallel(s)
fem.	feminine	par.	paragraph
frag.	fragments	*passim*	elsewhere
FS	*Festschrift,* volume written	pl.	plural
	in honor of	Pseudep.	Pseudepigrapha
ft.	foot, feet	Q	Quelle ("Sayings" source
gen.	genitive		for the Gospels)
Gr.	Greek	q.v.	*quod vide,* which see
hap. leg.	*hapax legomenon,* sole	rev.	revised by, reviser, revision
	occurrence	Rom.	Roman
Heb.	Hebrew	RVmg	Revised Version margin
Hitt.	Hittite	Sam.	Samaritan recension
ibid.	*ibidem,* in the same place	*sc.*	*scilicet,* that is to say
id.	*idem,* the same	Sem.	Semitic
i.e.	*id est,* that is	sing.	singular

Sumer.	Sumerian	UP	University Press
s.v.	*sub verbo,* under the word	u.s.	*ut supra,* as above
sy	Syriac	v, vv	verse, verses
Symm.	Symmachus	vg	Vulgate
Tg.	Targum	viz.	*videlicet,* namely
Theod.	Theodotion	v.l.	*varia lectio,* alternative
TR	Textus Receptus		reading
tr.	translator, translated by	vol.	volume
Ugar.	Ugaritic	x	times (2x = two times, etc.)

For abbreviations of Greek MSS used in *Notes,* see Nestle[26].

B. Abbreviations for Translations and Paraphrases

AmT	Smith and Goodspeed, *The Complete Bible, An American Translation*	NAB	The New American Bible
		NEB	The New English Bible
		NIV	The New International Version (1978)
ASV	American Standard Version, American Revised Version (1901)		
AV	Authorized Version = KJV	NJB	New Jerusalem Bible (1985)
GNB	Good News Bible = Today's English Version	NRSV	New Revised Standard Version (1989)
JB	Jerusalem Bible	Phillips	J. B. Phillips, *The New Testament in Modern English*
JPS	Jewish Publication Society, *The Holy Scriptures*	REB	Revised English Bible
		RSV	Revised Standard Version (NT 1946, OT 1952, Apoc. 1957)
KJV	King James Version (1611) = AV		
Knox	R. A. Knox, *The Holy Bible: A Translation from the Latin Vulgate in the Light of the Hebrew and Greek Original*	RV	Revised Version, 1881–85
		Wey	R. F. Weymouth, *The New Testament in Modern Speech*
		Wms	C. B. Williams, *The New Testament: A Translation in the Language of the People*
Moffatt	J. Moffatt, *A New Translation of the Bible* (NT 1913)		

C. Abbreviations of Commonly Used Periodicals, Reference Works, and Serials

AARSR	American Academy of Religion Studies in Religion	*AER*	*American Ecclesiastical Review*
		AfO	*Archiv für Orientforschung*
AAS	*Acta apostolicae sedis*	AGJU	Arbeiten zur Geschichte des antiken Judentums und des Urchristentums
AASOR	Annual of the American Schools of Oriental Research		
AB	Anchor Bible	AGSU	Arbeiten zur Geschichte des Spätjudentums und Urchristentums
AbrN	*Abr-Nahrain*		
ACNT	Augsburg Commentary on the New Testament	*AH*	F. Rosenthal, *An Aramaic Handbook*
AcOr	*Acta orientalia*		
ACW	Ancient Christian Writers	*AHW*	W. von Soden, *Akkadisches Handwörterbuch*
ADAJ	Annual of the Department of Antiquities of Jordan		
		AJA	*American Journal of Archaeology*

AJAS	American Journal of Arabic Studies	ArOr	Archiv orientální
AJBA	Australian Journal of Biblical Archaeology	ARW	Archiv für Religionswissenschaft
AJBI	Annual of the Japanese Biblical Institute	ASB	Austin Seminary Bulletin
		ASNU	Acta seminarii neotesta- mentici upsaliensis
AJP	American Journal of Philology	ASS	Acta sanctae sedis
AJSL	American Journal of Semitic Languages and Literature	AsSeign	Assemblées du Seigneur
		ASSR	Archives des sciences sociales des religions
AJT	American Journal of Theology	ASTI	Annual of the Swedish Theological Institute
ALBO	Analecta lovaniensia biblica et orientalia	ATAbh	Alttestamentliche Abhandlungen
ALGHJ	Arbeiten zur Literatur und Geschichte des hellenis- tischen Judentums	ATANT	Abhandlungen zur Theologie des Alten und Neuen Testaments
ALUOS	Annual of Leeds University Oriental Society	ATD	Das Alte Testament Deutsch
AnBib	Analecta biblica	ATDan	Acta theologica danica
AnBoll	Analecta Bollandiana	ATR	Anglican Theological Review
ANEP	J. B. Pritchard (ed.), Ancient Near East in Pictures	AusBR	Australian Biblical Review
ANESTP	J. B. Pritchard (ed.), Ancient Near East Supplementary Texts and Pictures	AUSS	Andrews University Seminary Studies
		BA	Biblical Archaeologist
ANET	J. B. Pritchard (ed.), Ancient Near Eastern Texts	BAC	Biblioteca de autores cristianos
ANF	The Ante-Nicene Fathers	BAGD	W. Bauer, A Greek-English Lexicon of the New Testament and Other Early Christian Literature, ET, ed. W. F. Arndt and F. W. Gingrich; 2d ed. rev. F. W. Gingrich and F. W. Danker (Univer- sity of Chicago, 1979)
AnnThéol	L'Année théologique		
AnOr	Analecta orientalia		
ANQ	Andover Newton Quarterly		
ANRW	Aufstieg und Niedergang der römischen Welt		
ANTF	Arbeiten zur Neutestament- lichen Textforschung		
ANTJ	Arbeiten zum Neuen Testament und zum Judentum	BARev	Biblical Archaeology Review
		BASOR	Bulletin of the American Schools of Oriental Research
Anton	Antonianum	BASP	Bulletin of the American Society of Papyrologists
AOAT	Alter Orient und Altes Testament	BBB	Bonner biblische Beiträge
AOS	American Oriental Series	BBET	Beiträge zur biblischen Exegese und Theologie
AP	J. Marouzeau (ed.), L'Année philologique	BCSR	Bulletin of the Council on the Study of Religion
APOT	R. H. Charles (ed.), Apocry- pha and Pseudepigrapha of the Old Testament	BDB	F. Brown, S. R. Driver, and C. A. Briggs, Hebrew and English Lexicon of the Old Testament
ARG	Archiv für Reformationsgeschichte		
ARM	Archives royales de Mari		

BDF	F. Blass, A. Debrunner, and R. W. Funk, *A Greek Grammar of the NT*	BNTC	Black's New Testament Commentaries
BDR	F. Blass, A. Debrunner, and F. Rehkopf, *Grammatik des neutestamentlichen Griechisch*	BO	*Bibliotheca orientalis*
		BR	*Biblical Research*
		BSac	*Bibliotheca Sacra*
		BSO(A) S	*Bulletin of the School of Oriental (and African) Studies*
BeO	*Bibbia e oriente*		
BETL	Bibliotheca ephemeridum theologicarum lovaniensium	BSR	Bibliothèque de sciences religieuses
		BT	*The Bible Translator*
BEvT	Beiträge zur evangelischen Theologie	BTB	*Biblical Theology Bulletin*
		BTS	*Bible et terre saint*
BFCT	Beiträge zur Förderung christlicher Theologie	BU	Biblische Untersuchungen
		BVC	*Bible et vie chrétienne*
BGBE	Beiträge zur Geschichte der biblischen Exegese	BW	*Biblical World*
		BWANT	Beiträge zur Wissenschaft vom Alten und Neuen Testament
BHH	*Biblisch-Historisches Handwörterbuch*		
BHK	R. Kittel, *Biblia hebraica*	BZ	*Biblische Zeitschrift*
BHS	*Biblia hebraica stuttgartensia*	BZAW	Beihefte zur *ZAW*
BHT	Beiträge zur historischen Theologie	BZNW	Beihefte zur *ZNW*
		BZRGG	Beihefte zur *ZRGG*
Bib	*Biblica*		
BibB	Biblische Beiträge	*CAD*	*The Assyrian Dictionary of the Oriental Institute of the University of Chicago*
BibLeb	*Bibel und Leben*		
BibNot	*Biblische Notizen*		
BibOr	Biblica et orientalia	*CAH*	*Cambridge Ancient History*
BibRev	*Bible Review*	CAT	Commentaire de l'Ancien Testament
BibS(F)	Biblische Studien (Freiburg, 1895–)		
		CB	*Cultura bíblica*
BibS(N)	Biblische Studien (Neukirchen, 1951–)	*CBQ*	*Catholic Biblical Quarterly*
		CBQMS	CBQ Monograph Series
BIES	*Bulletin of the Israel Exploration Society (= Yediot)*	CCath	Corpus Catholicorum
		CChr	Corpus Christianorum
BIFAO	*Bulletin de l'institut français d'archéologie orientale*	CGTC	Cambridge Greek Testament Commentary
BiTod	*The Bible Today*	CGTSC	Cambridge Greek Testament for Schools and Colleges
BJRL	*Bulletin of the John Rylands University Library of Manchester*		
		CH	*Church History*
		CHR	*Catholic Historical Review*
BJS	Brown Judaic Studies	*ChrTod*	*Christianity Today*
BK	*Bibel und Kirche*	*CIG*	*Corpus inscriptionum graecarum*
BKAT	Biblischer Kommentar: Altes Testament		
		CII	*Corpus inscriptionum iudaicarum*
BLE	*Bulletin de littérature ecclésiastique*		
		CIL	*Corpus inscriptionum latinarum*
BLit	*Bibel und Liturgie*		

CIS	Corpus inscriptionum semiticarum	DR	Downside Review
		DS	Denzinger-Schönmetzer,
CJT	Canadian Journal of Theology		Enchiridion symbolorum
CNT	Commentaire du Nouveau Testament	DTC	Dictionnaire de théologie catholique
ConB	Coniectanea biblica	DTT	Dansk teologisk tidsskrift
ConBNT	Coniectanea biblica, New Testament	DunRev	Dunwoodie Review
Concil	Concilium	EBib	Etudes bibliques
ConNT	Coniectanea neotestamentica	EBT	Encyclopedia of Biblical Theology
CQ	Church Quarterly		
CQR	Church Quarterly Review	EcR	Ecclesiastical Review
CRAIBL	Comptes rendus de l'Académie des inscriptions et belles-lettres	EDNT	H. Balz and G. Schneider (eds.), Exegetical Dictionary of the New Testament
CRev	Classical Review	EF	Études franciscaines
CrQ	Crozier Quarterly	EHAT	Exegetisches Handbuch zum Alten Testament
CSCO	Corpus scriptorum christianorum orientalium		
		EKKNT	Evangelisch-katholischer Kommentar zum Neuen Testament
CSEL	Corpus scriptorum ecclesiasticorum latinorum		
CTA	A. Herdner, Corpus des tablettes en cunéiformes alphabétiques	EKL	Evangelisches Kirchenlexikon
		EnchBib	Enchiridion biblicum
		EncJud	Encyclopedia judaica (1971)
CTJ	Calvin Theological Journal	EpR	Epworth Review
CTM	Concordia Theological Monthly	ER	Ecumenical Review
CTQ	Concordia Theological Quarterly	ErJb	Eranos Jahrbuch
		EstBib	Estudios bíblicos
CurTM	Currents in Theology and Mission	ETL	Ephemerides theologicae lovanienses
		ETR	Etudes théologiques et religieuses
DACL	Dictionnaire d'archéologie chrétienne et de liturgie	ETS	Erfurter Theologische Studien
DBSup	Dictionnaire de la Bible, Supplément	EV	Esprit et Vie
Diak	Diakonia	EvJ	Evangelical Journal
DISO	C.-F. Jean and J. Hoftijzer, Dictionnaire des inscriptions sémitiques de l'ouest	EvK	Evangelische Kommentar
		EvQ	Evangelical Quarterly
		EvT	Evangelische Theologie
DJD	Discoveries in the Judean Desert	EWNT	H. Balz and G. Schneider (eds.), Exegetisches Wörterbuch zum Neuen Testament
DJG	J. B. Green and S. McKnight (eds.), Dictionary of Jesus and the Gospels		
		Exp	Expositor
DL	Doctrine and Life	ExpTim	The Expository Times
DOTT	D. W. Thomas (ed.), Documents from Old Testament Times	FB	Forschung zur Bibel
		FBBS	Facet Books, Biblical Series

FC	Fathers of the Church	HNT	Handbuch zum Neuen
FRLANT	Forschungen zur Religion		Testament
	und Literatur des	HNTC	Harper's NT Commentaries
	Alten und Neuen	*HR*	*History of Religions*
	Testaments	HSM	Harvard Semitic Mono-
FTS	Frankfurter theologische		graphs
	Studien	HTKNT	Herders theologischer
FV	*Foi et Vie*		Kommentar zum Neuen
			Testament
GAG	W. von Soden, *Grundriss der*	*HTR*	*Harvard Theological Review*
	akkadischen Grammatik	HTS	Harvard Theological Studies
GCS	Griechische christliche	*HUCA*	*Hebrew Union College Annual*
	Schriftsteller	HUT	Hermeneutische
GKB	Gesenius-Kautzsch-		Untersuchungen zur
	Bergsträsser, *Hebräische*		Theologie
	Grammatik		
GKC	*Gesenius' Hebrew Grammar,* ed.	*IB*	*Interpreter's Bible*
	E. Kautzsch, tr. A. E.	*IBS*	*Irish Biblical Studies*
	Cowley	ICC	International Critical
GL	*Geist und Leben*		Commentary
GNT	Grundrisse zum Neuen	*IDB*	G. A. Buttrick (ed.), *Interpreter's*
	Testament		*Dictionary of the Bible*
GOTR	*Greek Orthodox Theological*	*IDBSup*	Supplementary volume to *IDB*
	Review	*IEJ*	*Israel Exploration Journal*
GPM	*Göttinger Predigtmeditation*	*Int*	*Interpretation*
GR	*Greece and Rome*	*ISBE*	G. W. Bromiley (ed.),
GRBS	*Greek, Roman, and Byzantine*		*International Standard Bible*
	Studies		*Encyclopedia,* rev. ed.
Greg	*Gregorianum*	*ITQ*	*Irish Theological Quarterly*
GTA	Göttinger Theologische		
	Arbeiten	*JA*	*Journal asiatique*
		JAAR	*Journal of the American*
HALAT	W. Baumgartner et al.,		*Academy of Religion*
	Hebräisches und	JAC	Jahrbuch für Antike und
	aramäisches Lexikon zum		Christentum
	Alten Testament	*JANESCU*	*Journal of the Ancient Near Eastern*
HAT	Handbuch zum Alten		*Society of Columbia University*
	Testament	*JAOS*	*Journal of the American*
HBT	*Horizons in Biblical*		*Oriental Society*
	Theology	*JAS*	*Journal of Asian Studies*
HDR	Harvard Dissertations in	*JBC*	R. E. Brown et al. (eds.), *The*
	Religion		*Jerome Biblical Commentary*
HeyJ	*Heythrop Journal*	*JBL*	*Journal of Biblical Literature*
HibJ	*Hibbert Journal*	*JBR*	*Journal of Bible and Religion*
HKAT	Handkommentar zum Alten	*JCS*	*Journal of Cuneiform Studies*
	Testament	JDS	Judean Desert Studies
HKNT	Handkommentar zum	*JEA*	*Journal of Egyptian Archaeology*
	Neuen Testament	*JEH*	*Journal of Ecclesiastical History*

JES	*Journal of Ecumenical Studies*	*KD*	*Kerygma und Dogma*
JETS	*Journal of the Evangelical Theological Society*	KlT	Kleine Texte
		KNT	Kommentar till Nya Testament
JHS	*Journal of Hellenic Studies*		
JIBS	*Journal of Indian and Buddhist Studies*	LCC	Library of Christian Classics
JIPh	*Journal of Indian Philosophy*	LCL	Loeb Classical Library
JJS	*Journal of Jewish Studies*	LD	Lectio divina
JMES	*Journal of Middle Eastern Studies*	*Leš*	*Lešonénu*
JMS	*Journal of Mithraic Studies*	*LexTQ*	*Lexington Theological Quarterly*
JNES	*Journal of Near Eastern Studies*	*LingBib*	*Linguistica Biblica*
JPOS	*Journal of the Palestine Oriental Society*	*LLAVT*	E. Vogt, *Lexicon linguae aramaicae Veteris Testamenti*
JQR	Jewish Quarterly Review	*LPGL*	G. W. H. Lampe, *Patristic Greek Lexicon*
JQRMS	Jewish Quarterly Review Monograph Series	*LQ*	*Lutheran Quarterly*
JR	*Journal of Religion*	*LR*	*Lutherische Rundschau*
JRAS	*Journal of the Royal Asiatic Society*	*LS*	*Louvain Studies*
		LSJ	Liddell-Scott-Jones, *Greek-English Lexicon*
JRE	*Journal of Religious Ethics*		
JRelS	*Journal of Religious Studies*	*LTK*	*Lexikon für Theologie und Kirche*
JRH	*Journal of Religious History*	*LTP*	*Laval théologique et philosophique*
JRS	*Journal of Roman Studies*		
JRT	*Journal of Religious Thought*	LUÅ	Lunds universitets årsskrift
JSJ	*Journal for the Study of Judaism*	*LumVie*	*Lumière et Vie*
JSNT	*Journal for the Study of the New Testament*	LumVieSup	Supplement to LumVie
		LVit	*Lumen Vitae*
JSNTSup	JSNT Supplement Series	*LW*	*Lutheran World*
JSOT	*Journal for the Study of the Old Testament*	*McCQ*	*McCormick Quarterly*
JSOTSup	JSOT Supplement Series	MDOG	Mitteilungen der deutschen Orient-Gesellschaft
JSS	*Journal of Semitic Studies*		
JSSR	*Journal for the Scientific Study of Religion*	MeyerK	H. A. W. Meyer, *Kritisch-exegetischer Kommentar über das Neue Testament*
JTC	*Journal for Theology and the Church*		
		MGWJ	*Monatschrift für Geschichte und Wissenschaft des Judentums*
JTS	*Journal of Theological Studies*		
Judaica	*Judaica: Beiträge zum Verständnis . . .*	MHT	J. H. Moulton, W. F. Howard, and N. Turner, *A Grammar of New Testament Greek*
KAI	H. Donner and W. Röllig, *Kanaanäische und aramäische Inschriften*	MM	J. H. Moulton and G. Milligan, *The Vocabulary of the Greek Testament*
KAT	Kommentar zum Alten Testament	MNTC	Moffatt NT Commentary
KB	L. Koehler and W. Baumgartner, *Lexicon in Veteris Testamenti libros*	*MPAIBL*	*Mémoires présentés a l'Académie des inscriptions et belles-lettres*

MScRel	*Mélanges de science religieuse*	NTD	Das Neue Testament Deutsch
MTS	Marburger theologische Studien	NTF	Neutestamentliche Forschungen
MTZ	*Münchener theologische Zeitschrift*	NTL	New Testament Library
MUSJ	*Mélanges de l'université Saint-Joseph*	NTR	*New Theology Review*
		NTS	*New Testament Studies*
MVAG	Mitteilungen der vorder-asiatisch-ägyptischen Gesellschaft	NTTS	New Testament Tools and Studies
		Numen	*Numen: International Review for the History of Religions*
NABPR	National Association of Baptist Professors of Religion	OBO	Orbis biblicus et orientalis
NB	*New Blackfriars*	ÖBS	Österreichische biblische studien
NCB	New Century Bible (new ed.)	*OCD*	*Oxford Classical Dictionary*
NCCHS	R. C. Fuller et al. (eds.), *New Catholic Commentary on Holy Scripture*	*OCP*	*Orientalia christiana periodica*
		OGI	W. Dittenberger (ed.), *Orientis graeci inscriptiones selectae* (1903–5)
NCE	M. R. P. McGuire et al. (eds.), *New Catholic Encyclopedia*	OIP	Oriental Institute Publications
NedTTs	*Nederlands theologisch tijdschrift*	OLP	Orientalia lovaniensia periodica
Neot	*Neotestamentica*		
NewDocs	*New Documents Illustrating Early Christianity, A Review of Greek Inscriptions, etc.*, ed. G. H. R. Horsley, North Ryde, NSW, Australia	*OLZ*	*Orientalische Literaturzeitung*
		Or	*Orientalia* (Rome)
		OrAnt	*Oriens antiquus*
		OrChr	*Oriens christianus*
NFT	New Frontiers in Theology	*OrSyr*	*L'orient syrien*
NHS	Nag Hammadi Studies	OTM	Oxford Theological Monographs
NIDNTT	*New International Dictionary of New Testament Theology*	*OTS*	*Oudtestamentische Studiën*
NICNT	New International Commentary on the New Testament	*PAAJR*	*Proceedings of the American Academy of Jewish Research*
NIBC	New International Biblical Commentary	*PCB*	M. Black and H. H. Rowley (eds.), *Peake's Commentary on the Bible*
NIGTC	New International Greek Testament Commentary		
NKZ	*Neue kirchliche Zeitschrift*	*PEFQS*	*Palestine Exploration Fund, Quarterly Statement*
NorTT	*Norsk Teologisk Tijdsskrift*		
NovT	*Novum Testamentum*	*PEQ*	*Palestine Exploration Quarterly*
NovTSup	Supplement to *NovT*		
NPNF	Nicene and Post-Nicene Fathers	*PG*	J. P. Migne, *Patrologia graeca*
		PGM	K. Preisendanz (ed.), *Papyri graecae magicae*
NRT	*La nouvelle revue théologique*		
NTA	*New Testament Abstracts*	*PhEW*	*Philosophy East and West*
NTAbh	Neutestamentliche Abhandlungen	*PhRev*	*Philosophical Review*
		PJ	*Palästina-Jahrbuch*

PLL	Papers on Language and Literature	RevScRel	Revue des sciences religieuses
PO	Patrologia orientalis	RevSém	Revue sémitique
POxy	Oxyrhynchus Papyri	RevSR	Revue des sciences religieuses (Strasbourg)
PRS	Perspectives in Religious Studies	RevThom	Revue thomiste
PRU	Le Palais royal d'Ugarit	RGG	Religion in Geschichte und Gegenwart
PSTJ	Perkins (School of Theology) Journal	RHE	Revue d'histoire ecclésiastique
PTMS	Pittsburgh (Princeton) Theological Monograph Series	RHPR	Revue d'histoire et de philosophie religieuses
PTR	Princeton Theological Review	RHR	Revue de l'histoire des religions
PVTG	Pseudepigrapha Veteris Testamenti graece	RivB	Rivista biblica
		RNT	Regensburger Neues Testament
PW	Pauly-Wissowa, Real-Encyklopädie der classischen Altertumswissenschaft	RR	Review of Religion
		RSO	Rivista degli studi orientali
		RSPT	Revue des sciences philoso-phiques et théologiques
PWSup	Supplement to PW	RSR	Recherches de science religieuse
QD	Quaestiones disputatae	RTL	Revue théologique de Louvain
QDAP	Quarterly of the Department of Antiquities in Palestine	RTP	Revue de théologie et de philosophie
		RTR	Reformed Theological Review
RA	Revue d'assyriologie et d'archéologie orientale	SacPag	Sacra Pagina
RAC	Reallexikon für Antike und Christentum	Sal	Salmanticensis
		SANT	Studien zum Alten und Neuen Testament
RB	Revue biblique	SAQ	Sammlung ausgewählter kirchen- und dogmengeschichtlicher Quellenschriften
RBén	Revue bénédictine		
RCB	Revista de cultura biblica		
RE	Realencyklopädie für protestantische Theologie und Kirche		
		SB	Sources bibliques
REA	Revue des études anciennes (Bordeaux)	SBF	Studii biblici franciscani
		SBJ	La sainte bible de Jérusalem
RechBib	Recherches bibliques	SBLASP	Society of Biblical Literature Abstracts and Seminar Papers
REg	Revue d'égyptologie		
REG	Revue des études grecques		
REJ	Revue des études juives	SBLDS	SBL Dissertation Series
RelS	Religious Studies	SBLMasS	SBL Masoretic Studies
RelSoc	Religion and Society	SBLMS	SBL Monograph Series
RelSRev	Religious Studies Review	SBLSBS	SBL Sources for Biblical Study
RES	Répertoire d'épigraphie sémitique		
		SBLSCS	SBL Septuagint and Cognate Studies
ResQ	Restoration Quarterly		
RevExp	Review and Expositor	SBLTT	SBL Texts and Translations
RevistB	Revista bíblica	SBM	Stuttgarter biblische Monographien
RevQ	Revue de Qumrân		

SBS	Stuttgarter Bibelstudien	*StimmZeit*	*Stimmen der Zeit* (Munich)
SBT	Studies in Biblical Theology	*STK*	*Svensk teologisk kvartalskrift*
SC	Sources chrétiennes	Str-B	[H. Strack and] P.
ScEccl	*Sciences ecclésiastiques*		Billerbeck, *Kommentar*
ScEs	*Science et esprit*		*zum Neuen Testament*
SCR	*Studies in Comparative Religion*	StudBib	Studia Biblica
Scr	*Scripture*	StudNeot	Studia neotestamentica
SD	Studies and Documents	SUNT	Studien zur Umwelt des
SE	*Studia Evangelica* 1, 2, 3, 4, 5, 6		Neuen Testaments
	(= TU 73 [1959], 87 [1964],	SVTP	Studia in Veteris Testamenti
	88 [1964], 102 [1968],		pseudepigrapha
	103 [1968], 112 [1973])	*SWJT*	*Southwestern Journal of*
SEÅ	*Svensk exegetisk årsbok*		*Theology*
Sef	*Sefarad*	SymBU	Symbolae biblicae
SeinSend	*Sein und Sendung*		upsalienses
Sem	*Semitica*		
SHT	Studies in Historical	*TantY*	*Tantur Yearbook*
	Theology	*TAPA*	*Transactions of the American*
SJLA	Studies in Judaism in Late		*Philological Association*
	Antiquity	*TBei*	*Theologische Beiträge*
SJT	*Scottish Journal of Theology*	*TBl*	*Theologische Blätter*
SKK	Stuttgarter kleiner	TBü	Theologische Bücherei
	Kommentar	TC	Theological Collection
SMSR	*Studi e materiali di storia delle*		(SPCK)
	religioni	*TCGNT*	B. M. Metzger, *A Textual*
SNT	Studien zum Neuen		*Commentary on the Greek*
	Testament		*New Testament*
SNTSMS	Society for New Testament	*TD*	*Theology Digest*
	Studies Monograph	TDNT	G. Kittel and G. Friedrich
	Series		(eds.), *Theological*
SNTU	*Studien zum Neuen Testament*		*Dictionary of the New*
	und seiner Umwelt		*Testament*
SNTUMS	SNTU Monograph Series	TextsS	Texts and Studies
SO	Symbolae osloenses	*TF*	*Theologische Forschung*
SOTSMS	Society for Old Testament	*TGeg*	*Theologie der Gegenwart*
	Study Monograph Series	*TGl*	*Theologie und Glaube*
SPap	*Studia papyrologica*	*Th*	*Theology*
SPAW	Sitzungsberichte der	THKNT	Theologischer
	preussischen Akademie		Handkommentar zum
	der Wissenschaften		Neuen Testament
SPB	Studia postbiblica	*TLZ*	*Theologische Literaturzeitung*
SR	*Studies in Religion/Sciences*	TNTC	Tyndale New Testament
	religieuses		Commentaries
SSS	Semitic Study Series	*TP*	*Theologie und Philosophie*
ST	*Studia theologica*	*TPQ*	*Theologisch-praktische*
STÅ	*Svensk teologisk årsskrift*		*Quartalschrift*
STDJ	Studies on the Texts of the	*TQ*	*Theologische Quartalschrift*
	Desert of Judah	*TRE*	*Theologische Realenzyklopädie*

TRev	*Theologische Revue*	WBC	Word Biblical Commentary
TRu	*Theologische Rundschau*	*WD*	*Wort und Dienst*
TS	*Theological Studies*	*WDB*	*Westminster Dictionary of the Bible*
TSK	*Theologische Studien und Kritiken*	*WHAB*	*Westminster Historical Atlas of the Bible*
TT	*Teologisk Tidsskrift*	WMANT	Wissenschaftliche Monographien zum Alten und Neuen Testament
TTh	*Tijdschrift voor theologie*		
TToday	*Theology Today*		
TTZ	*Trierer theologische Zeitschrift*		
TU	Texte und Untersuchungen	*WO*	*Die Welt des Orients*
TWAT	G. J. Botterweck and H. Ringgren (eds.), *Theologisches Wörterbuch zum Alten Testament*	*WortWahr*	*Wort und Wahrheit*
		WTJ	*Westminster Theological Journal*
		WUNT	Wissenschaftliche Untersuchungen zum Neuen Testament
TWNT	G. Kittel and G. Friedrich (eds.), *Theologisches Wörterbuch zum Neuen Testament*	*WW*	*Word and World*
		WZKM	*Wiener Zeitschrift für die Kunde des Morgenlandes*
TynB	*Tyndale Bulletin*		
TZ	*Theologische Zeitschrift*	*WZKSO*	*Wiener Zeitschrift für die Kunde Süd- und Ostasiens*
UBSGNT	United Bible Societies *Greek New Testament*		
		ZA	*Zeitschrift für Assyriologie*
UF	*Ugaritische Forschungen*	*ZAW*	*Zeitschrift für die alttestamentliche Wissenschaft*
UNT	Untersuchungen zum Neuen Testament		
		ZDMG	*Zeitschrift der deutschen morgenländischen Gesellschaft*
USQR	*Union Seminary Quarterly Review*		
UT	C. H. Gordon, *Ugaritic Textbook*	*ZDPV*	*Zeitschrift des deutschen Palästina-Vereins*
UUÅ	Uppsala universitetsårsskrift	*ZEE*	*Zeitschrift für evangelische Ethik*
		ZHT	*Zeitschrift für historische Theologie*
VC	*Vigilae christianae*		
VCaro	*Verbum caro*	*ZKG*	*Zeitschrift für Kirchengeschichte*
VChr	*Vigiliae Christianae*	*ZKT*	*Zeitschrift für katholische Theologie*
VD	*Verbum domini*		
VF	*Verkündigung und Forschung*	*ZMR*	*Zeitschrift für Missionskunde und Religionswissenschaft*
VKGNT	K. Aland (ed.), *Vollständige Konkordanz zum griech- ischen Neuen Testament*		
		ZNW	*Zeitschrift für die neutestamentliche Wissenschaft*
VS	Verbum salutis		
VSpir	*Vie spirituelle*	*ZRGG*	*Zeitschrift für Religions- und Geistesgeschichte*
VT	*Vetus Testamentum*		
VTSup	Vetus Testamentum, Supplements	*ZST*	*Zeitschrift für systematische Theologie*
		ZTK	*Zeitschrift für Theologie und Kirche*
WA	M. Luther, Kritische Gesamtausgabe (="Weimar" edition)		
		ZWT	*Zeitschrift für wissenschaftliche Theologie*

D. Abbreviations for Books of the Bible, the Apocrypha, and the Pseudepigrapha

OLD TESTAMENT

Gen	2 Chr	Dan
Exod	Ezra	Hos
Lev	Neh	Joel
Num	Esth	Amos
Deut	Job	Obad
Josh	Ps(s)	Jonah
Judg	Prov	Mic
Ruth	Eccl	Nah
1 Sam	Cant	Hab
2 Sam	Isa	Zeph
1 Kgs	Jer	Hag
2 Kgs	Lam	Zech
1 Chr	Ezek	Mal

NEW TESTAMENT

Matt	1 Tim
Mark	2 Tim
Luke	Titus
John	Philem
Acts	Heb
Rom	Jas
1 Cor	1 Peter
2 Cor	2 Peter
Gal	1 John
Eph	2 John
Phil	3 John
Col	Jude
1 Thess	Rev
2 Thess	

APOCRYPHA

1 Esdr	1 Esdras	Ep Jer	Epistle of Jeremiah
2 Esdr	2 Esdras	S Th Ch	Song of the Three Children (or Young Men)
Tob	Tobit		
Jdt	Judith	Sus	Susanna
Add Esth	Additions to Esther	Bel	Bel and the Dragon
Wis	Wisdom of Solomon	Pr Man	Prayer of Manasseh
Sir	Ecclesiasticus (Wisdom of Jesus the son of Sirach)	1 Macc	1 Maccabees
		2 Macc	2 Maccabees
Bar	Baruch		

E. Abbreviations of the Names of Pseudepigraphical and Early Patristic Books

Adam and Eve	*Life of Adam and Eve*	*Odes Sol.*	*Odes of Solomon*
Apoc. Abr.	*Apocalypse of Abraham* (1st to 2nd cent. A.D.)	*Pss. Sol.*	*Psalms of Solomon*
		Sib. Or.	*Sibylline Oracles*
2–3 Apoc. Bar.	Syriac, Greek *Apocalypse of Baruch*	*T. 12 Patr.*	*Testaments of the Twelve Patriarchs*
Apoc. Mos.	*Apocalypse of Moses*	*T. Abr.*	*Testament of Abraham*
As. Mos.	(See *T. Mos.*)	*T. Judah*	*Testament of Judah*
1–2–3 Enoch	Ethiopic, Slavonic, Hebrew *Enoch*	*T. Levi*	*Testament of Levi,* etc.
		T. Sol.	*Testament of Solomon*
Ep. Arist.	*Epistle of Aristeas*		
Jub.	*Jubilees*	*Gos. Eb.*	*Gospel of the Ebionites*
Mart. Isa.	*Martyrdom of Isaiah*	*Gos. Heb.*	*Gospel of the Hebrews*

Gos. Naass.	*Gospel of the Naassenes*	*Pol.*	Ignatius, *Letter to Polycarp*
Gos. Pet.	*Gospel of Peter*	*Rom.*	Ignatius, *Letter to the*
Barn.	*Barnabas*		*Romans*
1–2 Clem.	*1–2 Clement*	*Smyrn.*	Ignatius, *Letter to the*
Did.	*Didache*		*Smyrnaeans*
Diogn.	*Diognetus*	*Trall.*	Ignatius, *Letter to the*
Herm. Man.	*Hermas, Mandates*		*Trallians*
Sim.	*Similitudes*	*Mart. Pol.*	*Martyrdom of Polycarp*
Vis.	*Visions*	*Pol. Phil.*	Polycarp, *Letter to the*
Ign. Eph.	Ignatius, *Letter to the*		*Philippians*
	Ephesians	Irenaeus, *Adv.*	Irenaeus, *Against All*
Magn.	Ignatius, *Letter to the*	*Haer.*	*Heresies*
	Magnesians	Tertullian, *De*	Tertullian, *On the*
Phil.	Ignatius, *Letter to the*	*Praesc. Haer.*	*Proscribing of Heretics*
	Philadelphians		

F. Abbreviations of Names of Dead Sea Scrolls and Related Texts

CD	Cairo (Genizah text of the) Damascus (Document)	1QS	*Serek hayyahad (Rule of the Community, Manual of Discipline)*
Hev	Nahal Hever texts		
Mas	Masada texts	1QSa	Appendix A *(Rule of the Congregation)* to 1QS
Mird	Khirbet Mird texts		
Mur	Wadi Murabbaʿat texts	1QSb	Appendix B *(Blessings)* to 1QS
P	Pesher (commentary)		
Q	Qumran	3Q*15*	Copper Scroll from Qumran Cave 3
1Q, 2Q			
3Q, etc.	Numbered caves of Qumran, yielding written material; followed by abbreviation of biblical or apocryphal book	4QFlor	*Florilegium* (or *Eschatological Midrashim*) from Qumran Cave 4
		4QMess ar	Aramaic "Messianic" text from Qumran Cave 4
QL	Qumran literature	4QPrNab	Prayer of Nabonidus from Qumran Cave 4
1QapGen	*Genesis Apocryphon* of Qumran Cave 1	4QTestim	*Testimonia* text from Qumran Cave 4
1QH	*Hôdāyôt (Thanksgiving Hymns)* from Qumran Cave 1	4QTLevi	*Testament of Levi* from Qumran Cave 4
1QIsa*a,b*	First or second copy of Isaiah from Qumran Cave 1	4QPhyl	Phylacteries from Qumran Cave 4
1QpHab	*Pesher on Habakkuk* from Qumran Cave 1	11QMelch	*Melchizedek* text from Qumran Cave 11
1QM	*Milḥāmāh* (War Scroll)	11QtgJob	*Targum of Job* from Qumran Cave 11

G. Abbreviations of Targumic Material

Tg. Onq.	*Targum Onqelos*	*Tg. Ps. -J.*	*Targum Pseudo-Jonathan*
Tg. Neb.	*Targum of the Prophets*	*Tg. Yer. I*	*Targum Yerušalmi I**
Tg. Ket.	*Targum of the Writings*	*Tg. Yer. II*	*Targum Yerušalmi II**
Frg. Tg.	*Fragmentary Targum*	*Yem. Tg.*	*Yemenite Targum*
Sam. Tg.	*Samaritan Targum*	*Tg. Esth I,*	*First or Second Targum of*
Tg. Isa.	*Targum of Isaiah*	*II*	*Esther*
Pal. Tgs.	*Palestinian Targums*		
Tg. Neof.	*Targum Neofiti I*	*optional title	

H. Abbreviations of Other Rabbinic Works

ʾAbot R. Nat.	*ʾAbot de Rabbi Nathan*	*Pesiq. Rab Kah.*	*Pesiqta de Rab Kahana*
ʾAg. Ber.	*ʾAggadat Berešit*	*Pirqe R. El.*	*Pirqe Rabbi Eliezer*
Bab.	*Babylonian*	*Rab.*	*Rabbah* (following
Bar.	*Baraita*		abbreviation for biblical
Der. Er. Rab.	*Derek Ereṣ Rabba*		book: *Gen. Rab.* [with
Der. Er. Zuṭ.	*Derek Ereṣ Zuṭa*		periods] = *Genesis*
Gem.	*Gemara*		*Rabbah*)
Kalla	*Kalla*	*Sem.*	*Semahot*
Mek.	*Mekilta*	*Sipra*	*Sipra*
Midr.	*Midraš;* cited with usual	*Sipre*	*Sipre*
	abbreviation for biblical	*Soṗ.*	*Soperim*
	book; but *Midr. Qoh.* =	*S. ʿOlam Rab.*	*Seder ʿOlam Rabbah*
	Midraš Qohelet	*Talm.*	*Talmud*
Pal.	*Palestinian*	*Yal.*	*Yalqut*
Pesiq. R.	*Pesiqta Rabbati*		

I. Abbreviations of Orders and Tractates in Mishnaic and Related Literature

(Italicized *m., t., b.,* or *y.* used before name to distinguish among tractates in Mishnah, Tosepta, Babylonian Talmud, and Jerusalem Talmud.)

ʾAbot	*ʾAbot*	*Giṭ.*	*Giṭṭin*
ʿArak.	*ʿArakin*	*Hag.*	*Hagiga*
ʿAbod. Zar.	*ʿAboda Zara*	*Hal.*	*Halla*
B. Bat.	*Baba Batra*	*Hor.*	*Horayot*
Bek.	*Bekorot*	*Hul.*	*Hullin*
Ber.	*Berakot*	*Kelim*	*Kelim*
Besa	*Besa* (= *Yom Ṭob*)	*Ker.*	*Keritot*
Bik.	*Bikkurim*	*Ketub.*	*Ketubot*
B. Meṣ.	*Baba Meṣiʿa*	*Kil.*	*Kilʾayim*
B. Qam.	*Baba Qamma*	*Maʿaś.*	*Maʿaśerot*
Dem.	*Demai*	*Mak.*	*Makkot*
ʿEd.	*ʿEduyyot*	*Makš.*	*Makširin* (=*Mašqin*)
ʿErub.	*ʿErubin*	*Meg.*	*Megilla*

Meʿil.	Meʿila	Roš. Haš.	Roš Haššana
Menah.	Menahot	Sanh.	Sanhedrin
Mid.	Middot	Šabb.	Šabbat
Miqw.	Miqwaʾot	Šeb.	Šebiʿit
Moʿed	Moʿed	Šebu.	Šebuʿot
Moʿed Qat.	Moʿed Qatan	Šeqal.	Šeqalim
Maʿaś. Š.	Maʿaśer Šeni	Sota	Sota
Našim	Našim	Sukk.	Sukka
Nazir	Nazir	Taʿan.	Taʿanit
Ned.	Nedarim	Tamid	Tamid
Neg.	Negaʿim	Tem.	Temura
Nez.	Neziqin	Ter.	Terumot
Nid.	Niddah	Tohar.	Toharot
Ohol.	Oholot	T. Yom	Tebul Yom
ʿOr.	ʿOrla	ʿUq.	ʿUqsin
Para	Para	Yad.	Yadayim
Peʾa	Peʾa	Yebam.	Yebamot
Pesah.	Pesahim	Yoma	Yoma (= Kippurim)
Qinnim	Qinnim	Zabim	Zabim
Qidd.	Qiddušin	Zebah.	Zebahim
Qod.	Qodašin	Zer.	Zeraʿim

J. Abbreviations of Nag Hammadi Tractates

Acts Pet. 12 Apost.	Acts of Peter and the Twelve Apostles	Hyp. Arch.	Hypostasis of the Archons
Allogenes	Allogenes	Hypsiph.	Hypsiphrone
Ap. Jas.	Apocryphon of James	Interp. Know.	Interpretation of Knowledge
Ap. John	Apocryphon of John	Marsanes	Marsanes
Apoc. Adam	Apocalypse of Adam	Melch.	Melchizedek
1 Apoc. Jas.	First Apocalypse of James	Norea	Thought of Norea
2 Apoc. Jas.	Second Apocalypse of James	On Bap. A	On Baptism A
Apoc. Paul	Apocalypse of Paul	On Bap. B	On Baptism B
Apoc. Pet.	Apocalypse of Peter	On Bap. C	On Baptism C
Asclepius	Asclepius 21–29	On Euch. A	On the Eucharist A
Auth. Teach.	Authoritative Teaching	On Euch. B	On the Eucharist B
Dial. Sav.	Dialogue of the Savior	Orig. World	On the Origin of the World
Disc. 8–9	Discourse on the Eighth and Ninth	Paraph. Shem	Paraphrase of Shem
		Pr. Paul	Prayer of the Apostle Paul
Ep. Pet. Phil.	Letter of Peter to Philip	Pr. Thanks.	Prayer of Thanksgiving
Eugnostos	Eugnostos the Blessed	Prot. Jas.	Protevangelium of James
Exeg. Soul	Exegesis on the Soul	Sent. Sextus	Sentences of Sextus
Gos. Eg.	Gospel of the Egyptians	Soph. Jes. Chr.	Sophia of Jesus Christ
Gos. Phil.	Gospel of Philip	Steles Seth	Three Steles of Seth
Gos. Thom.	Gospel of Thomas	Teach. Silv.	Teachings of Silvanus
Gos. Truth	Gospel of Truth	Testim. Truth	Testimony of Truth
Great Pow.	Concept of our Great Power	Thom. Cont.	Book of Thomas the Contender
		Thund.	Thunder, Perfect Mind

Treat. Res.	*Treatise on Resurrection*	*Trim. Prot.*	*Trimorphic Protennoia*
Treat. Seth	*Second Treatise of the Great Seth*	*Val. Exp.*	*A Valentinian Exposition*
		Zost.	*Zostrianos*
Tri. Trac.	*Tripartite Tractate*		

Note: The textual notes and numbers used to indicate individual manuscripts are those found in the apparatus criticus of *Novum Testamentum Graece,* ed. E. Nestle and K. Aland et al. (Stuttgart: Deutsche Bibelgesellschaft, 1979[26]). This edition of the Greek New Testament is the basis for the *Translation* sections.

Commentary Bibliography

Albright, W. F., and **Mann, C. S.** *Matthew.* AB. Garden City, NY: Doubleday, 1971. **Allen, W. C.** *A Critical and Exegetical Commentary on the Gospel according to St. Matthew.* 3rd ed. ICC. Edinburgh: T. & T. Clark, 1912. **Argyle, A. W.** *The Gospel according to Matthew.* CBC. Cambridge: Cambridge University Press, 1963. **Barclay, W.** *The Gospel of Matthew.* Rev. ed. 2 vols. The Daily Study Bible. Philadelphia: Westminster, 1975. **Beare, F. W.** *The Gospel according to Matthew: A Commentary.* Oxford: Blackwell, 1981. **Bengel, J. A.** *Gnomon of the New Testament.* 7th ed. Edinburgh: T. & T. Clark, 1857. 1:71–490. **Benoit, P.** *L'Évangile selon saint Matthieu.* 3rd ed. La Sainte Bible. Paris: Letouzey et Ané, 1961. **Blomberg, C. L.** *Matthew.* New American Commentary. Nashville: Broadman, 1992. **Bonnard, P.** *L'Évangile selon saint Matthieu.* 2nd ed. CNT. Neuchâtel: Delachaux & Niestlé, 1970. **Bruner, F. D.** *The Christbook: A Historical/Theological Commentary: Matthew 1–12.* Waco, TX: Word, 1987. ————. *The Churchbook: A Historical/Theological Commentary: Matthew 13–28.* Dallas, TX: Word, 1990. **Calvin, J.** *Commentary on a Harmony of the Gospels.* 3 vols. Reprint. Grand Rapids: Eerdmans, 1956–57. **Carson, D. A.** "Matthew." In *The Expositor's Bible Commentary,* ed. F. E. Gaebelein. Grand Rapids: Zondervan, 1985. 8:1–599. **Dahl, N. A.** *Matteus Evangeliet.* 2 vols. 2nd ed. Oslo: Universitetsforlaget, 1973. **Davies, M.** *Matthew: Readings, a New Biblical Commentary.* Sheffield: JSOT, 1992. **Davies, W. D.,** and **Allison, D. C., Jr.** *A Critical and Exegetical Commentary on the Gospel according to Saint Matthew.* 2 vols. (1–7; 8–18). ICC. Edinburgh: T. & T. Clark, 1988, 1991. **Fenton, J. C.** *Saint Matthew.* Pelican Commentaries. Baltimore: Penguin, 1964. **Filson, F. V.** *A Commentary on the Gospel according to St. Matthew.* BNTC. London: A. & C. Black, 1960. **Fornberg, T.** *Matteusevangeliet 1:1–13:52.* KNT 1A. Uppsala: EFS, 1989. **France, R. T.** *The Gospel according to Matthew.* TNTC 1. Grand Rapids: Eerdmans, 1985. **Gaechter, P.** *Das Matthäus-Evangelium.* Innsbruck: Tyrolia, 1963. **Garland, D. E.** *Reading Matthew: A Literary and Theological Commentary on the First Gospel.* New York: Crossroad, 1993. **Gerhardsson, B.** "Ur Matteusevangeliet" (chaps. 1–2; 5–7; 26–28). In *Ur Nya Testamentet: Kommentar till valda texter,* ed. L. Hartman. Lund: Gleerup, 1970. **Gnilka, J.** *Das Matthäusevangelium.* 2 vols. HTKNT. Freiburg: Herder, 1986, 1988. **Green, H. B.** *The Gospel according to Matthew.* New Clarendon Bible. Oxford: Clarendon, 1975. **Grundmann, W.** *Das Evangelium nach Matthäus.* THKNT. Berlin: Evangelische Verlagsanstalt, 1968. **Gundry, R. H.** *Matthew: A Commentary on His Literary and Theological Art.* Grand Rapids: Eerdmans, 1982. **Harrington, D. J.** *The Gospel of Matthew.* SacPag. Collegeville, MN: Liturgical, 1991. **Hendricksen, W.** *The Gospel of Matthew.* Edinburgh: Banner of Truth, 1974. **Hill, D.** *The Gospel of Matthew.* NCB. London: Marshall, Morgan, and Scott, 1972. **Klostermann, E.** *Das Matthäusevangelium.* 2nd ed. HNT. Tübingen: Mohr, 1927. **Kvalbein, H.** *Matteus-Evangeliet.* 2 vols. Oslo: Nye Luther, 1989, 1990. **Lachs, S. T.** *A Rabbinic Commentary on the New Testament: The Gospels of Matthew, Mark and Luke.* Hoboken, NJ: Ktav, 1987. **Lagrange, M.-J.** *Évangile selon Saint Matthieu.* EBib. Paris: Gabalda, 1923. **Lenski, R. C. H.** *The Interpretation of St. Matthew's Gospel.* Columbus, OH: Wartburg, 1943. **Limbeck, M.** *Matthäus-Evangelium.* SKK NT 1. Stuttgart: Katholisches Bibelwerk, 1986. **Lohmeyer, E.** *Das Evangelium des Matthäus.* 4th ed. Ed. W. Schmauch. MeyerK. Göttingen: Vandenhoeck & Ruprecht, 1967. **Luz, U.** *Matthew 1–7: A Commentary.* Trans. W. C. Linss. Continental Commentaries. Minneapolis: Augsburg, 1989. ————. *Das Evangelium nach Matthäus.* Vol. 2, Matt 8–17. EKK. Neukirchen-Vluyn: Benzinger & Neukirchener, 1990. **Maier, G.** *Matthäus-Evangelium.* 2 vols. Bibel-Kommentar. Neuhausen-Stuttgart: Hänssler, 1979. **McNeile, A. H.** *The Gospel according to St. Matthew.* London: Macmillan, 1915. **Meier, J. P.** *Matthew.* NT Message 3. Wilmington, DE: Glazier, 1981. **Montefiore, C. G.** *The Synoptic Gospels.* Vol 2. 2nd ed. London: Macmillan, 1927. **Morris, L.** *The Gospel according to Matthew.* Pillar Commentary. Grand

Rapids: Eerdmans, 1992. **Mounce, R. H.** *Matthew.* NIBC. Peabody, MA: Hendrickson, 1991.
Patte, D. *The Gospel according to Matthew: A Structural Commentary on Matthew's Faith.* Philadelphia: Fortress, 1987. **Plummer, A.** *An Exegetical Commentary on the Gospel according to St. Matthew.* London: Stock, 1909. **Robinson, T. H.** *The Gospel of Matthew.* MNTC. Garden City, NY: Doubleday, 1928. **Sabourin, L.** *The Gospel according to St Matthew.* 2 vols. Bombay: St Paul, 1982. **Sand, A.** *Das Evangelium nach Matthäus.* RNT. Regensburg: Pustet, 1986. **Schlatter, A.** *Der Evangelist Matthäus.* 2nd ed. Stuttgart: Calwer, 1933. **Schmid, J.** *Das Evangelium nach Matthäus.* RNT. Regensburg: Pustet, 1965. **Schnackenburg, R.** *Matthäusevangelium.* 2 vols. Die neue echter Bibel. Würzburg: Echter, 1985, 1987. **Schniewind, J.** *Das Evangelium nach Matthäus.* 8th ed. NTD. Göttingen: Vandenhoeck & Ruprecht, 1956. **Schweizer, E.** *The Good News according to Matthew.* Atlanta: John Knox, 1975. **Smith, R. H.** *Matthew.* ACNT. Minneapolis: Augsburg, 1989. **Stendahl, K.** "Matthew." In *Peake's Commentary on the Bible,* ed. M. Black and H. H. Rowley. Rev. ed. New York: Nelson, 1962. 769–98. **Strack, H. L.,** and **Billerbeck, P.** *Kommentar zum Neuen Testament aus Talmud und Midrasch.* 4 vols. 3rd ed. Munich: Beck, 1951–56. **Tasker, R. V. G.** *The Gospel according to St. Matthew.* TNTC. London: Tyndale, 1961. **Trilling, W.** *The Gospel according to St. Matthew.* New York: Herder & Herder, 1969. **Viviano, B. T.** "The Gospel according to Matthew." In *The Jerome Biblical Commentary,* ed. R. E. Brown, J. A. Fitzmyer, and R. E. Murphy. Englewood Cliffs, NJ: Prentice Hall, 1990. 630–74. **Weiss, B.** *Das Matthäus-Evangelium.* 9th ed. Göttingen: Vandenhoeck & Ruprecht, 1898. **Zahn, T.** *Das Evangelium des Matthäus.* 2nd ed. Leipzig: Deichert, 1903.

General Bibliography

Abrahams, I. *Studies in Pharisaism and the Gospels.* 2 vols. Cambridge: Cambridge University, 1917, 1924. **Albertz, M.** *Die synoptischen Streitgespräche.* Berlin: Trowitzsch, 1921. **Allison, D. C., Jr.** *The End of the Ages Has Come: An Early Interpretation of the Passion and Resurrection of Jesus.* Philadelphia: Fortress, 1985. **Alsup, J. E.** *The Post-Resurrection Appearance Stories of the Gospel Tradition.* Stuttgart: Calwer, 1975. **Arens, E.** *The HΛΘON-Sayings in the Synoptic Tradition: A Historico-Critical Investigation.* OBO 10. Göttingen: Vandenhoeck & Ruprecht, 1976. **Aune, D. E.** *Prophecy in Early Christianity and the Ancient Mediterranean World.* Grand Rapids: Eerdmans, 1983. **Baarlink, H.** *Die Eschatologie der synoptischen Evangelien.* BWANT 120. Stuttgart: Kohlhammer, 1986. **Bacon, B. W.** *Studies in Matthew.* New York: Holt, 1930. **Balch, D. L.,** ed. *Social History of the Matthean Community: Cross-Disciplinary Approaches.* Minneapolis: Fortress, 1991. **Baltensweiler, H.** *Die Verklärung Jesu.* ATANT 33. Zürich: Zwingli, 1959. **Banks, R.** *Jesus and the Law in the Synoptic Tradition.* SNTSMS 28. Cambridge: Cambridge University, 1975. **Barrett, C. K.** *The Holy Spirit and the Gospel Tradition.* London: SPCK, 1966. ————. *Jesus and the Gospel Tradition.* Philadelphia: Fortress, 1968. **Barth, G.** "Matthew's Understanding of the Law." In *Tradition and Interpretation in Matthew,* ed. G. Bornkamm et al. Philadelphia: Westminster, 1963. 58–164. **Bauer, D. R.** *The Structure of Matthew's Gospel: A Study in Literary Design.* JSNTSup 31. Sheffield: JSOT, 1988. **Bayer, H. F.** *Jesus' Predictions of Vindication and Resurrection.* WUNT 2.20. Tübingen: Mohr, 1986. **Beasley-Murray, G. R.** *Jesus and the Kingdom of God.* Grand Rapids: Eerdmans, 1986. ————. *Jesus and the Last Days: The Interpretation of the Olivet Discourse.* Peabody, MA: Hendrickson, 1993. **Benoit, P.** *The Passion and Resurrection of Jesus Christ.* New York: Herder & Herder, 1969. **Berger, K.** *Die Amen-Worte Jesu: Eine Untersuchung zum Problem der Legitimation in apokalyptischer Rede.* BZNW 39. Berlin: de Gruyter, 1970. ————. *Die Gesetzesauslegung Jesu: Ihr historischer Hintergrund im Judentum und im Alten Testament: Teil I. Markus und Parallelen.* WMANT 40. Neukirchen-Vluyn: Neukirchener, 1972. **Betz, O.** *Jesus: Der Messias Israels.* WUNT 42. Tübingen: Mohr, 1987. ———— and **Grimm, W.** *Wesen und Wirklichkeit der Wunder Jesu.* Frankfurt: Lang, 1977. **Black, M.** *An Aramaic Approach to the Gospels and Acts.* 3rd ed. Oxford: Clarendon, 1967. **Blass, F., Debrunner, A.,** and **Funk, R. W.** *A Greek Grammar of the New Testament.* Chicago: University of Chicago Press, 1961. **Blair, E. P.** *Jesus in the Gospel of Matthew.* Nashville: Abingdon, 1960. **Blomberg, C. L.** *Interpreting the Parables.* Downers Grove, IL: InterVarsity, 1990. **Böcher, O.** *Christus Exorcista.* BWANT 90. Stuttgart: Kohlhammer, 1972. **Borgen, P.** *Paul Preaches Circumcision and Pleases Men and Other Essays on Christian Origins.* Trondheim: Tapir, University of Trondheim, 1983. **Boring, M. E.** *Sayings of the Risen Jesus: Christian Prophecy in the Synoptic Tradition.* SNTSMS 46. Cambridge: Cambridge University, 1982. **Bornkamm, G.** "The Authority to 'Bind' and 'Loose' in the Church in Matthew's Gospel." In *The Interpretation of Matthew,* ed. G. Stanton. Philadelphia/London: SPCK/Fortress, 1983. 85–97. ————. "End-Expectation and Church in Matthew." In *Tradition and Interpretation in Matthew,* ed. G. Bornkamm et al. Philadelphia: Westminster, 1963. 15–51. **Bornkamm, G., Barth, G.,** and **Held, H. J.** *Tradition and Interpretation in Matthew.* Philadelphia: Westminster, 1963. **Brandenburger, E.** *Das Recht des Weltrichters: Untersuchung zu Matthäus 25, 31–46.* SBS 99. Stuttgart: Katholisches Bibelwerk, 1980. **Bratcher, R. G.** *A Translator's Guide to the Gospel of Matthew.* New York: United Bible Societies, 1981. **Braun, H.** *Qumran und das Neue Testament.* 2 vols. Tübingen: Mohr, 1966. **Broer, I.** *Freiheit vom Gesetz und Radikalisierung des Gesetzes: Ein Beitrag zur Theologie des Evangelisten Matthäus.* SBS 98. Stuttgart: Katholisches Bibelwerk, 1980. **Brooks, S. H.** *Matthew's Community: The Evidence of His Special Sayings Material.* JSNTSup 16. Sheffield: JSOT, 1987. **Brown, R. E.** *The Birth of the Messiah.* Garden City, NY: Doubleday, 1977. ————. *The Gospel according to John.* 2 vols.

AB. Garden City, NY: Doubleday, 1966, 1970. ―――. *New Testament Essays.* Milwaukee: Bruce, 1965. ―――. *The Virginal Conception and Bodily Resurrection of Jesus.* New York: Paulist, 1973. ―――, **K. P. Donfried, J. A. Fitzmyer, and J. Reumann,** eds. *Mary in the New Testament.* Philadelphia: Fortress, 1978. ―――, **K. P. Donfried, and J. Reumann,** eds. *Peter in the New Testament.* Minneapolis: Augsburg, 1973. **Bultmann, R.** *History of the Synoptic Tradition.* 2nd ed. Oxford: Blackwell, 1968. **Burger, C.** *Jesus als Davidssohn.* FRLANT 98. Göttingen: Vandenhoeck & Ruprecht, 1970. **Burnett, F. E.** *The Testament of Jesus-Sophia: A Redaction-Critical Study of the Eschatological Discourse in Matthew.* Washington, DC: University Press of America, 1979. **Butler, B. C.** *The Originality of St. Matthew: A Critique of the Two Document Hypothesis.* Cambridge: Cambridge University, 1951. **Caird, G. B.** *The Language and Imagery of the Bible.* Philadelphia: Westminster, 1980. **Caragounis, C. C.** *Peter and the Rock.* BZNW 58. Berlin: de Gruyter, 1989. **Carlston, C. E.** *The Parables of the Triple Tradition.* Philadelphia: Fortress, 1975. **Chilton, B. D.** *God in Strength: Jesus' Announcement of the Kingdom.* SNTUMS B.1. Freistadt: Plöchl, 1979. **Cope, O. L.** *Matthew: A Scribe Trained for the Kingdom of Heaven.* CBQMS 5. Washington, DC: Catholic Biblical Association, 1976. **Crossan, J. D.** *In Fragments: The Aphorisms of Jesus.* San Francisco: Harper & Row, 1983. ―――. *In Parables: The Challenge of the Historical Jesus.* New York: Harper & Row, 1973. **Cullmann, O.** *Peter: Disciple, Apostle, Martyr.* 2nd ed. Philadelphia: Westminster, 1962. **Dahl, N. A.** *Jesus the Christ: The Historical Origins of Christological Doctrine.* Ed. D. H. Juel. Minneapolis: Fortress, 1991. **Dalman, G.** *Jesus-Jeshua: Studies in the Gospels.* 1929. New York: Ktav, 1971. ―――. *The Words of Jesus.* Edinburgh: T. & T. Clark, 1909. **Danby, H.** *The Mishnah.* Oxford: Oxford University, 1933. **Daube, D.** *The New Testament and Rabbinic Judaism.* London: Athlone, 1956. **Davies, W. D.** *The Setting of the Sermon on the Mount.* Cambridge: Cambridge University, 1966. **Davison, J. E.** "*Anomia* and the Question of an Antinomian Polemic in Matthew." *JBL* 104 (1985) 617–35. **Deutsch, C.** *Hidden Wisdom and the Easy Yoke: Wisdom, Torah and Discipleship in Matthew 11.25–30.* JSNTSup 18. Sheffield: JSOT, 1987. **Dibelius, M.** *From Tradition to Gospel.* New York: Scribner, 1965. **Didier, M.,** ed. *L'Évangile selon Matthieu: Rédaction et théologie.* BETL 29. Gembloux: Duculot, 1972. **Dobschütz, E. von.** "Matthew as Rabbi and Catechist." In *The Interpretation of Matthew,* ed. G. Stanton. Philadelphia/London: Fortress/SPCK, 1983. 85–97. **Dodd, C. H.** *The Parables of the Kingdom.* London: Nisbet, 1935/New York: Scribners, 1936. **Donaldson, T. L.** *Jesus on the Mountain: A Study in Matthean Theology.* JSNTSup 8. Sheffield: JSOT, 1985. **Dupont, J.** *Les Béatitudes: I. Le problème littéraire; II. La bonne nouvelle; III. Les Évangelistes.* Paris: Gabalda, 1958, 1969, 1973. **Edwards, J. R.** "The Use of ΠΡΟΣΕΡΧΕΣΘΑΙ in the Gospel of Matthew." *JBL* 106 (1987) 65–74. **Edwards, R. A.** *Matthew's Story of Jesus.* Philadelphia: Fortress, 1985. **Ellis, P. F.** *Matthew: His Mind and His Message.* Collegeville, MN: Liturgical, 1974. **Feldmeier, R.** *Die Krisis des Gottessohnes.* WUNT 2.21. Tübingen: Mohr, 1987. **Fiedler, M. J.** "Gerechtigkeit im Matthäus-Evangelium." *Theologische Versuche* 8 (1977) 63–75. **Fitzmyer, J. A.** *Essays on the Semitic Background of the New Testament.* SBLSBS 5. Missoula, MT: Scholars, 1974. ―――. *A Wandering Aramean.* SBLMS 25. Missoula, MT: Scholars, 1981. **Ford, D.** *The Abomination of Desolation in Biblical Eschatology.* Washington, DC: University Press of America, 1979. **France, R. T.** *Jesus and the Old Testament.* London: Tyndale, 1971. ―――. *Matthew: Evangelist and Teacher.* Grand Rapids: Zondervan, 1989. **Frankemölle, H.** "Amtskritik im Matthäus-Evangelium?" *Bib* 54 (1973) 247–62. ―――. *Jahwebund und Kirche Christi.* NTAbh n.s. 10. Münster: Aschendorff, 1974. **Freyne, S.** *Galilee, Jesus and the Gospels: Literary Approaches and Historical Investigations.* Philadelphia: Fortress, 1988. **Fuller, R. H.** *Interpreting the Miracles.* Philadelphia: Westminster, 1963. ―――. *The Mission and Achievement of Jesus.* SBT 1.12. London: SCM, 1967. **Gaechter, P.** *Die literarische Kunst im Matthäusevangelium.* SBS 7. Stuttgart: Katholisches Bibelwerk, 1965. **Gerhardsson, B.** *The Gospel Tradition.* ConBNT 15. Malmö: Gleerup, 1986. ―――. "Gottes Sohn als Diener Gottes: Agape und Himmelsherrschaft nach dem Matthäusevangelium." *ST* 27 (1973) 25–50. ―――. "'An ihren Früchten sollt ihr sie erkennen': Die Legitimitätsfrage in der matthäischen Christologie." *EvT* 42 (1982) 113–26. ―――. *Memory and Manuscript.* Tr. E. J. Sharpe.

ASNU 22. Lund: Gleerup, 1961. ————. *The Mighty Acts of Jesus according to the Gospel of Matthew.* Lund: Gleerup, 1979. ————. *Tradition and Transmission in Early Christianity.* ConBNT 20. Lund: Gleerup, 1964. **Giesen, H.** *Christliches Handeln: Eine redaktionskritische Untersuchung zum δικαιοσύνη-Begriff im Matthäus-Evangelium.* Frankfurt am Main: Lang, 1982. **Goulder, M. D.** *Midrash and Lection in Matthew.* London: SPCK, 1974. **Grässer, E.** *Das Problem der Parusieverzögerung in den synoptischen Evangelien und in der Apostelgeschichte.* 2nd ed. BZNW 22. Berlin: Töpelmann, 1966. **Gray, S. W.** *The Least of My Brothers: Matthew 25:31–46: A History of Interpretation.* SBLDS 114. Atlanta: Scholars, 1989. **Green, J. B.** *The Death of Jesus.* WUNT 2.33. Tübingen: Mohr, 1988. **Gundry, R. H.** *The Use of the Old Testament in St. Matthew's Gospel.* NovTSup 18. Leiden: Brill, 1967. **Hagner, D. A.** "Apocalyptic Motifs in the Gospel of Matthew: Continuity and Discontinuity." *HBT* 7 (1985) 53–82. ————. "Matthew, Gospel according to." In *The International Standard Bible Encyclopedia,* ed. G. W. Bromiley et al. Grand Rapids: Eerdmans, 1986. 3:280–88. ————. "Righteousness in Matthew's Theology." In *Worship, Theology and Ministry in the Early Church.* FS R. P. Martin, ed. M. J. Wilkins and T. Paige. Sheffield: JSOT, 1992. 101–20. ————. "The *Sitz im Leben* of the Gospel of Matthew." In *SBL 1985 Seminar Papers.* Atlanta: Scholars Press, 1985. 243–69. ————. *The Use of the Old and New Testaments in Clement of Rome.* NovTSup 34. Leiden: Brill, 1973. **Hahn, F.** *The Titles of Jesus in Christology.* New York: World, 1969. **Hare, D. R. A.** *The Theme of Jewish Persecution of Christians in the Gospel according to St. Matthew.* SNTSMS 6. Cambridge: Cambridge University, 1967. **Harrington, D. J.** "Matthean Studies Since Joachim Rohde." *HeyJ* 16 (1975) 375–88. **Hartman, L.** *Prophecy Interpreted.* ConBNT 1. Lund: Gleerup, 1966. **Harvey, A. E.** *Jesus and the Constraints of History.* Philadelphia: Westminster, 1982. **Hasler, V.** *Amen.* Zürich: Gotthelf, 1969. **Heil, J. P.** *The Death and Resurrection of Jesus: A Narrative-Critical Reading of Matthew 26–28.* Minneapolis: Fortress, 1991. **Held, H. J.** "Matthew as Interpreter of the Miracle Stories." In *Tradition and Interpretation in Matthew,* ed. G. Bornkamm et al. Philadelphia: Westminster, 1963. 165–299. **Hengel, M.** *The Atonement.* Philadelphia: Fortress, 1981. ————. *The Charismatic Leader and His Followers.* New York: Crossroad, 1981. ————. *Crucifixion in the Ancient World and the Folly of the Message of the Cross.* Philadelphia: Fortress, 1977. ————. *Judaism and Hellenism.* 2 vols. Philadelphia: Fortress, 1981. ————. *Property and Riches in the Ancient Church.* Philadelphia: Fortress, 1974. ————. *The Son of God.* Philadelphia: Fortress, 1976. **Hill, D.** *New Testament Prophecy.* Atlanta: John Knox, 1979. ————. "Some Recent Trends in Matthean Studies." *IBS* 1 (1979) 139–49. ————. "Son and Servant: An Essay on Matthean Christology." *JSNT* 6 (1980) 2–16. **Hoehner, H.** *Herod Antipas.* SNTSMS 17. Cambridge: Cambridge University, 1972. **Hoffmann, P.** *Studien zur Theologie der Logienquelle.* Münster: Aschendorf, 1972. ————, ed. *Orientierung an Jesus: Zur Theologie der Synoptiker.* Freiburg: Herder, 1973. **Houlden, J. L.** *Backward into Light: The Passion and Resurrection of Jesus according to Matthew and Mark.* London: SCM, 1987. **Hubbard, B. J.** *The Matthean Redaction of a Primitive Apostolic Commissioning: An Exegesis of Matthew 28:16–20.* SBLDS 19. Missoula, MT: Scholars, 1974. **Hübner, H.** *Das Gesetz in der synoptischen Tradition.* Witten: Luther-Verlag, 1973. **Hummel, R.** *Die Auseinandersetzung zwischen Kirche und Judentum im Matthäus-evangelium.* 2nd ed. BEvT 33. Munich: Kaiser, 1966. **Humphrey, H. M.** *The Relationship of Structure and Christology in the Gospel of Matthew.* New York: Fordham, 1977. **Iersel, B. M. F. van.** *"Der Sohn" in den synoptischen Jesusworten.* 2nd ed. NovTSup 3. Leiden: Brill, 1964. **Jeremias, J.** *Abba.* Göttingen: Vandenhoeck & Ruprecht, 1966. ————. *The Eucharistic Words of Jesus.* London: SCM, 1990. ————. *Jerusalem in the Time of Jesus.* 3rd ed. London: SCM, 1969. ————. *Jesus' Promise to the Nations.* 2nd ed. SBT 1.24. London: SCM, 1967. ————. *New Testament Theology: The Proclamation of Jesus.* New York: Macmillan, 1971. ————. *The Parables of Jesus.* New York: Scribner, 1972. ————. *The Prayers of Jesus.* Philadelphia: Fortress, 1978. **Johnson, M. D.** "Reflections on a Wisdom Approach to Matthew's Christology." *CBQ* 36 (1974) 44–64. **Juel, D.** *Messiah and Temple.* SBLDS 31. Missoula, MT: Scholars, 1977. ————. *Messianic Exegesis.* Philadelphia: Fortress, 1987. **Jülicher, A.** *Die Gleichnisreden Jesu.* 2 vols. 2nd ed. Tübingen: Mohr, 1911. **Käsemann, E.** *New Testament Questions of Today.*

Philadelphia: Fortress, 1969. **Kertelge, K.,** ed. *Der Tod Jesu.* QD 74. Freiburg: Herder, 1976. **Kilpatrick, G. D.** *The Origins of the Gospel according to St. Matthew.* Oxford: Clarendon, 1959. **Kingsbury, J. D.** *Jesus Christ in Matthew, Mark, and Luke.* Philadelphia: Fortress, 1981. ————. *Matthew.* Proclamation Commentaries. Philadelphia: Fortress, 1977. ————. *Matthew as Story.* Philadelphia: Fortress, 1986. ————. *Matthew: Structure, Christology, Kingdom.* Philadelphia: Fortress, 1975. ————. *The Parables of Jesus in Matthew 13.* Richmond: John Knox, 1969. ————. "The Title 'Kyrios' in Matthew's Gospel." *JBL* 94 (1975) 246–55. ————. "The Title 'Son of God' in Matthew's Gospel." *BTB* 5 (1975) 3–31. ————. "The Title 'Son of David' in Matthew's Gospel." *JBL* 95 (1976) 591–602. **Klauck, H.-J.** *Allegorie und Allegorese in synoptischen Gleichnistexten.* Münster: Aschendorff, 1978. **Kratz, R.** *Auferweckung als Befreiung: Eine Studie zur Passions- und Auferstehungstheologie des Matthäus.* SBS 65. Stuttgart: Katholisches Bibelwerk, 1973. **Kretzer, A.** *Die Herrschaft der Himmel und die Söhne des Reiches.* SBM 10. Stuttgart: Katholisches Bibelwerk, 1971. **Kruijf, T. de.** *Der Sohn des lebendigen Gottes.* AnBib 14. Rome: Biblical Institute, 1962. **Kümmel, W. G.** *Promise and Fulfilment.* SBT 23. London: SCM, 1961. **Künzel, G.** *Studien zum Gemeindeverständnis des Matthäus-Evangeliums.* Stuttgart: Calwer, 1978. **Kunzi, M.** *Das Naherwartungslogion Markus 9, 1 par.* BGBE 21. Tübingen: Mohr, 1977. **Kynes, W. L.** *A Christology of Solidarity: Jesus as the Representative of His People in Matthew.* Lanham, MD: University Press of America, 1991. **Ladd, G. E.** *The Presence of the Future.* Grand Rapids: Eerdmans, 1974. **Lange, J.** *Das Erscheinen des Auferstandenen im Evangelium nach Matthäus.* Würzburg: Echter, 1973. ————, ed. *Das Matthäus-Evangelium.* Wege der Forschung 525. Darmstadt: Wissenschaftliche Buchgesellschaft, 1980. **Lee, M. Y.-H.** *Jesus und die jüdische Autorität.* FB 56. Würzburg: Echter, 1986. **Lentzen-Deis, F.** *Die Taufe Jesu nach den Synoptikern.* FTS 4. Frankfurt: Knecht, 1970. **Léon-Dufour, X.** *Études d'Évangile.* Paris: Editions du Seuil, 1965. **Levine, A. J.** *The Social and Ethnic Dimensions of Matthean Salvation History: "Go nowhere among the Gentiles . . ." (Matt 10:5b).* Lewiston, NY: Mellen, 1988. **Lindars, B.** *New Testament Apologetic.* London: SCM, 1961. **Linnemann, E.** *Studien zur Passionsgeschichte.* FRLANT 102. Göttingen: Vandenhoeck & Ruprecht, 1970. **Ljungman, H.** *Das Gesetz erfüllen.* Lund: Gleerup, 1954. **Lohse, E.** *History of the Suffering and Death of Jesus Christ.* Philadelphia: Fortress, 1967. **Loos, H. van der.** *The Miracles of Jesus.* NovTSup 8. Leiden: Brill, 1965. **Lührmann, D.** *Die Redaktion der Logienquelle.* WMANT 33. Neukirchen-Vluyn: Neukirchener, 1969. **Luz, U.** "The Disciples in the Gospel according to Matthew." In *The Interpretation of Matthew,* ed. G. Stanton. Philadelphia/London: Fortress/SPCK, 1983. 98–128. ————. "Die Erfüllung des Gesetzes bei Matthäus (Mt 5.17–20)." *ZTK* 75 (1978) 398–435. ————. "Die Wundergeschichten von Mt 8–9." In *Tradition and Interpretation in the New Testament.* FS E. E. Ellis, ed. G. F. Hawthorne and O. Betz. Grand Rapids/Tübingen: Eerdmans/Mohr, 1987. 149–65. **Malina, B. J.,** and **Neyrey, J. H.** *Calling Jesus Names: The Social Value of Labels in Matthew.* Sonoma, CA: Polebridge, 1988. **Manson, T. W.** *The Sayings of Jesus.* 2nd ed. London: SCM, 1949. ————. *The Servant-Messiah.* Cambridge: Cambridge University, 1953. ————. *The Teaching of Jesus.* 2nd ed. Cambridge: Cambridge University, 1935. **Marcus, J.** *The Mystery of the Kingdom of God.* SBLDS 90. Atlanta: Scholars, 1986. **Marguerat, D.** *Le Jugement dans l'Évangile de Matthieu.* Geneva: Éditions Labor et Fides, 1981. **Martin, R. P.** "St. Matthew's Gospel in Recent Study." *ExpTim* 80 (1968–69) 132–36. **Massaux, E.** *The Influence of the Gospel of Saint Matthew in the Christian Literature before Saint Irenaeus.* Tr. N. J. Belval and S. Hecht. Ed. A. J. Bellinzoni. 2 vols. New Gospel Studies 5.1–2. Leuven/Macon, GA: Peters/Mercer, 1990, 1992. **Matera, F. J.** *Passion Narratives and Gospel Theologies.* New York: Paulist, 1986. **McConnell, R. S.** *Law and Prophecy in Matthew's Gospel.* Basel: Reinhardt, 1969. **McGuckin, J.** *The Transfiguration of Christ in Scripture and Tradition.* Lewiston, NY: Mellen, 1986. **Meier, J. P.** *Law and History in Matthew's Gospel.* AnBib 71. Rome: Biblical Institute, 1976. ————. *The Vision of Matthew: Christ, Church and Morality in the First Gospel.* New York: Paulist, 1979. **Merklein, H.** *Jesu Botschaft von der Gottesherrschaft.* SBS 11. Stuttgart: Katholisches Bibelwerk, 1983. **Metzger, B. M.** *A Textual Commentary on the Greek New Testament.* New York: United Bible Societies, 1971. **Meyer, B. F.** *The Aims of Jesus.* London: SCM, 1979. **Minear, P. S.**

Commands of Christ. Edinburgh: St. Andrew, 1972. ————. *Matthew: The Teacher's Gospel.* New York: Pilgrim, 1982. **Moffatt, J.** *An Introduction to the Literature of the New Testament.* 3rd ed. New York: Scribner's, 1922. **Mohrlang, R.** *Matthew and Paul: A Comparison of Ethical Perspectives.* SNTSMS 48. Cambridge: Cambridge University, 1984. **Montefiore, C. G.** *Rabbinic Literature and Gospel Teachings.* London: Macmillan, 1930. **Moo, D. J.** *The Old Testament in the Gospel Passion Narratives.* Sheffield: Almond, 1983. **Moore, A. L.** *The Parousia in the New Testament.* NovTSup 13. Leiden: Brill, 1966. **Moore, G. F.** *Judaism in the First Centuries of the Christian Era.* 3 vols. Cambridge, MA: Harvard University, 1955–58. **Moore, S. D.** *Literary Criticism and the Gospels: The Theoretical Challenge.* New Haven: Yale, 1989. **Moule, C. F. D.** *Essays in New Testament Interpretation.* Cambridge: Cambridge University, 1982. ————. *The Phenomenon of the New Testament.* SBT 2.1. London: SCM, 1967. **Neirynck, F.** *The Minor Agreements of Matthew and Luke against Mark.* BETL 37. Louvain: Louvain University, 1974. **Nepper-Christensen, P.** *Das Matthäusevangelium: Ein judenchristliches Evangelium?* Aarhus: Universitetsforlaget, 1954. **Newman, B. M.,** and **Stine, P. C.** *A Translator's Handbook on the Gospel of Matthew.* New York: United Bible Societies, 1988. **Nissen, A.** *Gott und der Nächste im antiken Judentum.* WUNT 15. Tübingen: Mohr, 1974. **Nolan, B.** *The Royal Son of God: The Christology of Mt 1–2.* OBO 23. Göttingen: Vandenhoeck & Ruprecht, 1979. **Ogawa, A.** *L'histoire de Jésus chez Matthieu: La signification de l'histoire pour la théologie matthéenne.* Frankfurt am Main: Lang, 1979. **Orton, D. E.** *The Understanding Scribe and the Apocalyptic Ideal.* JSNTSup 25. Sheffield: JSOT, 1989. **Overman, J. A.** *The Gospel of Matthew and Formative Judaism: A Study of the Social World of the Matthean Community.* Minneapolis: Fortress, 1990. **Percy, R.** *Die Botschaft Jesu.* Lund: Gleerup, 1953. **Pesch, R.** *Jesu ureigene Taten?* QD 52. Freiburg: Herder, 1970. ————. *Naherwartungen: Tradition und Redaktion in Mk 13.* Düsseldorf: Patmos, 1968. **Piper, J.** *"Love Your Enemies."* SNTSMS 38. Cambridge: Cambridge University, 1979. **Piper, R. A.** *Wisdom in the Q-Tradition: The Aphoristic Teaching of Jesus.* SNTSMS 61. Cambridge: Cambridge University, 1989. **Polag, A.** *Die Christologie der Logienquelle.* WMANT 45. Neukirchen-Vluyn: Neukirchener, 1979. ————. *Fragmenta Q.* Neukirchen-Vluyn: Neukirchener, 1979. **Przybylski, B.** *Righteousness in Matthew and His World of Thought.* SNTSMS 41. Cambridge: Cambridge University, 1980. **Reumann, J.** *Righteousness in the New Testament.* Philadelphia: Fortress, 1982. ————. *The Supper of the Lord.* Philadelphia: Fortress, 1985. **Riches, J.** *Jesus and the Transformation of Judaism.* New York: Seabury, 1980. **Ridderbos, H.** *Matthew's Witness to Jesus Christ.* New York: Association Press, 1958. **Riesenfeld, H.** *The Gospel Tradition and Its Beginnings.* London: Mowbray, 1961. **Riesner, R.** *Jesus als Lehrer.* WUNT 2.7. Tübingen: Mohr, 1981. **Rigaux, B.** *The Testimony of St. Matthew.* Chicago: Franciscan Herald, 1968. **Riley, H.** *The First Gospel.* Macon, GA: Mercer, 1992. **Robertson, A. T.** *A Grammar of the Greek New Testament in Light of Historical Research.* 4th ed. New York: Hodder & Stoughton, 1923. **Roloff, J.** *Das Kerygma und der irdische Jesus.* Göttingen: Vandenhoeck & Ruprecht, 1970. **Rothfuchs, W.** *Die Erfüllungszitate des Matthäus-Evangeliums.* BWANT 88. Stuttgart: Kohlhammer, 1969. **Sand, A.** *Das Gesetz und die Propheten: Untersuchungen zur Theologie des Evangeliums nach Matthäus.* Biblische Untersuchungen 11. Regensburg: Pustet, 1974. ————. *Das Matthäus-Evangelium.* Erträge der Forschung 275. Darmstadt: Wissenschaftliche Buchgesellschaft, 1991. ————. "Propheten, Weise, und Schriftkundige in der Gemeinde des Matthäusevangeliums." In *Die Kirche im Werden,* ed. J. Hainz. Munich: Schöningh, 1976. 167–85. **Schaberg, J.** *The Father, the Son and the Holy Spirit: The Triadic Phrase in Matthew 28:19b.* SBLDS 19. Chico, CA: Scholars, 1982. **Schenk, W.** *Die Sprache des Matthäus.* Göttingen: Vandenhoeck & Ruprecht, 1987. **Schenke, L.,** ed. *Studien zum Matthäusevangelium.* Stuttgart: Katholisches Bibelwerk, 1988. **Schlatter, A.** *Die Kirche des Matthäus.* Gütersloh: Bertelsmann, 1929. **Schmidt, T. E.** *Hostility to Wealth in the Synoptic Tradition.* JSNTSup 15. Sheffield: JSOT, 1987. **Schnackenburg, R.** "Petrus im Matthäusevangelium." In *À cause de l'Évangile: Études sur les Synoptiques et les Actes.* FS J. Dupont, ed. F. Refoulé. LD 123. Paris: Cerf, 1985. 107–25. ————. *Schriften zum Neuen Testament.* Munich: Kösel, 1971. ———— **et al.,** eds. *Die Kirche des Anfangs.* FS H. Schürmann. Freiburg: Herder, 1978. **Schottroff, L.** "Das geschundene Volk und die

Arbeit in der Ernte: Gottes Volk nach dem Matthäusevangelium." In *Mitarbeiter der Schöpfung: Bibel und Arbeitswelt*, ed. L. and W. Schottroff. Munich: Kaiser, 1983. **Schulz, S.** *Q: Die Spruchquelle der Evangelisten*. Zürich: Theologischer, 1972. ————. *Die Stunde der Botschaft*. Hamburg: Furche, 1967. **Schürer, E.** *The History of the Jewish People in the Age of Jesus Christ*. Rev. ed. Ed. G. Vermes et al. 3 vols. Edinburgh: T. & T. Clark, 1973–87. **Schürmann, H.** *Jesu ureigener Tod*. Freiburg: Herder, 1975. ————. *Traditionsgeschichtliche Untersuchungen zu den synoptischen Evangelien*. Düsseldorf: Patmos, 1968. **Schweizer, E.** "Gesetz und Enthusiasmus bei Matthäus." In *Beiträge zur Theologie des Neuen Testaments*, ed. E. Schweizer. Zürich: Zwingli, 1970. 49–70. ————. *Matthäus und seine Gemeinde*. SBS 71. Stuttgart: Katholisches Bibelwerk, 1974. ————. "Matthew's Church." In *The Interpretation of Matthew*, ed. G. Stanton. Philadelphia/London: Fortress/SPCK, 1983. 129–55. **Senior, D.** *Invitation to Matthew*. Garden City: Doubleday, 1977. ————. *The Passion of Jesus in the Gospel of Matthew*. Wilmington, DE: Glazier, 1985. ————. *What are they saying about Matthew?* New York: Paulist, 1983. **Shuler, P. L.** *A Genre for the Gospels: The Biographical Character of Matthew*. Philadelphia: Fortress, 1982. **Sigal, P.** *The Halakah of Jesus of Nazareth according to the Gospel of Matthew*. Lanham, MD: University Press of America, 1986. **Soares-Prabhu, G. M.** *The Formula Quotations in the Infancy Narrative of Matthew*. AnBib 63. Rome: Biblical Institute, 1976. **Solages, M. de.** *La composition des Évangiles de Luc et de Matthieu et leurs sources*. Leiden: Brill, 1973. **Stanton, G. N.** *A Gospel for a New People: Studies in Matthew*. Edinburgh: T. & T. Clark, 1992. ————. "The Origin and Purpose of Matthew's Gospel: Matthean Scholarship from 1945 to 1980." In *ANRW* 2.25.3 (1983) 1889–1951. ————, ed. *The Interpretation of Matthew*. Philadelphia/London: Fortress/SPCK, 1983. **Stendahl, K.** *The School of St. Matthew*. 2nd ed. Philadelphia: Fortress, 1968. **Stonehouse, N. B.** *The Witness of Matthew and Mark to Christ*. 2nd ed. Grand Rapids: Eerdmans, 1958. **Strauss, D. F.** *The Life of Jesus Critically Examined*. 1892. Philadelphia: Fortress, 1972. **Strecker, G.** "The Concept of History in Matthew." In *The Interpretation of Matthew*, ed. G. Stanton. Philadelphia/London: Fortress/SPCK, 1983. 67–84. ————. *Der Weg der Gerechtigkeit: Untersuchung zur Theologie des Matthäus*. FRLANT 82. Göttingen: Vandenhoeck & Ruprecht, 1962. **Stuhlmacher, P.** *Jesus von Nazareth—Christus des Glaubens*. Stuttgart: Calwer, 1988. ————, ed. *The Gospel and the Gospels*. Grand Rapids: Eerdmans, 1991. **Suggs, M. J.** *Wisdom, Christology and Law in Matthew's Gospel*. Cambridge, MA: Harvard University, 1970. **Suhl, A.** "Der Davidssohn im Matthäus-Evangelium." *ZNW* 59 (1968) 36–72. **Taylor, V.** *The Historical Evidence for the Virgin Birth*. Oxford: Clarendon, 1920. **Telford, W. R.** *The Barren Temple and the Withered Tree*. JSNTSup 1. Sheffield: JSOT, 1980. **Theissen, G.** *The Miracle Stories of the Early Christian Tradition*. Philadelphia: Fortress, 1983. **Thompson, W. G.** *Matthew's Advice to a Divided Community: Mt. 17,22–18,35*. AnBib 44. Rome: Biblical Institute, 1970. **Tilborg, S. van.** *The Jewish Leaders in Matthew*. Leiden: Brill, 1972. **Trilling, W.** "Amt und Amtsverständnis bei Matthäus." In *Mélanges bibliques*. FS B. Rigaux, ed. A. Descamps. Gembloux: Duculot, 1969. 29–44. ————. *Studien zur Jesusüberlieferung*. Stuttgarter biblische Aufsatzbände 1. Stuttgart: Katholisches Bibelwerk, 1988. ————. *Das wahre Israel: Studien zur Theologie des Matthäusevangeliums*. 3rd ed. Leipzig: St. Benno, 1975. **Turner, N.** *A Grammar of New Testament Greek: Vol. 3. Syntax*. Edinburgh: T. & T. Clark, 1963. **Verseput, D.** *The Rejection of the Humble Messianic King: A Study of the Composition of Matthew 11–12*. Frankfurt am Main: Lang, 1986. **Vögtle, A.** *Das Evangelium und die Evangelien*. Düsseldorf: Patmos, 1971. **Walker, R.** *Die Heilsgeschichte im ersten Evangelium*. FRLANT 91. Göttingen: Vandenhoeck & Ruprecht, 1967. **Walter, N.** "Zum Kirchenverständnis des Matthäus." *Theologische Versuche* 12 (1981) 25–46. **Weder, H.** *Die Gleichnisse Jesu als Metaphern*. FRLANT 120. Göttingen: Vandenhoeck & Ruprecht, 1984. **Weiser, A.** *Die Knechtsgleichnisse der synoptischen Evangelien*. SANT 10. Munich: Kösel, 1971. **Westcott, B. W.** *An Introduction to the Study of the Gospels*. London: Macmillan, 1875. **Westerholm, S.** *Jesus and Scribal Authority*. ConBNT 10. Lund: Gleerup, 1978. **White, R. E. O.** *The Mind of Matthew*. Philadelphia: Westminster, 1979. **Wilkins, M. J.** *The Concept of Disciple in Matthew's Gospel*. NovTSup 59. Leiden: Brill, 1988. **Wink, W.** *John the Baptist in the Gospel Tradition*. SNTSMS 7. Cambridge:

Cambridge University, 1968. **Wrede, W.** *The Messianic Secret.* Cambridge, MA: Clarke, 1971.
Zeller, D. *Die weisheitlichen Mahnsprüche bei den Synoptikern.* Würzburg: Echter, 1977.
Zumstein, J. *La condition du croyant dans l'Évangile selon Matthieu.* OBO 16. Göttingen:
Vandenhoeck & Ruprecht, 1977.

Introduction

Bibliography

France, R. T. *Matthew: Evangelist and Teacher.* Grand Rapids: Zondervan, 1989. **Guthrie, D.** *New Testament Introduction.* 4th ed. Leicester/Downers Grove: Apollos/InterVarsity, 1990. 28–60. **Harrington, D. J.** "Matthean Studies since Joachim Rohde." *HeyJ* 16 (1975) 375–88. **Hill, D.** "Some Recent Trends in Matthean Studies." *IBS* 1 (1979) 139-49. **Kümmel, W. G.** *Introduction to the New Testament.* Rev. ed. Nashville: Abingdon, 1975. 101–21. **Martin, R. P.** *New Testament Foundations.* Grand Rapids: Eerdmans, 1975. 1:224–43. —————. "St. Matthew's Gospel in Recent Study." *ExpTim* 80 (1969) 132–36. **Sand, A.** *Das Matthäus-Evangelium.* Erträge der Forschung 275. Darmstadt: Wissenschaftliche Buchgesellschaft, 1991. **Senior, D.** *What Are They Saying about Matthew?* New York: Paulist, 1983. **Stanton, G.** "The Origin and Purpose of Matthew's Gospel: Matthean Scholarship from 1945 to 1980." *ANRW* 2.25.3 (1985) 1889-1951. **Wikenhauser, A.**, and **Schmid, J.** *Einleitung in das Neue Testament.* 6th, new ed. Freiburg/Basel/Wien: Herder, 1973. 224–47.

ABOUT THE PRESENT COMMENTARY

Bibliography

Bauer, D. R. "The Major Characters of Matthew's Story: Their Function and Significance." *Int* 46 (1992) 357–67. **Edwards, R. A.** *Matthew's Story of Jesus.* Philadelphia: Fortress, 1985. —————. "Reading Matthew." *Listening* 24 (1989) 251–61. **Howell, D. B.** *Matthew's Inclusive Story: A Study in the Narrative Rhetoric of the First Gospel.* JSNTSup 42. Sheffield: JSOT, 1990. **Kingsbury, J. D.** *Matthew as Story.* 2nd ed. Philadelphia: Fortress, 1988. —————. "The Plot of Matthew's Story." *Int* 46 (1992) 347–56. **Moore, S. D.** *Literary Criticism and the Gospels: The Theoretical Challenge.* New Haven/London: Yale University, 1989. **Powell, M.** *What is Narrative Criticism?* Minneapolis: Fortress, 1990. —————. "Toward a Narrative-Critical Understanding of Matthew." *Int* 46 (1992) 341–46. **Thiselton, A. C.** *New Horizons in Hermeneutics: The Theory and Practice of Transforming Biblical Reading.* Grand Rapids: Zondervan, 1992.

It is not an exaggeration to say that a paradigm shift is currently taking place in the study of the Gospels (see the stimulating and insightful analyses of Moore and Thiselton). Whereas the Gospels have previously been approached mainly as historical documents, now they are being studied very deliberately as literature. Previously the Gospels were regarded as windows to the past through which one could look in order to gain historical or theological information about the earliest Christian communities and perhaps about events that occurred in the first century. Now they are increasingly regarded as documents worth studying in their own right, apart altogether from any referential aspect. They are stories with self-contained worlds; they are whole narratives with, among other things, plots, subplots, characters, narrators, implied authors, and implied readers. The study of these matters has given rise to a new discipline called *narrative criticism,* sometimes also called the new literary criticism (to distinguish it from earlier literary criticism that was a part of the historical approach).

This new approach to the Gospels is to be welcomed since unquestionably it enriches our understanding of these documents. At the same time, however, two unresolved problems face the proponents of narrative criticism. First, what are the implications of a non-referential approach to these writings so far as the importance of historical knowledge is concerned? Some narrative critics unfortunately would rule out historical interests altogether as being inappropriate, if not illegitimate. Second, what is the role of the actual reader in a narrative-critical understanding of the Gospels? Once these writings are viewed rather strictly as literature, as works of art, does not the reader have the right to see what he or she will—as in the reading of a great novel? That is, does not narrative criticism entail what is called a reader-response hermeneutic, wherein the reader constitutes the meaning of the text entirely apart from any consideration of the intention of the author?

There are without question valuable insights to be gained from narrative criticism. Many advocates rightly see that narrative criticism can be used together with historical exegesis in a complementary way and that its insights need not exclude the propriety of interest in an author's intended meaning. When work on this commentary was begun fifteen years ago, the concerns of narrative criticism were still relatively new and had not built up the head of steam they presently have. Even were I beginning today, however, I would not change the basic historical orientation of the commentary. The reason for this will become clear from the following remarks on the purpose of a commentary.

What the text meant. A commentator is someone who places herself or himself between the text—in this case an ancient text—and the current generation of readers of the text as a kind of mediator. The commentator thus looks in two directions: on the one hand—and primarily—to the text; on the other hand, to the readers of the text who will also become his or her readers. The goal of a commentary, simply put, is to help the reader understand the text. Although it will hardly occur to the average uninitiated reader, the exegete will almost immediately think of the distinction between what a text meant and what a text means.

The first and main purpose of a commentary is to help the reader to discover what the text meant in its original setting—that is, *exegesis*. The chief goal of the commentator is thus to arrive at the fruit of what has been known traditionally as grammatical-historical exegesis. The commentator must help the reader as much as possible to step into the past by providing at least the rudimentary knowledge necessary to comprehend what the original writer said to the original readers and then lead the readers to a line-by-line understanding and appreciation of that meaning as well as, of course, of the work as a whole. The supreme responsibility of the commentator is to the text as it is. For the exegete, the text is an autonomous datum. The autonomy of the text here does not mean that the text warrants any interpretation of it whatsoever. Such a view can only undermine the text. On the contrary, the text is meant to be sovereign over the interpreter, and the exegete is first and foremost the servant of the text—i.e., of the meaning of the text, or what the text wants to be and to say.

For all their similarity to the story form, the Gospels are intended as historical narratives and can be properly understood only when they are taken seriously as such. The evangelists—even the author of the Fourth Gospel—would be scandalized by non-referential approaches to their writings. And if strictly text-oriented approaches would have been unacceptable to them, much more would they be offended by strictly reader-oriented (i.e., reader-response) approaches. They would hardly have looked kindly upon the idea that readers have the right to make whatever they like of their Gospels as long as it is interesting, entertaining, or "relevant." The evangelists have a story to tell, yes. But the story concerns above all what happened in history. For this reason the historical-critical approach is both indispensable and of a higher order of importance than literary- or narra-tive-critical approaches.

The latter can, of course, be regarded as contributing to historical and theo-logical understanding of the Gospels. Historical and literary approaches should be regarded as complementary rather than mutually exclusive. Indeed, literary interests have always been a part of the historical approach itself. Thus, although the present commentary could not be considered a narrative-critical commen-tary, observations *are* made that are literary-critical in nature. For example, despite the fragmentary character of the pericope-by-pericope format, much attention is devoted to the flow of the narrative and the relationship between material that precedes and follows in the narrative as well as to material elsewhere in the Gos-pel, so that Matthew is treated as a unified and coherent document. Similarly, despite the attention devoted to redactional analysis, the finished form of the Gospel is of ultimate concern. Comments, furthermore, are made about such things as composition, characterization, turning points in the plot, and rhetori-cal features but without use of the technical jargon of narrative criticism.

Behind narrative-critical thinking, in the minds of some, is a pessimism con-cerning the very possibility of historical knowledge. There is, of course, much that we do not know about the Gospels. But we also possess a quite amazing amount of knowledge that may be judged as probable ("certainty" is not the lan-guage of historical research). Naturally there will be differences of opinion, but this should not be allowed to paralyze us or to keep us from evaluating argu-ments. If, for example, we are concerned with the life setting of the Gospel of Matthew and the relationship of his community to contemporary Judaism, there are two ways in which we may proceed. We may consider the constituent parts of the Gospel in light of the whole, and, second, we may observe the redactional changes Matthew makes in the use of his sources where the latter are available (Mark and indirectly Q). To be sure, there is a circularity in this process, whereby one conjectures a *Sitz im Leben* and then proceeds to interpret the text on the basis of the reconstruction to find, not surprisingly, that the texts support the hypothesis. There is a danger here, but it can also be overestimated. Every hy-pothesis, after all, involves a degree of circularity between explanatory theory and concrete data. It is often very difficult to advance in knowledge in any other way, especially when, as in the study of the Gospels, there is such a dearth of external data to help us. Consciousness of the danger and exegetical sensitivity will go a long way toward preventing abuse here.

What the text means. Of necessarily secondary importance, but still rightly within the purview of the commentator, is the problem of what the text means. But the question of what an ancient text may mean today—that is, what applications it may have—is, of course, a far more open-ended matter than what the text meant. Thus the commentator can hardly do more than indicate proper directions, and at times guard against improper ones, in which the text may be taken in modern application. Much here will depend on the interpretive community of which the commentator is a part and who the implied readers are thought to be.

With regard to our Gospels, we are in the very interesting and advantageous position of being able often to see how the writers took the traditions they received and applied them to the situation of *their* congregations, i.e., what they took the received tradition to mean to them. We have thus to keep in mind in reading the Gospels that we need to be sensitive to two life settings, the first being the time of Jesus itself and the second the time of the evangelist. What something came to signify in the second life setting may not be exactly what it signified in the first and original historical context. The interpretation of the event can, for example, have taken advantage of the light shed by the post-resurrection perspective that was, of course, not available in the original context. What the evangelists do with the traditions they received can accordingly serve as hermeneutical models for us in reaching for the kinds of significance the text may take on for our readers.

Matthew is particularly interesting here because of its widely admitted "transparency," wherein many individual narratives, without losing their historical character, are oriented toward the needs of the readers and indeed shaped accordingly. The disciples become paradigms for the Christians of Matthew's community: what is spoken to the former is spoken to the latter; what is demanded of and promised to the twelve is demanded of and promised to Matthew's church. Matthew's Gospel is above all a book for the church, not as merely the record of past history but as the handbook for the present experience of Christians. It is not difficult, even granting that the original readers were Jewish Christians, to find relevance for Christians at the end of the twentieth century.

The format of the Word Biblical Commentary lends itself well to accomplishing the purposes that have been referred to here. After a fresh translation with textual-critical and translation notes comes a section on Form/Structure/Setting, within which a variety of historical, formal, source, and redactional issues can be addressed. This is followed by verse-by-verse comment, concluding with a so-called explanation section, where specific, although necessarily brief, attention is given to the question of the present meaning of the text.

Objectivity and the commentator's perspective. Modern hermeneutical scholarship has shown that there is no such thing as an "objective" interpreter or interpretation. Every interpreter necessarily brings something to the text that affects the consequent interpretation. Worthy commentators will therefore be self-conscious, i.e., aware of their identity, background, and tradition—of all that goes into making them what they are—and how this in turn affects their perspective. Such an awareness will prevent them from too readily imposing preconceived opinions upon the text.

The problem, however, also has a positive aspect to it. Good commentators see their task as "theological exegesis." By this is meant exegesis that shares the faith commitment and priorities of the believing community, exegesis done, so to speak, "from within," exegesis concerned with the theological dimension and meaning of the text, and moreover, exegesis done within the context of the canon. Such exegesis can be very helpful in assisting readers to understand the text. Despite its dangers, we should hasten to add, theological exegesis does not mean uncritical exegesis.

The question of historicity. The purpose of a commentary, as we have seen, is to illuminate the text for the modern reader, *as it stands.* The historical question is another matter, although admittedly it does occasionally have a bearing on the exegesis of a text.

The present commentary presupposes without much argument that there is an essential historical core in every, or nearly every, pericope. The reasons for this can only be touched upon here. Matthew is relatively conservative in his handling of the traditional materials available to him (as can already be seen in his use of Mark). Furthermore, the oral tradition upon which Matthew depends for the sayings of Jesus was carefully transmitted and relatively stable (see below, "Oral Tradition in the Gospel of Matthew"). Had Matthew been in the habit of freely inventing material—sayings and narratives—we might expect quite a different Gospel from what we have. It is true that this means merely that Matthew relies upon tradition to which he has access. As to the historical reliability of that tradition, little more can be said than that this tradition is not far in time from the events themselves and that we choose to accept its integrity as a dependable account of the words and deeds of Jesus. There is furthermore, in addition to the questionability of the commentary as the appropriate forum for the debating of issues of historicity, the problem of space to consider. As a result, the present commentary discusses the question of historicity only in a handful of places where it is deemed absolutely necessary.

THE PAPIAS TRADITION CONCERNING MATTHEW

Bibliography

Black, M. "The Use of Rhetorical Terminology in Papias on Mark and Matthew." *JSNT* 37 (1989) 31–41. **Kennedy, G. A.** "Classical and Christian Source Criticism." In *The Relationships among the Gospels: An Interdisciplinary Dialogue*, ed. W. O. Walker, Jr. Trinity University Monograph Series in Religion 5. San Antonio: Trinity University, 1978. 125–55. **Körtner, U. H. J.** *Papias von Hierapolis: Ein Beitrag zur Geschichte des frühen Christentums.* FRLANT 133. Göttingen: Vandenhoeck & Ruprecht, 1983. **Kürzinger, J.** *Papias von Hierapolis und die Evangelien des Neuen Testaments.* Eichstätter Materialien 4, Abteilung Philosophie und Theologie. Regensburg: Pustet, 1983. **Meeks, W. A.** "Hypomnēmata from an Untamed Sceptic: A Response to George Kennedy." In *The Relationships among the Gospels: An Interdisciplinary Dialogue*, ed. W. O. Walker, Jr. Trinity University Monograph Series in Religion 5. San Antonio: Trinity University, 1978. 157–72. **Meredith, A.** "The Evidence of Papias for the Priority of Matthew." In *Synoptic Studies*, ed. C. M. Tuckett. JSNTSup 7. Sheffield: JSOT, 1984. 187–96. **Munck, J.** "Die Tradition über das Matthäusevangelium bei Papias." In *Neotestamentica et Patristica.* FS O. Cullmann, ed. W. C. van Unnik. NovTSup 6. Leiden: Brill, 1962. 249–60. **Schoedel, W. R.** "Papias." *ANRW* 2.27.1 (1992) 235–70. **Solages, B. de.** "Le témoignage de Papias." *Bulletin de littérature ecclésiastique* 71 (1970) 3–14. **Yarbrough, R. W.** "The Date of Papias: A Reassessment." *JETS* 26 (1983) 181–91.

The tantalizing statement of Papias from the first quarter of the second century (Körtner and Schoedel accept a date of 110; Yarbrough even earlier) is at once the earliest, most important, and most bewildering piece of early information we have concerning the origin of material associated with the name of the

Apostle Matthew. Some scholars believe that this testimony misled the entire early Church on the question of the origin of the Gospel of Matthew (cf. the statement of Irenaeus [c. 180] in *Adv. Haer.* 3.1.1, cited also by Eusebius in *H.E.* 5.8.2, who also refers to Matthew writing now "a gospel" [εὐαγγελίου] "for the Hebrews in their own dialect [τῇ ἰδίᾳ αὐτῶν διαλέκτῳ]," words clearly dependent upon Papias or a similar tradition; cf. too Eusebius, *H.E.* 5.10.3, for a similar statement from Pantaenus later in the second century, and *H.E.* 6.25.4, for the view of Origen as quoted by Eusebius; cf. *H.E.* 3.24.6).

Papias was the bishop of Hierapolis in Asia Minor and the author of a five-volume commentary entitled *Exegesis of the Oracles of the Lord* (Λογίων κυριακῶν ἐξηγήσεως [Eusebius, *H.E.* 3.39.1]). This work has not survived, however, and we know it only through the quotations that have been mediated to us by the fourth-century church historian Eusebius. In Book Three of his *History of the Church* (3.39.16), after recording Papias' statement of the testimony of John the Elder concerning the Gospel of Mark, Eusebius adds this comment of Papias concerning Matthew: "Matthew for his part compiled the oracles in the Hebrew [Aramaic] dialect and every person translated them as he was able" (Ματθαῖος μὲν οὖν Ἑβραΐδι διαλέκτῳ τὰ λόγια συνετάξατο, ἡρμήνευσεν δ᾽ αὐτὰ ὡς ἦν δυνατὸς ἕκαστος). Nearly every element in this sentence can be understood in more than one way (see France [*Matthew: Evangelist and Teacher*, 56–57] for a helpful display of the options).

Of key importance to the understanding of this passage is the meaning of λόγια (*logia*). The early Church soon took it to refer to the Gospel of Matthew itself and hence also to establish the priority of Matthew over the other Gospels. Those who "interpreted" became, on this view, the authors of Mark and Luke, for example, who made use of Matthew as their main source. Although *logia* means strictly "oracles," and thus most naturally an account of words rather than deeds, the word was also used by Papias in referring to the Gospel of Mark (*H.E.* 3.39.15). Further to be noted is its use in the title of Papias' own commentary, which was probably not restricted to the words of Jesus. There are two other options, however, that must be mentioned. More in keeping with a literal understanding of the word, *logia* could possibly refer to words of the OT, as is the case in the early fathers (e.g., *1 Clem.* 53:1; 62:3; Clement of Alexandria, *Stromata* 7.18). In view then might be the distinctive OT quotations in the Gospel of Matthew, the so-called messianic *testimonia* (thus J. R. Harris and V. Burch, *Testimonies*, 2 vols. [Cambridge: Cambridge University, 1916–20]; T. H. Robinson, xv). That these may have needed interpretation or explanation is obvious. A further possibility, however, is that *logia* refers only to the words of Jesus, in which case it could be taken, for example, as referring to an Aramaic version of Q (thus already Schleiermacher in 1892 ["Über die Zeugnisse des Papias von unsern beiden ersten Evangelien," *Theologische Studien und Kritiken* 5 (1892) 735–68]; more recently T. W. Manson, *Sayings of Jesus*, 28–30; B. de Solages; and M. Black).

The interpretation of the word *logia* is naturally dependent on the meaning of the other components of the Papias tradition. Two options present themselves so far as Ἑβραΐδι διαλέκτῳ is concerned. The most natural understanding of the words is "in the Hebrew language," by which is probably meant Aramaic. It is possible, however, that the word "dialect" is to be understood in a special sense, as documented among ancient technical rhetoricians, to mean "in a Semitic style" (thus Kürzinger, 9–32, 43–67; Gundry, 619–20), referring to the general Jewish "style" or character of the Gospel. In this view, the verb ἑρμηνεύειν must be taken in the sense of "to explain" rather than "to translate." But did the Jewish character of the Gospel of Matthew really need explanation? And would the task of explanation have been so challenging as to explain Papias' words "as each was able"? The combination of the term διάλεκτος with the verb ἑρμηνεύειν points, on the contrary, to the natural meaning "to translate a language" (thus rightly France, who regards it as "most unlikely" that the combination of terms would have been understood in any other way by a Greek reader [*Matthew: Evangelist and Teacher*, 57]; cf. Schoedel, 258).

If the conclusion is fairly secure that Papias (or John before him) spoke of something in Aramaic that was then translated into Greek, we may return to the discussion of the word *logia*. The major difficulties with the conclusion that it refers to the original Gospel of Matthew are that our Greek Matthew reveals no signs of having been translated from Aramaic (but note the caution of Davies-Allison [1:13], who indicate the difficulty of establishing this point) and that there is abundant evidence that Matthew's Greek is dependent upon Mark. Thus advocates of the priority of Matthew who appeal to the Papias testimony must also argue that the translator had Mark before him and that he simultaneously redacted Mark's Greek as he translated the putative Aramaic Matthew. Though not impossible, this solution remains improbable. There is, furthermore, as we have seen, the problem that *logia* is an improbable word (though again not an impossible one) to refer to a Gospel. The use of the word to refer to Mark in the Papias testimony concerning that Gospel does not necessarily guarantee that it means "gospel" in the Matthean reference. (The two passages, though consecutive in Eusebius, may have been from different contexts in Papias.) That there was at least one (perhaps more than one) Gospel in Aramaic or Hebrew known to the early Church (e.g., the Gospel of the Ebionites, the Gospel of the Nazoraeans, the Gospel according to the Hebrews) may have added to the confusion caused by Papias's statement, wrongly tempting the early church fathers to think of the Gospel of Matthew. (The recently published *The Gospel of Matthew according to a Primitive Hebrew Text* [Macon, GA; Mercer University, 1987], a fourteenth-century work, is regarded by its editor, G. Howard, as independent of, though perhaps in its old Hebrew substratum serving as the model for, the canonical Greek Gospel.)

What of the other two options for the meaning of *logia* mentioned above? We now have evidence of the collection of OT prophecies or prooftexts concerning the Messiah or messianic fulfillment (see at Qumran 4QTestimonia). That Matthew might have collected these together in the original Hebrew language seems feasible, especially given the conspicuous use of the OT in the Gospel (see below). Such a conclusion fits both the point about translation from Hebrew and also the use of the word *logia* to refer to the OT. The inference that what is in view in the Papias statement is a collection of *testimonia*, however, is purely speculative. The collection has not survived, except perhaps in the quotations of the Gospel itself, and there is no evidence of others having translated or interpreted such OT prooftexts.

More probable is the hypothesis that *logia* refers to sayings of Jesus. The term *logia*, rather than the more normal *logoi*, is used because of the veneration of the words of Jesus, which were treasured as the supreme authority of the early Church.

Already by the time of Clement of Rome they were put alongside the words of the OT, even superseding them in authority (cf. *1 Clem.* 13). The words of Jesus were no less "the oracles" of God than were the OT Scriptures. Matthew, then, may have collected the sayings of Jesus in their original Aramaic, and these were in turn translated by others "as each was able," which could nicely account for some differences among the Synoptic renderings of the sayings. It is conceivable that this collection was what we call Q or more precisely the Aramaic material that underlay Q. On the other hand, what Papias (or John) may have had in mind is the material contained in the five major discourses of the Gospel. These discourses are one of the major distinctives of Matthew. Perhaps the apostle was responsible for the collection of the core material of these discourses, the so-called M material (i.e., the special material or *Sondergut*). Such a collection would in effect be a proto-Matthew and could explain how the apostle Matthew's name eventually became attached to the Gospel (cf. Allen, lxxx–lxxxi). We are, of course, also here necessarily limited to speculation. But a solution such as this is most consistent with the testimony of Papias. And it seems better to take this early piece of evidence seriously rather than to dismiss it as being dead wrong. Papias had reasons for saying what he did, and although our knowledge now is partial, we do well to attempt to make sense of his testimony.

MATTHEW'S SOURCES

Bibliography

Butler, B. C. *The Originality of St. Matthew: A Critique of the Two-Document Hypothesis.* Cambridge: Cambridge University, 1951. **Chapman, J.** *Matthew, Mark, Luke: A Study in the Order and Interrelation of the Synoptic Gospels.* London/New York: Longmans, Green & Co., 1937. **Dungan, D. L.** "Mark—The Abridgement of Matthew and Luke." In *Jesus and Man's Hope,* ed. D. G. Miller. Pittsburgh: Pittsburgh Theological Seminary, 1970. 1:51–97. **Farmer, W. R.** *The Synoptic Problem: A Critical Analysis.* 2nd ed. Dillsboro, NC: Western North Carolina, 1976. ———, ed. *New Synoptic Studies.* Macon, GA: Mercer University, 1983. **Fitzmyer, J. A.** "The Priority of Mark and the 'Q' Source in Luke." In *Jesus and Man's Hope,* ed. D. G. Miller. Pittsburgh: Pittsburgh Theological Seminary, 1970. 1:131–70. **Goulder, M. D.** *Luke: A New Paradigm.* JSNTSup 20. Sheffield: JSOT, 1989. **Gundry, R. H.** "Matthean Foreign Bodies in Agreements of Luke with Matthew against Mark: Evidence that Luke Used Matthew." In *The Four Gospels 1992.* FS F. Neirynck, ed. F. Van Segbroeck, C. M. Tuckett, G. Van Belle, and J. Verheyden. Leuven: Leuven University, 1992. 1467–95. **Kümmel, W. G.** *Introduction to the New Testament.* Nashville: Abingdon, 1975. 38–80. **Longstaff, T. R. W.** *Evidence of Conflation in Mark? A Study of the Synoptic Problem.* Missoula, MT: Scholars, 1977. **Orchard, B.** *Matthew, Luke and Mark.* Manchester: Koinonia, 1976. ——— and **Riley, H.** *The Order of the Synoptics: Why Three Synoptic Gospels?* Macon, GA: Mercer University, 1987. **Reicke, B.** *The Roots of the Synoptic Gospels.* Philadelphia: Fortress, 1986. **Riley, H.** *The First Gospel.* Macon, GA: Mercer University, 1992. **Rist, J. M.** *On the Independence of Matthew and Mark.* SNTSMS 32. Cambridge: Cambridge University, 1978. **Stoldt, H. H.** *History and Criticism of the Markan Hypothesis.* Macon, GA: Mercer University, 1980. **Styler, G.** "The Priority of Mark." In C. F. D. Moule, *The Birth of the New Testament.* 3rd ed. San Francisco: Harper & Row, 1981. 285–316. **Tuckett, C. M.** "Arguments from Order: Definition and Evaluation." In *Synoptic Studies,* ed. C. M. Tuckett. JSNTSup 7. Sheffield: JSOT, 1984. ———. *The Revival of the Griesbach Hypothesis: An Analysis and Appraisal.* SNTSMS 44. Cambidge: Cambridge University, 1983. **Vaganay, L.** *Le problème synoptique: Une hypothèse de travail.* Tournai:

Desclée, 1954. **Wenham, J.** *Redating Matthew, Mark and Luke.* Downers Grove, IL: InterVarsity, 1992.

Over the last two or three decades there has been much discussion of the hypothesis of Markan priority. This has been stimulated largely by the efforts of W. R. Farmer, who has given new visibility to the alternate view of Synoptic relationships known as the Griesbach hypothesis, viz., that Matthew was the first of the canonical Gospels to have been written and that it served as the source of both Luke and Mark, which was the latest of the three. Those behind the revival of this hypothesis (from the above bibliography, in addition to Farmer, Dungan, Longstaff, Orchard, and Stoldt) point out with some relish the various weaknesses of the so-called two-document hypothesis (i.e., Mark and Q as the sources of Matthew and Luke), especially, for example, the "minor agreements" between Matthew and Luke against Mark in triple-tradition material and those particular passages, relatively few in number, where it seems easier to argue that Mark has redacted Matthew rather than vice versa.

This new crusade to establish the priority of Matthew has not succeeded, however, in persuading NT scholarship as a whole. It has reminded us that hypotheses concerning the sources of the Synoptics and their interrelationship fall short of proof and that no theory is without its problems. Yet, if the two-source hypothesis has its problems, the Griesbach hypothesis is even more problematic. We need not go into the weaknesses of the latter here (for a refutation see Tuckett), but we may at least look briefly at the strengths of the former.

Matthew reproduces some 90 percent of Mark, much of it verbatim. In single pericopes drawn from Mark, Matthew's version is almost consistently more terse. Matthew has edited out unnecessary words, improving the syntax considerably. It is most unlikely that Mark would have added so many redundancies to Matthew's syntax had he been dependent on Matthew. Matthew furthermore improves Mark's Greek at many points. Again, it is unlikely that Mark would have produced his Greek while looking at Matthew's Greek. It is also the case that in the vast majority of instances, it is easier to explain why and how Matthew may have redacted Mark than vice versa. The Markan sequence of pericopes, finally, seems normative for the Synoptics in that Matthew and Luke never agree against the order of Mark: where Matthew departs from the Markan order, Luke follows it; where Luke departs from the Markan order, Matthew follows it (see especially Tuckett, "Order"). These facts together with Mark's directness and vividness, which itself makes it very unlikely that Mark is simply an abbreviation of Matthew and Luke, suggest the priority of Mark and the probability of Matthew's dependence upon Mark. That there was no need for an abridgement of Matthew, such as Mark represents according to the Griesbach hypothesis, is clear from the neglect of Mark in the Church once Matthew became available.

We need not present further argument for the two-source hypothesis here (see Tuckett, Fitzmyer, Styler, Kümmel). Suffice it to say that despite the reopening of the question by advocates of Matthean priority, the hypothesis of Markan priority has hardly been overthrown. The present commentary presupposes that Mark was Matthew's major source. Consistent redactional analysis has only confirmed the rightness of this presupposition.

Because of the great differences between the Gospels, it is most unlikely that the author of Matthew knew the Gospel of Luke or that the author of Luke knew the Gospel of Matthew (*pace* Goulder and Gundry). The result of this is that a second source is needed to explain the considerable amount of material common to Matthew and Luke but not found in Mark. This hypothetical source, known as Q, may have been a written document, but more probably it existed in the form of oral tradition with some relatively minor variations in different geographical regions. This oral tradition, which did not cease with the production of written Gospels, may well be the missing link that could explain certain phenomena whose presence is often raised against the two-source hypothesis—for example, the so-called minor agreements between Matthew and Luke against Mark in the "triple-tradition" passages.

The author of Matthew thus probably had as his two main sources Mark and Q. In addition to the oral tradition, represented by the Q material, however, he also apparently had access to further oral tradition, which is reflected in the special (i.e., unique) material in his Gospel. This material, usually designated as M, is only with difficulty to be thought of as a discrete source. Rather, it was probably a part of a larger stream of tradition, no doubt overlapping with Q, that we may speculatively associate in its original Aramaic form with the Apostle Matthew.

ORAL TRADITION IN THE GOSPEL OF MATTHEW

Bibliography

Davids, P. H. "The Gospels and Jewish Tradition: Twenty Years after Gerhardsson." In *Gospel Perspectives*, ed. R. T. France and D. Wenham. Sheffield: JSOT, 1980. 1:75-99. **Dunn, J. D. G.** "Matthew's Awareness of Markan Redaction." In *The Four Gospels 1992*. FS F. Neirynck, ed. F. Van Segbroeck, C. M. Tuckett, G. Van Belle, and J. Verheyden. Leuven: Leuven University, 1992. 1349-59. **Gerhardsson, B.** *The Gospel Tradition.* Lund: Gleerup, 1986. ————. *Memory and Manuscript: Oral Tradition and Written Transmission in Rabbinic Judaism and Early Christianity.* ASNU 22. Lund: Gleerup, 1961. ————. *The Origins of the Gospel Traditions.* Philadelphia: Fortress, 1979. ————. "The Path of the Gospel Tradition." In *The Gospel and the Gospels*, ed. P. Stuhlmacher. Grand Rapids: Eerdmans, 1991. 75–96. ————. *Tradition and Transmission in Early Christianity.* ConBNT 20. Lund: Gleerup, 1964. **Goulder, M. D.** *Midrash and Lection in Matthew.* London: SPCK, 1974. 137–52. **Hagner, D. A.** "The Sayings of Jesus in the Apostolic Fathers and Justin Martyr." In *Gospel Perspectives*, ed. D. Wenham. Sheffield: JSOT, 1984. 5:233-68. **Henaut, B. W.** *Oral Tradition and the Gospels: The Problem of Mark 4.* JSNTSup 82. Sheffield: JSOT, 1993. **Jeremias, J.** *New Testament Theology: The Proclamation of Jesus.* SCM: London, 1971. 1–37. **Kelber, W. H.** *The Oral and the Written Gospel: The Hermeneutics of Speaking and Writing in the Synoptic Tradition, Mark, Paul, and Q.* Philadelphia: Fortress, 1983. **Lohr, C. H.** "Oral Techniques in the Gospel of Matthew." *CBQ* 23 (1961) 403–35. **Riesenfeld, H.** *The Gospel Tradition.* Philadelphia: Fortress, 1970. 1–29. **Riesner, R.** *Jesus als Lehrer.* WUNT 2.7. 2nd ed. Tübingen: Mohr, 1984. **Theissen, G.** *The Gospels in Context: Social and Political History in the Synoptic Tradition.* Minneapolis: Fortress, 1991. 1–22. **Wansbrough, H.,** ed. *Jesus and the Oral Gospel Tradition.* JSNTSup 64. Sheffield: JSOT, 1991.

To a very large extent, the shape of the sayings of Jesus in the Gospel of Matthew reflects the parallelism and mnemonic devices of material designed for easy memorization. It is estimated that 80 percent of Jesus' sayings are in the form of *parallelismus membrorum* (Riesner), often of the antithetical variety. The symmetry involved in this poetry is often pointed out in the present commentary (on the poetry, see Goulder, 70–94). In its Aramaic substratum, the teaching of Jesus regularly contains such things as rhythm, alliteration, assonance, and paronomasia (see Jeremias, 20–29), and the evangelists (esp. Matthew) try sometimes to reflect these phenomena in Greek dress. All this we take to be the sign not so much of Matthew's imitation of the oral tradition (although Lohr rightly indicates that this happens) as of the actual preservation of oral tradition very much in the form in which it was probably given by Jesus.

That the sayings of Jesus (and the narratives of his deeds) constituted a sacred tradition from the very beginning is clear. The words that had been uttered by the one who had risen from the dead and who was now at the right hand of God were cherished and assigned a very high authority. The Swedish scholars H. Riesenfeld and especially B. Gerhardsson have shown the plausibility not only of the existence of such a holy tradition and its derivation from Jesus but also of the existence of a first-century milieu where memorization was a fundamentally important pedagogical tool, in which the careful transmission of the tradition along the lines of rabbinic transmission of oral Torah can have taken place. Gerhardsson's work has unjustly been dismissed by some because of his early appeal to memorization of the gospel tradition on the analogy of a rabbi and his *talmidim* (pupils). One objection was that the rabbinic model only existed after A.D. 70. While technically this may be true, it is exceedingly improbable that the process of transmitting oral tradition began only after 70 and that there was no memorizing of oral tradition in the time of Jesus. To be sure, originally Gerhardsson may have overdrawn the analogy. But that Jesus and his disciples constituted a group at least similar to a rabbi and his disciples can hardly be doubted. A further objection was that Gerhardsson had originally overstated his case about the stability of the oral tradition since the phenomena of the synoptic Gospels do not substantiate such a view. It is not unusual for the same sayings of Jesus in the synoptic Gospels to exhibit differences. Gerhardsson's view, however, does not rule out such minor variations, which may well be expected to occur in oral tradition that is perpetuated in different geographical regions, for example, nor does it rule out redactional activity. What is given some measure of guarantee in Gerhardsson's perspective is the relative stability of the tradition of Jesus' teaching as it is maintained initially by the disciples. This we judge to be historically correct, and it is assumed in this commentary.

One of the key reasons Jesus hand-picked disciples and taught them was for the very purpose that they might pass on his teaching after he had departed. That they would have taken this responsibility seriously seems self-evident. In Matthew, Jesus is presented as the "one teacher" ($\kappa\alpha\theta\eta\gamma\eta\tau\dot{\eta}\varsigma$, 23:10), and the commission at the end of the Gospel stresses the responsibility of the disciples to hand on Jesus' teachings (28:20). The Lukan prologue refers to the accounts of events that were "handed on [$\pi\alpha\rho\acute{\epsilon}\delta o\sigma\alpha\nu$] to us by those who from the beginning were eyewitnesses and servants [$\dot{\upsilon}\pi\eta\rho\acute{\epsilon}\tau\alpha\iota$] of the word" (Luke 1:2). These passages presuppose a carefully transmitted oral tradition. Similarly, we encounter the technical language of oral tradition ($\pi\alpha\rho\acute{\epsilon}\lambda\alpha\beta o\nu$, "I received," and $\pi\alpha\rho\acute{\epsilon}\delta\omega\kappa\alpha$, "I handed on") in Paul's account of the Lord's Supper in 1 Cor 11:23–26 (cf. the same verbs in 1 Cor 15:3, referring to the faithful handing on of the kerygma).

The importance of the oral tradition containing the words and deeds of Jesus in the early Church did not cease with the appearance of the written Gospels.

Early in the second century, Papias (see above, "The Papias Tradition concerning Matthew") valued the oral tradition even above the available written material. This shows the confidence in the reliability of oral tradition in that culture. Finally, the continuing importance of oral tradition can be seen in the Apostolic Fathers and Justin Martyr (see Hagner). The significant degree of agreement between the written account of Jesus' words and the oral tradition later than the Gospels provides evidence both that the words of Jesus were treasured from the beginning and that they were handed down with the utmost care. We may accordingly have a high degree of confidence that the sayings of Jesus in our synoptic Gospels are true representations of what Jesus himself spoke.

THE STRUCTURE OF MATTHEW

Bibliography

Allison, D. C. "Matthew: Structure, Biographical Impulse and the *Imitatio Christi.*" In *The Four Gospels 1992.* FS F. Neirynck, ed. F. Van Segbroeck, C. M. Tuckett, G. Van Belle, and J. Verheyden. Leuven: Leuven University, 1992. 1203–21. **Bacon, B. W.** *Studies in Matthew.* New York: Holt, 1930. **Barr, D. L.** "The Drama of Matthew's Gospel: A Reconsideration of Its Structure and Purpose." *TD* 24 (1976) 349–59. **Bauer, D. R.** *The Structure of Matthew's Gospel.* Sheffield: Almond, 1988. **Combrink, H. J. B.** "The Structure of the Gospel of Matthew as Narrative." *TynB* 34 (1983) 61–90. **Fenton, J. C.** "Inclusio and Chiasmus in 'Matthew.'" *SE* 1 [= TU 73] (1959) 174–79. **Filson, F. V.** "Broken Patterns in the Gospel of Matthew." *JBL* 75 (1956) 227–31. **Gaechter, P.** *Die literarische Kunst im Matthäus-Evangelium.* Stuttgart: Katholisches Bibelwerk, 1966. **Gooding, D. W.** "Structure Littéraire de Matthieu XIII,53 à XVIII,35." *RB* 85 (1978) 227–52. **Goulder, M. D.** *Midrash and Lection in Matthew.* London: SPCK, 1974. **Green, H. B.** "The Structure of St. Matthew's Gospel." *SE* 4 [= TU 102] (1965) 47–59. **Humphrey, H. M.** *The Relationship of Structure and Christology in the Gospel of Matthew.* New York: Fordham, 1977. **Kilpatrick, G. D.** *The Origins of the Gospel according to St. Matthew.* Oxford: Clarendon, 1946. **Kingsbury, J. D.** *Matthew: Structure, Christology, Kingdom.* 2nd ed. Minneapolis: Fortress, 1989. **Krentz, E.** "The Extent of Matthew's Prologue: Toward the Structure of the First Gospel." *JBL* 83 (1964) 409–15. **Lohr, C. H.** "Oral Techniques in the Gospel of Matthew." *CBQ* 23 (1961) 403–35. **Neirynck, F.** "*ΑΠΟ ΤΟΤΕ ΗΡΞΑΤΟ* and the Structure of Matthew." *ETL* 64 (1988) 21–59. ————."La rédaction matthéenne et la structure du premier Évangile." In *De Jésus aux Évangiles: Tradition et rédaction dans les Évangiles synoptiques,* ed. I. de la Potterie. Gembloux: Duculot, 1967. 41–73. **Rolland, P.** "From the Genesis to the End of the World: The Plan of Matthew's Gospel." *BTB* 2 (1972) 155–76. **Standaert, B.** "L'Évangile selon Matthieu: Composition et genre littéraire." In *The Four Gospels 1992.* FS F. Neirynck, ed. F. Van Segbroeck, C. M. Tuckett, G. Van Belle, and J. Verheyden. Leuven: Leuven University, 1992. 1223–50. **Thompson, M. M.** "The Structure of Matthew: A Survey of Recent Trends." *Studia biblica et theologica* 12 (1982) 195–238.

Specially to be noted are two issues of the journal of the New Testament Society of South Africa: *Neotestamentica* 11 (1977) entitled "The Structure of Matthew 1–13—An Exploration into Discourse Analysis"; and *Neotestamentica* 16 (1982) entitled "Structure and Meaning in Matthew 14–28." To each volume there is also an addendum displaying the structure of the Greek text of Matthew.

Although much study has been devoted to the structure of Matthew in recent years, there has been little consensus as to the best analysis. The reason for this is not lack of data but rather that Matthew contains almost too large a variety of structural elements. There is apparently too much to comprehend under any single analysis of the structure.

The five discourses. Undoubtedly the most conspicuous structural marker in the Gospel is the statement (varying only slightly) with which each of the five major teaching discourses ends: "When Jesus finished all these sayings" (7:28; 11:1; 13:53; 19:1; and 26:1). As is the case in the Fourth Gospel, the evangelist alternates the teaching discourses with narrative blocks concerning the mighty deeds of Jesus. In Matthew, however, little attempt has been made to relate the discourses to the narratives. The discourses in their present form are the construction of the evangelist and have clearly catechetical interests: (1) the Sermon on the Mount, chaps. 5–7; (2) mission directives to the twelve, chap. 10; (3) parables of the kingdom, chap. 13; (4) discipleship and discipline, chap. 18; and (5) eschatology, chaps. 24–25. B. W. Bacon suggested that the evangelist intended the fivefold structure to correspond to the five books of the Pentateuch, with Jesus represented as a new Moses who is the giver of a new law (see, e.g., Kilpatrick). Although there is an implicit Moses typology at some points in the Gospel (see Davies-Allison), this hardly seems to provide sufficient warrant to accept Bacon's conclusion. It is furthermore true that a fivefold structure is found elsewhere in the canonical writings (e.g., the five books of Psalms; the five Scrolls).

Although these five discourses may be meant to include in each instance a preceding narrative (i.e., chaps. 3–4; 8–9; 11–12; 14–17; and 19–22), the fivefold structure hardly seems adequate to be considered the basic plan of the Gospel. The main reason for this is that certain parts of the Gospel do not fit into this structure at all. Chap. 23, with its criticism of the Pharisees, is only with difficulty to be considered a part of the eschatological discourse that follows; chap. 11 contains a considerable amount of Jesus' teaching that remains outside the fivefold discourse structure. More importantly, the fivefold structure excludes the infancy and passion narratives, which must therefore be relegated to prologue and epilogue. The narrative of the death of Jesus, however, is the goal and climax of the story, and any structural analysis must include it as a major element. Accordingly, the fivefold discourse structure should be recognized as a subsidiary structure rather than the primary one. For the latter, we are better advised to look to the major divisions of the Gospel.

Two major turning points. Two pivotal points in Matthew are noted with the repeated clause: ἀπὸ τότε ἤρξατο ὁ Ἰησοῦς, "from that time Jesus began" (4:17; 16:21). Already at the turn of the century J. C. Hawkins (*Horae Synopticae* [Oxford: Clarendon, 1899]) pointed out the significance of this formula for the structure of Matthew. More recently, J. D. Kingsbury, followed by D. R. Bauer, has understood these phrases as indicating the basic structure of the Gospel, which he accordingly describes under the following three headings: (1) the person of Jesus Messiah (1:1–4:16); (2) the proclamation of Jesus Messiah (4:17–16:20); and (3) the suffering, death, and resurrection of Jesus Messiah (16:21–28:20). Because these are such critical junctures in the narrative, they are obviously important to the general shape of the story. But whether they are in fact structural markers in the proper sense of the word is another question. F. Neirynck (*ETL* 64 [1988] 21–59) has shown how difficult it is *structurally* to divide 4:17 from 4:12–16 and 16:21 from the verses that precede it.

A chiastic structure. The symmetrical chiastic analysis of such scholars as Fenton, Lohr, Green, Gaechter, and Combrink is in some ways appealing, but one may only speculate whether such a structure was really in the evangelist's mind. This form of analysis builds on the alternation between narrative and teaching, as roughly in the following schema:

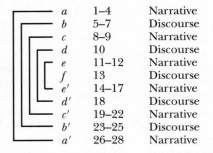

a	1–4	Narrative
b	5–7	Discourse
c	8–9	Narrative
d	10	Discourse
e	11–12	Narrative
f	13	Discourse
e'	14–17	Narrative
d'	18	Discourse
c'	19–22	Narrative
b'	23–25	Discourse
a'	26–28	Narrative

The chiastic approach can appeal to similar motifs in the content of the infancy and passion narratives and to the similar lengths of *b* and *b'* as well as *d* and *d'*. While similarity occasionally exists between other corresponding elements, this usually seems arbitrary and uncompelling. Green's analysis furthermore is not based on the narrative-discourse alternation and finds its center in chap. 11 rather than 13, while Gaechter finds seven major sections in Matthew with the central part of the Gospel in chaps. 13:1–16:20 (with 13:53–58 as the very center). In short, the evidence that can be gleaned from Matthew's text is ambiguous, and there has been no resultant consensus even among those who favor a chiastic analysis.

Other structural elements. Periodic markers in the flow of the narrative are provided by the capsule summaries of the ministry of Jesus placed by the evangelist at 4:23–25; 9:35; 11:1; 14:35–36; 15:29–31; 19:1–2; and 21:14. These point always to the healing of Jesus, often to his teaching, and in the first two instances specifically to Jesus' proclamation of "the good news of the kingdom." These summaries, however, are not similar enough to be thought of as deliberate macro-structural markers.

Within smaller sections of the Gospel, the author displays his literary artistry in the grouping of certain items. As examples, we may note his liking of groups of seven: e.g., the seven petitions of the Lord's Prayer (6:9–13); the seven parables in chap. 13; the seven woes in chap. 23; and the double sevens of the genealogy (1:1–17). He also favors groups of three: e.g., the three divisions of the genealogy (1:1–17); the three kinds of piety (6:1–18); and three polemical parables (21:28–22:14). Davies-Allison call attention to the importance of threes in Matthew and even propose a triadic outline of the macro-structure, with triadic subpoints and sub-subpoints. The evangelist has other groupings (multiples of three) in such instances as the six antitheses (5:21–48) and the nine benedictions (5:3–11).

The author of Matthew also apparently has a tendency to double items drawn from his sources, as in the two demoniacs of 8:28–34 (cf. Mark 5:1–20), the two blind men of 20:29–34 (cf. Mark 10:46–52), and the probable doublet of 20:29–34 in 9:27–31. This, like some of the threes in the Gospel, may well result from a concern to have the two or three witnesses required by the law (18:16; cf. 26:60). Many examples of the author's artistry could be multiplied by looking at such other literary devices as repetition, inclusio, chiasm, leitmotifs, and even poetry (on which see Goulder, 70–94).

The author of Matthew thus shows considerable skill and artistry in the narrative he has constructed. At the same time, as we have seen, it is very difficult to ascertain a unifying overall structure other than of a very general kind. As Filson has pointed out, Matthew has many "broken patterns," i.e., patterns that he begins but does not follow through. Also to be remembered in discussions of Matthew's structure is the fact that he is following the outline of Mark—indeed, following it very closely from chap. 12 onwards. In the final analysis, it may be that the evangelist really had no grand overall structure in mind (thus too Gundry, Thompson) other than of the general divisions marked by the alternation of narrative and discourse. Thus a good part of the time the Gospel appears to be a seamless succession of pericopes, alternating presentation of deeds and words of Jesus that have usually been collected and arranged topically—seldom is there an interest in chronology—for the sake of the impact on the reader.

With these facts in mind, D. C. Allison (1208) has proposed the following general outline:

1–4	N	Introduction: the main character (Jesus) introduced
5–7	D	Jesus' demands upon Israel
8–9	N	Jesus' deeds within and for Israel
10	D	Extension of ministry through words and deeds of others
11–12	N	Israel's negative response
13	D	Explanation of Israel's negative response
14–17	N	Establishment of the new people of God, the Church
18	D	Instructions to the Church
19–23	N	Commencement of the passion, the beginning of the end
24–25	D	The future: judgment and salvation
26–28	N	Conclusion: the passion and resurrection

In the present commentary no overall structural outline is offered. There is, of course, a de facto outline in the groupings of material that seem natural in the flow of the Gospel and that to some extent reflect a number of the issues that have been discussed here. With the prominence of Matthew's alternation of narrative and discourse, our approach results in a scheme very similar to Allison's. This may be seen in the listing of material in the Contents of each volume of the present commentary.

MATTHEW'S USE OF THE OLD TESTAMENT

Bibliography

France, R. T. "The Formula-Quotations of Matthew 2 and the Problem of Communication." *NTS* 27 (1980–81) 233–51. ———. *Jesus and the Old Testament.* London: Tyndale, 1971. **Gärtner, B.** "The Habakkuk Commentary (DSH) and the Gospel of Matthew." *ST* 8 (1954) 1–24. **Gundry, R. H.** *The Use of the Old Testament in St. Matthew's Gospel, with special reference to the Messianic Hope.* NovTSup 18, Leiden: Brill, 1967. **Hagner, D. A.** "The Old Testament in the New Testament." In *Interpreting the Word of God,* ed. S. J. Schultz and M. A.

Inch. Chicago: Moody, 1976. 78–104. ————. "When the Time Had Fully Come." In *Dreams, Visions and Oracles*, ed. C. E. Armerding and W. W. Gasque. Grand Rapids: Baker, 1977. 89–99. **Hartman, L.** "Scriptural Exegesis in the Gospel of St. Matthew and the Problem of Communication." In *L'Évangile selon Matthieu*, ed. M. Didier. Gembloux: Duculot, 1972. 131–52. **Moo, D. J.** *The Old Testament in the Gospel Passion Narratives*. Sheffield: Almond, 1983. **Rothfuchs, W.** *Die Erfüllungszitate des Matthäus-Evangeliums*. Stuttgart: Kohlhammer, 1969. **Soares Prabhu, G. M.** *The Formula Quotations in the Infancy Narrative of Matthew*. Rome: Biblical Institute, 1976. **Stanton, G. N.** "Matthew's Use of the Old Testament." In *It is Written: Scripture Citing Scripture*, ed. D. A. Carson and H. M. G. Williamson. Cambridge: Cambridge University, 1988. 205–19 (reprinted in G. N. Stanton, *A Gospel for a New People: Studies in Matthew* [Edinburgh: T & T. Clark, 1992] 346–63). **Stendahl, K.** *The School of St. Matthew and Its Use of the Old Testament*. 2nd ed. Philadelphia: Fortress, 1968. **Van Segbroeck, F.** "Les citations d'accomplissement dans l'Évangile selon saint Matthieu." In *L'Évangile selon Matthieu*, ed. M. Didier. Gembloux: Duculot, 1972. 107–30.

Matthew contains well over sixty explicit quotations from the OT (not counting a great number of allusions), more than twice as many as any other Gospel. This heavy dependence on the OT reflects Matthew's interest in the gospel of the kingdom as the fulfillment of the OT expectation. Of particular interest in this regard are the so-called fulfillment quotations, one of the most distinctive features of Matthew. These quotations represent Matthew's own creative interpretation of his narrative. Their reflective character has led to the designation *Reflexionszitate*, "reflection citations."

Ten quotations employ a specialized introductory formula containing the verb πληροῦν, "fulfill":

Matthew	Introductory Formula	OT Quotation (LXX)
1:22–23	ἵνα πληρωθῇ τὸ ῥηθὲν ὑπὸ κυρίου διὰ τοῦ προφήτου λέγοντος "in order that the word of the Lord through the prophet might be fulfilled which says"	Isa 7:14
2:15	(identical with preceding)	Hos 11:1
2:17–18	τότε ἐπληρώθη τὸ ῥηθὲν διὰ Ἰερεμίου τοῦ προφήτου λέγοντος "then the word through Jeremiah the prophet was fulfilled which says"	Jer 31:15
2:23b	ὅπως πληρωθῇ τὸ ῥηθὲν διὰ τῶν προφητῶν ὅτι "so that the word through the prophets might be fulfilled that"	(Isa 11:1?)
4:14–16	ἵνα πληρωθῇ τὸ ῥηθὲν διὰ Ἡσαΐου τοῦ προφήτου λέγοντος "in order that the word through Isaiah the prophet might be fulfilled saying"	Isa 8:23–9:1
8:17	ὅπως πληρωθῇ τὸ ῥηθὲν διὰ Ἡσαΐου τοῦ προφήτου λέγοντος	Isa 53:4

"so that the word through Isaiah the prophet
might be fulfilled saying"

| 12:17–21 | (identical with formula for 4:14–16) | Isa 42:1–4 |

13:35 ὅπως πληρωθῇ τὸ ῥηθὲν διὰ   Ps 78(77):2
       τοῦ προφήτου λέγοντος
       "so that the word through the prophet might be
       fulfilled saying"

21:4–5 ἵνα πληρωθῇ τὸ ῥηθὲν διὰ   Isa 62:11; Zech 9:9
        τοῦ προφήτου λέγοντος
        "in order that the word through the prophet
        might be fulfilled saying"

27:9–10 (identical with formula for 2:17–18) Zech 11:12–13
                                                (cf. Jer 32:6–15)

To these may be added a further formula quotation that employs the synonymous ἀναπληροῦν rather than πληροῦν:

13:14–15 καὶ ἀναπληροῦται αὐτοῖς ἡ προφητεία   Isa 6:9–10
          Ἡσαΐου ἡ λέγουσα
          "and the prophecy of Isaiah is fulfilled in them
          which says"

One further related formula quotation stresses fulfillment without using the word "fulfill":

3:3 οὗτος γάρ ἐστιν ὁ ῥηθεὶς διὰ Ἡσαΐου   Isa 40:2(LXX)
     τοῦ προφήτου λέγοντος
     "This is what was spoken through Isaiah the
     prophet saying"

Other quotations employing the word γέγραπται, "it is written," in the introductory formula can also stress fulfillment, as in 2:5; 11:10; and 26:31. Also to be noted is the general fulfillment formula without any actual quotation in 26:56 (cf. 26:54) with reference to the events of the passion narrative: ἵνα πληρωθῶσιν αἱ γραφαὶ τῶν προφητῶν, "in order that the writings of the prophets might be fulfilled."

The introductory formulae of Matthew's fulfillment quotations are unique among the synoptic Gospels, although, of course, the emphasis on fulfillment is itself ubiquitous. The placement of the quotations in the book does not help us to discern the structure of the Gospel; their distribution is not uniform, four occurring in the first two chapters. The importance of the quotations is theological. They are Matthew's own way of undergirding the manner in which the events of his narrative, indeed its totality, are to be understood as the fulfillment of what God had promised in the Scriptures.

The most difficult challenge of these quotations for the modern reader is to understand the hermeneutical basis upon which the majority of them rests. Although the word "fulfill" is used, the quoted texts themselves are as a rule not even predictive of future events. Nor therefore can we say that the evangelist does exegesis of the texts, i.e., that he understands them the way their original authors intended them. Instead, we encounter in our author's practice, as throughout the NT, the use of what has been dubbed *sensus plenior,* i.e., a fuller or deeper sense within the quoted material not understood by the original author but now detectable in the light of the new revelatory fulfillment. This is not an arbitrary, frivolous misuse of the texts, as is sometimes claimed, but a reasoned practice that assumes a divinely intended correspondence between God's saving activity at different times in the history of redemption. The understanding of texts through *sensus plenior* was not the invention of Christians but had already long been practiced by the Jews. Together, Jews and Christians shared such convictions as the sovereignty of God, the inspiration of the Scriptures, and the unity of God's saving purpose resulting in the interconnectedness of his redemptive acts. To these the Christians added the one supreme conviction that Jesus was the *telos,* the goal, of what the OT had promised. With these presuppositions, Christians like Matthew saw correspondences between events of the past and the time of Jesus not as coincidental, as we moderns might, but as divinely intended, with the earlier foreshadowing the latter, much in the sense of prophecy and fulfillment.

What needs to be stressed is that these quotations are not to be understood as prooftexts that would in themselves persuade, for example, Jews who had rejected the gospel. The quotations have as their foundation christological convictions—they are, indeed, christocentric. They take as their *starting point* that Jesus is the One promised by the OT Scriptures. The quotations are thus addressed to Christians, and their compelling power is only evident to those who have been confronted with the fact of the risen Christ. Given the truth of Matthew's narrative, the quotations find their rightful place as interpretive support and as a demonstration of the unity of God's plan exhibited in promise and fulfillment.

The special formula quotations of Matthew are furthermore distinctive in that whereas the other OT quotations, drawn from Mark or Q, are consistently septuagintal in text type, they exhibit a mixed text form (except for the quotation in 13:14–15) that reflects dependence upon the Hebrew (Masoretic) text together with other text types, including also septuagintal influence (see Gundry). The explanation of this fact together with the question of the source of these quotations has been much debated.

It is possible, but highly conjectural, that the formula quotations originally formed part of a collection of *testimonia* (such as now found at Qumran [4QTestim]) that Matthew drew upon, or even perhaps collected himself. If this is true, however, Matthew has made the quotations his own by the distinctive way in which he utilizes them in his narrative. But other explanations are also available. Thus K. Stendahl has proposed that the quotations are the product of a Matthean school that interpreted OT texts in a manner similar to the *pesher* hermeneutic (i.e., pointing to fulfillment by arguing "this is that") practiced at Qumran. B. Gärtner has disputed this hypothesis, denying that Matthew's fulfillment quotations are similar to those of Qumran since they do not expound a continuous text (such as Habakkuk). Gärtner proposes instead that the quotations were derived from the missionary preaching of the early Church (so too Rothfuchs) and were possibly directed against Jewish opponents.

Opinion has remained divided regarding whether the formula quotations are the evangelist's own creation or are derived from some particular source. Because they so clearly reflect the evangelist's theology, with its strong emphasis on fulfillment, it is clear that he at least made the quotations his own in his portrayal of Jesus as the Messiah.

THE GENRE AND PURPOSE OF MATTHEW

Bibliography

Allison, D. C. "Matthew: Structure, Biographical Impulse and the *Imitatio Christi.*" In *The Four Gospels 1992.* FS F. Neirynck, ed. F. Van Segbroeck, C. M. Tuckett, G. Van Belle, and J. Verheyden. Leuven: Leuven University, 1992. 1203–21. **Burridge, R. A.** *What Are the Gospels? A Comparison with Graeco-Roman Biography.* SNTSMS 70. Cambridge: Cambridge University, 1992. **Carrington, P.** *The Primitive Christian Calendar.* Cambridge: Cambridge University, 1952. **Davies, W. D.** *The Setting of the Sermon on the Mount.* Cambridge: Cambridge University, 1963. **Gärtner, B.** "The Habakkuk Commentary (DSH) and the Gospel of Matthew." *ST* 8 (1954) 1–24. **Goulder, M. D.** *The Evangelists' Calendar.* London: SPCK, 1978. ————. *Midrash and Lection in Matthew.* London: SPCK, 1974. **Guelich, R. A.** "The Gospel Genre." In *The Gospel and the Gospels,* ed. P. Stuhlmacher. Grand Rapids: Eerdmans, 1991. 173–208. **Kilpatrick, G. D.** *The Origins of the Gospel according to St. Matthew.* Oxford: Clarendon, 1946. **McConnell, R. S.** *Law and Prophecy in Matthew's Gospel.* Basel: Reinhardt, 1969. **Minear, P. S.** *Matthew: The Teacher's Gospel.* New York: Pilgrim, 1982. **Schweizer, E.** "Observance of the Law and Charismatic Activity in Matthew." *NTS* 16 (1969–70) 213–30. **Shuler, P. L.** *A Genre for the Gospels: The Biographical Character of Matthew.* Philadelphia: Fortress, 1982. **Stanton, G. N.** "Matthew: *ΒΙΒΛΟΣ, ΕΥΑΓΓΕΛΙΟΝ,* or *ΒΙΟΣ*? In *The Four Gospels 1992.* FS F. Neirynck, ed. F. Van Segbroeck, C. M. Tuckett, G. Van Belle, and J. Verheyden. Leuven: Leuven University, 1992. 1187–1201. **Stendahl, K.** *The School of St. Matthew and Its Use of the Old Testament.* 2nd ed. Philadelphia: Fortress, 1968. **Talbert, C. H.** *What Is a Gospel? The Genre of the Canonical Gospels.* Philadelphia: Fortress, 1977. **Thompson, W. G.** *Matthew's Advice to a Divided Community: Mt. 17,22–18,35.* Rome: Biblical Institute, 1970. **Trilling, W.** *Das wahre Israel: Studien zur Theologie des Matthäusevangeliums.* 3rd ed. Munich: Kösel, 1964.

The genre, or literary character and form, of a document is vitally related to the purposes of its author. How can the Gospel of Matthew be described so as to account for its unique emphases and its peculiar formal elements? Several possible answers must be considered.

Gospel. Matthew is of course preeminently a Gospel, i.e., an account of the life of Jesus, an ancient type of biography though not a biography in the modern sense. It is increasingly realized that Matthew is a βίος ("life") that bears sufficient resemblance to Greco-Roman biographies to be classified as such (see Talbert, Stanton; cf. Shuler who, however, too specifically identifies Matthew's portrait of Jesus as an encomium or "laudatory biography"). Matthew, like the other Gospels, is an expansion of the kerygma concerning the fulfillment brought by Jesus, especially through his death and resurrection. Fundamentally, a Gospel proclaims the good news concerning the saving activity of God. That saving activity of God manifests itself climactically in the death and resurrection of Jesus, the heart of the Gospel. In addition, however, its special characteristics have raised the question of whether Matthew may also be seen to possess the traits of other more specific genres. The following categories are not necessarily parallel and are by no means mutually exclusive.

Midrash. The word, a noun derived from the Hebrew verb דָּרַשׁ (*dāraš*), "to seek, inquire," has been used with various meanings by scholars who have applied it to Matthew. In Jewish literature, it came to refer specifically to the interpretation of biblical texts. In its broader meaning, when applied to Matthew, it refers to the setting forth of an edifying, theological interpretation of Jesus in, or under the form of, historical narrative. In its proper, more restricted meaning, midrash refers to such "historicizing" done in connection with specific OT quotations. Many scholars argue that Matthew contains much midrash, in both the narrower and the wider sense of the word. According to M. D. Goulder, Matthew is a midrashic or "interpretive" expansion of the Gospel of Mark, to be compared to the Chronicler's treatment of Kings. R. H. Gundry argues for the midrashic character of much of Matthew and maintains that Matthew's readers would have had no difficulty in distinguishing the midrashic material from straightforward historical narrative or in accepting it for what it was. It cannot be denied that the evangelist works midrashically with some of his OT quotations, but it does not follow from this that whatever appears as historical narrative in Matthew is without any historical basis. Matthew contains narratives (e.g., the infancy narrative) that make much use of OT quotations, and these indeed appear to have had their effect on the wording of the narratives. But this does not mean that the author created historical narratives at will for his own convenience.

Lectionary. Following G. D. Kilpatrick and P. Carrington, Goulder (*Midrash*, 171–98) has argued not merely that the composition of the Gospel of Matthew was determined by the lectionary year but also that it was written to be used liturgically by supplying consecutive readings based on the Jewish festal year. For Goulder, the genre of Gospel is liturgical rather than strictly literary.

Catechesis or catechetical manual. The collection of the sayings of Jesus into the five discourses, one of the most obvious characteristics of Matthew, has led many scholars to conclude that it should be thought of as a catechetical document for the upbuilding of Christian discipleship. It is clear that in the early Church the sayings of Jesus were supremely authoritative and that they played a great role in the instruction of new converts as well as older members of the church. The view of the Gospel as catechesis is in keeping with the importance of teaching throughout the Gospel (see esp. 28:20). K. Stendahl extends this view of Matthew as catechesis to the hypothesis of a Matthean school, modeled on the the rabbinic schools, that produced a kind of teacher's manual, a Christian equivalent to the Qumran community's Manual of Discipline. Particular evidence of the school's work, according to Stendahl, is seen in the use of the OT quotations throughout the Gospel.

Church correctives. Some have seen Matthew as providing correctives to a community facing serious difficulties and find in the negative material a clue to the purpose of the Gospel. W. G. Thompson, in a study of 17:22–18:35, argues that Matthew's community was seriously divided and that scandal was commonplace. It is, of course, also possible to argue that behind every positive instruction of the Gospel is a corresponding vice in the community. Kingsbury (*Parables*) finds indications in chap. 13 that Matthew's community was troubled not only by internal strife but also by a spiritual malaise that manifested itself in materialism, secularism, and a disregard for the law. Others (e.g., Minear and Trilling) detect a special concern for the leaders of Matthew's community, who were in danger of becoming false prophets or falling into hypocrisy. Still others (e.g., E. Schweizer) have called attention to the polemic in Matthew against false prophets and certain charismatics in the community who did not keep the law (7:15–23). Although the evangelist accepts the place of prophecy and charismatic healings in the Church, he has no tolerance for the exercise of these gifts apart from the Christian virtues that are exemplified preeminently in the keeping of the law.

Missionary propaganda. Since one of the main intentions of Matthew is to demonstrate that Jesus is the Messiah, it is possible to see the Gospel as primarily a tool to be used in the Church's mission to the Jews. B. Gärtner and R. S. McConnell have explained the unique quotations in Matthew as derived from the missionary preaching directed to the Jews. The great stress on fulfillment throughout the Gospel can be taken as support of this hypothesis.

Polemic against the rabbis. That Jesus debates and criticizes the Pharisees so frequently through the course of the Gospel (see esp. chap. 23) leads naturally to the conclusion that the author and his readers faced a continuing problem in their defense of the gospel against the claims of the synagogue. The debate concerned the question of who possessed the true interpretation of the Torah. In this view, the Gospel draws on the traditions about Jesus and the Pharisees and uses this material in the struggle with the Pharisaic Judaism of a later time. W. D. Davies (256–315) regards Matthew as a Jewish-Christian counterpart of, and response to, the rabbinic activity at Yavneh (Jamnia).

This variety of options concerning the genre of Matthew indicates something of its multifaceted character. Several of these explanations may well be equally true. The evangelist could have had several purposes. This much at least is clear: Matthew is a "community book," written to a considerable extent in order to meet the immediate needs of the evangelist's church or churches during the interim period between the historical events narrated and the return of Christ. In particular, as we will argue below ("The *Sitz im Leben* ['Life Setting'] of Matthew's Community"), the evangelist intends to help his Jewish-Christian readers understand their new faith as in continuity with the faith of their ancestors, as the fulfillment of the Scriptures, and as the beginning of the realization of the hope of Israel. The author wrote, above all, for the Church to interpret the Christ-event but also to instruct and edify the Christians of his own and future generations.

MATTHEW'S THEOLOGY

Bibliography

Barth, G. "Matthew's Understanding of the Law." In G. Bornkamm, G. Barth, and H. J. Held, *Tradition and Interpretation in Matthew.* Philadelphia: Fortress, 1963. 58–164. **Bornkamm, G.** "End-Expectation and Church in Matthew." In G. Bornkamm, G. Barth, and H. J. Held, *Tradition and Interpretation in Matthew.* Philadelphia: Fortress, 1963. 15–51. **Broer, I.** "Versuch zur Christologie des ersten Evangeliums." In *The Four Gospels 1992.* FS F. Neirynck, ed. F. Van Segbroeck, C. M. Tuckett, G. Van Belle, and J. Verheyden. Leuven: Leuven University, 1992. 1251–82. **Carlston, C. E.** "Christology and Church in Matthew." In *The Four Gospels 1992.* FS F. Neirynck, ed. F. Van Segbroeck, C. M. Tuckett, G. Van Belle, and J. Verheyden. Leuven: Leuven University, 1992. 1283–1304. **Gibbs, J. M.** "The Son of God as the Torah Incarnate in Matthew." *SE* 4 [= TU 102] (1968) 38–46. **Hagner, D. A.** "Apocalyptic Motifs in the Gospel of Matthew: Continuity and Discontinuity." *HBT* 7 (1985)

53–82. ————. "Righteousness in Matthew's Theology." In *Worship, Theology and Ministry in the Early Church.* FS R. P. Martin, ed. M. J. Wilkins and T. Paige. Sheffield: JSOT, 1992. 101–20. **Hamerton-Kelly, R. G.** *Pre-Existence, Wisdom and the Son of Man.* SNTSMS 21. Cambridge: Cambridge University, 1973. **Hummel, R.** *Die Auseinandersetzung zwischen Kirche und Judentum im Matthäusevangelium.* 2nd ed. Munich: Kaiser, 1966. **Kingsbury, J. D.** *Matthew: Structure, Christology, Kingdom.* 2nd ed. Minneapolis: Fortress, 1989. **Luz, U.** "Eine thetische Skizze der Matthäischen Christologie." In *Anfänge der Christologie.* FS F. Hahn, ed. C. Breytenbach and H. Paulsen. Göttingen: Vandenhoeck & Ruprecht, 1991. 221–35. **Meier, J. P.** *The Vision of Matthew: Christ, Church and Morality in the First Gospel.* New York: Paulist, 1979. **Przybylski, B.** *Righteousness in Matthew and His World of Thought.* SNTSMS 41. Cambridge: Cambridge University, 1980. **Schweizer, E.** "Observance of the Law and Charismatic Activity in Matthew." *NTS* 16 (1969–70) 213–30. **Strecker, G.** *Der Weg der Gerechtigkeit.* 3rd ed. Göttingen: Vandenhoeck & Ruprecht, 1971. **Suggs, M. J.** *Wisdom, Christology and Law in Matthew's Gospel.* Cambridge, MA: Harvard University, 1970. **Trilling, W.** *Das wahre Israel: Studien zur Theologie des Matthäusevangeliums.* 3rd ed. Munich: Kösel, 1964. **Wilkins, M. J.** *The Concept of Disciple in Matthew's Gospel.* NovTSup 59. Leiden: Brill, 1988.

Since Matthew takes over so much of Mark, we may expect that he shares Mark's theology. At the same time, by seeing how Matthew redacts the Markan material, we gain insight into Matthew's particular theological interests. Even more, we may determine Matthew's perspective by the material that is unique to his Gospel, the material drawn from his special source. We now look at some of the major theological emphases in the Gospel.

Fulfillment: the kingdom of heaven. The theme of fulfillment is clearly one of Matthew's favorites. The central emphasis of the book is found in what is designated (uniquely in the Gospels) as τὸ εὐαγγέλιον τῆς βασιλείας, "the gospel of the kingdom" (4:23; 9:35; 24:14; cf. 26:13), namely, the good news that the reign or rule of God has begun to be realized in history through the presence of Jesus Christ. Matthew may fairly be described as practically a demonstration of the reality of the presence of the kingdom through the words and deeds of Jesus. The evangelist prefers the Jewish expression ἡ βασιλεία τῶν οὐρανῶν, "the kingdom of heaven" (lit. "of the heavens"), a circumlocution for ἡ βασιλεία τοῦ θεοῦ, "the kingdom of God" (which, however, does occur in 12:28; 19:24; and 21:31, 43). The importance of the kingdom for the evangelist is obvious from the fact that he uses the word much more frequently than does any one of the other Gospels, and nearly three times as often as Mark. The message of Jesus, like that of John the Baptist (3:2), is the coming of the kingdom (4:17), and this in turn becomes the message of the disciples (10:7). Everything in the Gospel relates in some way to this controlling theme. It is true that the kingdom has come presently as a mystery in an unexpected way, as we learn especially from the parables of chap. 13. In particular, the fulfillment brought by Jesus involves a delay in the judgment of the wicked (13:36–42, 47–50). Nevertheless, the excitement of what *has* come is not to be missed: "blessed are your eyes because they see, and your ears because they hear. For truly I say to you that many prophets and righteous persons desired to see what you are seeing, and they did not see it, and to hear what you are hearing, and they did not hear it" (13:16–17). Matthew's special interest in the theme of fulfillment is also clearly seen in his frequent quotation of the OT and particularly in the so-called fulfillment quotations (see preceding section).

There is also a sense, of course, in which the kingdom is a future expectation for Matthew. If the kingdom is presently inaugurated in and through the work of Christ, it remains to be consummated through his parousia (see below on "Eschatology").

Christology. Matthew's doctrine of Jesus as the Christ is fundamentally important to every theological emphasis in the Gospel, for it is the identity of Jesus that determines such things as fulfillment, authoritative exposition of the law, discipleship, ecclesiology, and eschatology. Matthew heightens the Christology of the material drawn from Mark, making it more explicit (e.g., the important confession of Mark 8:29, "You are the Christ," becomes in Matt 16:16, "You are the Christ, the Son of the living God"; cf. Matt 19:17 with Mark 10:18; and Matt 9:3 with Mark 2:7). It is in Matthew's unique material, moreover, that the evangelist's emphasis on Christology is most apparent.

Kingsbury argues that the key christological title in Matthew is υἱὸς τοῦ θεοῦ, "Son of God." The importance of this title can be seen not only where it is used (e.g., 8:29; 14:33; 16:16; cf. 3:17 and 17:5) but also in places where it is implied, such as in 1:23, "'and they shall name him Emmanuel,' which means 'God is with us'"; 14:27, ἐγώ εἰμι, "it is I" (cf. Exod 3:14); and the passages promising the future presence of Jesus with his disciples (18:20 and 28:20). Matthew also stresses the sonship of Jesus by having him refer to God as his Father some twenty-three times, fifteen of which are unique to Matthew (eight in original material; seven in redactional alteration). For Matthew, the most exalted confession, which alone expresses the mystery of Jesus' identity, is that he is the Son of God (16:16; esp. 11:27). This confession in Matthew is made only by believers (except where it is blasphemy) and only by revelation (16:7; 11:27; cf. 13:11).

The second major title, Son of Man, is regularly used by Jesus and thus serves as the public counterpart to the confessional title. In references to the parousia and the eschatological judgment, it tends to coincide with Son of God. Kingsbury finds no material difference between the titles. J. P. Meier has argued for the equal importance of the two titles.

The important title κύριος, "Lord," is analogous to Son of God, being found almost exclusively on the lips of the disciples. The titles Χριστός, "Christ," and υἱὸς τοῦ Δαυίδ, "Son of David," being closely linked with stress on fulfillment, are also very important in Matthew. Kingsbury, however, is probably correct in arguing that these titles support the title Son of God. The same is true of such lesser titles or categories as Son of Abraham, the Coming One, Teacher (Rabbi), Shepherd, and Servant, although, of course, each has its own meaning. Some scholars (esp. M. J. Suggs; cf. J. M. Gibbs; R. G. Hamerton-Kelly) have found the key to Matthew's Christology in the concept of Jesus as the incarnation of Wisdom (e.g., 11:19, 25–27; 23:34–39) and Torah (e.g., 11:28–30). These analyses are consistent with Matthew's emphasis on a Son-of-God Christology, i.e., "God with us."

It should also be remembered that there is also a powerful Christology in Matthew that can be described as indirect, that is, as manifested in the deeds and words of Jesus altogether apart from the titles we have examined.

Righteousness and discipleship. A key term for the evangelist is δικαιοσύνη, "righteousness," which occurs among the synoptic Gospels only in Matthew (except for Luke 1:75). Although it had been argued by others earlier (e.g., Strecker, Dupont [*Les Béatitudes*, 3:211–305]), the view that all seven occurrences of the word refer to the righteousness of ethical demand seems to be winning the day since the important work of B. Przybylski(see, for example, the commentaries of Luz and Davies-Allison). Although it is clear that several of the seven occurrences of the word in Matthew refer unmistakably to the call to personal righteousness associated with discipleship (e.g., 5:20; 6:1) and other instances are probably so to be interpreted (e.g., 5:10; and possibly 6:33), the word in some instances can be understood in a salvation-historical sense, i.e., as God's righteousness active in the saving of his people (3:15, 5:6; and 21:32; also possibly 6:33). For support of this conclusion, see Hagner, "Righteousness." See further the discussion of law and grace below.

The cognate word δίκαιος, "just" or "righteous," occurs seventeen times in Matthew, more than all the references in the other three Gospels combined. This righteousness finds its definition and standard in the law, especially as authoritatively interpreted by Jesus. The righteousness to which Jesus calls his disciples, according to Matthew, is a better or higher righteousness (cf. 5:20). In the final analysis, it is a call to the doing of the will of the Father (7:21; 12:50; 21:31).

The evangelist emphasizes the importance of discipleship. The noun μαθητής, "disciple," occurs much more often in Matthew (seventy-three times) than in the other synoptic Gospels, and the verb μαθητεύειν, "to make disciples," occurs only in Matthew among all four Gospels (13:52; 27:57; 28:19). Disciples are called υἱοὶ τοῦ θεοῦ, "sons of God" (5:9, 45), but more frequently by terms meant to emphasize humility, e.g., ἀδελφοί, "brothers" (esp. 12:49–50; 18:15, 21, 35; 23:8; 25:40; 28:10) and, most distinctively, μικροί, "little ones" (10:42; 18:6, 10, 14). Discipleship involves following in the steps of the Lord, which entails self-denial and taking up one's cross (10:38–39; 16:24–26), the suffering of persecution (5:10–12; 10:16–25; 24:9–13), and the humility of a servant (20:26–27; 23:11–12) or child (18:1–4).

Law and grace. Matthew is well known for its emphasis upon Jesus' faithfulness to the law, particularly as expressed in 5:17–18: "Do not think that I have come to abolish the law or the prophets; I have come not to abolish but to fulfill. For truly I tell you, until heaven and earth pass away, not one letter, not one stroke of a letter, will pass from the law until all is accomplished" (NRSV). Jesus' teaching about righteousness and the doing of the will of the Father (7:21; 12:50; 21:31) is understood throughout the Gospel as nothing other than the explication of the true meaning of the law. For the sake of his Jewish-Christian readers, the evangelist portrays Jesus as less radical toward the law than does Mark (compare 15:1–20 against Mark 7:1–23, where Matthew avoids the conclusion that Jesus "declared all foods clean" and emphasizes only the issue of handwashing). Jesus is, moreover, shown to agree in principle with the Pharisees (23:2–3), that is, to the extent that they truly expound the meaning of the Mosaic law. Even in Matthew, however, Jesus transcends not only the teachings of the Pharisees (see 9:10–17; 15:1–20) but also the letter of the law while penetrating to its inner spirit (see 5:31–42; 12:1–14; 15:11; 19:3–9). This uniquely authoritative interpretation of the law is possible only because of who Jesus is (the messianic Son of God) and what he is in the process of bringing (the kingdom, i.e., the rule of God). Accordingly, the Pharisees are no match for Jesus in their interpretation of the law, and at the same time the author's Jewish-Christian church—and not the synagogue—is shown to be in true succession to Moses. The emphasis upon the law in Matthew is thus much more probably due to the Jewish-Christian orientation of the Gospel than to a direct attempt to counteract a "Pauline" antinomianism, as some (e.g., G. Barth) have thought.

The law as expounded by Jesus is not a "new" law (note Matthew's omission of Mark's reference to "a new teaching" [1:27]) but the "true" or intended meaning of the Mosaic law. Matthew's stress on the law, however, occurs in the context of the good news of the presence of the kingdom. The announcement of grace is antecedent to the call to live out the righteousness of the law (e.g., the beatitudes precede the exposition of the law in the Sermon on the Mount). Thus, alongside the stern calls to righteousness (e.g., 5:19–20; 7:21–27; 25:31–46) is also a clear emphasis upon grace (e.g., 5:3–12; 9:12–13; 10:7–8; 11:28–30; 18:23–35; 20:1–16; 22:1–10; 26:26–28). The grace of the kingdom and the demands of the law as interpreted by the messianic king stand in dynamic tension throughout the Gospel, but it is clear that the former precedes the latter.

Community (church). The Greek word ἐκκλησία, "church," occurs among the Gospels only in Matthew (16:18; 18:17, twice). In chap. 16, at Peter's confession that Jesus is "the Messiah, the Son of the living God," Jesus promises to build his new community (as the underlying Aramaic would have to be translated) upon Peter. The authority bestowed on Peter in 16:19 (singular verbs) is extended to the church in a disciplinary context in 18:18 (plural verbs). Here Matthew's church receives its commission to exercise discipline over believers in the full knowledge that it is being led by the Lord (see esp. 18:19, "if two of you agree on earth about anything you ask, it will be done for you by my Father in heaven"). Matthew can appropriately be called an "ecclesiastical" Gospel for other reasons as well. We have already noted that the evangelist has collected and shaped the major discourses particularly for the instruction and edification of the Church. The disciples and their experiences serve as models for the evangelist's contemporaries; Peter is a prototype of Christian leadership.

The evangelist addresses some urgent matters in his Gospel. His community was probably experiencing division, lawlessness, and even apostasy. He accordingly stresses that the church is a mixed community that includes both true and false disciples (e.g., 13:29–30, 47–50; 22:11–14). He gives severe warnings concerning "false prophets," that is, charismatic enthusiasts who prophesy, cast out demons, and heal—all in the name of Jesus—who come "in sheep's clothing but inwardly are ravenous wolves" (7:15–23). The fault in these false prophets is that they are "evildoers" who bear "evil fruit"; they do not observe the law (cf. E. Schweizer). Elsewhere (10:41) the author can encourage hospitality to the itinerant prophet. He urges leaders to avoid the pride and hypocrisy of the Pharisees (23:8–12), who also fail to keep the law. He repeatedly uses the words of Jesus to address the needs of his own church.

Eschatology. Matthew's special interest in eschatology can be seen simply from the length of the apocalyptic discourse compared with that of Mark 13. Not only is chap. 24 longer than its Markan source (including the warning pericopes in 24:37–51, drawn from Q), but the author adds a whole chapter of material not found in Mark, centering on the reality of eschatological judgment. (The parables of the ten virgins [25:1–13] and the last judgment [25:31–46] are unique to Matthew.) Other unique eschatological material in Matthew is found in 13:24–30, 36–43; 20:1–16; and 22:1–14. But apocalyptic threads run throughout the Gospel (see Hagner). The technical word παρουσία (*parousia*), which refers to the eschatological return of Christ, is found only in Matthew (24:3, 27, 37, 39) among the Gospels. G. Bornkamm has furthermore shown that the evangelist's eschatology is vitally important to his ecclesiology, Christology, and view of the law. As is true throughout the NT, the primary purpose of eschatological teaching for Matthew is not so much to provide information concerning the future as to motivate the church to conduct that is appropriate in the light of imminent judgment. Thus in Matthew, eschatology is important not only to theology but also to discipleship. The promise of future judgment and deliverance makes perseverance in the present both a possibility and a necessity.

Salvation history. Much debate has centered on the structure of Matthew's salvation-history perspective. That is, does the author conceive of three epochs (Israel, Jesus, and the Church) or two (Israel and Jesus, with the Church understood as the extension of the latter)? Kingsbury (25–37) has argued in favor of two because of the greater importance of Christology as compared to ecclesiology in the Gospel. In this view, the epoch of the Church is regarded as a subcategory of the epoch of Jesus. The threefold analysis (e.g., as in Strecker, Trilling, and Walker), however, may be held without concluding that ecclesiology is the dominant theme in the Gospel. A threefold analysis, moreover, can give proper emphasis to Christology (the time of Jesus as the central epoch) and the schema of promise and fulfillment, while at the same time finding a place for the obvious importance of the transition from Israel to the Church, the limitations of the time of Jesus (cf. the restriction of the mission to Israel), and the determinative significance of the cross and resurrection for Matthew (cf. Meier, 26–39). See below ("The *Sitz im Leben* ['Life Setting'] of Matthew's Community") for a discussion of the problem of Israel and the Church.

THE ORIGINAL READERS OF MATTHEW

Bibliography

Balch, D. L., ed. *Social History of the Matthean Community: Cross-Disciplinary Approaches.* Minneapolis: Fortress, 1991. **Clark, K. W.** "The Gentile Bias in Matthew." *JBL* 66 (1947) 165–72. **Meier, J. P.** *The Vision of Matthew: Christ, Church and Morality in the First Gospel.* New York: Paulist, 1979. 15–25. **Nepper-Christensen, P.** *Das Matthäusevangelium: Ein judenchristliches Evangelium?* Aarhus: Universitetsforlaget, 1954. **Tagawa, K.** "People and Community in the Gospel of Matthew." *NTS* 16 (1969–70) 149–62.

The data of the Gospel of Matthew are again and again explained most satisfactorily on the hypothesis that the first readers were Jewish Christians. Among various key items to be mentioned here are: the stress throughout the Gospel on fulfillment of the OT and especially the distinctive formula quotations (see above) that point to Jesus as the Messiah and his ministry as the dawning of the messianic age; the importance of Jesus' fidelity to the law (not only 5:17–19, but cf. Matthew's redactional changes of Mark 7 in chap. 15) and his call to righteousness; Matthew's omission of Mark's explanation of Jewish customs (cf. 15:2 with Mark 7:3–4); and his formulation of several discussions in typical rabbinic patterns (e.g., 19:3–9 on divorce). Also worth noting are the apologetic motifs of the infancy narrative (against early Jewish claims of the illegitimacy of Jesus' birth) and the resurrection narrative (explicitly against the Jewish claim that the body was stolen; 28:12–15).

It is, of course, not impossible that Matthew was written to a mixed community or even to Gentiles by a gentile author. Gentile Christians, after all, were also interested in the fulfillment of the OT and in Jesus as Messiah; they may further-more have been in need of the emphasis on law to counter antinomian tendencies, perhaps stemming from a Paulinist enthusiasm. But these explana-tions seem less natural and are hence less probable. There is, in fact, little in the Gospel that is effectively explained as finding its raison d'être in a supposed gen-tile readership. Moreover, the hypothesis of a gentile life setting leaves other aspects of the Gospel, and especially the particularist sayings, unaccounted for.

A further probability is that both the original readers and the final redactor (see below on "Authorship") were Hellenistic Jews and Jews of the Diaspora rather than Palestinian Jews. This follows not only from the fact that the Gospel was written in Greek but from the apparent proximity of the readers to a gentile Christianity.

Although apparently addressed specifically to Jewish Christians, Matthew has a magisterial and universal character that transcends that specific readership. And if the problem of continuity and discontinuity with the revelation of the earlier cov-enant may not be a relevant one for gentile Christians in the same way that it is for Jewish Christians, they too may profit from Matthew's treatment of this issue.

THE *SITZ IM LEBEN* ("LIFE SETTING") OF MATTHEW'S COMMUNITY

Bibliography

Brown, S. "The Matthean Community and the Gentile Mission." *NovT* 22 (1980) 193–221. ————. "The Two-Fold Representation of the Mission in Matthew's Gospel." *ST* 31 (1977) 21–32. **Davies, W. D.** *The Setting of the Sermon on the Mount.* Cambridge: Cambridge University, 1966. **Hagner, D. A.** "The *Sitz im Leben* of the Gospel of Matthew." In *SBL 1985 Seminar Papers.* Atlanta: Scholars, 1985. 243–69. **Hare, D. R. A.,** and **Harrington, D. J.** "'Make Disciples of All the Gentiles' (Mt. 28.19)." *CBQ* 37 (1975) 359–69. **Hummel, R.** *Die Auseinandersetzung zwischen Kirche und Judentum im Matthäusevangelium.* 2nd ed. Munich: Kaiser, 1966. **Kimelman, R.** "*Birkat Ha-Minim* and the Lack of Evidence for an Anti-Chris-tian Jewish Prayer in Late Antiquity." In *Jewish and Christian Self-Definition,* ed. E. P. Sanders et al. Philadelphia: Fortress, 1981. 2:226–44, 391–403. **Levine, A.-J.** *The Social and Ethnic Dimensions of Matthean Salvation History.* Lewiston/Queenston: Mellen, 1988. **Meier, J. P.** "Antioch." In R. E. Brown and J. P. Meier, *Antioch and Rome: New Testament Cradles of Catho-lic Christianity.* New York: Paulist, 1983. 11–86. **Menninger, R.** *Israel and the Church in the Gospel of Matthew.* American University Studies 7. Theology and Religion. New York: Lang, 1994. **Stanton, G. N.** *A Gospel for a New People: Studies in Matthew.* Edinburgh: T. & T. Clark, 1992. **Thompson, W. G.** "A Historical Perspective in the Gospel of Matthew." *JBL* 93 (1974) 243–62. ———— and **Laverdière, E. G.** "New Testament Communities in Transition: A Study of Matthew and Luke." *TS* 37 (1976) 567–97. **Trilling, W.** *Das wahre Israel: Studien zur Theologie des Matthäusevangeliums.* 3rd ed. Munich: Kösel, 1964.

The challenge that has always faced Matthean studies is to posit a convincing *Sitz im Leben* for the Gospel that can account for its varied perspectives and em-phases. Of great importance among these are especially the tension between particularism and universalism within the Gospel and the closely related prob-lem of Israel and the Church. The extent to which any proposed *Sitz im Leben* is able to explain the diverse material in the Gospel (without, for example, alleging that some material was included by the evangelist simply because it was there in his tradition) should be an important measure of its plausibility.

Particularism and universalism. Matthew is the only Gospel that records Jesus' startling words that restrict his and his disciples' immediate ministry to Israel. According to 10:5–6 (cf. 10:23, "all the towns of Israel"), when Jesus sends the twelve out on their mission, he begins with a stern prohibition: "Go nowhere among the Gentiles, and enter no town of the Samaritans, but go rather to the lost sheep of the house of Israel." Later in the narrative (15:24), when Jesus himself is entreated by a gentile woman, he not only ignores her request (initially) but responds by saying: "I was sent only to the lost sheep of the house of Israel." So contradictory is this attitude to that of the evangelist's day, when the gentile mission was an undeniable reality, that these passages excellently satisfy the criterion of dissimilarity (so far as the early Church is concerned, but not, of course, so far as Judaism is concerned), and hence most scholars accept these sayings as authentic.

On the other hand, and seemingly against this particularism, there is an implicit universalism throughout the Gospel (i.e., the good news of the gospel is for Gentiles too). Thus, e.g., there is emphasis on gentile response to the gospel in the genealogy of Christ, which contains gentile names (Ruth and Rahab; 1:5); the magi from the East (2:1–12); the Roman centurion ("Truly I tell you, in no one in Israel have I found such faith"; 8:5–13); The statements "and in his name the Gentiles will hope" (12:21; cf. Isa 42:4) and "the field is the world" (13:38); the Canaanite woman (15:21–28); the parable of the tenants (21:33–43); the parable of the marriage feast (22:1–10); and the Roman soldiers' confession (27:54). What is implicit earlier becomes explicit in 24:14, where Jesus says, "And this good news of the kingdom will be proclaimed throughout the world, as a testimony to all the nations; and then the end will come"; and, of course, most impressively in the commission of 28:19: "Go therefore and make disciples of all nations, baptizing them in the name of the Father and of the Son and of the Holy Spirit."

Israel and the Church. The tension between particularism and universalism is obviously bound up with another polarity in the Gospel, that involving Israel and the Church. In Matthew, we encounter an apparent polemic against the Jews that is all the more striking because of the favored position of the Jews already noted and because of the generally Jewish tone of the Gospel. Probably most conspicuous here are the passages referring to a transference of the kingdom from Israel to those who believe in the gospel (the Church). Thus in 8:11–12, just following the compliment given to the Roman centurion for his faith, we read "I tell you, many will come from east and west and will eat with Abraham and Isaac and Jacob in the kingdom of heaven, while the heirs of the kingdom will be thrown into the outer darkness, where there will be weeping and gnashing of teeth." And in 21:41, at the end of the parable of the tenants, the tenants pronounce their own judgment: "He will put those wretches to a miserable death and lease the vineyard to other tenants who will give him the produce at the harvest time." This is followed by Jesus' words (21:43), "Therefore I tell you, the kingdom of God will be taken away from you and given to a people that produces the fruits of the kingdom." Agreeing with this emphasis is the parable of the marriage feast, where those invited "would not come" (22:3), and thus the invitation is extended to all: "Go therefore into the main streets, and invite everyone you find to the wedding banquet" (22:9).

To these passages may be added others that speak of the judgment of unbelieving Israel. Upbraiding the cities of Galilee where his miracles had been done

(11:20–24), Jesus concludes, "But I tell you, on the day of judgment it will be more tolerable for Tyre and Sidon . . . and the land of Sodom than for you." In 12:45 he refers to "this evil generation"; in 13:10–15 Matthew alone gives the full quotation of the judgment oracle of Isa 6:9–10: "With them indeed is fulfilled the prophecy of Isaiah that says: 'You will indeed listen, but never understand, and you will indeed look, but never perceive. For this people's heart has grown dull, and their ears are hard of hearing, and they have shut their eyes; so that they might not look with their eyes, and listen with their ears, and understand with their heart and turn—and I would heal them" (cf. Acts 28:26–27). In the parable of the marriage feast it is noted that "those invited were not worthy" (22:8). In 23:38 Jesus, lamenting over Jerusalem, states, "See, your house is left to you, desolate." And finally we may note the bitter and fateful words of 27:25, unique to Matthew: "Then the people as a whole answered: 'His blood be on us and on our children!'" words that have tragically and unjustifiably been used to promote anti-Semitism (see below "On Matthew's 'Anti-Judaism'").

By contrast, in these passages the kingdom is transferred to those who believe, a "nation" (ἔθνος) producing the fruit of the kingdom (righteousness), those who repent, those whose eyes are blessed and whose ears hear what "many prophets and righteous people longed to see and hear" (13:16–17). In view, of course, is the new community, called with deliberate anachronism the ἐκκλησία, the Church.

The Church and Israel thus stand in obviously painful tension in Matthew. Also reflecting this tension are the references to "*their* synagogues" (4:23; 9:35; 10:17; 12:9; 13:54), "*your* synagogues" (23:34), "*their* scribes" (7:29), and "the Jews to this day" (28:15)—most references unique to Matthew and the last comparable to the well-known derogatory use of "the Jews" in the Fourth Gospel. Throughout the book, moreover, it is the Pharisees, those whose viewpoint dominates Judaism after the destruction of Jerusalem in A.D. 70, that are the main antagonists of Jesus and who are repeatedly shown to be inferior to Jesus in their understanding of the Torah. Thus "when Jesus had finished saying these things, the crowds were astounded at his teaching, for he taught them as one having authority, and not as their scribes" (7:28–29). And at the end of the bitter denunciation of the scribes and Pharisees in chap. 23, Jesus can say, "Fill up, then, the measure of your ancestors. You snakes, you brood of vipers! How can you escape being sentenced to hell?" (23:32–33). Finally, the evangelist speaks explicitly of Jewish persecution of the Church: "Beware of them, for they will hand you over to the councils and flog you in their synagogues" (10:17); and "Therefore I send you prophets, sages, and scribes, some of whom you will kill and crucify, and some you will flog in your synagogues and pursue from town to town" (23:34).

Redaction-critical study of these passages shows that Matthew has given these motifs much greater prominence than have the other Synoptic writers. Much of the material is unique to this Gospel; and where Matthew depends upon Mark or Q, Matthew usually intensifies the tone of hostility. Matthew indeed is second only to the Fourth Gospel in apparent animosity toward the Jews.

Here, then, we have what is probably the major puzzle in the Gospel of Matthew. On the one hand, we have the particularism that limits Jesus' and his disciples' ministry to Israel. Together with this exclusivism—the normal Jewish viewpoint—is the generally Jewish tone of the Gospel with, among other things, its stress on the abiding validity of the law, the necessity of righteousness, and the fulfillment of messianic prophecy. On the other hand, however, standing in rather sharp contrast to the preceding, are the universalism of the Gospel, its striking transference of the kingdom motif to a new community, and the particularly harsh sayings against the Jews.

The relation of Matthew's church to contemporary Judaism. A key issue in defining the life setting of Matthew's community is whether by the time of the writing of the Gospel a clear break between the church and synagogue had taken place. In view here is the decision, which may have been made at Yavneh (Jamnia) around A.D. 85, to force Jewish Christians out of the synagogue by an addition of a curse against the *minim* or "heretics" to the liturgy of the synagogue (the *Birkat ha-Minim* in the twelfth of the Eighteen Benedictions, the *Shemoneh Esreh*).

A number of scholars have argued that the break with the synagogue had already happened by the time Matthew wrote and that this fact accounts for the hostility toward the Jews in the Gospel (e.g., Strecker, Trilling, and Meier). On this hypothesis, the pro-Jewish elements in the Gospel, the stress on the law and fulfillment of prophecy and especially the exclusivistic or particularistic sayings, are understood as remnants of earlier tradition that the evangelist did not assimilate to his own viewpoint. Some who hold this view also argue for a gentile readership and perhaps even a gentile author.

Other influential scholars, on the other hand, are convinced that Matthew reflects a time *prior* to the separation of church and synagogue, i.e., the Yavneh decision of 85 (e.g., Bornkamm, G. Barth, Hummel, Davies, S. Brown). They point to the Gospel's argument concerning Jesus as Messiah as evidence that the mission to the Jews had not ceased. They further note marks of a Jewish Christianity in such things as the positive note about the Pharisees in 23:2, the concern to avoid offense by the payment of the temple tax (17:24–27), and Matthew's view of the law (5:17–19). These data, together with those already mentioned in the preceding section, point to the continuing relationship between Jewish Christians and their non-Christian Jewish brethren.

Matthean scholarship thus finds itself in the strange circumstance of having been forced into two camps by emphasizing one side of the data in the Gospel to the neglect, not to say exclusion, of data on the other side. In the instance of Strecker and Trilling, certain Jewish motifs are pronounced anachronistic and hence essentially irrelevant to the life setting of the evangelist. In the case of Bornkamm, Barth, and Hummel, such things as the hostility toward the Jews and the transference of the kingdom motif find no convincing place in the life setting of the Jewish Christianity represented by the evangelist and his community.

Too much weight has been put upon Yavneh by many Matthean scholars in their attempt to understand Matthew and its life setting. This is all the more remarkable given how little we actually know about what transpired there, for our knowledge of what took place at Yavneh is tenuous at best. It may well be that Yavneh had no significance for the relationship between Jews and Jewish Christians (thus R. Kimelman). Matthean scholars have tended to work with two false presuppositions about Yavneh: (1) that there was no exclusion of Jewish Christians from the synagogue before this date and (2) that after Yavneh the mission to the Jews ceased. In fact, however, there is sufficient evidence of an early and continuing hostility between Jews who did not accept the gospel and those who did, including forceful exclusion from the synagogue (cf. Acts 6:12–14; 7:57–8:1;

and Paul's frequent experiences). If any specific date is to be mentioned as a clear turning point for the worse in the relationship between Jews and Christians, it would have to be 70, but even this date does not mark the beginning of hostility between the two groups. Thus the *Birkat ha-Minim*, even on the traditional understanding, amounts only to a formalizing and standardizing of practice, perhaps indeed as the result of mounting hostility, but it should by no means be thought of as an absolute beginning of the hostility or of the practice of exclusion. Furthermore, despite the argument of Hare and Harrington, there is no need to conclude that Matthew's community had abandoned the mission to the Jews (see commentary on 28:19). Because a mission to the Jews *within* the synagogue must have been abandoned after 85—again, on the traditional understanding—the end of the Jewish mission itself is hardly necessitated. Christian Jews would have continued to meet their unbelieving brothers and sisters in the community, where discussions, however tense, undoubtedly continued. It is in the final analysis unthinkable both psychologically and theologically that the Jewish-Christian community addressed by the evangelist could have altogether abandoned the mission to members of their own former community. The Apostle Paul can speak in no uncertain terms about the judgment of unbelieving Israel and the new reality of the Church that now stands in the place of national Israel, just as he can wrestle with the actual shift from Jews to Gentiles in the church, without for a moment losing his zeal for the conversion of his people (cf. Rom 9–11).

It seems unlikely, then, that the year 85 (or 90) should be thought of as a watershed providing a radically altered situation that can be used to explain the complex and apparently contradictory data of the Gospel. There is no solid reason why the phenomena assigned so confidently to the post-85 era by some scholars cannot equally well find a place before that time. Thus the universalism, the sayings about the transference of the kingdom, and the hard sayings against Israel are hardly impossible in the earlier decades. Jesus could have spoken about the future (i.e., the post-resurrection period), envisioning a mission to the Gentiles and thus justifying the transference sayings. All of this would have been quite meaningful in a context where the gentile mission was thriving, as would be the sayings against the Jews, which would have reflected the unbelief of the Jews as well as the continuing and probably growing hostility between the church and the synagogue.

The special situation of Matthew's community. As we have seen in the preceding section, Matthew's readers were almost certainly Jewish Christians. To begin with, it is worth noting that Jewish Christians have always found themselves in a difficult situation, not least in the first century. When Jews become Christians they are forced to cope, on the one hand, with their non-Christian Jewish brothers and sisters from whom they have separated themselves and, on the other hand, with a largely gentile Christianity among whom they now exist as a minority but as members of the family nonetheless. To their Jewish brothers and sisters, Jewish Christians have always had to answer such charges as disloyalty to the religion of Israel, disloyalty to the Mosaic law (or at least of association with others who fail to observe it), and affiliation with an alien, if not pagan, religion, the large majority of whose adherents are Gentiles. In short, Jews are naturally put on the defensive by their non-Christian Jewish community, and probably more so if they have insisted on preservation of their Jewishness and have resisted assimilation, thus making at least the implicit claim of being the true Israel. So far as the gentile

Christians are concerned, Jewish Christians are always under a subtle pressure to minimize the significance of their Jewishness; their continued observance of the Jewish law and customs can easily become a theological problem for gentile Christians and a hindrance to fellowship and a sense of unity. The gentile Christians in Matthew's day may have rejoiced in (and may have insisted upon) discontinuity between the old and new covenants much more readily than many Jewish Christians would have. Jewish Christians were thus forced to work out their relationships with gentile Christianity and their understanding of the newness contained in and implied by the reality of Christ.

Matthew's original readers were in this unenviable position, in a kind of "no man's land" between their Jewish brothers and sisters, on the one hand, and gentile Christians, on the other, wanting to reach back for continuity with the old and at the same time to reach forward to the new work God was doing in the largely gentile church—simultaneously answerable, so to speak, to both Jews and Gentiles. Finding themselves in this dilemma, Matthew's readers needed an account of the story of Jesus that would enable them to relate both to unbelieving Jews and to gentile Christians. In particular, the increasing success of the gentile mission and the overall failure of the mission to Israel raised questions not only in the readers' minds but also among their Jewish opponents. Thus the Gospel was written to confirm Jewish believers in the truth of Christianity as the fulfillment of the promises to Israel, which entails the argument that Jesus is the Messiah, that he was loyal to the law, and that he came to the Jews. Through this material, the readers could gain confidence in the correctness of their faith as something standing in true succession to the Scriptures and at the same time be in a better position to answer their unbelieving Jewish brothers and sisters in the synagogues. (See now esp. Stanton, who convincingly argues for a view similar to this, buttressing the conclusion with sociological insights.)

If this is true, we may well also find here the reason for the preservation of the particularist sayings in Matthew. It was important for the author to be able to stress that Jesus came specifically—indeed, exclusively—to the Jews in order to underline God's faithfulness to his covenant people, i.e., to stress the continuity of God's salvific promises and the actuality of their fulfillment in the first instance to Israel, as the Scriptures promised. In the face of an increasingly gentile church, which must have given its Jewish opponents the embarrassing opportunity to argue that Christianity was an alien religion, the readers were thus able to realize that they, unlike the Gentiles, had a place in the ministry of Jesus from the beginning. They, as Jewish Christians, were important in the fulfillment of God's plan as a righteous remnant attesting the faithfulness of God to his covenant promises. Matthew thus affirms the rightful place of Jewish Christianity as the true Israel. Far from renouncing Judaism, as K. W. Clark maintains, Matthew finds in Christianity a perfected or fulfilled Judaism, brought to its goal by the long-awaited Christ.

The particularist sayings, then, are not simply relics of the historical tradition without relevance for the readers of the Gospel, but neither do they indicate a contemporary limitation upon the mission of Matthew's community. They refer historically to what once was the case, during the pre-resurrection ministry of Jesus and his disciples, but have special relevance to the readers as a theological justification of the faithfulness of God to his people Israel and thus of the propriety of Jewish-Christian faith.

If Jesus was sent "only to the lost sheep of the house of Israel," it remains true, however, that Israel largely failed to respond. The Jewish-Christian readers of this Gospel would have been painfully aware of the lack of response among the Jewish community. What had happened already in the time of Jesus was happening in their time. Inevitably and by reason of their unbelieving and hostile brothers and sisters, Jewish-Christian congregations must early have begun to think of themselves as separate from, and even as opposed to, unbelieving Judaism—as a righteous remnant against the rabbinic Judaism represented in the Gospel by the Pharisees. It is not at all unthinkable that Jewish Christians could have appreciated the harsh sayings in the Gospel against the Jews, the judgment against unbelieving Israel, and could have referred, for example, to "their synagogues" (9:35) or "their scribes" (7:29). The familiar biblical pattern, denounced so frequently by the prophets, would have been seen in Israel's rejection of God, followed by God's rejection of Israel. And from the latter it is only a step to the sayings about the transference of the kingdom. In the case of these sayings, however, our Jewish-Christian readers would, of course, have identified themselves as among those nations (ἔθνη, "gentiles," largely but not exclusively), the new people of God to whom the kingdom was being transferred. Similarly, the record of Jesus' words about the Jewish persecution of Christians (23:34; 10:23) would have been especially relevant to the readers. The considerable polemics against the Jews— and the distancing from the Jews—in Matthew are by no means unimaginable within a Jewish-Christian context.

The evangelist's community thus shared in two worlds, the Jewish and the Christian. Although the members of this community saw their Christianity as the true fulfillment of Judaism, they were also very conscious that they had broken with their unbelieving brothers and sisters. They were struggling to define and defend a Jewish Christianity to the Jews, on the one hand, and to realize their identity with gentile Christians, on the other. This twofold challenge explains the basic tensions encountered in the Gospel.

And it is for these reasons that Matthew writes that "new wine is put into fresh wineskins and so both are preserved" (9:17). Matthew's redactional addition of the last words "and so are both preserved," found neither in Mark or Luke, is congruent with his emphasis on the abiding validity of the law. The new wine of the gospel is preserved together with the new skins, i.e., the law as definitively interpreted by Jesus the Messiah. Here we see the evangelist reaching in both directions to stress continuity with Moses and the Torah and yet at the same time to affirm the radical newness of the gospel. Similarly, he writes in what some think is an autobiographical allusion: "Therefore every scribe who has been trained for the kingdom of heaven is like the master of a household who brings out of his treasure what is new and what is old" (13:52).

ON MATTHEW'S "ANTI-JUDAISM"

Bibliography

Garland, D. E. *The Intention of Matthew 23.* NovTSup 51. Leiden: Brill, 1979. **Johnson, L. T.** "The New Testament's Anti-Jewish Slander and the Conventions of Ancient Rhetoric." *JBL* 108 (1989) 419–41. **Mason, S.** "Pharisaic Dominance before 70 C.E. and the Gospels'

Hypocrisy Charge." *HTR* 83 (1990) 363–81. **McKnight, S.** "A Loyal Critic: Matthew's Polemic with Judaism in Theological Perspective." In *The New Testament and Anti-Semitism*, ed. C. A. Evans and D. A. Hagner. Minneapolis: Fortress, 1993. 55–79. **Niedner, F. A.** "Rereading Matthew on Jerusalem and Judaism." *BTB* 19 (1989) 43–47. **Russell, E. A.** "'Antisemitism' in the Gospel of Matthew." *IBS* 8 (1986) 183–96.

This is not the place to deal fully with this important subject. Our purpose is merely to alert readers to the problem and to put them on their guard against the anti-Semitic potential of the material.

We have already spoken in the above paragraphs (see under "The *Sitz im Leben* ['Life Setting'] of Matthew's Community") concerning the harshness of Matthew's polemic against the Jews. In some instances the material is shared, such as the Q passage of 3:7 where those coming to John the Baptist (the Pharisees and Sadducees according to Matthew) are addressed as "you brood of vipers." But in the majority of instances the harsh passages are unique to Matthew. By way of illustration, we may point out the following.

In 6:1–18, religious practices of Jews (i.e., probably the Pharisees) make them ὑποκριταί, "hypocrites." The kingdom is taken away from the Jews in 21:43, and they are designated "not worthy" in 22:8. The Pharisees are, of course, repeatedly described as hypocrites in the infamous denunciation of the Pharisees and scribes in chap. 23. They are blasted with such names as "child(ren) of hell" (v 15), "blind fools" (v 17), "blind guides" (v 24), and "snakes" and "brood of vipers" (v 33) and described as "full of hypocrisy and lawlessness" (v 28). Perhaps worst of all is the responsibility Matthew puts squarely upon the Jews for the death of Jesus, seen most vividly in the shocking statement of 27:25, only in Matthew, "His blood be on us and on our children."

It is very important to understand that this language is not anti-Semitic. These words are written by a Jew concerning Jews and are therefore to be understood as intramural Jewish polemic not unlike the blistering criticism of the Jews that is frequently delivered by the classical OT prophets. This kind of inflated language is furthermore typical of the polemical rhetoric used in the ancient world (see Johnson). It is also even wrong, strictly speaking, to refer to this material as anti-Judaic. None of the Jewish Christians of the NT would have thought of Christianity as an anti-Judaism. To believe in the gospel of the kingdom and Jesus as the messianic king was for them to enter into the beginning of the fulfillment of the Jewish hope (cf. Acts 28:20), to be true Jews, and to form the remnant of the true Israel.

Yet, tragically, the hostile words of Matthew have through the centuries provided many with a pretext for anti-Semitism. At the end of our century, which has witnessed in the Holocaust the most horrific result of anti-Semitism, Christians must be responsible in their handling of these passages in Matthew as well as in the rest of the NT. It is thus important for all who study and teach the Gospel of Matthew to understand the historical character of this material, its first-century context, its rhetorical nature, and the intramural nature of the polemic and to be vigilant against every misunderstanding or misuse of these texts. Because of the tragic history of the relation between the synagogue and the church, we are now under permanent obligation to explain carefully what these texts do *not* mean.

We have positive material elsewhere in the NT to help counteract anti-Semitic thinking. Paul, who can at times engage in the harshest polemic against his fellow

Jews who reject the gospel, regards them still as beloved of God (Rom 11:28) and believes that they too shall yet receive mercy (Rom 11:12, 15, 23–24, 26, 29, 32). But even in Matthew we have Jesus the Jew who comes to save his people (1:22), who goes only to "the lost sheep of the house of Israel" (15:24; cf. 10:5–6), and who at the end of the hostile denunciation of the Pharisees laments with utmost tenderness the unresponsiveness of his people, referring to a time when they will finally welcome him (23:37–39). And it is Matthew above all for whom the whole law and the prophets are summarized in the two supreme commandments: "You shall love the Lord your God with all your heart, and with all your soul, and with all your mind," and "You shall love your neighbor as yourself" (22:37–40).

DATE AND PROVENANCE

Bibliography

Balch, D. L., ed. *Social History of the Matthean Community: Cross-Disciplinary Approaches.* Minneapolis: Fortress, 1991. **Gundry, R. H.** *Matthew: A Commentary on His Literary and Theological Art.* Grand Rapids: Eerdmans, 1982. 599–609. **Kilpatrick, G. D.** *The Origins of the Gospel according to St. Matthew.* Oxford: Clarendon, 1946. **Meier, J. P.** "Antioch." In R. E. Brown and J. P. Meier, *Antioch and Rome.* New York: Paulist, 1983. 11–86. **Osborne, R.** "The Provenance of St. Matthew's Gospel." *SR* 3 (1973) 220–35. **Reicke, B.** *The Roots of the Synoptic Gospels.* Philadelphia: Fortress, 1986. ————. "Synoptic Prophecies on the Destruction of Jerusalem." In *Studies in New Testament and Early Christian Literature,* ed. D. Aune. Leiden: Brill, 1972. 121–34. **Rengstorf, K. H.** "Die Stadt der Mörder (Matt. 22.7)." In *Judentum, Urchristentum, Kirche.* FS J. Jeremias, ed. W. Eltester. BZNW 26. Berlin: Töpelmann, 1960. 106–29. **Robinson, J. A. T.** *Redating the New Testament.* Philadelphia: Westminster, 1976. 86–117. **Slingerland, H.** "The Transjordanian Origin of St. Matthew's Gospel." *JSNT* 3 (1979) 18–28. **Viviano, B.** "Where Was the Gospel according to St. Matthew Written?" *CBQ* 41 (1979) 533–46. **Wenham, J.** *Redating Matthew, Mark and Luke.* Downers Grove, IL: InterVarsity, 1992. **Zumstein, J.** "Antioche sur l'Oronte et l'Évangile selon Matthieu." *SNTU* A5 (1980) 122–38.

Date. Two key questions that pertain to the dating of Matthew are (1) whether the relationship between church and synagogue indicates that the final break, usually dated at A.D. 85 or 90, had already occurred when the Gospel was written and (2) whether the Gospel reflects a knowledge of the fall of Jerusalem (A.D. 70). We have noted above that we know little about the Yavneh decisions of 80 or 85, and we have argued that Yavneh is hardly to be conceived of as a watershed in relations between the church and the synagogue (see under "The *Sitz im Leben* ['Life Setting'] of Matthew's Community"). Alienation, competition, and hostility were not unusual before the alleged break, and the mission to the Jews did not cease after it.

The second question is not as easy to answer as many have thought. Matthew does allude to the destruction of Jerusalem in 24:2 (cf. 24:15–28), but this can be naturally explained as a record of the prophecy of Jesus, unless the possibility of foretelling the future is ruled out a priori. The reference in 22:7 to the parable of the king who, being angry because those invited to the marriage feast did not come, "sent his troops, destroyed those murderers, and burned their city" is more problematic. The reference to "troops" who "burned the city," unnecessary and alien to the context, seems to point to the destruction of Jerusalem. Even if it does, however, the possibility remains that Jesus prophesied the event through the parable or that the words were added to the Gospel later, after the event had occurred. Thus 22:7 cannot itself be proof that Matthew as a whole is to be dated after 70. It is furthermore true that the language of the parable under consideration is hyperbolic and not necessarily to be taken literally. K. H. Rengstorf has indicated the possibility that the language is a conventional stereotype for punitive expeditions. Gundry (*Matthew*, 436) shows that the language could be an allusion to Isa 5:24–25 (cf. too Judg 1:8; 1 Macc 5:28; *T. Jud.* 5:1–5). B. Reicke has also indicated the weakness of the usual explanation of 22:7. In short, far too much weight has been put on this text in the confident post-70 dating of Matthew.

Other common objections to an early date of the Gospel need consideration at this point. First, if it is true that Matthew is dependent on Mark, as we have argued above, and Mark was written in the late 60s, as the consensus holds, must not Matthew be post-70? The false assumption here is that one needs a decade between Mark and Matthew. In actuality, Matthew needs only to be written after Mark—and there is no reason why this needs to have been more than a year or two later, if that. Second, a more "developed" Judaism and a considerably heightened hostility between the church and the synagogue than existed before 70 are needed to account for the content in Matthew. This objection presupposes, on the one hand, more knowledge of pre-70 Judaism than we possess and, on the other, that there was only limited hostility between church and synagogue before 70. Third, some have thought Matthew's doctrine too developed to be before 70, e.g., in its Christology (11:27–30), ecclesiology (16:18–19; 18:15–20), and trinitarian formula (28:19). Yet the letters of Paul have similar, developed perspectives several years before the destruction of Jerusalem.

Matthew's redaction of the Markan eschatological discourse makes no attempt to disentangle the references to the fall of Jerusalem and the end of the age (chap. 24). Luke very deliberately does so in his redaction of Mark 13, and we might expect Matthew to do the same had it been written after 70. Indeed, the evangelist aggravates the problem considerably by his insertion of εὐθέως, "immediately," in 24:29, which leaves the clear impression that he expected the parousia of the Son of Man to occur in close succession to the fall of Jerusalem.

Among other evidence that seems to point to an early date of the Gospel, the following should be mentioned. Unique to Matthew are several redactional additions connected with the temple: the reference to offering and leaving one's "gift" at the altar (5:23–24), the passage on the rightness of paying of the temple tax (17:24–27), and the reference to "swearing by the sanctuary" (23:16–22). It is more difficult to believe that these are anachronisms deliberately added by the evangelist after the temple had been destroyed than it is to believe that they have relevance because the temple was still standing when the Gospel was written. Similarly, Matthew's redactional addition of the words "pray that your flight may not be in winter or on a sabbath" (24:20) make little sense if the destruction of Jerusalem had already occurred.

There is thus good reason to take seriously the possibility of an early (i.e., pre-70) dating of the Gospel (with, for example, Gundry, Reicke, Robinson, and Wenham). The inclination toward an early date taken here, however, is just that

and no more. It needs to be re-emphasized that the dogmatism of critical ortho-
doxy concerning a post-70 date is unwarranted. But this is no reason to give rein
to a similar dogmatism concerning a pre-70 date. We need to remind ourselves
how very difficult the dating of the Gospels is and how necessarily speculative
our conclusions are.

Provenance. We are in equal straits when it comes to knowing where the Gospel
of Matthew was written. The only evidence we have is indirect: a document written in Greek in a group of Jewish Christians in the neighborhood of a Jewish
community and perhaps near gentile Christians as well. There are also signs in
the Gospel that may point to a prosperous community in an urban context.

Even if we look for a city with a Jewish population where the lingua franca was
Greek and where there were also gentile churches, we have not narrowed the
possibilities very much. H. D. Slingerland's hypothesis of a Transjordanian origin
(Pella) of Matthew depends altogether on the phrase "across the Jordan" in 4:15
and 19:1, which can be explained in other ways. Caesarea Maritima has been favored by Viviano; the Phoenician cities of Tyre or Sidon by Kilpatrick. Other cities
have also been suggested.

One of the most popular options for a long time was a Palestinian origin, with
support derived from the numerous Jewish characteristics of the Gospel and especially the idea (from Papias) of an original Aramaic Gospel. With the modern
consensus that the Gospel was written originally in Greek, the likelihood of a
Palestinian origin diminishes considerably. Diaspora Judaism, moreover, can
readily account for the Jewishness of the Gospel.

Of Diaspora cities that might fit what is required, Syrian Antioch has been the
clear favorite. Given the population of cosmopolitan Antioch, just the kind of
problems that the Gospel addresses can easily be imagined as occurring. That is,
Jewish Christians would have had to defend their views against the charges of the
Jewish community while at the same time relating to the gentile Christian community. There are furthermore some links between the Gospel of Matthew and
the *Didache,* which has been related to Syria. And the letters of Ignatius, bishop of
Antioch, are the first to indicate a probable knowledge of the Gospel of Matthew.

It may be, on the other hand, that Antioch is such an attractive hypothesis
simply because we happen to know so much more about it than about most other
cities. It is worth reminding ourselves that Antioch is only a good guess. On this
point it is worth quoting a summary of the view held by contributors to a recent
important symposium on the "Social History of the Matthean Community." J. D.
Kingsbury (in D. L. Balch, ed., *Social History*) summarizes the opinion concerning the location of the Matthean community in these words: "[it] was situated in
an urban environment, perhaps in Galilee or perhaps more toward the north in
Syria but, in any case, not necessarily Antioch" (264).

AUTHORSHIP

Bibliography

Abel, E. L. "Who Wrote Matthew?" *NTS* 17 (1970-71) 138–52. **Clark, K. W.** "The Gentile
Bias in Matthew." *JBL* 66 (1947) 165–72. **Gundry, R. H.** *Matthew: A Commentary on His Literary and Theological Art.* Grand Rapids: Eerdmans, 1982. 609–22. **Meier, J. P.** *The Vision of*

Matthew: Christ, Church and Morality in the First Gospel. New York: Paulist, 1979. **Nepper-Christensen, P.** *Das Matthäusevangelium: Ein judenchristliches Evangelium?* Aarhus: Universitetsforlaget, 1958. **Strecker, G.** *Der Weg der Gerechtigkeit.* 3rd ed. Göttingen: Vandenhoeck & Ruprecht, 1971.

Matthew, like all the Gospels in the NT, is an anonymous document. The title κατὰ Μαθθαῖον, "according to Matthew," was affixed to the Gospel sometime in the second century. From early in the second century, the unanimous tradition of the Church supports Matthew as the author (e.g., Papias, who received the tradition from the Elder [Apostle?] John, Pantaenus, Irenaeus, Origen, Eusebius, Jerome). The only clues within the text of the Gospel itself are the substitution of the name Matthew (9:9) for Levi in the calling of the tax collector to be a disciple (Mark 2:13; cf. Luke 5:27) and the addition of the words "the tax collector" to the name Matthew in the listing of the twelve in 10:3 (cf. Mark 3:18; Luke 6:15). For some reason the evangelist wants to show that Levi is the Matthew listed among the twelve. Is this because he believes that Levi was or should have been one of the twelve, or is it perhaps because in writing of himself he preferred the name Matthew to his own pre-conversion name, Levi?

The real question concerns the reliability of the tradition about the authorship of the Gospel. It is possible, although uncertain, that the whole tradition derives from, and is thus dependent upon, the testimony of one man, Papias (as recorded in Eusebius, *H.E.* 3.39.16). In any event, the tradition appears to have been unchallenged. It is difficult to believe that the Gospel would have been attributed to Matthew without good reason, since, so far as we can tell from the available data, Matthew was not otherwise a leading figure among the apostles or in the early Church (his name being mentioned only once outside the Gospels in Acts 1:13). A key objection often set against the traditional ascription of the Gospel to Matthew is the difficulty of believing that one of the twelve, an eyewitness of the events, could have depended so much upon the account of Mark, a non-participant in the narrated events. According to the tradition handed on by Papias (Eusebius, *H.E.* 3.39.15), however, Mark is essentially the preaching of Peter, and it is not at all inconceivable that Matthew might depend upon a Petrine account represented by Mark.

But can Matthew the apostle have written the Greek document that goes by his name, a document that contains such developed and "late" perspectives? Here it is more difficult to be confident. The tradition about Matthean authorship may be compatible with a conclusion that the Gospel contains traditions stemming from the apostle (who as a former tax collector may well have kept records of Jesus' ministry), perhaps now recognizable particularly in the Gospel's special material, e.g., in the formula quotations or the material underlying the five discourses. A disciple (or disciples) of Matthew may later have translated and adapted these materials, combined them with the Markan and Q traditions, and reworked the whole to produce our present Gospel. Such a hypothesis, speculative though it must be, could account for the Gospel in the form we have it.

The argument of some (e.g., Clark, Meier, Nepper-Christensen, Strecker) that the author was a Gentile rather than a Jew is not convincing. The typical problems that are raised in this connection have better explanations. Thus, for example, the linking of the Sadducees with the Pharisees (e.g., in 16:1, 6, 11–12) is not the result of ignorance concerning the great differences between the two groups but probably only the indication of a united front of opposition against Jesus based upon the agreement that Jesus was not the Messiah. The mention of two animals in 21:1–9 is by no means necessarily a misunderstanding of the synonymous parallelism of Zech 9:9 (see commentary). The hostility against the Jews in Matthew is not at all unthinkable from the hand of a Jewish Christian; on the contrary, it points to a Jewish author and is exactly what one might expect in the circumstances. Few recent commentators on the Gospel have been inclined to accept the view that the author was a Gentile.

Matthew the apostle is thus probably the source of an early form of significant portions of the Gospel, in particular the sayings of Jesus, but perhaps even some of the narrative material. One or more disciples of the Matthean circle may then have put these materials into the form of the Gospel we have today. The final editing probably was done by a Hellenistic Jewish Christian, who in transmitting the tradition addressed Jewish fellow believers who, like himself, had come to accept Jesus as the Messiah and now had to articulate that new faith in such a way as to show its continuity with the past as well as to affirm all the newness of the gospel of the kingdom.

Matthew 1:1–13:58

The Birth and Infancy Narratives   (1:1–2:23)

Bibliography

Bornhäuser, K. *Die Geburts- und Kindheitsgeschichte Jesu.* BFCT 2.23. Gütersloh: Bertelsmann, 1930. **Bourke, M.** "The Literary Genus of Matthew 1–2." *CBQ* 22 (1960) 160–75. **Box, G. H.** "The Gospel Narratives of the Nativity and the Alleged Influence of Heathen Ideas." *ZNW* 6 (1905) 80–101. **Brown, R. E.** *The Birth of the Messiah.* Garden City, NY: Doubleday, 1977. **Daniélou, J.** *The Infancy Narratives.* New York: Herder & Herder, 1968. **Derrett, J. D. M.** "Further Light on the Narratives of the Nativity." *NovT* 17 (1975) 81–108. **Down, M. J.** "The Matthean Birth Narratives: Matt. 1:18–2:23." *ExpTim* 90 (1978) 51–52. **Elderen, B. van.** "The Significance of the Structure of Matthew 1." In *Chronos, Kairos, Christos.* FS J. Finegan, ed. J. Vardaman and E. M. Yamauchi. Winona Lake, IN: Eisenbrauns, 1989. 3–14. **Goodman, F. W.** "Sources of the First Two Chapters in Matthew and Luke." *CQR* 162 (1961) 136–43. **Kattenbusch, F.** "Die Geburtsgeschichte Jesu als Haggada der Urchristologie." *TSK* 102 (1930) 454–74. **Leaney, R.** "The Birth Narratives in St. Luke and St. Matthew." *NTS* 8 (1961–62) 158–66. **Mann, C. S.** "The Historicity of the Birth Narratives." In *Historicity and Chronology in the New Testament.* Theological Collection 6. London: SPCK, 1965. 46–58. **Milton, H.** "The Structure of the Prologue to St. Matthew's Gospel." *JBL* 81 (1962) 175–81. **Minear, P. S.** "The Interpreter and the Birth Narratives." *SymBU* 13 (1950) 1–22. **Nellessen, E.** *Das Kind und seine Mutter: Struktur und Verkündigung des 2. Kapitels im Matthäusevangelium.* SBS 39. Stuttgart: Katholisches Bibelwerk, 1969. ————. "Zu den Kindheitsgeschichten bei Matthäus und Lukas." *TTZ* 78 (1969) 305–9 (a survey of German literature). **Nolan, B. M.** *The Royal Son of God: The Christology of Matthew 1–2 in the Setting of the Gospel.* OBO 23. Göttingen: Vandenhoeck & Ruprecht, 1979. **Pesch, R.,** ed. *Zur Theologie der Kindheitsgeschichten: Der heutige Stand der Exegese.* Munich: Katholische Akademie Freiburg, 1981. **Reicke, B.** "Christ's Birth and Childhood." In *From Faith to Faith.* FS D. G. Miller, ed. D. Y. Hadidian. Pittsburgh: Pickwick, 1979. 151–65. **Riedl, J.** *Die Vorgeschichte Jesu: Die Heilsbotschaft von Mt 1–2 und Lk 1–2.* Biblisches Forum 3. Stuttgart: Katholisches Bibelwerk, 1968. **Stendahl, K.** "Quis et Unde? An Analysis of Mt. 1–2." In *Judentum—Urchristentum—Kirche.* FS J. Jeremias, ed. W. Eltester. BZNW 26. Berlin: Töpelmann, 1964. 97–105. **Thompson, P. J.** "The Infancy Gospels of St. Matthew and St. Luke Compared." *SE* 1 [TU 73] (1959) 217–22. **Vögtle, A.** "Die Genealogie Mt 1,2–16 und die matthäische Kindheitsgeschichte." *BZ* 8 (1964) 45–58, 239–62; 9 (1965) 32–49. ————. *Messias und Gottessohn: Herkunft und Sinn der matthäischen Geburts- und Kindheitsgeschichte.* Düsseldorf: Patmos, 1971. **Wickings, H. F.** "The Nativity Stories and Docetism." *NTS* 23 (1977) 457–60.

ON THE OT FORMULA QUOTATIONS:

France, R. T. "The Formula Quotations and the Problem of Communication." *NTS* 27 (1981) 233–51. **Friggens, M. A.** "Further Light on the Narratives of the Nativity." *NovT* 17 (1975) 81–108. **Gundry, R. H.** *The Use of the Old Testament in St. Matthew's Gospel.* NovTSup 18. Leiden: Brill, 1967. **Hartman, L.** "Scriptural Exegesis in the Gospel of St. Matthew and the Problem of Communication." In *L'Evangile selon Matthieu: Rédaction et Théologie,* ed. M. Didier. Gembloux: Duculot, 1972. **McConnell, R. S.** *Law and Prophecy in Matthew's Gospel: The Authority and Use of the Old Testament in the Gospel of Matthew.* Theologische Dissertationen 2. Basel: Basel University, 1969. **O'Rourke, J.** "The Fulfillment Texts in Matthew." *CBQ* 24 (1962) 394–403. **Pesch, R.** "Eine alttestamentliche Ausführungsformel im Matthäus-Evangelium." *BZ* 10 (1966) 220–45; 11 (1967) 79–95. ————. "Der Gottessohn im matthäischen Evangelienprolog (Mt 1–2): Beobachtungen zu den Zitationsformeln der Reflexionszitate." *Bib* 48 (1967) 395–420. **Rothfuchs, W.** *Die Erfüllungszitate des Matthäus-*

Evangeliums. BWANT 88. Stuttgart: Kohlhammer, 1969. **Soares Prabhu, G. M.** *The Formula Quotations in the Infancy Narrative of Matthew.* AnBib 63. Rome: Biblical Institute, 1976. **Stendahl, K.** *The School of St. Matthew.* 2nd ed. Philadelphia: Fortress, 1968.

Introduction

Since the ministry of Jesus begins only after his baptism by John (chap. 3) and the temptation (4:1–11), the opening two chapters of Matthew are in a sense the preparation for the main narrative. The preparation that Matthew provides, however, is far from simply the supplying of some helpful background information. The first two chapters constitute a work of art that makes a statement of its own and that anticipates the theological richness of the total Gospel.

The question of the historicity of chaps. 1–2 is very often posed in terms of history and theology conceived of as polar opposites, as though what is theological cannot be historical and vice versa. That is, one has here *either* theology *or* history. The idea of a historical core with theological elaboration is hardly considered. Yet that may very well be the case here in what is admittedly material of a special character. Matthew has taken his historical traditions and set them forth in such a way as to underline matters of fundamental theological importance. Thus he grounds his narrative upon several OT quotations and provides a strong sense of fulfillment. The literary genre of these chapters, as we shall see, is that of midrashic haggadah, designed to bring out the deeper meaning of the present by showing its theological continuity with the past. Matthew's procedure is to set the scene theologically by identifying the who (*quis*) and the how (*quomodo*) in chap. 1, and the where (*ubi*) and whence (*unde*) in chap. 2 (Stendahl, "Quis," and Brown, *Birth*). To some extent Matthew may have apologetic or polemical concerns here, but in the main these chapters are a statement of the theological significance that may be perceived even in the preliminaries (see Van Elderen, "Significance," on theological aspects of chap. 1). In this instance the prolegomena articulate the gospel before the main narrative.

The Ancestry of Jesus   (1:1–17)

Bibliography

Abel, E. L. "The Genealogies of Jesus *Ho Christos.*" *NTS* 20 (1973–74) 203–10. **Blair, H. A.** "Matthew 1, 16 and the Matthean Genealogy." *SE* 2 [TU 87] (1964) 149–54. **Davis, C. T.** "The Fulfillment of Creation: A Study of Matthew's Genealogy." *JAAR* 41 (1973) 520–35. **Freed, E. D.** "The Women in Matthew's Genealogy." *JSNT* 29 (1987) 3–19. **Gibbs, J. M.** "The Gospel Prologues and Their Function." *SE* 2 [TU 112] (1973) 154–58. **Godet, F.** *A Commentary on the Gospel of St. Luke.* Tr. E. N. Shields. 2 vols. 1887, 1889. Repr. Edinburgh: T. & T. Clark, 1976. **Hanson, A. T.** "Rahab the Harlot in Early Christian Tradition." *JSNT* 1 (1978) 53–60. **Heffern, A. D.** "The Four Women in St. Matthew's Genealogy of Christ." *JBL* 31 (1912) 68–81. **Hood, R. T.** "The Genealogies of Jesus." In *Early Christian Origins.* FS H. R. Willoughby, ed. A. Wikgren. Chicago: Quadrangle, 1961. 1–15. **Jeremias, J.** *Jerusalem* *in the Time of Jesus.* Philadelphia: Fortress, 1969. 272–97. **Johnson, M. D.** *The Purpose of the Biblical Genealogies with Special Reference to the Setting of the Genealogies of Jesus.* SNTSMS 8. Cambridge: Cambridge University, 1969. **Krentz, E.** "The Extent of Matthew's Prologue." *JBL* 83 (1964) 409–14. **Kuhn, G.** "Die Geschlechtsregister Jesu bei Lukas und Matthäus, nach ihrer Herkunft untersucht." *ZNW* 22 (1923) 206–28. **Lerle, E.** "Die Ahnenverzeichnisse Jesu." *ZNW* 72 (1981) 112–17. **Lindblom, J.** "Matteusevangeliets Överskrift." In *Teologiska Studier.* FS E. Stave. Uppsala: Almquist & Wiksells, 1922. 102–9. **Masson, J.** *Jésus fils de David dans les généalogies de Saint Matthieu et de Saint Luc.* Paris: Téqui, 1982. **Metzger, B. M.** "The Text of Matthew 1.16." In *Studies in New Testament and Early Christian Literature.* FS A. P. Wikgren, ed. D. E. Aune. Leiden: Brill, 1972. 16–24. **Moore, R. F.** "Fourteen Generations—490 Years." *HTR* 14 (1921) 97–103. **Moreton, M. J.** "The Genealogy of Jesus." *SE* 2 [TU 87] (1964) 219–24. **Newman, B. M., Jr.** "Matthew 1:1–18: Some Comments and a Suggested Restructuring." *BT* 27 (1976) 209–12. **Nineham, D. E.** "The Genealogy in St. Matthew's Gospel and Its Significance for the Study of the Gospel." *BJRL* 58 (1975–76) 421–44. **Quinn, J. D.** "Is 'Rachab' in Mt. 1.5 Rahab of Jericho?" *Bib* 62 (1981) 224–28. **Schnider, F.,** and **Stenger, W.** "Die Frauen im Stammbaum Jesu nach Matthäus: Strukturale Beobachtungen zu Mt. 1,1–17." *BZ* 23 (1979) 187–96. **Schöllig, H.** "Die Zählung der Generationen im matthäischen Stammbaum." *ZNW* 59 (1968) 261–68. **Stegemann, H.** "'Die des Uria': Zur Bedeutung der Frauennamen in der Genealogie von Matthäus 1,1–17." In *Tradition und Glaube: Das frühe Christentum in seiner Umwelt.* FS K. G. Kuhn, ed. G. Jeremias, H.-W. Kuhn, and H. Stegemann. Göttingen: Vandenhoeck & Ruprecht, 1971. 246–76. **Tatum, W. B.** "The Origin of Jesus Messiah (Matt. 1:1, 18a): Matthew's Use of the Infancy Traditions." *JBL* 96 (1977) 523–35. **Vögtle, A.** "Die Genealogie Mt 1, 2–16 und die matthäische Kindheitsgeschichte." In *Das Evangelium und die Evangelien.* Düsseldorf: Patmos, 1971. 57–102. **Waetjen, H. C.** "The Genealogy as the Key to the Gospel according to Matthew." *JBL* 95 (1976) 205–30. **Wilson, R. R.** *Genealogy and History in the Biblical World.* New Haven: Yale, 1977. **Zakowitch, Y.** "Rahab als Mutter des Boas in der Jesus-Genealogie (Matth. I 5)." *NovT* 17 (1975) 1–5.

Translation

1   *A record of the origin of Jesus Christ, the son of David, the son of Abraham:*
2   *Abraham was the father of Isaac,*
      Isaac the father of Jacob,
      Jacob the father of Judah and his brothers,
3   *Judah was the father of Perez and Zerah by Tamar,*
      Perez the father of Hezron,
      Hezron the Father of Aram,[a]
4   *Aram the father of Amminadab,*
      Amminadab the father of Nahshon,
      Nahshon the father of Salmon,
5   *Salmon the father of Boaz by Rahab,*
      Boaz the father of Obed by Ruth,
      Obed the father of Jesse,
6   *and Jesse the father of David the king.*

      And David became the father of Solomon by the wife of Uriah,
7   *Solomon the father of Rehoboam,*
      Rehoboam the father of Abijah,
      Abijah the father of Asaph,[b]

8   *Asaph the father of Jehoshaphat,*
      Jehoshaphat the father of Joram,
      Joram the father of Uzziah,
9   *Uzziah the father of Jotham,*
      Jotham the father of Ahaz,
      Ahaz the father of Hezekiah,
10   *Hezekiah the father of Manasseh,*
      Manasseh the father of Amos,[c]
      Amos the father of Josiah,
11   *and Josiah the father of Jechoniah*[d] *and his brothers, at the time of the exile to*
      Babylon.

12   *And after the exile to Babylon, Jechoniah became the father of Salathiel,*[e]
      Salathiel the father of Zerubbabel,
13   *Zerubbabel the father of Abiud,*
      Abiud the father of Eliakim,
      Eliakim the father of Azor,
14   *Azor the father of Zadok,*
      Zadok the father of Achim,
      Achim the father of Eliud,
15   *Eliud the father of Eleazar,*
      Eleazar the father of Matthan,
      Matthan the father of Jacob,
16   *Jacob was the father of Joseph, the husband of Mary*
      of whom God brought forth[f] *Jesus who is called "Christ."*[g]

17   *All the generations, therefore, are reckoned as follows:*[h]
      from Abraham to David fourteen generations,
      and from David to the Babylonian exile fourteen generations,
      and from the Babylonian exile to the Christ fourteen generations.

Notes

ᵃ The reading of the Gr. text and KJV. Other English translations beginning with RV use the short-ened spelling Ram. Cf. 1 Chr 2:10 (LXX).

ᵇ The TR reads Asa; apparently early scribes altered Asaph (the psalmist of the titles of Pss 50 and 73–83) to the more appropriate royal name Asa. The textual evidence for Asaph is strong, including Alexandrian (p^lvid ℵ B), Caesarean (f^{1,13} 700 1071), and Western witnesses, as well as some Eastern versions (co arm aeth geo).

ᶜ Very much as in the preceding note, the TR reads Amon, reflecting a scribal alteration to pro-duce the name of the Davidic king. The textual evidence favoring Amos, however, is about the same as it is for Asaph in the preceding note.

ᵈ Several late uncials (M U Θ Σ) and other witnesses (e.g., f¹ 33 661 sy^h pal geo) add τὸν Ἰωακίμ, Ἰωακίμ δὲ ἐγέννησεν. This insertion of Jehoiakim as the father of Jechoniah brings the list into har-mony with 1 Chr 3:15–16, but produces fifteen names against Matthew's tabulation of fourteen (see v 17).

ᵉ Σαλαθιηλ (Salathiel) is the LXX spelling for שְׁאַלְתִּיאֵל (Shealtiel) in 1 Chr 3:17. ASV and RSV use the latter spelling in their translation at this point; NRSV uses the former.

ᶠ ἐγεννήθη, lit. "was born." The passive, however, reflects the divine agency.

ᵍ Variant readings of this verse fall into two categories: (1) where Mary is explicitly referred to as a betrothed virgin and her role is expressed actively, e.g., ᾧ μνηστευθεῖσα παρθένος Μ. ἐγέννησεν Ἰησοῦν τὸν λεγόμενον χριστόν, "to whom being betrothed the virgin Mary begot [some MSS have ἔτεκεν, "bore," instead of ἐγέννησεν] Jesus the one called Christ" (Θ, *f*¹³ it); (2) where Joseph is explicitly said to have begotten (ἐγέννησεν) Jesus, although Mary is still called a betrothed virgin (the reading is found only in the Sinaitic Syriac version but is possibly also alluded to in a few late sources). The first category has only relatively slight MS support and may have arisen to avoid misunderstanding of the text as translated above. If it were the correct reading, it is difficult to know how it was displaced. The second category of variants has extremely weak attestation and probably arose from the mechanical blunder of repeating Joseph's name. See the full discussion in *TCGNT*, 2–7.

ʰ "Are reckoned as follows" is added to complete the sense.

Form/Structure/Setting

A. βίβλος γενέσεως may be taken as referring to (1) the entire Gospel, hence functioning as a title for the entire book (Zahn, Klostermann, Lindblom, Davies-Allison); (2) 1:1–4:16, that is, up to the formula of 4:17, "From that time on, Jesus began to preach" (Krentz; Kingsbury, *Structure*; D. Bauer, *Structure*, 73–77); (3) the first two chapters (Allen, Carson; chap. 1 only: Luz); or (4) only vv 1–17 (McNeile; Brown, *Birth*; Gundry, *Matthew*). Although it is clear that vv 1–17 are closely related to 18–25, that there is a sense in which chaps. 1 and 2 belong together (as distinct from the following chapters), and that the first two chapters are also related to 3:1–4:16, and indeed the remainder of the Gospel, it is nevertheless arguable that the words refer only to vv 1–17. Although unquestionably related to what immediately follows, these verses constitute a recognizably independent unit as can readily be seen from the chiastic inclusio in v 17:

> v 1 Χριστοῦ ... Δαυίδ ... Ἀβραάμ
> v 17 Ἀβραάμ ... Δαυίδ ... Χριστοῦ.

B. V 17 also indicates the carefully devised structure of the pericope by its reference to three groups of fourteen. Note the deliberate repetition of the threefold γενεαὶ δεκατέσσαρες. The passage itself, however, is not as symmetrical as v 17 might lead us to believe. The data may be set forth as follows:

> I. (vv 2–6a) Ἀβραάμ ⟶ Δαυίδ: ἐγέννησεν (13x); names inclusive: 14
> II. (vv 6a–11) Δαυίδ ⟶ Ἰεχονίας: ἐγέννησεν (14x); names inclusive: 15 (repeating Δαυίδ)
> III. (vv 12–16) Ἰεχονίας ⟶ Ἰωσήφ: ἐγέννησεν (12x); names inclusive: 13 (repeating Ἰεχονίας)
> ἐξ [Μαρίας] ἐγεννήθη (1x) Ἰησοῦς

Since the first two groups contain fourteen names each (if we discount the repetition of David at the beginning of the second group), the problem centers in the third group. Because Jechoniah is repeated at the beginning of the third group (following the pattern established) and is therefore not to be counted again, we are left with only twelve names. Adding Jesus, we get thirteen, one short of the needed fourteen.

A variety of explanations has been offered. (1) If Mary is counted, the total comes to fourteen; but it is impossible that both Joseph and Mary are to be counted as separate generations (γενεαί). (2) Some (e.g., Stendahl) have suggested that, if Jesus is the thirteenth name, then Christ—i.e., the risen or returning Christ—would be the fourteenth. Against this, however, is the fact that, for Matthew, the climax lies in the Jesus of his narrative, not only in the Christ of the Gospel's epilogue or eschatological discourse. (3) Much more likely is the explanation that focuses on the end of the second group and beginning of the third group, marked by the Babylonian exile. When, at the end of the second group, Matthew says, "Josiah was the father of Jechoniah and his brothers," he departs from the OT (cf. 1 Chr 3:15–16), which indicates that Jeconiah (the spelling with a simple *c* reflects the Heb. ב) was the grandson of Josiah, but the son of Jehoiakim. While Matthew is under no obligation to include every name contained in his source, in this case the second group may well have originally ended with Jehoiakim. This conjecture is supported by the fact that in 1 Chr 3:15 the brothers of Jehoiakim are mentioned (Zedekiah and Shallum), whereas in 1 Chr 3:16 there is reference to only a single brother of Jeconiah. A further cause of confusion is that according to the same verse Jeconiah had a son also named Zedekiah. Moreover, Jeconiah's regnal name was Jehoiachin (cf. 2 Kgs 24:8), which in the LXX is spelled the same as Jehoiakim (i.e., Ἰωακίμ; see, e.g., the LXX of 2 Kgs 23:36; 24:8). If we accept Jehoiakim as the last name of the second group, then the Jechoniah of the beginning of the third group in Matthew's genealogy is not a repeated name, as with the case of David at the beginning of the second group, but a new name which, when counted, gives us thirteen, with Jesus then as the fourteenth. By this explanation, Matthew has fourteen names in each of the three groups. His listing lacks symmetry in that whereas he repeated the last name of the first group (David, perhaps because of self-evident importance), he did not repeat the last name of group two at the beginning of group three. Indeed, here a sharp break seems natural given the tragedy of the exile (cf. also the reference to Jeconiah the captive in 1 Chr 3:17, who is therefore hardly to be included in the list of those who were ἐπί [up to] τῆς μετοικεσίας, Βαβυλῶνος, "the Babylonian Exile"). Some scribe, expecting symmetry in structure and perhaps confused by the identical LXX spelling for Jehoiachim and Jehoiachin (Jeconiah), assumed that the Jechoniah of the beginning of Matthew's third group was also the name with which the second group should end and so changed Ἰωακίμ to Ἰεχονίας. The minority reading recorded in *Note* d above may therefore reflect the original reading but has gone astray in attempting to include the reference to Jehoiachim begetting Jechoniah. Jechoniah stands at the head of group three without reference to his father, even as Abraham stands at the beginning of group one. Thus, despite the lack of structural symmetry, Matthew does have fourteen names in each group (David *not* counted twice, Jechoniah counted twice).

C. The structure of three fourteens is regarded as significant by Matthew, and probably for more than pedagogical reasons. Indeed, Matthew or his source has deliberately arranged the fourteens by not inconsiderable omissions. Pressed into three equal segments are unequal historical periods of approximately 750, 400, and 600 years (so Brown, *Birth*). If we take the three fourteens as multiples of seven (i.e., six sevens), then with the coming of Christ we are about to enter the seventh seven, the period of perfection and fulfillment. Alternatively, we may be about to enter the tenth week of years, as in 1 Enoch 93:1–10 (cf. 91:12–17), if, as there, we allow three weeks of years to be reckoned for the period prior to Israel (Jacob). Another possibility is that the number fourteen alludes to Daniel's reference to seventy weeks of years (Dan 9:24), since by reckoning a generation at thirty-five years, the same number, 490, is reached (Moore). Thus, after three periods of seventy weeks of years, God sends his Messiah into the world.

Many commentators have called attention to the fact that the numerical value of the Hebrew letters spelling David is fourteen (דוד = 4, 6, 4) and that, given David's importance to his purpose, Matthew may have structured the genealogy with this in mind (Davies-Allison). But the Book of Matthew, it should be remembered, is written in Greek, and the numerology of the Hebrew name would not at all be evident to Greek readers without explanation. That David's name in Hebrew is equal to fourteen may well be only a coincidence; in any event, it can hardly be determinative in a Greek text.

Another theory about the use of fourteens has to do with the waxing and waning of the moon (twenty-eight-day cycles); this in turn related to the alternating high and low points in the dividing points of the genealogy—i.e., the Davidic kingdom, the Babylonian exile, the appearance of Christ. Yet, in the genealogy there is no idea of gradual growing or diminishing of Israel's fortunes. This too is to be regarded as an interesting coincidence, as are other such conjectures— e.g., that 3 x 14 = 42 and there are forty-two months of evil in Rev 13:5 before the intervention of God (Moreton). For the possible apocalyptic significance of the number fourteen and of four ages, see Waetjen.

We are unable conclusively to discern Matthew's intent in the 3 x 14 structure. It seems likely that there is significance in the veiled notion of multiple sevens. The fact that Matthew uses three "fourteens," rather than six "sevens," is possibly the result of the form of the genealogical list he used or (if Matthew composed the list) because the two key turning points of David and the Babylonian exile facilitated such a division. (For parallel configurations, see 1 Enoch 91:12–17; 93:1–10.) More certainly, however, Matthew intends to convey the providential design behind the history of Israel, which has structured the periods between pivotal eras (Abraham, David, the Exile) in more or less equal segments of time (Matthew surely knew they were not exactly equal), leading now appropriately, and in due course, to the goal of all that preceded, the coming of the promised Messiah. (See the full discussion and similar conclusion of Johnson, 189–208.)

D. Matthew's source for much of the genealogy offered is either directly or indirectly the LXX:

MATTHEW	LXX
I. (vv 2–6a) 14 names	1 Chr 1:28, 34: Abraham, Isaac
	1 Chr 2:1–15: Israel (Jacob)—→David, 14 names
	(cf. Ruth 4:18–22: Perez—→David)
II. (vv 6b–11) 14 names	1 Chr 3:10–15:
(not counting the repeated David)	Solomon—→Jehioakim, 17 names

Matthew's first group coincides exactly with 1 Chronicles and the partial list in Ruth. Matthew's second group is also in exact agreement, except for the omission of three kings. This involves a skip from Joram to Uzziah, which may have been caused by a confusion of Ahaziah (Ὀχοζίας or Ὀζείας according to Codex B) with Uzziah (Ὀζίας), although the main LXX tradition employs Uzziah's birth name Azariah (Ἀζαρία[ς]) rather than the regnal name (except for the Lucianic recension, which reads Ὀζίας). An alternate explanation of the omission of the three kings, Ahaziah, Jehoash, and Amaziah, is that a curse was upon them through Athaliah, the daughter of Ahab, who became the wife of Joram and the mother of Ahaziah; if the curse lasted to the fourth generation (as it seems from the narrative in 2 Chr 22–25), it would have included the three kings missing from Matthew's list. We have no known source for Matthew's third group, which, apart from the first three names (found in 1 Chr 3:17–19, but not consecutively), is completely unknown until the names of Joseph and Jesus.

There is much evidence that genealogical lists existed and were treasured in Matthew's day. Brown argues that Matthew used two genealogical lists (pre-monarchical and monarchical) already in existence and partially dependent upon the LXX, and already containing the omissions in group two. While this complicated conjecture is a possibility, there seems to be no reason, on the other hand, that Matthew could not himself have constructed the lists, making direct use of the LXX for the first two groups and of family records for the third group. Indeed, as Vögtle indicates (*BZ* 9 [1965] 48), the unity of concept and the theological agreement with the rest of the Gospel suggest that the genealogy is the work of the evangelist himself. For the similarities between the genealogy and the Gospel itself, see Johnson (210–28), who points to numerical structure, language, and theology. Matthew may have devised the concept of three fourteens when he found fourteen names in the first group (Matthew wants, above all, to point back to Abraham and David, the termini of group one), and then accordingly he may have abbreviated the second and third lists to conform them to the pattern.

E. Unlike Matthew, Luke (3:23–38) presents the genealogy going backward from Jesus past Abraham to Adam, "the son of God." Between Abraham and Jesus, Luke has fifty-six names, compared to Matthew's forty-one. Of Matthew's forty-one, Luke has only seventeen, thirteen of which are in the period between Abraham and David (all except Ram or Aram), and the remaining four in Matthew's last section (Shealtiel, Zerubbabel, Joseph, and Jesus). The major cleavage in the two genealogies is caused by the fact that, whereas Luke traces the lineage of Jesus through David's son, Nathan, Matthew chooses to follow the royal lineage from David through Solomon. There are two major ways (each reversible) of accounting for the extensive differences between the two genealogies: (1) one (Luke is more often favored here) traces Mary's ancestry (so Luther; Bengel; Godet, 128–32) while the other traces Joseph's; (2) both refer to Joseph, but one (in modern times Luke is more commonly favored) traces actual biological descent, while the other traces legal descent. It seems unlikely that either genealogy is to be regarded as Mary's, since lineage was always reckoned through the male line in Jewish culture, and Luke's Gospel presents the genealogy as Joseph's (3:23). Most probably, given Matthew's concern for the kingly line, the second explanation is closest to the truth (so Zahn; Taylor, 89; Westcott, 312–13; Allen; Moffatt, 250–51).

One point bears emphasis. In these genealogies we must not expect accuracy by our modern standards. Omissions, variant spellings, and even variant names (i.e., some persons with two names) may be expected in genealogies, with many of these alterations motivated theologically. But to admit the theological interest in and impact upon these genealogies need not lead to the conclusion that they are not in any sense meant to be taken as factual. Both Matthew and Luke are concerned to represent the facts contained in their sources; they are hardly creating lists out of thin air. These genealogies, like much of the content of the Gospels, are to be taken as interpreted history—i.e., factual and not fictional data, conceived and set forth with theological goals, these in turn informed by the eschatological fullness now inescapably present to these writers.

Comment

1 βίβλος γενέσεως, lit. "book of the origin," or "genealogical scroll," is deliberately an allusion to the formulaic title used in the LXX (Gen 2:4; 5:1; the Heb. word underlying γενέσεως is *tôlĕdôt*, "generations"), which can be used to introduce both genealogies and historical narratives. The words reflect the Heb. סֵפֶר תּוֹלְדֹת, *sēper tôlĕdôt*, which in Gen 5:1 means "genealogical register" (BDB, 707a). Although here the expression refers, as argued above, only to Matt 1:1–17, it is obvious that by this beginning Matthew wishes to call attention to the momentous, even sacred, character of the genealogy and therefore also of the narrative to follow. Even as the story of creation began with the use of this formula in referring to "the generations of the heavens and the earth" or "the book of the generations of Adam," so now we are at the fulfillment of God's plan in matters of corresponding importance. In this sense the opening words of Matthew are similar in impact to Mark's ἀρχὴ τοῦ εὐαγγελίου, "beginning of the gospel."

We should not, however, go so far in this view as to take the words Ἰησοῦ Χριστοῦ as a subjective genitive, i.e., to mean that the γενέσεως is "a bringing into being" (a new creation) accomplished by Jesus. It is, rather, the origin of Jesus himself that is in view. Whether "Christ" (= "Anointed") here is employed as a proper name or as a title can be debated. The initial impression is that it is a proper name. But since it is followed immediately by "son of David," and with an eye on the titular use in v 16, it must be said that here the meaning of the name cannot be far from Matthew's mind. (See *Comment* on v 16 for the significance of the title.)

It is very important to notice that genealogies in the OT and Jewish tradition always take their name from the progenitor, the first name of the list. Here, however, the genealogy is designated according to the last member of the list. The teleological orientation is unmistakable.

The names υἱοῦ Δαυὶδ υἱοῦ Ἀβραάμ, "son of David, son of Abraham," signify much more than simply pointing to two of the most important persons in the history of Israel who were among the ancestors of Jesus. "Son of David" had become, by the first century, a title for the messianic deliverer who would assume the throne of David in accordance with the promise of 2 Sam 7:4–17 (the Davidic covenant), thereby inaugurating a kingdom of perfection and righteousness that would last forever. Jesus is *that* promised Son of David, and already Matthew's great stress on fulfillment is anticipated (see Nolan, *Royal Son of God*, 224–34). This title is a favorite of Matthew's, occurring ten times, compared to four times each in Mark and Luke. On the title, see *Comment* on 9:27.

"Son of Abraham" also carries a note of promise and fulfillment. Although David, rather than Jesus, could be referred to here as "the son of Abraham," the focus of this opening sentence and passage is clearly on Jesus himself. The Abrahamic covenant (Gen 12:1–3, etc.) speaks of blessing through Abraham for "all the families of the earth." In Jesus, through the line of Abraham, that promise is fulfilled.

Only anticipated in the Gospel, narrative itself (e.g., 8:11; 21:43), it comes to full expression in the climactic passage at the end of the Gospel, where Jesus commands μαθητεύσατε πάντα τὰ ἔθνη ("make disciples of all nations," 28:19).

2 The genealogy begins with Abraham since he serves as the beginning of salvation history and of God's election of a people. The first break in the regular rhythm of the genealogy, καὶ τοὺς ἀδελφοὺς αὐτοῦ, "and his brothers," points to the twelve tribes of Israel. The goal of the genealogical list, Jesus the Christ, provides the historical culmination and theological fullness that inevitably refer to all Israel (cf. the continued importance of the twelve tribes in an eschatological sense in 19:28).

3 The two names τὸν Φάρες καὶ τὸν Ζάρα, "Perez and Zerah," are listed rather than one because Tamar was the mother of twins (cf. Gen 38:27–30). The addition to the genealogy of ἐκ τῆς Θαμάρ, "by Tamar," is clearly the work of Matthew, as are the special references to Rahab (v 5), Ruth (v 5), and the wife of Uriah (Bathsheba, v 6b).

> Matthew's purpose in adding these women to the genealogy, rare in Jewish genealogical lists, has been much discussed. The possible reasons for their inclusion (see esp. Johnson, 152–79; Brown, *Birth*, 71–74) are as follows. (1) The four women were regarded as notorious sinners, all specifically involved in sexual sins; Matthew intends by their inclusion either (a) to point generally to Jesus as the Savior of sinners (cf. 1:21), or (b) to answer Jewish claims about Mary's alleged adultery by these reminders of the sexual sins of those associated with the lineage of David (Freed). An obstacle to this option, apart from the fact that Ruth is not so immediately implicated in sexual transgression as are the others, is that rabbinic tradition shows considerable discussion of and disagreement about the sinfulness of these women (see especially Johnson). The identity of the Rahab mentioned here has also been questioned (see below on v 5). Johnson conjectures that the presence of the four women in Matthew's genealogy reflects the polemic between the Pharisees, who looked for a Davidic Messiah, and the Sadducees, Essenes, and others, who expected a Levitical Messiah and who therefore were inclined to stress the sinfulness of the four in order to demean the Davidic lineage. Matthew's deliberate inclusion of the four thus suggests his acceptance of the Pharisee's notion of a Davidic Messiah. That Matthew is a champion of the Davidic descent of the Messiah is more than obvious from the genealogy, but that this alone accounts for their inclusion is doubtful. The suggestion that the Jewish slander against Mary is countered by the reference to the immorality of women in the Davidic lineage makes little sense and implies acceptance of the charge against her. (2) The four women were Gentiles, so Matthew intends to underline the propriety of the ultimate inclusion of the Gentiles in God's purposes by showing that the Messiah has Gentiles among his ancestors (Stegemann). It is, however, not fully clear that Tamar and "the wife of Uriah" were Gentiles, although the compiler of the genealogy may well have regarded them as such (Johnson). There is evidence from post-biblical Jewish literature, moreover, that refers to Rahab and Tamar as Jewish proselytes—which would leave their status unclear and could raise uncomfortable questions in the minds of Matthew's readers (Brown, *Birth*). (3) The third and most appealing option utilizes a little from each of the first two options but centers on the way in which the women prefigure Mary by calling attention to the abundant presence of both surprise and scandal in the Messiah's lineage. The sovereign plan and purpose of God are often worked out in and through the most unlikely turn of events, and even through women who, though Gentiles or harlots, are receptive to God's will. The virgin birth and the importance of Mary are just such surprising and scandalous (though in Mary's case only seemingly scandalous) ways through which God brings his purposes to realization in the story of Jesus. The women then serve as reminders that God often works in the most unusual ways and that to be open to his sovereign activity is to be prepared for the surprising.

As for the names listed in the remainder of v 3 through v 4 (Perez to Salmon), the OT provides no information.

5 Σαλμὼν δὲ ἐγέννησεν τὸν Βόες ἐκ τῆς Ῥαχάβ, "Salmon was the father of Boaz by Rahab." The reference to Rahab has been added to the genealogical list apparently by Matthew himself (no Rahab is mentioned in the OT lists, which probably serve as source; cf. 1 Chr 2:12; Ruth 4:21). If the Rahab of the conquest narrative is in view, as most commentators agree, then Rahab appears several generations, or something like two centuries, too late. In Jewish literature, Rahab is said to have married Joshua (Str-B 1:23). Though possible, it seems very improbable that we have another Rahab here (contra Quinn), of whom nothing is known from any other source—this despite the variant spelling of Ῥαχάβ (LXX, Ῥαάβ), which actually is closer to the Hebrew רָחָב, *Rāḥāb*, for the Rahab of Jericho. Further support that this Rahab is meant is the tainted character of at least two other of the four women added by Matthew. For a discussion of this, see *Comment* above, v 3, Θαμάρ. For the discussion of ἐκ τῆς Ῥούθ, "by Ruth," see also the discussion under Θαμάρ, v 3.

6 The addition of the words "the king" in τὸν Δαυὶδ τὸν βασιλέα serves to strengthen the link between David and Jesus as the Davidic, messianic king, an important motif in Matthew. In the words ἐκ τῆς τοῦ Οὐρίου, "by the wife of Uriah," the name of Bathsheba is deliberately avoided. Davis argues that Matthew's purpose is to call attention to Uriah's righteousness in contrast to David. See discussion under Θαμάρ, v 3.

7–8 Ἀσάφ, "Asaph." In this list of the kings of Judah, one expects to find Asa rather than Asaph and, in v 10, Amon rather than Amos. Asaph is known to us as a psalmist (cf. titles of Pss 50, 73–83; 1 Chr 16:5–37; 2 Chr 29:30); Amos is probably the prophet. Matthew, or an intermediate source (standing between him and the LXX), appears to be responsible for the lapses. Some have argued that the alterations are deliberate, having the intention of representing both wisdom and prophecy in the lineage of Jesus. But this is very unlikely since, for Matthew, the former was already present in David the royal psalmist, and the latter, given the overwhelming prophetic witness to the Christ according to Matthew, hardly seems necessary. It is possible that the Textus Receptus preserves the original reading (with correct names) and that the critical text is actually the result of scribal alteration. Yet it is more likely that the more difficult readings are original and that scribes are responsible for correcting, rather than inserting, the errors.

8 Ἰωράμ δὲ ἐγέννησεν τὸν Ὀζίαν, "Joram was the father of Uzziah." For the omission of three kings of Judah between Joram and Uzziah (Ahaziah, Jehoash, and Amaziah), see the discussion above (*Form/Structure/Setting* §D). Omissions in genealogies are not uncommon.

10 Ἀμώς, "Amos." See discussion under Ἀσάφ in *Comment* on vv 7–8 above.

11 Ἰωσίας δὲ ἐγέννησεν τὸν Ἰεχονίαν καὶ τοὺς ἀδελφοὺς αὐτοῦ, "Josiah was the father of Jechoniah and his brothers." For Jechoniah we are probably to substitute Jehoiachin. See discussion above (*Form/Structure/Setting* §B). In this instance, the reference to "his brothers" derives from 1 Chr 3:15, where three brothers of Jehoiakim are named.

12 μετὰ δὲ τὴν μετοικεσίαν Βαβυλῶνος (lit. "after the exile to Babylon") refers to after the beginning of the exile, not to the time after it was over. Ἰεχονίας, "Jeconiah" (= Jehoiachin of 2 Kgs 24:15), was the first king to be deported to

Babylon and hence receives the title "the captive" in 1 Chr 3:17. Ἰεχονίας, Σαλαθιήλ, Ζοροβαβέλ, "Jechoniah, Salathiel, Zerubbabel," follows the LXX of 1 Chr 3:19, rather than the MT, where Zerubbabel is the son of Pediah (cf. Ezra 3:2).

13 Ἀβιούδ, "Abiud." The names from Abiud (not listed among the sons of Zerubbabel in 1 Chr 3:19–20) to Jacob the father of Joseph are not known to us from any other source.

16 In the words τὸν Ἰωσὴφ τὸν ἄνδρα Μαρίας, ἐξ ἧς ἐγεννήθη Ἰησοῦς, lit. "Joseph the husband of Mary, of whom was born Jesus," we encounter the biggest surprise in the genealogy. Having brought the genealogy down to Joseph, the evangelist identifies him as the husband of Mary, and the attention shifts to her (ἐξ ἧς, "from whom"). The repeated active verb ἐγέννησεν gives way to a divine passive (i.e., God is the active agent). Joseph is important—it is his genealogy, after all, that is traced—but as the extraordinary change in the syntax indicates, he is not important as the physical father of Jesus but rather (as argued above, *Form/Structure/Setting* §E) as his legal parent. This notion of legal parentage is commonplace in rabbinic thought. The explanation of this surprising sentence is, of course, to be found in the account of the virgin birth contained in the next pericope.

ὁ λεγόμενος Χριστός, "the one called 'Christ.'" The lack of the definite article suggests that Christ is used as a name rather than a title, even as in 1:1 (cf. 27:17, 22, where the same phrase is found on the lips of Pilate). Again, however, the titular meaning is not far from the author's thoughts, as can be seen from τοῦ Χριστοῦ of v 17.

17 This verse not only summarizes but, in so doing, points out the structure and teleological momentum of the preceding verses. Climactic fulfillment is reached in the phrase ἕως τοῦ Χριστοῦ, "to the Christ." The Christ has now appeared, rounding out and bringing to fruition the earlier history of Israel. For the significance of the groups of "fourteen," see the discussion above (*Form/Structure/Setting* §C).

Explanation

The "book of the origin of Jesus Christ," far from being simply the recitation of historical data for their own sake, is above all an artistically devised theological statement. The data are important in providing the vehicle for the initial presentation of Jesus as the fulfillment of the promises to Abraham and David. Indeed, the responsibilities and hopes of Israel, bound up as they are with the preparation of the past, receive their realization in the one who is the subject of Matthew's narrative. There is, moreover, a certain appropriateness about the timing of this fulfillment, coming as it does at the end of three segments of time that can be expressed as 3 x 14, segments marked by Abraham, David, and the Babylonian captivity. Behind these events, the highest and lowest points in the history of Israel, stands the sovereignty of God, who works out all things in accordance with his purpose and timing. Further evidence of that remarkable sovereignty and its salvific intent can be seen in the surprising inclusion of irregular and sometimes scandalous events, as reflected in the four women of the genealogy, which prepare for the actual circumstances of Jesus' birth. Matthew has in this opening pericope anticipated the fulfillment theme that is so prominent in the Gospel. And concluding this skillful presentation of the genealogy of Jesus, he turns to events surrounding the birth itself.

The Birth and Naming of Jesus (1:18–25)

Bibliography

Boslooper, T. *The Virgin Birth.* London: SCM, 1962. **Box, G. H.** *The Virgin Birth of Christ.* London: Pitman & Sons, 1916. **Bratcher, R. G.** "A Study of Isaiah 7:14." *BT* 9 (1958) 97–126. **Broer, I.** "Die Bedeutung der 'Jungfrauengeburt' im Matthäusevangelium." *BibLeb* 12 (1971) 248–60. **Brown, R. E.** *The Virginal Conception and Bodily Resurrection of Jesus.* New York: Paulist, 1973. ——— **et al.,** eds. *Mary in the New Testament.* Philadelphia: Fortress, 1978. **Conrad, E. W.** "The Annunciation of Birth and the Birth of the Messiah." *CBQ* 47 (1985) 656–63. **Edwards, D.** *The Virgin Birth in History and Faith.* London: Faber & Faber, 1943. **Fenton, J. C.** "Matthew and the Divinity of Jesus: Three Questions Concerning Matthew 1:20–23." In *Studia Biblica 1978: II. Papers on the Gospels,* ed. E. A. Livingstone. Sheffield: JSOT, 1979. 79–82. **Fitzmyer, J.** "The Virginal Conception of Jesus in the New Testament." In *To Advance the Gospel.* New York: Crossroad, 1981. 41–78. **Gärtner, B.** "The Habakkuk Commentary (DSH) and the Gospel of Matthew." *ST* 8 (1954) 1–24. **Graystone, J. M.** "Matthieu 1:18–25: Essai d'interprétation." *RTP* 23 (1973) 221–32. **Hill, D.** "A Note on Matthew i.19." *ExpTim* 76 (1964–65) 133–34. **Kilian, R.** *Die Verheissung Immanuels Jes 7,14.* SBS 35. Stuttgart: Katholisches Bibelwerk, 1968. **Kotze, P. P. A.** "The Structure of Matthew One." *Neot* 11 (1977) 1–9. **Krämer, M.** "Die Menschwerdung Jesu Christi nach Matthäus (Mt 1)." *Bib* 45 (1964) 1–50. **Léon-Dufour, X.** "L'annonce à Joseph." In *Études.* 65–81. **Machen, J. G.** *The Virgin Birth of Christ.* New York: Harper & Row, 1930. **Milavec, A.** "Matthew's Integration of Sexual and Divine Begetting." *BTB* 8 (1978) 108–16. **Orr, J.** *The Virgin Birth of Christ.* London: Hodder & Stoughton, 1907. **Raatschen, J. H.** "Empfangen durch den Heiligen Geist: Überlegungen zu Mt 1, 18–25." *TBei* 11 (1980) 262–77. **Spicq, C.** "'Joseph, son mari, étant juste . . .' (Mt. 1,19)." *RB* 71 (1964) 206–14. **Stauffer, E.** "Jeschu ben Mirjam." In *Neotestamentica et Semitica.* FS M. Black, ed. E. E. Ellis and M. Wilcox. Edinburgh: T. & T. Clark, 1969. 119–28. **Taylor, V.** *The Historical Evidence for the Virgin Birth.* Oxford: Clarendon Press, 1920. **Tosata, A.** "Joseph, Being a Just Man (Matt. 1:19)." *CBQ* 41 (1979) 547–51. **Trilling, W.** "Jesus, der Messias und Davidssohn (Mt 1,18–25)." In *Christusverkündigung in den Synoptischen Evangelien.* Munich: Kösel, 1969. 13–39. **Vögtle, A.** "Matthew 1,25 und die Virginitas B. M. Virginis post partum." *TQ* 147 (1967) 28–39. **Willis, J. T.** "The Meaning of Isaiah 7:14 and Its Application in Matthew." *ResQ* 21 (1978) 1–18. **Winter, P.** "Jewish Folklore in the Matthaean Birth Story." *HibJ* 53 (1954–55) 34–42. **Wright, D. F.,** ed. *Chosen by God: Mary in Evangelical Perspective.* London: Marshall Pickering, 1989.

Translation

[18]*Now the birth[a] of [Jesus][b] Christ happened like this. When his mother, Mary, was engaged to Joseph, before the marriage was consummated she was found to be with child—by the agency of the Holy Spirit.[c]* [19]*But Joseph, her husband, a righteous man, yet not wanting to disgrace her publicly, planned to divorce her privately.* [20]*And while he was considering these things, behold, an angel of the Lord appeared to him in a dream, saying, "Joseph, son of David, do not be afraid to take Mary as your wife. For what has been conceived in her is of the Holy Spirit.* [21]*But she will bear a son, and you shall call his name Jesus [= Yahweh is salvation], for he will save his people from their sins."* [22]*This whole state of affairs had come about in order that what was spoken by the Lord through the prophet[d] might be fulfilled when he says,* [23]*Behold, a virgin shall conceive and shall bear a son,*

and they shall call his name Emmanuel,
which translated is "God with us."
²⁴ *And Joseph arose from his sleep and did as the angel of the Lord had ordered him,*
and he took his wife. ²⁵ *And he did not have intercourse with her until she had given*
*birth to a son.*ᵉ *And he gave him the name Jesus.*

Notes

ᵃ L *f*¹³ TR Ir Or Epiph have γέννησις rather than the γένεσις of the earliest witnesses. Although
both words can mean "birth," the latter also carries a wider connotation ("history," "origin," etc.).
γένεσις picks up the same word as in 1:1, but here it refers specifically to the birth. The γέννησις of
the later MSS is no doubt the substitution of the very similar, but more usual, word for "birth." See
TCGNT, 8.

ᵇ Only a few relatively unimportant MSS have either Χριστοῦ (71 lat syˢ·ᶜ Ir) or Ἰησοῦ (W and a few
others) rather than Ἰησοῦ Χριστοῦ (as in the overwhelming majority of MSS; B has names reversed).
Yet textual critics are dubious about the reading because of the oddity of having the double name
prefixed by the definite article (which elsewhere occurs in only three places, all in inferior MSS). The
addition of either name is readily explainable as the result of scribal industry.

ᶜ Following Brown's translation (*Birth*), the dash is used to indicate that this inserted phrase is a
preliminary explanation and not to be understood as known to Joseph.

ᵈ Some relatively unimportant witnesses insert the name of Isaiah here, following the usual
Matthean pattern (e.g., 3:3; 4:14; 8:17; 12:17).

ᵉ C D W TR vg syᵖ·ʰ read τὸν υἱὸν αὐτῆς τὸν πρωτότοκον, "her first-born son," apparently derived
from Luke 2:7.

Form/Structure/Setting

A. This pericope is closely related to the preceding one, as is evident from the
opening sentence, including the specific use of the word γένεσις. Indeed, the
passage intends to explain in some detail the surprise encountered in v 16, namely
that ἐγέννησεν, "he begat," gives way to ἐγεννήθη, "he was begotten," and that
Mary accordingly becomes the focus of attention. In the account of how Jesus
was born, Matthew is able to make several important theological statements about
the central figure of his narrative.

B. We cannot say anything about Matthew's sources other than that he relies
upon tradition circulating in the early Church—indeed he is probably quite se-
lective in his use of it. He is hardly to be thought of as creating material out of
nothing, nor is he composing the story with some imagination from Isa 7:14.
What he has done is to take items from the tradition (deriving perhaps ultimately
from the participants) and set them forth in his narrative in such a way as to
maximize coincidence with Isa 7:14, thereby underlining the resultant theological fulfillment of God's purposes in Jesus. The latter is indeed Matthew's
controlling motif in the Gospel generally, but particularly in the infancy narrative. Brown's complex argument about pre-Matthean sources (*Birth*, 154–63) is
plausible enough but highly conjectural, involving the conflation of an angelic
dream tradition with an annunciation tradition, joined perhaps already before
Matthew utilized the material.

Given the very few contacts between Matthew and Luke in the present pericope,
it must be concluded that they are making use of different traditional materials,
or at least making different selections from a common fund of tradition. Luke
focuses on Mary, Matthew on Joseph. There is nothing incompatible, or even

implausible, about divine revelations to *both* Mary and Joseph. Still, it is unnecessary to take an excessively harmonistic approach. Each evangelist, while using a formalized birth announcement pattern, has his own artistic method of shaping and presenting the materials of the tradition(s), and in so doing reflects individualized theological interests. The parallels that do exist, however, point to fixed traditional elements. With Matthew, compare Luke's stress on Joseph's Davidic descent, ἐξ οἴκου Δαυίδ, "from the house of David" (Luke 1:27; 2:4); Mary's betrothal, ἐμνηστευμένην (Luke 1:27; 2:5); the angelic revelation, καὶ ἰδοὺ συλλήμψῃ ἐν γαστρὶ καὶ τέξῃ υἱὸν καὶ καλέσεις τὸ ὄνομα αὐτοῦ Ἰησοῦν . . . κληθήσεται υἱὸς θεοῦ, "and behold you will conceive in your womb and you will give birth to a son and you shall call his name 'Jesus' . . . he will be called 'Son of God'" (Luke 1:31, 35); and the fulfillment καὶ ἔτεκεν τὸν υἱὸν αὐτῆς τὸν πρωτότοκον, "and she gave birth to her first-born son" (Luke 2:7). Parallels found in *Prot. Jas.* 14.2 and Justin, *Apol.* 1.33.5, are dependent upon Matthew.

C. The unity of the pericope is evident from the opening and closing words (which form an inclusio): τοῦ δὲ Ἰησοῦ [Χριστοῦ] . . . Ἰησοῦν. The contents follow this outline: (1) the problematic situation and Joseph's plan, vv 18b–19; (2) the angel's revelation to Joseph, vv 20–21; (3) fulfillment quotation, vv 22–23; (4) Joseph's obedience and the resultant fulfillment, vv 24–25. Except for the fulfillment quotation, a similar pattern is found again in the two other angelic revelations by dream found in the infancy narrative (2:13–14, 19–21). Common to these three are the following: (a) an initial genitive absolute; (b) the appearance of the ἄγγελος κυρίου, "angel of the Lord," marked by ἰδού, "behold," and κατ' ὄναρ, "in a dream"; (c) the revelation itself, introduced by λέγων, "saying," and including a command and supporting reason (γάρ, "for"); (d) Joseph's obedience, introduced by ἐγερθείς, "arose." The fixed features seen in these three narratives suggest Matthew's use of a stereotypical format in presenting the stories. Therefore, they need not be taken in an overly literal sense. What they convey above all is the realization by the participants, in whatever way, of God's superintendence of their affairs, of his gracious provision of salvation in and through what happens, and of the appropriate action in response.

D. The fulfillment quotation (see *Introduction*) is of central importance in the passage. It does not seem probable, as some have argued, that it was added later to an earlier existing story, unless we allow that the whole has been thoroughly reworked by the evangelist. Matthew's wording of the narrative on either side of the quotation depends closely upon the wording of the quotation (Isa 7:14 LXX).

Isa 7:14 LXX = Matt 1:23	Matt 1
ἐν γαστρὶ ἕξει	ἐν γαστρὶ ἔχουσα, v 18
καὶ τέξεται υἱόν	(a) τέξεται δὲ υἱόν, v 21
	(b) ἔτεκεν υἱόν, v 25
καὶ καλέσουσιν (LXX: καλέσεις)	(a) καὶ καλέσεις
τὸ ὄνομα αὐτοῦ Ἐμμανουήλ	τὸ ὄνομα αὐτοῦ Ἰησοῦν, v 21
	(b) καὶ ἐκάλεσεν
	τὸ ὄνομα αὐτοῦ Ἰησοῦν, v 25

Matthew deliberately constructs his narrative around the quotation in midrashic fashion so that the wording of the quotation is reflected in the angelic revelation and in the fact of fulfillment (contra Brown, *Birth*, who argues the quotation is a later insertion). It is also to be noted that the location of this quotation in the middle of the pericope is unlike the pattern of 2:13–15; 2:16–18; and 2:19–23, where the quotation uniformly occurs at the end of the pericope.

Further obvious parallelism within the pericope is to be found between the angelic revelation and Joseph's obedience: μὴ φοβηθῇς παραλαβεῖν Μαρίαν τὴν γυναῖκά σου, "Do not be afraid to take Mary (as) your wife" (v 20); καὶ παρέλαβεν τὴν γυναῖκα αὐτοῦ, "and he took his wife" (v 24); καλέσεις τὸ ὄνομα αὐτοῦ Ἰησοῦν, "and you shall call his name Jesus" (v 21); καὶ ἐκάλεσεν τὸ ὄνομα αὐτοῦ Ἰησοῦν, "and he called his name Jesus" (v 25). The angelic announcement of the birth reflects a pattern of birth announcements found in the OT (e.g., Ishmael, Gen 16:7–12; Isaac, Gen 17:1–19; cf. John the Baptist, Luke 1:11–20).

E. While not strictly midrash, the genre of the passage is best labeled "midrashic haggadah"—i.e., *midrashic* in the sense that the OT quotation is of key importance and phrases of it are utilized in the surrounding narrative; *haggadah* in the sense that the story is not told for the sake of facts alone, but in order to illustrate their deeper meaning, that is, the theological significance of Jesus as the fulfillment of OT promises. The point is that Matthew's approach in the pericope is highly stylized and has very evident theological purposes.

The question of whether the virgin birth itself actually happened in history is of course something the historian can say nothing about, but this does not make it a matter that rests absolutely upon faith. Matthew and Luke present it as a central part of their narratives, and this to an extent does constitute historical evidence. Where the question of faith *does* enter in is in one's *a priori* world view, which either does or does not have room for God's acts in history. If one's world view does not prohibit it, there is no compelling reason not to take the testimony of Matthew and Luke seriously on this point. And that testimony should be taken seriously for its own sake (the deity of Christ is not necessarily at stake in the issue).

F. Some scholars dispute whether this pericope is a birth story at all (e.g., Stendahl, "Quis"; Waetjen, *JBL* 95 [1976] 205–30), since no details are given, nor indeed is the actual birth recorded. Nevertheless, the pericope is properly regarded as a birth narrative for the following reasons: γένεσις can mean "birth" (see BAGD and F. Büchsel, *TDNT* 1:682–83); the passage begins with reference to Mary's pregnancy, and the following pericope (2:1–12) assumes the birth; the pattern of angelic revelation and obedience (esp. the naming) suggests the full accomplishment of what was promised. The details of place and time are not important to Matthew's purpose nor, apparently, for the early tradition. The fact that no actual reference to the birth occurs is the result of its presence in the temporal clause ἕως οὗ ἔτεκεν υἱόν, "until she had given birth to a son," which is joined to οὐκ ἐγίνωσκεν αὐτήν, lit. "he did not know her" (v 25). Matthew consequently avoids repeating (καὶ) ἔτεκεν υἱόν, "(and) she gave birth to a son," as an independent clause. That he means to imply the clause is evident from the words that follow, καὶ ἐκάλεσεν τὸ ὄνομα αὐτοῦ Ἰησοῦν, "and he gave him the name Jesus" (v 25). It remains true, however, that the focus of the passage is on matters other than the actual birth itself. Especially to be noticed is the emphasis on the naming of Jesus (vv 21, [23], 25), which underlines the appropriateness of Stendahl's analysis ("Quis") of chap. 1 as focusing on the who (*quis*), or the identity of Matthew's central figure.

Comment

18 ἡ γένεσις, "the birth," picks up the γενέσεως, "origin," of 1:1 and suggests that the βίβλος γενέσεως, "record of origin," now reaches its goal. The initial position of the words τοῦ δὲ Ἰησοῦ Χριστοῦ, "of Jesus Christ," makes them emphatic. His birth is the focus of attention, the account of which is especially an unraveling of the mystery and surprise of v 16.

μνηστευθείσης ("betrothal") involves a more serious matter than our Western notion of "engagement." It was a formal pre-nuptial contract entered into before witnesses, which gave the man legal rights over the girl and which could only be broken by a formal process of divorce (cf. *m. Ketub.* 1:2; 4:2). This would take place, for example, if the girl had been guilty of adultery during the betrothal period. She would then face the penalty for being an adulteress. It is short of "marriage," which involved a second and final public ceremony, in that sexual relations between the partners were not allowed and the girl had not yet left her own family to live with the man. The terminology "husband" and "wife," which we reserve for marriage, may already have been employed for the time between betrothal and marriage (see vv 16, 19, 20, 24). If one of the partners died before the marriage, the other was a "widow" or "widower." (On the other hand, see *Comment* below on v 20.) Betrothal usually took place when a girl was between twelve and thirteen, and by arrangement between the parents; the second part, the marriage proper, usually took place about a year later (cf. *m. Ketub.* 5:2; *m. Ned.* 10:5). The word μνηστεύω is also used in reference to Mary in Luke 1:27; 2:5. πρὶν ἢ συνελθεῖν αὐτούς, lit. "before they came together," refers, in agreement with the above, to the marriage itself and the beginning of sexual relations.

The phrase ἐκ πνεύματος ἁγίου, "by the Holy Spirit," repeated in v 20, is of great theological importance to the narrative. Mary's pregnancy is attributed to the agency of God's Spirit (the lack of the definite article in the Greek is not significant; BDF §257 [2]). We do not have here the pagan notion (for a catalog, see Nellessen, *Kind*, 97–109) of a god having sexual relations with a woman but rather of the creative power of God at work within Mary in order to accomplish his purposes. (It has rightly been pointed out by commentators that the whole tenor of this passage is Jewish rather than Hellenistic. See Machen.) The divine origin of Mary's baby in turn marks him out as the Son of God, a christological title that, although not used here, is very important to Matthew. The relation between Jesus' divine sonship and the Holy Spirit is evident at two other key junctures in the story of Jesus, viz., his baptism (3:16–17) and his resurrection (Rom 1:4).

In addition to the divine origin of the child, the reference to the Holy Spirit here suggests that God is about to act graciously through this child. The promised deliverance and fulfillment of the promises rest upon the coming of an era marked above all by the presence of the Spirit; thus this little phrase sounds a distinctively eschatological note. Hill's argument that the reference to the Spirit here is an allusion to the new creation (the counterpart to the role of the Holy Spirit in Gen 1:1–2) is therefore theologically sound, although it may be more

than Matthew means to say. This salvation perspective, including the special preliminary role of God's Spirit, is of course brought out emphatically in Luke's
nativity narrative (e.g., Luke 1:15, 41, 67; 2:26). Luke's own counterpart to this
Matthean phrase, also spoken by an angel (but to Mary), is πνεῦμα ἅγιον
ἐπελεύσεται ἐπὶ σὲ καὶ δύναμις ὑψίστου ἐπισκιάσει σοι, "the Holy Spirit will come
upon you, and the power of the Most High will overshadow you" (Luke 1:35).
This is in agreement with the interpretation of ἐκ πνεύματος ἁγίου given above.

19 In δίκαιος ὢν καὶ μὴ θέλων αὐτὴν δειγματίσαι, "being righteous and not
wanting to make a public example of her," the exegetical question is the relationship between the two participial clauses, which in turn relates to the sense in
which Joseph is to be regarded as δίκαιος, "righteous." There are two main explanations:

(1) There is a tension between the two clauses, so that one should translate
"*although* being righteous," or "and *yet* not willing to make an example of her."
Here Joseph's righteousness, in the sense of obedience to the law, is set over against
his own wishes (McNeile; Tasker; Brown, *Birth*; Luz; Davies-Allison). (2) The two
clauses are in harmony, and so the translation should run "and *therefore* not willing." Here Joseph's righteousness is seen as expressed in his benevolent attitude
to Mary (Pesch, "Das Weihnachtsevangelium (Lk 2, 1–21)," in *Zur Theologie*, 97–
118; Spicq). A third option also sees harmony in the two clauses; it assumes that
Joseph already knew that Mary's pregnancy was ἐκ πνεύματος ἁγίου and that
Joseph's unwillingness to expose Mary was the result of his righteous awe, i.e., his
saintly attitude toward the divine origin and salvific purpose in the sending of
the child (Schlatter, Léon-Dufour). The first option is most consonant with
Matthew's narrative and understanding of δίκαιος as right behavior according to
the law. Joseph's righteousness impels him to act faithfully, which by the law's
standard meant that Mary should be exposed as an adulteress and suffer the punishment (death by stoning, according to Deut 22:20–21, 23–24, but probably not
insisted upon in the NT era; cf. John 8:3–11).

Joseph did not want to expose Mary as an adultress, yet neither would he marry
one so obviously guilty of sin. He therefore chose the one other option open to
him, formal divorce proceedings in relative privacy, λάθρᾳ (two witnesses were
required; see Str-B 1:51–52). Thus Joseph's plan expresses simultaneously his righteousness and his charitable kindness. (δειγματίζειν, "make public example of,"
occurs elsewhere in the NT only in Col 2:15.)

20 While Joseph ponders "these matters" (ταῦτα), no doubt including how
he will bring his plan to realization, an ἄγγελος κυρίου, "angel of the Lord," appears to him in a dream with a revelation that overturns his strategy by casting an
entirely new light on Mary's pregnancy. The protestations of innocence that Mary
had doubtless made to Joseph were now seen indeed to be true (ἰδού is Matthew's
favorite device for calling attention to something extraordinary that is about to
occur; sixty-two occurrences, thirty-four of which are insertions into parallel material and nine of which are in material unique to Matthew).

The deliberate reference to Joseph as υἱὸς Δαυίδ, "son of David" (the only place
in the Gospel where this designation is applied to someone other than Jesus),
underlines what Matthew has forcefully asserted through the genealogy of vv 1–
17. Jesus, the legal son of Joseph, as he shall become through Joseph's obedience,
is therefore reckoned as of Davidic descent with the concomitant note of

eschatological fulfillment. Several other very important elements of this and the next verse reinforce this, as we shall see.

μὴ φοβηθῇς παραλαβεῖν Μαρίαν τὴν γυναῖκά σου, "do not be afraid to take Mary (as) your wife." While the terms husband and wife were apparently used for betrothed couples, they are anachronistic in the sense that the marriage proper, the "taking home," had not yet occurred. Thus, they are only "husband and wife" in a special sense. This prompts us to translate "Do not be afraid to take Mary *as* your wife." Others would translate παραλαβεῖν as "take home": "Do not be afraid to take Mary your wife home." The difference is not significant once the background is known. ἐκ πνεύματος ἁγίου, "by the Holy Spirit," is the revelation of what was mentioned in v 18 only by anticipation (see *Comment* there). The clause τὸ γὰρ ἐν αὐτῇ γεννηθέν, "for what has been conceived in her," underlines the passive roles of both Joseph and Mary (cf. v 16). God initiates the action in all of this.

21 τέξεται δὲ υἱόν, καὶ καλέσεις τὸ ὄνομα αὐτοῦ Ἰησοῦν, "she will give birth to a son, and you shall name him Jesus," depends directly upon the LXX of Isa 7:14, which is quoted in v 23. The naming of a male child took place formally at the time of circumcision on the eighth day after birth (cf. Luke 2:21). Names held far more importance in that culture than in ours, being thought of as linked with or pointing to the actual character and destiny of the individual (see H. Bietenhard, *TDNT* 5:254). The name Ἰησοῦς is not the name mentioned in the quotation of Isa 7:14 (see below, v 23). The reason for the name Jesus is spelled out in the second part of the verse (γάρ). That it is already known is in accord with the rabbinic view that the Messiah was named before the creation of the world (*b. Pesaḥ* 54a; Str-B 1:64).

αὐτὸς γὰρ σώσει τὸν λαὸν αὐτοῦ ἀπὸ τῶν ἁμαρτιῶν αὐτῶν, "for he will save his people from their sins." The αὐτός is emphatic: it is *he* who will save his people. The introduction of Jesus thus far in Matthew's narrative has been as the Son of David, the Christ (Messiah), the one who has come to fulfill the promises of God. The natural expectation regarding the significance of σώσει, "will save," would be that it refers to a national-political salvation, involving in particular deliverance from the Roman occupation. Jesus had indeed come to save his people—the very meaning of his name in Hebrew, *Yeshua*, a shortened form of "Joshua" (Heb.: יְהוֹשֻׁעַ, *Yĕhôšuaʿ*), is "Yahweh is salvation." The reader's knowledge of the meaning of Ἰησοῦς via its Hebrew meaning is assumed by the γάρ without further explanation, indicating that this early Hebrew etymology had already become a part of the common tradition of the Greek-speaking church. (Cf. also the same etymology applied to "Joshua" [i.e., Ἰησοῦς] in the Greek Sir 46:1.) The surprise is in the content of the salvation that the Son of David will bring, namely, that he will save his people, ἀπὸ τῶν ἁμαρτιῶν αὐτῶν, "from their sins." Although it was possible to associate even this with a national-political deliverance, Matthew and his readers could not easily have made this association after A.D. 70. The deliverance from sins is in a much more profound, moral sense and depends finally upon the pouring out of Jesus' blood (26:28). Matthew and his readers knew well the kerygmatic significance of this verse. Ps 130:8, which probably is in Matthew's mind (indeed, he may be giving a targumic rendering of it), provides similar language and finds its fulfillment here. In the same way, whereas τὸν λαὸν αὐτοῦ, "his people," leads one to think initially of God's people, Israel, both Matthew and his readers were capable of a deeper understanding of the expression wherein it includes both Jews and Gentiles, i.e., as the people of the messianic king (αὐτοῦ, "his") who is both Son of David and Son of Abraham. We may thus finally equate this λαός, "people," with the ἐκκλησία, "Church," of which Jesus speaks in 16:18.

22 Vv 22–23 are best regarded as an aside by the evangelist rather than a continuation of the words spoken by the angel. This, as Grundmann points out, reveals the evangelist in his role as teacher. He will not only tell the story but also convey its significance. τοῦτο δὲ ὅλον γέγονεν, lit. "this whole has happened." All that had thus far transpired (this is the force of the perfect) was in exact accord with, indeed the very fulfillment of, God's sovereign purpose (cf. v 20c) as expressed through the prophet. This stress on the fulfillment of God's promises (πληρωθῇ) is of central importance to Matthew's perspective. τὸ ῥηθὲν ὑπὸ κυρίου διὰ τοῦ προφήτου, "what was spoken by the Lord through the prophet" (as also in 2:15), accurately expresses the evangelist's and the early Church's view of the Scriptures as stemming from God and mediated to human beings by the agency of prophets. In only half of Matthew's ten fulfillment quotations is the prophet named (see table in *Introduction*). The occurrence of ὑπὸ κυρίου, "by the Lord," here and in 2:15 may emphasize the divine sonship of Jesus (despite the lack of the title "Son of God"), as Pesch ("Das Weihnachtsevangelium [Lk 2, 1–21]," in *Zur Theologie*) and Gundry (*Matthew*) correctly argue.

23 The words of Isa 7:14, ἰδοὺ ἡ παρθένος ἐν γαστρὶ ἕξει καὶ τέξεται υἱόν, "behold the virgin shall conceive and bear a son," have their own historical context and primary level of meaning. The prophet there promises as a sign to King Ahaz and the House of David the birth of a royal son (perhaps Hezekiah) during whose infancy the two kings dreaded by Ahaz (i.e., of Syria and Israel) would suffer ruin. Fulfillment is thus required in the immediate future. While all this may seem relatively uncomplicated and of not very great significance, a deeper meaning in the promise was apparent to Jews of later centuries (on the *sensus plenior* of the fulfillment quotations, see *Introduction*). Two things in particular were responsible for the later perception of this secondary level of meaning: the name given to the child, "Emmanuel" (עִמָּנוּ אֵל, lit. "God with us"; cf. Isa 8:8, 10), and the surrounding passages, which speak of the dawn of the promised golden age with the judgment of the wicked and the blessing of the righteous (e.g., Isa 2:2–4; 9:2–7; 11:1–16). This was the ultimate sense in which God's presence was to be manifested in Israel. The promised son of Isa 7:14 thus became readily identifiable as that son of David who would bring the expected kingdom of security, righteousness, and justice. Accordingly, probably sometime in the third century B.C., the Greek translators of Isa 7:14 apparently regarded the passage as having a deeper meaning, as yet unrealized. In agreement with this interpretation, they chose to translate the Hebrew word עַלְמָה, ʿalmâ (which means "young woman," who may or may not be a virgin), with the Greek word παρθένος (specifically "virgin") rather than νεᾶνις ("young woman," used by the later Jewish translations of Theodotion, Aquila, and Symmachus) in order to stress the supernatural associations brought to mind by the identity and work of this son. Such an interpretation of the word is congruent with the larger picture. Matthew, unquestionably delighted with the agreement between the tradition about Jesus' birth and the words of Isaiah, not only prefaces the quotation with a formula of fulfillment but even conforms the wording of the surrounding narrative to that of the quotation (see *Form/Structure/Setting* §D).

This quotation, unlike the other formula quotations of Matthew, is in verbatim agreement with the LXX text (LXX, according to B, has λήμψεται for ἕξει). The one slight difference is Matthew's καλέσουσιν ("they shall call") for LXX's καλέσεις ("you shall call"). This is probably Matthew's alteration of the text rather than a variant (Matthew has "she"), made in order to avoid the conflict between the command to Joseph to name the child Jesus and the statement of Isaiah that the child shall be named Emmanuel.

There is no problem in referring the names Jesus and Emmanuel to the same person. This may well be the reason Matthew spells out the meaning of the name Emmanuel, μεθ' ἡμῶν ὁ θεός, "God with us" (LXX Isa 8:8, 10). Indeed this is not a personal name but rather a name that is descriptive of the task this person will perform. Bringing the presence of God to man, he brings the promised salvation—which, as Matthew has already explained, is also the meaning of the name Jesus (v 21b). "They" who will call him Emmanuel are those who understand and accept the work he has come to do. Matthew probably intends the words of Jesus at the end of his Gospel—"Behold I am with you always, until the end of the age" (28:20)—to correspond to the meaning of Emmanuel. Jesus is God, among his people to accomplish their salvation (see Fenton, "Matthew," 80–82).

24 Following the pattern of angelic revelations, Matthew carefully records Joseph's obedience in stylized language (see *Form/Structure/Setting* §C).

παρέλαβεν τὴν γυναῖκα αὐτοῦ, "he took his wife," means he completed the second stage of the marriage process, presumably by proceeding with a second formal ceremony and then taking Mary to live with him. She was now his "wife" in the sense of being fully married. (See *Comment* on v 20.)

25 καὶ οὐκ ἐγίνωσκεν αὐτὴν ἕως [οὗ] ἔτεκεν υἱόν, lit. "and he did not know her until she had given birth to a son," i.e., Joseph did not have sexual relations with Mary before the son was born. Matthew records this obviously as a guarantee that Jesus was virgin born. It is most natural to assume that the verse implies that after the birth of Jesus, Joseph and Mary had sexual relations as did any other husband and wife; Brown is surely correct that the later question of Mary's perpetual virginity is very far from Matthew's mind.

Joseph's obedience in completing his marriage to Mary and in naming Jesus (καὶ ἐκάλεσεν τὸ ὄνομα αὐτοῦ Ἰησοῦν, "and he named him Jesus") is also indicative of his formal adoption of Jesus and hence the establishment of his Davidic lineage. It becomes evident, then, how effectively the pericope extends the point of the genealogical table of vv 1–17. The repetition of the name Jesus serves to remind the reader both of the purpose for which he has come (v 21) and of the consequent accomplishment of the sovereign plan of God (v 20c).

Explanation

The story of the birth of Jesus is filled with the surprise and excitement that one might expect when God begins to act in fulfillment of the promise and preparation of the past. In particular, it portrays the wonderful mixing of the miraculous and the ordinary, the divine and the human. The surprising turn in v 16 finds its explanation in the remarkable birth of a son to a virgin—this by the agency of the Holy Spirit, in the accomplishment of God's saving purposes for his people. The focus of attention is, of course, not on the birth itself but on the significance of the child, on the role he will play in fulfilling God's will—as is seen particularly in the importance of the naming in the passage, as well as in the content of the names themselves, Jesus and Emmanuel. The one who is born embodies both God's presence and his saving efficacy. As we have been prepared to understand from the genealogy, the history of God's people has now reached its long-awaited goal. The person of whom Isaiah (among others) wrote is now entering history and the era of fulfillment has now begun. The evangelist, as he tells the story contained in the tradition he received, is thus also its interpreter, centering the narrative around the quotation of Isa 7:14, using its phraseology and prefacing it with an introductory formula that stresses fulfillment.

The story is thus both simple and profound, told with enthusiasm and restraint. Joseph appears as a very real person, confronted with an understandable dilemma. Yet this righteous man, of such little significance to the narrative on the one hand and such great significance on the other (bestowing Davidic descent upon Jesus), receives a revelation to which he is submissive and obedient. Not only is there an artistry in the way the evangelist has set forth his traditional material, using stylized formats and the OT quotation, but there is a poetry, too, about his narrative. And evident throughout his midrashic haggadah, as we have described it above, is his concern that the theological import of his story come alive to the reader.

The Magi Worship the Newborn King   (2:1–12)

Bibliography

Böcher, O. "Matthäus und die Magie." In *Studien zum Matthäusevangelium.* FS W. Pesch, ed. L. Schenke. Stuttgart: Katholisches Bibelwerk, 1988. 11–24. **Brown, R. E.** "The Meaning of the Magi: The Significance of the Star." *Worship* 49 (1975) 574–82. **Bruns, J. E.** "The Magi Episode in Matthew 2." *CBQ* 23 (1961) 51–54. **Ferrari-D'Occhieppo, K.** "The Star of the Magi and Babylonian Astronomy." In *Chronos, Kairos, Christos.* FS J. Finegan, ed. J. Vardaman and E. M. Yamauchi. Winona Lake, IN: Eisenbrauns, 1989. 41–53. **Gaechter, P.** "Die Magierperikope (Mt 2.1–12)." *ZTK* 90 (1968) 259–95. **Hagner, D. A.** "Sun, Moon, Stars." In *NIDNTT* 3:730–737. **Heater, H.** "Matthew 2:6 and Its Old Testament Sources." *JETS* 26 (1983) 395–97. **Hengel, M.,** and **Merkel, H.** "Die Magier aus dem Osten und die Flucht nach Ägypten (Mt 2) im Rahmen der antiken Religionsgeschichte und der Theologie des Matthäus." In *Orientierung an Jesus.* FS Josef Schmid, ed. P. Hoffmann. Freiburg: Herder, 1973. 139–69. **Hoehner, H. W.** *Chronological Aspects of the Life of Christ.* Grand Rapids: Zondervan, 1977. 11–28. **Mann, C. S.** "Epiphany—Wise Men or Charlatans?" *Theology* 61 (1958) 495–500. **McNamara, M.** "Were the Magi Essenes?" *IEJ* 110 (1968) 305–28. **Metzger, B. M.** "Names for the Nameless in the New Testament." In *Kyriakon.* FS J. Quasten, ed. P. Granfield and J. Jungmann. Münster: Aschendorf, 1970. 79–99. **Nellessen, E.** *Das Kind und seine Mutter: Struktur und Verkündigung des 2. Kapitels im Matthäusevangelium.* SBS 39. Stuttgart: Katholisches Bibelwerk, 1969. **Petrotta, A. J.** "A Closer Look at Matt. 2.6 and Its Old Testament Sources." *JETS* 28 (1985) 47–52. **Richards, H. J.** "The Three Kings (Mt ii.1–12)." *Scr* 8 (1956) 23–38. **Rosenberg, R. A.** "The 'Star of the Messiah' Reconsidered." *Bib* 53 (1972) 105–9. **Stuhlmacher, P.** "Epiphanias: Matthäus

2, 1–12." *GPM* 27 (1972) 63–70. **Yamauchi, E. M.** "The Episode of the Magi." In *Chronos, Kairos, Christos.* FS J. Finegan, ed. J. Vardaman and E. M. Yamauchi. Winona Lake, IN: Eisenbrauns, 1989. 15–39.

Translation

[1]*After Jesus had been born in Bethlehem of Judea, in the days of Herod the King, look, magi from the east arrived in Jerusalem,* [2]*saying, "Where is the one born King of the Jews? For we saw his star rising above the eastern horizon,*[a] *and we have come to worship him."* [3]*When King Herod heard this, he was troubled, as was all of Jerusalem with him.* [4]*And he gathered all the chief priests and scribes of the people and asked them, "Where is the Messiah to be born?"* [5]*And they said to him, "In Bethlehem of Judea, for thus it has been written by the prophet:*[b]

[6] *And you, Bethlehem, land of Judah,*[c]
by no means are you the least among the princes of Judah.
For from you shall come forth a ruler
who will shepherd my people Israel."

[7]*Then Herod secretly summoned the magi and carefully ascertained from them the time when the star became visible,* [8]*and when he had sent them to Bethlehem, he said, "Go, search carefully for the little child. But as soon as you have found him, tell me, so that I too may come and worship him."* [9]*And, when they had listened to the King, they departed. And look, the star which they had seen in the eastern sky* [d] *kept going before them until it came and stood above the place where the baby was.*[e] [10]*When they saw the star they rejoiced with a very great joy.* [11]*And when they had come into the house, they saw the infant with Mary his mother and fell to the ground and worshiped him. And they opened their treasure chests and offered to him gifts, gold and frankincense and myrrh.* [12]*And because they had been warned in a dream not to return to Herod, they departed by another road to their own country.*

Notes

[a] ἐν τῇ ἀνατολῇ, lit. "in the east," i.e., "at its rising."
[b] sy co add "Micah"; it[a] adds "Isaiah." The overwhelming silence of the other witnesses certifies the conclusion that these are late additions designed to identify the prophet as Matthew usually does.
[c] D it read τῆς Ἰουδαίας, thereby producing agreement with vv 1 and 5. The majority of witnesses preserves the more difficult reading γῇ Ἰούδα. Perhaps this reading results from the influence of the Ἰούδα at the end of the second line of the citation.
[d] ἐν τῇ ἀνατολῇ, lit. "in the east."
[e] A somewhat awkward construction in Gr. The western text (D it) therefore omits οὗ ἦν and reads τοῦ παιδίου, governed by ἐπάνω, "stood above the child."

Form/Structure/Setting

A. Chap. 2 is quite independent of chap. 1. To some extent, as Stendahl ("Quis") and others have noted, it serves to place the narrative in geographical context by calling attention to place names. We now reach the "whence?" (*unde*) in contrast with the "who?" (*quis*) of chap. 1. Perhaps even more important, however, is the stress on the *opposite reactions* to the Christ from his earliest days, as exhibited in the magi and Herod. The two stories are, of course, linked via the announcement of the magi (v 2) and their subsequent meeting with Herod (v 7). Chap. 2 is therefore a unity consisting of a story of acceptance and rejection. It is linked to chap. 1 only by the references to the birth: γεννηθέντος (v 1); τεχθείς (v 2); γεννᾶται (v 4). A gap of some thirty years exists between the end of chap. 2 and the beginning of chap. 3. It would thus be possible to skip from chap. 1 to chap. 3 without any loss of continuity. Nevertheless, as Schlatter points out, chap. 1 may raise in the reader's mind how this announcement of a new king is taken by the existing king.

B. Some have seen chap. 2 as structured around the four (or five, so Hengel and Merkel) OT quotations, which are in turn related to the four place names:

Matthew 2	OT Citation	Place Name
vv 1–6	v 6 (Mic 5:1, 3)	Bethlehem
vv 7–12	v 11 (Ps 72:10–11; Isa 60:6)	
vv 13–15	v 15 (Hos 11:1)	Egypt
vv 16–18	v 18 (Jer 31:15)	Rama
vv 19–23	v 23 (Isa 11:1?)	Nazareth

N.B. The OT citation comes at the end of every pericope except in the first instance, where it occurs in the middle (v 6).

Four OT citations, each involving a different place name, are certainly an interesting feature of chap. 2. Nevertheless, the quotations give the impression of being added to an already formulated story line rather than giving rise to it. Moreover, granted the obvious importance of Bethlehem and Nazareth and the symbolic significance of Egypt (see below), Rama has no importance as a place name *per se* (although one might mention the exilic association of this passage from Jeremiah). Chap. 2 naturally divides into two parts: (1) the worship of the magi (vv 1–12) and (2) the wrath of Herod (vv 13–23).

Within vv 1–12 Lohmeyer finds six components arranged in a parallelism, i.e., vv 1–2 match vv 9–10 (the leading of the star); vv 3–6 match v 11 (place of birth); and vv 7–8 match v 12 (command and failure to return). This analysis seems unconvincing because of the weakness of some of the suggested correspondences, and a simpler outline such as the following may be suggested: (1) the arrival and message of the magi (vv 1–2); (2) the troubled reaction of Herod (vv 3–8); and (3) the completion of the journey of the magi in the worship of the child (vv 9–12).

The OT citation in v 6, although of central importance, does not have much impact on the actual wording of the surrounding narrative, perhaps because in the narrative the quotation comes from the lips of the high priests and scribes. For this reason, it is not prefaced by an introductory formula stressing fulfillment—which is Matthew's usual practice elsewhere in the Gospel and especially in the opening two chapters. The most interesting structural feature in this pericope is found in vv 11–12, where Matthew concisely presents the climax of the story through three aorist verbs (προσεκύνησαν, "they worshiped"; προσήνεγκαν, "they offered" [gifts]; ἀνεχώρησαν, "they departed"), each with an accompanying adverbial participle (πεσόντες, "having fallen to the ground"; ἀνοίξαντες, "having opened" [their treasure chests]; χρηματισθέντες, "having been warned"). Thus with a concise forcefulness, the evangelist recounts the fulfillment of the mission of the magi.

C. Although it need not be denied that a historical tradition underlies the passage, the genre of this pericope continues in the vein of haggadah wherein the historical narrative finds its primary purpose in the conveying of theological truth. The way in which the story is told is calculated to bring the reader to further theological comprehension of the significance of Jesus as well as to anticipate a number of themes or motifs that are to recur repeatedly in the Gospel before the story is over. For the midrashic aspects, see *Form/Structure/Setting* §C on the second half of chap. 2.

D. In spite of the widespread hesitancy concerning the historicity of this pericope (e.g., Brown, *Birth;* Hill; Luz), there is no insuperable reason why we must deny that the tradition used by Matthew is historical at its core (see E. M. Yamauchi, "Episode"). We do not know the source of Matthew's narrative; Luke apparently did not know the story or else he deliberately ignored it (cf. Luke 2:39).

There are some possible contacts with similar OT stories (e.g., the Queen of Sheba's visit to Solomon), especially involving Balaak and Balaam (Num 22–24). Balaak is the wicked king of Moab who wants to destroy Moses (for a comparison of the contents of Matt 2 with the story of Moses, see the next pericope); Balaam is a gentile wizard from the east, called a $\mu\acute{\alpha}\gamma o\varsigma$ by Philo (*Vit. Mos.* 1.50), who surprisingly ended up saying good things about Israel rather than cursing her, thus frustrating the king's evil intentions. Balaam furthermore refers in one of his oracles to the rising of a star ($\acute{\alpha}\sigma\tau\rho o\nu$; cf. Matthew's $\acute{\alpha}\sigma\tau\acute{\eta}\rho$) out of Jacob (Num 24:17; cf. Gen 49:10), which is to rule over many nations and possess a kingdom that will increase (Num 24:7). The elements in common with our pericope are striking: the wicked, threatened king; the strange non-Israelite "medium" who yet recognizes God's presence in Israel; and the talk of a coming king together with the star symbolism. Yet, since Matthew makes no deliberate attempt to draw wording from the episode in Numbers, nor does he cite or allude to the OT passages, it may be that the similarities are coincidental. We cannot know with certainty that Matthew had the Balaak/Balaam material in his mind when he wrote this narrative. Brown (*Birth)* speculates that the source used by Matthew here is separate from the basic source (depending on Joseph in Egypt and Moses) used elsewhere in the first two chapters because of the lack of any reference to Joseph or to dreams. The two pre-Matthean stories came to be associated by the view that scribes who advised Pharaoh were magi (so Philo, *Vit. Mos.* 1.16). This, however, is to say much more than we can know.

E. Hellenistic parallels to various aspects of our pericope exist. It was commonly held that the birth (and death) of great men was heralded by the appearance of a star or a similar heavenly phenomenon. (See Rosenberg. Recorded examples are Alexander the Great, Mithridates, and Alexander Severus. For rabbinic examples referring to Abraham, Isaac, and Moses, see Str-B 1:77–78.) Virgil relates how Aeneas was guided by a star to the place where Rome was to be founded (*Aeneid* 2.694). The giving of homage to a king by those from a distant country is, of course, a common motif in the ancient world. A striking parallel to our story is the coming of Tiridates, the king of Armenia, with representatives of other eastern kingdoms (described as magi by Pliny, *Nat. Hist.* 30.1.16–17; cf. Dio Cassius 63.1–7; Suetonius, *Nero* 13) to pay homage ($\pi\rho o\sigma\kappa\upsilon\nu\epsilon\widehat{\iota}\nu$, as in our passage) to Nero in A.D. 66, and their return by another route. Parallels such as these show that Matthew's narrative was not as alien to his age as it is to ours. We may allow for some indirect influence of these parallels upon Matthew's formulation of his narrative without concluding that it therefore contains nothing historical. Parallels in *Prot. Jas.* 21.1–4 and Justin Martyr, *Dialogue* 77.4–78.2, are dependent on Matthew (so too Ign. *Eph.* 19:1–3).

F. The Lukan counterpart to Matthew's narrative about the magi appears to be the story of the shepherds (Luke 2:8–20). The few superficial similarities can be explained by the similar circumstances. Otherwise, the passages and the respective underlying tradition are completely independent (contrary to Gundry's [*Matthew*] argument that Matthew's narrative is a transmutation of the Lukan tradition).

Comment

1   The use of the genitive absolute τοῦ δὲ Ἰησοῦ γεννηθέντος, "after Jesus had been born," enables the name of Jesus to occur first (as it also did at the beginning of 1:18). γεννηθέντος links with chap. 1, especially the ἐγέννησεν of 1:16. The aorist participle indicates that the birth had already occurred when the magi arrived in Jerusalem.

ἐν Βηθλέεμ τῆς Ἰουδαίας, "in Bethlehem of Judea," is the first indication of a place name in Matthew's narrative; its theological importance can be seen in the way it anticipates the quotation of Mal 5:1 in v 6 (cf. also vv 5, 8), despite the slight difference between τῆς Ἰουδαίας and the γῆ Ἰούδα of the quotation. Bethlehem of Judea is located about five miles south of Jerusalem and is to be distinguished from Bethlehem of Zebulon, far to the north (Josh 19:15). It had strong Davidic associations through David's ancestors (Judah) and his own anointing by Samuel; hence, it is elsewhere called "the city of David" (Luke 2:4, 11), a designation we might have expected Matthew to use here. But for Matthew the same theological purpose is accomplished through the designation "Judea." In addition to the geographical location, the evangelist provides a general date with the words ἐν ἡμέραις Ἡρῴδου τοῦ βασιλέως, "in the days of Herod the king" (Luke is more precise in dating; see Luke 2:1). Herod the Great is in view here, and since his death occurred in 4 B.C., the birth of Jesus must be placed earlier. (The discrepancy with the numbering of years by the designation A.D. results from an error of the sixth-century scholar Dionysius Exiguus, who was responsible for the calculations that moved the Western world away from dating according to the year after the foundation of Rome.) The specification "king," here and in v 3, stands in deliberately marked contrast to the magi's reference to the "king of the Jews" (v 2) whom they seek.

ἰδού, "look," is a favorite device of emphasis in Matthew, especially in chaps. 1 and 2. "Magi" (μάγοι) has four general meanings according to G. Delling (*TDNT* 4:356–58): (1) members of a Persian priestly class; (2) possessors of supernatural knowledge and power; (3) magician; and (4) deceiver or seducer. In the NT, the word refers to possessors of secret wisdom, and in our passage it probably connotes astrologers, that is, men who gained special insight into world affairs from their observation of the planets and stars (hence, the common translation "wise men"). Some (e.g., W. K. L. Clarke, *Divine Humanity* [London: SPCK, 1936]; Mann) have seen a veiled polemic against occultism and magic in the magi's worship of the newborn king (cf. Ign. *Eph.* 19). This is at best an undertone of the passage, since Matthew gives no hint that this was in his mind. What *is* in Matthew's mind is that Gentiles, those considered alien to God's purposes, exhibit an openness to God's purposes (even through the instrumentality of their own craft) and an eager receptivity toward the newborn king. This is obviously a sign of what Matthew will repeatedly call attention to in his narrative (e.g., 8:11; 21:43). The argument of some (e.g., Mann) that the magi were Jews rather than Gentiles is not convincing. The whole tenor of the passage, and not simply the designation "magi," suggests non-Israelites. Matthew would have to indicate that they were Jews for his readers to draw this conclusion. Their knowledge about the messianic king, however, was certainly gained from prior Jewish contact. Only later Christian tradition designates the magi as kings (cf. Isa 60:3), three in number (corresponding to the three gifts), and assigns them names (see Metzger) and personal characteristics.

ἀπὸ ἀνατολῶν, "from the east," is perhaps deliberately vague because of the prototypical character of the magi. If we presume a historical kernel to the narrative, four areas may be mentioned as possibilities: (1) Parthia; (2) Babylon; (3) Arabia (for a detailed survey, see Brown, *Birth*, 168–70, who, however, regards the magi and the east as idealizations); and (4) Egypt. Since the magi in Matthew's narrative have some knowledge of Jewish messianic expectation, they must have had some contact with Jewish thinking. While this could have occurred in Persia or Arabia, Babylon had a settled Jewish community and seems the most likely candidate (cf. Dan 2:48; 5:11).

The magi, apparently unfamiliar with the Micah passage cited by the high priests and scribes, make the natural assumption that the new king was to be born in the capital city. Hence they go εἰς Ἱεροσόλυμα, "to Jerusalem." They do not go to Herod but are only summoned to him (v 7) after he has heard of their purpose (v 3). The fact that they come to Jerusalem rather than Bethlehem suggests that we misunderstand the reference to the star if we take it to mean that they were actually led by and "followed" the star in the most literal sense (cf. *Comment* on v 9).

2 The only other occurrences of the title βασιλεὺς τῶν Ἰουδαίων, "king of the Jews," in Matthew are in the passion narrative, where it is used in mockery of Jesus and always in the mouths of Gentiles (27:11, 29, 37). Here it has obvious messianic significance, as can be seen from Herod's rephrasing of the question "Where is the Christ to be born?" (v 4) and in the scriptural answer (v 6). But, as in the passion narrative, so also here in the context of references to "King Herod," the title has political overtones. This is true because of Jewish expectation, but it goes against Jesus' own understanding of his kingship.

The star is seen ἐν τῇ ἀνατολῇ, "at its rising," rather than "in the east" (for which we might expect the plural, as in v 1). Although we cannot be certain, it may well be that in τὸν ἀστέρα, "the star," we are to understand a "natural" astronomical phenomenon such as a conjunction of planets (Jupiter and Saturn, for example, came in line in 7–6 B.C. in the constellation of Pisces; on this theory, see Ferrari-D'Occhieppo), a comet (Halley's passed in 12–11 B.C.), or a supernova (i.e., an exploding star). In this phenomenon, whatever it was, the magi-astrologers perceived the sign of the fulfillment of the Jewish eschatological expectation concerning the coming king and so would have set off on their journey toward Jerusalem. For an elaboration of the star tradition, cf. Ign. *Eph.* 19.1–3.

Elsewhere in the NT, Jesus is himself referred to as the rising star (cf. Luke 1:78; 2 Pet 1:19; Rev 22:16). With this, compare Matt 4:16.

The most natural meaning of προσκυνῆσαι αὐτῷ in the historical setting (with the reference to a king) is "to pay homage to him." "To worship him" may also be used in the looser sense, referring to the divinity claimed by ancient monarchs. But Matthew's readers know the real meaning of what the magi have come to do better than the magi themselves knew, namely, "worship" in its proper sense. That is, Jesus is the manifestation of God's presence (1:23), the son of God (2:15) in a unique sense, and thus one to be worshiped.

3 ὁ βασιλεὺς Ἡρῴδης ἐταράχθη, "King Herod was troubled." The repetition of βασιλεύς, "king" (cf. v 1), underlines the obvious reason that Herod is deeply troubled when he hears of the magi's quest. This response, of course, prepares the reader for the second part of chap. 2. Schlatter entitles chap. 2 "The Battle of the King against the Christ." Herod cannot tolerate homage being paid to another as "king of the Jews."

It is unclear why the populace (πᾶσα Ἱεροσόλυμα, "all Jerusalem") is troubled μετ᾽ αὐτοῦ, "with him." They may be afraid of Herod's reaction (Grundmann) or of the expected trouble that was immediately to precede the reign of the Messiah. On the other hand, one expects them to rejoice at the possibility of the experience of the long-awaited deliverance. Some (e.g., Gerhardsson, Luz) have therefore seen the μετ᾽ αὐτοῦ as associating the Jerusalemites (or Jewish leaders, Davies-Allison) with Herod's rejection and persecution of the Messiah, thus anticipating the rejection of Jesus by Jerusalem and Israel in the Gospel (cf. 23:37–39; 27:25). Later, the whole city is "shaken" by Jesus' triumphal entry (21:10).

4 It is unlikely that the neutral word for "gathering," συναγαγών, connotes in any sense the synagogue, as some have argued. To capitalize in this way on the identical root is to over-interpret. Nor is this gathering sinister, except in the case of Herod himself. The plural ἀρχιερεῖς, "chief priests," is common and explainable: it includes living past high priests and members of the family of the ruling high priest as well as leading priests in charge of the large corps of priests employed in the temple cult and related activities. The γραμματεῖς, "scribes," are the learned scholars of Scripture. τοῦ λαοῦ, "of the people," which modifies both nouns, refers to the Jewish nation over which Herod ruled. These experts are precisely the people one would expect Herod to consult. They would certainly have composed an important part of the Sanhedrin, but a meeting of that body itself is not meant (cf. the lack of reference to the elders). The imperfect tense of ἐπυνθάνετο, lit. "were asking," is regularly used for this verb. See BDF §328. ὁ χριστός, "the Messiah," is the correct interpretation of the king sought by the magi (v 2) as being the eschatological king of the Jews.

5 The answer of the experts, ἐν Βηθλέεμ τῆς Ἰουδαίας, "in Bethlehem of Judea," agrees with the fact recorded in v 1. The difference between τῆς Ἰουδαίας, "Judea" (the common expression), and γῆ Ἰούδα, "land of Judah" (the quotation), is not significant. Since the formula introducing the quotation is not the same as those employed by the evangelist elsewhere (see *Introduction*), it and the quotation that follows are probably meant by Matthew to be understood as a part of the answer given by the experts. But the use of the quotation is also obviously consonant with Matthew's purpose (as is his own apparent alteration of the text-form). The report that some of the crowd in John 7:41–42 know that the Messiah is to be born in Bethlehem should be no surprise. The knowledge is not limited to the experts, yet Herod understandably wishes to have the most authoritative answer possible (and perhaps also to get their reaction to the entire affair). The fact, however, that Jesus' hometown was Nazareth rather than Bethlehem constituted a problem, as can be seen from the Johannine passage. This problem was certainly still raised by Jews in Matthew's day and probably accounts for Matthew's emphasis on Bethlehem in chap. 2 and the inclusion of the explanation of how Jesus came to dwell in Nazareth. But this does not mean that the early Christians found it necessary to invent a tradition about Jesus' birth in Bethlehem (cf. Luke 2:4, 15).

6   The form of Matthew's citation of Mic 5:2 is distinctive, agreeing neither with the LXX nor with the MT. Matthew's own work is to be seen in the shape of the quotation. Most of the differences are minor. Thus, Matthew omits the reference to Ephrathah and substitutes γῆ Ἰούδα. The reason for this difficult reading, which stands in apposition to Βηθλέεμ, is unclear. It is possibly a theological alteration to remind the reader of Jesus' descent from Judah (with the messianic implication) as in 1:1, 2. On the other hand, it may simply have been caused by the use of Ἰούδα at the end of line 2 in the citation. In any event, in this instance Matthew has not let the reading of the citation affect the surrounding references to "Bethlehem of Judea." A second minor difference is in Matthew's use of ἡγεμόσιν, "princes," and ἡγούμενος, "a ruler," in lines 2 and 3, where the LXX has χιλιάσιν, "thousands," and ἄρχοντα, "ruler," respectively. Behind χιλιάσιν is the Hebrew אֶלֶף, ᵓlp, which with different vowels can alternatively be rendered ἡγεμῶν (as LXX does in other places); obviously Matthew prefers the notion of "ruler." ἡγούμενος may then be explained as a synonym for ἄρχοντα, chosen to agree with the ἡγεμόσιν of the previous line.

The most significant change by far is Matthew's reversal of the statement of both LXX and MT that Bethlehem *is* small among the thousands of Judah. Given Matthew's sense of the fulfillment that has occurred in Bethlehem, the initial statement of the prophet must now paradoxically be reversed: hence, οὐδαμῶς ἐλαχίστη, "by no means the least." But the change may involve more than simply a liberty on the evangelist's part. If in the MT the initial ל were read as the negative particle (לֹא, lōᵓ) i.e., with the slight change of לִהְיוֹת, lihyôt, to לֹא־הֱיוֹת, lōᵓhĕyôt, a reading is produced that coincides with Matthew's Greek rendering of the passage. This reading, given its appropriateness in a reference to the birth of the coming ruler, could possibly already have been circulating in Matthew's time. (See Allen, Lohmeyer-Schmauch, Klostermann.)

The last line of the quotation is similar to Mic 5:3 (LXX), "and he will shepherd his flock in the strength of the Lord," but probably is dependent upon 2 Sam 5:2 (cf. 1 Chr 11:2), where the Lord says to David that he "will shepherd my people Israel" (Matthew's wording is in verbatim agreement with the LXX of the latter). It was rabbinic practice to combine quotations referring to the same thing, particularly when linked by a key word or common concept, in the present instance "ruling" and "shepherding." The messianic king, the Son of David, would shepherd his people. The special appropriateness of a Davidic context for Matthew is obvious. In Luke's narrative, the fulfillment of the Davidic covenant is more explicit (Luke 1:32–33, using the language of 2 Sam 7:12–16).

The application of the quotation, unlike the formula quotations of the first two chapters, is straightforward, involving no dimension of *sensus plenior* or deeper fulfillment. Its meaning is obvious: the Messiah (the verse was understood as messianic by the Jews) is to be born in Bethlehem, the very place where Jesus' birth had already occurred. The Messiah is to "shepherd my people Israel," which recalls the statement in 1:21 that "he will save his people." The people of the Lord are thus the people of the Messiah.

7 τότε, "then," is a very common connective introducing new sections of narrative in Matthew (e.g., 2:16; 3:13; 4:1; it is so used sixty-one times according to McNeile). Herod's secrecy (λάθρᾳ, "in secret") may be designed to keep the Jews from warning the magi of Herod's treachery. Has he already determined his course of action? The verb ἠκρίβωσεν, "ascertained exactly," suggests special care or exactness in ascertaining the time of the star's appearance. It reflects Herod's high personal interest in the report of the magi because of the implicit threat to his own regime. The report of the star apparently involves a symbolism familiar to Herod, and he does not challenge what the magi say.

8 The unnecessary adverb ἀκριβῶς, "diligently," reflects the same high concern found in the previous verse. For the meaning of ἐξετάζειν, "search carefully for," see BAGD, 275b. Jesus is referred to as τὸ παιδίον (the diminutive of παῖς), "the very young child," throughout the chapter (cf. vv 9, 11, 13, 14, 20, 21); in the Lukan infancy narrative the word occurs only three times.

ὅπως κἀγὼ ἐλθὼν προσκυνήσω αὐτῷ, "so that I too may come and worship him." It is difficult to believe that the magi had not heard of Herod's reputation or that they were unable to estimate his character so as to surmise the guile and pretense behind these words.

9 This verse makes difficult the explanation of the star as a strictly "natural" astronomical phenomenon (see *Comment* on v 2). If the "natural" explanation of the star is accepted nevertheless, then the present verse (esp. προῆγεν αὐτούς, lit. "it was going before them," and ἕως ἐλθὼν ἐστάθη, "until it came and stood," above where the child was) must be understood either as a touch of romantic myth growing out of the historical kernel or else as referring to something actually experienced by the magi and interpreted in terms of the leitmotif of the star that first "led" them from the east to Jerusalem. The real point is that by divine guidance they are able to complete their quest and find the child. The arrival thus corresponds to the departure (ὁ ἀστήρ, ὃν εἶδον ἐν τῇ ἀνατολῇ, "the star which they had seen rising in the eastern sky"; cf. v 2).

10 Having thus experienced divine guidance from beginning to end (as the star motif suggests) and now about to see the child, the magi were filled with great joy. This is emphatically expressed by Matthew in a redundant conjunction of words: ἐχάρησαν χαρὰν μεγάλην σφόδρα, lit. "they rejoiced with a great joy exceedingly." (The sentence could end with ἐχάρησαν; the cognate accusative χαράν, emphatic by itself, is in turn modified by μεγάλην and σφόδρα. The structure is a Hebraism. See BDF §153.) This statement of an extremely heightened joy is typical in a context of messianic fulfillment (cf. Luke, who uses much more of this kind of language in the nativity narrative; cf. Luke 1:14, 44, 46; 2:10 [χαρὰν μεγάλην, "great joy"], 14, 20).

11 The words εἰς τὴν οἰκίαν, "into the house," show that Matthew apparently does not know of the Lukan tradition that the child was born in a stable (Luke 2:7), just as he does not appear to know of a previous residence of Mary and Joseph in Nazareth (Luke 1:26). The little infant is described as μετὰ Μαρίας τῆς μητρὸς αὐτοῦ, "with Mary his mother." The silence concerning Joseph is in keeping with Mary's central importance (cf. 1:16). πεσόντες προσεκύνησαν graphically portrays the Eastern custom of obeisance: falling to the ground with head to the ground, signifying homage and submission. See further in *Comment* on v 2. Having opened their "treasure boxes" (the meaning of θησαυρός here, in contrast with its meaning in 6:21), the magi make their offering of "gifts" (δῶρα): χρυσὸν καὶ λίβανον καὶ σμύρναν, "gold and frankincense and myrrh." The presentation of gifts to the King of Israel by representatives of the nations is mentioned in the OT in several places. Although Matthew does not capitalize on this by means of a fulfillment quotation, his language may show influence from these passages. Ps 72:10–11 refers to all kings falling down before *the* king, all nations serving him, and the offering of "gifts" (δῶρα), with "gold" (χρυσόν) mentioned specifically in v 15. Isa 60:1–6 (in a more obviously eschatological context) refers to all nations and kings coming to the light (of fulfillment), with the wealth of the nations offered as well as "gold" and "frankincense" (χρυσόν, λίβανον). Apart from the specific language, theologically these passages are saying in part the same thing that Matthew says: the newborn king is king of all the world, and the appropriate homage shall be paid to him by all nations (yet in Matthew Israel, who rejects her king, stands in conspicuous contrast to the gentile nations).

The fact that these OT parallels refer to kings offering gifts is responsible for the later idea that the magi were themselves kings. The offering of gold and precious spices is not extraordinary but does suggest that the magi who could give these gifts were of some wealth. The "decoding" of the three gifts—that gold reflects Christ's kingship, frankincense his deity, and myrrh his suffering—is irrelevant to Matthew's intention (C. Hemer, *The Letters to the Seven Churches of Asia* [Sheffield: JSOT, 1986] 64).

12 The magi are still privileged recipients of divine leading. They are thus χρηματισθέντες κατ' ὄναρ, "warned in a dream," not to return to Herod. χρηματίζειν is commonly used in reference to divine revelations, injunctions, and warnings. κατ' ὄναρ, "in a dream," recalls the continuing control of divine providence in the entire sequence of events (cf. 1:20; 2:13). The magi return "to their own country" (εἰς τὴν χώραν αὐτῶν), the unknown place from which they came.

Explanation

The awe and wonder of the extraordinary events surrounding the birth of the messianic king continue in the present passage. The striking story of magi coming from the distant East calls attention to the significance of the royal infant. In their paying homage to the newborn king, they anticipate the propriety of the worship of the Son of God in the early Church. Moreover, it is obvious that the magi symbolize the Gentiles who, unlike the Jews, prove receptive to the king and God's purposes in him. The realization of eschatological salvation means blessing for all the nations and not simply Israel—this in accord with God's promise to Abraham and the universalism of the prophets. The Church, in the West at least, did not miss the import of the magi, and before they began to celebrate Christmas, they already celebrated Epiphany (Jan. 6), the manifestation of Christ to the Gentiles.

Already in this passage we see a motif that occurs throughout the Gospel: the presence of the messianic king demands decision and therefore causes division between those who accept and those who reject him. This accounts for the glaring contradiction in this passage in the presence of two kings. The extent to which Herod understands his own status as threatened becomes the terrifying subject of the following pericope. But the opposite reactions of Herod and the magi are an important feature of chap. 2.

The significance of Jesus finds further underlining in the agreement between his birth in Bethlehem and the words of the prophet Micah. Although his home was Nazareth (explained in the following passage), he was born in Bethlehem, in fulfillment of prophecy and in further substantiation of his Davidic descent. Again the reader senses the constancy of divine providence throughout the narrative.

The Massacre of the Innocents and the Flight to Egypt (2:13–23)

Bibliography

Albright, W. F. "The Names 'Nazareth' and 'Nazorean.'" *JBL* 65 (1946) 397–401. **France, R. T.** "Herod and the Children of Bethlehem." *NovT* 21 (1979) 98–120. ———. "The 'Massacre of the Innocents'—Fact or Fiction?" In *Studia Biblica 1978: II. Papers on the Gospels,* ed. E. A. Livingstone. Sheffield: JSOT, 1980. 83–94. **Gärtner, B.** *Die rätselhaften Termini Nazoräer und Iskariot.* Horae Soederblomianae 4. Uppsala: Gleerup, 1957. Esp. 5–36. **Menken, M. J. J.** "The References to Jeremiah in the Gospel according to Matthew (Mt 2, 17; 16, 14; 27, 9)." *ETL* 60 (1984) 5–24. **Moore, G. F.** "Nazarene and Nazareth." In *The Beginnings of Christianity,* ed. F. J. Foakes Jackson and K. Lake. London: Macmillan, 1920–33. 1:426–32. **Sanders, J. A.** "Ναζωραῖος in Matt. 2:23." *JBL* 84 (1965) 169–72. **Schaeder, H. H.** "Ναζαρηνός, Ναζωραῖος." *TDNT* 4:874–79. **Schweizer, E.** "'Er wird Nazoräer heissen' (zu Mc 1, 24; Mt 2, 23)." In *Judentum, Urchristentum, Kirche.* FS J. Jeremias, ed. W. Eltester. BZNW 26. Berlin: Töpelmann, 1960. 90–93. **Tatum, W. B.** "Matthew 2.23—Wordplay and Misleading Translations." *BT* 27 (1976) 135–38. **Zuckschwerdt, E.** "Ναζωραῖος in Matth. 2, 23." *TZ* 31 (1975) 65–77.

Translation

^{13}*After they had departed,*[a] *look, an angel of the Lord appeared to Joseph in a dream, saying, "Rise, take the child and his mother, and flee to Egypt, and stay there until I tell you. For Herod is about to look for the child in order to destroy him."* ^{14}*And he rose and took the child and his mother by night and departed for Egypt.* ^{15}*And he was there until the death of Herod, in order that what was spoken by the Lord through the prophet*[b] *might be fulfilled when he says, "Out of Egypt I called my son."*

^{16}*Then when Herod saw that he had been deceived by the magi, he became very angry and he sent and murdered all the male infants in Bethlehem and in the surrounding region two years old and younger, in keeping with the time which he had ascertained from the magi.* [17] *Then what was spoken by the Lord[c] through Jeremiah the prophet was fulfilled when he says,*

[18] *A voice was heard in Rama,*
   much weeping and lamentation.[d]
   Rachel weeping for her children,
   and she would not be comforted, because they are no more.

[19] *But after Herod died, behold, an angel of the Lord appeared in a dream to Joseph in Egypt, saying,* [20] *"Rise, take the child and his mother, and go to the land of Israel. For they who were seeking the life of the child have died."* [21] *And he rose and took the child and his mother and he went to the land of Israel.* [22] *But when he heard that Archelaus was reigning over Judea in place of his father Herod, he was afraid to go there. And being warned in a dream he departed to the region of Galilee.* [23] *And he came and dwelt in the city called Nazareth,[e] so that what was spoken through the prophets was fulfilled that he shall be called a "Nazarene."*

Notes

[a] B has εἰς τὴν χώραν αὐτῶν, "to their own country," probably through the influence of v 12.

[b] sy[s] inserts τοῦ στόματος Ἡσαίου, "through the mouth of Isaiah."

[c] "By the Lord" added to complete the sense. D aur add ὑπὸ κυρίου, "by the Lord."

[d] TR C D L W *f*[13] and sy[s.c], among others, include a third word, θρῆνος (a synonym of the other two), this apparently by way of harmonization with the text of LXX.

[e] *Ναζαρέτ* is the spelling in א B D L. Other MSS (C K N W Γ (Δ) *f*[(1) 13] lat co) have the alternate spelling *Ναζαρέθ*. p[70vid] has *Ναζαρά*.

Form/Structure/Setting

A. This passage is closely connected with the preceding passage, which indeed serves as its preparation. The recurrence of the dream revelations to Joseph provides some continuity with chap. 1, although the stories of chap. 2 are quite independent. Herod's attempt to destroy the child leads to the flight of the holy family to Egypt, his death allows their return to Israel, and the rule of his son Archelaus accounts for their eventual residence in Nazareth of Galilee. This brings Matthew's nativity narrative to a close, and chap. 3 constitutes a new beginning in the story.

B. This pericope is unique to Matthew and is probably drawn from his special source. Two structural features of the pericope are striking. First, the passage divides readily into three separate frames, each ending with an OT quotation: (1) vv 13–15, the dream warning and flight to Egypt (Hos 11:1); (2) vv 16–18, the slaughter of the innocents (Jer 31:15); (3) vv 19–23, the return to Israel and settlement in Nazareth (Isa 11:1?).

Second, there is a remarkable parallelism in the opening of the first and third frames. Apart from the genitive absolutes that begin both frames, we have nearly verbatim agreement in (1) the account of the revelation; (2) the initial imperatives of the angel; and (3) the obedient response of Joseph (which, in each instance, mirrors the angelic commands of the same frame).

C. The genre here is again midrashic haggadah—the narrative carries great theological significance, which is related to OT texts, not simply in the quotations employed but also in the indirect dependence upon the story of Moses. Much of the narrative indeed can be perceived as a Christian midrash on the biblical narrative of Moses' birth and may have been influenced by Jewish midrash on the same narrative.

The parallels to Matthew's narrative in the opening chapters of Exodus are as follows (with further Jewish midrashic similarities, as witnessed by Josephus and Philo, given in parentheses): the Pharaoh killed all male Hebrew infants, Exod 1:22 (he had been forewarned, either by scribes or through a dream, of a newborn Hebrew who was a threat to his kingdom, and this possibility filled him and all Egypt with terror); at a later time, Moses fled Egypt because his life was threatened by the Pharaoh, Exod 2:15 (the infant Moses' deliverance is due to his parents' actions); at the death of Pharaoh, Moses was directed to return, and he obeyed, Exod 4:19–20. In addition to these general similarities, there are some striking agreements in language: in Exod 2:15, ἐζήτει ἀνελεῖν, "he was seeking to kill," is close to Matthew's (2:13) ζητεῖν . . . ἀπολέσαι, and ἀνεχώρησεν, "he fled," is identical (Matt 2:14); in Exod 2:23, ἐτελεύτησεν ὁ βασιλεὺς Αἰγύπτου, "the king of Egypt died," is close to Matthew's τελευτήσαντος δὲ τοῦ Ἡρῴδου (2:19); most impressive of all, however, is the nearly verbatim agreement between Exod 4:19, τεθνήκασιν γὰρ πάντες οἱ ζητοῦντές σου τὴν ψυχήν, "for all those who sought your life have died," and Matt 2:20, which lacks the πάντες, "all," and for σου, "you," substitutes τοῦ παιδίου, "the child" (but after, instead of before, τὴν ψυχήν). Clearly, Matthew has in mind the story of Moses as he narrates the story of Jesus: Herod is the antitype of Pharaoh; Jesus is the antitype of Moses.

To this we must add the exodus typology involved in the citation of Hos 11:1 at the end of the first frame: "Out of Egypt I called my son" (2:15). Although Matthew does not capitalize on the Moses-Christ typology, it is certainly not far from his thinking. The one who has come to "save his people from their sins" (1:21) is the eschatological counterpart to the one who saved his people from the bondage in Egypt. We may add that while the phrase τῷ Ἰωσὴφ ἐν Αἰγύπτῳ, "Joseph in Egypt" (Matt 2:19), turns our thoughts immediately to patriarchal Joseph, the resemblance between the two Josephs is not particularly convincing, nor is it important to Matthew—although both Josephs were concerned with dreams and kings, and for a time both lived in Egypt out of necessity. Matthew's typology focuses on Jesus, who, to be sure, resembles his people in their sojourn in Egypt in the time of Joseph, even as he does in their exodus from Egypt in the time of Moses. For Matthew, all Israel's history finds its recapitulation in the life of Jesus.

This last statement is further substantiated by Matthew's introduction of an exilic motif in Jeremiah's reference to Rachel's weeping for her children, the OT citation at the end of the second frame (2:18–19). The story of Jesus, even at its beginning, sums up and presents the ultimate significance of all that has preceded, both good and evil. This is especially true of the major events such as the slavery/exodus and the exile/return—which are already related in the later writings of the OT as being theologically of one fabric. As Brown points out, the first three quotations of Matthew, involving the city of David, the land of the exodus, and the mourning of the exile, "offer a theological history of Israel in geographical miniature" (*Birth*, 217). The suggestion of the haggadic account of Laban's persecution of Jacob/Israel as further background to Matthew's narrative (M. Bourke, *CBQ* 22 [1960] 160–75; D. Daube, *The NT and Rabbinic Judaism*) has little to commend it. (See Appendix VI, in Brown, *Birth*.)

In ever-increasing specificity, the third frame refers to a return to Israel (2:20–21), Galilee (2:22), and Nazareth (2:23). The first two are by divine direction; the last is in fulfillment of Scripture. Regardless of what is meant by 2:23 (see *Comment* below), the point is the realization of messianic fulfillment. Although from one perspective the move to the north, rather than to Judea, seems to be the result of the reign of Archelaus in his father's stead, divine providence is obviously at work at the same time. It is precisely in this way that the Scripture quoted in 4:15–16 about the light that is to shine upon the darkness of Gentile-inhabited Galilee finds its fulfillment. Thus the third frame, like the first two, is permeated with theological overtones and is far from being a simple historical narrative. In the events that Matthew records, the Scriptures concerning Israel's experience—its suffering as well as expectation—are both reflected and find their fulfillment.

D. To argue that Matthew has been influenced by the OT story of Moses and perhaps by later midrashic expressions of that story does not necessitate the conclusion that his narrative depends directly or solely on those sources rather than on any historical tradition. The story is consistent with what we know of Herod and reflects the way he would have responded to the announcement of the magi. The fact that there are no other unquestionable references among contemporary historians to the killing of the infants may not be surprising if, as seems probable, the number killed was around twenty. Among the atrocities of Herod, this event in a small unimportant village would hardly have demanded the attention of historians. (The reference in Macrobius, *Saturnalia* 2.4.11, is almost certainly derived from Matthew.) It is also very unlikely that in this narrative we are to see the influence of similar motifs in mythology involving the persecution of divine children by evil persons. On the historicity of the pericope, see especially France.

Luke's narrative makes no mention of a journey to Egypt but has the holy family move directly from Bethlehem to Nazareth, which is, moreover, "their own city" (Luke 2:29). But Luke was presumably under no obligation to write his own narrative in such a way that it could be harmonized with other historical traditions, even if he knew about them. In short, disagreement (which is different from formal contradiction) between the evangelists says nothing about the historical value of the traditions, since neither writes with the expectation that readers will eventually be concerned to fit everything together into one harmonious whole.

Comment

13 ἰδοὺ ἄγγελος κυρίου φαίνεται κατ' ὄναρ, "Look, an angel of the Lord appeared in a dream," is typical of the Matthean infancy narrative (cf. 1:20; 2:19–20). The historical present tense of φαίνεται, lit. "appears" (along with ἰδού, "look!"), adds vividness to the narrative. The pattern of the narrative is stereotyped (see above on 1:18–25, *Form/Structure/Setting* §A). τὸ παιδίον καὶ τὴν μητέρα αὐτοῦ, "the infant and his mother," becomes a stock phrase in chap. 2 (cf. 2:11, 14, 20, 21). The threat to the child is imminent: μέλλει γὰρ Ἡρῴδης ζητεῖν, "for Herod is about to seek." This draws attention to the importance of both the angelic revelation and Joseph's obedience. Herod's purpose is τοῦ ἀπολέσαι αὐτό, "to destroy him." This intent is in full accord with what is known of Herod's character and reflects his perception of his threatened status. The verb ἀπολέσαι, "to destroy," anticipates its recurrence in the passion narrative (27:20), where, in that instance, it is the chief priests and elders who are the acting subjects.

14 The account of Joseph's obedience echoes closely the wording of the angelic command in the preceding verse. Egypt is chosen because it is convenient and removed from Herod's power (and perhaps for the exodus typology it makes possible). It does not seem very likely, contrary to Brown (*Birth*), that Egypt here shows the influence upon Matthew of a "flight to Egypt" tradition (two OT instances are given: 1 Kgs 11:40 and Jer 26:21 [LXX 33:21]; and one instance from Jos. *Ant.* 12.9.7). Later rabbinic tradition knows of Jesus' sojourn in Egypt and attributes his supernatural powers to the magic he learned there. This story probably stems from a passing acquaintance with the Christian tradition rather than from direct dependence upon Matthew. The suggestion, on the other hand, that Matthew writes to counter the Jewish tradition (McNeile, Allen, Grundmann) is unlikely.

15 The fulfillment quotation (see *Introduction*) anticipates the narrative and belongs properly at the end of v 21, after the account of Herod's death and Joseph's return to the land of Israel. Its occurrence here lends symmetry to the structure of chap. 2 (see above, *Form/Structure/Setting* §B), where vv 19–23 focus on Nazareth. More importantly, the premature quotation serves as the signal of the theological import of the presence of the holy family in Egypt by its explicit reference to the exodus. This placing of the quotation also has the advantage of putting the exodus motif prior to the exilic motif (vv 16–18). Gundry denies that the exodus motif is present, arguing instead that what is meant is only the preservation of God's Son in Egypt and that this explains the placing of the quotation after v 14. This hypothesis, however, is strained in view of the actual content of the quotation.

In the formula quotations, ὑπὸ κυρίου, "by the Lord," occurs only here and in 1:22, where in both cases the quotation speaks of the Son of God. See *Comment* on 1:22. The quotation here is from Hos 11:1, but in a form agreeing more with the MT than with the LXX (which has μετεκάλεσα, "I summoned," for Matthew's ἐκάλεσα, "I called," and τὰ τέκνα αὐτοῦ, "his children" [i.e., Ἰσραήλ, "Israel"] for Matthew's τὸν υἱόν μου, "my Son"). Matthew has altered the LXX text for his own purposes, made use of a Greek text more faithful to the MT (which reads לִבְנִי, *libnî*, "my son"), or here reflects knowledge and use of the Hebrew text. No serious problem exists here since there is no essential difference between the collective singular and the plural, and Israel's sonship is assumed throughout the OT.

Hosea is, of course, alluding to the historical exodus and not making a prophecy about the future. How then can Matthew say that the quotation is "fulfilled" (πληρωθῇ)? What we have here is a matter of typological correspondence—that is, a substantial similarity is seen to exist between two moments of redemptive history, and therefore the two are regarded as interconnected, forming one larger continuity; the earlier is thus seen to foreshadow or anticipate the latter, which then becomes a kind of realization or fulfillment of the former. The fulfillment motif is of course central to Matthew's whole perspective, given the eschatological significance of the Christ, here seen as God's unique Son. Thus, in the similarity of the son of God, Israel, and the Son of God, Jesus, both in Egypt of necessity and both delivered by divine provision, Matthew sees Jesus as living out and summing up the history of Israel. In Egypt, in the exodus, and in the wilderness (see 4:1–11), Jesus is the embodiment of Israel, not only anticipating her victories but also participating in her sufferings (cf. Isa 63:8–9).

To round out Matthew's perspective, we must add that since Israel's history has now reached its goal, which gathers together all previous threads, the earlier exodus now finds its counterpart and its climax in the eschatological deliverance of God's people from their sins (1:21; cf. the Greek text of Luke 9:31 for the most obvious exodus typology in the Gospels). This conception of the final salvation in exodus terminology is found in the OT (e.g., Isa 11:11; Hos 2:15; 12:9; Mic 7:15) as well as in rabbinic tradition (see Str-B). It is certainly also in Matthew's mind, given the obvious parallels between Moses and Christ in our passage. Another passage that may be in Matthew's mind is Num 23:22 (and 24:8), where, in Balaam's oracles, God is said to bring the promised one out of Egypt.

16 Despite the preceding clause, Herod's excessive anger (ἐθυμώθη λίαν, "he became very angry") does not rest solely upon the failure of the magi to return. His evil intent remains constant from the first report of the birth of the purported messianic king; he will brook no rival. But his anger was no doubt intensified when the magi did not return. Unable now to determine whether the child existed and, if so, where in Bethlehem he might be found, the unscrupulous Herod would take no chances and thus "sent" (ἀποστείλας has no express object) his henchmen to destroy all the "male infants" (τοὺς παῖδας, masculine gender) two years and younger, in keeping with the time of the observance of the star by the magi. We may thus conclude that the magi may have first observed the star long before their arrival in Jerusalem (2:7), perhaps even as much as nearly two years, although of course Herod's allowance for a margin of error must be taken into consideration. The birth of Jesus accordingly is probably to be placed not much later than 6 B.C. Herod murdered πάντας τοὺς παῖδας τοὺς ἐν Βηθλέεμ καὶ ἐν πᾶσι τοῖς ὁρίοις αὐτῆς, "all the children in Bethlehem and the surrounding districts," who were ἀπὸ διετοῦς καὶ κατωτέρω, "two years and under." Herod thus gives himself an extra measure both of temporal and of geographical assurance. Even within these expanded boundaries, the number of infants under two in a population of 1,000, given the birth and infant mortality rates of the time, has been reckoned at less than twenty (see Zahn, 109, n. 6). The early Church tended to exaggerate the number (Byzantine tradition sets it at 14,000; Syrian at 64,000; some have even equated it with the 144,000 of Rev 14). That Herod could perpetrate such a horrendous act is consistent with what history has recorded about him. His ruthlessness knew no bounds when it came to protecting his throne, as can be seen in the oft-mentioned example of the execution of his wife Mariamne and his own sons Alexander and Aristobulus in A.D. 6 or 7, and thereafter his son Antipater (Jos. *Ant.* 16.11.7; 17.7). And this is but a token of his atrocities. So that there would be widespread mourning at the time of his own death, mad Herod ordered that a member of every family was to be killed when he died (Jos. *Ant.* 17.6.6).

17 The quotation is introduced with a fulfillment formula, τότε ἐπληρώθη, "then was fulfilled," but with this notable exception: it lacks either of the strong conjunctions expressing purpose, ἵνα, "in order that," and ὅπως, "so that." All the other formulae (see *Introduction*) have one or the other except for 27:9–10, which interestingly is the only other quotation referring to something evil (Judas' betrayal money). This seems to reflect Matthew's reluctance to ascribe evil to the purposes of God. In Matthew's perspective, God's providence overrules evil in the working out of his gracious will.

18 The quotation drawn from Jer 31:15 (LXX 38:15) agrees closely with the LXX in the first two lines, the only difference being Matthew's employment of the adjective πολύς, "much," and the omission of a third noun (θρήνου), a synonym of the other two, thus agreeing more with the MT, which has only the two nouns. In the LXX the nouns are in the genitive case, modifying φωνή, "voice," whereas Matthew has nominatives in apposition to φωνή. (The LXX according to A has τῇ ὑψηλῇ, "on high," as a translation of Rama.) In lines 3 and 4 Matthew is quite close to the LXX according to A, except for υἱοί, "sons," where Matthew has τέκνα, "children." The LXX according to B is fairly similar, but has παύσασθαι, "stop," for παρακληθῆναι, "be comforted," in addition to υἱοί. The MT is close both to the LXX^A and to Matthew, with one important difference at the very end: the awkward אֵינֶנּוּ, ʾênennû, "he is no more," although the plural בָּנֶיהָ, bānêhā, "sons," occurs in the preceding line. Unless he is quoting from memory, Matthew is either using the LXX in a rendition more like A than B, or else a translation even closer to the MT but with the correction οὐκ εἰσίν, "they are no more." Had Matthew translated the Hebrew himself (so Stendahl, School, 102–3), he would probably have used παῖδες (to agree with v 16) instead of τέκνα, as Brown points out (Birth, 222). None of the variations is of great theological interest or significance.

The citation seems strange here because of its exilic connotation as it stands in Jeremiah. Rachel, in her tomb at Rama (cf. 1 Sam 10:2) about six miles north of Jerusalem on the road the exiles would have taken, weeps bitterly because of the fate of those taken into exile (it is uncertain whether Assyrian or Babylonian captivity [or both] is in view)—"they are no more," they are reckoned as dead. With Isa 10:29 and Hos 5:8 together with Jer 31:15 in mind, Davies-Allison refer to Ramah as "a city of sadness par excellence." The larger context in Jeremiah is nevertheless one of hope, deliverance, and fulfillment (chaps. 30–31 form a "book of consolation" and include the statement of the new covenant, 31:31–34). References to messianic joy surround Jer 31:15. In a similar way, Matthew's story of messianic joy and fulfillment is marred by the shadow of the death of the innocent children of Bethlehem. Further strengthening the parallel is the alternate tradition, probably current also in Matthew's day, that Rachel's tomb was on the outskirts of Bethlehem, five miles south of Jerusalem (cf. Gen 35:19; 48:7; to this day, what is called Rachel's tomb is located there). Rachel might well weep there for the infants of Bethlehem, even within the larger context of messianic joy through the birth of the Christ in that same village. Matthew's point rests on typological correspondence and is in no way affected by the actual correctness or incorrectness of the tradition concerning Rachel's burial place near Bethlehem. Apparently, however, that tradition was initially responsible for his utilization of the quotation.

Just as there was a deliverance from the exile, patterned on the deliverance from Egypt in the exodus, so God now brings definitive messianic deliverance. The typological correspondence between Rachel's weeping for the exiles and the weeping of the mothers of Bethlehem, both in larger contexts of deliverance, is more than coincidental for Matthew (see above on v 15). Again, in Matthew's perspective, Jesus is understood as summarizing the whole experience of Israel as well as bringing it to fulfillment. Every strand of hope and trial in the OT is woven together in the eschatological appearance of the Promised One. To see in this passage the consequences of the rejection of Jesus by Jewish leaders, as Gundry does, is to bring in something quite extraneous to Matthew's text.

19 Herod, whose long reign began in 37 B.C., died in 4 B.C. His death signaled the possibility of return, not only of the holy family (cf. v 15) but also of others who had fled from his tyranny, such as the Qumran community. Cf. the similar language in the reference to the death of Pharaoh in Exod 2:23. Following the stereotyped pattern (see above on 1:18–25, *Form/Structure/Setting* §A), this verse agrees nearly verbatim with v 13 (cf. 1:20). An opening genitive absolute is thus followed by the words ἰδοὺ ἄγγελος κυρίου φαίνεται κατ' ὄναρ τῷ Ἰωσήφ, "Look, an angel of the Lord appeared to Joseph in a dream." On τῷ Ἰωσήφ ἐν Αἰγύπτῳ, "Joseph in Egypt," see above, *Form/Structure/Setting* §C.

20 The first part of the verse further maintains the pattern by being in verbatim agreement with v 13. The words εἰς γῆν Ἰσραήλ, "into the land of Israel," constitute an obvious echo of the exodus narrative. The delay of the further revelation, i.e., to go to Galilee (v 22), also "by a dream," is necessary to underline the exodus typology.

The sentence τεθνήκασιν γὰρ οἱ ζητοῦντες τὴν ψυχὴν τοῦ παιδίου, "for they who were seeking to kill the child died," agrees nearly verbatim with Exod 4:19 (see above, *Form/Structure/Setting* §C), and this may account for the plural. More probably the plural is meant to refer to Herod's servants (who after Herod's death were no longer in power) rather than to the chief priests and scribes of 2:4 (as Brown, *Birth,* and Gundry, *Matthew,* argue). ψυχή is regularly used in the NT for "life."

21 The recording of the obedience mirrors the wording of the command in v 20 (cf. v 14, mirroring v 13). On εἰς γῆν Ἰσραήλ, "into the land of Israel," see *Comment* on the preceding verse.

22 The present tense of Ἀρχέλαος βασιλεύει, "Archelaus reigns," reflects the direct discourse of the original report. Joseph's fear of Archelaus appears to have been well grounded, as the son of Herod tended to follow the ways of his father. His subjects managed eventually to have him deposed by the Romans in A.D. 6.

The same words, χρηματισθεὶς δὲ κατ' ὄναρ, "having been warned in a dream," are found in v 12. By means of this last occurrence of the dream motif, Matthew again stresses the continuing divine protection of the child (cf. 1:20; 2:13). It was God's will that they go to Galilee. To be sure, another son of Herod, Herod Antipas, ruled as ethnarch over Galilee and Perea. But he was a more tolerant ruler, and Galilee in his day became known for revolutionary sentiments that would never have been tolerated by his father.

In the statement ἀνεχώρησεν εἰς τὰ μέρη τῆς Γαλιλαίας, "he departed to the region of Galilee," the narrative reaches its last stage. As pointed out above (*Form/Structure/Setting* §C), in the sequence Israel-Galilee-Nazareth (v 23), we move from the general to the more specific. It is in keeping with this sequence that Matthew, employs τὰ μέρη, lit. "the regions," in referring to Galilee. The mention of Galilee is theologically important for Matthew as we shall see in 4:12–16. There he again writes, now of Jesus, ἀνεχώρησεν εἰς τὴν Γαλιλαίαν, "he departed into Galilee" (4:12). It is in Galilee that he inaugurates his ministry in fulfillment of Isa 9:1 (which Matthew then cites). Galilee's large population of Gentiles symbolizes the universal significance Matthew sees in Jesus.

23 κατῴκησεν εἰς πόλιν λεγομένην Ναζαρέτ, "he dwelt in a city called Nazareth." The "city" is unknown from the OT or any sources earlier than the NT documents. Popular opinion in the metropolis of Jerusalem concerning this northern town may well be summarized by the question put by Nathaniel in John 1:46: "Can anything good come out of Nazareth?" Matthew now faces the difficulty that the Messiah was brought up in such an unpromising location. But he is able, by some rabbinic wordplay, to turn an apparent disadvantage into an advantage. In Matthew's affirmations of Nazareth with its negative connotation, Grundmann and Tasker (depending on Jerome) see a deliberate allusion to Jesus as the despised servant of God, but the connection is not compelling. A further possibility (Lindars, *NT Apologetic*, 195–96; Hill) related to the servant theme is found in the revocalizing of the consonants *nsr* (נצר) in Isa 49:6 (cf. 42:6, with *nsr* in the sense of "protect") with the resultant reading "branch" (see below) or even "Nazorean." This is an attractive speculation and has the added advantage of an obviously messianic context, but it remains at best a guess.

ὅπως πληρωθῇ τὸ ῥηθὲν διὰ τῶν προφητῶν, "so that what was spoken through the prophets was fulfilled." In the fourth fulfillment formula quotation (and fifth OT quotation) of the nativity narrative, Matthew presents words not found in the OT or indeed in any pre-Christian extrabiblical writings known to us. It cannot be accidental that the introductory formula here is the most general of all the formulae used by Matthew (see *Introduction*). In five of the ten formulae quotations, Matthew gives a prophet's name; in the remaining five he invariably refers to "*the* prophet" (τοῦ προφήτου). Only here among the formula quotations does he use the plural τῶν προφητῶν, perhaps implying that he has in view a motif common to several prophets (cf. 26:54, 56), although the specific wording is found in none (cf. the same phenomenon in Ezek 9:10–12; for rabbinic parallels, see Str-B 1:92–93). The proposal that Matthew quotes a source unknown to us, although possible, is hardly necessary. What is found in the prophets is generally ὅτι Ναζωραῖος κληθήσεται, "that he shall be called a Nazarene." Matthew's introductory formula, lacking the expected λεγόντων, "saying," does not in fact point to a specific quotation consisting of the words "he shall be called a Nazarene." The ὅτι, "that," is thus not, as it is elsewhere (e.g., 4:6), a recitative ὅτι that introduces quoted words. If Matthew is able eventually to account for Galilee (4:12–16) as the place of Jesus' ministry, he is able also to account for Nazareth as the place where Jesus lived. Here Matthew's ingenuity is impressive. The key to understanding what he says lies in the similarity between Ναζαρέτ, "Nazareth," and Ναζωραῖος, "Nazarene." The difficulty lies in discerning his intent behind Ναζωραῖος; and this is further compounded by the serious uncertainty about the spelling of Nazareth.

The end of the name is uncertain; in the NT the name occurs mainly in the form Ναζαρέτ or Ναζαρέθ, but twice as Ναζαρά (cf. Matt 4:13). More problematic is the fact that the middle consonant is rendered by a ζ in Greek. Is this meant to reflect a צ? (The usual Greek rendering of צ is by ς.) During his ministry Jesus acquired the title "the Nazarene" (Mark regularly uses the form Ναζαρηνός; Matthew always uses Ναζωραῖος, even in passages drawn from Mark; Luke uses both forms). Matthew therefore means at least that Jesus was called "the Nazarene" (as were his followers after him: Acts 24:5, τῆς τῶν Ναζωραίων αἱρέσεως, "the sect of the Nazarenes"). It is doubtful that the omission of the definite article by Matthew is significant. Matthew thus associates the title with the name of Jesus' hometown Nazareth, despite the phonetic difficulty of transliterating the צ with a ζ, instead of the usual ς (thus Albright, Schaeder, Moore, Schlatter, Str-B, Luz).

But Matthew almost certainly means more than this. We may presume that the reference to "the prophets" has something to say theologically. Two possibilities have been favored by scholars—namely, Matthew means to allude to (1) Jesus as a "Nazirite," or (2) Jesus as the promised *nēṣer* (נצר), the messianic branch.

(1) The meaning of "Nazirite" (favored by Bonnard, Sanders, Schweizer, Schaeder, Zuckschwerdt, Davies-Allison) is dependent on the passage in Num 6:1–21 (cf. Judg 13:5, 7), where a person separates himself from others through a special vow involving abstinence from strong drink, not cutting his hair, and avoiding contact with the dead. Although the description may fit John the Baptist (cf. Luke 1:15), it seems singularly inappropriate for Jesus, who, according to Matthew, was accused of being "a glutton and a drunkard, a friend of tax collectors and sinners" (11:19) and who raised the dead by touching them (9:23–26). Because of a reference in Epiphanius (*Haer.* 29.6) to a Jewish sect of *Nasaraioi* deriving from the disciples of John the Baptist (and a related self-designation of the Mandaeans, *nāṣōrayyā*), it has been argued that Matthew's word originally described a larger movement ("observants"; from נָצַר, *nāṣar,* "to guard, protect, observe"), out of which Christianity eventually came; they were called Nazarenes because of the similarity of their perspective to that of John the Baptist (see Black, *Aramaic Approach,* 2nd ed., 198–200). But it is highly doubtful that this is what Matthew meant by the word since he hardly presents Jesus as primarily an observant (cf. 11:12). Since *Nāzîr* becomes synonymous with "holy," it has also been argued that it is therefore an appropriate designation for Jesus. Thus Brown (*Birth;* see too Schweizer and Zuckschwerdt) explains 2:23 by a combination of two texts involving a synonymity between "holy one" and "Nazirite." Isa 4:3 (LXX), "they [MT "he"] will be called holy," is thought to be combined with Judg 16:17 (LXX), "I am a holy one [MT and LXX^A, "Nazirite"] of God." Matthew then understood Nazirite for "holy" in Isa 4:3. But while "holy one" is an appropriate description of the Messiah (cf. Mark 1:24; Luke 4:34), this cannot be construed as "holiness" in the Nazirite sense. Appeal has been made to the extraordinary birth of Jesus and his consecration to the service of God in his mother's womb as further parallels. But if this is what Matthew had in mind, the "quotation" should have appeared in the birth narrative of chap. 1. A further difficulty in this view is the LXX spelling of Nazirite (Ναζιραῖος) which leaves the ω of Matthew's spelling unaccounted for, although this is not insurmountable given the phonetic liberties that were allowable. The suggestion of some that the ω is to be traced back to the vowels of *Qādôš,* which were put with the consonants *nṣr,* is only clever speculation.

(2) The most likely play on words in Matthew's mind is the similarity between the Hebrew word for "branch," *nēṣer,* and Nazareth. This view (Black, *Aramaic Approach;* Stendahl, *School;* Luz; Davies-Allison, but as a "secondary allusion") traces Matthew's "quotation" back to Isa 11:1: "There shall come forth a shoot from the stump of Jesse and a branch [*nēṣer;* LXX ἄνθος] shall grow out of his roots." The distinct advantage of this view is the messianic content of the Isaiah passage, which in turn should be related to the quotation of Isa 7:14 in Matt 1:23. The messianic figure of Isa 11:1 is the Emmanuel of Isa 7:14. Phonetically, the Hebrew of *Nasrat* (Nazareth) and *nēṣer* have the same middle consonant; that consonant is reflected in the ζ of the two words in our verse. To be sure, the ω of Ναζωραῖος remains without satisfactory explanation, as in every reckoning. The word *nēṣer,* although only occurring in Isa 11:1, became an important designation of the Messiah in the rabbinic literature and targums, and was also interpreted messianically by the Qumran community (1QH 6:15; 7:6, 8, 10, 19). Other prophets also spoke similarly of a messianic "branch" or "shoot," although using different words (cf. Jer 23:5; 33:15; Zech 3:8; 6:12). These words form a unified concept in looking to the fulfillment of the promises, and the mention of one doubtless brought the others to mind automatically (see Str-B 1:94). This may well be the explanation of the plural "prophets" in Matthew's introductory formula.

If this theory is correct, then we must believe that Matthew's Greek readers did not realize the wordplay until they became acquainted with the meaning of *nēṣer* in Hebrew. This, however, is precisely the kind of material that is quickly passed on orally and may have become common knowledge in the community. In this connection it should also be remembered that this is a secondary meaning. The primary meaning, Nazareth/Nazarene, is evident to every Greek reader. If this messianic *nēṣer* underlies Matthew's Ναζωραῖος, it is doubtful that further parallels with the verb *nāṣar* ("watch, observe, keep" in Isa 42:6; 49:6), as argued by Gärtner, were really in Matthew's mind. They point rather to the exegete's ingenuity as much as to the complex interrelationship of messianic ideas in the prophets.

Explanation

The response of Herod to the infant Christ stands in intentionally sharp contrast with that of the magi in the preceding passage (2:1–12). The message of the gospel demands decision and necessitates a division between those who accept and reject that message—a motif that will occupy Matthew throughout his narrative. In Herod's attempt to kill the infant King, we encounter evil for the first time in the narrative. In Matthew's perspective, evil continually stands in opposition to the purposes of God, who in Christ brings the kingdom. The resistance to the Christ comes to a climax in the crucifixion narrative of which, to some extent, our passage is an anticipation. At the same time, abundantly evident in our passage is the protection of the holy child by divine guidance. The gracious purposes of God cannot be thwarted; neither the bondage of Egypt nor the tragedy of the exile could thwart them. In the history of Israel, God repeatedly brought salvation to his people, and he has now brought them to the time of fulfillment— eschatological fulfillment in one who relives, sums up, and brings to fruition all the history and experience of his people. Thus the events that surround this child are related to all that preceded, as fulfillments of earlier anticipations. The messianic Branch, the promised descendant of David, toward whom all pointed, is now in the world. He comes, as did his people, out of Egypt to the promised land, through the trauma of the exile, to Galilee, breaking forth light to those sitting in darkness, as the prophet had foretold, to dwell in the unlikely town of Nazareth and so to be known as the Nazarene. Thus, according to Matthew, the plan of God unfolds. Nothing has happened by accident—all is in its proper place as it must be when the sovereign God brings salvation.

The Preparation for the Ministry (3:1–4:11)

Introduction

Having the important prolegomena of chaps. 1–2 in place, the evangelist begins the story of Jesus with an account of the work of John the Baptist (3:1–12), followed by two significant episodes in the life of Jesus, his baptism (3:13–17) and the following temptation (4:1–11). Only then does the record of Jesus' ministry itself begin (4:12–17). The last verse (4:17), which may also be construed as the first verse of the following section, signals a major turning point in the Gospel: "From that time Jesus began to proclaim, 'Repent, for the kingdom of heaven has come near.'" This verse constitutes an inclusio in relation to precisely the same statement of John the Baptist in 3:2. (See the arguments of D. Bauer [*Structure*, 73–84] for the unity of 1:1–4:16.)

The material of this section of the Gospel is particularly important since the baptism of Jesus serves as the occasion of his special anointing by the Holy Spirit for the ministry that follows, but it is also christologically significant in that his divine Sonship is confirmed and the non-triumphalist nature of the present phase of that Sonship is indicated (3:17c and 4:1–11). Thus Matthew provides information that is vitally important to an understanding of the narrative that follows: what Jesus does in his ministry he does by the power of the Spirit; yet Jesus will not act in the manner of a triumphalist messiah, in accordance with popular expectation, but in his own unique way, in obedience to the will of his Father. With the end of the work of John, the work of Jesus begins, announced by the evangelist as the fulfillment of prophecy (4:12–16).

John the Baptist (3:1–12)

Bibliography

Bammel, E. "The Baptist in Early Christian Thought." *NTS* 18 (1971) 95–128. **Beasley-Murray, G. R.** *Baptism in the New Testament.* Grand Rapids: Eerdmans, 1962. 31–44. **Best, E.** "Spirit-Baptism." *NovT* 4 (1960) 236–43. **Böcher, O.** "Johannes der Täufer in der neutestamentlichen Überlieferung." In *Kirche in Zeit und Endzeit.* Neukirchen-Vluyn: Neukirchener, 1983. 70–89. **Cullmann, O.** "Ο ΟΠΙΣΩ ΜΟΥ ΕΡΧΟΜΕΝΟΣ." *ConNT* 11 (1947) 26–32. **Dunn, J. D. G.** "Spirit-and-Fire Baptism." *NovT* 14 (1972) 81–92. **Funk, R. W.** "The Wilderness." *JBL* 78 (1959) 205–14. **Gnilka, J.** "Die essenischen Tauchbäder und die Johannestaufe." *RevQ* 3 (1961–62) 185–207. **Hughes, J.** "John the Baptist: the Forerunner of God Himself." *NovT* 14 (1972) 191–218. **Lindeskog, G.** "Johannes der Täufer: Einige Randbemerkungen zum heutigen Stand der Forschung." *ASTI* 12 (1983) 55–83. **Manson, T. W.** "John the Baptist." *BJRL* 36 (1954) 393–412. **Mauser, U. W.** *Christ in the Wilderness.* SBT 39. London: SCM, 1963. **Meier, J. P.** "John the Baptist in Matthew's Gospel." *JBL* 99 (1980) 383–405. **Merklein, A.** "Die Umkehrpredigt bei Johannes dem Täufer und Jesus von Nazaret." *BZ* 25 (1981) 29–46. **Nepper-Christensen, P.** "Die Taufe im Matthäusevangelium." *NTS* 31

(1985) 189–207. **Pryke, J.** "John the Baptist and the Qumran Community." *RevQ* 4 (1964) 483–96. **Reicke, B.** "Die jüdischen Baptisten und Johannes der Täufer." In *Jesus in der Verkündigung der Kirche*, ed. A. Fuchs. SNTU MS A.1. Freistadt: F. Plöchl, 1976. 62–75. **Schlatter, A.** *Johannes der Täufer*, ed. W. Michaelis. Basel: Reinhardt, 1956. **Scobie, C. H. H.** *John the Baptist.* London: SCM, 1964. **Trilling, W.** "Die Täufertradition bei Matthäus." *BZ* 3 (1959) 271–89. **Wink, W.** *John the Baptist and the Gospel Tradition.* SNTSMS 7. Cambridge: Cambridge University, 1968.

Translation

[1] *In those days John the Baptist came, preaching in the wilderness of Judea,* [2] *[and] saying, "Repent, for the kingdom of heaven has come near."* [3] *For this was the one spoken about through the prophet Isaiah when he says,*

> *The voice of one crying in the wilderness:*
> *Prepare the way of the Lord.*
> *Make straight his paths.*

[4] *John himself had his garment of camel hair and a leather belt around his waist. And his food was locusts and wild honey.* [5] *Then Jerusalem and all Judea and all the surrounding region of the Jordan began coming out to him,* [6] *and they were baptized by him in the Jordan river,*[a] *confessing their sins.* [7] *And when he saw the multitudes of the Pharisees and Sadducees coming to the baptism,*[b] *he said to them, "Brood of vipers, who warned you to flee from the wrath about to come?* [8] *Produce, therefore, fruit in keeping with*[c] *repentance,* [9] *and do not consider saying among yourselves, 'We have Abraham as father.' For I say to you that God is able to raise up children to Abraham from these stones.* [10] *Already the axe is laid to the root of the trees. Therefore every tree not producing good fruit is cut down and is cast into fire.* [11] *I myself am baptizing you in water, a baptism*[d] *associated with*[e] *repentance. But he who is coming after me is stronger than I am, whose sandals I am not worthy to bear. He will himself baptize you in the Holy Spirit and fire,* [12] *whose winnowing fork is in his hand, and he will clean his threshing floor, and he will gather his wheat into the barn,*[f] *but the chaff he will burn with unquenchable fire."*

Notes

  a TR D lat omit ποταμῷ. There is no reason for the word to have been added, if it were not in the original.

  b TR C D add αὐτοῦ ("his baptism"), apparently to improve the style. The pronoun is omitted only in ℵ* B cop^{sa} Or Hil.

  c Gr.: ἄξιον, lit. "worthy of."

  d "A baptism," added to translation.

  e Gr.: εἰς μετάνοιαν, lit. "to repentance."

  f Some MSS have αὐτοῦ after ἀποθήκην ("his barn") rather than after σῖτον ("wheat"); some have the pronoun after both nouns; others have the pronoun in neither place. External evidence (MSS) favors the present reading of the text; moreover, placement of the pronoun after ἀποθήκην is probably by influence of Luke 3:17.

Form/Structure/Setting

A. Matthew gives no hint of the number of years that have elapsed between the end of chap. 2 and the beginning of chap. 3. This is indeed the beginning of the story proper, and Jesus appears in v 13 as an adult about to embark upon his ministry. It is assumed as self-evident that "in those days" refers now to the beginning of the story of Jesus. John the Baptist was in Matthew's day already well known as the forerunner of Jesus the Messiah (cf. Acts 13:24; 19:4). To mention him was to signal the beginning. Matthew, who could have begun his story at this point (cf. Mark), began his narrative with the account of how Jesus was born. Now he turns to the account of how Jesus embarked upon the path God had marked out for him.

B. For the first time in the Gospel, we have access to some of Matthew's sources, directly in the case of Mark, indirectly (through comparison with Luke) in the case of Q. This does not mean we know everything that Matthew is using—e.g., we do not know the shape, content, or mode of the hypothetical special source called M, nor do we have any access to oral traditions, which also undoubtedly influenced him.

In the first section (vv 1–6) Matthew is dependent on Mark. With Luke (and thus by means of Q), however, Matthew begins with only the Isaiah quotation, placing the Mal 3:1 quotation in a later context (11:10). Matthew is close to Mark in content, if not wording, except for his insertion of the statement that the kingdom of heaven is at hand (v 2). The other major difference is in Matthew's shifting of the description of John's lifestyle from after the report of the crowds who came to be baptized (as in Mark) to a more logical position before that account. (The description of John is omitted altogether by Luke.) This enables an easy transition from the crowds to the preaching of John in the second section. The first part of this second section (vv 7–10) agrees verbatim with Luke 3:7–9 for the most part and thus is drawn from Q. (We cannot say whether Luke 3:10–15, the discussion between John and the crowd, was in Q and omitted by Matthew, although this is a good possibility since Matthew desires to keep the Baptist subordinate to Christ. See 3:14.) Vv 11–12 are largely drawn from Q except for John's reference to one coming who is stronger than he, which is probably drawn from Mark. The reference to that one baptizing in the Holy Spirit is probably an instance of where Mark and Q overlap (cf. A. Polag, *Fragmenta Q*, 28).

C. The passage consists of two major sections: (1) the ministry of John (vv 1–6); and (2) the preaching of John (vv 7–12). In the first section, vv 1–4 find their center in the citation of Isa 40:3, which, though lacking the stereotyped introductory formula, nonetheless stresses the reality of fulfillment. The importance of the quotation is especially apparent in the words ἐν τῇ ἐρήμῳ, "in the wilderness," of v 1 and the theological connection between the exhortation to "prepare the way of the Lord" and that of John to "repent" (v 2). The description of John in v 4 apparently finds its stimulus in the earlier references to the wilderness. The second section stresses the imminence of judgment (vv 7, 10), the futility of the appeal to Abrahamic descent (v 9), and the consequent need for the fruit of repentance (vv 8, 10). Two different metaphors of judgment are used: the tree barren of good fruit (v 10) and the separation of the chaff from the wheat (v 12). Between these two metaphors occurs the important announcement of the one to follow John who will baptize with the Holy Spirit and fire (v 11).

The genre of the pericope, more apparently than in the preceding sections, is that of historical narrative in that for the first time we encounter nothing extraordinary—that is, nothing that is not conceivable within the regular process of history. This is not to deny the spectacular nature of John's announcement but merely to say that with our knowledge of the historical context (see below) the events of this particular pericope require nothing supernatural. At the same time, Matthew continues to write theological history, being concerned to do more than to convey information or facts. In the sense that Matthew writes out of theological conviction and with post-resurrection clarity, there is no radical difference between the infancy narrative and the chapters that follow.

D. There is a deliberate attempt on Matthew's part to portray John in terms parallel to Jesus. Both are announced with παραγίνεται (3:1; 3:13); John's preaching anticipates that of Jesus (cf. 3:2 with 4:17; 3:10 with 7:19; 3:12 with 13:30; and the "offspring of vipers" of 3:7 with 12:33–34; 23:33). John, as well as Jesus, thus has a message for Matthew's church. At the same time, John's inferiority to Jesus, as the forerunner to the Messiah, is also obvious in the narrative (3:11, 14–15).

E. The background of the passage is to be found in the expectation of Jewish apocalyptic (cf. Dan 2:44; 7:14–27). John, the appointed forerunner, announces that the promised kingdom is on the verge of dawning. The promises of a new, golden age are about to be realized. This means not only the experience of blessing for the righteous but the overthrow and judgment of the wicked, the enemies of Israel. To a larger extent, therefore, John's announcement is readily intelligible to his listeners, who eagerly await their God to act. Extrabiblical evidence (e.g., *Pss. Sol.* 17–18) indicates that such expectations were at a high level in first-century Palestine. At the same time, John's message entails some surprises, as will be seen below.

F. The source of John's practice of baptism remains uncertain. While similarities have been noted in proselyte baptism and ceremonial lustrations, neither is sufficient in itself to explain John's baptism. More likely, but still uncertain, is the possibility of direct or indirect links between John and the community of Qumran, which was located in just the area where John began his ministry. Qumran shared not only a heightened eschatological expectation but, in that connection, emphasized repentance and saw itself as preparing (in the wilderness, and depending on Isa 40:3) for the appearance of two messiahs (of the line of David and Aaron) and the realization of the promise to Israel. This "community of the prepared" practiced baptism, which for them, however, was an oft-repeated process as well as a self-administered rite (1QS 1:24ff.; 5:13–25). John's baptism, by contrast, had an eschatological definiteness because of its connection with the announcement of fulfillment brought by John's successor. This definiteness marks off John and his baptism from Qumran in a decisive manner. Further differences may also be noted, such as John's failure to call his followers to a monastic separatism or intensive study of Torah (cf. 1QS 8:12–16). John's baptism, with its call to righteousness, is at least to be regarded as a kind of prophetic action, wherein the message (and response to it, in this instance) is given symbolic portrayal, for the sake of both participants and observers. The symbolism of washing related to the removal of spiritual uncleanness is a natural one and is found frequently in the OT (e.g., Ps 51:7; Isa 4:4; Jer 4:14; Ezek 36:25; Zech 13:1). Despite the parallels that can be collected, John's baptism thus preserves a high degree of originality (see Gnilka, *RevQ* [1961–62] 185–207).

Comment

1 Although the time reference ἐν δὲ ταῖς ἡμέραις ἐκείναις, "in those days," is not specific, it does indicate a special time (cf. the language of the prophets when they speak of eschatological matters in such passages as Zeph 1:15; Amos 9:11; Zech 12:3–4; Isa 10:20; Jer 37:7 [LXX]). This little phrase in this context functions as a pointer to a special time of revelation (Strecker, *Weg*, 90–91). Matthew's vivid historical present παραγίνεται, lit. "comes," is used also to describe the appearance of Jesus in v 13. Although the title ὁ βαπτιστής, "the Baptist," is used by Mark and Luke, it is used much more frequently by Matthew. Here it serves as a kind of nickname. The word is found only in Christian writings, except for one reference in Josephus (*Ant.* 18.5.2), and in all three Synoptics, and always in reference to John. Matthew says that John came κηρύσσων, "preaching." The essential message of that preaching is given in the following verse. "The wilderness of Judea" (τῇ ἐρήμῳ τῆς Ἰουδαίας) includes the area just west of the Dead Sea and the banks of the lower Jordan; hence it is not far from where the Qumran community was located, on the northwest shore of the Dead Sea. The reference to the desert deliberately picks up the language of Isa 40:3, which Matthew is about to quote. The desert has an eschatological connotation and was associated with messianic deliverance. (See Funk; Mauser; Kittel, *TDNT* 2:658–59.)

2 Only Matthew puts John's message in direct discourse: μετανοεῖτε· ἤγγικεν γὰρ ἡ βασιλεία τῶν οὐρανῶν, "Repent, for the kingdom of heaven has come near." Mark and Luke summarize the message as concerning a βάπτισμα μετανοίας εἰς ἄφεσιν ἁμαρτιῶν ("a baptism of repentance with a view to the forgiveness of sins"), words lacking in Matthew. Matthew, on the other hand, is the only one to mention the nearness of the kingdom at this point. In preaching repentance, John takes up the message of the prophets. In anticipation of God's activity, which involves judgment as well as redemption, there can be only one clarion call: to turn, to return to the God of Israel. In view is a basic change not unlike conversion. Only then will there be the required preparedness (for John as a preacher of righteousness, cf. Jos. *Ant.* 18.5.2 §§116–19). This is a centrally significant Jewish theme from the time of the prophets onward. The Qumran community especially regarded itself as participants in a covenant of repentance (CD 19:16; 4:2; 6:5). John's message is repeated by Jesus in the same words in 4:17 (cf. also the message that the disciples are sent to proclaim in 10:7). John and Jesus therefore stand in continuity, and the message of John to the Jews is equally a message to Matthew's church. Although repentance here is not explicitly linked with the forgiveness of sins as in Mark and Luke, forgiveness of sins has been alluded to in 1:21, and Matthew mentions it again in 26:28, in connection with the blood of the covenant. The forgiveness of sins is furthermore presupposed by the reference in v 6 to the confessing of sins. Cf. too the commission to baptize in 28:19.

The verb ἤγγικεν means literally to "draw near." The fact that Jesus uses the same verb in referring to the kingdom in 4:17 (cf. Mark 1:15) but elsewhere (12:28) can use ἔφθασεν, "has come," led Dodd (*Parables*) to argue that ἐγγίζω here means "is present." The meaning of the verb, however, refers normally to that which is at the point of arriving (see K. W. Clark, "Realized Eschatology," *JBL* 59 [1940] 367–83). The perfect tense here results in the nuance "having drawn near and remaining near." ἡ βασιλεία τῶν οὐρανῶν, "the kingdom of heaven," is a Jewish circumlocution for ἡ βασιλεία τοῦ θεοῦ, "the kingdom of God," to avoid unnecessary use of the word "God" (cf. Mark 11:30–31; Luke 15:18, 21). Matthew favors the phrase (thirty-three occurrences), and it is used only by him in the NT (but he can on occasion also use "kingdom of God"; cf. 12:28; 19:24; 21:31, 43). There is no difference between the two expressions (cf., for example, 19:23–24). The phrase means "God's reign," i.e., his sovereign rule with the concomitant blessings now about to be experienced by humanity (see G. E. Ladd, *The Presence of the Future* [Grand Rapids: Eerdmans, 1974]). That which God had promised from the earliest days, which reached its fullest expression in the prophets' glowing description of a golden age of blessing, is now on the verge of being realized and experienced, at least to a degree, by those whose preparedness of mind and heart make them receptive to the message (see Davies-Allison's excellent discussion, 1:389–92).

3 A fixed feature of the early Christian tradition, Isa 40:3 is quoted in all four Gospels (John lacks the last line) to describe the function of John the Baptist. All four Gospels identify the words as those of Isaiah the prophet. The use of the quotation by Matthew is consonant with his stress on fulfillment; although he does not here employ a characteristic fulfillment formula, he does make use of a pesher-type formula ("this is that"), which points to fulfillment (cf. Acts 2:16). Of the Synoptics, however, Matthew most emphatically calls attention to the identity of John as the one spoken of by Isaiah with οὗτος γάρ ἐστιν, "this is the one." The quotation itself follows the LXX verbatim except for the last pronoun, αὐτοῦ, "his," where the LXX reads τοῦ θεοῦ ἡμῶν, "of our God." The simple pronoun may have been regarded as more appropriate in referring to Jesus and has the advantage of avoiding the mention of God, in keeping with Jewish sympathies. At the same time, it is clear that the κυρίου, "Lord," whose way is to be prepared, refers in the first instance to Yahweh. The words in Isaiah occur in a context of comfort and deliverance from the exile, but they also allude to messianic fulfillment. The preparation is for the fulfillment that is shortly to be experienced. This is indeed the announcement of good news (εὐαγγελίζεσθαι, "proclaim good tidings," occurs twice in Isa 40:9; cf. 52:7; 60:6; 61:1). ἐν τῇ ἐρήμῳ, "in the desert," in the parallelism of the Hebrew text, is a part of the message of the voice; that is, the preparation is to be made in the wilderness. (This is a major reason the Qumranites chose to locate their community on the shore of the Dead Sea.) But by either understanding, John fulfills the passage. His was a voice crying in the wilderness, and it was in the wilderness that he offered the baptism of preparation (cf. v 1). John's message of repentance and his call to righteousness correspond to preparing the way of the Promised One or, using Isaiah's metaphor, "making his paths straight."

4 The emphatic pronoun αὐτός, "himself" (BDF §277[3]), indicates that John's manner of living was in accord with the prophecy of the forerunner. Indeed, more explicitly, John is deliberately presented as resembling Elijah in the reference to a garment of hair (cf. Zech 13:4) and "a leather belt around his waist" (cf. 2 Kgs 1:8, where the words just quoted are in nearly verbatim agreement with Matthew). The actual identification of John with Elijah is not made by Matthew until 11:14 (cf. also 17:12–13), but it is certainly also in view here. (This is more apparent in Mark because of the Malachi quotation in 1:2, which Matthew defers until chap. 11.) John's unusual demeanor associates him with Elijah and gives to him the aura of a holy man (a *Nāzîr*, cf. Luke 1:15), and this in itself makes John the subject of special attention among his contemporaries. But more than that, John symbolizes the breaking of the centuries of prophetic silence recognized by the Jews themselves (cf. 1 Macc 4:46; 9:27; 14:41). Here then is a new thing: a voice from God out of the silence, self-authenticating by its power and message, as well as by its unusual mediator. Prophecy appears again in the midst of Israel, the people of God.

5 Matthew does not say "all the Jerusalemites" came out to be baptized by John, as does Mark, perhaps because he recognizes Jerusalem as the center of opposition to Jesus' later ministry, and perhaps also because of the opposition his own church is experiencing from the Jews. With Mark, however, he does say "all of Judea" ($\pi\hat{a}\sigma\alpha\ \dot{\eta}\ \text{'}Iov\delta\alpha i\alpha$) and adds "all the region surrounding the Jordan," $\pi\hat{a}\sigma\alpha\ \dot{\eta}\ \pi\epsilon\rho i\chi\omega\rho os\ \tau o\hat{v}\ \text{'}Io\rho\delta\acute{a}\nu ov$ (possibly drawn from Q; cf. Luke 3:3), a natural fact that could be presumed. The result is the deliberate impression of a great response to John's preaching. (Note the imperfect tense of $\dot{\epsilon}\xi\epsilon\pi o\rho\epsilon\acute{v}\epsilon\tau o$, "they were coming out," describing a repeated process over some time.) The forerunner indeed appears to enjoy as much or even more success than will the one whom he precedes.

6 The imperfect tense of $\dot{\epsilon}\beta\alpha\pi\tau i\zeta o\nu\tau o$, "were being baptized," matches $\dot{\epsilon}\xi\epsilon\pi o\rho\epsilon\acute{v}\epsilon\tau o$, "were coming out," of the preceding verse and underlines the success of John's mission. On the source of John's baptism, see above *Form/Structure/Setting* §F. The confession of sins is the point of John's baptism, being fundamental to repentance and the accompanying new orientation. It cannot be definitely concluded from the present participle in $\dot{\epsilon}\xi o\mu o\lambda o\gamma o\acute{v}\mu\epsilon\nu o\iota\ \tau\grave{a}s\ \dot{a}\mu\alpha\rho\tau i\alpha s\ \alpha\dot{v}\tau\hat{\omega}\nu$, "confessing their sins," that this was done during the actual baptism (i.e., "while confessing their sins"). It was, however, clearly done in connection with the baptism (cf. Jos. *Ant.* 8.4.6). Remarkably, Jews came to submit themselves to a rite that for them had the association of the initiation of gentile proselytes into Judaism. But the announcement of the imminent end of the age no doubt seemed to justify confession of sins and the cleansing symbolism of the baptism.

7 Matthew's $\pi o\lambda\lambda o\grave{v}s\ \tau\hat{\omega}\nu\ \Phi\alpha\rho\iota\sigma\alpha i\omega\nu\ \kappa\alpha\grave{\iota}\ \Sigma\alpha\delta\delta ov\kappa\alpha i\omega\nu$, "the multitudes of the Pharisees and Sadducees," takes up the opportunity to identify the opponents who will be encountered later in the narrative. But this by no means makes Matthew's account unhistorical. To be sure, the scholarly and priestly authorities were separated by some major differences, but nonetheless they come together toward the end of the Gospel narrative in their opposition to Jesus (cf. 16:1, 11–12; 21:45–46) and rather remarkably are also mentioned together here at the beginning of the story. Their common interest in John hardly requires agreement between them, nor does it point to the evangelist's ignorance of their differences. Their motives in coming were no doubt mixed. A few may have been sincere in believing John's message; others probably came more out of curiosity (the lack of belief is pointed out in 21:25–27, 32); but many may have been so angered at John's preaching that they did not submit to his baptism (see Luke 7:29–30). For this reason Matthew has simply $\dot{\epsilon}\rho\chi o\mu\acute{\epsilon}\nu ovs\ \dot{\epsilon}\pi\grave{\iota}\ \tau\grave{o}\ \beta\acute{a}\pi\tau\iota\sigma\mu\alpha$, "coming to the baptism," rather than Luke's $\beta\alpha\pi\tau\iota\sigma\theta\hat{\eta}\nu\alpha\iota\ \dot{v}\pi'\alpha\dot{v}\tau o\hat{v}$ (Luke 3:7), "to be baptized by him" (which suggests actual baptism; in Luke, however, the reference is to "the crowds"). The Pharisees, as proponents of a legal righteousness through the observance of oral tradition, are the main competitors of Jesus throughout the Gospel and are the subjects of repeated attacks culminating in chap. 23. (The Qumran community also attacked the Pharisees.) The Sadducees are of much less importance until the end of the Gospel when, through their control of the cultic hierarchy and the high priesthood, they play a major role in condemning Jesus to death. Thus Matthew calls attention in this reference to the Jewish leaders to the presence of the enemies of Jesus from the beginning of the narrative. The initially positive response to John's message, even if partial, stands in sharp contrast to the final rejection of Jesus.

The expression γεννήματα ἐχιδνῶν, "offspring of vipers," is used three times by Matthew (see also 12:34; 23:33), always in reference to the Pharisees. The only other occurrence in the Gospels is in the parallel passage in Luke (3:7, applied to "the crowds"). Parallels to this figurative use of "viper" can be found in classical Greek authors (see BAGD, 331b).

John's apocalyptic message involves an imminent judgment of the unrighteous in τῆς μελλούσης ὀργῆς, "the coming wrath." This eschatological wrath, associated with fulfillment, is further alluded to in vv 10–12. Abundant parallels indicate that this was a fixed component in the Jewish apocalyptic expectation (see esp. Dan 7:9–11; Isa 13:9; Zeph 1:15; 2:2–3; Mal 4:1). The construction (φυγεῖν with ἀπό) is a Hebraism (BDF §149). What frightened John's listeners was the insistence that the judgment was about to occur (μελλούσης). The fleeing (as from a burning field) is particularly appropriate to the figurative mention of vipers. (For the notion of coming wrath in the early Church, see 1 Thess 1:10; Eph 5:6; Col 3:6.)

8   In requiring καρπὸν ἄξιον τῆς μετανοίας, lit. "fruit worthy of repentance," i.e., fruit befitting repentance, John asks for concrete evidence of repentance (cf. also Acts 26:20) from those who come to him, and he thus protects against mere outward participation in his baptism. Matthew's singular καρπόν, "fruit," is a collective singular, perhaps caused by the singular of v 10. Repentance and good works are very frequently associated in rabbinic thought (see Str-B 1:170–72).

9   μὴ δόξητε λέγειν ἐν ἑαυτοῖς, "do not consider saying among yourselves," reflects an understanding of what would have been a typical objection to John's baptism of Jews. (For the construction, see BDF §392.) In their appeal πατέρα ἔχομεν τὸν Ἀβραάμ, "we have Abraham as father," they made the mistake of thinking that physical descent from Abraham granted them an automatic immunity from God's eschatological wrath. John, however, by no means allowed them to entertain such a presumption. (For the appeal to descent from Abraham, cf. John 8:33, 39.) The statement that ἐκ τῶν λίθων τούτων, "from these stones," God was able to raise up τέκνα τῷ Ἀβραάμ, "children to Abraham," is John's way of underlining the fundamental insufficiency of Abrahamic descent in itself. While it is unlikely that John had in mind the mission to the Gentiles (though he could have had in mind the universalism of the prophets), we may safely assume that Matthew and his church did understand the words as pointing in that direction. God's work cannot be limited by the disobedience of his people. For the prominence of this motif of a new people in Matthew, see esp. 8:10–11; 21:43; 28:19. John here also anticipates the later arguments of Paul (Rom 2:28–29; 4:11; 9:6–8; Gal 3:7, 29). John's statement appears to be a play on words, since in Aramaic (and Hebrew too) the word for "children" (בְּנַיָּא, běnayyāʾ) is similar to that for "stones" (אַבְנַיָּא, ʾabnayyāʾ).

10   The imminence of judgment is stressed not only by the initial adverb ἤδη, "already," but also by the vivid present tenses of this verse. The metaphor of an unfruitful tree being cut down and thrown into the fire is not uncommon in

Jewish literature (see Str-B). It is repeated verbatim in the words of Jesus in 7:19 (cf. 13:40; John 15:6). The words καρπὸν καλόν, "good fruit" (the same concept is found in 7:17–20; 12:33; cf. 21:43), are analogous to καρπὸν ἄξιον τῆς μετανοίας, "fruit worthy of repentance," in v 8. Judgment based on good works is also an important theme in the teaching of Jesus according to Matthew (cf. 7:21–23; 25:45–46).

11 Although Matthew, unlike Mark, does not directly conjoin the two parallel clauses ἐγὼ μὲν ὑμᾶς βαπτίζω, "I baptize you," and αὐτὸς ὑμᾶς βαπτίσει, "he will baptize you," inserting between them the parenthetical statement of John's unworthiness compared with the mightier one who is to follow him, the contrast is still very apparent. John describes his own baptism as εἰς μετάνοιαν, by which is not meant that repentance is the goal or result of baptism (as "to repentance" might be taken), since the baptism itself presupposes the existence of repentance. Hence, εἰς μετάνοιαν is best understood as "with reference to," "associated with," or "in agreement with" (for this meaning of εἰς, see BAGD, s.v. εἰς, 5; p. 230a). This phrase, only in Matthew, heightens the contrast between John and Jesus. The stress on repentance reminds the reader of the preparatory function of John; although there is no counterpart to this phrase in the clause describing Jesus' baptism, it is clear that his baptism is rather one of fulfillment having to do with the inauguration of the kingdom. ὁ δὲ ὀπίσω μου ἐρχόμενος, "the one coming after me," is probably also an allusion to "the coming one," i.e., pointing to a technical term for the Messiah (cf. 11:3; 21:9; 23:39; cf. Heb 10:37, and for OT background, Ps 118:26). No further identification is needed; the forerunner precedes the one who will bring the kingdom. (Cf. the exact parallel in John 1:27.) While the Baptist expects a triumphant Messiah, it is probably going too far to conclude that he regards the coming one as none other than Yahweh (as Hughes claims). The words that immediately follow are only appropriate to a human agent such as the Messiah. Common to the three Synoptics, the phrase ἰσχυρότερός μου, "stronger than me," is probably to be associated with the powerful impact of the kingdom that the Messiah brings. The noun form of this same root is applied to the Messiah, the Son of David, in *Pss. Sol.* 17:37. While Mark, followed by Luke, has John express his unworthiness by referring to the loosening of the strap of the sandals, Matthew puts it in terms of τὰ ὑποδήματα βαστάσαι, "to bear his sandals" (MM and BAGD, however, state that βαστάσαι here means "to take off"; s.v.). This is possibly Matthew's heightening of the contrast between John and Jesus, although both metaphors describe a slave-master relationship. In αὐτὸς ὑμᾶς βαπτίσει, "he himself will baptize you," the αὐτός is intensive and contrasting. John draws the contrast by describing the work of the one to come as also a baptism, though metaphorical rather than literal. There is thus continuity and discontinuity between John and Jesus.

Jesus will baptize ἐν πνεύματι ἁγίῳ καὶ πυρί, "with the Holy Spirit and fire." Were the words καὶ πυρί known to Mark and deliberately omitted (Mark lacks any reference to John's message of the coming wrath), or are they a secondary addition in Q? Related to this question is the actual meaning of the words.

That is, are the words καὶ πυρί (1) further describing ἐν πνεύματι ἁγίῳ, and hence epexegetical, or (2) do they refer to a different aspect of the baptism altogether? (1) If πνεύματι and πυρί refer to the same thing, they may both describe either judgment or blessing. (a) The majority of scholars accept that John preached only a message of judgment and that therefore πνεύματι ἁγίῳ is to be understood as a destroying wind that works together with the fire. (C. K. Barrett [*The Holy Spirit in the Gospel Tradition* (London:

SPCK, 1970) 126] suggests that the wind that blows away the chaff is in view; cf. v 12.) Thus John's message is regarded as consistently pessimistic and in full agreement with the urgency of his call to repentance. (b) Some (e.g., Lagrange) have followed Chrysostom, on the other hand, in seeing the statement as referring only to the blessing experienced in the outpouring of the Holy Spirit at Pentecost. In this view, the words καὶ πυρί refer to the tongues of fire that symbolized the Holy Spirit in that event (cf. Acts 2:3). A major difficulty with this interpretation of the reference to fire is that in the following verse (cf. v 10) fire is so forcefully a metaphor of judgment (for its background, see Scobie, 68–69). (2) Many (e.g., Lohmeyer, Schmid, Filson, Luz) have therefore followed Origen in seeing this sentence as referring to a twofold baptism—that is, blessing for the righteous (ἐν πνεύματι ἁγίῳ) and judgment for the wicked (καὶ πυρί). What may be regarded as a proper refinement of this view (Beasley-Murray, *Baptism;* Hill; Dunn) insists that there is but *one* baptism (the two nouns are governed by one preposition, ἐν, and the ὑμᾶς allows no distinctions), which is experienced either as judgment or blessing (cf. v 12). The blessing, on this interpretation, is more indirect, being experienced as a kind of refinement or purging (Davies-Allison; Carson); this process, however, is concomitant with the arrival of the kingdom and thus is positive in the final analysis. Beasley-Murray refers to Isa 4:2–5 as an analogous passage. Further OT passages may be mentioned (Isa 44:3; Ezek 36:25–27; 39:29; Joel 2:28), and Hill calls attention to a remarkable parallel in 1QS 4:20–21. There is no reason why John may not have contemplated the positive effects of the coming of the Promised One, as well as the negative effects that are so prominent in his urgent call to repentance. The latter, to be sure, seem to have dominated his thinking (according to Matthew and Luke, not Mark). But later in Matthew's narrative, Jesus' response to John's question, asked through his disciples, suggests that John was expected also to have thought of the positive consequences of the arrival of fulfillment (11:4–5). Those who responded to his message in repentance and baptism were surely to experience the baptism of Jesus finally as blessing, and that mediated by the Spirit he was to bestow (cf. 10:20; 28:19). See the excursus in R. A. Guelich, *Mark 1–8:26,* WBC 34A (Dallas: Word, 1989) 27–28.

12   The second metaphor of judgment (cf. v 10) is drawn from a common scene in Palestine. The "winnowing fork" (πτύον), here found in the hand of the coming Messiah, is used to throw the mixed wheat and chaff into the air. This is usually done on high ground during a good wind, which separates the lighter chaff from the heavier wheat. The threshing floor is "cleaned" (διακαθαριεῖ), the wheat is put into storage (cf. 13:30), and the chaff becomes fuel. The only other reference to "unquenchable" (ἄσβεστος) fire in the Synoptic tradition (besides the parallel to our passage in Luke 3:17) occurs in Mark 9:43, where it stands in apposition to Gehenna, the place of final punishment. Abundant parallels to this metaphor exist both in the OT (e.g., Isa 34:10; 66:24; Jer 7:20) and in the rabbinic literature (references in Str-B 4:1075–6).

Explanation

The story of the central figure of Matthew's narrative, Jesus of Nazareth, the Son of David, must begin with the divinely sent forerunner, John. In agreement with prophecy, the voice of John thundered forth in the wilderness. John knew well the role he had to perform. The fulfillment of the promises—the dawning of the kingdom of God—was at hand, for the Agent who would bring this to pass, the Promised One to come, was about to make his appearance. John was called to make urgent preparation for the judgment that would surely ensue. Only a radical repentance would suffice, and those who thought they could find shelter in their Abrahamic pedigree needed to be told that God's purposes could not be restricted to them. So John preached and baptized, anticipating the preaching and "baptizing" activity of the one who would follow.

But this straightforward account does not do justice to the full significance that Matthew and his readers saw in all of this. For them the judgment of which John spoke—and Jesus, too, in the following narrative—lay in the future (though perhaps already anticipated in the destruction of Jerusalem). Still, the positive aspects of the kingdom had begun to be experienced in the ministry of Jesus and now, through the resurrected Christ, in the Church. They themselves had been taught to baptize disciples in the name of Father, Son, and Holy Spirit (28:19). But this was no longer a baptism of preparation, as was John's, but rather an extension of that baptism "in the Holy Spirit," which John had prophesied. In short, the church of Matthew now knows the reality of what John announced in its beginnings. It sees itself as bringing forth the proper response of "fruit in agreement with repentance" (v 8), and it sees its present adversaries as already typified in the Jewish leaders who came to John but were inclined to rest in their Abrahamic lineage. For them was reserved the unhappy prospect of the judgment to come.

The Baptism of Jesus   (3:13–17)

Bibliography

Beasley-Murray, G. R. *Baptism in the New Testament.* Grand Rapids: Eerdmans, 1962. 45–67. **Coggan, F. D.** "Note on St. Matthew iii.15." *ExpTim* 60 (1948–49) 258. **Cothenet, E.** "Le baptême selon S. Matthieu." *SNTU* 9 (1984) 79–94. **Cullmann, O.** *Baptism in the New Testament.* Tr. J. K. S. Reid. London: SCM, 1950. **Dunn, J. D. G.** *Baptism in the Holy Spirit.* SBT 2.15. London: SCM, 1970. 23–37. **Eissfeldt, O.** "Πληρῶσαι πᾶσαν δικαιοσύνην in Matthäus 3, 15." *ZNW* 61 (1970) 209–15. **Feuillet, A.** "Le baptême de Jésus." *RB* 71 (1964) 321–52. **Garnet, P.** "The Baptism of Jesus and the Son of Man Idea." *JSNT* 9 (1980) 49–65. **Gerhardsson, B.** "Gottes Sohn als Diener Gottes." *ST* 27 (1973) 73–106. **Gero, S.** "The Spirit as Dove at the Baptism of Jesus." *NovT* 18 (1976) 17–35. **Jeremias, J.** *New Testament Theology: Vol. 1. The Proclamation of Jesus.* Tr. J. Bowden. London: SCM, 1971. 43–55. **Hill, D.** "Son and Servant: An Essay on Matthean Christology." *JSNT* 6 (1980) 2–16. **Keck, L. E.** "The Spirit and the Dove." *NTS* 17 (1970) 41–67. **Lentzen-Deis, F.** *Die Taufe Jesu nach den Synoptikern: Literarkritische und gattungsgeschichtliche Untersuchungen.* FTS 4. Frankfurt am Main: Knecht, 1970. **Ljungman, H.** *Das Gesetz Erfüllen: Matth. 5, 17ff. und 3, 15 Untersucht.* Lund: Gleerup, 1954. 97–126. **Lövestam, E.** *Son and Saviour.* Lund: Gleerup, 1961. 88–112. **Sabbe, M.** "Le baptême de Jésus." In *De Jésus aux Evangiles,* ed. I. de la Potterie. BETL 25. Gembloux: Duculot, 1967. 184–211. **Turner, C. H.** "Ο ΥΙΟΣ ΜΟΥ Ο ΑΓΑΠΗΤΟΣ." *JTS* 27 (1926) 113–29.

Translation

[13] *Then Jesus came from Galilee to the Jordan to John, in order to be baptized by him.* [14] *But John tried to hinder him, saying, "I have need to be baptized by you, and yet do you come to me?"* [15] *But Jesus answered and said to him, "Let it be, for now. For it is fitting for us thus to fulfill all righteousness." Then he permitted him.*[a] [16] *And when*

Jesus had been baptized, he came up immediately[b] *out of the water. And look, the heavens were opened [to him],*[c] *and he saw [the] Spirit of God*[d] *descending,*[e] *as a dove might, [and]*[f] *coming upon him.* [17]*And behold, there was a voice from heaven saying,*[g] *"This is*[h] *my beloved son, in whom I am well pleased."*

Notes

[a] At this point OL MSS (a [g¹]) add that a great light shone from the water and filled the spectators with fear. Though not in any Gr. MSS, the addition is early, being possibly found in the Diatesseron (cf. Ephr), Ju and Epiph (quoting the *Gos. Eb.*). See *TCGNT*, 10–11.

[b] A few MSS including sy⁵ omit εὐθύς, "immediately."

[c] Important MSS (ℵ* B vg^mss sy^s,c sa) do not contain αὐτῷ, "to him." It is possible, however, that the word was originally a part of the text (as in ℵ¹ C D⁵ L W f¹·¹³ TR lat sy^p,h mae bo) and was omitted because it was regarded as unnecessary. The brackets reflect the uncertainty. See *TCGNT*, 11.

[d] The important MSS ℵ and B lack definite articles before πνεῦμα, "spirit," and θεοῦ, "God." The words do not thereby become indefinite in this instance, and the meaning is not affected.

[e] A few MSS (D it vg^mss [sy^h]) have καταβαίνοντα ἐκ τοῦ οὐρανοῦ, "coming down [the participle is masc. gender] from heaven."

[f] ℵ* B lat omit καί, "and," while the majority of MSS (ℵ² C D L W f¹·¹³ TR vg^cl sy) include it.

[g] A few MSS (D sy^s,c) add πρὸς αὐτόν, "to him."

[h] D a sy^s,c replace οὗτός ἐστιν, "this is," with σὺ εἶ, "you are," undoubtedly by the influence of the parallel in Mark 1:11 and Luke 3:22.

Form/Structure/Setting

A. In all four Gospels, Jesus shares in John's baptism. There is no small tension between the fact that Jesus identifies with and participates in John's baptism and the fact that Jesus, as the goal of what John proclaims, transcends that baptism. The baptism of Jesus, indeed, serves as a kind of transition between the work of preparation and the appearance upon center stage of the one who brings fulfillment. Only the temptation narrative that immediately follows stands between the baptism and the ministry of Jesus.

B. Matthew appears to be dependent upon Mark for the main content of the passage although he does not at all follow Mark closely. Vv 14–15, on the other hand, are drawn from Matthew's private source (M), unless we are to attribute them to his own historicizing of a theological point (see below). The occurrence of non-Matthean vocabulary in the passage suggests that Matthew here is to some extent dependent upon oral tradition (thus Strecker, *Weg*, 150).

C. The form of the pericope is straightforward historical narrative but, as always, with important theological information conveyed at the same time. The supernatural occurrences of vv 16–17 are apparently not witnessed by the crowds. Therefore, we are probably to think of a subjective experience. The content of the passage readily divides into (1) the arrival of Jesus (v 13), (2) the dialogue with John (vv 14–15), and (3) the descent of the Spirit upon Jesus after his baptism, including the climactic divine attestation (vv 16–17). Thus the events associated with the baptism are the center of attention, rather than the baptism itself.

D. The setting of Jesus' baptism within the Baptist's ministry is problematic because of the implication that Jesus, too, needed to repent. Matthew alone among the Synoptics protects against this in vv 14–15. But the real point of the passage is not the baptism of Jesus itself but the threads of continuity and discontinuity between John and Jesus. Only through contact with the forerunner can Jesus be launched into his own ministry. That contact and the formal beginning of Jesus' ministry are filled with theological significance.

Comment

13 The adverb τότε, "then," favored by Matthew as a connective at the beginnings of new sections, has no time significance. παραγίνεται, lit. "arrives," is the same word (in the historical present for vividness) used to introduce John in v 1. Now the main figure of the Gospel comes upon the stage. It is strange that Matthew omits Mark's reference to Nazareth (Mark 1:9). He may do so because of his mention of it in 2:23; repetition of it here, however, could have strengthened his point. The purpose of Jesus in coming to John, τοῦ βαπτισθῆναι ὑπ' αὐτοῦ, "to be baptized by him," is so forcefully stated in this way only by Matthew. This in turn sets the scene for the following discussion between John and Jesus.

14 διεκώλυεν is a conative imperfect, "he tried to hinder," reflecting John's (unsuccessful) attempt to avoid baptizing Jesus (see BDF §326). The pronouns ἐγώ, "I," and καὶ σύ, "and you," are emphatic and underline John's protest. The prepositional phrase ὑπὸ σοῦ, "by you," receives emphasis by being placed before the infinitive (contrast βαπτισθῆναι ὑπ' αὐτοῦ in v 13). What causes John's recognition of his need to be baptized by Jesus and his consequent reluctance to baptize Jesus? The text does not tell us what John concluded about Jesus. The implication, however, is that John recognized Jesus as the one whose way he was preparing. That is certainly the conclusion that Matthew's church was meant to draw. Probably we are to understand some previous contact (Schlatter suggests a conversation prior to the baptism) between John and Jesus, in contrast to the Fourth Gospel (1:29–34), which seems to assert that John did not know the identity of Jesus until the baptism. This in turn would necessitate Jesus' own consciousness of his messianic identity, which (despite objections, e.g., by Klostermann) is a natural assumption if the events immediately following the baptism (i.e., the divine voice, the temptations) were to have meaning for Jesus (see Beasley-Murray, *Baptism;* Schlatter, 86). The suggestion that John's reluctance to baptize Jesus is the result of his intuition of a high degree of righteousness in Jesus, rather than the recognition of Jesus' messianic identity (so Tasker), has little to commend it. It is unlikely that John allowed for exceptions to his call for preparation. That John did recognize Jesus as the Messiah is evident from his question in 11:3, even if that question stems from disenchantment. The present verse fits perfectly with v 11, which stresses John's comparative unworthiness. How should the one who prepares the way with a baptism of repentance baptize the one for whom preparation is made? Surely the reverse must be true, and John must submit to the baptism of the Holy Spirit and fire. In these terms, the objection is perfectly understandable. The words are precisely what we would expect John to say (*pace* Schweizer). This passage was hardly constructed as a polemic against the disciples of John who persisted as such during and after the time Matthew wrote (cf. Acts 19:1–7). Its content is of course inconsistent with a continued commitment to John, especially after the crucifixion and resurrection; Matthew does not, however, like the Fourth Gospel, purposely belittle John, but holds him in the highest esteem (see 11:7–15).

15 Jesus' answer is given with messianic authority: an imperative verb ἄφες, "permit (it)," and an adverb ἄρτι, meaning "at once" or "immediately," but also in a weaker sense meaning "now." If we accept the latter meaning, the strange turnabout is to be allowed for the time being, although it will later (when the Son has embarked upon his ministry) have become an impossibility. "It is fitting" (πρέπον ἐστίν) or "right and proper" for this baptism to take place. The rightness of course points to the accomplishment of God's will, as is apparent from the important clause that follows. The words themselves bear the notion of divine necessity in Hellenistic idiom (cf. Grundmann). Matthew's church may well have seen itself included in the ἡμῖν, "for us" (thus Strecker, *Weg*, 180–81, 216), it too having been baptized and called to "all righteousness." Yet the ἡμῖν here focuses on John and Jesus, who in this event have a unique function to fulfill, defined in the words πληρῶσαι πᾶσαν δικαιοσύνην, "to fulfill all righteousness."

Righteousness is a key concept in Matthew (seven occurrences). It is preeminently the goal of discipleship (5:20; 6:1, 33), that is, the accomplishing of God's will in its fullness. It is accordingly closely associated with the coming of the kingdom (cf. 5:6, 10). Thus John's appearance to make preparation is described by Jesus as his coming ἐν ὁδῷ δικαιοσύνης, "in the way of righteousness" (21:32; cf. 21:25). It is in the latter sense, as a part of the process of salvation-history, that we are probably to understand the present clause.

Matthew's use of δικαιοσύνη has been the cause of much disagreement. In a full study of the subject (*Righteousness in Matthew*), B. Przybylski concludes that all seven occurrences involve God's demand upon human beings, i.e., proper conduct before God. While, however, it does seem incontestable that in some instances (5:20; 6:1; perhaps 5:10; 6:33) ethical conduct is in view, this is not necessarily so in every case. No writer is obligated to use a word consistently; the meaning of a word must be determined from its immediate context and not be imposed upon a text in the name of lexical consistency. If δικαιοσύνη has a range of meanings, there is then no reason why Matthew may not have used the word in different senses (as we shall argue for its occurrence, not only here but in 5:6 and 21:32; see A. Sand, *Gesetz*, 197–205). In the present instance, several reasons may be offered for accepting a salvation-history understanding of δικαιοσύνη: (1) It is difficult to understand submission to John's baptism as submitting to God's demand. There is no divine commandment either in the OT or in the Gospels to submit to John's baptism. Submission to that baptism then can hardly in itself be thought of as an act of righteousness. And even more difficult is the idea that it can be thought of as fulfilling *all* righteousness. The attempt of Eissfeldt (213–14) to draw a parallel with the temple tax and the tax paid to Caesar, both of which Jesus accepted responsibility for, though in fact he was not obligated, is not convincing. In the present instance the act is positively described as the fulfilling of all righteousness. (2) Since Matthew, as nearly all admit, has a salvation-historical perspective, there is no reason to exclude the possibility that he can understand δικαιοσύνη here not as moral goodness but as the will of God in the sense of God's saving activity. That is, by the baptism and its main point—the accompanying anointing by the Spirit— John and Jesus together ("for us") inaugurate the fulfillment of God's saving purposes, "the saving activity of God" (see Meier, *Law*, 79; idem, *Matthew*, 27; cf. McConnell, *Law*, 19–22; France, 95; Hagner, "Righteousness in Matthew's Theology"; see also the note of F. D. Coggan: "Only by His very literal standing-in with His people will they see the saving activity of God completely brought about"; see too the similar view of Ljungman, *Gesetz*, 104–21).

In this act of baptism, John will obediently bring his preparatory mission to its climax (cf. John 1:31) by accomplishing the transition to the Promised One. The reception of the baptism by Jesus in obedience to the will of his Father, on the other hand, proves to be the occasion of the formal beginning of his ministry.

Thus, in his first words in the Gospel, Jesus refers to the fulfilling of God's will in nothing less than the establishing of the salvation he has promised (hence πληρῶσαι and πᾶσαν) through what now begins to take shape (cf. G. Barth, in G. Bornkamm, *Tradition,* 137–41).

But why does Jesus need to be baptized by John at all? Not because he was himself a sinner (Strauss, *Life of Jesus;* B. Weiss), nor simply to identify with John's movement (Loisy; Manson, *Servant-Messiah*). Beasley-Murray (*Baptism*) correctly argues that Jesus thereby shows his solidarity with his people in their need. The Messiah is a representative person, the embodiment of Israel, whether as King or righteous Servant (cf. Isa 53:11; both concepts emerge in v 17). As such, he identifies with his people fully and, obediently acting out this role, receives the anointing of the Spirit in order to accomplish his mission. That mission and that identification with his people ultimately involve the death of the Servant on behalf of his people (cf. 1:21), but it is nevertheless unlikely that we are to see in this pericope—in the baptism of Jesus—a reference to the sacrificial death of Jesus, as Cullmann argues.

16 When Jesus had been baptized, εὐθὺς ἀνέβη ἀπὸ τοῦ ὕδατος, "immediately he came up out of the water." Matthew probably draws εὐθύς from Mark, where it modifies εἶδεν, "immediately he saw," functioning as a device to capture the reader's attention. Since Matthew has his own word, ἰδού, to do this, εὐθύς is pushed earlier to become the modifier of ἀνέβη, "immediately he came up." Most probably Matthew means that the events next to be described happened immediately after Jesus' baptism, i.e., in connection with it. The suggestion that here Matthew means literally that Jesus did not stay in the water to confess his sins but came out immediately (Gundry) seems farfetched.

The metaphorical expression ἠνεῴχθησαν οἱ οὐρανοί, "the heavens were opened," is not uncommon in the OT (Ezek 1:1; Isa 64:1) and refers (as here) to key episodes of revelation and provision (cf. Acts 7:56; 10:11; John 1:51). The verb is a "divine" passive, God being understood as the acting subject. Matthew and Luke have the same verb against Mark's σχιζομένους, "dividing," perhaps by the influence of Q or oral tradition (although Matthew and Luke do not agree closely in wording). Only Matthew explicitly writes that Jesus εἶδεν [τὸ] πνεῦμα [τοῦ] θεοῦ, "saw the Spirit of God," coming upon him; the other evangelists of course imply this. The Synoptics do not indicate whether the crowds witnessed the event, but the silence is probably to be interpreted as meaning they did not; in the Fourth Gospel, however, John the Baptist is explicitly made a witness (but not in Matthew, contra Grundmann). Matthew's [τὸ] πνεῦμα [τοῦ] θεοῦ, "the Spirit of God" (Luke, τὸ πνεῦμα τὸ ἅγιον, "the Holy Spirit"; Mark, simply τὸ πνεῦμα, "the Spirit"), with and without the articles, is common in Paul's epistles and occurs elsewhere in the Gospel (12:28; cf. 10:20). It is essentially interchangeable with τὸ πνεῦμα τοῦ κυρίου, "the Spirit of the Lord" (cf. Acts 5:9; 8:39; cf. BAGD, s.v. πνεῦμα 5a), and is here very probably intended as an allusion to the anointing of the Servant by the Spirit in Isa 42:1, quoted in the words of v 17 and in the citation of 12:18. (Cf. also the anointing of the Son of David by the Spirit of the Lord in Isa 11:2.) The age about to begin is preeminently the age of the Spirit according to the prophets (cf. Isa 61:1), and therefore the one who is to baptize with the Spirit must himself experience the formal anointing of the Spirit. To be sure, Jesus was ἐκ πνεύματος ἁγίου, "from the Holy Spirit," from his conception (1:20). The present anointing, however, has to do with the formal inauguration of his ministry, marked by the baptism and its aftermath, which is itself based on the dual pattern of the king's coronation and the servant's commission.

The Spirit is described as καταβαῖνον ὡσεὶ περιστεράν, "descending as a dove." The participle καταβαῖνον is accompanied by ἐρχόμενον in Matthew alone, "descending and coming upon him." The reference to the dove is found in all four Gospels. Here (cf. John 1:32) ὡσεὶ περιστεράν appears to be adverbial: the Spirit descended as a dove might. In Luke 3:22, ὡς περιστεράν is adjectival, and this is emphasized by σωματικῷ εἴδει: the Spirit descended "in bodily form" as a dove. Either way the common burden of the evangelists is to convey that a literal or real descent of the Spirit upon Jesus occurred. The symbolism contained in the reference to the dove is unclear. Most promising are the following two possibilities: (1) since the rabbis likened the Spirit's brooding over the waters in Gen 1:2 to a bird nestling her young (and in one instance specifically to a dove: *b. Hag.* 15a), the dove here signals the beginning of a new creation (Davies-Allison); (2) parallel to the dove that returned to Noah's ark (Gen 8:8–12), the dove signifies the end of judgment (cf. John's message) and the beginning of an age of blessing in the presence of the Promised One. The former seems preferable. (For other possibilities in the symbolism, such as Israel, Divine Wisdom, etc., see Keck and the full discussion in Davies-Allison.) The dove as the symbol of the Holy Spirit occurs only in relatively late rabbinic literature (*Tg. Cant.* 2:12). H. Greeven calls attention to the frequent association of the dove and deity in the ancient world (*TDNT* 6:68–69).

17 καὶ ἰδού, "and look," parallels the same words in v 16. With the opening of the heavens comes not only the symbolic outpouring of the Spirit but also a divine revelation of the identity of the one who has thus received the Spirit. The significance of Jesus and the present event is conveyed by means of a vision shared with the readers; this interpretive schema has rabbinic parallels (see Lentzen-Deis, 200–202). The reference to φωνὴ ἐκ τῶν οὐρανῶν, "a voice from heaven," means a divine voice. After the exile, when prophecy was regarded as dead in Israel, the rabbis developed the concept of *baṭ qôl*, "the daughter [or 'echo'] of the voice," as a way of accounting for continued revelation from God, but thereby designating it as indirect and not of binding authority. Ordinarily, in the NT period a voice from heaven would be regarded as a *baṭ qôl*. Here, however (contra Hill), Matthew means something that transcends rabbinic allowances and expectations: with the presence of the Messiah, the Spirit of God is again abundantly active, and God speaks from heaven with directness and authority. The message conveyed by the divine voice is οὗτός ἐστιν ὁ υἱός μου ὁ ἀγαπητός, ἐν ᾧ εὐδόκησα, "this is my Son, the beloved, in whom I am well pleased." While Mark and Luke have this sentence as a direct statement to Jesus—"You are my son"—Matthew has it in the third person (cf. also John 1:34), thereby objectifying it and making it more suitable as catechetical material for the church. With this alteration, however, Matthew also departs from the wording of the OT passage being cited, Ps 2:7 (υἱός μου εἶ σύ, "you are my son," LXX). The affirmation of Jesus as God's Son partakes of messianic associations through the use of Ps 2. Jesus, now anointed with the Spirit (cf. Ps 2:2), is through this ceremony of inauguration (cf. the coronation of the king as the background of Ps 2) about to enter into his ministry whereby the nations shall become his heritage (cf. Ps 2:8). This affirmation has already been anticipated in 2:15 (cf. 1:23); hence we are not to think of adoption here. Jesus is now marked out formally as the Son of God in conjunction with the beginning of his work. The designation is presupposed in the temptation narrative that follows (cf. 4:3, 6). The argument of Jeremias (*NT Theology*, 1:53–55), that υἱός, "son," here was originally παῖς (which can mean "servant" as well as "son") and that therefore the passage originally in view was not Ps 2 but Isa 42:1 (see next clause), is thus not persuasive.

That the title "Son of God" had clear messianic significance in Judaism prior to the NT period is evident from Qumran (4QFlor 10–14; 4QpsDanA[a]). ὁ ἀγαπητός probably modifies υἱός, "son," in the sense not merely of "beloved" but of "only beloved" (cf. Gen 22:2 where Isaac is referred to as τὸν ἀγαπητόν; see BAGD 6b; cf. LXX). It can thus clearly be related to Ps 2:7. On the other hand, ἀγαπητός may bear the connotation of "elect" or "chosen" (cf. its occurrence in 12:18 as the translation of בָּחִיר, *bāḥîr*, and the substitution of ἐκλελεγμένος for ἀγαπητός in Luke 9:35). In that case it may refer to the following words and Isa 42:1. In fact, the term is suitable for both passages. ἐν ᾧ εὐδόκησα, "in whom I am well pleased," is an allusion to Isa 42:1, the servant passage that refers to the coming of the Spirit upon the servant enabling him to accomplish his mission. Not all MSS of the LXX have εὐδοκεῖν (Θ does), but evidence that Matthew related this verb to Isa 42 is found in his quotation of vv 1–4 in 12:18–21. It is obvious that Isa 42 is of basic importance to Matthew's understanding of Jesus. There is evidence that Ps 2:7 and Isa 42:1 were linked in Jewish messianic thought (see Lövestam). God is well pleased (cf. Tasker) in his "only beloved" Son, who in obedience takes upon himself the mission of the Servant who brings salvation to the nations (Isa 42:1, 4) and who ultimately in his death bears the iniquity of his people (Isa 53). The aorist tense is probably gnomic, reflecting a Hebrew stative perfect.

Thus in this passage we already encounter the paradoxical nature of the central figure of Matthew's narrative: he is declared the unique Son, the powerful anointed one (in the analogy of triumphant king) *and* the humble Servant who obediently accomplishes the will of God, eventually through suffering and death (as the reader of Matthew is to learn in the climax of the narrative). This dual picture is found again later in the Gospel, through the verbatim repetition of the same words (17:5), this time most suitably in conjunction with the transfiguration narrative that immediately follows Jesus' first announcement (to his disciples) of his imminent suffering and death.

Explanation

Since Jesus is the one for whom John prepares the way, he cannot remain unrelated to the work of John. But it comes as a great surprise to John, as to the readers of the Gospel, that Jesus will submit himself to John's baptism. The apparent inappropriateness is obvious: John, like all others, needs the baptism of fulfillment that the Messiah has come to bring, while Jesus himself, as the Holy One of God, needs no baptism of repentance. Nevertheless, when Jesus undergoes the rite, it becomes a matter of great significance both for him and for the Church. It serves as the occasion of the formal beginning of his ministry, wherein he receives the anointing of the Spirit together with the divine attestation of his unique Sonship (the early Church would not have missed the trinitarian associations). All of this is in keeping with the will of God, who will now bring salvation to the world. Thus John and Jesus perform their respective roles, fulfilling "all righteousness" as the salvific will of God now receives expression in the inauguration of the kingdom and the arrival of a new and crucial stage of salvation-history. The Agent of the kingdom, the Son of David and the Son of God, holds through his identity a position of strength and authority. Yet paradoxically he is at the same time described as the humble, obedient Servant of the Lord whom we meet in the Servant Songs of Isaiah (chaps. 42–53), the Servant who is instrumental in bringing the kingdom to fruition, not by the exertion of power but through the mystery of his suffering and eventual death. This indeed is the goal of the Gospel narrative, but already we are given a hint of its appropriateness. And here preeminently the meaning of Jesus' baptism is discovered. In this identification with his people, Jesus shows himself to be one with them in all that they experience. It is *as* representative of Israel that he gives his life *for* Israel and so completes the task of the Servant. Matthew's church may well have seen some parallels between the baptism of Jesus and the baptism they themselves experienced (cf. 28:19), but they would also have been conscious of the uniqueness of this complex of events in the life of Jesus, with all of its undertones for the fulfillment of salvation-history. With this insight into the secret of Jesus, the readers are being prepared to read the narrative of Jesus' ministry with deeper understanding.

The Temptation of Jesus (4:1–11)

Bibliography

Donaldson, T. L. *Jesus on the Mountain.* JSNTSup 8. Sheffield: JSOT, 1985. 87–104. **Dupont, J.** *Die Versuchungen Jesu in der Wüste.* SBS 37. Stuttgart: Katholisches Bibelwerk, 1969 (German tr. of *Les tentations de Jésus au désert.* StudNeot 4. Bruges: Desclée de Brouwer, 1968). **Fitzgerald, J. T.** "The Temptation of Jesus: The Testing of the Messiah in Matthew." *ResQ* 15 (1972) 152–60. **Gerhardsson, B.** *The Testing of God's Son (Matt 4:1–11 & Par.).* ConBNT 2.1. Lund: Gleerup, 1966. **Hoffmann, P.** "Die Versuchungsgeschichte in der Logienquelle." *BZ* n.s. 13 (1969) 207–23. **Hyldahl, N.** "Die Versuchung auf der Zinne des Tempels." *ST* 15 (1961) 113–27. **Kelly, H. A.** "The Devil in the Desert." *CBQ* 26 (1964) 190–220. **Kirk, J. A.** "The Messianic Role of Jesus and the Temptation Narrative." *EvQ* 44 (1972) 11–29; 91–102. **Mahnke, H.** *Die Versuchungsgeschichte im Rahmen der synoptischen Evangelien: Ein Beitrag zur frühen Christologie.* BBET 9. Frankfurt am Main: P. Lang, 1978. **Neugebauer, F.** *Jesu Versuchung: Wegentscheidung am Anfang.* Tübingen: Mohr, 1986. **Pokorný, P.** "The Temptation Stories and Their Intention." *NTS* 20 (1973–74) 115–27. **Przybylski, B.** "The Role of Matthew 3:13–4:11 in the Structure and Theology of the Gospel of Matthew." *BTB* 4 (1974) 222–35. **Robinson, J. A. T.** "The Temptations." In *Twelve New Testament Studies.* SBT 34. London: SCM, 1962. 53–60. **Schnackenburg, R.** "Der Sinn der Versuchung Jesu bei den Synoptikern." *TQ* 132 (1952) 297–326 (also in idem. *Schriften zum Neuen Testament.* Munich: Kösel, 1971. 101–28). **Stegemann, W.** "Die Versuchung Jesu im Matthäusevangelium: Mt 4, 1–11." *EvT* 45 (1985) 29–44. **Stegner, W. R.** "Wilderness and Testing in the Scrolls and in Mt 4:1–11." *BR* 12 (1967) 18–27. **Thomson, H. P.** "Called-Proved-Obedient: A Study in the Baptism and Temptation Narratives of Matthew and Luke." *JTS* n.s. 11 (1960) 1–12. **Wilkens, W.** "Die Versuchung Jesu nach Matthäus." *NTS* 28 (1982) 479–89.

Translation

[1] *Then Jesus was led up into the wilderness by the Spirit to be tested by the devil.* [2] *And when he had fasted forty days and forty nights, he was afterwards hungry.* [3] *And the tempter came and said to him, "If you are the Son of God, speak so that these stones become bread."* [4] *But he answered and said, "It is written, 'Not by bread alone shall one live, but by every word proceeding out of the mouth[a] of God.'"* [5] *Then the devil took[b] him to the holy city, and he set[c] him upon the pinnacle of the temple,* [6] *and said[d] to him, "If you are the Son of God, cast yourself down. For it is written that*

> *He will command his angels around you*
> *and with their hands they will bear you,*
> *lest you should strike your foot against a stone."*

[7] *Jesus said to him, "Again it is written, 'You shall not test the Lord your God.'"* [8] *Again the devil took[e] him to a very high mountain and he showed[f] him all the kingdoms of the world and their glory,* [9] *and he said[g] to him, "All these things I will give you, if you fall down and worship me."* [10] *Then Jesus said[h] to him, "Get away from me,[i] Satan. For it is written, 'The Lord your God shall you worship and him alone shall you serve.'"* [11] *Then the devil left[j] him, and look, angels came to him and were ministering to him.*

Notes

[a] D lacks "proceeding out of the mouth," ἐκπορευομένῳ διὰ στόματος. This constitutes a "Western non-interpolation" in D, which generally includes the fullest reading.

[b] The Gr. has a historical present here: παραλαμβάνει.

[c] TR has apparently harmonized the aorist tense of the earlier MSS (ἔστησεν) to agree with the historical presents on either side of it, by substituting the present tense ἵστησιν (cf. the same phenomenon in v 9).

[d] The Gr. text has a historical present tense here: λέγει.

[e] The Gr. text has a historical present tense here: παραλαμβάνει.

[f] The Gr. text has a historical present tense here: δείκνυσιν.

[g] TR apparently again substitutes a historical present (λέγει) to agree with the other historical presents, against the earliest MSS, which here have the aorist.

[h] The Gr. text has a historical present tense here: λέγει.

[i] TR and the Western text (D, it) and sy^c add ὀπίσω μου, apparently by influence of 16:23. As Metzger notes, no good reason can be found for its omission if it were the original reading (*TCGNT*, 11).

[j] The Gr. text has a historical present tense here: ἀφίησιν.

Form/Structure/Setting

A. The narrative of the testing of Jesus is closely related to the preceding narrative concerning the baptism of Jesus. The specific connective is found in the key term of this narrative, "God's Son" (so Gerhardsson, *Testing*). Jesus is proclaimed Son of God in the events immediately following the baptism, and his sonship is vitally important to his mission. But how does he stand with relation to that sonship, especially in circumstances of testing? Does the Son exhibit those qualities that are called for in sonship to Yahweh, as for example those required of God's son, Israel, e.g., trust, obedience, faithfulness? Indeed, in this passage we encounter a most interesting parallel to the experience of Israel in the wilderness. After the experience of her deliverance from Egypt and the establishment of the covenant relationship, Israel experienced a season of testing in the wilderness. The sequence in Matthew's account of Jesus is similar: following the return from Egypt, we have the baptism (likened, by some scholars, to Israel's crossing of the Sea of Reeds), the divine declaration of Jesus as God's son, and the time of testing in the wilderness. The parallel is heightened by the fact that all of Jesus' answers to the tempter are drawn from Deut 6–8, the very passage that describes Israel's experience in the wilderness. Thus Jesus, the embodiment of Israel and the fulfiller of all her hopes, repeats in his own experience the experience of Israel—with, of course, the one major difference, that whereas Israel failed its test in the wilderness, Jesus succeeds, demonstrating the perfection of his own sonship. This account is placed here deliberately because it serves as an important prolegomenon to the ministry of Jesus. Although the motif of the testing of Jesus' commitment to the will of his Father (the real criterion of true sonship) occurs again later in the Gospel narrative, the issue must be confronted at the beginning, as it is here, in a definitive and tone-setting manner.

B. The pericope is apparently not the work of Matthew since it is found also in Luke and is thus to be regarded as derived from Q. The agreement with Luke is very close, with four exceptions. The first is, of course, that Luke's order of the temptations, compared to Matthew's, is a, c, b. Matthew's order is probably the original order (contra Grundmann), since in Matthew the two "Son of God" temptations occur together and the response of Jesus, ὕπαγε σατανᾶ (v 10), is most suitable in the final temptation (though the words are lacking in Luke). On the other hand, Luke may well have placed the "temple" temptation last in order to stress Jesus' final victory in Jerusalem (Dupont, Grundmann). The second exception is that in segment c Luke has the devil say that the kingdoms of this world are in his power to give to whomever he wants, which Matthew has deleted (from Q material) probably because he regarded it as objectionable. Third, Jesus' quotation of Scripture in segment a is longer in Matthew than in Luke, including the words "but by every word that proceeds out of the mouth of God." Luke has either abbreviated the quotation from what it was in Q, or else Matthew has extended the quotation of Q in order to include the positive aspect in Jesus' response. Fourth, the actual wording of segment c is quite different throughout in Matthew and Luke. This may suggest different recensions of Q (see McNeile) or the influence of a variant oral tradition. It is difficult to know whether Mark knew the full account as contained in Q and greatly abbreviated it or he simply records all that is known to him. Matthew may show the influence of Mark in the concluding reference to angels ministering to Jesus (not found in Luke); both Matthew and Luke omit Mark's introductory reference to Jesus' being with the wild beasts (Mark 1:13).

C. The pericope consists of three temptation segments, framed by an introductory sentence (vv 1–2) and a concluding sentence (v 11): (1) to turn stones into bread (vv 3–4); (2) to jump from the pinnacle of the temple (vv 5–7); and (3) to receive the kingdom of the world by worshiping the devil (vv 8–10). The most characteristic feature common to the three segments is the quotation of Scripture by Jesus (in all three cases from Deuteronomy and introduced with γέγραπται, "it is written") in response to the devil's words. The temptations have a common pattern: (a) the setting (briefest in segment a, προσελθών); (b) the words of Satan; and (c) the response of Jesus. The remarkable parallelism of the passage, however, is broken at two points: first in the surprising quotation of Scripture by Satan in segment b (v 6) and second in the lack of εἰ υἱὸς εἶ τοῦ θεοῦ, "if you are the Son of God," in segment c (v 9), where furthermore the main clause is not an imperative but the promise "I will give you all these things."

D. The genre of the passage is again that of haggadic midrash (see esp. Gerhardsson, *Testing*). The four OT quotations are of central significance to the whole passage. The account of Jesus' testing is set forth and interpreted in terms of the quotations and by means of a stream of rabbinic exegesis with which the author was familiar. In this way the key items, such as Jesus' own identity as Son of God, his consistent obedience to and trust in his father, the nature of his messiahship, and the parallelism with Israel's own experience, receive theological emphasis. This does not, however, necessitate the conclusion that the story has no historical basis. Haggadic midrash here, as elsewhere, is not necessarily incompatible with the respect for and use of historical tradition by the author.

E. All three Synoptics agree in locating the temptation experience of Jesus in the wilderness—almost certainly the wilderness of Judea, probably not far from where John was baptizing. The baptism and temptation of Jesus belong together, as we have seen (cf. Mark's εὐθύς, "immediately": Mark 1:12). Whereas the time of Jesus' testing is understood as occurring in the wilderness, two of the temptations speak of other locations: segment b, the pinnacle of the temple in "the holy city" (v 5), and segment c, a very high mountain (v 8). This suggests that the temptations are to be regarded as subjective experiences of Jesus rather than involving the literal transportation of Jesus to other places (however miraculously); this conclusion is further supported by the fact that no high mountain enables one to see "the kingdoms of the world and their glory" (v 8). There is furthermore a natural connection between fasting and the experience of visions (cf. Dan 10:3; 4 Ezra 5:20; *2 Apoc. Bar.* 20:5–6). It should be realized, of course, that to designate the temptations as a subjective experience does not lessen their reality or significance. It is not impossible that the Church created the temptation narrative for theological reasons, although the suggestion that we are to see here the reflection of a common motif of testing of heroes or divine figures found in other religious contexts is highly improbable (see Klostermann). There is no reason, on the other hand, why we may not have here a historical tradition that Jesus himself mediated to the disciples, perhaps as a means of encouragement in the face of the testing they were to confront.

Comment

1 Matthew uses his favorite connective τότε, "then" (for Mark's εὐθύς, "immediately"), to introduce the pericope. ἀνήχθη εἰς τὴν ἔρημον, "led up to the desert," refers probably to the highlands of the Judean wilderness west of the Jordan and the Dead Sea (it hardly refers to a vision, as Grundmann argues). The purpose of the leading into the desert is its particular suitability as a place of testing. The leading of the Son of God ὑπὸ τοῦ πνεύματος, "by the Spirit," is in direct continuity with the descent of the Spirit upon him in the preceding pericope; the Spirit indeed is sovereignly active in and through Jesus' life and ministry from the baptism onward. That it is the Spirit of God who leads Jesus into this period of testing should not be regarded as unduly strange. It is explained by the Jewish belief that God is behind all that happens as an ultimate cause (see Gerhardsson, 38–41). In the parallel account of the testing of Israel in the wilderness, it is Yahweh who leads Israel into the wilderness for testing (Deut 8:2: "the Lord your God has led you these forty years in the wilderness, that he might humble you, testing you to know what was in your heart, whether you would keep his commandments or not"). In the case of Jesus, the testing is under the ultimate aegis of the Spirit (for important background, cf. Job 1:6–12). As the Son of God, Jesus proves to be triumphant in the testing, which in turn confirms his endowment with the Spirit as the obedient Son of God.

In the words πειρασθῆναι ὑπὸ τοῦ διαβόλου, "to be tempted by the devil," the second ὑπό phrase of the verse occurs. Whereas it is the Spirit who leads Jesus into the wilderness, it is the devil (διάβολος, lit. "slanderer," occurs in Matthew outside the present pericope only in 13:39 and 25:41) who does the testing. The Spirit's role is thus prior to that of the devil. The infinitive πειρασθῆναι expresses purpose in the sentence. Only Matthew expresses so strongly that the Spirit led Jesus into the wilderness in order that he might be tested by the devil.

2 νηστεύσας ἡμέρας τεσσεράκοντα καὶ νύκτας τεσσεράκοντα, "having fasted forty days and forty nights." The testing takes place in conjunction with fasting, which is to be understood as commanded by God. The rabbinic notion of atonement through fasting (suggested by Grundmann) is far from Matthew's mind. Several OT parallels are readily available. Both Moses (Exod 34:28) and Elijah (1 Kgs 19:8) fasted for forty days and nights. Parallels have already been drawn between Jesus and Moses in chap. 2; the reference to Moses' fasting for forty days and nights in Deut 9:9 occurs moreover in the context of Deut 6–8, which serves as the basis of the passage. Matthew, who alone among the Synoptists refers to forty nights, may show the influence of this language, but more probably the number forty itself (common to the Synoptics), which is of course a round rather than an exact number, goes back to the basic parallelism with Israel's wandering in the wilderness for forty years (Deut 8:2).

> The shift from forty years to forty days is not difficult in rabbinic typology (in the OT, cf. Num 14:34; Ezek 4:6). Hunger (ἐπείνασεν, "he became hungry") is also mentioned in the account of Israel's experience (Deut 8:3), and, as Gerhardsson points out, the Hebrew עִנָּה, ʿnh, in the piel can have the special sense of "cause to fast." Matthew's aorist participle νηστεύσας (and ὕστερον, "afterwards") puts the testing explicitly after the forty days and nights, unlike the accounts of Mark and Luke, who set forth the entire period as a period of testing. This may suggest that Matthew conceived of the forty days and nights as a time of communion with God (cf. G. Kittel, *TDNT* 2:58). The evangelist thus reserves the actual temptations for Jesus' weakest moment.

3 Only now does "the tempter" (ὁ πειράζων) come to Jesus to accomplish his purpose (cf. Gen 3:1–7). For the importance of προσέρχεται, "come to," in Matthew, see *Comment* on 5:1. The key clause in the pericope, εἰ υἱὸς εἶ τοῦ θεοῦ, "If you are the Son of God," is repeated in segment b (v 6) and assumed in segment c (v 9). υἱός lacks the definite article because it precedes the verb, not because it is indefinite. The question has been prepared for in the baptism narrative, where Jesus is designated the Son of God (see *Comment* on 3:17). In the temptation pericope the relation of the Son to the will of his Father is called into question (cf. the likening of Israel to a son in Deut 8:5). The testing is accomplished here by the suggestion of something that, looked at from another perspective or in a different context, is within the power and prerogative of the Messiah. The tempter does not suggest uncertainty on his part concerning the divine sonship of Jesus by use of εἰ, "if" (in a first-class condition). Indeed, the situation here is like the narrative about the demons, e.g., in Mark 1:24, where, with the invasion of their realm, the demons have an intuitive knowledge of the true identity of Jesus. Thus, from the perspective of the devil, we might well translate εἰ here as "since." (The same words are spoken in unbelief in 27:40.) McNeile is hardly correct when he says that the temptation to Jesus was to see if he had the power to work a miracle—i.e., a testing of Jesus' own confidence in his identity. The question is one of obedience to the will of the Father.

ἵνα οἱ λίθοι οὗτοι ἄρτοι γένωνται, "that these stones might become bread." It is unlikely that the plural οἱ λίθοι οὗτοι . . . ἄρτοι, "these stones . . . bread," implies the feeding of multitudes in a messianic sense (so Lohmeyer-Schmauch). Since there is nothing intrinsically sinful about turning stones into bread, the meaning of the temptation must be explored more deeply. Fundamental to any correct understanding of this particular testing of Jesus is the realization that the fasting and hunger are, at this stage, the will of the Father for the Son. To turn the stones into bread would be in effect to refuse God's will and would involve a disobedience that would belie Jesus' sonship. But is there more significance than this in the testing? Given that the testing specifically involves the testing of the Son of God and that miraculous feeding is a messianic deed, perhaps an improper or ill-timed expression of messianic power is involved. If this is probably true, it still is a matter that involves only Jesus and his obedience to his Father's will since there are no witnesses to the testing and no multitude to be fed. The testing then amounts to this: shall Jesus exercise his messianic power for his own ends in a way that avoids difficulty and pain, or shall he accept the path of suffering (and death) that is his Father's will? In this sense the testing is different from the testing of Israel, who did not have it in her power to turn stones into bread. It is, however, going too far to suggest that this testing involves the Messiah's repetition of the manna-miracle of Israel's wilderness experience, as expected by late rabbinic literature (see Str-B 2:481–2). That background is more appropriate to the miracle of the feeding of the multitude (cf. 14:15–21).

4 Jesus answers the command of the devil with an OT quotation introduced by the common formula of introduction in the perfect tense, γέγραπται, with the thrust "it stands written." The quotation itself agrees exactly with the LXX of Deut 8:3 except for the omission of the article τῷ before ἐκπορευομένῳ. The context of that quotation—the wilderness wandering of Israel—is centrally important to the understanding of this pericope, wherein the Son of God relives the experience of God's son, Israel, but in victory rather than in defeat. The words οὐκ ἐπ' ἄρτῳ μόνῳ, "not by bread alone," allow the necessity of bread for life but imply that bread alone is insufficient. Fundamentally important to life, as the next clause reveals, is one's relation to the will of God. This is the point of the saying of Jesus recorded in John 4:34: "My food is to do the will of him who sent me, and to accomplish his will" (cf. John 6:35).

For ἀλλ' ἐπὶ παντὶ ῥήματι, "but by every word," the Hebrew text has literally "everything." Matthew's longer quotation (this clause is lacking in Luke) may be the work of his own extension of the quotation in Q. The effect is to give positive teaching concerning obedience by suggesting the reason for Jesus' conduct (for a closely related statement, cf. Wis 16:26). This positive note supports Gerhardsson's claim that the temptations are related to the Shema (Deut 6:5) with its threefold exhortation to love God with heart, soul, and might. In this instance Jesus shows that he loves God with his whole heart. Thus the Son will not exercise his messianic power to satisfy his own desires; he remains steadfastly obedient to the Father and to the fulfillment of a messianic role involving deprivation and suffering (cf. Heb 5:8). It should be noted here that Jesus serves as a paradigm for the Church when he subjects himself, as the human Son of God, to a commandment that specifically refers to a human being (ὁ ἄνθρωπος) living by the word of God.

5 As in v 1, Matthew again begins with τότε, "then." Here, in παραλαμβάνει, "takes," and in λέγει, "says," of v 6, he shifts to the historical present, but not consistently (ἔστησεν, "placed," is again aorist, like the verbs in vv 1–4). If Q had the narrative in the historical present, Luke has been more consistent in changing the verbs to aorist; more probably, however, Matthew inconsistently alters some of the verbs to the historical present (by influence of oral tradition?). He now also picks up ὁ διάβολος, "the devil" (cf. v 1), the counterpart to ὁ πειράζων, "the tempter," in v 3. τὴν ἁγίαν πόλιν, "the holy city," is a common designation for Jerusalem (so in Luke) and is so used in 27:53 (cf. Isa 52:1; Neh 11:1, 18; Dan 3:28 [LXX]; Rev 11:2; 21:2, 10; 22:19). In his trance-like vision Jesus sees himself perched upon one of the highest points of the temple.

> Despite much discussion, exactly what is meant by the phrase τὸ πτερύγιον τοῦ ἱεροῦ, "the pinnacle of the temple," remains unclear. πτερύγιον is the diminutive of πτέρυξ, "wing," and may refer to the tip, end, or edge of something (BAGD, 727a). Suggestions have included the following: the (east) corner of the south wall of the temple, which overlooked a deep ravine (Josephus refers to its height, *Ant.* 15.11.5 §§411–412); the roof of the temple or a projection thereof (a rabbinic tradition expects the Messiah to appear on the roof of the temple, Str-B 1:151); the "lintel" or "superstructure" of a temple gate (for which another Greek word, ὑπέρθυρον, would be expected, according to BAGD, 727a); a tower in the temple precincts. Gerhardsson suggests that whatever it refers to, the unusual word πτερύγιον may deliberately have been chosen in order to play on the idea of safety in God (cf. reference to the "wings" of God in Ps 91:4, the very psalm quoted in the next verse)—a plausible suggestion, given the occurrence of the idea in the context of Ps 91 and the rabbis' penchant for such minute correspondences. The temple is portrayed as the location of this particular testing not because it is envisaged as a public spectacle but because the temple precinct always served as a very special place of divine protection. Moreover, as Gerhardsson (*Testing*, 56–58) points out, there are many common associations between protection in the wilderness and protection in the temple. Hegisippus' account of the martyrdom of James the Just (Eusebius, *H.E.* 2.23.11) refers to him being thrown from the πτερύγιον of the temple in conjunction with his being stoned. Whatever that may say about the location of the "wing of the temple," Hyldahl applies this to Jesus' experience and argues that Jesus is commanded to submit himself to stoning as the sentence of judgment for the blasphemy of considering himself to be the Son of God—if he really were, he would receive the protection promised by God to his Son. But this is only interesting speculation.

6 The words εἰ υἱὸς εἶ τοῦ θεοῦ, "if you are the Son of God," are in verbatim agreement with v 3 (see *Comment* there). In the first test, Jesus is commanded by the devil to provide food for himself—i.e., to save himself by exercising his messianic power. Here, by contrast, he is commanded to put himself in mortal danger (βάλε σεαυτὸν κάτω, "cast yourself down") and thus to force God to save him (i.e., through the agency of angels). It is important to note that the test involves a jump to safety, i.e., to rescue by God, and not to destruction. By refusing to jump, therefore, Jesus chooses the path of continuing danger and hardship. This testing should be understood as involving a struggle between Jesus and Satan. There is no mention of and no need of witnesses for the passage to make sense. Again he is called not to capitalize upon his identity as the Son of God but to yield in obedience to the Father and to trust in his will.

The devil uses the same introductory formula, γέγραπται, "it is written," used by Jesus in his three replies (see on v 4). Only here is recitative ὅτι used. That the devil quotes Scripture here is, of course, paradoxical. This is, however, hardly an example of *Streitgespräch* (controversy dialogue), a contest wherein the devil tries to outdo Jesus in his use of Scripture. The point of the command, βάλε σεαυτὸν κάτω, "cast yourself down," is beyond comprehension without the accompanying quotation to supply the significance of what is asked. To see the scriptural warrant is to set forth the justification that could be legitimately claimed by Jesus for jumping to safety, and accordingly to sharpen the struggle that goes on within him. The quotation is from Ps 91[LXX, 90]:11–12 and is in verbatim agreement with the LXX except for the omission after the first clause of the words τοῦ διαφυλάξαι σε ἐν πάσαις ταῖς ὁδοῖς σου, "to guard you in all your ways" (of which Luke has the first three words). There is probably no significance in the omission (contra Tasker). The use of Ps 91 may presuppose a messianic understanding of the psalm, although there is nothing overtly messianic in it. More likely, the psalm is understood to apply to any faithful Israelite and thus *a fortiori* to the Son of God, who serves as the representative of Israel. The message of the psalm is simply that God protects the faithful. The force of the particular verses quoted here is the same. The reference to protecting angels anticipates Jesus' statement at the time of his arrest that he could receive the help of twelve legions of angels if he asked for it (26:53). There is no specific messianic element here (contra Hill) but only the test of obedience and trust. Again no observers are mentioned to witness a messianic act.

7 With πάλιν γέγραπται, "again it is written" (see on v 4), Matthew continues to stress the importance of Scripture. The quotation is in verbatim agreement with the words as found in the LXX of Deut 6:16. The MT has "you" in the plural against the singular "you" of the LXX and Matthew, but the difference is of no significance. The LXX verse goes on to say, "as you tested him in the Testing (ἐν τῷ Πειρασμῷ)" (MT: "at Massah" = "testing"; cf. Exod 17:1–7). Israel in the wilderness failed in obedience and tested God (cf. 1 Cor 10:9). But where Israel failed, the Son is obedient. In quoting Deut 6:16, Jesus asserts that he will not test God on this (or any other) issue. The words are not meant as a command to the devil not to test Jesus. At stake again is Jesus' implicit trust in and obedience to his Father; Jesus will be obedient and will not fail as did God's son Israel (cf. esp. Ps 95:9). To act otherwise—i.e., to jump to safety—would be to act only out of self-interest and to act against the will of God on the matter of testing. The Son, however, trusts the Father's will and provision, though that trust may involve the risk of life (cf. 26:53–54; 27:40). The Son accordingly loves God with all of his life or soul (Deut 6:5).

8 πάλιν παραλαμβάνει αὐτὸν ὁ διάβολος, "again the devil takes him," is in verbatim agreement with the beginning of v 5, except for πάλιν (cf. v 7); the syntactical structure of the testings is very similar (see above, *Form/Structure/Setting* §C).

εἰς ὄρος ὑψηλὸν λίαν, "to a very high mountain," is probably not to be taken literally, as can be seen from the following clause. (For evidence concerning a mythical mountain with similar panoramas, cf. Rev 21:10; 2 *Apoc. Bar.* 76:3. See Foerster, *TDNT* 5:486.) The reference, however, does have literal associations. Moses was commanded to go to the top of Pisgah (Mount Nebo) and from there not only to survey the promised land (Deut 34:1–4) but to look in every direction (Deut 3:27)—which the rabbis took symbolically to mean to survey the whole world (references in Gerhardsson, *Testing*, 63). In this connection Moses also warns the people not to be tempted by the riches of Canaan, for it is God who gives wealth (Deut 8:18). A secondary significance of the "very high mountain" may be the association with idolatry (see, e.g., Deut 12:2), which is of course pertinent to the devil's words in the next verse. δείκνυσιν αὐτῷ, "shows to him," continues the historical present tense (following παραλαμβάνει), against Luke's aorist. πάσας τὰς βασιλείας τοῦ κόσμου καὶ τὴν δόξαν αὐτῶν, "all the kingdoms of the world and their glory," means "this world and all its wealth" or "all that this world has to offer." The πάσας is all inclusive from the writer's perspective. For δόξα in the sense of worldly splendor, see BAGD, 204a (s.v. 2).

9 The aorist εἶπεν, "he said," is surprisingly used after two successive historical present tenses in the preceding verse. Further historical present tenses are used in vv 10 (λέγει, "he says") and 11 (ἀφίησιν, "leaves"). The main clause in this third testing by the devil contains not an imperative, as in the preceding two (vv 3, 6), but a promise: ταῦτά σοι πάντα δώσω, "I will give you all these things." Therefore, the conditional clause that follows, unlike the two previous conditional clauses (vv 3, 6), involves an actual condition to be met (cf. the use of ἐάν in a third-class condition in place of εἰ). The devil's offer of all the kingdoms of the world is a parody in that God has already promised the messianic king, the Son of God, "Ask of me, and I will make the nations your heritage, and the ends of the earth your possession" (Ps 2:8; cf. Ps 72:8; Rev 11:15). Again the devil tries to detour Jesus away from the will of the Father, offering him something within his rights (cf. 28:18), but, as the following clause shows, at the cost of idolatry: ἐὰν πεσὼν προσκυνήσῃς μοι, "if you fall down and worship me." What Jesus received from the magi (the same combination of participle and verb occurs in 2:11), Satan desires from Jesus. In this conditional clause, we have the key to the testing of Jesus, and indeed to all such testing. As in the very first account of testing, failed by Adam and Eve (Gen 3:1–7), the question centers on a choice between the will of Satan or the will of God, which involves implicitly the rendering of worship to the one or the other. Satan indeed vaunts himself as god in place of the only God. Thus, at stake here is the fundamental issue addressed by the first of the commandments: "I am the Lord your God . . . you shall have no other gods before me" (Deut 5:6–7).

10 The response of Jesus is direct and unwavering: ὕπαγε, σατανᾶ, "get away from me, Satan." Only here at the end of the three testings does Jesus respond with a command (cf. the similar words and same address in 16:23). Satan is the transliteration of the Aramaic שָׂטָנָא, *stn'* (alternately spelled שָׂטָן, *śtn'*), "the Adversary" (cf. 1 Chr 21:1; Job 1:6–12; 2:1–7; Zech 3:1–2), and is essentially the equivalent of διάβολος (the common LXX translation). Satan has tested Jesus and has failed. Jesus sends him away with a command that calls attention simultaneously to his victory and to his authority.

For the third time (cf. vv 4, 6), Jesus answers Satan with a quotation from Deuteronomy (6:13), introduced with the γέγραπται formula. The quotation is exact except for two slight changes (found also in Luke, hence derived from Q): προσκυνήσεις, "you shall worship," replaces LXX's φοβηθήσῃ, "you shall fear"; and μόνῳ, "only," is inserted before λατρεύσεις, "you shall serve." The former may be chosen to echo the words of the devil in v 9, "if you worship me," and is not far from the meaning of φοβηθήσῃ in this context (i.e., "reverence" or "respect"); the μόνῳ simply underlines what is evident in the following verse of Deuteronomy (6:14). Jesus thus employs a verse of Scripture that addresses the issue right at its heart. We may also note (with Gerhardsson, *Testing*) that when Jesus refused the world and all its wealth, he demonstrated that he loved God with all his might (wealth) and so perfectly fulfilled the commandment of Deut 6:5, in its third and final component as in the first two (see above). Again Jesus succeeds where Israel failed (cf. Exod 32). What Jesus declines to exploit on the mount of temptation, his messianic power and authority, he proclaims as his on the mount of the commission at the end of the Gospel (28:16; cf. Donaldson, 103, following Allen).

11 Again Matthew begins with his favorite initial τότε, "then" (as above, 4:1, 5). The historical present tense appears (ἀφίησιν, "leaves"), followed by an aorist and an imperfect. Matthew lacks Luke's ἄχρι καιροῦ, "until an opportune time," which is probably a Lukan addition rather than a Matthean omission since Matthew indeed knows of the reappearance of the tempter (cf. 16:23 and 27:40, both in relation to "Son of God"). For a similar association of ideas, see Jas 4:7 (cf. *T. Naph.* 8:4).

The motif expressed in ἰδοὺ ἄγγελοι προσῆλθον καὶ διηκόνουν αὐτῷ, "look, angels came to him and were ministering to him," has a Jewish background. More than ministering to Jesus' physical needs (e.g., hunger) is to be seen here. The angels come not simply to minister to a faithful Israelite (as promised in v 6) but to call special attention to the victory of the obedient Son (cf. Heb 1:6). The verse is thus symbolic of the true identity of the Son (cf. 26:53), which is again affirmed at this point. It also underlines God's faithfulness to the obedient.

Explanation

Just as the baptism of Jesus represents an identification with the people of God, so also does the narrative of the testing of Jesus. The newly adopted son of God, Israel, experienced testing in the wilderness for forty years; the newly proclaimed Son of God, Jesus, experienced testing in the wilderness for forty days and nights. That testing was real for Jesus, and the narrative must not be taken as a charade. But Jesus exhibits the faithful obedience of the Son to the Father where Israel failed. The things offered to Jesus—bread, safety, and the kingdoms of this world—are rightfully his by virtue of his sonship and messianic identity. Yet, as we see in the words spoken from heaven after the baptism, Jesus is called to be obedient not only as Son but also as Servant. He thereby is called to exemplify obedience to the will of the Father under the pressure of severe testing and at the cost of self-denial. He will, in particular, express his messianic identity only in accord with the will of the Father.

In this pericope we encounter a theme that is vital in the theology of the Gospels. The goal of obedience to the Father is accomplished, not by triumphant self-assertion, not by the exercise of power and authority, but paradoxically by the way of humility, service, and suffering. Therein lies true greatness (cf. 20:26–28). In fulfilling his commission by obedience to the will of the Father, Jesus demonstrates the rightness of the great commandment (Deut 6:5) as well as his own submission to it. In his faithful adherence to the teaching of the law, he reveals the fundamental consistency of his own teaching and ministry with the law rightly understood (cf. 5:17) and serves as a paradigm of conduct for the early Church. The sonship of Christians, too, must be expressed in full obedience to the will of God, involving, as it will, difficulties and testings (cf. 10:22, 24). Those testings will not be the same as those faced by Jesus, which relate to his unique identity and mission. But they will in principle be similar in that Christians too are called to self-sacrifice, and for them, too, obedience to the will of the Father alone is the measure of true discipleship.

Galilean Ministry (4:12–25)

Jesus Begins His Ministry in Galilee (4:12–17)

Bibliography

Romaniuk, K. "Repentez-vous, car le Royaume des Cieux est tout proche (Matt. iv.17 par.)." *NTS* 12 (1965–66) 259–69. **Rothfuchs, W.** *Die Erfüllungszitate des Matthäus-Evangeliums.* Stuttgart: W. Kohlhammer, 1969. 67–70. **Slingerland, H. D.** "The Transjordanian Origin of St. Matthew's Gospel." *JSNT* 3 (1979) 18–28.

Translation

[12]*When he heard that John was taken into custody, he departed into Galilee.* [13]*And he left Nazareth, and he came and dwelt in Capernaum beside the sea, in the regions of what had been Zebulun and Naphtali,* [14]*in order that what was spoken through Isaiah the prophet might be fulfilled, saying,*
[15] *Land of Zebulun and land of Naphtali,*
   The way of the sea, across the Jordan, Galilee of the Gentiles:
[16] *The people sitting in darkness*[a] *have seen a great light,*
   and upon those sitting in the realm and shadow of death,
   on them a light has dawned.
[17]*From that time Jesus began to preach and to say, "Repent, for the kingdom of Heaven has come near."*

Notes

[a] For σκοτία (B D), the majority of MSS read σκότει, probably by harmonization with the LXX of Isa 9:1.

Form/Structure/Setting

A. This short pericope serves as a transition and introduction to the narrative of the Galilean ministry of Jesus. The brief notice about the arrest of John rounds out the account of the time of preparation. Jesus' own work, which now begins, is prefaced by an OT quotation with a fulfillment formula (see *Introduction*). This quotation serves as a rubric for the entire Galilean ministry of Jesus. The final verse clearly marks a dividing point in the entire narrative and finds its counterpart in another major dividing point that is introduced with the very same words, ἀπὸ τότε ἤρξατο ὁ Ἰησοῦς (16:21). There Jesus announces his imminent suffering and death in Jerusalem. Despite the importance of the present dividing point, it is a mistake to suggest that the opening words of Matthew, βίβλος γενέσεως, are meant to include 1:1–4:16 (see discussion above on 1:1–17, *Form/Structure/Setting* §A).

B. The tradition concerning Jesus' residence in Capernaum at the beginning of his ministry is found in all four Gospels. Matthew here seems to depend on his own source rather than being dependent upon Mark or Q. When Mark and Luke refer to Jesus' coming to Capernaum, it is in connection specifically with his teaching in the synagogue (Mark 1:21; Luke 4:31). Matthew alone quotes Isa 8:23–9:1 (the only other brief use of the passage in the NT is found in Zechariah's Benedictus in Luke 1:79). Jesus' teaching is summarized in v 17, in verbatim agreement with the summary of John's preaching in 3:2, stressing the continuity between the two.

C. The quotation from Isa 9:1–2, the significance attributed to it, and its impact on the wording of the preceding verses give this passage a midrashic flavor. It is obvious that Matthew understands Jesus to be the fulfillment of the Isaiah passage (cf. esp. Isa 9:6–8, which Matthew would clearly have taken to refer to Jesus) and therefore interprets the move of Jesus to Galilee and Capernaum as corresponding to the specific words of Isaiah. The light referred to in the quotation is the presence of the kingdom in and through Jesus. The passage may be outlined as follows: (1) Jesus' arrival in Galilee (v 12); (2) the fulfillment of the Isaiah prophecy (vv 13–16); and (3) the beginning of Jesus' proclamation of the kingdom (v 17).

Comment

12 While we read of John in prison in 11:2, we must wait until 14:3–4 to find out what lies behind the Ἰωάννης παρεδόθη, "John was taken into custody." This was apparently a piece of tradition so familiar to the Church that it could stand here without explanation (as it does also in Mark 1:14). Like Mark, Matthew notes that it was after John's arrest that Jesus began his ministry in Galilee. If there was a causal connection (cf. ἀκούσας, "when he had heard") between the two events, we cannot be sure what it was. With no mention of a Judean ministry in Matthew or Mark, the problem of a rivalry between John and Jesus is avoided (cf. John 3:22–24; 4:1–3). For almost identical wording in reference to Jesus' reaction to the news of John's death, see 14:13. The παρεδόθη may be intended to anticipate Jesus' betrayal (17:22; 20:18–19; 26:2; etc.), thus drawing a parallel between the suffering of John and of Jesus (so Grundmann). The reason for the return to Galilee is not simply that Jesus went home to Nazareth. This is ruled out by the opening words of v 13.

13 The reason for leaving Nazareth is not given. Before the mention of Capernaum, Luke has Jesus rejected by the people of his hometown (Luke 4:16–30); this motif occurs in Matthew much later (13:53–58). Jesus has not returned to Galilee to be at home as before but, by the will of God, to begin the work he was commissioned to do. The ministry of Jesus had better possibilities in Galilee, which was far removed from the Pharisees' center of power (note the reference to them in John 4:1) and provided a much more tolerant atmosphere than Jerusalem. Capernaum may have been chosen as a base of operations because it was home for some of the disciples. (In Mark the disciples are chosen before any reference to Capernaum, 1:16–21.) Matthew's deliberate description of Capernaum as τὴν παραθαλασσίαν, "beside the sea," anticipates ὁδὸν θαλάσσης, "way of the sea," in the Isaiah quotation that follows. This of course is true also of the reference to Zebulun and Naphtali.

14 ἵνα πληρωθῇ τὸ ῥηθέν, "in order that what was spoken might be fulfilled," introduces the fifth of ten fulfillment quotations used by Matthew (see *Introduction*). The correspondence between events in the life of Jesus and words of the prophet, even though the latter may initially have been referring to something different, is seen not as coincidental but as divinely foreordained. Especially prominent in Matthew are the quotations from Isaiah. Matthew does not hesitate to stress that what Isaiah talks about as the future hope of his people (cf. "in the latter time"; Isa 9:1 MT) has now come in Jesus.

15 The quotation here is close to the LXX of Isa 8:23–9:1 (= versification of MT), except for the following: in referring to Zebulun, Matthew has γῆ, "land," for χώρα, "district"; following θαλάσσης, Matthew omits the LXX's καὶ οἱ λοιποὶ οἱ τὴν παραλίαν κατοικοῦντες καί, "and the others who inhabit the seacoast and"; and after ἐθνῶν, "Gentiles," Matthew omits τὰ μέρη τῆς Ἰουδαίας, "the regions of Judea." The former omission is an unimportant abbreviation of the text; the latter is obviously omitted because Matthew wants to make another point (but cf. the reference to Judea in v 25). According to the LXX, Isaiah addresses the message to all Israel (but with emphasis on the regions to the north); Matthew wants to stress the way in which Jesus, by beginning his ministry at Capernaum in Galilee, fulfills Isaiah's expectation.

γῆ Ζαβουλὼν καὶ γῆ Νεφθαλίμ, "the land of Zebulun and the land of Naphtali," refers to two northern tribes of Israel bordering on the Sea of Galilee, Zebulun to the south (where Nazareth lies) and Naphtali to the north (where Capernaum lies). The fact that in the Hebrew text (Isa 9:1) the places named are not specifically addressees (as in the LXX) is not significant; the plain meaning of the context is that the words spoken in Isa 9:2 are meant for those previously named.

The "way of the sea" (ὁδὸν θαλάσσης) was the Roman road (the *via maris*) connecting Damascus with Caesarea on the Mediterranean coast, a branch of which went along the west bank of the Sea of Galilee through Bethsaida and Capernaum, key towns in the ministry of Jesus. Capernaum, of course, is not "beyond the Jordan," πέραν τοῦ Ἰορδάνου, i.e., east of the Jordan, but Jesus' ministry in Galilee does extend into the region of the Decapolis across the Jordan (cf. 4:25), and Matthew may well have this in mind. It is unlikely that "across the Jordan" refers to Galilee and thus reflects the perspective of a writer located east of the Jordan, even despite the lack of the LXX's καί before the phrase (Slingerland). The phrase reflects too standard an expression to describe anything other than the trans-Jordan territory (cf. esp. v 25). The phrase Γαλιλαία τῶν ἐθνῶν, "Galilee of the Gentiles," was a common designation for Galilee, resulting from what had historically been a rather large gentile population. Matthew does not refer to a mission of Jesus to the Gentiles, but Matthew's readers may well have seen in these words a foreshadowing of what would occur after the resurrection (28:19; cf. 24:14). It is again for Matthew no accident that despite his limitation of his ministry to the Jews, Jesus began his ministry in a region that had gentile associations.

16 Agreement with the LXX continues to be close, with only the following significant differences: Matthew has ὁ καθήμενος, "sitting," for LXX's ὁ πορευόμενος ("walking"), a variant that may emphasize the plight of the addressees. He repeats the nuance by means of the parallel τοῖς καθημένοις, "those sitting," which is substituted for the LXX's οἱ κατοικοῦντες ("those dwelling"). Matthew's aorist ἀνέτειλεν, "dawned," supplants LXX's future λάμψει, "will shine," reflecting the

Hebrew perfect tense, but also Matthew's own perspective. ὁ λαὸς ὁ καθήμενος ἐν σκότει, "the people sitting in darkness," refers probably to the Jewish people (λαός is elsewhere in Matthew used only for Israel)—living in conditions of frustration and despair, and among pagan Gentiles—who are the first to be privileged to see the fulfillment of God's promises. The "great light" (φῶς . . . μέγα) which has shined upon them is the presence and ministry of the messianic king. This is emphasized by the following verse, which summarizes Jesus' message and mission. For the same imagery of light, see Luke 1:78–79; John 1:4–5, 9; 8:12.

17 The formulaic ἀπὸ τότε ἤρξατο ὁ Ἰησοῦς, "from that time Jesus began," signals a turning point in the narrative (see *Form/Structure/Setting* §A); it is repeated verbatim in 16:21, another major turning point of the Gospel. Jesus, like John (cf. 3:1), functions as a herald (κηρύσσειν, "to proclaim") proclaiming good news (cf. v 23). The theme of the proclamation of the gospel occurs throughout the narrative (cf. 9:35; 11:1) and is a responsibility committed in turn to the disciples (cf. 10:7, 27; 24:14; 26:13). καὶ λέγειν, "and to say," introduces the essential content of the kerygma: μετανοεῖτε· ἤγγικεν γὰρ ἡ βασιλεία τῶν οὐρανῶν, "repent, for the kingdom of Heaven has come near." Jesus' words echo John's message recorded in 3:2 (see *Comment* there). The drawing near of the kingdom is the ground (γάρ, "for") of the call to repentance and as such is more important than the call to repentance (contra Luz, Davies-Allison).

Explanation

This passage serves as an important transition, bringing Jesus to Galilee where his ministry is to have its formal beginning. Jesus has been prepared by the baptism and the temptation in the wilderness, the stage is fully set, and now comes the word that John has been arrested: the work of the forerunner is complete. Jesus comes to Nazareth and to Capernaum beside the sea, and in these regions, so significant in their correspondence to the prophecy of Isaiah, Jesus begins to proclaim the presence of the kingdom by word and deed: a great light appears to those who sit in darkness. Thus, as G. Dalman (*Sacred Sites and Ways* [London: SPCK, ET 1935] 183) puts it, "the loveliest lake of Palestine remains the place where God's redeeming power appeared to men for the first time on earth in a new guise, like a light, and thus was the prophetic word (Isa 8:23; 9:1) concerning the great light in the land of Zebulun and Naphtali abundantly fulfilled." The gospel in its essence is the proclamation of the good news of the dawning of God's rule. With that rule begins a new frame of salvation-history, one closely related to the eschaton itself.

The Calling of the Disciples   (4:18–22)

Bibliography

Abogunrin, S. O. "The Three Variant Accounts of Peter's Call: A Critical and Theological Examination of the Texts." *NTS* 31 (1985) 587–602. **Betz, O.** "Donnersöhne,

Menschenfischer und der davidische Messias." *RevQ* 3 (1961) 41–70. **Franzmann, M. H.** *Follow Me: Discipleship according to Saint Matthew.* St. Louis: Concordia, 1961. **Freyne, S.** *The Twelve: Disciples and Apostles.* London: Sheed & Ward, 1968. **Kingsbury, J. D.** "The Verb *Akolouthein* ("To Follow") as an Index of Matthew's View of His Community." *JBL* 97 (1978) 56–73. **Mánek, J.** "Fishers of Men." *NovT* 2 (1958) 138–41. **Smith, C. W. F.** "Fishers of Men: Footnotes on a Gospel Figure." *HTR* 52 (1959) 187–203. **Wuellner, W. H.** *The Meaning of 'Fishers of Men.'* Philadelphia: Westminster, 1967.

Translation

¹⁸ *Walking beside the Sea of Galilee, he saw two brothers, Simon, called Peter, and Andrew his brother,*[a] *casting a net into the sea; for they were fishermen.* ¹⁹ *And he said to them, "Come after me and I will make you fishers of human beings."* ²⁰ *And they left their nets immediately and followed him.* ²¹ *And when he went a little further, he saw two other brothers, James the son of Zebedee and John his brother, in the boat with Zebedee their father, putting their nets in order.* ²² *And he called them. And they immediately left the boat and their father and followed him.*

Notes

a Because Matthew has added the words δύο ἀδελφούς, "two brothers," the Markan reference to Andrew as τὸν ἀδελφὸν αὐτοῦ, "his brother," although preserved by Matthew, becomes redundant.

Form/Structure/Setting

A. Matthew follows Mark in putting this passage after the initial statement of the message of Jesus (cf. Mark 1:15) and before any reporting of the actual ministry of Jesus (but in Mark a summary of Jesus' ministry precedes). This logical order stands in contrast to Luke, where the calling comes only in chap. 5, after an account of Jesus' ministry in Capernaum and after a reference to Simon for which there has been no preparation (Luke 4:38). The Lukan account of the calling (5:1–11) is given in connection with the miracle of a great catch and contains no reference to Andrew, but does include the reference to "catching people," although with a different verb (ζωγρεῖν), as well as the response following (5:10–11). Luke furthermore has Jesus get into one of the boats in order to teach the large crowd, something that occurs later in Matthew and Mark in connection with the teaching of the parables of the kingdom (Matt 13:1–2; Mark 4:1–2).

B. Matthew's redactional changes of Mark reveal his concern for parallelism (contra Schniewind, cited approvingly by Grundmann, who argues that the changes have no special intention). Thus Matthew adds the words δύο ἀδελφούς, "two brothers," both in v 18 and v 21; but most conspicuously of all, in v 22 he moves Mark's εὐθύς, "immediately" (changing it to εὐθέως), from before ἐκάλεσεν, "he called," to before the participle ἀφέντες, "having left," thus producing verbatim agreement with v 20. Matthew furthermore abbreviates the ending of the final verse of the pericope (v 22), omitting Mark's reference to Zebedee being in the boat with his hired servants as well as changing the words concerning the disciples' response to the simple ἠκολούθησαν αὐτῷ, "they followed him," which agrees verbatim with v 20.

C. The passage consists of two sections that are obviously parallel: (1) the calling of Peter and Andrew (vv 18–20) and (2) the calling of James and John (vv 21–22). Each section contains (a) reference to the movement of Jesus, (b) his observing of two brothers, (c) the activity of the latter, in each case connected with fishing, (d) an invitation to discipleship (much fuller in the first instance, v 19), and (e) the response of the brothers, given in verbatim language except for the object left behind (v 20, "the nets"; v 22, "the boat and their father"). This striking parallelism is deliberate in Matthew, who enhances the parallelism that already existed in Mark.

D. Only four disciples are called here, the two pairs of brothers: Simon Peter and Andrew, and James and John. Besides Matthew, who is called in 9:9, there is no further account of the calling of the disciples. At 10:2 we are presented with twelve names, seven of which are completely new in the narrative. The Fourth Gospel alone gives an account of the calling of two additional disciples, Philip and Nathanael (= Bartholomew?). The point of the present passage in Matthew is to account for Jesus' disciples prior to the teaching discourse of chaps. 5–7, which is primarily addressed to them (cf. 5:1). The calling of the four thus in a sense represents the calling of the others.

E. Despite the opinion of some (e.g., Bultmann, *History*), there is no reason to question the basic historical character of this passage. To be sure, it is stylized and not directly connected with what precedes or follows. But Matthew intends neither a complete nor even necessarily a chronological narrative. For this reason, he gives no hint of any prior acquaintance of the disciples with Jesus or any explanation of their immediate response to the call. (It may be that Luke, in delaying the call until chap. 5, implies such previous contact; cf. John 1.)

Comment

18 The reference to the Sea of Galilee (called the Lake of Gennesaret in Luke 5:1 and the Sea of Tiberias in John 21:1) is a reminder of the fulfillment of Isa 8:23–9:1, which has just been quoted. Simon is identified by Matthew as τὸν λεγόμενον Πέτρον, "the one called Peter" (cf. 10:2), anticipating the very important role of Peter in this Gospel (Andrew is mentioned again in Matthew only in the list of the twelve in 10:2). The significance of the name Peter is not mentioned until 16:18. Here alone in the NT does the technical word ἀμφίβληστρον occur (Mark uses the cognate verb). It describes a circular casting net used in fishing. The call of the disciples constitutes the only place in the Gospels where the word "fishermen" (ἁλιεῖς) is used. Here the word prepares the way for the saying of v 19.

19 The invitation of Jesus amounts to a demand based on electing grace. That is, the disciples have been chosen by Jesus to follow after him (cf. the same use of δεῦτε, "come," in 11:28; 22:4; 25:34). The invitation is accompanied by the promise that Jesus will equip them (ποιήσω, "make") for the new work to which he calls them; their obedience is followed by the promise of provision (Luke makes this point more clearly by means of the conjoining of the calling with the miraculous catch). The idea of "following after" another stems from the Jewish background of the rabbis and their disciples, where imitation of the master's example, and not only his teaching, is given great importance. The crucial difference from the rabbinic practice is that here the master, not the would-be disciple, takes the initiative to establish the relationship.

Jesus frames the invitation to follow him using the image of fishing. Hitherto these men had been fishermen by occupation (cf. preceding verse); when they follow Jesus they will continue to be fishermen, but now metaphorically as ἁλιεῖς ἀνθρώπων, "fishers of human beings." That is, by joining Jesus in his mission of the proclamation of the kingdom, they will be laboring to encourage the response of those who listen, thus enabling them to enter that kingdom. It may well have been the former occupation of the disciples that prompted Jesus later to liken the kingdom to a "dragnet" (σαγήνη, a different kind of net from that referred to in the present passage) that gathered in fish of every kind (13:47–48).

> It is a mistake, however, in considering the metaphor of the disciples as "fishers of human beings," to focus on the aspect of eschatological judgment, as Smith has done, or upon the sea as a mythological symbol of evil from which men are to be rescued (thus Mánek). The focus here is not the crisis of judgment faced by the fish (separation of good from bad) or the situation in which they are found—indeed the fish are not in view at all—but simply the activity of the disciples in their new calling, here set forth in an analogy drawn from their former career. It is thus a mistake to press the expression allegorically so as to focus upon the fate of the fish and to see the disciples appointed here as ministers of eschatological judgment. Fishers of people in a negative sense does occur in Jer 16:16, but this is not the background of the present verse. The simplest and most convincing understanding of the phrase, for which no genuine parallels exist, is that it refers in a general way to the work of the new disciples, who are now to be concerned with drawing men and women into the kingdom of God. This is true also of the related expression of Luke 5:10: "from now on you will catch people" (cf., too, the miraculous catch of John 21:1–13 as also a picture of the mission of the Church).

20 The brothers' immediate response is significant for Matthew, as can be seen from its redactional repetition in v 22. He apparently sees in this verse the pattern of true discipleship: the leaving behind of past preoccupations and the unhesitating and unconditional response of following. The verb ἀκολουθεῖν, "to follow" (a technical term), is important for the stress on discipleship throughout the Gospel (see Kingsbury). It occurs more often in Matthew than in Mark or Luke, and in eight instances it is redactionally inserted in material drawn from Mark or Q (cf. 4:22; 8:22; 8:23; 10:38; 19:28). Although ἀκολουθεῖν can at times be neutral (e.g., 8:19, 23), it is the special word for discipleship, as can be seen in Jesus' use of the word (e.g., 8:22; 10:38; 16:24; 19:21, 28). Peter and Andrew here are said to leave their nets, and in v 22 John and James leave their boat and their father. The point to be understood is that they left everything behind, as they themselves later will assert in the question of 19:27 (cf. Luke 5:11 where "they left everything").

21 Matthew's interest in parallelism is evident in his addition of the words ἄλλους δύο ἀδελφούς, "two other brothers" (cf. v 18). He alone notes, in anticipation of v 22, that it was with Zebedee their father that they were in the boat. James and John too were fishermen καταρτίζοντας τὰ δίκτυα αὐτῶν, "putting their nets in order" (i.e., from a previous outing), and when Jesus called them, the dictum "I will make you fishers of human beings," although not repeated, is clearly implied. James and John are mentioned again in Matthew, not only in the list of the twelve in 10:2 but also in connection with their mother in 20:20 and 27:56. For καλεῖν, "to call," in the sense of a call to discipleship, see also 9:13; 22:3–4, 8–9; 25:14.

22 Except for the object that is mentioned as left behind, the words of this verse are in verbatim agreement with v 20. In the latter, the nets are left behind; here, although James and John were busy preparing the nets (v 21), it is the boat and the father that are left behind. The discipleship of the kingdom often involves separation from loved ones (cf. 10:35–37), and thus in Matthew, John and James leave both "the boat and their father," although this is perhaps a softening of Mark's more direct "having left their father Zebedee in the boat." Mark, on the other hand, by the words "with the hired hands" may have meant to indicate that the father had not been left alone or abandoned and thus eases somewhat the responsibility of the sons. Matthew's omission of this reference to the hired hands is caused by his interest in the parallelism with v 20, which consequently produces a heightened emphasis on discipleship. James and John, like the first pair of brothers, are paradigms of Christian discipleship: they too "immediately" (Matthew's added εὐθέως) left their old way of life for service in the cause of the kingdom.

Explanation

Matthew follows Mark in placing this narrative after the initial statement about the preaching of Jesus. The disciples must be on the scene at the beginning as witnesses of the ministry of Jesus and recipients of his teaching. But for Matthew, the placement of the passage is also important in that it fits in with his emphasis on the importance and nature of discipleship, something he will stress in the major discourse that follows the brief description of the ministry of Jesus in vv 23–25. Thus the evangelist uses the tradition for historical purposes, showing the way in which Jesus gathered disciples, but also for pastoral purposes directly relevant to his readers. That is, the calling of these disciples serves as a model of the nature of true discipleship generally. The call of God through Jesus is sovereign and absolute in its authority; the response of those who are called is to be both immediate and absolute, involving a complete break with old loyalties. The actual shape of this break with the past will undoubtedly vary from individual to individual, but that there must be a fundamental, radical reorientation of a person's priorities is taken for granted. As the first disciples were called and responded, so are Matthew's readers called to respond. Such response is of primary importance if they are to participate in the new reality of the kingdom. And with discipleship comes the task of bringing others into the kingdom—a task for which Jesus equips those whom he calls (cf. 28:18–20).

The Ministry of Jesus Encapsulated   (4:23–25)

Bibliography

Duling, D. C. "The Therapeutic Son of David." *NTS* 24 (1978) 393–99. **Gerhardsson, B.** *The Mighty Acts of Jesus according to Matthew.* Lund: Gleerup, 1979. **Lohfink, G.** "Wem gilt die Bergpredigt? Eine redaktionskritische Untersuchung von Mt 4, 23f und 7, 28f." *TQ*

163 (1983) 264–84. **Parker, S. T.** "The Decapolis Reviewed." *JBL* 94 (1975) 437–41. **Ross, J. M.** "Epileptic or Moonstruck?" *BT* 29 (1978) 121–28.

Translation

[23]*And he*[a] *was going about the whole of Galilee, teaching in their synagogues and preaching the gospel of the kingdom and healing every disease and every malady among the people.* [24]*And his fame spread into the whole of Syria. And they brought to him all those who were ill, who were tormented with various diseases and pains, the demon-possessed, those subject to seizures, and the paralyzed, and he healed them.*[b] [25]*And large crowds followed him from Galilee and the Decapolis, as well as Jerusalem and Judea and across the Jordan.*

Notes

[a] The revised text of ℵ (ℵ[1]), the Western text (D), and Syriac (sy[s.p]) have ὁ Ἰησοῦς. B witnesses to the shorter and more difficult syntax with no specified subject.

[b] D it sy[s.c] read καὶ πάντας ἐθεράπευσεν, "and he healed them all."

Form/Structure/Setting

A. The stage has now been carefully set. Jesus has been fully prepared through the baptism and temptations; he has moved to the north, where the prophet Isaiah said the fulfillment would begin; the summarizing rubric of the kingdom of heaven over all of Jesus' work has been spoken by him as it had by John the Baptist (v 17); and the disciples have been called. Now we encounter what is simultaneously a programmatic and summarizing statement of the ministry of Jesus before we embark upon Matthew's proper account of that teaching and healing ministry in detail.

B. It is remarkable that v 23 is repeated almost verbatim in 9:35. The only differences (besides the addition of ὁ Ἰησοῦς in 9:35) are that 9:35 has "all the cities and villages" for "the whole of Galilee" and omits the final words "among the people." At the same time, the contacts with Mark (Mark 1:39) are slight (viz., ἦλθεν κηρύσσων εἰς τὰς συναγωγὰς αὐτῶν εἰς ὅλην τὴν Γαλιλαίαν, "he went preaching in their synagogues in the whole of Galilee"). If in 9:35 Matthew is not copying his own earlier summary, he may reflect a traditional summary of the ministry of Jesus such as might have been contained in oral tradition. The summary of 9:35 may function as an inclusio with the present passage, enclosing the account of Jesus' teaching in chaps. 5–7 and his healing in chaps. 8–9. Matthew includes a number of other such summaries, e.g., 8:16–17; 12:15–16; 14:13–14, 36; 15:29–31; 19:1–2; 21:14 (see Gerhardsson).

V 24 finds no parallel in Mark or Luke, whereas v 25 finds a few contacts in the summary of Mark 3:7–8 (cf. Luke 6:17–19), especially in the reference to larger crowds from Galilee who followed him and in the formulaic "Jerusalem, Judea, and across the Jordan." But only Matthew here refers to the Decapolis (cf. Mark 5:20), whereas Mark refers also to the coastal cities of Tyre and Sidon.

C. Each of the three verses in this pericope contains a list. The second and third point to the rapid growth of the ministry of Jesus. V 23 tersely describes the ministry of Jesus using three parallel participles, διδάσκων, κηρύσσων, and θεραπεύων, "teaching," "preaching," and "healing." V 24 describes the result by referring to the spread of his fame and then listing the various types of maladies he removed from the people. V 25 in turn refers to the growing number of followers Jesus gained, listing the regions from which they came. In the last list, references to Galilee and "across the Jordan" remind us of the citation of Isa 8:23–9:1 in vv 15–16.

The summary in v 23 reflects the structure of Matthew, if we put teaching and preaching together over against healing, for Matthew consists of blocks of teaching and healing material, an alternation of the words and deeds of Jesus.

Comment

23   The Gospel of Matthew stresses the teaching of Jesus (διδάσκων), and here the evangelist mentions it even before "preaching the good news of the kingdom" (κηρύσσων τὸ εὐαγγέλιον τῆς βασιλείας). (For this phrase, see also 9:35, 24:14; cf. 26:13; on the kingdom, see 4:17 and esp. 3:2.) The teaching referred to is probably the exposition of Torah, of which Matthew provides an example in chaps. 5–7 (note ἐν ταῖς συναγωγαῖς αὐτῶν, "in their synagogues," which may reflect the distancing of Matthew's community from the synagogues). But such teaching is inseparable from the preaching of "the good news of the kingdom." Thus διδάσκων and κηρύσσων here belong together, and no important difference is to be seen between the words (see the excursus in Luz, 1:206–8). (They are also apparently interchangeable in Luke 4:15, 44.) The latter is but the foundation of the former. It is, of course, also the foundation for the healing (θεραπεύων) ministry of Jesus, for the words and deeds of Jesus also belong together. Jesus healed πᾶσαν νόσον καὶ πᾶσαν μαλακίαν ἐν τῷ λαῷ, "every disease and every malady among the people." In 8:17, Matthew will quote Isa 53:4 as being fulfilled in the ministry of Jesus: "he bore our diseases," where the word for "diseases" (νόσους) is the same as that used here. Although the phrase "every disease and malady," which occurs also in 10:1 in the commissioning of the twelve just prior to their mission, is hyperbolic rather than literal, it is clear that Jesus healed multitudes of their illnesses. The language is absolute because it describes something of absolute importance. Note too, in v 24, "they brought to him *all*" their sick, with the implication that Jesus healed them all (although there the evangelist avoids using πάντας, "all," with ἐθεράπευσεν, "he healed"). As further illustration of this absolute perspective, note "the whole of Galilee" and "the whole of Syria" (v 24). ἐν τῷ λαῷ refers to the "people" of Israel, as the word λαός is regularly used in Matthew (e.g., 1:21; 4:16; 13:15; 21:23).

24   The report concerning the healings performed by Jesus spread quickly throughout Syria. Syria was a Roman province that included Palestine (cf. Luke 2:2–5), and it may mean that here (as v 25 might confirm, with its reference to Jerusalem and Judea). On the other hand, "Syria" here could have a more restricted meaning, as it also sometimes had, referring to the region north of the Sea of Galilee. It is possible, but no more than a guess, that the unexpected reference to Syria here reflects the evangelist's own community and the frequently argued Syrian provenance of the Gospel. ἀκοή, referring to the "fame" of or "report" concerning Jesus, is used in the same way in 14:1. The list of sicknesses healed by Jesus is comprehensive, beginning with the general (cf. v 23)—"those who were ill [τοὺς κακῶς ἔχοντας; cf. 8:16; 9:12; 14:35], those tormented with various diseases [ποικίλαις νόσοις; cf. 8:17; 9:35; 10:1] and pains [καὶ βασάνοις; only here in Matthew]"—and then proceeding to the particular and more spectacular healings of the demon possessed (δαιμονιζομένους; cf. 8:16, 28, 33; 9:32; 12:22), those subject to seizures (σεληνιαζομένους), and the paralyzed (παραλυτικούς; cf. 8:6; 9:2, 6). σεληνιαζομένους, lit. "moonstruck," in the NT occurs only in Matthew and may refer to epilepsy (cf. the RSV translation "epileptics"; cf. 17:15). That this can be closely associated with demon possession is indicated in 17:14–21, where a person suffering this disease is cured of it by the exorcism of a demon. Specific examples of the curing of the demon possessed (cf. 8:28–34; 9:32–34; 12:22–24; and 15:22–28) and the paralyzed (cf. 8:5–13; 9:2–8) occur later in Matthew. The verb θεραπεύειν, "to heal," occurs sixteen times in Matthew, more than in any other NT book.

25   ὄχλοι πολλοί, "large crowds," refers to the large number who "followed" him (same verb, ἀκολουθεῖν, used in vv 20 and 22), some of whom, but not all, were genuine in their discipleship. This is also the case elsewhere in the Gospel where ὄχλοι, "crowds," is linked with the verb ἀκολουθεῖν, "to follow" (as in 8:1; 12:15; 14:13; 19:2; 20:29; and 21:9). It is clear that among the crowds there were true disciples in addition to the twelve special disciples. The list of places from which these followers came is comprehensive: Galilee, where the ministry was centered, comes first; the Δεκάπολις, "Decapolis," referring to the area south and east of the Sea of Galilee; and also from further south, namely Jerusalem and Judea (where apparently his fame had already spread), as well as Transjordan. Galilee and "across the Jordan" (πέραν τοῦ Ἰορδάνου) echo the original citation of Isa 8:23–9:1 in vv 15–16. If we add to this list Syria as the northern area, we have a rather full and symbolic representation of that region of the world, i.e., the whole of Israel.

Explanation

Before recounting any of the details of Jesus' healing ministry, the evangelist wants to present a major teaching discourse of Jesus. But the teaching of Jesus must be set in the larger context of his ministry, and thus at the outset it is necessary for him to encapsulate the ministry of Jesus. Jesus' teaching and preaching were done in the context of a healing ministry that, as will be emphasized later in the Gospel, pointed to the validity of his message. Jesus thus heals the multitudes of every kind of disease, including those stemming from the spiritual world of the demons. Consequently, he gathers a large following, at least initially, from the surrounding, and even somewhat distant, areas. The evangelist wants us quickly to sense the great excitement surrounding Jesus at the beginning of his ministry, where he began to preach "the good news of the kingdom," before presenting him in more detail as the master teacher (chaps. 5–7) and charismatic healer (chaps. 8–9).

The First Discourse:
The Sermon on the Mount   (5:1–7:29)

General Bibliography

Allison, D. C. "The Structure of the Sermon on the Mount." *JBL* 106 (1987) 423–55. **Bauman, C.** *The Sermon of the Mount: The Modern Quest for Its Meaning.* Macon, GA: Mercer University, 1985. **Berner, U.** *Die Bergpredigt: Rezeption und Auslegung im 20. Jahrhundert.* 2nd ed. Göttingen: Vandenhoeck & Ruprecht, 1983. **Betz, H. D.** *Essays on the Sermon on the Mount.* Philadelphia: Fortress, 1984. **Bligh, J.** *The Sermon on the Mount: A Discussion on Matthew 5–7.* Slough: St. Paul Publications, 1975. **Bornkamm, G.** "Der Aufbau der Bergpredigt." *NTS* 24 (1978) 419–32. **Brooks, O. S.** *The Sermon on the Mount.* Lanham, MD: University Press of America, 1985. **Davies, W. D.** *The Setting of the Sermon on the Mount.* Cambridge: Cambridge University, 1964. ——— and **Allison, D. C.** "Reflections on the Sermon on the Mount." *SJT* 44 (1991) 283–309. **Derrett, J. D. M.** *The Ascetic Discourse: An Explanation of the Sermon on the Mount.* Eilsbrunn: Ko'amar, 1989. **Friedländer, G.** *The Jewish Sources of the Sermon on the Mount.* 1911. New York: Ktav, 1969. **Guelich, R. A.** *The Sermon on the Mount.* Waco, TX: Word, 1982. **Hendrickx, H.** *The Sermon on the Mount.* London: Geoffrey Chapman, 1979. **Hengel, M.** "Zur matthäischen Bergpredigt und ihrem jüdischen Hintergrund." *TRu* 52 (1987) 327–400. **Hill, D.** "The Meaning of the Sermon on the Mount in Matthew's Gospel." *IBS* 6 (1984) 120–33. **Jeremias, J.** *The Sermon on the Mount.* Tr. N. Perrin. FBBS 2. Philadelphia: Fortress, 1963. **Kissinger, W. S.** *The Sermon on the Mount: A History of Interpretation and Bibliography.* Metuchen, NJ: Scarecrow & ATLA, 1975. **Kodjak, A.** *A Structural Analysis of the Sermon on the Mount.* New York: de Gruyter, 1981. **Lambrecht, J.** *The Sermon on the Mount: Proclamation and Exhortation.* Wilmington, DE: Michael Glazier, 1985. **Lapide, P.** *The Sermon on the Mount: Utopia or Program for Action?* Tr. A. Swidler. Maryknoll, NY: Orbis, 1986. **Matera, F. J.** "The Ethics of the Kingdom in the Gospel of Matthew." *Listening* 24 (1989) 241–50. **McArthur, H. K.** *Understanding the Sermon on the Mount.* New York: Harper, 1960. **McEleney, N. J.** "The Principles of the Sermon on the Mount." *CBQ* 41 (1979) 552–70. **Schweizer, E.** *Die Bergpredigt.* Göttingen: Vandenhoeck & Ruprecht, 1982. **Songer, H. S.** "The Sermon on the Mount and Its Jewish Foreground." *RevExp* 89 (1992) 165–77. **Stanton, G.** "The Origin and Purpose of Matthew's Sermon on the Mount." In *Tradition and Interpretation in the New Testament.* FS E. E. Ellis, ed. G. F. Hawthorne and O. Betz. Grand Rapids/Tübingen: Eerdmans/Mohr, 1987. 181–92. **Strecker, G.** *The Sermon on the Mount: An Exegetical Commentary.* Tr. O. C. Dean, Jr. Nashville: Abingdon, 1988. **Stuhlmacher, P.** "Jesu vollkommenes Gesetz der Freiheit: Zum Verständnis der Bergpredigt." *ZTK* 79 (1982) 283–322. **Syreeni, K.** *The Making of the Sermon on the Mount: A Procedural Analysis of Matthew's Redactional Activity.* Part One: *Methodology and Compositional Analysis.* Annales Academiae Scientiarum Fennicae, Dissertationum Humanarum Litterarum 44. Helsinki: Suomalainen Tiedeakatemia, 1987. **Thurneysen, E.** *The Sermon on the Mount.* Tr. W. C. Robinson and J. M. Robinson. Richmond: John Knox, 1964.

Introduction

The Sermon on the Mount (chaps. 5–7) is the first and lengthiest of the five Matthean discourses. It presents the first and main example of the ethical teaching of Jesus. The righteousness of the kingdom of God (cf. 6:33) expounded in the sermon is presented as being in continuity with the righteousness of the OT law (5:17–19), yet also as surpassing it (cf. the antitheses of 5:21–48). The evangelist's placement of this first discourse toward the beginning of the Gospel indicates he attached importance to this material. Indeed, the content of the sermon would have had special relevance for the Jewish-Christian readers of the Gospel.

The "sermon" is clearly a compilation of the sayings of Jesus by the evangelist, rather than something spoken by Jesus on a single occasion. The parallel material in Luke (hence, Q material) is found at different places. Luke's "Sermon on the Plain" (Luke 6:17–49) does contain parallels to Matt 5:1–12, 38–48 and 7:1–5, 12, 16–21, 24–27. But other material is sprinkled throughout Luke (cf. 5:13 in Luke 14:34–35; 5:14 in Luke 11:33; 5:18 in Luke 16:17; 5:25–26 in Luke 12:57–59; 5:31–32 in Luke 16:18; 6:9–13 in Luke 11:2–4; 6:19–21 in Luke 12:33–34; 6:21–23 in Luke 11:34–36; 6:24 in Luke 16:13; 6:25–34 in Luke 12:22–32; 7:7–11 in Luke 11:9–13; 7:13–14 in Luke 13:23–24; and 7:22–23 in Luke 13:25–27).

The contents of the sermon are as a whole fundamentally Jewish (cf. Friedländer; Montefiore), while at some points they admittedly go beyond what is typically Jewish teaching and reflect the originality of Jesus (e.g., 5:39–42, 44; 7:12, which puts in positive form what Judaism expressed negatively).

Much debated has been the question of the practicability of the sermon at a number of points. Do we have here an interim ethic, applicable only during the (short) interval between the first coming of Christ and his imminent return (thus Schweizer), or is the ethic for the long haul of what we call the church age, a description of "ordinary" Christian discipleship? Do the radical demands of the sermon point only to the level of personal ethics, or do they intend a social dimension as well? Does the sermon represent a "realistic utopianism" (Lapide), or is the sermon an invitation to asceticism (Derrett)? Is the idealism of the sermon mainly intended to demonstrate the need of grace and hence to drive us to the gospel (the "Lutheran" view)? Does the sermon present in reality a salvation by works, or does it presuppose a framework of grace? These issues deserve fuller discussion than can be given here (see Davies and Allison, *SJT* 44 [1991] 283–309, and esp. Kissinger on the history of interpretation of the sermon). We assume the perspective that the sermon describes *the ethics of the kingdom,* thus explaining its idealism. An adequate understanding of the sermon is thus hardly possible apart from the context of the Gospel and the proclamation of the good news of the now dawning kingdom of God. The grace of God is fundamental to all, as the beatitudes that preface the sermon clearly show. (For a defense of the sermon as an integral part of the Gospel, against the argument of Betz [*Sermon*], see Stanton ["Origin"].) The righteousness described here is to be the goal of the Christian in this life, although it will only be attained fully in the eschaton proper. It is primarily an ethics concerning the individual, but it is not without implications for social ethics (see Strecker, *Sermon*). The radical nature of the sermon must not be lost in a privatization of its ethics. Some of the practical issues will receive discussion in the commentary as we proceed.

The structure of Matthew's sermon is not easy to discern. A variety of proposals has been made. Jeremias *(Sermon),* for example, proposed that 5:3–19 was the introduction; 5:20 the "theme" of the sermon; and that this was followed by the discussion of three types of righteousness: that of the scribes, 5:21–48; that of the Pharisees, 6:1–18; and that of the disciples, 6:19–7:27. Grundmann, on the other hand, attempted to structure the sermon in relation to the Lord's Prayer, which is at the center of the sermon. The beatitudes and 5:13–16 correspond to "Thy kingdom come" and "Hallowed be thy name," while 5:17–48 correspond to "Thy will be done." The material following the sermon he then understood to correspond to the remaining petitions. Thus, 6:19–34 relates to "our daily bread," 7:1–5 to "forgive us our debts," and 7:13–27 to "deliver us from evil." In an influential article (*NTS* 24 [1978] 419–32), Bornkamm modified this hypothesis, focusing on the material following the Lord's Prayer, with the following resultant analysis: the first three petitions of the prayer correspond to 6:19–24; the fourth petition to 6:25–34; the fifth petition to 7:1–5; and the sixth and seventh petitions to 7:6. Bornkamm is followed by Guelich (*Sermon*, 324–25) and to a lesser extent by Lambrecht (155–64). See too K. Syreeni's discussion (168–84). At least a few things seem clear: 5:3–16 constitute a kind of introduction; 5:17–7:12 the body of the sermon, with the reference to "the law and the prophets" in 7:12 serving as an inclusio corresponding to 5:17; and 7:13–27 the admonitory conclusion of the sermon. The Lord's Prayer does indeed stand at the approximate center of the sermon, and its content is related generally to some of the themes in the material that follows, though it seems doubtful that deliberate structural correspondence is intended. To a considerable extent, the sermon consists of an arbitrary gathering of ethical materials available to the evangelist. This is not to deny, however, the presence of considerable and impressive structure in the individual components that make up the whole.

As one possible outline, the following may be suggested:

    I. Introduction (5:3–16)
       A. The Foundation of Righteous Living: The Beatitudes (5:3–12)
       B. The Essence of Discipleship: Salt and Light (5:13–16)
    II. The Main Body of the Sermon (5:17–7:12)
       A. The Relation between the Old and the New Righteousness (5:17–48)
          1. Continuity with the Old (5:17–20)
          2. The Surpassing of the Old: The Six Antitheses (5:21–48)
       B. Outward vs. Inward Righteousness (6:1–18)
          1. Almsgiving (6:1–4)
          2. Prayer and the Lord's Prayer (6:5–15)
          3. Fasting (6:16–18)
       C. Dependence upon God (6:19–34)
          1. Serving God Rather Than Wealth (6:19–24)
          2. The Disciple and Anxiety (6:25–34)
       D. Various Teachings and the Golden Rule (7:1–12)
    III. Conclusion (7:13–27)
       A. The Two Ways (7:13–14)
       B. The False and the Genuine (7:15–23)
          1. Warning concerning False Prophets (7:15–20)
          2. The Insufficiency of the Charismata (7:21–23)
       C. The Parable of the Two Builders (7:24–27)

The Setting of the Sermon   (5:1–2)

Bibliography

Allison, D. C. "Jesus and Moses (Mt 5.1–2)." *ExpTim* 98 (1987) 203–5. **Black, D. A.** "The Translation of Matthew 5.2." *BT* 38 (1987) 241–43. **Donaldson, T. L.** *Jesus on the Mountain:*

A Study in Matthean Theology. JSNTSup 8. Sheffield: JSOT, 1985. 105–21. **Edwards, J. R.**
"The Use of *ΠΡΟΣΕΡΧΕΣΘΑI* in the Gospel of Matthew." *JBL* 106 (1987) 65–74. **Keegan,
T. J.** "Introductory Formulae for Matthean Discourses." *CBQ* 44 (1982) 415–30. **Manek, J.**
"'On the Mount—On the Plain' (Mt. v 1–Lk. vi 17)." *NovT* 9 (1967) 124–31.

Translation

¹ *When he saw the crowds, he went up to the mountain. And when he had sat down,
his disciples came to him.*ᵃ ² *And he opened his mouth and began to teach them, saying:*

Notes

ᵃ B and a few other MSS omit *αὐτῷ*, "to him."

Form/Structure/Setting

A. These introductory verses indicate that Jesus addresses primarily the disciples in the sermon. The crowds prompt him to go to the mountain where he can teach his disciples in relative privacy. Yet from the way in which Matthew ends the great sermon, "the crowds" too had gathered and heard the teaching and were amazed at the authority of his teaching (7:28–29). The Lukan counterpart to the Sermon on the Mount reflects the same situation. There we read of "a great crowd of his disciples and a great multitude of people . . . who came to hear him and to be healed of their diseases" (Luke 6:17), but in the immediate introduction to the sermon, Luke writes "And he lifted up his eyes on his disciples and said." And at the end of the Lukan sermon are the words "After he had ended all his sayings in the hearing of the people" (Luke 7:1).

B. Matthew's reference to "the mountain" (*ἀνέβη εἰς τὸ ὄρος*) is possibly related to Mark's *ἀναβαίνει εἰς τὸ ὄρος* (Mark 3:13), but there the words introduce the calling of the twelve, after which it is said "he went home" (Mark 3:19b). Luke also has Jesus go "to the mountain" (*ἐξελθεῖν αὐτὸν εἰς τὸ ὄρος*) to pray before calling the twelve (Luke 6:12). This immediately precedes the Sermon on the Plain, which is introduced with the words "And he came down [*καταβάς*] with them and stood on a level place [*ἐπὶ τόπου πεδινοῦ*]" (Luke 6:17). In Matthew the calling of the twelve is not found until 10:1–4 and does not occur in conjunction with a mountain. Obviously Matthew has a special purpose in the setting of the sermon by locating it on "the mountain."

C. Matthew has carefully constructed this introduction of the sermon out of the following: (1) Jesus goes up to the mountain (a special place for a special event); (2) he sits down and his disciples come to him (as to a rabbinic master); and (3) in v 2, Matthew introduces the elaborate "he opened his mouth and taught them, saying," a construction that points to the weighty significance of what he is about to say.

Comment

1 In two other places Jesus goes up to "the mountain" (14:23, to pray; 15:29, where he "sat down" and healed multitudes). Mountains in Matthew are clearly places where special events occur (4:8, the mountain of temptation; 17:1, the mountain of the transfiguration; 28:16, the mountain of the resurrection appearance and the great commission; see Donaldson). In 8:1 Jesus goes down from the mountain, as he does from the mount of transfiguration in 17:9. The setting of the Olivet discourse in 24:3 is very similar to the present passage: Jesus sits down, his disciples come to him (but κατ' ἰδίαν, "privately"), and he begins to teach them (24:3). Since Matthew emphasizes mountains in special narratives usually having to do with revelation, τὸ ὄρος, "the mountain," here functions as a literary device. Matthew may well have in mind the parallel of Moses going up to Mount Sinai to receive the law (Exod 19–20; 34; cf. ʾAbot 1:1; Pirqe R. El. 46; see too Matt 23:2). Donaldson (111–18) links the mountain with a Zion eschatology background, providing the scene for the Messiah's renewal of Torah for his eschatological people. For a discussion of a possible location for an original sermon (i.e., containing elements or the nucleus of the present sermon), see C. Kopp, The Holy Places of the Gospels (Tr. R. Walls; New York: Herder & Herder, 1963) 204–13.

Jesus went to the mountain apparently in the hope of escaping the crowds who pressed upon him to be healed (cf. 4:23–25). But this was to be a special time of teaching for his disciples, who "came to him." προσῆλθαν, a favorite verb of Matthew in this connection, has cultic connotations and itself points to the messianic character of Jesus (see J. R. Edwards). It was customary in Judaism for the rabbi to teach from a seated position. Thus Jesus sat down (καθίσαντος αὐτοῦ) before he began to teach (cf. 13:2; 24:3). Jesus, somewhat like a new Moses, goes up to the mount to mediate the true interpretation of the Torah.

2 The phrase ἀνοίξας τὸ στόμα αὐτοῦ, "he opened his mouth," is a Semitic idiom used at the beginning of a public address (see Black for the OT background; cf. Acts 8:35; 10:34). ἐδίδασκεν is an inceptive imperfect, "he began to teach."

Explanation

The evangelist carefully sets the stage for the first and most impressive of the five discourses that he will present. There is probably a deliberate attempt on the evangelist's part to liken Jesus to Moses, especially insofar as he is about to present the definitive interpretation of Torah, just as Moses, according to the Pharisees, had given the interpretation of Torah on Sinai to be handed on orally. The evangelist, however, does not press the Moses typology. For him, Jesus is far more than a new Moses, and his teaching is not to be construed as a new law. Indeed, Jesus can teach as he does because of his unique identity as the Messiah, the Son of God. His teaching alone, and not that contained in the Pharisaic oral tradition, penetrates to the full meaning of God's commandments. Thus Jesus majestically assumes his authority as teacher and begins in a definitive manner to expound the way of righteousness to his disciples.

Introduction (5:3–16)

The Foundation of Righteous Living: The Beatitudes (5:3–12)

Bibliography

Barré, M. L. "Blessed Are the Poor of Heart." *BiTod* 22 (1984) 236–42. **Best, E.** "Matthew 5, 3." *NTS* 6 (1960–61) 255–58. **Betz, H. D.** "Die Makarismen der Bergpredigt (Matthäus 5, 3–12)." *ZTK* 75 (1978) 1–19. **Böhl, F.** "Die Demut (ʿnwh) als höchste der Tugenden: Bemerkungen zu Mt 5.3, 5." *BZ* 20 (1976) 217–23. **Broer, I.** *Die Seligpreisungen der Bergpredigt.* BBB 61. Bonn: Peter Hanstein, 1986. **Dodd, C. H.** "The Beatitudes: A Form-critical Study." In *More New Testament Studies.* Grand Rapids: Eerdmans, 1968. 1–10. **Dupont, J.** *Les béatitudes.* 3 vols. Paris: J. Gabalda, 1958–73. ———. "Les πτωχοὶ τῷ πνεύματι de Matthieu 5,3 et les רוח ענוי de Qumran." In *Neutestamentliche Aufsätze.* FS J. Schmid, ed. J. Blinzer et al. Regensburg: Pustet, 1963. 53–64. **Flusser, D.** "Blessed Are the Poor in Spirit." *IEJ* 10 (1960) 1–13. **Frankemölle, H.** "Die Makarismen (Mt 5,1–12; Luke 6,20–23)." *BZ* 15 (1971) 52–75. **Guelich, R. A.** "The Matthean Beatitudes: 'Entrance Requirements' or Eschatological Blessings?" *JBL* 95 (1976) 415–34. **Holmes, M. W.** "The Text of Matthew 5.11." *NTS* 32 (1986) 283–86. **Kertelge, K.** "'Selig, die verfolgt werden um der Gerechtigkeit willen' (Mt 5,10)." *Internationale katholische Zeitschrift/Communio* 16 (1987) 97–106. **Kieffer, R.** "Wisdom and Blessing in the Beatitudes of St. Matthew and St. Luke." *SE* 6 [= TU 112] (1973) 291–95. **Kirchschläger, W.** "Die Friedensbotschaft der Bergpredigt: Zu Matthew 5,9, 17–48; 7,1–5." *Kairos* 25 (1983) 223–37. **Lapide, P.** "The Beatitudes." *Emmanuel* 92 (1986) 322–29, 355. **McEleney, N. J.** "The Beatitudes of the Sermon on the Mount/Plain." *CBQ* 43 (1981) 1–13. **Rodzianko, V.** "The Meaning of Matthew 5,3." *SE* 2 [= TU 87] (1964) 229–35. **Schnackenburg, R.** "Die Seligpreisung der Friedensstifter (Mt 5,9) im matthäischen Kontext." *BZ* 26 (1982) 161–78. **Schweizer, E.** "Formgeschichtliches zu den Seligpreisungen." *NTS* 19 (1972–73) 121–26. **Stenger, W.** "Die Seligpreisung der Geschmähten (Mt 5,11–12; Lk 6,22–23)." *Kairos* 28 (1986) 33–60. **Strecker, G.** "Die Makarismen der Bergpredigt." *NTS* 17 (1970–71) 255–75. **Trilling, W.** "Heilsverheissung und Lebenslehre des Jüngers (Mt 5, 3–12)." In *Christusverkündigen in den synoptischen Evangelien.* Munich: Kösel, 1969. 64–85. **Trites, A. A.** "The Blessings and Warnings of the Kingdom (Matthew 5:3–12; 7:13–27)." *RevExp* 89 (1992) 179–96. **Tuckett, C. M.** "The Beatitudes: A Source-Critical Study: With a Reply by M. D. Goulder." *NovT* 25 (1983) 193–216. **Walter, N.** "Die Bearbeitung der Seligpreisungen durch Matthäus." *SE* 4 [= TU 102] (1968) 246–58. **Zimmerli, W.** "Die Seligpreisungen der Bergpredigt und das Alte Testament." In *Donum Gentilicium.* FS D. Daube, ed. E. Bammel, C. K. Barrett, and W. D. Davies. Oxford: Clarendon, 1978. 8–26.

Translation

Beatitude

3 *"Happy are the oppressed,*[a] *because* to them *belongs the kingdom of heaven.* (1)
4 *Happy are they who grieve,*[b] *for* they *shall be comforted.*[c] (2)
5 *Happy are those who have been humbled,*[d] *for* they *will inherit the earth.* (3)

6 *Happy are those who hunger and thirst after justice,*[c] *for* they *shall be satisfied.* (4)

7 *Happy are those who show mercy, for* they *shall be shown mercy.* (5)

8 *Happy are the pure in heart, for* they *will see God.* (6)

9 *Happy are those who are peacemakers, for* they [f] *shall be called children of God.* (7)

10 *Happy are those who are persecuted for righteousness' sake, for* theirs *is the kingdom of heaven.* (8)

11 *Happy are you whenever they*[g] *reproach you and persecute you and [lying]*[h] *speak all kinds of evil*[i] *concerning you for my*[j] *sake.* (9)

12 *Be joyful and be glad because in heaven your reward is great. For in the same way they*[k] *persecuted the prophets*[l] *who came before you."* [m]

Notes

ª οἱ πτωχοὶ τῷ πνεύματι, lit. "the poor in spirit." See *Comment.*

ᵇ Some witnesses (א¹ 33 vgᵐˢˢ saᵐˢ bo) add νῦν, "now," thereby emphasizing the contrast between the present time and future eschatological blessings.

ᶜ A few witnesses (D 33 vg syᶜ boᵐˢ) put v 4 after v 5, in order to put οἱ πραεῖς, "the meek" (v 5a), immediately after οἱ πτωχοὶ τῷ πνεύματι, "the poor in spirit" (v 3a), as well as thereby juxtaposing the reference to τῶν οὐρανῶν, "heaven" (v 3b), and τὴν γῆν, "earth" (v 5b). See *TCGNT*, 12.

ᵈ οἱ πραεῖς, lit. "the meek."

ᵉ Or "righteousness" (δικαιοσύνην).

ᶠ Some important MSS (א C D f¹³ it vgᶜˡ·ˢᵗ syᵖ) omit the intensive pronoun αὐτοί, "they."

ᵍ A few witnesses (0133, vgˢ syˢ·ᶜ) insert οἱ ἄνθρωποι, "people," by the influence of the parallel in Luke 6:22.

ʰ The critical text places ψευδόμενοι, "lying," in brackets because of uncertainty about whether the word (which is omitted in D it syˢ) should be included. The word was possibly omitted in the Western textual tradition by way of harmonization with Luke 6:22. On the other hand, the word may be a scribal addition designed to clarify the text. See *TCGNT*, 12–13.

ⁱ Many MSS (C W Θ f¹·¹³ TR syᵖ·ʰ mae) insert ῥῆμα, "word," which appears to be the addition of a natural complement to the verb εἴπωσιν, "speak."

ʲ D it read δικαιοσύνης, "righteousness," in place of ἐμοῦ, "my." syˢ·ᶜ has in the same place τοῦ ὀνόματος μου, for the sake of "my name."

ᵏ U syˢ·⁽ᶜ⁾ add the subject οἱ πατέρες αὐτῶν, "their fathers," through the influence of the parallel in Luke 6:26.

ˡ D adds ὑπάρχοντας, "who ruled," i.e., the prophets in charge before you.

ᵐ syᶜ omits τοὺς πρὸ ὑμῶν, "who came before you."

Form/Structure/Setting

A. The opening of this discourse, with its decisive pronouncements of the blessedness of those who receive the kingdom, befits the setting of the discourse as well as the material that follows. The form of these affirmations, the so-called beatitudes, is found with many minor variations in Hellenistic literature but is also well known in the OT and was taken up by the rabbis. The same form—an initial μακάριος, "blessed" or "happy," without the copula—is thus found frequently in the LXX (e.g., Pss 1:1; 2:12; 105[106]:3; 118[119]:1; Isa 30:18; for the OT background, see esp. Zimmerli). For rabbinic parallels, see *b. Hag.* 14b; *b. Yoma* 87a (see further Str-B 1:189). The beatitude form is also common in the NT. Outside the Sermon on the Mount (and Luke's Sermon on the Plain), see Matt 11:6; 13:16; 16:17; 24:46; Luke 1:45; 11:27–28; 12:37–38; 14:14–15; 23:29; John 13:17;

20:29. See, too, Rom 14:22; Jas 1:12; Rev 1:3; 14:13; 16:15; 19:9; 20:6; 22:7, 14. Although other NT beatitudes employ the ὅτι clause, it is rare outside the NT, and Matthew's consistent use of it is unique.

B. Only four of the beatitudes are paralleled in Luke, where they also occur at the beginning of the sermon (Luke 6:20b–23). Luke gives the first, fourth, second, and ninth beatitudes, in that order, although none of these is in verbatim agreement with Matthew. The major difference is that the second part of Luke's first three beatitudes is in the second person plural rather than in the third person plural as in Matthew. The first two beatitudes in Luke (i.e., Matthew's first and fourth) are closest in form, but Luke lacks Matthew's ἐν πνεύματι, "in spirit," in the first, where Luke also has "kingdom of God" (not "heaven"), and the words καὶ διψῶντες τὴν δικαιοσύνην, "and thirst for righteousness," in the second. Luke's third beatitude is similar in thought rather than vocabulary, and the fourth contains numerous differences in wording. Luke furthermore has four corresponding woes (Luke 6:24–26) that follow the beatitudes directly and serve as their counterparts.

The explanation of this state of affairs remains unclear. Both the Matthean beatitudes and the Lukan beatitudes/woes reflect careful, artistic construction. It seems unlikely that they used the same source here, for then one or the other omitted what would appear to be irresistible material (Luke, several beatitudes; Matthew, the woes). It may well be that each evangelist follows an independent, though overlapping, oral tradition. This material, as it is found in both of the Gospels, exhibits content and form that the early Church very likely would have committed to memory.

C. It is clear that the evangelist has carefully structured this passage with its nine successive sentences beginning with the word μακάριοι, "blessed." Each of the first eight beatitudes consists of (1) the initial μακάριοι; (2) designation of those called "happy"; and (3) a ὅτι clause describing the reason or ground of the predication of happiness. At the same time, however, the structure is not altogether rigid. The ninth and last beatitude (vv 11–12) is by far the most different in form, shifting as it does from the third to the second person plural ("happy are you"), adding the lengthy ὅταν ("whenever") clause, and delaying the ὅτι ("for") clause by the insertion of the verbs at the beginning of v 12 ("be joyful and be glad"). Indeed, because of this distinctiveness, the ninth appears not to have been a part of the original collection. Such a conclusion also finds support in the verbatim agreement of the ὅτι clause of the eighth beatitude (v 10), ὅτι αὐτῶν ἐστιν ἡ βασιλεία τῶν οὐρανῶν, "because theirs is the kingdom of heaven," with that of the first (v 3), thereby forming an inclusio.

Other slight modifications of the parallelism can be seen in the addition of defining datives in the first and sixth beatitudes, vv 3 (πνεύματι, "in spirit") and 8 (τῇ καρδίᾳ, "in heart"), as well as the more expanded subjects of the fourth and eighth beatitudes in vv 6 ("those who hunger and thirst after righteousness") and 10 ("those who are persecuted for righteousness' sake"). The strict parallelism of the simple future passive in the ὅτι clause is found only in the second, fourth, and fifth beatitudes, vv 4, 6, and 7 (but cf. also the seventh beatitude, v 9). One further parallel of note occurs in the ἕνεκεν δικαιοσύνης, "for righteousness' sake," of the eighth beatitude (v 10) and the ἕνεκεν ἐμοῦ, "for my sake," of the ninth beatitude (v 11).

D. It is difficult to determine the extent to which the Matthean form of the beatitudes is the creation of the evangelist.

A number of scholars (e.g., Guelich, *Sermon*; Davies-Allison) have concluded for a variety of reasons (see Davies-Allison) that Matthew has derived eight (Gundry: four) of the nine beatitudes from his sources (the exception being the eighth, which is regarded as a Matthean creation), though some argue that Matthew has also created the third (or even the second four; thus Gundry). The argument (e.g., E. Bammel, *TDNT* 6:904) that the third beatitude was created as a gloss on the first (in some MSS it is reversed with the second beatitude) depends too much on an unjustified presupposition that originally there were seven beatitudes in the collection. A further conclusion (Luz; Guelich, *Sermon*; Schweizer; Gnilka; Davies-Allison) is that only three of these nine go back to Jesus himself (i.e., the first, second, and fourth), namely, three of the four found in Luke and thus presumably in Q (Luke's fourth, "blessed are you when people hate you, and when they exclude you, revile you, and defame you on account of the Son of Man" [= Matthew's ninth], is said to exhibit secondary characteristics; thus Guelich, *Sermon*). There seems little reason, however, not to accept that all nine beatitudes are derived from tradition by Matthew (without denying his redactional hand, as, e.g., in vv 3, 6). Why would he create a beatitude (i.e., the eighth) that simply reduplicated the thought of the ninth rather than creating an entirely new one? Moreover, the Matthean vocabulary (e.g., "righteousness") does not guarantee that this beatitude could not be derived from tradition. To assert that only three go back to Jesus assumes criteria that are too restrictive and presumes to know more than we can know.

Although we are limited to speculation in this regard, it may well be the case that the beatitudes were transmitted through oral tradition essentially as they appear in the Gospel. The essential structure of the beatitudes can indeed go back to Jesus himself. If we allow ourselves a further guess, based upon the form of Matthew's beatitudes, the following may be said. It appears that the first eight beatitudes are a unity in themselves, with the ending of the eighth forming an inclusio with the ending of the first and serving as an appropriate conclusion: "for theirs is the kingdom of heaven." The ninth beatitude, on the other hand, not only repeats the thought of the eighth concerning persecution but shifts to the second person plural, "Happy are you." It may be that the evangelist has added this beatitude to the eighth, possibly drawing it from another tradition (which we may say because of the shift in person and Luke's similar fourth beatitude) but also shaping it in his own way. More probably Jesus originally spoke the beatitudes using the second person plural form that we see in Luke, and the evangelist, or someone before him, has altered the form to the third person plural to objectify these teachings and hence make clear their universal significance. (For the beatitude form using the second person plural form, see Ps 127[128]:2 and Luke 14:4, as well as the Lukan parallel to the present pericope.)

E. It is also difficult to ascertain much significance in the order of the beatitudes. The first and eighth (and ninth) beatitudes set the tone for the entire collection, referring to those who are "poor in spirit" or oppressed and those who are persecuted. Closely related to this emphasis are the second ("those who mourn"), third ("those humbled"), and fourth ("those who hunger for justice") beatitudes. Thus, the first four beatitudes form a more or less single unit of thought focusing on the needy. On the other hand, there is some relationship in thought between the fifth and seventh beatitudes, in which those who are designated as blessed are described in relation to others as "merciful" and "peacemakers." These two beatitudes together with the sixth, concerning "the pure in heart," come closest to being of the ethical exhortation type, characteristic of the wisdom tradition, over against the apocalyptic type of declarative statement concerning the future (see Guelich, *Sermon*, 64–65). Although all the beatitudes can be said to involve implicit commands, this aspect of the beatitudes is decidedly secondary to the clear and grace-filled affirmation of the deep happiness of the recipients of the kingdom (cf. Broer, 52). Some beatitudes describe the unenviable position of the needy, who have become the blessed recipients of the kingdom, and some describe their demeanor in these circumstances. This leaves only the sixth beatitude ("the pure in heart"), which could be related to the condition described in either of these two groups but which alone focuses on the inner motivation of those who are the blessed ones.

Comment

3 Although the word μακάριοι, which appears as the first word in each of the nine beatitudes, occurs in Hellenist literature, where it describes those of good fortune, the true background to the NT use of the word is in the OT (Zimmerli finds forty-six instances in the Hebrew canon). The LXX often uses the word as a translation of אַשְׁרֵי (deeply "happy, blessed"). The word is of course especially appropriate in the NT in such contexts as the present one, where it describes the nearly incomprehensible happiness of those who participate in the kingdom announced by Jesus. Rather than happiness in its mundane sense, it refers to the deep inner joy of those who have long awaited the salvation promised by God and who now begin to experience its fulfillment. The μακάριοι are the deeply or supremely happy.

οἱ πτωχοὶ τῷ πνεύματι, lit. "the poor in spirit," the subject of the first beatitude, refers to the frame of mind characteristic of the literally poor. Thus, by the added "in spirit," Matthew or the tradition before him has not "spiritualized" the Lukan (and probably original) form of the beatitude (so too Guelich, *Sermon*). He too means the literally poor, but he focuses on their psychological condition or frame of mind. The poor are almost always poor in spirit; the poor in spirit are almost always the poor (cf. Broer [71], who notes that the two phrases were synonymous in the Judaism of Jesus' time). In Israel, especially in the post-exilic period, poverty and piety often went together, the poor (Luz refers to the "déclassé") having no other recourse than their hope in God. The poor were driven to complete reliance upon God, and the righteous poor were thought especially to be the objects of God's special concern (cf. Pss 9:18; 33[34]:18; 40:18; Isa 57:15; Jas 2:5). The poor were particularly in view in expressions of eschatological hope. In a passage alluded to in Matt 11:5, Isaiah (61:1) writes:

> The Spirit of the Lord GOD is upon me,
>   because the LORD has anointed me
> to bring good tidings to the afflicted [poor];
>   he has sent me to bind up the brokenhearted,
> to proclaim liberty to the captives, and the opening of the prison
>   to those who are bound.

This passage is almost certainly the basis for the present beatitude. The good news that has now come to the poor is that the kingdom is *"theirs"* ($αὐτῶν$ is in an emphatic position). Thus this opening beatitude points to eschatological fulfillment (cf. the citation of Isa 61:1–2 and the beginning of Jesus' Galilean ministry in Luke 4:18–19). The exact expression "poor in spirit" (עֲנָוֵי רוּחַ, *ʿnwy rwḥ*) is found in the War Scroll from Qumran (1QM 14:7), where the community describes itself, the "sons of light," as those who are poor in spirit. Although membership in the community entailed a voluntary poverty, this reference indicates how the literally poor were identified as the righteous. Zimmerli (19) finds the equivalent concept in the combination of passages in Isaiah referring to the poor (Isa 61:1) and the contrite in spirit (Isa 57:15; 66:2). On "kingdom of heaven," see *Comment* on 3:2. It is important to note that the present tense is used, $ἐστίν$, "*is* theirs," rather than the future tense. Because Jesus is present, the kingdom is already present, already theirs despite contradictory appearances (cf. too v 10b). There is, however, at the same time an awareness of an eschatology that is future, hence the future tenses, especially "they will inherit the earth" (v 5), "they will see God" (v 8), and the future orientation of "great is your reward in heaven" (v 12). F. Hauck thus rightly calls the beatitudes "sacred paradoxes" (*TDNT* 4:368) in that they point both to present and to future blessedness.

4 In the second beatitude we have an even more striking allusion to the words of Isa 61. In the LXX of Isa 61:2, the one anointed by the Spirit says he has come $παρακαλέσαι\ πάντας\ τοὺς\ πενθοῦντας$, "to comfort all those who mourn." Here the key word ($πενθοῦντας$) is exactly the same as in the beatitude. Thus again we find the eschatological expectation of the downtrodden and poor, those who suffer. The rabbis accordingly referred to the Messiah as the "Comforter" (*Měnaḥēm*) because of his mission in the messianic age (cf. Str-B 1:195). Those who mourn do so because of the seeming slowness of God's justice. But they are now to rejoice, even in their troubled circumstances, because their salvation has found its beginning. The time draws near when they shall be comforted (cf. Rev. 7:17; 21:4), but they are already to be happy in the knowledge that the kingdom has arrived. Their salvation is at hand. The verb $παρακληθήσονται$ is a so-called divine passive, which assumes God as the acting subject (so too in the fourth, fifth, and seventh beatitudes).

5 The third beatitude is practically a quotation of the LXX of Ps 36[37]:11: $οἱ\ δὲ\ πραεῖς\ κληρονομήσουσιν\ τὴν\ γῆν$, "the meek will inherit the earth." The Hebrew word underlying $πραεῖς$ is עֲנָוִים, *ʿănāwîm*, the same word that occurs in Isa 61:1, which the LXX there translates $πτωχοί$, "poor." Therefore we have approximately the same thought here as in the first beatitude. In view are not persons who are submissive, mild, and unassertive, but those who are humble in the sense of being oppressed (hence, "have been humbled"), bent over by the injustice of the ungodly, but who are soon to realize their reward. Those in such a condition have no recourse but to depend upon God. The Qumran community revered Ps 37 and saw themselves as those about to experience the vindication that would come with messianic fulfillment (4QpPs 37). The "earth" ($τὴν\ γῆν$) originally referred to the land of Israel, i.e., what was promised to the Jews beginning with the Abrahamic covenant (cf. Gen 13:15). But in the present context of messianic fulfillment it connotes the regenerated earth (19:28; cf. Rom 4:13, where $κόσμος$, "world," replaces $γῆ$), promised by the eschatological passages in the prophets (e.g., Isa 65–66). This beatitude stands in parallel with the assertion of the first beatitude that the kingdom of heaven belongs to the poor in spirit. It is possible, though we cannot be certain, that the third beatitude originally followed the first in synonymous parallelism and that the evangelist broke the couplet by inserting the beatitude concerning those who mourn, in order to follow the lead of Isa 61:1–2 (thus Guelich, *Sermon*, 82). See *Form/Structure/Setting* §E, above. It should be noted that the LXX of Isa 61:7 also contains the words κληρονομήσουσιν τὴν γῆν, "they will inherit the land (earth)."

6 In keeping with the preceding, the fourth beatitude names the literally hungry and thirsty, i.e., the downtrodden and oppressed, who especially hunger and thirst after the justice associated with the coming of God's eschatological rule. There is, then, no significant difference between the Matthean and Lukan versions of the beatitude, despite the additional words καὶ διψῶντες τὴν δικαιοσύνην, "and thirst for justice," in Matthew. That δικαιοσύνη here means "justice" rather than "personal righteousness" is clear from the context. The poor, the grieving, and the downtrodden (i.e., those who have experienced injustice) are by definition those who long for God to act. They are the righteous who will inherit the kingdom. Yet this interpretation does not altogether exclude the sense of δικαιοσύνη as personal righteousness. The justice of God's eschatological rule presupposes the δικαιοσύνη of those who enjoy its blessings (cf. 2 Pet 3:13). Thus, albeit to a slight degree, this verse may anticipate the stress on δικαιοσύνη in v 20 and 6:33. This beatitude seems to reflect the language of Ps 107 (LXX: 106), where, after a reference to the hungry and thirsty (v 5), the psalmist writes, "Then they cried to the LORD in their trouble, and he delivered them from their distress" (v 6), and then a few verses later continues, "For he satisfies the thirsty and the hungry he fills with good things" (v 9), where the LXX contains the same verb χορτάζειν, "to fill," as in Matthew. This is the language of messianic fulfillment: he has filled the hungry soul with good things (cf. Luke 1:53). It is the language of those who at long last have been "redeemed from trouble" (cf. Ps 107:2; for a similar sense of "thirsting" for salvation, cf. Pss 42:1–3; 63:1). In the first instance it is God's righteousness that satisfies (cf. the "divine passive") these hungry and thirsty souls (cf. John 6:35; Rev 7:16–17). (On "righteousness" in Matthew, see *Comment* on 3:15.)

7 The fifth beatitude marks a new emphasis in the beatitudes. Whereas the first four find their focus primarily in a state of mind or an attitude (and imply conduct only secondarily), this beatitude refers to the happiness of those who act, namely, those who are merciful toward others. This beatitude again has strong biblical overtones. Prov 14:21b reads ἐλεῶν δὲ πτωχοὺς μακαριστός, "blessed is the one who has mercy on the poor" (cf. Prov 17:5c, a phrase only in the LXX text: ὁ δὲ ἐπισπλαγχνιζόμενος ἐλεηθήσεται, "the one who has compassion will be shown mercy"). Showing mercy to the needy became a key element in rabbinic ethics (see *b. Šabb.* 151b; *t. B. Qam.* 9.30[366]; cf. Str-B 1:203–5 and the excursus in 4:559–610). For the importance of mercy to Matthew's presentation of the Christian ethic, cf. 9:13; 12:7; 23:23. What the poor and oppressed have not received from the rich and powerful, they should nevertheless show others. The point is analogous to that made somewhat differently in 18:33; there a servant who had been forgiven a great debt refused to have mercy on his debtor, whereupon his master said, "Should not you have had mercy on your fellow servant, as I had mercy on you?" Implicit in this beatitude is the judgment upon the wicked oppressors, i.e., the ones who have *not* shown mercy: to them mercy will not be shown (cf. Jas 2:13).

8 The sixth beatitude bears strong similarity to the thought of Ps 24[LXX: 23]:3–4, where the LXX refers, as does the present text, to the καθαρὸς τῇ καρδία, "the pure in heart" (cf. Pss 51:10; 73:1; linked here with "guiltless hands"), who will go up to the mountain of the Lord and stand in his holy place. "Pure in heart" refers to the condition of the inner core of a person, that is, to thoughts and motivation, and hence anticipates the internalizing of the commandments by Jesus in the material that follows in the sermon. It takes for granted right actions but asks for integrity in the doing of those actions, i.e., a consistency between the inner springs of one's conduct and the conduct itself. Another way of putting this is in terms of "single-mindedness" (cf. Jas 4:8, where it is the "double-minded" who are exhorted to "purify [their] hearts"). Purity of heart and purity of conscience are closely related in the pastoral Epistles (cf. 1 Tim 1:5; 3:9; 2 Tim 1:3; 2:22; cf. 1 Pet 1:22). The reference to seeing God in the present passage is again eschatological in tone. In contrast to the strong OT statement that no one can see the face of God and live (e.g., Exod 33:20), the righteous in the eschatological age will experience the beatific vision; they will see the face of God (cf. too Rev 22:4). Although one might have expected in the second clause something more in line with the first, such as "for they will be granted peace," Matthew describes the greatest possible eschatological reward, one that by its nature includes all else. This beatitude is the most difficult to relate to the others. Perhaps it is meant to indicate that even for the downtrodden and oppressed, for those to whom the good news of the kingdom comes, an inner purity is also required and is not something that can be presupposed.

9 The substantive εἰρηνοποιοί, "peacemakers," of the seventh beatitude occurs only here in the NT (the verb of the same stem occurs in Col 1:20). In the context of the beatitudes, the point would seem to be directed against the Zealots, the Jewish revolutionaries who hoped through violence to bring the kingdom of God. Such means would have been a continual temptation for the downtrodden and oppressed who longed for the kingdom. The Zealots by their militarism hoped furthermore to demonstrate that they were the loyal "sons of God." But Jesus announces the kingdom entirely apart from human effort and indicates that the status of υἱοὶ θεοῦ, "children of God" (cf. Rom 9:26), belongs on the contrary to those who live peaceably. It is the peacemakers who will be called the "children of God." Later in the present chapter, Jesus will teach the remarkable ethic of the love of even one's enemies (vv 43–48). This stress on peace becomes a common motif in the NT (cf. Rom 14:19; Heb 12:14; Jas 3:18; 1 Pet 3:11).

10–12 The paradoxes of the beatitudes reach a climax in the eighth and ninth beatitudes, in which not simply the poor and oppressed are declared to be happy, but also those who experience active persecution precisely for their righteousness. Here ἕνεκεν δικαιοσύνης, "on account of righteousness," points to the character of the recipients of the kingdom as it has hitherto been described in the beatitudes. That is, their loyalty to God and his call upon their lives become in turn the cause of their further suffering. To be identified with Jesus and the kingdom is to be in "the way of righteousness" (cf. 21:32); hence ἕνεκεν δικαιοσύνης, "on account of righteousness," finds its counterpart in the ἕνεκεν ἐμοῦ, "on account of me" (cf. 10:22), of the following verse. (See further in *Comment* on 3:15.)

The theme of persecution is particularly important in Matthew, very probably reflecting the situation of the community for whom the Gospel was written. As they experienced persecution, especially from their Jewish brethren, they needed to know what Jesus had said about it, how to regard it and how to endure it (cf. the perfect tense of the participle δεδιωγμένοι). Hence we have the present verse and the following two verses, all unique to Matthew, which encourage the readers not to be alarmed by the experience of persecution. We may note how 1 Pet 4:12–14 (cf. 3:14) makes use of the same underlying material used by Matthew. We find similar motifs in Matt 5:44, where the readers are told to pray even for their persecutors, and 10:23, where they are told to flee. All of these passages are found only in Matthew.

V 10 could well be the closing beatitude of the collection used by Matthew, since it rounds out the collection by an inclusio, i.e., concluding with the same ending as in the first beatitude: "for theirs is the kingdom of heaven" (cf. v 3). The poor and the persecuted, precisely the most unlikely candidates, are proclaimed the happy or blessed ones who receive the kingdom.

The ninth beatitude, vv 11–12, is in effect an elaboration of the preceding beatitude. Its original independence from the preceding collection of eight is indicated not only by its different form but also by the use of the second person pronoun rather than the third. Matthew probably received it in the form in which it stands and added it to the collection he had received from another source. Added now to persecution are "reproach" (cf. 27:44, where Christ is reproached) and the speaking of "all evil concerning you." This is exactly the kind of behavior one would expect from Jewish opponents, first toward the disciples, and then later toward the Jewish-Christian readers. It is obvious, whether the word ψευδόμενοι ("lying") is authentic or not (see *Note* h above), that the persecutors do not speak the truth. What they say is motivated by hatred (cf. Luke 6:22). Luke here has the more Semitic expression "cast out your name as evil."

The opening words of v 12 serve as a parenthetic expansion of μακάριοι in v 11. The happiness referred to in the beatitudes is nothing other than a deep and exuberant joy. The evangelist heightens the paradox with the redundant χαίρετε καὶ ἀγαλλιᾶσθε, "rejoice and be glad," which can only be seen as exceptionally remarkable in connection with persecution (the same verbs are joined in Rev 19:7). These words are followed by the delayed ὅτι clause, giving the reason for such joy: "great is your reward [μισθός] in heaven." It is self-evident that, in any persecution context, the reward spoken of must lie in the future, which is the meaning of ἐν τοῖς οὐρανοῖς, "in heaven." That holds true here, too, but it is confidence about the future that can and should produce joy in the present in full contradiction of the present, painful circumstances. The kingdom is already theirs, hence the appropriateness of the happy rejoicing in advance of the consummation. If this is a reward for their faithfulness under testing, it is also a reward that stems primarily not from their merit but from the grace of God, who gives the kingdom both in the present and the future. The idea of μισθός, "reward," is much more important in Matthew (ten occurrences; cf. 6:1–16; 10:41–42) than in any other Gospel. Despite its importance, the actual content of the reward is left vague. The concept of reward is important even when the word is not used, as for example in 25:31–46, where the content is described generally as inheriting "the kingdom" and entering into "eternal life." (Cf. too passages with the verb ἀποδιδόναι; see *Comment* on 6:4.)

The suffering of the righteous at the hands of persecutors is nothing new in the history of God's dealings with Israel, as the evangelist reminds his readers. It is an honored tradition they stand in when they suffer persecution. τοὺς προφήτας τοὺς πρὸ ὑμῶν, "the prophets before you," should not be taken narrowly to mean only the literary or canonical prophets, but broadly as referring to all God's earlier spokespersons (cf. 2 Chr 36:16; Matt 23:35). This motif is important to Matthew as the unique material in 23:31 also shows; it is found also in Acts 7:52 and Jas 5:10.

Explanation

The beatitudes are a bold, even daring, affirmation of the supreme happiness of the recipients of the kingdom proclaimed by Jesus. They are thus based upon—their truth depends upon—the fulfillment brought by Jesus and already stressed by the evangelist. Indeed, it is a part of this fulfillment that the good news comes to the poor and oppressed, the grieving and humbled, those who hunger so much for the revelation of God's justice. A turning point has been reached. The time is at hand, and these needy people, so dependent upon God, will now have their needs met. For this reason they are pronounced happy, blessed. The reality of the kingdom causes this new, unexpected joy. And that kingdom sets these people upon the way of righteousness, peacemaking, and inner purity.

What must be stressed here, however, is that the kingdom is presupposed as something given by God. The kingdom is declared as a reality apart from any human achievement. Thus the beatitudes are, above all, predicated upon the experience of the grace of God. The recipients are just that, those who *receive* the good news. Because they are the poor and oppressed, they make no claim upon God for their achievements. They do not merit God's kingdom; they but await his mercy. This emphasis on God's mercy is essential at the beginning of Jesus' teaching, especially at the beginning of the present discourse with its description of the righteousness of the kingdom, which has all too often been taken as involving a new nomism. But here, as throughout God's dealings with humanity, grace precedes requirements. It is true that the beatitudes contain implied ethical exhortations (becoming more explicit in the case of the fifth and seventh beatitudes). Indeed, the traits of those who are proclaimed "happy" could well be taken as a description of the behavior of Jesus himself. Yet this ethical side of the beatitudes remains distinctly subordinate to the indicative aspect that is directly related to the announcement of the kingdom.

These declarations of happiness are to some extent a manifestation of realized eschatology. The remarkable tension throughout is, of course, caused by the temporary delay of the final consummation. In this interim period those who may appear to enjoy anything but the favor of God are paradoxically pronounced blessed. In their present condition, and even as they experience intense persecution, they are already accounted as supremely happy. Salvation has begun; their time has come, and this assurance of the future is meant to transform their present existence.

The Essence of Discipleship: Salt and Light (5:13–16)

Bibliography

Campbell, K. M. "The New Jerusalem in Matt. 5:14." *SJT* 31 (1978) 335–63. **Cullmann, O.** "Das Gleichnis vom Salz." In *Vorträge und Aufsätze 1925–1962*. Tübingen: Mohr, 1966. 192–201. **Gerhardsson, B.** "Mysteriet med Saltet: Ett kryptiskt Jesusord (Matt. 5:13a)." In *Kyrka och Universitet*. FS C.-G. Andrén, ed. L. Eckerdal et al. Stockholm: Verbum, 1987. 113–20. **Hutton, W. R.** "The Salt Sections." *ExpTim* 58 (1946–47) 166–68. **Jeremias, J.** "Die Lampe unter dem Scheffel." In *Abba*. Göttingen: Vandenhoeck & Ruprecht, 1966, 99–102 (ET in *Soli Deo Gloria*. FS W. C. Robinson, ed. J. M. Richards. Richmond: Knox, 1968, 83–87). **Nauck, W.** "Salt as a Metaphor in Instructions for Discipleship." *ST* 6 (1953) 165–78. **Schnackenburg, R.** "Ihr seid das Salz der Erde, das Licht der Welt." In *Schriften zum Neuen Testament*. Munich: Kösel, 1971. 177–200. **Schneider, G.** "Das Bildwort von der Lampe: Zur Traditionsgeschichte eines Jesus-Wortes." *ZNW* 16 (1970) 183–209. **Souček, J. B.** "Salz der Erde und Licht der Welt: Zum Exegese von Matth. 5,13–16." *TZ* 19 (1963) 169–79. **Wood, W. S.** "The Salt of the Earth." *JTS* 25 (1924) 167–72.

Translation

[13] *"You yourselves are the salt of the earth. But if salt loses its taste, how[a] can it become salty again? It is worth nothing anymore except to be thrown out and[b] to be trampled upon by people.* [14] *You yourselves are the light of the world. It is not possible for a city positioned on a hill to be hidden.* [15] *Nor do people light a lamp and put it under a measuring vessel; they put it upon a lampstand, and it shines upon everyone in the house.* [16] *Thus let your light shine before others so that they may see your good deeds[c] and glorify your Father who is in heaven."*

Notes

[a] ἐν τίνι, lit. "with what."

[b] A great number of MSS (D W Θ *f*[13] TR) have βληθῆναι ἔξω καί, "to be thrown out and." The better text, however, is βληθὲν ἔξω, lit. "having been thrown out." The translation above is only a different way of translating and does not imply acceptance of the inferior text. See *TCGNT*, 13.

[c] B* omits ἔργα, "works," perhaps through homoioteleuton. The noun, however, can be implied by the adjective καλά, "good (things, deeds)."

Form/Structure/Setting

A. With the tone of the sermon now set by means of the beatitudes and their proclamation of the blessedness of the kingdom, the evangelist next presents two comprehensive statements about the necessity of living in a way that reflects the good news of the kingdom. Now following the introductory beatitudes is a statement concerning the ethical demand of the kingdom, the very essence of discipleship. These are, in short, "kingdom" ethics—instructions for how those who are recipients of the kingdom are to live. The emphatic ὑμεῖς, "you yourselves," in each maxim brings out this emphasis. It is particularly important to note that the kingdom precedes the ethics; there is no insistence that people are to live this way *in order to* receive the kingdom. The disciples are first identified as salt and light, and even here being precedes doing. It is because they are salt and light that they are expected to behave in appropriate ways. The two maxims about salt and light thus serve as an introductory rubric for what is given in considerable detail in the material that follows.

B. Matthew is unique among the Gospels in placing these two main metaphors side by side in the form of maxims in parallel structure. The salt metaphor, however, is found also in Mark 9:50 and Luke 14:34–35. Luke 14:34 seems dependent on the Markan parallel, although, in one word ($\mu\omega\rho\alpha\nu\theta\hat{\eta}$, "loses its taste"), Luke agrees with Matthew against Mark. Luke's second verse (14:35) is not found in Mark but is similar in content to Matt 5:13c, especially in the reference to "casting out" tasteless salt. Mark alone has the corresponding comment: "Have salt in yourselves and be at peace with one another" (9:50).

The metaphor of a lamp upon a lampstand is found in Mark 4:21 and Luke 8:16 (and 11:33). In Mark 4:21 and Luke 8:16, however, it occurs in reference to the mission of Jesus. Luke 11:33 is followed, on the other hand, by material that occurs in Matt 6:22–23. Thus, despite the similarity of language, the Markan and Lukan passages utilize the metaphor of the lamp on the lampstand in quite a different way. Matthew alone has the imperative about letting your light shine. The wording in all three Synoptic parallels, moreover, varies considerably.

Rather than literary dependence between the Synoptics here, we probably have an example of independently developed oral traditions, at least in the light on the lampstand metaphor, originating from a common starting point. That metaphor, by its nature, found different applications, either in the pre-synoptic tradition or in the work of the individual evangelists.

C. The two declarative maxims of this pericope (vv 13 and 14) are exactly parallel in form: $\tau\grave{o}$ $\mathring{\alpha}\lambda\alpha\varsigma$ $\tau\hat{\eta}\varsigma$ $\gamma\hat{\eta}\varsigma$, "the salt of the earth," is parallel to $\tau\grave{o}$ $\phi\hat{\omega}\varsigma$ $\tauo\hat{v}$ $\kappa\acute{o}\sigma\mu ou$, "the light of the world." The discussion following each maxim is parallel in content, though not in form, focusing on the uselessness of salt that is not salty and light that is hidden. The second maxim is followed by another metaphor (v 14b) that makes the same point as the discussion that follows: "a city on a hill cannot be hidden." V 16 contains the imperative application of the second maxim (and the first by implication). This imperative is the subject of the entire sermon: to belong to the kingdom necessitates reflecting the light of the kingdom through one's good deeds. The imperative, however, receives its force from the indicative: i.e, you are the light; let your light shine.

D. Matthew's material is probably drawn from oral tradition. It is impossible to know the extent to which the evangelist is responsible for the present form of the pericope. V 14b is a somewhat awkward mixing of metaphors interpreting the argument about light. It may therefore be a later accretion to the original material, but at what time we cannot say. If the sermon is essentially the construction of the evangelist using pieces of oral tradition, then his creativity may be seen in his placement of this passage here, immediately following the beatitudes and prior to the detailed instruction provided by the sermon. The parallel structure of the pericope argues for the evangelist's having taken over material from the oral tradition.

Comment

13 Jesus describes his disciples (the ὑμεῖς, "you," is emphatic) as τὸ ἅλας τῆς γῆς, "the salt of the earth." It is difficult to know which specific natural quality of salt (e.g., preserving [Carson], purifying, seasoning [Luz], fertilizing[Gundry]), if any, he intends. There is, moreover, the possibility of salt as a metaphor for wisdom (Nauck), as well as various other associations—sacrificial (Lev 2:13a; Ezek 43:24; see Cullmann, Souček, and Gerhardsson), covenantal (Num 18:19; Lev 2:13b), and moral. Plausible arguments can be made for each of these associations in explaining the present salt metaphor, but to emphasize a single association is to surpass the text itself and to allegorize it. Since it is virtually impossible now to know which of its several associations would have come most readily to the minds of the disciples when they heard these words, it may be best simply to take the metaphor broadly and inclusively as meaning something that is vitally important to the world in a religious sense, as salt was vitally necessary for everyday life (cf. Sir 39:26; Sop. 15:8; Pliny, Nat. Hist. 31.102). Thus, the disciples are vitally significant and necessary to the world in their witness to God and his kingdom. The meaning is not fundamentally different from the second maxim (v 14), which describes the disciples as the "light of the world." For other references to "salt" in connection with discipleship, see Mark 9:50; Luke 14:34–35; and Col 4:6.

The reference to salt losing its saltiness (which has a proverbial character; cf. b. Bek. 8b) is sometimes regarded as problematic, given the chemical stability of salt. The salt in view here, however, is probably that derived from the Dead Sea by evaporation, the residue of which also contains crystals of another mineral (gypsum) that can easily be mistaken for salt, which is hence regarded as having lost its saltiness (cf. F. Hauck, TDNT 1:229). Less convincing is the suggestion that in view are cakes of salt that are no longer effective as an aid in the burning of dung as fuel. This is an unnecessarily complicated explanation that goes beyond what the text says or requires.

The verb μωραίνειν means "to become or to make foolish" (e.g., Sir 23:14; Rom 1:22; 1 Cor 1:20). The unusual use of it here to describe what has lost its saltiness goes back to the underlying Hebrew root, תפל, tpl, a word that had both meanings (see Black, Aramaic Approach, 166–67). A Greek translator then chose the Greek word μωραίνειν because it applied more readily to the disciples. For the disciples, the salt of the earth, to lose their saltiness was equivalent to becoming foolish. It would in effect be to lose their identity.

The suggestion (cf. N. Hillyer, NIDNTT 3:445) that the subject of the verb ἁλισθήσεται is γῆ rather than ἅλας, i.e., that Jesus questions how the earth will be salted, makes good sense in itself. Against it, however, is the fact that τὸ ἅλας (salt) is the nearest antecedent and the natural subject of ἁλισθήσεται. Furthermore, the Markan parallel (9:50) is quite specific in making ἅλας the subject of the related verb ἀρτύσετε: "with what shall it [the salt] be seasoned." καταπατεῖσθαι, "trampled upon," an infinitive expressing result, occurs in Matthew in only one other place, 7:6, where swine trample upon pearls offered to them. ἀνθρώπων is a general term here referring to people.

14 Light is a very important metaphor in the Bible. "God is light" according to 1 John 1:5, and Christ is described in the Fourth Gospel as "the light of the world" (John 8:12; 9:5; 12:46; cf. 1:7–8). God is also described as light in eschatological contexts (e.g., Isa 60:19–20; cf. Rev 21:10–11). God, moreover, has come in Christ to bring light into the darkness (John 1:4–5, 9; 12:46; cf. Ps 27:1), a point Matthew has already emphasized in his quotation of Isa 9:2 (9:1, LXX) in 4:16 ("the people sitting in darkness have seen a great light"). In Paul, the metaphor also extends to Christians, who are described as "children of light" (Eph 5:8; 1 Thess 5:5). Another community on the edge of eschatology, the Qumran covenanters, also referred to themselves as the "sons of light." In Isa 42:6, Israel's mission is to be a "light to the Gentiles" (cf. Isa 51:4–5). Light is thus associated with God, his Messiah, his people, the law, the temple, Jerusalem, and the accomplishment and experience of salvation (see Str-B 1:237). Paul writes of "the light of the glorious gospel of Christ" (2 Cor 4:4; cf. 4:6). Of Christians he writes that in this fallen world they "shine as lights" (Phil 2:15). For Matthew, the metaphor of light is applied specifically to God's new people represented by the disciples.

When Jesus declares that the disciples are τὸ φῶς τοῦ κόσμου, "the light of the world," he means that they, as recipients of the kingdom, represent to the world the truth of the salvation that has come. Thus, as in the preceding maxim about the salt of the earth, here too the message is that the disciples are (and will continue to be) indispensable. If the world is not to be left in darkness, the disciples must fulfill their calling to represent the kingdom. They now are the light (cf. v 16), whose shining thus becomes the hope of the world.

It is as unthinkable that a city set on a hill (a metaphor that has unavoidable associations with Jerusalem on Mount Zion; see Campbell) can be hid as that light would be put under a measuring vessel. A version of the same saying is found in *Gos. Thom.* 32, but the emphasis there is different, focusing on the point that such a fortified city situated on a mountain cannot fall.

15 The purpose of a lamp is to give light, and thus it is placed upon a stand. πᾶσιν τοῖς ἐν τῇ οἰκίᾳ, "to all who are in the house," should not be understood in a restrictive sense but as parallel in meaning to the general τῶν ἀνθρώπων ("the people") of vv 13 and 16. That is, all are in view. λύχνος refers to an ordinary oil-burning household lamp (cf. Luke 15:8). When the lamp was lit, it was placed upon or hung from a stand so as to provide maximum benefit from the light. The μόδιος was a common vessel used in measuring grain (about one peck, or 8.75 liters). The suggestion that the measuring vessel was used to extinguish a burning lamp and that the point of the saying is "one does not light a lamp to put it out" (Jeremias) is not persuasive. The issue is whether that light is seen or not seen.

16 This verse serves as the climax of the entire pericope. Since the disciples are the light of the world (v 15), they are now exhorted to let their light shine— that is, they are to let the light accomplish its purpose. There are no known parallels to this imperative use of λάμπειν, "shine," in the OT or rabbinical literature (although Isa 42:6 could be the background of the metaphor). The verb furthermore is surprisingly never used in NT ethical parenesis (but cf. Luke 12:35). The ὅπως clause spells out the result of such a shining of the light and thus provides a most welcome aid to the interpretation of the metaphor. To let one's light shine is to live in such a way as to manifest the presence of the kingdom. This conclusion can be drawn not only because of the context but also because the good works entailed (τὰ καλὰ ἔργα) are connected with the glorifying of the Father in heaven. Letting one's light shine is living according to the perfection of the kingdom and thus manifesting the righteousness of the Torah according to its correct interpretation, examples of which are shortly to emerge. The love commandment provides the foundation for these good works (cf. 22:37–40).

The emphasis here on doing one's good works ἔμπροσθεν τῶν ἀνθρώπων, "before people," so that they will see them appears to stand in some tension with the warning in 6:1–6 *not* to do one's good works ἔμπροσθεν τῶν ἀνθρώπων, "before people" (6:1). In the latter instance, however, it is obvious that the almsgiving and praying are performed deliberately for self-glorification. But to let one's light shine is to call attention not to oneself but to the kingdom's presence and thus to glorify God for his gracious fulfillment of the promises (Jews primarily are in view here, whereas in 1 Pet 2:12, which depends on this saying of Jesus, Gentiles are in view). Thus within the ὅπως clause, ἴδωσιν ὑμῶν τὰ καλὰ ἔργα ("that they may see your good works"; cf. Phil 1:11) stands exactly parallel to δοξάσωσιν τὸν πατέρα ὑμῶν ("that they may glorify your father"; cf. John 15:8). The expression τὸν πατέρα ὑμῶν τὸν ἐν τοῖς οὐρανοῖς, "your father in heaven," is very common in Matthew and in the Sermon on the Mount. The Greek plural οὐρανοῖς, "heavens," is the result of translation from Aramaic and Hebrew, where the word is regularly a plural. Fundamental to the manifestation of the righteousness in view here is the disciples' unique relation to their heavenly Father. "A 'signal' which points to the relationship to God, so critical to the practice of the Sermon on the Mount, flashes like a beacon in v 16" (Luz 1:253).

> God is referred to as πατήρ, "Father," forty-five times in Matthew, and in nearly half the occurrences (nineteen times) it is modified, as here, by the words "in heaven" or "heavenly." The expression "heavenly Father" or "Father in heaven" occurs in the rabbinic literature, but in the NT it is distinctively Matthean; outside Matthew it occurs only in Mark 11:25. Only John uses "Father" for God more than Matthew does. God is referred to as Father seventeen times in the Sermon on the Mount; in seven instances the modifier, which occurs in the context, is not repeated. Although the Greeks, as well as the Jews, referred to God as Father, the NT makes a new and greater use of the title in referring to God. In the NT, the fatherhood of God is experienced at a new level of intimacy (cf. the Aramaic term *Abba*). The reason for this is that the kingdom (reign) of God announced by Jesus involves the possibility of a new relationship with God. One key way of expressing that new relationship in the NT is in the believer's ability to refer to God as *Abba*, or as "Father" in the most personal sense (Mark 14:36; Rom 8:15; Gal 4:6). Thus, the emphasis in the Gospels on God as "Father" rests directly upon the announcement of the eschatological salvation that brings about this new relationship between God and his people. The expression "Father in heaven" is remarkable in that it combines the personal, or immanent, element of fatherhood with the transcendental element of God's otherness, "in heaven."

Explanation

This key pericope is virtually a programmatic or summarizing statement for the importance of living according to the righteousness of the newly arrived kingdom. It is first of all an affirmation of the unique identity of the disciples, an identity that depends on the gracious activity of their heavenly Father. They and they alone are the salt of the earth and the light of the world. The emphatic "you yourselves" deliberately excludes all other groups claiming to have the truth, especially the Pharisees in Jesus' time but also their rabbinic successors in the time of the evangelist. The disciples—the blessed recipients of the kingdom—are thus of vital importance for the accomplishment of God's purpose in the world. They constitute the salt and light without which the earth cannot survive and remains in darkness. Their mission is accomplished, however, not only in word (cf. 10:7; 28:19–20) but in the deeds of their daily existence. Others observing their conduct will know that the priorities of these persons have changed—that before them is something of inestimable value, something that gives light and results in the glorifying of God. But to accomplish their purposes, salt must be salt and light, light. It is inconceivable that salt can be non-salt or light not serve its purpose of illuminating. The kinds of good deeds that enable light to be seen as light are now to be elaborated in the course of the sermon that follows. They are shown to be nothing other than the faithful living out of the commandments, the righteousness of the Torah as interpreted by Jesus.

The Main Body of the Sermon   (5:17–7:12)

The Relation between the Old and the
New Righteousness   (5:17–48)

Continuity with the Old   (5:17–20)

Bibliography

Banks, R. "Matthew's Understanding of the Law: Authenticity and Interpretation in Matthew 5:17–20." *JBL* 93 (1974) 226–42. ————. *Jesus and the Law in the Synoptic Tradition.* SNTSMS 28. Cambridge: Cambridge University, 1975. **Berger, K.** *Die Gesetzesauslegung Jesu. Teil I: Markus and Parallelen.* WMANT 40. Neukirchen-Vluyn: Neukirchener, 1972. 209–27. **Broer, I.** *Freiheit vom Gesetz und Radikalisierung des Gesetzes.* SBS 98. Stuttgart: Katholisches Bibelwerk, 1980. **Davies, W. D.** "Matthew 5:17, 18." In *Christian Origins and Judaism.* London: Darton, Longman & Todd, 1962. 31–66. ————. *Torah in the Messianic Age and/or the Age to Come.* JBLMS 7. Philadelphia: SBL, 1952. **Hahn, F.** "Mt 5,17—Anmerkung zum Erfüllungsgedanken bei Matthäus." In *Die Mitte des Neuen Testaments.* FS E. Schweizer, ed. U. Luz and H. Weder. Göttingen: Vandenhoeck & Ruprecht, 1983. 42–54. **Hamerton-Kelly, R. G.** "Attitudes to the Law in Matthew's Gospel: A Discussion of Matthew 5, 18." *BR* 17 (1972) 19–32. **Hübner, H.** *Das Gesetz in der synoptischen Tradition.* Witten: Luther, 1973. 15–39. **Ljungman, H.** *Das Gesetz erfüllen: Matth. 5,17ff. und 3,15 untersucht.* LUÅ n.s. 50.6. Lund: Gleerup, 1954. **Luz, U.** "Die Erfüllung des Gesetzes bei Matthäus (5,17–20)." *ZTK* 75 (1978) 398–435. **McConnell, R.** *Law and Prophecy in Matthew's Gospel.* Basel: Reinhardt, 1969. **Meier, J. P.** *Law and History in Matthew's Gospel.* AnBib 71. Rome: Biblical Institute, 1976. **Moo, D. J.** "Jesus and the Authority of the Mosaic Law." *JSNT* 20 (1984) 3–49. **Moule,**

C. F. D. "Fulfillment Words in the New Testament: Use and Abuse." *NTS* 14 (1967–68) 293–320. **Sand, A.** *Das Gesetz und die Propheten.* Regensburg: F. Pustet, 1974. **Schweizer, E.** "Matthäus 5,17–20: Anmerkungen zum Gesetzverständnis des Matthäus." In *Neotestamentica.* Zürich: Zwingli, 1963. 399–406. ————. "Noch einmal Mt 5,17–20." In *Matthäus und seine Gemeinde.* Stuttgart: Katholisches Bibelwerk, 1974. 78–85. **Snodgrass, K.** "Matthew and the Law." *SBLSP* (1988) 536–54. **Wenham, D.** "Jesus and the Law: An Exegesis on Matthew 5:17–20." *Themelios* 4 (1979) 92–96.

Translation

[17] "*Do not think I have come to destroy the law or the prophets. I did not come to destroy them but to bring them to their intended goal.* [18] *Truly I say to you: As long as heaven and earth last, not the slightest aspect of the law*[a] *will fail until everything has been accomplished.*[b] [19] *Whoever, therefore, breaks one of the least of these commandments and teaches others so shall be called the least in the kingdom of heaven. But whoever shall do and teach them, this person shall be called great in the kingdom of heaven.*[c] [20] *For I tell you that unless your righteousness surpasses that of the scribes and Pharisees, you will in no way enter the kingdom of heaven.*"[d]

Notes

[a] A few MSS (Θ *f*[13]) add καὶ τῶν προφητῶν, "and the prophets," in imitation of v 17.
[b] A Latin MS (c) adds *caelum et terra transibunt, verba autem mea non praeteribunt,* "heaven and earth will pass away, but my words will not pass away," an insertion drawn from 24:35.
[c] The last sentence in v 19 is omitted by ℵ* D W bo[ms] clearly through homoioteleuton, since the previous sentence also ends in ἐν τῇ βασιλείᾳ τῶν οὐρανῶν, "in the kingdom of heaven."
[d] The entire verse is omitted by D, again through the homoioteleuton in the words τῶν οὐρανῶν, "of heaven." Cf. previous note.

Form/Structure/Setting

A. This passage is placed here for a very important reason. The ethical teaching of Jesus that follows in this sermon, as well as later in the Gospel, has such a radical character and goes so much against what was the commonly accepted understanding of the commands of the Torah that it is necessary at the outset to indicate Jesus' full and unswerving loyalty to the law. Only when this is set clearly before the listeners or readers will they be in a position to understand correctly Jesus' teaching about the righteousness of the kingdom. This is especially the case given the six contrasts drawn in the remainder of this chapter, which begin with the words "you have heard it said" (5:21, 27, 31, 33, 38, 43). Jesus' corrections of the mistaken understandings involve the presentation of the true meaning of the Torah, not its cancellation as might at first seem to be the case.

B. In this pericope, only v 18 finds a partial Synoptic parallel. Luke 16:17 reads, "It is easier for heaven and earth to pass away, than for one stroke of a letter in the law to be dropped." Obviously, these are different renditions of the same saying. Matthew's version adds the reference to "one jot," which may be an elaboration occurring in the tradition. Matthew's final ἕως ("until") clause, finding no parallel in the Lukan version, gives the strong appearance of having been added by the evangelist as an explanation and a strengthening of his point. One other related saying, which refers to the passing away of heaven and earth in contrast to the permanence of Jesus' words, occurs in verbatim agreement in all three Synoptics (Matt 24:35; Mark 13:31; Luke 21:33).

C. The four verses of this pericope, although related in theme, are not inter-related or interdependent in such a way that they form a single entity. Instead, they are readily separable without any loss of meaning and thus could have come initially from different contexts. On the other hand, the verses did cohere in the evangelist's mind, and every attempt should be made to consider them as a unified whole. The key statement in the pericope is, of course, v 17. The stress of the passage is evident from the repetition in the words "I did not come to destroy" after the words "think not that I came to destroy." V 18, which describes the permanent authority of the law, is prefaced by the formula "verily I say to you" and contains a double ἕως ἄν ("until") clause, chiastically constructed, making it both awkward in structure and difficult to understand. V 19 contains a beautiful symmetry of form in the contrast between the one who fails to keep the commandments and the one who keeps them. The repetition and symmetry make this verse ideal for memorization; it could well have circulated as an independent logion used to introduce or to conclude ethical teachings of Jesus. V 20 has the "I say unto you" formula again, emphatically pointing to the righteousness that is the subject of the following verses. The reference to entering the kingdom of heaven binds this verse to the preceding one, so that it serves as a bridge between what precedes and what follows.

D. Without question, the perspective contained in this pericope is especially useful to the evangelist in his presentation of the gospel to his Jewish-Christian audience. This need not mean, however, that he has composed this material. Even the partial Synoptic parallel indicated above in §B points to the presence of material in the tradition that made the same point (see esp. Luke 16:17). The evangelist, on the other hand, was hardly a passive transmitter of the tradition available to him. He is responsible at least for the present juxtaposition of these four separate verses, a juxtaposition that lends emphasis to the whole. The evangelist, moreover, has probably put his own stamp on the traditional material, shaping it so as to make the strongest possible impact upon his Jewish-Christian readers.

Comment

17 μὴ νομίσητε ὅτι ἦλθον, "do not think that I came," presupposes the existence of the opinion that is denied (the same four words occur verbatim in 10:34, where the mistaken opinion is that the Messiah comes to bring peace). Although it is unlikely that we are to suppose that, like James, Matthew here opposes Paul (contra Manson, *Sayings*, 25, 154) or an explicitly Pauline group (contra Beare, 141), it may well be that the law-free gospel of the gentile church aggravated the claim of non-Christian Jews that Jesus' teaching, and hence the Christian faith, was antinomian. Here it is fair to assume that Jesus' sovereign interpretation of the law was so out of step with contemporary interpretation (e.g., the Pharisees) that it seemed to many that Jesus was going against the law. (Indeed, at one level, we shall see that he does.) The form of his teaching in the remainder of chap. 5 (the contrasts "you have heard . . . but I say to you") also makes necessary the present passage. Jesus here emphatically denies (twice, and thus with the greatest emphasis) that he has come καταλῦσαι, "to destroy," the law or the prophets. The infinitive here has the sense of "to abolish," "annul," or "repeal" (cf. its use in 24:2; 26:61; and 27:40 in reference to the destruction of the temple; in reference to the law, cf. 2 Macc 2:22; 4:11; 4 Macc 5:33; and Jos. *Ant.* 16.2.4 §35; 20.4.2 §81). Jesus, therefore, denies that he has come to cancel or to do away with the law or the prophets. The verb ἦλθον, "I came," in itself hints at the authority of Jesus (cf. Arens, *HΛΘON-Sayings*, 114–16). "Jesus is not the servant but the Lord of the law" (Luz, 271). Matthew contains, in addition to the two ἦλθον sayings in this verse, similar sayings in 9:13; 10:34, 35.

The words τοὺς προφήτας, "the prophets," probably a Matthean addition, are significant, especially since the subject under consideration is primarily the Mosaic law. Although the "prophets" here may in the first instance refer to the further stipulation of the requirements of righteousness, i.e., of the will of God (thus Berger, *Gesetzesauslegung*, 1:224), an added dimension with the implication of fulfillment is introduced by these words. The reference to "the prophets" suggests that the significance of Jesus for the Mosaic law can only be understood as part of a larger picture, namely, the fulfillment of the entire Torah, understood in its broad sense, including the prophets (cf. the inclusio in 7:12). (The entire OT can be referred to as "the law and the prophets.") This elevation of the prophets to the eternal worth of the law was not a view held by the Jews of Jesus' day (see Str-B 1:246–47). The messianic age has dawned in history, and with it comes the fulfillment of the prophetic expectation. Consequently, the way in which the law is "fulfilled" is inseparable from the total mission of Jesus.

The precise meaning of πληρῶσαι, "to fulfill," is a difficult question that has produced much debate. The verb means literally "to fill to the full" (from Aramaic מלא, *mēlā'*, "fulfill," rather than קם, *qûm*, "establish," which is never translated by πληροῦν in the LXX). From this basic meaning comes such derivative meanings as "accomplish," "complete," "bring to its end," "finish." "Fulfill" here hardly means "to do," although Jesus in his conduct is faithful to the true meaning of the Torah. "Complete" is congruent with the stress on fulfillment in and through Jesus but wrongly connotes that Jesus has come simply to add something to the law. The meaning in this instance cannot be determined by word study alone but must be established from the context and in particular must be consonant with the statement of v 18.

The options may be simplified into the following: (1) to do or obey the commandments of the OT (Luz, Bruner, Zahn, Schlatter, Schniewind); (2) a reference to Jesus' life and/or the accomplishment of the salvific acts of Jesus' death and resurrection ("fulfillment of prophecy"; Meier, 46; idem, *Law*, 76; Ljungman, 60; Guelich, *Sermon*, 142; Gundry; Carson); (3) teaching the law in such a way as to (a) "establish" or "uphold" the law (Wenham, *Themelios* 4 [1979] 93; Dalman, *Jesus-Jeshua*, 56–66; Daube, *Rabbinic*, 60), (b) add to and thus "complete" the law (Jeremias, *Theology*, 83–4), or (c) bring out the intended meaning of the law through definitive interpretation (with some differences: Davies-Allison; Broer, *Freiheit*, 34; Moo, *JSNT* 20 [1984] 3–49; T. W. Manson, *Sayings*, 153; Allen; McNeile; Green). A major decision is thus whether the verb refers to the deeds of Jesus or to the teaching of Jesus, although some scholars want to find both (e.g., Banks, *JBL* 93 [1974] 231; Sand, *Gesetz*, 186; cf. Moo, *JSNT* 20 [1984] 25; Carson). The first option is unsatisfactory because the word πληροῦν, "to fulfill," is never used in Matthew to describe obedience to the law, it misses the nuance of fulfillment that is associated with the word in Matthew, and it is not at all appropriate to the context, vv

21–48, which refer to Jesus' teaching. The second option is again unrelated to the context, where the deeds of Jesus are not in view, and in some forms presupposes a questionable exegesis of v 18 (see below). The third option is the most appropriate, not in the sense of simply establishing the law as is, nor of supplementing it, but in the sense of bringing it to its intended meaning in connection with the messianic fulfillment (together with πληροῦν, note "the law *and* the prophets") brought by Jesus. This interpretation has the advantage of fitting the context well, of maintaining the commitment to the law reflected in v 18, and at the same time of affirming the new definition that comes with fulfillment. In Matthew's view, the teaching of Jesus by definition amounts to the true meaning of the Torah and is hence paradoxically an affirmation of Jesus' loyalty to the OT.

Since in 5:21–48 Jesus defines righteousness by expounding the true meaning of the law as opposed to wrong or shallow understandings, it is best to understand πληρῶσαι here as "fulfill" in the sense of "bring to its intended meaning"—that is, to present a definitive interpretation of the law, something now possible because of the presence of the Messiah and his kingdom. Far from destroying the law, Jesus' teachings—despite their occasionally strange sound—penetrate to the divinely intended (i.e., the teleological) meaning of the law. Because the law and the prophets pointed to him and he is their goal, he is able now to reveal their true meaning and so to bring them to "fulfillment." This view is consonant with the expectation that the Messiah would not only preserve the Torah but also bring out its meaning in a definitive manner (see Davies, *Setting*, 161–72; idem, *Torah*).

18 ἀμὴν γὰρ λέγω ὑμῖν, "Truly I say to you." As an introductory formula ("amen" is the transliteration of the Hebrew אָמֵן, ʾāmēn, meaning "verily" or "truly," i.e., something to be relied upon), these words stress the gravity of what follows. This prefatory usage of "amen" is found neither in the OT nor in the rabbinic literature, where the word occurs consistently as a response to a preceding statement. ἀμήν occurs no less that thirty-one times in Matthew, far more than in any other of the Gospels (the Fourth Gospel uses the double ἀμήν, ἀμήν, which never occurs in Matthew).

The important declaration introduced by this formula is that not a "jot or tittle" (to use the now traditional language) of the law will pass away (for a rabbinic parallel, cf. *Exod. Rab.* 1:6). This, then, is a further and more forceful statement that Jesus has not come to destroy the law (v 17). The repetition of "one" (ἕν, μία) in the chiastic formulation ἰῶτα ἓν ἢ μία κεραία, "one iota or one mark," provides extra emphasis on the absoluteness of the saying (cf. BDF §474[1]). ἰῶτα ("iota") is the smallest letter of the Greek alphabet but translates an underlying reference to the smallest Hebrew letter, the yod ('). The κεραία ("tittle," lit. "horn" or "hook") refers to minute markings of the written text, either those that distinguish similar Hebrew letters (as between ה and ח) or, more probably, the ornamental marks customarily added to certain letters. We have here thus a deliberate hyperbole—an overstatement that is designed to drive home the main point that the law be fully preserved. Jesus' words stress that the law is to be preserved not as punctiliously interpreted and observed by the Pharisees (although the language apart from the context could suggest such a perspective) but as definitively interpreted by Jesus the Messiah. That is, to follow the authoritative teaching of Jesus is to be faithful to the whole meaning of the law. Figuratively speaking, it is to uphold every "jot and tittle."

This verse contains two ἕως clauses, which indicate the law's continuing validity "until" something occurs. One clause precedes and one follows the main clause just examined. Are the two clauses synonymous in meaning? And why are there two such clauses in the same sentence?

Again there has been extensive debate concerning these questions. We may summarize the options for each ἕως clause before considering their relation. The first ἕως clause, "until heaven and earth pass away," is by far the easier of the two, although even here some disagreement exists. The most common view is that the clause refers straightforwardly to (1) the end of the present age, viz., the time of the parousia (the majority of commentators), but some advocate (2) a way of saying "never" (Allen; Klostermann; Montefiore; Strecker, *Sermon*, 55; Dupont, *Béatitudes*, 116) or (3) a rhetorical figure indicating difficulty (Banks, *JBL* 93 [1974] 234; cf. France). The second ἕως clause, "until everything is accomplished" (πάντα γένηται), has been taken to refer to the following: (1) the accomplishment of the ministry of Jesus, including his death and resurrection in fulfillment of prophecy (Jeremias, *Sermon*, 24; Davies, "Matthew 5:17, 18," 60–64 [but not Davies-Allison]; Guelich, *Sermon*, 148; Hendrickx, *Sermon*, 51; Lenski; Meier, *Law*, 63–64; Hamerton-Kelly, *BR* 17 [1972] 30; France); (2) the complete fulfilling of the commandments (Ljungman, *Gesetz*, 40–41; Strecker, *Sermon*, 56; Broer, *Freiheit*, 48; G. Barth, in Bornkamm et al., *Tradition*, 70; Grundmann; Sand, *Gesetz*, 38; Hill) or the fulfillment of all the prophecies of Scripture (Carson; Moo, *JSNT* 20 [1984] 27); and (3) the equivalent of the first ἕως clause, i.e., the end of the age, marked by the return of Christ (Allen; McNeile; Klostermann; T. W. Manson, *Sayings*, 154; and Davies-Allison, who refer to synonymous parallelism).

The two clauses may thus be taken as referring to different things or as being synonymous or nearly so. Since there is widespread agreement concerning the meaning of the first clause, the question remains regarding how to understand the second in relation to it. The trouble with taking the second clause as referring to what is accomplished by the ministry of Jesus is that this plainly contradicts the meaning of the first clause, which refers to the ongoing validity of the law until the end of the age. (Meier [*Law*, 60–61] and Hendrickx [*Sermon*, 51] admit the contradiction but argue that in the second clause Matthew deliberately corrects the traditional view reflected in the first clause. But why then, it may be asked, did he include the first clause at all?) Against the second explanation is the fact that the verb γένηται normally means "to happen" rather than "to do" and that the main clause of v 18 and the context refer to the law, i.e., the doing of the commandments, rather than to the fulfillment of prophecy. Despite the disagreement of some, the easiest solution is the third option, i.e., to take the clauses as essentially synonymous. The explanation of Matthew's addition of a tautologous clause is that the repetition emphasizes a most important point for the evangelist: the law remains in place until the consummation of the age. We must reiterate, however, that the way in which the law retains its validity for Matthew is in and through the teaching of Jesus.

The words of the first clause, ἕως ἂν παρέλθῃ ὁ οὐρανὸς καὶ ἡ γῆ, "until heaven and earth pass away," are not simply a popular way of saying "never" (contra Montefiore; Strecker, *Sermon*). They refer instead to the end of time as we know it and the beginning of eschatology proper, that is, the time of the regeneration of the created order (cf. 2 Pet 3:7, 13; Rev 21:1). In other words, the law, as interpreted by Jesus, will remain valid until the close of this age. The same point is made, though differently, in the Lukan parallel: "it is easier for heaven and earth to pass away" (Luke 16:17). With this we may compare the similar statement in 24:35: "Heaven and earth will pass away, but my words will not pass away." The words of Jesus are here elevated even above those of the law, for they endure eternally, even beyond the existence of heaven and earth.

ἕως ἂν πάντα γένηται, "until all is accomplished," the second of these clauses, is probably synonymous with the first (see discussion above) and may well have been added by the evangelist for clarification of the former clause and for emphasis of the point. It is interesting to note, in support of the synonymity of the clauses, that in Luke 21:32–33 the same clause as in Matthew, ἕως ἂν πάντα γένηται, "until all has occurred," is found just before the words ὁ οὐρανὸς καὶ ἡ γῆ παρελεύσονται, "the heaven and the earth will pass away." The Matthean clauses are equivalent in that they both point to the coming eschatological era. The law as interpreted by Jesus remains valid until all the events between the present and the full enjoyment of the eschatological era have occurred. This is fully in keeping with the Jewish and rabbinic view of Torah (see Str-B 1:245–6, and cf. Bar 4:1; 4 Ezra 9:37). But again, as we have said, this is the law as understood in the context of the fulfillment of God's purposes announced by Jesus (hence the law *and* the prophets). For Jesus is the goal of the law and prophets, the bringer of the kingdom, and hence the final interpreter of the law's meaning. The law as *he* teaches it is valid for all time, and thus in effect the law is upheld.

19   The key problem of this verse hinges on the meaning of the phrase τῶν ἐντολῶν τούτων τῶν ἐλαχίστων, "the least of these commandments." A number of scholars have concluded that the phrase refers to the teaching of Jesus as given, for example, in vv 21–48 (Banks, *JBL* 93 [1974] 239; Lohmeyer; Schweizer). But in keeping with the emphasis of the preceding verses, it is more naturally taken as a reference to the Mosaic law, and the equivalent of the "jot and tittle" of v 18 (the majority of commentators). What is in view is not the least in importance but the easiest to fulfill (cf. Montefiore, *Rabbinic Literature*). If the commandments of the OT are in view here, we must regard this statement as hyperbolic. As in the preceding verse, a literal understanding is not consistent with Jesus' own treatment of the law, nor indeed with the emphasis in v 20. What is being emphasized in this way are not the minutiae of the law that tended to captivate the Pharisees but simply a full faithfulness to the meaning of the law *as it is expounded by Jesus.* Thus, the phrase "the least of these commandments" refers to the final and full meaning of the law, but taken up and interpreted by Jesus, as for example in the material that begins in v 21 (cf. too the description of the "great commandment" in 22:36–40 and Jesus' ability to find the heart of the law in the double love commandment; cf. Schweizer, "Matthäus 5:17–20," 402). Thus, the language of this verse, like that of the preceding verse, is familiar to the Jews, and especially to the Pharisees (a "sentence of holy law," in which human action is followed by divine action). Now, however, it has new connotations, given the larger context in which it is uttered—the fulfillment brought by Jesus. These new connotations and a fuller picture of Jesus' intention concerning the Mosaic law will emerge as we progress through the Gospel.

The addition of the word διδάξῃ, "teach," in both halves of the verse stresses the responsibility of the disciples, not simply to observe the law as interpreted by Jesus but also to teach it faithfully. Teaching receives great emphasis in the Gospel of Matthew, and the evangelist obviously regarded it as of the highest importance for his church (cf. 28:20).

The ranking of persons as ἐλάχιστος, "least," or μέγας, "great," in the kingdom of heaven is in keeping with the Jewish and rabbinic perspective (see Str-B

1:249–50). It is directly related to the idea of rewards as a motivation for correct conduct (cf. 5:12 and 18:4). The "least" has presumably been essentially faithful to the law, though not having reached or taught the ideal championed by Jesus. Matthew could well have in mind more liberal Jewish Christians or especially gentile Christians who tolerated more laxity regarding the law than he wished to (or could) promote among his particular Jewish-Christian congregation. It is unlikely that "least" refers to those excluded from the kingdom (contra Luz, Schweizer). The assumption is that although they were guilty of the smallest commandments, they had kept the law for the most part. Their reward will be proportionately less (for rabbinic parallels, cf. Str-B 1:249–50; 4:1138–43). It is highly improbable that Paul, the "least" of the apostles, is being alluded to (contra Manson, *Sayings*, 25, 124; Betz, *Essays*, 21–22, 49). On "kingdom of heaven," see *Comment* on 3:2.

20 Again, as in v 18, the formulaic λέγω γὰρ ὑμῖν, "I say to you," stresses the great importance of the words that follow. This verse points to the essence of the matter and provides a clarification of the meaning of v 18, as well as a confirmation of our interpretation of the pericope. The δικαιοσύνη, "righteousness," in view must exceed that of the scribes and Pharisees (πλεῖον, "more," provides emphasis when added to περισσεύσῃ, "abound"; cf. BDF §246). But it is clear, especially from what follows in the sermon, that despite the language used this is not to be understood quantitatively (contra Luz)—that is, that the righteousness Jesus speaks of does not come through a greater preoccupation with the minutiae of the law that outdoes even the Pharisees! The ethical teaching presented by Jesus in the Gospel can hardly be said to do that. Instead, Jesus expects, as the antitheses to follow show, a new and higher kind of righteousness that rests upon the presence of the eschatological kingdom he brings and that finds its definition and content in his definitive and authoritative exposition of the law. Thus Jesus clearly calls his disciples to a way of righteousness, but it is a new way that rests upon the true meaning of the Torah now delivered by the Messiah. To follow that teaching is to follow the path that leads to perfection (5:48).

The larger context of the verse (e.g., the grace of the beatitudes) forbids us to conclude that entrance into the kingdom depends, in a cause-effect relationship, upon personal moral attainments. The verse is addressed, it must be remembered, to those who are the recipients of the kingdom. Entrance into the kingdom is God's gift; but to belong to the kingdom means to follow Jesus' teaching. Hence, the kingdom and the righteousness of the kingdom go together; they cannot be separated. And it follows that without this righteousness there can be no entrance into the kingdom (cf. 6:33).

δικαιοσύνη is a word of special significance in the Gospel (see *Comment* on 3:15). The γραμματεῖς, "scribes," were the professional scholars of the law who spent much of their time in detailed study of its minutiae. The Pharisees were the sect who attempted to fulfill the requirements of the Torah through an elaborate oral tradition that was meant to explicate its demands. The scribes and Pharisees are mentioned together several times in Matthew (cf. 12:38; 15:1; 23:2, 13–15). See discussion of 16:5–12.

Explanation

The ethical teaching of Jesus the Messiah, the one who in his person brings the fulfillment that indicates the kingdom's presence, is nothing other than the true meaning of the Torah. As the Messiah, Jesus has come to bring both the law and the prophets to their intended fulfillment. Jesus' view of the law as valid until the end of time means that the fulfillment he brings is in true continuity with the past, a fulfillment toward which the law and prophets pointed. God's purposes have a unity; yet a new stage in his purposes has been reached. Jesus alone and not the Pharisees can interpret the Torah finally and authoritatively. This is the explanation of the radical-sounding teaching of Jesus that cuts through the casuistry and mystification of the scribes and Pharisees. Jesus' commitment to the whole law is no less serious than theirs, but he alone is in a position to penetrate to the intended meaning of the Torah. In this connection, it is absolutely important to note that the understanding of the Torah and the attainment of the righteousness of the law are thus vitally linked with the presence of the kingdom. Where the kingdom has come, there exists the possibility of the realization of the righteousness of the law.

Thus Jesus' language about the "jot and tittle" and the "least of these commandments" is justified only in connection with his final and authoritative exposition of the meaning of the law. If he is what the law and the prophets point to, then his exposition of the law is absolutely true, and it is as though his teaching satisfies every minute aspect of the law that so worried the Pharisees. Thus, Jesus is using the language of the Pharisees in these verses. And the language is justified in one sense because Jesus as the infallible expounder of the truth of the Torah has indeed outdone the Pharisees. The depth and truth of his understanding of the law is such that it comprehends the totality—and thus in effect the minutest aspects—of the Torah.

Only an interpretation of the present pericope such as this is compatible with the bearing of Jesus toward the law throughout the Gospel. These words do not contradict what is said elsewhere in the Gospel nor do they involve a misunderstanding of the ministry of Jesus. Although they unmistakably reflect the idiom of the Pharisees, and to that extent may be misleading if taken literally, they make a valid point concerning Jesus and his attitude toward the law. The words may not have been adequately understood at their first hearing, but in retrospect, given the whole sweep of events recorded in the Gospels, their meaning would have become clear to the early Church. The evangelist is of course delighted to seize these sayings and incorporate them into this discourse on the righteousness of the kingdom. His Jewish-Christian readers needed to know—especially in the light of repeated counter-claims—that the pattern for righteousness taught by Jesus reflects the true meaning of the Torah, and thus that the Torah in its entirety is preserved in and through the ethical teaching of the Church.

The Surpassing of the Old: The Six Antitheses (5:21–48)

General Bibliography

Barton, G. A. "The Meaning of the 'Royal Law,' Matt. 5:21–48." *JBL* 37 (1918) 54–65. **Broer, I.** "Die Antithesen und der Evangelist Matthäus." *BZ* 19 (1975) 50–63. **Descamps, A.**

"Essai d'interprétation de Mt. 5, 17–48." In *SE* 1 [= TU 73] (1959) 156–73. **Dietzfelbinger, C.** *Die Antithesen der Bergpredigt.* Theologische Existenz heute 186. Munich: Kaiser, 1975. ————. "Die Antithesen der Bergpredigt im Verständnis des Matthäus." *ZNW* 70 (1979) 1–15. **Guelich, R. A.** "The Antitheses of Matthew v. 21–28: Traditional and/or Redactional?" *NTS* 22 (1976) 444–57. **Hasler, V.** "Das Herzstück der Bergpredigt: Zum Verständnis der Antithesen in Matth. 5, 21–48." *TZ* 15 (1959) 90–106. **Levison, J. R.** "A Better Righteousness: The Character and Purpose of Matthew 5.21–48." *Studia Biblica et Theologica* 12 (1982) 171–94. ————. "Responsible Initiative in Matthew 5:21–48." *ExpTim* 98 (1987) 231–34. **Lohse, E.** "Ich aber sage euch." In *Der Ruf Jesu und die Antwort der Gemeinde.* FS J. Jeremias, ed. E. Lohse et al. Göttingen: Vandenhoeck & Ruprecht, 1970. 189–203. **Percy, E.** "Die Forderungen Jesu und das Gesetz (Die Antithesen der Bergpredigt: Mt. 5, 21–48)." In *Die Botschaft Jesu.* Lund: Gleerup, 1953. 123–64. **Schmahl, G.** "Die Antithesen der Bergpredigt." *TTZ* 83 (1974) 284–97. **Strecker, G.** "Die Antithesen der Bergpredigt (Mt 5.21–48 par.)." *ZNW* 69 (1978) 36–72. **Suggs, M. J.** "The Antitheses as Redactional Products." In *Essays on the Love Commandment,* ed. R. H. Fuller. Philadelphia: Fortress, 1978. 93–107. **Wrege, H. T.** *Die Überlieferungsgeschichte der Bergpredigt.* WUNT 9. Tübingen: Mohr, 1968.

Introduction

By means of six bold antitheses representing the teaching of Jesus, Matthew now contrasts Jesus' exposition of the true and ultimate meaning of the Torah with the more common, rabbinic understandings of the commandments. In this way the incomparable ethical demands of the kingdom are set forth, and in this way examples are provided showing how the righteousness of the Pharisees is to be exceeded (v 19). The antitheses are thus at the very heart of the sermon (Hasler). Having assured his readers that the radical-sounding teaching of Jesus involves no annulment of the law but represents the goal and fulfillment of its intended meaning, the evangelist now proceeds to record some examples of this authoritative and definitive teaching. The antitheses, which consist basically of the material introduced directly by the repeated twofold formula ("you have heard . . . but I say to you"), are accompanied in each instance by illustration, application, or clarification of some kind (the first antithesis includes the most such material, the third the least). In this way the radical significance of the antithesis and the extent to which it involves a departure from common understandings of the law are dramatically clarified.

The form ἠκούσατε ὅτι ἐρρέθη, "you have heard that it was said" (vv 21, 27, 33, 38, 43; v 31 has the abbreviated form ἐρρέθη, "it was said"), prior to the setting forth of a truer interpretation of the law, was a device used by the rabbis (see Daube, *New Testament,* 55). Although by no means unparalleled in rabbinic Judaism (cf. Lohse, 196–97), the second half of the comparison used by Jesus, ἐγὼ δὲ λέγω ὑμῖν, "but I say to you" (in all six antitheses: vv 22, 28, 32, 34, 39, and 44), involves an authority that is alien to the spirit of the rabbis—especially, of course, where the new interpretation seems to stand in tension with the direct statement of Scripture. The rabbis, who never would pit their views against Scripture, preferred to support differing interpretations by appealing to other earlier representatives of the rabbinic tradition. Jesus' remarkable use of the "but I say to you" formula is to be explained by his identity as the messianic bringer of the kingdom (Hengel points out that the element "to you," which gives each antithesis the tonality of a kerygmatic statement, is lacking in the rabbinic parallels [*TRu* 52 (1987) 376]). It is the Messiah's interpretation of the Torah that is finally authoritative.

In this connection it is important to note, however, that the "antithesis," the "but I say to you" element, opposes not so much the law itself but a shallow and inadequate understanding of what the commandment entails. It should be self-evident that although Matthew stresses the supreme authority of Jesus, he does not regard the antitheses as contradicting the strong statement of 5:17–19 about Jesus' faithfulness to the law. Thus although Jesus goes against a strict interpretation of the letter of the law in the third, fourth, and fifth antitheses—i.e., in disallowing divorce, oath-taking, and just retaliation, all of which find their place in the OT (see below)—it is also the case that he at the same time penetrates to the deeper spirit of the law in a quite remarkable way. What tension may exist between Jesus' teaching and the law here, as elsewhere in the Gospel, is to be understood not as the violation of the law but as the eschatological fulfillment of the law brought about by the authoritative teaching of the Messiah. This does not mean that the contrasting, antithetical element should be minimized (as does Levison [*Studia Biblica et Theologica* 12 [1982] 176], who would translate the second element "*and* I say to you," thus avoiding the contrastive "*but* I say to you"). Despite his affirmation of the continuity between Jesus and the law, Matthew at the same time stresses the authority of Jesus as the eschatological Messiah who in bringing the law to a new, definitive interpretation can also transcend it. Messianic transcending of the law is not understood as involving a violation of it. All commentary on this material in Matthew that attempts to avoid this necessary dialectic is less than fair to the text and thus inadequate.

The first two of the antitheses involve commandments concerning murder and adultery, drawn from the ten commandments of Exod 20:1–17 (cf. Deut 5:6–21). Jesus deepens these commandments by internalizing them, i.e., by emphasizing the underlying thoughts, which themselves condemn a person. The final four antitheses involve a similarly high ethical idealism; again, they are descriptive of the righteousness of the kingdom. The fourth and fifth antitheses, concerning oaths and the *lex talionis* ("an eye for an eye," etc.), involve direct commandments in the OT; the third and sixth, those concerning divorce and hatred of enemies, involve, on the other hand, implications drawn from the Torah more than direct commands. The antitheses thus move from the weightiest items, those contained in the ten commandments, to other commandments in the Torah and finally to an apparent implication of the Torah. They constitute what amounts to a representative sampling of what we may call *kingdom ethics*. It is no accident that the final antithesis concerns the love commandment (Lev 19:18), leading even to the love of enemies, and that this is followed immediately by the reference to the perfection entailed by the presence of the kingdom that rounds out this section of the sermon. The love commandment is the quintessential aspect of the new righteousness proclaimed by Jesus (see esp. Stuhlmacher, *ZTK* 79 [1982] 287–88; cf. Hengel, *TRu* 52 [1987] 394).

Since antitheses 3, 5, and 6 contain material paralleled in Luke (see below), although not in antithesis form, Matthew is here usually thought to be dependent on Q, the material of which he reshaped in the form of the antitheses. Antitheses 1, 2, and 4, on the other hand, are usually regarded as from Matthew's special source and often as going back to Jesus more or less in their present form. Based on this hypothesis, Matthew formed antitheses 3, 5, and 6 (thus Strecker, *ZNW* 69 [1978] 47, following Bultmann) according to the pattern of antitheses 1,

2, and 4 (so too, Guelich, *Sermon*; Davies-Allison; and Luz). There are, of course, exceptions to this analysis, ranging on the one hand from that of Wrege (*Überlieferungsgeschichte*, 57–94) and Jeremias (*Theology* 1:251–53), who argue that Matthew inherited all six antitheses from the tradition, to that of Suggs ("Antitheses") and Broer (*BZ* 19 [1975] 56, 62–3; cf. Gundry), who contend that Matthew is responsible for the formulation of all six antitheses in keeping with his intention of stressing the authority of Jesus. It is, of course, not at all impossible that the evangelist modeled some of the material at his disposal into the shape of antitheses according to the pattern of those he received from the tradition. Such conclusions are, however, necessarily speculative. It seems far less likely that Matthew himself is responsible altogether for the creation of the form of the antitheses. In all likelihood the form goes back to Jesus. Given Matthew's conservative stance toward the tradition, it may well be that all the antitheses in some form may be traced back to Jesus.

On Murder (5:21–26)

Bibliography

Caird, G. B. "Expounding the Parables: I. The Defendant (Matthew 5.25f.; Luke 12.58f.)." *ExpTim* 77 (1965) 36–39. **Dalman, G.** *Jesus-Jeshua: Studies in the Gospels.* New York: Ktav, 1971. **Guelich, R. A.** "Matthew 5, 22: Its Meaning and Integrity." *ZNW* 64 (1973) 39–52. **Köhler, K.** "Zu Mt 5, 22." *ZNW* 19 (1920) 91–95. **Moule, C. F. D.** "'The Angry Word': Mt 5, 21f." *ExpTim* 81 (1969) 10–13. **Trilling, W.** "Die neue und wahre 'Gerechtigkeit' (Mt 5, 20–22)." In *Christusverkündigung in den synoptischen Evangelien.* Munich: Kösel, 1969. 86–107.

Translation

[21] *"You have heard that it was said to those of early times: You shall not murder, and whoever murders shall be guilty in the judgment.* [22] *But I say to you that everyone who is filled with wrath against his brother or sister*[a,b] *shall be guilty in the judgment. And whoever says to his brother or sister, 'Raka,'*[c] *shall be liable to the sanhedrin. And whoever says,*[d] *'Fool,' shall be liable to fiery Gehenna.* [23] *If, therefore, you bear your gift to the altar, and then remember that your brother or sister has something against you,* [24] *leave your gift there before the altar and go and first be reconciled to that person, and then go and offer your gift.* [25] *Be well disposed to your adversary, and do so quickly, while you are still with that one on the road, lest your adversary hand you over to the judge, and the judge*[e] *to the servant,*[f] *and you be thrown into prison.* [26] *I say to you, emphatically, you will never get out from there, until you have paid the last quarter-penny."*

Notes

[a] "Or sister" added to translation.

[b] Many MSS (א[2] D L W Θ *f*[1,13] TR it sy co) add εἰκῇ, "without reason," here, in an obvious attempt to soften the teaching of the passage. P[67] א* B lack the word.

Form/Structure/Setting

A. The first of the antitheses addresses a basic commandment, the meaning of which would hardly have seemed debatable. This antithesis, like the one that follows, involves one of the ten commandments of Exod 20:1–17 (cf. Deut 5:6–21). The horizon of what is addressed by the commandment not to murder is broadened to include even the harboring of anger against another. Here, as elsewhere in the antitheses, Jesus' interpretation deepens the commandment, making the demand greater than it was usually understood to be.

B. The antithesis proper (vv 21–22) is without parallel in the Gospels and is thus from Matthew's own source rather than from Mark or Q. The first illustration (vv 23–24) finds a parallel, more in content than in wording, in Mark 11:25, where the context concerns praying and receiving one's requests (cf. Matt 21:22). According to Mark, Jesus speaks of the necessity of forgiving "if you have anything against someone" in order to receive the forgiveness of the Father in heaven (this point is also made in Matt 6:14). Obviously, for Jesus reconciliation and forgiveness are closely related. Moreover, the motif of the forgiveness of trespasses is related also to the second illustration in our pericope (vv 25–26), which finds a close parallel in Luke 12:58–59. The latter passage refers to being ἐν τῇ ὁδῷ, "on the road," μετὰ τοῦ ἀντιδίκου σου, "with your adversary," and to ὁ κριτής, "the judge," and to being cast into "prison" (εἰς φυλακήν). But there are also some intriguing differences: Luke refers to a "magistrate" (ἄρχων), using the verb "to be reconciled" (ἀπηλλάχθαι; cf. the related διαλλάγηθι of Matt 5:24) and a different word for "servant" (πράκτωρ, or "official"). The final saying of the Lukan passage agrees nearly verbatim with v 26 except for the lack of the ἀμήν formula and the use of λεπτόν, a small copper coin, worth even less than Matthew's κοδράντης. We have here what must be described as Q material, but perhaps stemming from different Greek translations or different oral traditions. The content of this illustration (vv 25–26), however, makes much better sense in the Lukan context, which seems to concern eschatological judgment, than Matthew's, which concerns reconciliation and forgiveness.

Matthew thus appears to have composed the present pericope using the various materials available to him: his own, probably oral, source (cf. the symmetrical form) for vv 21–22; traditional material bearing some relationship to Mark 11:25, albeit somewhat remote, for vv 23–24; and some version of Q for vv 25–26. In the last instance, Matthew uses material that may well have had its primary application in a context concerning judgment but, with its reconciliation theme, has some relevance to the first antithesis. Jeremias correctly points out that the outlook, language, and parallelism are all distinctly Palestinian (*TDNT* 6:976).

C. The present pericope consists of three parts: (1) the antithesis proper (vv 21–22), which, however, also includes some clarifying material (v 22b, c); (2) a specific illustration involving ὁ ἀδελφός σου, "your brother" (vv 23–24); and (3) a specific illustration involving τῷ ἀντιδίκῳ σου, "your adversary" (vv 25–26). The illustrations clarify the radical nature of the antithesis and the extent to which it involves a departure from the common understanding of the law. The two illustrations involve a shift from the second person plural (in the antithesis proper) to the second person singular (through to the end of v 26). The last section gives the appearance of having been adapted for the present application. Thus, the saying with which the pericope ends (v 26), introduced moreover by the formula of emphasis ("I say to you"), has little to do with the point of the original antithesis. The last illustration including the final warning is, as we have seen, found in Luke 12:58–59 in an entirely different context involving eschatological judgment— a context in which the illustration is much more comfortable (see *Comment* below). The first section of the pericope is carefully structured around the fourfold ἔνοχος ἔσται, "he is liable (or subject) to." The last two occurrences (v 22b, c) are particularly symmetrical in structure, involving the parallel "Raka" and "Fool," on the one hand, and "sanhedrin" and "the Gehenna of fire," on the other.

Comment

21 τοῖς ἀρχαίοις, "to those of early times," which occurs also in the fourth antithesis (v 33), is probably meant to refer to the original recipients of the Mosaic law (thus the majority of commentators). Although this phrase does not occur with the other four antitheses, it is probably presupposed, as the consistent use of ἐρρέθη, "it was said" (*sc.* "God said," divine passive), confirms. This appropriately includes not only those commandments that are drawn verbatim from the OT (such as here and in vv 27, 38) but also those that involve interpretation or inference going beyond the letter of the OT, particularly the sixth antithesis (vv 43–47). This interpretation and inferential understanding of the law is thus also regarded as ancient tradition. It is not differentiated from the actual content of the law itself. The formulaic ἠκούσατε, "you have heard," occurs in five of the six antitheses; it is lacking (but assumed) only in the third (v 31). The repeated formula means "you have received as tradition" (cf. Str-B 1:253). The commandment οὐ φονεύσεις, "you shall not murder," is drawn verbatim (LXX) from the catalogue of ten commandments as found in both Exodus (20:15) and Deuteronomy (5:18). Matthew again cites it in 19:18. The words that follow, however, are not a part of the original commandment but reflect other statements in the Mosaic law (see below).

ἔνοχος ἔσται τῇ κρίσει, "shall be liable to the judgment," occurs identically in v 22. But two further occurrences of ἔνοχος ἔσται ("shall be liable to") in v 22 are linked with "the sanhedrin" and "the Gehenna of fire." It is difficult to solve the exegetical puzzle regarding whether the four references are essentially synonymous or the last two are meant to involve higher penalties (as Str-B argue, 1:276), and whether we move through three different courts, the local, the sanhedrin, and the divine. Jeremias, however, is probably correct when he argues that the passage simply contains "three expressions for the death penalty in a kind of crescendo" (*TDNT* 6:975). This, however, is a rhetorical device and the differences have no literal significance (just as the offense of anger is essentially the same in the three instances). Here in both occurrences $\tau\hat{\eta}$ $\kappa\rho\acute{\iota}\sigma\epsilon\iota$ may mean initially the judgment of the religious authorities, in this case of the local sanhedrins (composed of twenty-three members; cf. *m. Sanh.* 1:4) found in larger cities, which handled murder cases. The penalty for murder was death (cf. Lev 24:17; Exod 21:12; Num 35:16–17). The $\sigma\upsilon\nu\acute{\epsilon}\delta\rho\iota\upsilon$, "sanhedrin" (cf. v 22), was the highest court in Jerusalem (composed of seventy-one members). The eschatological reference to "the Gehenna of fire" in the fourth sentence (v 22) is undoubtedly climactic. And since the judgment of the local and main sanhedrins would have been anticipations of the final judgment, we are probably justified in hearing an echo of this in the first two references to "judgment." This is especially true if, as we have argued, v 22b, c are illustrative of 22a. The point in all four cases is that anger, as the root of murder, deserves in principle the same penalty. The use of this language of the courts points by deliberate irony to the impossibility of understanding this material casuistically (thus Guelich, *Sermon*, following Zahn).

22   The first part of this verse, introduced by the formula $\dot{\epsilon}\gamma\dot{\omega}$ $\delta\dot{\epsilon}$ $\lambda\dot{\epsilon}\gamma\omega$ $\dot{\upsilon}\mu\hat{\iota}\nu$, "but I [emphatic by initial position] say to you [plural]," is the key statement of the pericope. The formula points to the unparalleled authority of Jesus. According to Jesus, anger alone—what may perhaps be described as murdering your brother in your heart (cf. 1 John 3:15)—is a violation of God's law and puts a person in danger of judgment. The radical character of Jesus' teaching apparently allows for no exception (despite the insertion of $\epsilon\iota\kappa\hat{\eta}$, "without reason," in some MSS [see *Note* b]). (On the meaning of the three $\check{\epsilon}\nu o\chi o\varsigma$ $\check{\epsilon}\sigma\tau\alpha\iota$ ["shall be liable to"] clauses, see the discussion of the preceding verse.) For Jesus the inner attitude is thus of supreme importance. (Cf. the teaching of Jesus in 15:19, where a catalogue of sins is said to have its beginning "from the heart.") And even as that inner attitude expresses itself in apparently trivial acts of unkindness, such as referring to one's brother as a "Fool," one shows that, according to God's standard of righteousness, one has begun down the wrong path and is already worthy of condemnation (cf. 12:34, where "the mouth speaks out of the abundance of the heart"). The reference to "brother" here may seem to limit this command to the community of faith. But since in the last antithesis Jesus breaks through such group loyalty by teaching love, even of one's enemies (v 44), this point should not be pressed here (cf. v 16). The ethical injunction against anger is directed to those who receive the kingdom—but in their relations with all other human beings. The question concerning the illustrative material of v 22b, c is whether the strictly parallel forms are synonymous. Are $\dot{\rho}\alpha\kappa\acute{\alpha}$, "Raka," and $\mu\omega\rho\acute{\epsilon}$, "Fool," equivalents?

$\dot{\rho}\alpha\kappa\acute{\alpha}$, "Raka," an Aramaic word (רֵיקָא, *rêqā'*) transliterated directly into Greek letters, occurs frequently as an insult in the rabbinic literature (see Str-B 1:278–89). According to Jeremias (*TDNT* 6:974), the retention of $\dot{\rho}\alpha\kappa\acute{\alpha}$ in a Greek document points to a Syrian provenance for the Gospel, since only there were Greeks found in an oriental milieu where the word would be understandable. The word means something like "blockhead" or "idiot," but in that culture conveying a much more objectionable insult than in modern Western society. Name calling was a much more serious affair in biblical times, because of the importance attached to names (cf. Elisha, 2 Kgs 2:23–24; for the rabbinic period, cf. *b. Qidd.* 28a), than in our day when names, like labels, can be readily exchanged (see H. Bietenhard, *TDNT* 5:253–54). On the high importance of shaming another publicly, see *m. 'Abot* 3:12.

$\mu\omega\rho\acute{\epsilon}$, "Fool," could also be a transliteration of the Aramaic word מורא, *môrā'*, or the Hebrew word מורה, *môreh*, "rebel" (or even "heretic"). On the other hand,

and more probably, it could derive from the Greek μωρός (meaning "foolishness"), and thus mean simply "Fool." This too in that culture was much more insulting than it seems to our ears (cf. Pss 14:1; 53:1; Proverbs, *passim*). The words ῥακά and μωρέ are thus roughly equivalent, with the latter involving no escalation of offense (contra Lambrecht, *Sermon*; cf. Köhler, who argued the second was the Greek translation of the former). On the gravity of insulting another person, cf. *2 Enoch* 44:2–3.

τὴν γέενναν τοῦ πυρός, "the Gehenna of fire." Matthew refers to Gehenna seven times, more than twice as often as any other evangelist (cf. in the context, vv 29, 30). The expression "Gehenna of fire" is used only by Matthew and occurs once again in 18:9. The name Gehenna is from the Aramaic words גֵּי הִנֹּם, *gê hinnām*, for the "valley of Hinnom" (cf. Josh 15:8; 18:16), a despised place to the southwest of Jerusalem where at one time human sacrifices were offered to the god Molech (cf. 2 Kgs 23:10; Jer 7:31) and where in later times the city's refuse was burned. The constant burning there made the valley a particularly suitable metaphor for eternal punishment (cf. 4 Ezra 7:36; *Sib. Or.* 1.103; 2.292; Str-B 4.2:1029–1118).

23–24 In this section and to the end of the pericope, the pronouns shift to the second person singular. This may be accounted for by the illustrative nature of the material and its character as personal application. This first illustration involves the offering (the verb προσφέρειν is regularly so used) of a gift (δῶρον), a sacrifice at the altar (θυσιαστήριον), i.e., in the temple. So important is the issue of anger toward a member of the community and so urgent is the need for reconciliation before one's offering to God can be acceptable that one is to interrupt the act, "leave the gift there before the altar," and immediately seek reconciliation. (For parallel instances of the grave seriousness attached to anger, see *2 Enoch* 44:2–3 and 1QS 6:24–7:14.) In our context, the statement "your brother has something against you" must be taken to imply some degree of anger in the person offering the sacrifice. (We would expect "you have something against your brother," as in Mark 11:25.) Perhaps we are to understand a reciprocal resentment. The key here is the imperative διαλλάγηθι, "be reconciled." This is the only occurrence of the verb διαλλάσσεσθαι in the NT. When reconciliation has been made, "then" (τότε) the gift may be offered (and, the implication is, then God will accept it; cf. Mark 11:25). In Judaism, reconciliation was required before an acceptable sacrifice (Sir 34:23; *m. Yoma* 8:9; cf. Str-B 1:287–88). The theme of reconciliation, under somewhat different circumstances, again appears in vv 25–26. A similar point, but in starker clarity, is made in 6:12, 14–15.

25–26 The second illustration of the main statement in v 22a is added here apparently because of the reconciliation theme (cf. the preceding illustration), although the utilitarian conclusion (v 26) seems to complicate rather than clarify the main point of the pericope. The second person singular continues, as in the preceding two verses, in contrast to the plural of v 22. εὐνοεῖν, which occurs only here in the NT, means to "make friends with." The ἀντίδικος, "adversary," is some kind of opponent (to whom money is owed; cf. v 26) who is apparently in a position to take legal action, but no further specific information is given. ἐν τῇ ὁδῷ, "on the road," is also not specific but makes obvious the emphasis on the urgency of a reconciliation. Without the latter, the legal process is set in motion, wherein the judge passes sentence and hands the person over to the officer, who in turn casts the person into prison (the background here seems to be non-Jewish since the Jews did not imprison for debt). The point of v 20, emphasized with the ἀμήν

λέγω σοι, "I say to you," formula, is that full punishment will be exacted once the
sentence has been passed. κοδράντην, "quarter-penny," is from a Latin word
(*quadrans*), found also in the rabbinic literature. From Mark 12:42 we know that
one κοδράντης equals two λεπτά (thus the Lukan parallel with its single λεπτόν
refers to an eighth of a penny; see Luke 12:59). Probably the illustration of these
two verses provides some practical wisdom that the evangelist deems appropriate
to his argument against anger. It is a mistake to allegorize the details and to identify the adversary or the judge with God. At the same time, however, since God's
judgment is in view in vv 21–22, it is impossible to avoid at least the suggestion of
the same in the present passage (cf. 18:34–35; cf. too the context of the passage
in Luke 12:57–59). In this illustration, as in the preceding one, the need to overcome the effects of anger requires a certain urgency.

Explanation

In his exegesis of the truest meaning of the Mosaic commandment—and presentation of the level of righteousness required by the kingdom—Jesus goes far
beyond the letter of the text (where some may have been inclined to stop). By his
explication of "thou shalt not murder," Jesus penetrates to the spirit of the commandment. Since the spring of a person's conduct is the heart, or inner person, the
transforming power of the kingdom must be especially experienced there. Anger
and insults spoken from anger are evil and corrupting, and they therefore call
forth God's judgment, just as the act of murder itself does. Accordingly, the worship and service of God cannot be performed as long as anger infects the soul.
Thus, the recipient of the grace of the kingdom is one who initiates and seeks
reconciliation, both with members of the community of faith and with adversaries (cf. 5:9). The underlying and key message of these astonishingly authoritative
words is that a person is held accountable for his or her angry thoughts, not merely
for external acts of violence against others. Here, as in the beatitudes, the truly
revolutionary character of the kingdom and its ethics makes itself felt.

It is a mistake to treat these stipulations casuistically and thus to fall into a new
and harsh nomism. While they are meant to be taken seriously, calling attention to
the relation between the root of a tree and its fruit (to use other Matthean metaphors),
they, like the antitheses that follow, function more as exhortations to a life that perfectly reflects the reality of the kingdom. This teaching is not necessarily incompatible
with the display of righteous anger by Jesus in Mark 3:5 (cf. Eph 4:26) or his calling
the Pharisees "Fools" in 23:17 (where Matthew uses the same word as here).

On Adultery   (5:27–30)

Bibliography

Basser, H. W. "The Meaning of 'Shtuth,' Gen. R. 11 in Reference to Matthew 5.29–30 and
18.8–9." *NTS* 31 (1985) 148–51. **Haacker, K.** "Der Rechtssatz Jesu zum Thema Ehebruch
(Mt 5,28)." *BZ* n.s. 21 (1977) 113–16. **Plessis, P. J. du.** "The Ethics of Marriage according

to Matt 5:27–32." *Neot* 1 (1967) 16–27. **Stauffer, E.** *Die Botschaft Jesu damals und heute.* Bern: Francke, 1959. 82–85.

Translation

[27] *"You have heard that it was said,[a] 'You shall not commit adultery.'* [28] *But I say to you that everyone who looks at a woman with the purpose of lusting after her[b] has in his heart already committed adultery with her.* [29] *But if your right eye causes you to stumble, pluck it out and cast it from you. For it is better for you that one of your members perish than that your whole body be thrown[c] into Gehenna.* [30] *And if your right hand causes you to stumble, cut it off and cast it from you. For it is better for you that one of your members perish than that your whole body depart[d] into Gehenna."[e]*

Notes

[a] Many MSS (L Δ Θ *f*[13] 33 lat sy[c,h**]) insert τοῖς ἀρχαίοις, "to those of old," according to the pattern of vv 21 and 33.

[b] p[67] and ℵ* omit αὐτήν, "(after) her."

[c] D it sy[s,c] (mae) bo have ἀπέλθῃ, "depart," for βληθῇ, "be cast," probably by the influence of the parallel in Mark 9:43. Cf. v 30. See next note.

[d] The majority of MSS ([L] W Θ *f*[13] TR vg[ms] sy[p,h] sa) have βληθῇ, "be thrown," for ἀπέλθῃ, "depart."

[e] D vg[ms] sy[s] bo[ms] omit v 30 in its entirety, perhaps by homoioteleuton with v 29.

Form/Structure/Setting

A. The second antithesis quotes again one of the ten commandments. In both lists (Exod 20:13; Deut 5:17) this commandment concerning adultery precedes that concerning murder. The fact that the evangelist (or Jesus) has reversed the order indicates—as do the remaining antitheses —that the present section of the sermon is no attempt to present a systematic or thorough exegesis of the commandments. What we encounter instead is a sampling of the way in which Jesus' interpretation cuts through to the inner meaning of the law.

B. Almost the same material as in vv 29–30 is found in 18:8–9 (cf. Mark 9:43–48). The first elements ("If your . . . causes you to stumble") are in verbatim agreement except that in 18:8–9, where the hand is referred to first, the word δεξιός ("right") is omitted in both instances, and the word πούς ("foot") is added to the reference to the hand. Although the second elements ("it is well for you") of 18:8 and 18:9 are worded a little differently, the thought is practically identical: "it is well for you to enter into life with one eye [maimed or lame] than to have two eyes [two hands or two feet] and to be cast into the Gehenna of fire [eternal fire]." The parallelism of the passage in 18:8–9 is thus nearly as strong as in the present pericope. The context there, as in the Markan parallel (Mark 9:42–48), concerns not sexual morality but the causing to stumble of "one of the little ones who believe in me." This leads in turn to the more general comments on various possible stumbling blocks to oneself ("you").

It seems probable that vv 29–30 of the present pericope and the parallel in 18:8–9 (and Mark 9:42–48) represent variant transmissions of the same original teaching of Jesus. It is not improbable that Jesus spoke the same or nearly the same words on different occasions in different contexts. But here the evangelist seems to have applied and perhaps adapted this material (which contains no reference to sexual sins and is easily separable from the preceding verses) to the discussion concerning adultery. The impressive structure suggests the strong possibility that the material was handed on orally in this form and presented itself in this way to the evangelist. Another oral form of the same material is probably reflected in 18:8–9, which, however, is borrowed directly from Mark 9:43–48.

C. The structure of this antithesis is similar to the preceding one. Again we have (1) at the beginning (vv 27–28) the basic contrast between the prohibition of the external deed and Jesus' emphasis on the thoughts of the inner person ("in his heart," v 28). This is followed by (2) material that illustrates the gravity of the offending thoughts. Vv 29 and 30 are exactly parallel in structure and nearly verbatim (especially in the second element of each verse ["For it is better . . ."]; only one word differs at the end of v 30).

Comment

27–28 The formulaic introduction (see above) is nearly identical with its form in v 21, lacking only the τοῖς ἀρχαίοις, "to the ancients." The commandment οὐ μοιχεύσεις, "you shall not commit adultery," is in verbatim agreement with its occurrence in Exod 20:14 and Deut 5:18. (It is found again in Matt 19:18.) With no further addition (such as reference to the penalty of death; Deut 22:22; Lev 20:10), Jesus gives his interpretation of the commandment in light of the perfection of the kingdom. On the "but I say to you" formula, see above. The sin of adultery, like other sins, finds its root in a person's inner thoughts. Thus, to look deliberately at a woman lustfully, i.e., desiring or imagining a sexual relationship with her, is to commit adultery in one's heart and thus to violate the deepest intention of the law as now revealed by Jesus. The idea of sinning in the heart through one's desires (for a rabbinic parallel, cf. *b. Yoma* 29a; *b. Hal.* 1) is already contained in the ten commandments, where one is forbidden to covet, among other things, the wife of a neighbor (Exod 20:17; Deut 5:21). Although in the OT and Jewish contexts lusting after the wife of another man was forbidden, in the present passage γυναῖκα is probably to be understood more broadly to mean any "woman" and not simply the wife of another (*pace* Luz; Guelich, *Sermon*; if a more restrictive understanding were in view, one might expect the noun to be modified, e.g., τοῦ πλησίου [σου], "your neighbor's"). The argument that in the clause πρὸς τὸ ἐπιθυμῆσαι αὐτήν, "with the purpose of lusting after her," αὐτήν, "her," is the subject rather than the object of the infinitive, thus "with the purpose of getting her to lust" (Haacker), goes against both Matthean usage and the normal sense of the man lusting after the woman. The importance of the eyes in lusting is vividly caught in the phrase of 2 Pet 2:14: "eyes full of adultery" (cf. 1 John 2:16; Sir 9:8; for rabbinic statements paralleling v 28, cf. Str-B 1:298–301). The key verb μοιχεύειν, "commit adultery," is found again in the next antithesis, v 32 (and in 19:9), in connection with the divorcing of one's wife.

29–30 The use of ὁ βλέπων ("the one who looks") in the preceding verse probably suggested to the evangelist the appropriateness of adding here the saying of Jesus concerning the eye as a cause of stumbling. And because in the tradition that saying was linked with one concerning the hand, exactly parallel in structure, it too was included by the evangelist. The specification of the "right [δεξιός]" eye" and "right hand" is probably meant to indicate that which is preferred or more skilled and, therefore, the most valuable (the left eye can lust as well as the right can). The right eye is to be plucked out ($\check{\epsilon}\xi\epsilon\lambda\epsilon$), the right hand to be cut off ($\check{\epsilon}\kappa\kappa o\psi o\nu$), if they are the cause of stumbling. The reason given in both cases is the same (and verbatim): it is better for one member of the body to perish than for the whole to suffer damnation. For "Gehenna," see *Comment* on v 22. The slight alteration of word order and the use of the verb $\dot{\alpha}\pi\acute{\epsilon}\lambda\theta\eta$, "depart to," for $\beta\lambda\eta\theta\hat{\eta}$, "be cast," in the second sentence are only stylistic variations and are thus not significant. The point of these admonitions is clear without pressing for a literal understanding of the words. Because of the importance of obeying God's standard of righteousness, radical action should be taken to avoid the cause of the temptation. The discipleship of the kingdom sometimes requires drastic measures. The literal plucking out of an eye or cutting off of a hand, however, will not at all necessarily rid one of the problem. The culprit lies elsewhere, in the heart, the inner person. This is the language of hyperbole (contra Gundry) used to make a significant point.

Explanation

Jesus again deepens the OT commandment by interpreting it to include what occurs "in the heart," prior to and as the foundation of the external act. Thus, again, he shifts the attention from the external act to the inner thought. There, in the inner person, lie the real problem and the initial guilt. To lust after someone sexually is to nurture a burning desire for that person in one's heart. Such lust has a consuming effect. Where lust exists, the discipleship of the kingdom requires dramatic and determined action to rid oneself of the cause. Without pressing the literal meaning of the words in vv 29–30, we may conclude that it is better to suffer minor losses willingly than to suffer the ultimate loss unwillingly. The discipleship of the kingdom is a serious matter that requires true, i.e., unreserved, absolute, commitment. Disciples are called to a standard of conduct that includes even the realm of their thinking.

On Divorce   (5:31–32)

Bibliography

Baltensweiler, H. *Die Ehe im Neuen Testament.* Zürich: Zwingli, 1967. ————. "Die Ehebruchsklauseln bei Matthäus." *TZ* 15 (1959) 340–56. **Bauer, J. B.** "Bemerkungen zu den matthäischen Unzuchtklauseln (Mt 5,32; 19,9)." In *Begegnung mit dem Wort.* FS H. Zimmermann, ed. J. Zmijewski et al. BBB 53. Bonn: Hanstein, 1980. 23–33. **Bockmuehl, M.** "Matthew 5.32; 19.9 in the Light of Pre-Rabbinic Halakhah." *NTS* 35 (1989) 291–95. **Catchpole, D. R.** "The Synoptic Divorce Material as a Traditio-Historical Problem." *BJRL* 57 (1974) 92–127. **Down, M. J.** "The Sayings of Jesus about Marriage and Divorce." *ExpTim* 95 (1984) 332–34. **Dupont, J.** *Mariage et divorce dans l'Évangile.* Bruges: Desclée de Brouwer, 1959. **Fitzmyer, J.** "The Matthean Divorce-Texts and Some New Palestinian Evidence." In

To Advance the Gospel. New York: Crossroad, 1981. 79–111. **Geldard, M.** "Jesus' Teaching on Divorce: Thoughts on the Meaning of *porneia* in Mt 5:32 and 19:9." *Churchman* 92 (1978) 134–43. **Greeven, H.** "Ehe nach dem Neuen Testament." *NTS* 15 (1968–69) 365–88. **Harrington, W.** "Jesus' Attitude towards Divorce." *ITQ* 37 (1970) 199–209. **Holzmeister, U.** "Die Streitfrage über die Ehescheidungstexte bei Mt 5,32; 19,19." *Bib* 26 (1945) 133–46. **Isaksson, A.** *Marriage and Ministry in the New Temple.* ASNU. Lund: Gleerup, 1965. **Jensen, J.** "Does *porneia* Mean Fornication? A Critique of Bruce Malina." *NovT* 20 (1978) 161–84. **Kilgallen, J. J.** "To What Are the Matthean Exception Texts (5.32 and 19.9) an Exception?" *Bib* 61 (1980) 102–5. **Lövestam, E.** "Divorce and Remarriage in the New Testament." *The Jewish Law Annual* 11 (1981) 47–65. **Lohfink, G.** "Jesus und die Ehescheidung: Zur Gattung und Sprachintention von Mt 5,32." In *Biblische Randbemerkungen.* FS R. Schnackenburg, ed. H. Merklein et al. 2nd ed. Würzburg: Echter, 1974. 207–17. **Malina, B.** "Does *Porneia* Mean Fornication?" *NovT* 14 (1972) 10–17. **Moingt, J.** "Le divorce 'pour motif d'impudicité' (Mt 5,32; 19,9)." *RSR* 56 (1968) 337–84. **Mueller, J. R.** "The Temple Scroll and the Gospel Divorce Texts." *RevQ* 10 (1980) 247–56. **O'Rourke, J. J.** "A Note on an Exception." *HeyJ* 5 (1964) 299–302. **Reicke, B.** "Ehe, Eherecht, Ehescheidung: IV. Neues Testament." *TRE* 9:318–25. **Sabourin, L.** "The Divorce Clauses (Mt 5:32; 19:9)." *BTB* 2 (1972) 80–86. **Sigal, P.** *The Halakah of Jesus of Nazareth according to the Gospel of Matthew.* Lanham, MD: University Press of America, 1986. 83–118. **Smith, D. T.** "The Matthean Exception Clauses in the Light of Matthew's Theology and Community." *Studia Biblica et Theologica* 17 (1989) 55–82. **Stein, R. H.** "Is It Harmful for a Man to Divorce His Wife?" *JETS* 22 (1979) 115–21. **Stock, A.** "Matthean Divorce Texts." *BTB* 8 (1978) 24–33. **Vawter, B.** "Divorce and the New Testament." *CBQ* 39 (1977) 528–48. ———. "The Divorce Clauses in Mt 5.32 and 19.9." *CBQ* 16 (1954) 155–67. **Wenham, G. J.** "Matthew and Divorce: An Old Crux Revisited." *JSNT* 22 (1984) 98–100. ———. "May Divorced Christians Remarry?" *Churchman* 95 (1981) 150–61. **Witherington, B.** "Matt. 5.32 and 19.9—Exception or Exceptional Situation?" *NTS* 31 (1985) 571–76.

Translation

[31] *"And it was said, 'Whoever divorces his wife must give her a certificate of divorce.'* [32] *But I say to you that everyone who divorces his wife, except on the grounds of sexual infidelity,*[a] *causes her to commit adultery. And whoever marries a divorced woman commits adultery."*[b]

Notes

[a] The meaning of the word πορνεία (*porneia*), translated here "sexual infidelity," is difficult. See *Comment.*

[b] D it[a,b,d,k] omits καὶ ὃς ἐὰν ἀπολελυμένην γαμήσῃ, μοιχᾶται, "and whoever marries a divorced woman commits adultery," perhaps regarding the words as superfluous in light of the preceding sentence (*TCGNT,* 14). B and perhaps sa have ὁ . . . γαμήσας for ὃς ἐὰν . . . γαμήσῃ, which does not affect the meaning but brings about syntactical parallelism with the participle in the first clause of the verse.

Form/Structure/Setting

A. This antithesis is related to the preceding antithesis by its reference to adultery (in the use of the verb μοιχεύειν). It may indeed have suggested itself to the evangelist if, as is likely, he is responsible for the coupling, because of the relationship between divorce and adultery. This antithesis, however, is unlike the first two since it involves acts rather than thoughts—as indeed do all the remaining antitheses.

B. This antithesis must be read together with 19:3–12 (cf. Mark 10:2–12), where the Pharisees precipitate a discussion of the specific question of divorce and Moses' allowance of it. The present pericope indeed contains nothing that is not found in 19:3–12. Moreover, 19:7 corresponds to v 31, and v 32 is in nearly verbatim agreement with 19:9. This suggests the likelihood that the evangelist has constructed the present antithesis using the material he borrowed from Mark 10:2–12 and used in chap. 19. The similarity between Luke 16:18 and v 32 is not sufficient to argue that the latter should be regarded as derived from Q. (More likely Luke 16:18 is derived from Mark 10:11.)

C. The structure of the present passage is somewhat simpler than that of the preceding antitheses, because it concerns action rather than inner thoughts, and thus no practical illustration or application is added as in the preceding antitheses. This antithesis, moreover, has the shortest of opening formulas: only ἐρρέθη δέ ("it was spoken") remains of the full formula found in v 21, although the full formula is also to be understood here. The present antithesis lacks the strong parallelism in form that characterizes the earlier antitheses. This adds to the conclusion that, rather than deriving this antithesis from oral tradition as in the earlier antitheses, the evangelist has constructed the antithesis from the material he uses in 19:7 and 9.

D. It seems probable that in the antithesis before us Matthew has added the exception clause (παρεκτὸς λόγου πορνείας, "except for sexual infidelity") of v 32 (and that of 19:9), unless it had already been added in the tradition he depends upon (as Luz argues). There are three reasons that it is extremely unlikely that the exception clauses go back to Jesus himself: (1) elsewhere, including in Matthew, the ethics of the kingdom are set forth in absolute terms (cf. the absolute prohibition of divorce in the parallel passage, Mark 10:11; Luke 16:18; cf. 1 Cor 7:11); (2) the clause is an accommodation to the common understanding of Deut 24:1, which probably reflects the practice of Matthew's community; and (3) the addition of the exception clause nullifies the antithesis and in the case of the parallel in 19:3–12 weakens the logic of the passage, where Jesus appears no different from the Pharisees of the Shammaite persuasion.

Comment

31–32 In 19:6, when Jesus makes a strong statement against divorce, the Pharisees refer to the commandment of Moses in Deut 24:1 about giving the wife who is being divorced a "writ" thereto (ἀποστάσιον, a technical term referring to a legal document of certification, in this case stipulating a relinquishing of rights) before sending her out of the house (divorce was exclusively the husband's prerogative; contrast Mark 10:23). This is the Mosaic commandment referred to here under the words "it was said." It is clear that Deut 24:1 allows divorce; Jesus addresses that problem in 19:8. Here, in his antithetical interpretation of the law, he disallows divorce on the ground that it causes adultery, first on the part of the divorced woman and secondly on the part of any man who marries her. The latter idea, of a *man* committing adultery by marrying a divorced woman, seems to have been an innovation in that era. The theological premise for these views is not presented here, as it is in 19:4–6. The bald antithesis here (as in the opposition to the Pharisees in 19:3–12) is that, whereas Moses allowed divorce, Jesus disallows it (cf. too Mark 10:9; 1 Cor 7:10). For the introductory formula ἐγὼ δὲ λέγω ὑμῖν, "but I say to you," see *Comment* on v 22.

At this point, however, Matthew has added an exception clause, παρεκτὸς λόγου πορνείας ("except for a matter of *porneia*"), the equivalent of which is found also in 19:9 (μὴ ἐπὶ πορνείᾳ, "except for *porneia*"). These exception clauses are unique to Matthew. (For a statement of the claim that the clauses are the evangelist's additions, see above *Form/Structure/Setting* §D.) Some have tried to deny that the clauses in question involve any exception. Against Holzmeister's view that the clauses are inclusive is the fact that the παρεκτὸς of 5:32 cannot so be understood and that the μή of 19:9 must be altered to μηδ(ὲ) to mean "not even." The argument of Vawter in favor of the preteritive view, i.e., that the phrase means "passing over," could work for 19:9 but is much less natural for the meaning of παρεκτός in 5:32.

The meaning of the exception clauses hinges, of course, on the meaning of the word *porneia*. The word regularly refers to sexual sins, such as fornication and adultery (cf. Acts 15:20, 29), and is taken in this way in the present instance by many scholars (e.g., Allen; Schweizer; Grundmann; Gundry; Carson; Luz; Davies-Allison; Strecker, *Sermon*; France; Gnilka; Harrington; Morris). If Matthew's added reference to *porneia* here means either sexual sins before marriage or extramarital intercourse, then, as we have seen, v 32 presents no antithesis to v 31, or to Deut 24:1, which lies behind it. It amounts instead only to an affirmation of "what was said"—and is thus in effect a siding with the Pharisaic school of Shammai, which interpreted Deut 24:1 to refer only to sexual sins (cf. *m. Giṭ.* 9:10), against the school of Hillel, which understood the allowance of divorce much more broadly, indeed for the most trivial of reasons (see Str-B 1:313–15). The debate among the Pharisees concerned the meaning of the phrase עֶרְוַת דָּבָר, *ʿerwat dābār*, lit. "nakedness of a thing," i.e., "some uncleanness" (LXX, ἄσχημον πρᾶγμα, "shameful thing") in Deut 24:1. The Shammaites regarded it as referring to the discovery of sexual sins (whether occurring before marriage or after); the Hillelites stressed the earlier words of Deut 24:1, "finds no favor in his eyes" (cf. 24:3, where the second husband "hates her" [which could, however, mean sexually; cf. *TDNT* 6:591, n. 75] and gives her a writ of divorce).

A second major interpretation of *porneia* has been gaining ground in the last decade or more, especially among Roman Catholic scholars (e.g., Baltensweiler; Fitzmyer; Lambrecht; Gaechter; Mueller; Stock; Jensen; Sabourin [in his commentary, but not in his article]; Meier; so too Bonnard; Guelich, *Sermon*; Fornberg; Witherington). In this view *porneia* refers not to sexual immorality but rather to the specific problem of incestuous marriage, i.e., marriage within the forbidden degrees stipulated in Lev 18:6–18. In 1 Cor 5:1 the word may be so used, although "sexual immorality" may be the connotation (cf. Acts 15:29, where, however, the meaning is also debatable). This interpretation has made its way into the translation of the NJB: "except for the case of an illicit marriage" (so too, 19:9). In this way the passage makes good sense, and problems associated with the alternate interpretation are avoided. According to this view, Matthew's Jewish-Christian readers, apprehensive about the influx of large numbers of Gentiles into the church, would have considered it important that those who had married within the forbidden degrees of kinship, allowed by pagan law, be divorced since they had unknowingly violated the law revealed by God.

For a number of reasons, the former view is to be preferred (see esp. Lövestam; Sigal, *Halakah*, 83–118; cf. Bockmuehl). Particularly telling is the point made by Sigal that an illicit marriage would not have been recognized as a true marriage and thus would not have required a divorce. Further worth noting is the fact that the word *porneia* is not used in the LXX of Lev 17–18. Most importantly, would Matthew have inserted ethical material that had no direct relevance to his Jewish-Christian readers, and could they have read that material without thinking of its relevance to their own lives (with Deut 24:1 in mind)? What evidence, in fact, do we have that Matthew's community was specifically concerned with the lives of gentile converts to Christianity?

As for the objection that Matthew would have used μοιχεία rather than πορνεία had he been thinking of adultery, it is well known that the latter term is a broad one that can also be used to refer to adultery (cf. Sir 23:23; see F. Hauck and S. Schulz, *TDNT* 6:592).

Although Matthew's exception clause reflects such concerns, Jesus himself did not engage in the intramural debate of the Pharisees. The radical character of the righteousness of the kingdom demands a return to the standards of the Garden of Eden. The attitude of Jesus in 19:6 (cf. Mark 10:11, which lacks the exception clause) is absolute; it is indeed so stern that the disciples (who were hardly of a Hillelite persuasion on the subject) wonder who can tolerate such a high standard (19:10–11). Here is the antithesis to Deut 24:1.

The husband who divorces his wife causes her to commit adultery because in the culture of that day, unlike ours, a single woman could hardly survive on her own, except through prostitution. She was therefore bound to take another husband and so be made into an adulteress. And the man who married such a divorced woman himself committed adultery in so doing, because he has married the wife of another man. This viewpoint presupposes the permanent character of the marriage bond. For Jesus, not even divorce can change that fact.

Explanation

The Mosaic law allowed divorce, making provision for the divorced woman by the certificate of divorce. Later in the Gospel, Jesus will comment on the reason for this legislation (19:3–12). In the present passage Jesus introduces the new and shocking idea that even properly divorced people who marry a second time may be thought of as committing adultery. The OT, allowing divorce, does not regard those who remarry as committing adultery. This new and dramatic way of speaking is directly related to the absolute prohibition of divorce by Jesus. Marriage was meant to establish a permanent relationship between a man and a woman, and divorce should therefore not be considered an option for the disciples of the kingdom. As will appear in 19:3–12, the original ideal for man and woman was one of permanent marriage. The fulfillment brought by the present existence of the kingdom demands a return of the disciples to that original standard. Divorce is therefore to be shunned. The ethics of the kingdom do not balk at the idealism of such a standard (cf. 5:48).

The point of speaking of remarriage as involving "adultery" is simply to emphasize the wrongness of divorce. The conclusion is drawn by some interpreters that while divorce may be allowable for the Christian, on the basis of this passage remarriage is prohibited because it involves adultery. A divorce without the possibility of remarriage is, however, in the context of this discussion really only a separation and not a divorce. Moses allowed divorce *and* remarriage—it must be noted, without designating the remarried as adulterers—because of the hardness of the hearts of the people. If, as we shall argue in the explanation of the parallel passage in chap. 19, followers of Jesus, recipients of the kingdom, are still not in this new era rid of their hard hearts, divorce and remarriage will continue to occur among them, just as it did among the people of God in the OT (see further

Comment on 19:3–12). Matthew's own insertion of the exception clauses, modifying the absolute teaching of Jesus, is just such an admission in the church of his day. Still, however, it is worth adding that conceding the hard realities of our continuing fallenness and the reality of forgiveness for those who fail must not allow us to weaken our commitment to continue to strive after the ideal.

On Oaths   (5:33–37)

Bibliography

Bauernfeind, O. "Der Eid in der Sicht des Neuen Testaments." In *Eid, Gewissen, Treuepflicht,* ed. H. Bethke. Frankfurt: Stimme, 1965. 79–112. **Dautzenberg, G.** "Ist das Schwurverbot Mt 5,33–37; Jak 5,12 ein Beispiel für die Torakritik Jesu?" *BZ* n.s. 25 (1981) 47–66. **Ito, A.** "Matthew's Understanding of the Law with Special Reference to the Fourth Antithesis." Diss., Oxford, 1989. ————. "The Question of the Authenticity of the Ban on Swearing (Matthew 5.33–37)." *JSNT* 43 (1991) 5–13. **Kutsch, E.** "Eure Rede aber sei ja ja, nein, nein." *EvT* 20 (1960) 206–18. **Minear, P. S.** *Commands of Christ.* Edinburgh: St. Andrew, 1972. 30–46. ————. "Yes or No: The Demand for Honesty in the Early Church." *NovT* 13 (1971) 1–13. **Stählin, G.** "Zum Gebrauch von Beteuerungsformeln im Neuen Testament." *NovT* 5 (1962) 115–43.

Translation

[33] *"Again, you have heard that it was said to those of early times,*[a] *'You shall not swear falsely,*[b] *but you shall fulfill your oaths as to the Lord.'* [34]*But I say to you, do not take an oath at all, not by heaven, because it is the throne of God,* [35]*nor by the earth, for it is the footstool of his feet, nor with reference to Jerusalem, because it is the city of the great king;* [36]*nor should you swear by your own head, because you are unable to make one hair white or black.* [37]*But let your word be such that a yes is a yes and a no is a no.*[c] *But the rest of these practices are from the evil one."*

Notes

[a] τοῖς ἀρχαίοις, "to those of early times," is omitted by k sy[s] in order to bring more agreement with the formula introducing the other antitheses (only the first of which has τοῖς ἀρχαίοις).

[b] The verb οὐκ ἐπιορκήσεις could be translated "you shall not break an oath" (see *EDNT* 2:31). Cf. REB; NJB; NIV.

[c] Lit. "Let your word be yes, yes, no, no [ναὶ ναί, οὒ οὔ]." L adds καί, "and," between the yeses and noes; Θ refers to "the yes, yes and the no, no" [τὸ ναὶ ναὶ καὶ τὸ οὒ οὔ], as to something well known.

Form/Structure/Setting

A. The fourth antithesis involves again, as in the preceding antithesis, a denial of what was allowed in the Mosaic legislation. But whereas in the preceding antithesis we have a contradiction of Moses, here the contradiction is only at the level of the letter of the text, not its spirit. That is, Jesus pursues the same goal as does the law: integrity of word. But Jesus insists on the latter altogether outside of the context of oath taking, in keeping with the high ethics of the new reality of the presence of the kingdom.

B. This material on oath taking, like the related material in 23:16–22, finds no parallels in any of the other Gospels. Its stylized form suggests that the evangelist has probably taken the material from oral tradition. It is difficult to know what relationship, if any, exists between the material in the third woe against the Pharisees in 23:16–22 and the present passage. There Jesus criticizes the Pharisees for subtle and unwarranted distinctions in oath taking. The focus is on the temple and the altar. In the final verse (23:22), however, which falls outside the basic structure of the passage, Jesus says, "whoever swears by heaven swears by the throne of God and by the one sitting upon it." This bears a close relationship to v 34 in the present passage, from which indeed it may have been borrowed. The main difference, of course, is that in Matt 23 Jesus does not prohibit oath taking as he does here. Probably the strong view against oath taking here is the direct result of the clear abuse of the practice that Jesus encountered (cf. 23:16–22). Possibly the evangelist has added the material of vv 34b–36 from a different context where it was conceivably more pertinent than here.

C. The form of the passage follows in a general way the pattern of the earlier antitheses: (1) the received view (v 33); (2) Jesus' new perspective (v 34a); (3) the grounds for that perspective (vv 34b–36); and (4) the fundamental principle (v 37). The introductory formula in v 33 is in the full form that is found elsewhere only in the first antithesis (v 21). But now Jesus expresses his perspective in terms of a prohibition (so too the fifth antithesis [v 39]; the sixth consists of a positive command [v 44]). Most striking is the form of the antithetical material of vv 34–36, where four μήτε phrases occur, each with a ὅτι clause giving the ground for the avoidance of that particular oath. This repetitious form makes the material ideal for memorization. Only the end of v 36 breaks the pattern somewhat by the different syntax of the ὅτι clause. V 37 provides both a positive statement about integrity of word and a summary statement about the evil nature of oath taking.

Comment

33 After the full introductory formula (cf. v 21), the evangelist presents not a quotation from the OT, as in the first two antitheses, but a crystallization of the OT teaching on the subject (cf. Lev 19:12; Num 30:2; Deut 23:21–23; cf. Zech 8:17). The OT clearly emphasizes that oaths have a binding character. The verb ἐπιορκεῖν, "swear falsely," can also mean "break an oath" (cf. *Did.* 2:3). The more clearly promissory oath is in view in the sentence: "you shall fulfill your oaths as unto the Lord." Exod 20:7 may also lie behind these imperatives.

34–36 With his authoritative "But I say to you" (see *Comment* on v 22), Jesus denies altogether the need for oaths. μὴ ὀμόσαι ὅλως, "do not swear at all." In the explanation that follows, i.e., particularly in the ὅτι ("because") clauses, it seems to be assumed that oath taking is in practice more often a means of avoiding what is promised than of performing it (cf. the polemic specifically against the Pharisees in 23:16–22). (For examples of rabbinic casuistry in the matter of oaths, cf. *m. Ned.* 1:3; *m. Šeb.* 4:13. See the continuing importance of oaths in rabbinic

Judaism as shown in Str-B 1:321–28.) Thus, one should not swear by heaven, for it is the throne of God. That is, the oath is of a binding character, and to swear by heaven—or anything else one might care to mention —is much more significant than it may initially sound. Each of the four "because" clauses finally evokes God himself: heaven is his throne and earth is his footstool (these are biblical metaphors; cf. Isa 66:1; Pss 11:4; 99:5; Lam 2:1); Jerusalem is the city of the great King (cf. Ps 48:2, and "the city of our God" in 48:1); and finally even one's own head, or the hairs thereof, is outside of one's control (but subject to God's control, as the text implies; cf. the same point in 10:30). Each of these examples of objects sworn by can be paralleled in the rabbinic literature (see Str-B 1:332–34). All oath taking implicates God, is in effect to swear in his name, and thus all oath taking is to be understood as possessing an absolute character. But whereas this might well have served the point Jesus wanted to make, i.e., the necessity of an absolute integrity (as stressed for example in Sir 23:7–11), he goes further to the quite shocking initial statement that oath taking is altogether unnecessary, and since it serves no purpose, it should be avoided. Therein lies the real antithesis. Josephus (*J.W.* 2.8.6 §135), describing the Essenes, writes: "Any word of theirs has more force than an oath; swearing they avoid, regarding it as worse than perjury, for they say that one who is not believed without an appeal to God stands condemned already." Philo (*Prob.* 84) also notes of the Essenes that they show their love of God among other ways "by abstinence from oaths, by veracity." Criticism of oaths is found elsewhere in Philo (see esp. *Decal.* 84; other references in Luz).

37 The strong affirmative statement that alone makes sense of Jesus' repudiation of oath taking is the imperative that one's word—whether a yes or a no—be sufficient. "Let your word be ναὶ ναί, οὒ οὔ [lit. 'yes, yes, no, no']" should not be regarded as an oath or asseveration formula (in *b. Šeb.* 36a "yes" and "no" can be regarded as an oath, or each said twice; cf. *2 Enoch* 49:1–2) but as a fully sincere yes or no. The absolute reliability of one's word renders an oath superfluous. And indeed, because in the contemporary situation oaths so often suggested not commitment but untruthfulness by the creation of loopholes, Jesus strongly condemns anything beyond the simple, genuine yes or no as being ἐκ τοῦ πονηροῦ, "from the evil one," the one associated preeminently with deception (cf. John 8:44). In the ethics of the kingdom, there is no need for the taking of oaths. For an example of how this teaching was used in early Christian parenesis, see Jas 5:12, which depends on the same logia of Jesus (cf. 2 Cor 1:17–18). Matthew refers to "the evil one," i.e., Satan or the Devil (cf. 6:13; 13:19, 38), more than does any other evangelist or any other NT book except 1 John.

Explanation

Although in the OT the practice of oath taking was encouraged, or at least allowed, as a means of strengthening one's personal resolution to do something, as it evolved it apparently often became a way by which some persons avoided responsibility. Jesus affirms the binding character of oaths and implicitly denies the subtle distinctions that some used to invalidate their oaths (cf. Matt 23:16–22). Yet at the same time, he lifts the entire matter to a new level by denying the necessity of oaths altogether. The ethics to which Jesus calls his disciples are those of the kingdom and its perfection. Here a person's word can be relied upon without qualification and without need of the further guarantee an oath might afford. Oaths are thereby rendered superfluous. With the dawn of the new era comes a wholly new standard of righteousness, one in which a yes is really a yes and a no is really a no. It is a mistake, however, to take a biblicist approach to this passage that would disallow Christians from taking an oath, say in a court of justice. The issue is nothing less than and nothing more than truthfulness.

On Retaliation (5:38–42)

Bibliography

Clavier, H. "Matthieu 5,39 et la non-résistance." *RHPR* 37 (1957) 44–57. **Currie, S.** "Matthew 5,39f.—Resistance or Protest?" *HTR* 57 (1964) 140–45. **Daube, D.** "Matthew v.38f." *JTS* 45 (1944) 177–87. **Donelson, L. R.** "'Do Not Resist Evil' and the Question of Biblical Authority." *HBT* 10 (1988) 33–46. **Fiebig, P.** "ἀγγαρεύω." *ZNW* 18 (1917–18) 64–72. **Horsley, R. A.** "Ethics and Exegesis: 'Love Your Enemies' and the Doctrine of Non-Violence." *JAAR* 54 (1986) 3–31. **Lambrecht, J.** "The Sayings of Jesus on Nonviolence." *LS* 12 (1987) 291–305. **Lührmann, D.** "Liebet eure Feinde (Lk 6,27–36; Mt 5,39–48)." *ZTK* 69 (1972) 412–38. **Neugebauer, F.** "Die dargebotene Wange und Jesu Gebot der Feindesliebe: Erwägungen zu Lk 6,27–36/Mt 5,38–48." *TLZ* 110 (1985) 865–76. **Rausch, J.** "The Principle of Nonresistance and Love of Enemy in Mt 5,38–48." *CBQ* 28 (1966) 31–41. **Sahlin, H.** "Ett svart ställe i Bergspredikan (Mt 5:39–42)." *SEÅ* 51–52 (1986–87) 214–18. ———. "Traditionskritische Bemerkungen zu zwei Evangelienperikopen." *ST* 33 (1979) 69–84. **Sauer, J.** "Traditionsgeschichtliche Erwägungen zu den synoptischen und paulinischen Aussagen über Feindesliebe und Wiedervergeltungsverzicht." *ZNW* 76 (1985) 1–28. **Schottroff, L.** "Gewaltverzicht und Feindesliebe in der urchristlichen Jesustradition (Mt 5,38–48; Lk 6,27–36)." In *Jesus Christus in Historie und Theologie.* FS H. Conzelmann, ed. G. Strecker. Tübingen: Mohr, 1975. 197–221. **Tannehill, R. C.** "The 'Focal Instance' as a Form of New Testament Speech: A Study of Matthew 5,39b–42." *JR* 50 (1970) 372–85. **Theissen, G.** "Gewaltverzicht und Feindesliebe (Mt 5,38–48; Lk 6, 27–38) und deren sozialgeschichtlichen Hintergrund." In *Studien zur Soziologie des Urchristentums.* WUNT 19. Tübingen: Mohr, 1979. 160–97. **Wink, W.** "Beyond Just War and Pacifism: Jesus' Nonviolent Way." *RevExp* 89 (1992) 197–214.

Translation

[38] *"You have heard that it was said, 'An eye for an eye and* [a] *a tooth for a tooth.'* [39] *But I say to you, do not resist evil.* [b] *But whenever anyone insults you by slapping your right cheek, turn your other cheek to that person.* [c] [40] *And to anyone who takes you to court to get your garment, give that person even your coat.* [41] *And whenever some soldier compels you in public service to go one mile, go with him two.* [42] *And give to anyone who asks anything of you; and do not turn away anyone who wants to borrow from you."*

Notes

[a] D *f* [13] it mae omit καί, "and."

[b] τῷ πονηρῷ, "evil," could be rendered as "the evil one" (cf. 6:13).

[c] Lit. "him" (αὐτῷ), as also in v 40.

Form/Structure/Setting

A. The fifth antithesis contrasts two patterns of conduct. The first is based on the strict justice of the OT code; the second is based on a totally new set of priorities wherein the disciples sacrifice their own rights and make themselves available to the needs and demands of others. The behavior called for in this antithesis brings us close to the next and final antithesis with its command to love one's enemies.

B. Parallel material in the Lukan sermon, 6:29–30, where Jesus teaches love for one's enemies (cf. the sixth antithesis), seems to represent essentially the same content but in rather different words, reflecting quite possibly a variant oral tradition (rather than the common source, Q). In addition to the different wording, Luke 6:29 transposes "garment" ($\chi\iota\tau\acute{\omega}\nu$) and "cloak" ($\acute{\iota}\mu\acute{\alpha}\tau\iota o\nu$) so that one who is asked for his cloak should also give his garment (and not vice versa, as in Matthew). Luke appears to have in mind robbery that occurs on a road; hence the cloak is taken first. Matthew, on the other hand, envisages a court scene or lawsuit where the inner garment is initially demanded. (Matthew's order appears to have been a problem to the author of the *Didache*, however, who, although quoting the tradition underlying Matthew, transposes the two words [1:4]; cf. Justin, *Apol.* 1.16.1.)

C. In form, the pericope again gives us the threefold pattern of the preceding antitheses: (1) the OT teaching, in this case through verbatim citation (v 38); (2) the antithetical perspective offered by Jesus (v 39a); and (3) illustration of the point (vv 39b–42). The last verse of the pericope (v 42), although somewhat similar in form to v 40, seems to broaden the application beyond the initial statement not to resist evil. Here we seem to move to a general spirit of charity to anyone who asks or who wishes to borrow, not simply behavior toward those who have treated one unjustly or in an evil manner.

Again we encounter strong parallelism of form, especially between v 39b and 41, but also to a lesser degree between v 40 and 42a. If the latter parallelism were a little stronger, an *a b a b* pattern would be clear, but as the text stands we have only a suggestion of this. Nevertheless, the passage again shows sufficient parallelism to make it probable that the evangelist here draws again upon oral tradition.

Comment

38 The introductory formula, as in the second and sixth antitheses, lacks only the reference to "the ancients" ($\tauo\hat{\iota}\varsigma$ $\dot{\alpha}\rho\chi\alpha\acute{\iota}o\iota\varsigma$). The material cited is again drawn verbatim (as in the first two antitheses), except for the $\kappa\alpha\acute{\iota}$, "and," from the OT (LXX), where it occurs identically in Exod 21:24; Lev 24:20; and Deut 19:21. In these passages, it should be noted, the *lex talionis* is presented more as a way of limiting the degree of personal vengeance that one may take upon another than as a positive teaching about what a person must or should do. By the time of Jesus, monetary recompense was apparently often substituted for the literal application of *lex talionis*.

39 The command of Jesus, again introduced with the authoritative "but I say to you," is shocking in its contrast to the principle of justice defended by the OT texts. Jesus says simply $\mu\grave{\eta}$ $\dot{\alpha}\nu\tau\iota\sigma\tau\hat{\eta}\nu\alpha\iota$ $\tau\hat{\omega}$ $\pio\nu\eta\rho\hat{\omega}$, "do not resist evil" at all, i.e., as we learn from the context, do not render evil for evil. The articular $\tau\hat{\omega}$ $\pio\nu\eta\rho\hat{\omega}$ here clearly does not mean "the evil one," i.e., Satan (as in v 37; cf. 6:13). If an evil person were in view, one would expect an anarthrous noun. It is much more likely that the evangelist has in mind "the evil deed." This is interpreted first in terms of nonretaliation, as in the first illustration, then in terms of compliance with unreasonable requests (vv 40–41), and finally in terms of simple charity (v 42). The first illustration refers to someone striking "the right [δεξιάν] cheek." This is apparently more than merely a physical slap of the cheek (for this imagery see Lam 3:30). The specifying of the right cheek (which is lacking in the parallel in Luke 6:29) may mean a blow with the back of the hand (assuming the striker is righthanded), and thus make the personal insult even more serious (cf. *m. B. Qam.* 8:6). στρέψον αὐτῷ καὶ τὴν ἄλλην, "turn to that person the other cheek," means to avoid retaliation (a perspective already found in Prov 20:22; 24:29; at Qumran, cf. 1QS 10:18–19) and instead to put oneself intentionally in a condition of continuing vulnerability. Jesus, of course, supremely modeled this attitude in the passion narrative (cf. 26:67–68; 27:30; 1 Pet 2:23). For the place of similar teaching in early Christian parenesis, see Rom 12:19, 21; 2 Cor 11:20; and 1 Thess 5:15, where since vengeance is the Lord's (cf. Deut 32:35), one should not render evil for evil.

40–41 The second illustration refers to legal action (κριθῆναι, "to be judged," i.e., in a court), the result of which could be the loss of one's χιτών ("tunic" or "inner garment"). Jesus teaches not only that one should give up what one is sued for but that one should also voluntarily give up one's ἱμάτιον (the more essential "outer garment," i.e., robe or cloak) as well. Cf. 1 Cor 6:7 for Paul's similar attitude. Along the same lines, in the third illustration, when one is pressed into service by the military authorities to assist in bearing a load (this is the meaning of the semi-technical term ἀγγαρεύειν; cf. its use in 27:32), one should not simply go the required mile but an extra one too. Thus, these unjustifiable requests should be complied with—indeed, the response should considerably exceed the requests. Again the perspective of the kingdom of God is alien to the perspective of the world.

42 This verse takes further the line of thought in the preceding verses by teaching a charitable response to all who may ask for something or who may ask to borrow. In these illustrations, it is no longer a matter of response to mistreatment, or even to forced conduct, but to straightforward requests. Again, OT precedent can be found (cf. Deut 15:7–8). The only other passage in the NT where the verb δανίζειν ("to borrow, lend") occurs is in Luke 6:34–35 (material that finds no parallel in Matthew), where the point is emphasized that one should lend to those from whom one does not expect to receive repayment. And this teaching occurs in connection with the command to "love your enemies," which is the form of Matthew's next antithesis. Quite probably, then, the present verse teaches not simply to give and lend but to do so even to one's enemies, to those from whom one has no hope of repayment. This interpretation is consistent with both preceding and following contexts in Matthew.

Explanation

Jesus again expounds the ethics of the kingdom. What he presents is ethics directed more to conduct at the personal, rather than the societal, level. These directives are for the recipients of the kingdom, not for governmental legislation.

Rather than demanding strict justice, or allowing for retaliation of any kind, the disciple of the kingdom defers to others. The disciple does not insist on personal rights. Furthermore, the true disciple does more than is expected. He or she is free from society's low standards of expectation, being subject only to the will of the Father. The conduct of the disciple is filled with surprise for those who experience it. This element of surprise relates closely to and reflects the grace that is central to the gospel. It is the unworthy who have experienced the good things of the kingdom; and as they have experienced the surprise of unexpected grace, so they act in a similar manner toward the undeserving among them (cf. Luke 6:34–35). Jesus himself provides the supreme example of the fulfillment of this ethic (cf. passion narratives and 1 Pet 2:23), and the disciples are called to follow in his path. Kingdom ethics demands not mechanical compliance to rules but a lifestyle governed by the free grace of God.

On Loving One's Enemies   (5:43–48)

Bibliography

Bauer, W. "Das Gebot der Feindesliebe und die alten Christen." In *Aufsätze und kleine Schriften*. Tübingen: Mohr, 1967. 235–52. **Borchert, G. L.** "Matthew 5:48—Perfection and the Sermon." *RevExp* 89 (1992) 265–69. **Dible, A.** *Die goldene Regel.* Göttingen: Vandenhoeck & Ruprecht, 1962. **Dupont, J.** "L'appel à imiter Dieu en Matthieu 5,48 et Luc 6,36." *RivB* 14 (1966) 137–58. ————. "'Soyez parfaits' (Mt 5,48), 'soyez miséricordieux' (Lc 6,36)." In *Sacra Pagina.* Vol. 2. BETL 12–13. Gembloux: Duculot, 1959. 150–62. **Huber, W.** "Feindschaft und Feindesliebe." *ZEE* 26 (1982) 128–58. **Linton, O.** "St. Matthew 5,43." *ST* 18 (1964) 66–79. **Piper, J.** *"Love Your Enemies": Jesus' Love Command in the Synoptic Gospels and the Early Christian Paraenesis.* SNTSMS 38. Cambridge: Cambridge University, 1979. **Reuter, R.** "Liebet eure Feinde." *ZEE* 26 (1982) 159–87. **Schnackenburg, R.** "Die Vollkommenheit des Christen nach den Evangelien." *GL* 32 (1959) 420–33. **Seitz, O. J. F.** "Love Your Enemies." *NTS* 16 (1969–70) 39–54. **Strecker, G.** "Compliance—Love of One's Enemy—The Golden Rule." *AusBR* 29 (1981) 38–46. **Yarnold, E.** "Teleios in St. Matthew's Gospel." In *SE* 4 [= TU 102] (1968) 269–73.

See also *Bibliography* on 5:38–42.

Translation

[43] *"You have heard that it was said, 'Love your neighbor and hate your enemy.'* [44] *But I say to you, love your enemies*[a] *and pray for those who persecute you,* [45] *in order that you may be children of your heavenly Father, because he makes his sun rise upon both evil and good people and he makes it rain upon both the just and the unjust.* [46] *For if you love those who love you, what reward do you have? Don't even the tax collectors do the same thing?*[b] [47] *And if you greet only the members of your community,*[c] *what rewardable thing have you done? Do not even the Gentiles*[d] *do the same thing?*[e,f] [48] *You, therefore, be perfect as*[g] *your heavenly*[h] *Father is perfect."*

Notes

 a The majority of MSS (D L W Θ *f* ¹³ TR lat sy⁽ᵖ⁾ʰ) insert the following with occasional slight modifications: εὐλογεῖτε τοὺς καταρωμένους ὑμᾶς, καλῶς ποιεῖτε τοῖς μισοῦσιν ὑμᾶς, "bless those who curse you, do well to those who hate you," and after the verb "pray for" the words ἐπηρεαζόντων ὑμᾶς καί, "those who abuse you." This material is quite obviously borrowed from the Lukan parallel to the "love your enemies" passage in Luke 6:27–28. Favoring the shorter text are ℵ B among others. See *TCGNT,* 14.

b D Z syˢ·ᶜ have οὕτως, "thus." Cf. *Note* e.

c ἀδελφοὺς ὑμῶν, lit. "your brothers." The majority of later MSS (L W Θ TR syʰ) have φίλους ὑμῶν, "your friends." 1424 has ἀσπαζομένους ὑμᾶς, "those who greet you," on the model of v 46a.

d The majority of later MSS (L W Θ *f* ¹³ TR syᵖ) have τελῶναι, "tax collectors," as in v 46c.

e K L Δ Θ TR syᶜ·ʰ have οὕτως, "thus." Cf. *Note* b.

f Two witnesses (k syˢ) omit v 47 in its entirety through homoioteleuton.

g A majority of later MSS (D K W Δ Θ TR) have for ὡς the slightly more emphatic ὥσπερ, "just as."

h Some MSS ([D*] K Δ Θ it) read ἐν τοῖς οὐρανοῖς, "in heaven" (cf. v 45).

Form/Structure/Setting

A. This final antithesis is climactic in its emphasis on loving one's enemies and in its concluding call to the perfection of the Father. The practice of love is the most fundamental element of the Christian ethic (cf. 22:37–40). Here the call to love is extended even to one's enemies. There is thus a summarizing aspect to this antithesis that includes all the ethical teaching of the preceding antitheses.

B. Luke, in the Sermon on the Plain, has material parallel to the present passage but in quite different order and wording. Therefore, it is unlikely that Matthew and Luke are dependent upon the same source (Q); more likely they are dependent upon different traditions that contain material probably stemming originally from Jesus himself. Thus, Luke contains the command to "love your enemies" in verbatim agreement with Matthew (Luke 6:27–28) but includes other expressions of the same thought that are lacking in Matthew. Luke further includes the call to "pray for those who abuse you," but he uses different vocabulary. Luke lacks any equivalent to v 45 (but cf. καὶ ἔσεσθε υἱοὶ ὑψίστου, "and you will be children [lit. 'sons'] of the Highest"; Luke 6:35). The closest parallel in Luke is to vv 46–47 (Luke 6:32–33). There Luke uses slightly different wording, in particular substituting (for his gentile readers) οἱ ἁμαρτωλοί, "the sinners," for Matthew's οἱ τελῶναι, "the tax collectors," and again for οἱ ἐθνικοί, "the Gentiles," and having ἀγαθοποιῆτε, "do good to," for Matthew's ἀσπάσησθε, "greet." Luke has a third example pertaining to lending money (Luke 6:34) that is not found in Matthew. Finally, the concluding statement in Matt 5:48 is paralleled in Luke 6:36, where, however, Luke has "be merciful [οἰκτίρμων] as your Father is merciful."

C. The structure of this antithesis follows that of the earlier antitheses in the inclusion of illustrative material, here in two exactly parallel statements (vv 46–47). But, unlike the earlier antitheses, the antithetical teaching of Jesus is supported by a statement of both the goal and grounds (in two parallel statements) of acting in accordance with Jesus' teaching (v 45). Further, the concluding challenge (v 48), in addition to rounding off the present pericope, also serves as the conclusion to this portion of the sermon (i.e., the antitheses). The structure is as follows: (1) the received view (v 43); (2) Jesus' correction (vv 44–45a); (3) two supporting statements (v 45b–c); (4) two illustrative parallels (vv 46–47); and

(5) a concluding exhortation (v 48). The parallelism in Matt 5:46–47, but also in vv 44 and 45, points to the strong probability that Matthew uses oral tradition in the present pericope. Although this oral tradition overlaps to a degree with that used by Luke, the two Gospels have probably used independent oral traditions that developed from a common source.

Comment

43 On the formula "you have heard that it was said," see *Comment* on v 21. The first element of the OT tradition, ἀγαπήσεις τὸν πλησίον σου, "you shall love your neighbor," is drawn verbatim from Lev 19:18 (this passage is quoted again, more fully, in 22:39). The words "as yourself" (ὡς σεαυτόν) are probably omitted here in order to form a more exact parallel with the second member, μισήσεις τὸν ἐχθρόν σου, "you shall hate your enemy." The latter, though not taught in the OT, is an inference that was commonly drawn, for example, from such passages as Pss 139:21–22; 26:5; or Deut 7:2; 30:7. On the basis of such passages, the Qumranites explicitly taught hatred of those regarded as enemies (1QS 1:4, 10–11; 9:21–26). Clearly, neither Jesus' listeners nor Matthew's readers would have been surprised by the added words, since the traditional interpretation had become regularly associated with the text. The "neighbor" meant fellow Jew; the "enemy" meant Gentile.

44–45 The antithesis, on the other hand, must have startled those who first heard it. Again, with the characteristic and emphatic ἐγὼ δὲ λέγω ὑμῖν, "but I say to you," Jesus commands ἀγαπᾶτε τοὺς ἐχθροὺς ὑμῶν, "love your enemies," and προσεύχεσθε ὑπὲρ τῶν διωκόντων ὑμᾶς, "pray for those who persecute you" (cf. 5:10–12). This is revolutionary in its newness, having no exact parallel in the Jewish tradition. (Perhaps the OT comes closest to this in its attitude toward the alien [גֵּר, *gar*], as expressed in Lev 19:34, but other passages may also be mentioned: e.g., Exod 23:4–5; Prov 25:21; cf. Str-B 1:369–70; for Hellenistic parallels, cf. Piper.) But such an attitude of love toward all, even one's enemies, is of crucial importance to the very identity of the disciple; thus Jesus stresses that such an unrestricted love must be manifested ὅπως, "in order that," you may be υἱοὶ τοῦ πατρὸς ὑμῶν, "children [lit. 'sons'] of your Father" (cf. 5:9). To participate in the kingdom relates the disciple to the Father in a unique way, and that unique relationship involves doing his will. This is also the point of v 48. The children of the kingdom are called to reflect the character of their heavenly Father (cf. Eph 5:1), who has brought to them the kingdom. The early Church picks up the emphasis of this teaching in such passages as Rom 12:14; 1 Cor 4:12; 1 Pet 3:9. One important foundation for the unheard-of command to love one's enemies is the very fact that God gives his good gifts of sunshine and rain both to good and to bad. The different words for "good" (ἀγαθούς, "good," and δικαίους, "just") and "bad" (πονηρούς, "evil," and ἀδίκους, "unjust") represent stylistic variation, as does the chiastic order of the nouns. The "bad" are, from the context, analogous to the "enemies" of God. To love one's enemies is, then, to treat them as God treats those who have rebelled against him. Thus the children, the disciples, should imitate their heavenly Father.

46–47 The illustrative rhetorical questions make the point that nothing wonderful has been accomplished when one returns good for good. This is but the standard of the world, which even "tax collectors" (τελῶναι) and "Gentiles" (ἐθνικοί) are able to fulfill. (On "tax collector," see *Comment* on 9:9.) It is thus no achievement to love those who love you (the words ἀγαπήσητε and ἀγαπῶντας reflect the initial verb ἀγαπήσεις, "you shall love" [v 43], as well as the command of v 44). The ethical standard of the kingdom calls the disciples to a much more radical love that includes even one's enemies—the unrighteous and the evil.

Matthew also links tax collectors and Gentiles in 18:17 ("tax collectors" is linked with "sinners," ἁμαρτωλοί, in 9:10, 11; 11:19; in 21:31–32 the word is twice linked with πόρναι, "harlots"). This negative use of ἐθνικοί, "Gentiles," is found elsewhere in Matthew (e.g., 6:7; 18:17) and reflects the Jewish orientation of the evangelist's community.

ἀσπάσησθε, "salute," "greet," in parallelism with "love," means something like "wish peace and blessing upon" or "show favor toward" (the only other use of the word in Matthew occurs in 10:12). μισθόν, "reward," is far more important in Matthew than in any other Gospel (cf. esp. 5:12; 6:1–16; and 10:41–42), again reflecting the evangelist's Jewish framework.

48 This verse confirms the argument of v 45 and properly forms the conclusion of the pericope. The disciples (ὑμεῖς, "you," is emphatic) are to be "perfect" (τέλειος)—that is, they are to be like their Father in loving their enemies. This view is supported by the context as well as by the Lukan parallel (Luke 6:36), which employs the word οἰκτίρμων, "merciful" or "compassionate," in place of Matthew's τέλειος. There is a sense, however, in which this verse also serves as the logical conclusion to all the preceding antitheses. The righteousness of the kingdom, which altogether exceeds that of the Pharisees, involves a call to be like the Father.

τέλειος is the Greek equivalent of the Hebrew word תָּמִים (*tāmîm*), used often in the OT to refer to perfection in the sense of ethical uprightness (e.g., Gen 6:9; 17:1; 2 Sam 22:24–27; frequently in the Psalms and in the Qumran scrolls) and animals without blemish (esp. Leviticus, Numbers, and Ezekiel). The word can also have the connotation of completeness (e.g., Lev 23:15, 30; Josh 10:13). τέλειος here may have the connotation of "whole" or "total" (thus Delling, *TDNT* 8:74), as it does elsewhere (cf. 19:21; and Col 4:12; Jas 1:4), but it should be emphasized that in the sphere of ethics this entails perfection. This call does not differ from that in the OT: "Be holy for I, the LORD God, am holy" (Lev 19:2; cf. 1 Pet 1:16). The LXX even uses the same word (τέλειος, translating תָּמִים) at one point (Deut 18:13): "Be perfect before the LORD your God." The perfection here is the fulfillment of the Mosaic law (*pace* Guelich, *Sermon*), but now according to its definitive interpretation by the Messiah who brings the kingdom. Love for God and one's neighbor (and particularly, love of one's enemies) will be described by Matthew as the commandments upon which thus all the law and the prophets depend (22:40). For Matthew, to be τέλειος means to fulfill the law through the manifestation of an unrestricted love (including even enemies) that is the reflection of God's love. This unrestricted love preeminently embodies ethical perfection. This perfection, and nothing less, is that to which Jesus calls his disciples. As the kingdom Jesus brings is "of heaven" (see on 3:2), so also the Father in Matthew is οὐράνιος, "heavenly," i.e., transcendent. This way of referring to God as ὁ πατὴρ ὁ οὐράνιος is unique to Matthew in the NT (see 6:14, 26, 32; 15:13; 18:35; 23:9) and again reflects Matthew's Jewish milieu. The expression beautifully combines God's divine transcendence ("heavenly") with his immanence in love and grace, which can only be described adequately in the intimate term "Father."

Explanation

The final, climactic antithesis turns to the great love commandment of the OT. Jesus, interpreting the law in the light of the dawning kingdom, extends the application of that commandment so as to include even one's enemies. The love he describes, of course, is not an emotion (*pace* Carson) but volitional acts for the benefit and well-being of others, even those we may dislike. In this love that knows no boundaries, the disciples are to reflect the generosity of God, who sends blessing upon both the righteous and the unrighteous and who has brought the kingdom to the unworthy. Through the coming of the kingdom, the disciples are thus called to be "perfect" as their Father is perfect. The righteousness of the kingdom can be satisfied by nothing less. And as the disciples live out this righteousness, they confirm their identity as "children of the heavenly Father." This is an ethic that will startle those who experience it; it is an ethic that will inevitably shine like light in a dark place and cause the Father to be glorified (v 16). It should be added that the perfection in view here is a goal toward which disciples are called to strive, but not one they will fully achieve in this life. The Christian will thus always have occasion to pray for the forgiveness of sins, as Jesus taught his disciples to pray (6:12). The call to perfection is quite like the Pauline call for Christians to be what they are in Christ. Here it is a matter of being children of the Father.

Outward vs. Inward Righteousness   (6:1–18)

Almsgiving   (6:1–4)

Bibliography

Betz, H. D. "A Jewish-Christian Cultic *Didache* in Matt. 6:1–18: Reflections and Questions on the Historical Jesus." In *Essays on the Sermon on the Mount*. Philadelphia: Fortress, 1985. 55–69. **Büchler, A.** "St Matthew VI 1–6 and Other Allied Passages." *JTS* 10 (1909) 266–70. **Dietzfelbinger, C.** "Die Frömmigkeitsregeln von Mt 6:1–18 als Zeugnisse frühchristlicher Geschichte." *ZNW* 75 (1984) 184–200. **George, A.** "La justice à faire dans le secret (Matthieu 6,1–6 et 16–18)." *Bib* 40 (1959) 509–98. **Gerhardsson, B.** "Geistiger Opferdienst nach Matth 6,1–6.16–21." In *Neues Testament und Geschichte*. FS O. Cullmann, ed. H. Baltensweiler and B. Reicke. Zürich: Theologischer, 1972. 69–77. **Klostermann, E.** "Zum Verständnis von Mt 6,2." *ZNW* 47 (1956) 280–81. **McEleney, N. J.** "Does the Trumpet Sound or Resound? An Interpretation of Matthew 6,2." *ZNW* 76 (1985) 43–46. **Minear, P. S.** "Keep It Secret." In *Commands of Christ*. 47–68. **Nagel, W.** "Gerechtigkeit—oder Almosen? (Mt 6,1)." *VC* 15 (1961) 141–45. **Oakley, I. J. W.** "'Hypocrisy' in Matthew." *IBS* 7 (1985) 118–38. **Schweizer, E.** "Der Jude im Verborgenen . . . , dessen Lob nicht von Menschen, sondern von Gott kommt." In *Matthäus und seine Gemeinde*. 86–97.

Translation

[1] *"Be careful not to practice your piety [a] before others in order to be seen by them. Otherwise you have no reward with your heavenly Father.* [2] *When you give alms, therefore, do not blow a trumpet to attract attention,[b] as do the hypocrites in the synagogues and in the streets, so that they may be glorified by others. Truly [c] I say to you, they are having their reward at that moment.* [3] *But as for you, when you give alms, do not let your left hand know what your right hand is doing,* [4] *so that your almsgiving may be in secret. And your Father, who sees in secret, will [d] reward you."* [e]

Notes

[a] δικαιοσύνην, lit. "righteousness." The majority of (late) MSS (L W Z Θ *f*[13] TR sy[p.h] mae) have ἐλεημοσύνην, "almsgiving," perhaps by the influence of v 2. א[1] sy[c] bo have δόσιν, "giving."

[b] ἔμπροσθέν σου, lit. "before you."

[c] א* and a few other late MSS insert a second ἀμήν, "truly."

[d] D W *f*[1] TR sy[p.h] add αὐτός before the verb, producing a slightly emphatic "he."

[e] A majority of late MSS (L W Θ TR it sy[s,p,h]) add ἐν τῷ φανερῷ, "in the open," as a counterbalance to ἐν τῷ κρυπτῷ, "in secret." As Metzger points out, however, the superiority of the Father's reward to human approval is important, not its public or nonpublic character (*TCGNT*, 15). Cf. *Note* e on v 6.

Form/Structure/Setting

A. We now come to a new section of the sermon (6:1–18) devoted to three important exercises of the religious life (H. D. Betz refers to the passage as "a Jewish-Christian cultic *Didache*"): almsgiving (vv 2–4), prayer (vv 5–6), and fasting (vv 16–18). These practices do not themselves come under criticism, nor are they regulated, but rather the motivation underlying them is scrutinized. The entire section is introduced by the general principle enunciated in v 1, a *kělāl* sentence, i.e., a form introducing the themes of the following section. The formal parallelism of the sections indicates that these three sections constitute one entity in the sermon despite the lengthy parenthetical section containing the Lord's Prayer (vv 7–15).

B. These three main sections (vv 2–4, 5–6, 16–18) are without Synoptic parallels and, as their stylized form suggests, probably were derived as a unit from the special oral tradition available to the evangelist. Into the second member of this unit, however, the evangelist has inserted other traditional material having to do with prayer, including the Lord's Prayer (vv 7–15). Only here do we encounter parallel Synoptic material. The traditional Jewish linking of the three items— almsgiving, prayer, and fasting—is found (but in reverse order) in POxy 654.5 (cf. *Gos. Thom.* 6).

C. The parallelism of the three sections is readily apparent from the verbatim recurrence of the words ἀμὴν λέγω ὑμῖν ἀπέχουσιν τὸν μισθὸν αὐτῶν, "truly I say to you, they have their reward" (vv 2, 5, and 16), as well as the repetition of the concluding formula, τῷ πατρί σου τῷ ἐν τῷ κρυπτῷ, "to your Father who is secret" (vv 6 and 18, but the latter has the synonym κρυφαίῳ for κρυπτῷ; v 4 has only the last three words ἐν τῷ κρυπτῷ, "in secret," which are applied to the giving of alms rather than to the Father), followed by the sentence in verbatim agreement (except again for the use of κρυφαίῳ in v 18): καὶ ὁ πατήρ σου ὁ βλέπων ἐν τῷ κρυπτῷ ἀποδώσει σοι, "and your Father who sees in secret will reward you" (vv 4, 6, 18). In addition to these verbatim parallels, there is considerable similarity in the structure of the three passages. Each (i.e., vv 2–4; 5–6; 16–18) contains the following, with only slight variations: (1) an introductory ὅταν with the subjunctive, "whenever you . . ." (singular in v 2; plural in vv 5 and 16), followed by a negative imperative, "do not" (formed using successively the subjunctive, future indicative, and imperative moods), a ὡς clause "as (or like) the hypocrites," and a ὅπως, "so that," clause that describes the intent of the hypocrites; (2) the "they have their reward" saying in the present tense, addressed to a plural "you"; (3) a strongly adversative clause beginning with the words σὺ δέ, "but you" (always in the singular), in which the proper way to act is described, followed by a ὅπως, "so that," clause (but lacking in v 6) emphasizing "in secret"; and (4) the concluding saying, introduced by the ἀμὴν λέγω ὑμῖν formula ("truly I say to you"): "your Father who sees in secret will reward you" (singular). For wordplay in a possible Aramaic tradition underlying the passage, see M. Black (*Aramaic*, 176–78). As an outline of the present pericope the following may be suggested: (1) a general warning about doing righteous deeds to be seen by others (v 1); (2) the specific example of almsgiving (v 2); and (3) the proper performance of almsgiving: "in secret" (vv 3–4).

Comment

1   The opening verse stands almost as a rubric over the entire passage of vv 1–18. The warning (προσέχετε, "beware," "be careful") here admonishes the readers to avoid performing their righteousness in order to be seen by others. The expression "to do righteousness" (δικαιοσύνην . . . ποιεῖν) is Hebraic (e.g., Gen 18:19; Ps 106:3; Isa 56:1) and is found also in the NT in 1 John 2:29; 3:7, 10; and Rev 22:11. The word δικαιοσύνη here is to be understood in the broad sense of "righteousness" (cf. 5:20), of which three basic aspects of Jewish piety (cf. Tob 12:8–10)—almsgiving, prayer, and fasting—are specific examples (on "righteousness," see *Comment* on 3:15). Again, as in the antitheses (5:21–48), the supreme importance of motive or inner thought emerges. Although δικαιοσύνη can also mean "almsgiving" and thus some have tried to associate this verse with vv 2–4, the formal analysis (see above, *Form/Structure/Setting* §C) shows that v 1, rather than being a part of the section that follows, is better understood as an introduction to all three sections (vv 2–4; 5–6; 16–18). The deeds may be thought of as the Christian's self-offering in "spiritual service" and may correspond to the demand of the Shema (Deut 6:4–5) to love God with all your heart (prayer), soul (fasting), and might (almsgiving), with the order changed to move from the easier to the harder (thus Gerhardsson). The phrase ἔμπροσθεν τῶν ἀνθρώπων, "before others," is intensified by the following πρὸς τὸ θεαθῆναι αὐτοῖς, "to be seen by them." This is an emphasis found in all three following sections: cf. ὅπως δοξασθῶσιν ὑπὸ τῶν ἀνθρώπων, "so that they might be glorified by others" (v 2); ὅπως φανῶσιν τοῖς ἀνθρώποις, "so that they might be seen by others" (in verbatim agreement in vv 5 and 16; cf. the corresponding negative ὅπως μὴ φανῇς τοῖς ἀνθρώποις, "so that you may not be seen by others," in v 18). Those who do their righteous deeds in order to be observed by others are described as "hypocrites" (ὑποκριταί) in each of the three following sections (vv 2, 5, and 16). Matthew almost certainly

has in mind the Pharisees, who are repeatedly described as "hypocrites" in chap. 23 and of whom it is also said (23:5) that "they do all their works" πρὸς τὸ θεαθῆναι τοῖς ἀνθρώποις, "to be seen by others"—almost exactly the same language as in the present passage.

If the disciples perform acts of righteousness "to be seen by others," Jesus says to them, μισθὸν οὐκ ἔχετε παρὰ τῷ πατρὶ ὑμῶν τῷ ἐν τοῖς οὐρανοῖς, "you do not have a reward with your Father who is in heaven." This anticipates the considerable stress on reward in the three following sections, in each of which Jesus says concerning those who display their piety "they have their reward" (vv 2, 5, and 16), and of those who practice their piety in secret that "your Father will reward you" (vv 4, 6, and 18). For the expression "your Father in heaven," see 5:16. On μισθός, which occurs more often in Matthew than any other Gospel, see 5:12.

2 Here, "whenever you give alms" (ὅταν . . . ποιῇς ἐλεημοσύνην) is in the second person singular, unlike in the second and third sections where the "whenever" clause is addressed to the second person plural (vv 5 and 16). The words ποιεῖν ἐλεημοσύνην (also in v 3) mean literally "to do an act of mercy," but by the intertestamental period they had become a technical expression for almsgiving (cf. Tob 1:3, 16; 4:7–8; Sir 7:10; in the NT, see Acts 9:36; 10:2; 24:17). Performing deeds of mercy, or doing kindness, was one of the pillars of Judaism (m. ʾAbot 1:2). It is difficult to know whether the reference to blowing a trumpet is intended literally or metaphorically.

> Luz denies rather strongly that a trumpet was actually blown at the giving of a major gift, taking the words as a metaphor of irony (so too, Gnilka; Gundry; Guelich, *Sermon;* France; Davies-Allison are somewhat less confident in their denial). It is still possible—despite the lack of solid evidence—that a trumpet was blown to draw attention to very large gifts (thus Schlatter; Bonnard; Hill), in order perhaps to encourage others to do similarly; on the other hand, perhaps the association was made because trumpets were blown at fasts (see Büchler), at a time when large gifts were given to avert disaster (see G. Friedrich, *TDNT* 7:87–88). Or perhaps the sound is that of coins being thrown into the six trumpet-shaped money chests placed in the temple specifically for the collection of alms (the "Shofar-chests" of m. Šeqal. 2:1; see Danby's note [*The Mishnah*] on that text) in order to attract the attention of others (so McEleney). The point, in any case, is clear: the hypocrites did all they could to draw attention to their generosity.

The sense in which these persons are ὑποκριταί, "hypocrites," is that their real motivation in their apparently pious conduct is self-glorification (ὅπως δοξασθῶσιν ὑπὸ τῶν ἀνθρώπων, "so that they might be glorified by others") ἐν ταῖς συναγωγαῖς καὶ ἐν ταῖς ῥύμαις, "in the synagogues and in the streets," i.e., in the places of worship and in public (cf. the similar phrase in v 5).

> The word ὑποκριτής in Hellenistic Greek commonly meant "actor," i.e., one who performs in front of others, pretending to be something he or she is not. In the NT it is used consistently in a negative sense. Matthew captures the duplicity inherent in hypocrisy when he juxtaposes the word with the quotation of Isa 29:13, "this people honors me with their lips, but their heart is far from me" (15:8). In addition to the three references in this section of Matthew (vv 2, 5, 16), the word occurs in 7:5; 15:7; 22:18; and 24:51. Note especially too the six occurrences in chap. 23, directed against the Pharisees, 23:13, 15, 23, 25, 27, 29. See U. Wilckens, *TDNT* 8:559–71.

The response of Jesus to this self-glorifying activity is introduced with the formula of emphasis: ἀμὴν λέγω ὑμῖν, "truly I say to you [plural]" (cf. vv 5 and 16). This formula, which previously occurred in 5:18 and 26, is found some thirty-two times in Matthew, more than twice as often as in any other Gospel. The use of the present tense in ἀπέχουσιν τὸν μισθὸν αὐτῶν, "they are having their reward," implies that this temporary praise from others is all the reward they will receive, in deliberate contrast to the statement at the end of each of the three sections that promises a future, eschatological reward (vv 4, 6, 18). In the rabbinic doctrine concerning rewards, almsgiving is promised a high return (see Str-B 4:552–53). Jesus' remark that those who give alms for the praise of others already have their reward must have had a shocking effect on his hearers.

3–4 In the strong adversative sentence, Jesus says to the disciples ("when you [here and in all three applications in the singular] give alms") that almsgiving must not be an act done to draw the attention and admiration of others (for Jewish parallels, cf. Str-B 1:391–92). Far from almsgivers calling attention to their act, they should do so unself-consciously, with the left hand taking no heed of what the right hand does (cf. *Gos. Thom.* 62). The speculation that the left hand stands for one's best friend, as in a contemporary Arabic proverb (Grundmann), is hardly convincing; the same must be said for Gundry's suggestion that giving with one and not two hands indicates unobtrusive giving.

Jesus emphasizes, "so that" (ὅπως), the disciple's almsgiving must be ἐν τῷ κρυπτῷ, "in secret." This is the point of the pericope and of all three sections. Righteous deeds are to be done in secret, beyond the attention of any onlookers. These deeds will not escape the attention of God (cf. 1 Sam 16:7): "your Father who sees in secret [ὁ πατήρ σου ὁ βλέπων ἐν τῷ κρυπτῷ] will reward [ἀποδώσει] you." Schweizer ("Der Jude") finds a direct connection between this teaching and Paul's reference in Rom 2:28–29 to being a Jew ἐν τῷ κρυπτῷ, "in secret." The reward motif is more important in Matthew than in any other Gospel (see *Comment* on 5:12). On ἀποδιδόναι, the verb underlying "to reward" in this verse (and vv 6, 18), see especially 16:27 and 20:8.

Explanation

The sermon has been concerned thus far with the defining of true righteousness by a correct understanding of the law. Now specific deeds of piety come into the picture of true righteousness. The practice of righteous deeds—here specifically almsgiving—in order to capture the attention and admiration of others cancels the possibility of any reward from God. The only reward such deeds receive is in the momentary applause of the onlookers. "They were not giving, but *buying*. They wanted the praise of men, they paid for it" (Davies-Allison, 1:582). True deeds of righteousness, by contrast, are done "in secret" where only God, "who sees in secret," knows of them. The deeds of righteousness performed by the Christian *will* of course be seen by others. According to 5:16, followers of Jesus should let their light shine "before others [precisely the language of our pericope], so that they may see your good works." Although this may seem at first to be a contradiction, 5:16 goes on to say "that they might glorify your Father who is in heaven," which is in bold contrast to the desire of the hypocrites that "they might be glorified by others" (v 2). Only deeds done for God's glory will receive an eschatological reward. This stress is in keeping with the emphasis on the inner obedience to God's commandments, which we encountered in chap. 5. God is concerned with the heart, with the motivation behind a person's deeds, as much as with the external deeds themselves. The application of the passage is clear and timeless in its bearing upon Christians.

Prayer and the Lord's Prayer   (6:5–15)

The Setting of Prayer   (6:5–6)

Bibliography

See *Bibliography* for 6:1–4.

Translation

⁵ *"And when you pray, do not be like the hypocrites, because they love to pray*ᵃ *positioning themselves conspicuously*ᵇ *in the synagogues and on the corners of the main roads so that they will be observed by others. Truly I say to you, they are having their reward at that moment.*ᶜ ⁶ *But as for you,*ᵈ *when you pray, go into your closet, shut the door, so that you pray to your Father who is in secret. And your Father, who sees in secret, will reward you."*ᵉ

Notes

ᵃ The Western tradition (D it) inserts στῆναι, "to stand," after the verb φιλοῦσιν, "love," and alters the infinitive προσεύχεσθαι, "to pray," to the participle προσευχόμενοι, "praying," coordinate with ἐστῶτες, "standing." The resulting construction avoids the statement "love to pray."

ᵇ "Positioning themselves conspicuously" is a paraphrase of ἐστῶτες, "standing," drawing out the sense of the participle from the context.

ᶜ syˢ inadvertently omits the entirety of v 5, probably as the result of the similar beginning of vv 5 and 6 (homoioarcton).

ᵈ "But as for you" reflects the emphatic σὺ δέ, lit. "but *you.*"

ᵉ Many MSS (L W Θ *f*¹³ TR it syᵖ·ʰ) add ἐν τῷ φανερῷ, "in the open." See *Note* e on v 4.

Form/Structure/Setting

See the corresponding section to the preceding pericope. Syntactically the one major difference between this and the preceding pericope is found in the ὅτι, "because," clause in v 5 (which, however, finds a counterpart in the γάρ, "for," clause in the third section, v 16).

Comment

5 Again Jesus tells the disciples to avoid being like the hypocrites (cf. vv 2 and 16) who do their utmost to attract attention to themselves when they pray.

They "love" to position themselves where they can be most noticed as they pray. (φιλεῖν is used again of Pharisees in 23:6 [cf. Luke 11:43], where it is said they love the places of honor at feasts and the best seats in the synagogues.) The perfect participle, ἑστῶτες, has the nuance of having taken a position and continuing to stand in it, and this implies the enjoyment of public attention. Standing was the common position for prayer. Again, as in v 2, places of worship, "the synagogues," and public places, "the corners of the main roads," are in view. The phrase ἐν ταῖς γωνίαις τῶν πλατειῶν refers literally to "the corners of the wide (streets)" and in the NT occurs only here. (Matthew's earlier word ῥύμαι is combined with πλατεῖαι in Luke 14:21.) The usual ὅπως or purpose clause (cf. vv 2 and 16) follows, indicating here (and in v 16) "so that they will be observed" (cf. "so that they will be glorified by others" in v 2). Again, Jesus indicates that in this way they receive their only reward (cf. the same logion in verbatim agreement in vv 2 and 16). See *Comment* on v 2.

6   σύ, "you" (singular), in the strong adversative sentence is emphatic: "but when *you* pray . . ." (cf. the same formula in v 17). τὸ ταμεῖον refers to an inner room of a house (cf. Matt 24:26, the only other Matthean occurrence), sometimes secret or hidden (cf. Luke 12:3, "private room," RSV; "behind closed doors," NRSV) and often used as a storeroom (cf. Luke 12:24). It would be a room that allowed privacy; the reference to shutting the door adds emphasis to this aspect. The LXX of Isa 26:20 refers to entering τὰ ταμίεια, "the closets," and shutting the door, but this is to escape the wrath of the Lord. More relevant as OT background is the reference to Elisha shutting the door upon Gehazi and the Shunammite woman to pray (2 Kgs 4:33), but in this case the privacy is also for the miracle of raising the dead. The goal of the command to the disciple is to pray to the Father in secret. Here (and in v 18) one expects ἐν τῷ κρυπτῷ after τῷ πατρί σου to refer to the activity of praying (and fasting in v 18). The slightly awkward reference to τῷ πατρί σου τῷ ἐν τῷ κρυπτῷ, "to your Father who is in secret," may initially have been caused by the words of the next sentence, ὁ βλέπων ἐν τῷ κρυπτῷ, "who sees in secret." The main points are nevertheless quite clear: the activity in question is to be done in secret before the God who sees in secret because he is everywhere (i.e., in secret as well as in public). The final words ἐν τῷ κρυπτῷ could conceivably go with ἀποδώσει σοι, i.e., "he will reward you in secret," but it is more natural to take the words with ὁ βλέπων, "who sees in secret." This key statement is found virtually verbatim at the close of each of the three sections (cf. vv 4 and 18). See *Comment* on v 4.

Explanation

The comments of the preceding *Explanation* apply equally well here since the same point is being made about praying as was made about almsgiving. Prayer (even if offered in the context of public worship or a prayer gathering) is to be directed to God in secret and not to be made a public spectacle to display the "righteousness" of the one who prays. A true reward for prayer will come only when prayer is God oriented, genuine, and not for display—only when prayer is directed to God and not to others.

On the Right Way to Pray: "The Lord's Prayer" (6:7–15)

Bibliography

Abrahams, I. "The Lord's Prayer." In *Studies in Pharisaism and the Gospels.* 2:93–108. **Balz, H.** "Βατταλογέω." *EDNT* 1:209. **Burkitt, F. C.** "As we have forgiven (Mt 6,12)." *JTS* 33 (1932) 253–55. **Brocke, M., Petuchowski, J. J.,** and **Stroly, W.,** eds. *Das Vaterunser—Gemeinsames im Beten von Juden und Christen.* Freiburg: Herald, 1974. **Brown, R. E.** "The Pater Noster as an Eschatological Prayer." *TS* 22 (1961) 175–208 (reprinted in idem, *New Testament Essays,* 275–320). **Buchan, W. M.** "Research on the Lord's Prayer." *ExpTim* 100 (1989) 336–39. **Bussby, F.** "A Note on ῥακά (Matthew v 22) and βατταλογέω (Matthew v 7) in the Light of Qumran." *ExpTim* 76 (1964–65) 26. **Carmignac, J.** *Recherches sur le 'Notre Père.'* Paris: Letourzey & Ané, 1969. **Dalman, G.** *Die Worte Jesu.* 2nd ed. Leipzig: Hinrichs, 1930. 283–365. **Delling, G.** "Βατταλογέω." *TDNT* 1:597–98. **Dewailly, L.-M.** "'Donne-nous notre pain': quel pain? Notes sur la quatrième demande du Pater." *RSPT* 64 (1980) 561–88. **Evans, C. F.** *The Lord's Prayer.* London: SPCK, 1963. **Finkel, A.** "The Prayer of Jesus in Matthew." In *Standing before God.* FS J. M. Oesterreicher, ed. A. Finkel and L. Frizzell. New York: Ktav, 1981. 131–69. **Gerhardsson, B.** "The Matthaean Version of the Lord's Prayer (Matt 6:9b–13): Some Observations." In *The New Testament Age.* FS B. Reicke, ed. W. C. Weinrich. Macon, GA: Mercer University, 1984. 1:207–20. **Goulder, M. D.** "The Composition of the Lord's Prayer." *JTS* n.s. 14 (1963) 32–45. **Harner, P.** *Understanding the Lord's Prayer.* Philadelphia: Fortress, 1975. **Hemer, C.** "ἐπιούσιος." *JSNT* 22 (1984) 81–94. **Higgins, A. J. B.** "Lead Us Not into Temptation." *ExpTim* 58 (1946–47) 250. **Hill, D.** "'Our Daily Bread' (Matt 6.11) in the History of Exegesis." *IBS* 5 (1983) 2–11. **Hultgren, A. J.** "The Bread Petition of the Lord's Prayer." In *Christ and His Communities.* FS R. H. Fuller, ed. A. J. Hultgren and B. Hall. ATR Supplementary Series 11. Cincinnati, OH: Forward Movement Publications, 1990. 41–54. **Jeremias, J.** *The Lord's Prayer.* Philadelphia: Fortress, 1964. ————. *The Prayers of Jesus.* SBT 2.6. London: SCM, 1967 (includes a revised version of *The Lord's Prayer* [Philadelphia: Fortress, 1964]). **Kistemaker, S. J.** "Lord's Prayer in the First Century." *JETS* 21 (1978) 323–28. **Lightfoot, J. B.** *On a Fresh Revision of the English NT.* London: Macmillan, 1872. 195–242. **Lohmeyer, E.** *Our Father: An Introduction to the Lord's Prayer.* New York: Harper & Row, 1966. **Manson, T. W.** "The Lord's Prayer." *BJRL* 38 (1955–56) 99–113, 436–48. **Meinertz, M.** "Das Vaterunser." *TRev* 45 (1949) 1–6. **Metzger, B. M.** "How Many Times Does 'EPIOUSIOS' Occur outside the Lord's Prayer?" *ExpTim* 69 (1957) 52–54. **Moule, C. F. D.** "'. . . As we forgive . . .': A Note on the Distinction between Deserts and Capacity in the Understanding of Forgiveness." In *Essays in New Testament Interpretation.* Cambridge: Cambridge University, 1982. 278–86. ————. "An Unresolved Problem in the Temptation Clause in the Lord's Prayer." *RTR* 33 (1974) 65–76. **Orchard, B.** "The Meaning of *ton epiousion* (Mt 6:11/Lk 11:3)." *BTB* (1973) 274–82. **Petuchowski, J. J.,** and **Brocke, M.** *The Lord's Prayer and Jewish Liturgy.* New York: Seabury, 1978. **Schürmann, H.** *Praying with Christ: The "Our Father" for Today.* New York: Herder & Herder, 1964. **Schwarz, G.** "Matthäus VI 9–13; Lukas XI 2–4." *NTS* 15 (1968–69) 233–47. **Scott, E. F.** *The Lord's Prayer: Its Character, Purpose, and Interpretation.* Toronto: Saunders, 1962. **Swetnam, J.** "Hallowed Be Thy Name." *Bib* 52 (1971) 556–63. **Sykes, M. H.** "And Do Not Bring Us to the Test." *ExpTim* 73 (1962) 189–90. **Thompson, G. H. P.** "Thy Will Be Done in Earth, as It Is in Heaven (Mt 6,11): A Suggested Reinterpretation." *ExpTim* 70 (1958–59) 379–81. **Tilborg, S. van.** "A Form-Criticism of the Lord's Prayer." *NovT* 14 (1972) 94–105. **Trudinger, P.** "The 'Our Father' in Matthew as Apocalyptic Eschatology." *DR* 107 (1989) 49–54. **Vögtle, A.** "Der eschatologische Bezug der Wir-Bitten des Vaterunsers." In *Jesus und Paulus.* FS W. G. Kümmel, ed. E. E. Ellis and E. Grässer.

Göttingen: Vandenhoeck & Ruprecht, 1975. 344–62. **Yamauchi, E. M.** "The 'Daily Bread' Motif in Antiquity." *WTJ* 28 (1966) 145–56.

For full bibliography on the Lord's Prayer, see M. Dorneich, ed., *Vater-Unser Bibliographie— The Lord's Prayer, a Bibliography*, Veröffentlichungen der Stiftung Oratio Dominica (Freiburg im Breisgau: Herder, 1982).

Translation

⁷ *"And when you pray, do not babble as do the Gentiles,*[a] *for they think that they will be heard merely because of the abundance of their words.* ⁸*Do not be like them in this regard,*[b] *for your Father*[c] *knows the things you need before you ask him.*[d] ⁹*Therefore you are to pray in this manner:*[e]
> *Our Father in heaven*
> *Set apart your holy name.*
> ¹⁰ *Bring your eschatological kingdom.*
> *Cause your will to be fulfilled on earth as*[f] *it is in heaven.*
> ¹¹ *Give us today the eschatological*[g] *bread that will be ours in the future.*
> ¹² *And forgive us our offenses*[h] *as we ourselves also have forgiven*[i] *those who offend us.*
> ¹³ *And do not bring us into testing, but deliver us from the Evil One.*[j,k]
> ¹⁴ *For*[l] *if you forgive other people's sins, your heavenly Father will also forgive you.*[m]
> ¹⁵ *But if you do not forgive others,*[n] *neither will your Father forgive your sins.*

Notes

[a] B 1424 syᶜ mae substitute ὑποκριταί, "hypocrites," for "Gentiles," in order to avoid the offense for gentile readers (cf. too "hypocrites" in v 5).

[b] "In this regard" added to complete sense.

[c] אⁱ B sa mae read ὁ θεὸς ὁ πατὴρ ὑμῶν, "God your Father," a Pauline idiom, which is foreign to Matthew (cf. *TCGNT*, 15). A few later MSS read ὁ πατὴρ ὑμῶν ὁ οὐράνιος, "your heavenly Father" (cf. vv 9, 14).

[d] D has ἀνοῖξαι τὸ στόμα, "open your mouth."

[e] The following translation of the well-known prayer is deliberately paraphrastic and interpretive. For explanation and support, see *Comment* section.

[f] D* boᵐˢˢ and a few other witnesses omit ὡς, "as," resulting in "cause your will to be fulfilled in heaven and on earth."

[g] The difficult word ἐπιούσιον is rendered differently in the versions: it has *cottidianum*, "daily"; vg has *supersubstantialem*, "supersubstantial"; syᶜ has (the equivalent of, as in the remaining variants) *perpetuum*, "perpetual"; sy⁽ᵖ⁾ʰ *necessarium*, "necessary"; sa *venientem*, "future"; and mae bo *crastinum*, "tomorrow's."

[h] D has the singular τὴν ὀφειλήν, "debt," or "guilt." Origen has τὰ παραπτώματα, "transgressions."

[i] The majority of later MSS (אⁱ D (L) W Δ Θ *f*¹³ TR and possibly syᶜ and co) have the present tense (ἀφίομεν or ἀφίεμεν), "forgive" (cf. Luke 11:4). Supporting the aorist tense ἀφήκαμεν, "have forgiven," see א* B Z *f*¹ vgˢᵗ syᵖ·ʰ. See *TCGNT*, 16.

[j] τοῦ πονηροῦ may also be translated "evil."

[k] A variety of later endings have been added to the prayer in the MS tradition (*without* such additions are א B D Z *f*¹ lat mae boᵖᵗ). Codex 1424 (ninth/tenth century) actually includes a note explicitly indicating that "the 'because yours is the kingdom' to 'amen' is not found in some copies." These additions, made obviously for liturgical purposes, are probably based on 1 Chr 29:11–13. A few late MSS (157 225 418 1253) add a trinitarian closing to the original prayer: ὅτι σοῦ ἐστιν ἡ βασιλεία τοῦ πατρὸς καὶ τοῦ υἱοῦ καὶ τοῦ ἁγίου πνεύματος εἰς τοὺς αἰῶνας· ἀμήν, "because yours is the kingdom of the Father and of the Son and of the Holy Spirit forever, Amen" (cf. 28:19). A few MSS add simply ἀμήν, "amen" (17 vgᶜˡ). The best-known addition is ὅτι σοῦ ἐστιν ἡ βασιλεία καὶ ἡ δύναμις καὶ ἡ δόξα

εἰς τοὺς αἰῶνας [+ τῶν αἰώνων, 2148 k sa^ms] · ἀμήν, "for yours is the kingdom and the power and the glory forever (and ever). Amen" (with slight variations: L W Θ 0233 f^13 TR sy sa bo^pt; *Did.* 8:2).

[1] D* L sa^ms omit γάρ, "for," thereby detaching somewhat the logion of vv 14–15 from the prayer itself.

^m Some MSS (L f^1 lat co) add the specific τὰ παραπτώματα ὑμῶν, "your sins," perhaps by the influence of the end of v 15 (cf. Mark 11:26).

^n The majority of MSS (B L W Θ f^13 TR sy^c,h sa bo^pt) insert τὰ παραπτώματα αὐτῶν, "their sins," perhaps in imitation of v 14a. See *TCGNT,* 17.

Form/Structure/Setting

A. The evangelist has here inserted further traditional material stemming from Jesus on the subject of prayer, thereby breaking the smooth sequence of the three parallel sections on the practice of righteousness (vv 2–4; 5–6; 16–18). This entire pericope would hardly be missed if it were omitted from the present context. Vv 9–15 in particular do not fit well their present context.

B. Vv 9–13 present "The Lord's Prayer" in a more developed form than is found in the parallel in Luke 11:1–4. Matthew's form contains seven petitions following the opening vocative (which in Luke is the simple "Father") compared to Luke's five (Luke lacks Matthew's third petition about the will of God being accomplished on earth as in heaven and Matthew's seventh petition, "deliver us from the Evil One"). The first two petitions are in verbatim agreement. Matthew's fourth petition is in close agreement with the Lukan form except only for Luke's present imperative for Matthew's aorist and Luke's τὸ καθ᾽ ἡμέραν, "for each day," for Matthew's simple σήμερον, "today." Matthew's fifth petition is basically the same as in Luke except for his use of τὰ ὀφειλήματα ἡμῶν, "our debts," where Luke has τὰς ἁμαρτίας ἡμῶν, "our sins." Matthew's sixth petition is in verbatim agreement with Luke's fifth.

Because this prayer is such an important piece of liturgical tradition, it is unnecessary to argue for common dependence upon Q to explain the common material. Quite probably the prayer was handed down in slightly differing versions in churches of different geographical regions. Thus Matthew and Luke may well have received it independently from different sources (thus Harner), despite both the agreements and disagreements. Jeremias is almost certainly correct in his conclusion that Luke preserves an earlier form of the prayer (expansions are more likely than omissions), whereas Matthew's language at a number of points is the more original (e.g., ὀφειλήματα, "debts," for Luke's ἁμαρτίας, "sins"; σήμερον, "today," for Luke's τὸ καθ᾽ ἡμέραν, "the daily"). Luke's setting for the prayer differs from Matthew's. Luke presents the prayer in response to a specific request from one of the disciples, who asks to be taught to pray as John (the Baptist) taught his disciples to pray. The prayer is also found in the early Christian document the *Didache* (8:2) in nearly verbatim agreement with the Matthean version (probably dependent on Matthew) and set forth in contrast to the improper prayer of "the hypocrites." Immediately after the prayer the *Didache* adds: "Pray thus three times a day" (8:3).

Vv 14–15 form a logion that the evangelist appends to the prayer because of its close association to the content of the fifth petition. The fact that it interrupts the flow of the larger passage (vv 1–18) suggests that the evangelist regarded its content as of great importance, not only for the offering of acceptable prayer but perhaps for its practical relevance for certain tensions with his Jewish-Christian community (cf. 5:23–24). This logion consists of two parallel parts, the second of which restates the first in negative form. No parallel to this material is found in the other Gospels (Mark 11:26 in the TR is the result of the influence of Matthew upon early copyists). Matt 18:35 contains the same thought as vv 14–15 but is probably an independent logion belonging to the parable that it concludes.

C. This pericope is itself divided into three parts: (1) the nature of true prayer, vv 7–8; (2) a model prayer ("The Lord's Prayer"), vv 9–13 (see outline below); and (3) an appended statement about the importance of forgiving others, vv 14–15. Vv 7–8 resemble to a certain extent the pattern of the three main sections (cf. *Form/Structure/Setting* §C on 6:1–4): the equivalent of the ὅταν clause in the temporal participle προσευχόμενοι, "when you pray"; a negative imperative; a comparative clause using ὥσπερ, "as," but with οἱ ἐθνικοί, "the Gentiles," for "the hypocrites"; a clause describing the cause of the unacceptable behavior (cf. v 5); the reason for behaving differently; and finally, positive advice about the correct performance of the deed in question. This form of the material is probably the result of the evangelist's work (cf. his use of ἐθνικοί in v 7; cf. 5:47; 18:17; *Did.* 8:2 preserves what is probably the original ὑποκριταί) and the influence of the three main sections of the larger passage. But he has only partially adapted the material and has not made it conform entirely to the passages on either side. Material closely related to v 8 is found in Q (Matt 6:32; Luke 12:30), but the similarity is probably due to a similar point being made independently rather than Q being the source of, or dependent upon, the present passage.

The prayer itself in Matthew begins with (1) a typically Matthean formula as the invocation: "our Father in heaven" (v 9b). This is followed by (2) three petitions quite parallel in form, all of which end in σου, "your" (hence often called "you petitions") and employ divine passives, thus referring to the agency of God in the fulfillment of the petition (vv 9c–10). The third of these is slightly expanded by the prepositional phrase, "on earth as in heaven." (The argument that the third petition is a later creation based on Jesus' Gethsemane prayer [26:36]—thus Schweizer [cf. van Tilborg]—can be no more than speculation.) These brief petitions are in turn followed by (3) two lengthier petitions that also reveal some parallelism (vv 11–12). (4) Matthew's final two petitions, although adversative, are again parallel in structure (v 13). The last four petitions involve so-called we petitions. The traditional ending of the Lord's Prayer is, of course, not found in the earliest MSS of the NT. See *Note* k above.

D. This entire passage (vv 7–15), although it interrupts the three sections on the practice of righteousness—being added to the second of these—and although it is obviously shaped to some extent by the evangelist, has good claim as traditional material stemming ultimately from Jesus. As to the petitions in the Lord's Prayer, it is arguable, though it must remain uncertain, that Matthew's third petition is not original but had probably been modeled upon the first two before the evangelist's writing. It is clearly in harmony with the teaching of Jesus. The sixth and seventh petitions appear to be an insertion between vv 12 and 14–15. But because the sixth is paralleled in Luke, it is to be regarded as tradition. The seventh petition is possibly an early elaboration of the sixth but could go back to Jesus himself since such parallelism is consistent with what seems to have been his teaching style.

Comment

7–8 These verses are relevant to the ἐθνικοί, "Gentiles," much more than to the "hypocrites," who are the bad examples in the three major illustrations. In view is the attempt to manipulate God through repetitive, perhaps even magical, phrases, as the verb βατταλογεῖν, "babble," and the noun πολυλογία, "much speaking," suggest. βατταλογεῖν, an onomatopoeic word, is probably derived from the cognate noun meaning "stammerer" or "stutterer." The verb here, however, refers not to a speech impediment but to the repetition of meaningless syllables. πολυλογία seems to have in mind vain repetition and lengthiness. They "think" (δοκοῦσιν) they will be heard by means of their devices, but in this they are mistaken. The disciples are to avoid this kind of "praying" but are to realize that what they need is already known to God. Prayer does not inform God about their needs. The stress on economy of words in prayer is already found in the OT (cf. Eccl 5:1 [MT]; Isa 1:15; Sir 7:14). V 8 presupposes that God will grant them what they need. The sermon emphasizes again in 6:32 (cf. Luke 12:30) that God knows the needs of his people. There, as here, the favorite Matthean phrase "your heavenly Father" is used.

9 οὕτως οὖν προσεύχεσθε ὑμεῖς, "therefore you are to pray in this manner." ὑμεῖς makes "you" emphatic and distinguishes the prayer of the disciples from that of others. Matthew sets forth the short prayer as a model to be followed; Luke ("when you pray, say"), on the other hand, seems to suggest the repetition of the actual words of this prayer (as was already done in the early Church). According to the *Didache* (8:3), the prayer is to be said three times a day following the regular Jewish pattern. Set liturgical prayers were already a common thing in the contemporary Jewish milieu (on the Jewish background of this prayer, see Abrahams). The Lord's Prayer, in its eschatological orientation, is similar in a number of ways to the Qaddish prayer of the synagogue. This is true not only of the spirit of the entire prayer but especially of the content of the first three petitions. Cf. especially the opening of the Qaddish:

> Exalted and hallowed be His great Name
> in the world which He created
> according to His will.
> May He establish His kingdom
> in your lifetime and in your days,
> and in the lifetime of the whole household of Israel,
> speedily and at a near time.
> And say, Amen.
>
> (from Petuchowski and Brocke, *The Lord's Prayer and Jewish Liturgy*, 37)

In a similar way other petitions in the Lord's Prayer find parallels in various Jewish prayers.

Invocation. πάτερ ἡμῶν ὁ ἐν τοῖς οὐρανοῖς, "our Father in heaven [i.e., who transcends all that is on earth]." Juxtaposed in this address are the contrasting phrases, "Father," pointing to the intimate relationship between God and his children, and "in heaven," pointing to his transcendent nature. Underlying the simple πάτηρ (as in Luke) in the probable Aramaic original, is the word אַבָּא (ʾabbā), a term of special affection and intimacy used by children in addressing their earthly fathers.

Jesus' use of ʾabbā is unique (Jeremias; Luz; Davies-Allison regard it as only "characteristic" and "distinctive," 602). The phrase "Father in heaven" is one of the evangelist's favorites (see on 5:48). The address provides the basis of the possibility of such a prayer: as Father, God is concerned for the needs of his children; as the One in heaven, he is all-powerful.

First Petition. ἁγιασθήτω τὸ ὄνομά σου, "set apart your holy name." This is an appeal to God to act in vindication of his name. The relationship between name and person is much closer in Hebraic thought than for us today (see *Comment* on 5:22). The name of God is virtually indistinguishable from the person of God (cf., for example, Mal 1:6; Isa 29:23; Ezek 36:23; John 12:28; 17:6). Thus God is called upon to vindicate himself. In a Jewish context, this petition refers to God acting in fulfillment of the promises to Israel, and thus to the silencing of the taunts of her enemies. In short, God's name will only be properly honored when he brings his kingdom and accomplishes his will on earth (cf. the Qaddish). Thus, the first three petitions of the prayer are closely linked, referring essentially to the same salvation-historical reality. The similar form of these three petitions, employing the divine passive and the aorist tenses in each case, also points to this conclusion. Gerhardsson refers to the three petitions as "one prayer in a three-part *parallelismus membrorum*" ("Matthaean Version," 210). There are at the same time ethical implications for the disciples in this petition (see *Comment* on next verse).

10   *Second Petition.* ἐλθέτω ἡ βασιλεία σου, "bring your eschatological kingdom." This refers to the eschatological rule of God (cf. Harner) expected and longed for by the Jewish people (cf. the central petition of the Qaddish, above v 9). It involves the consummation of God's purposes in history, the fulfillment of the prophetic pictures of future bliss (cf. Acts 1:6). The gospel is itself, above all, the announcement that God's promised rule has now begun in and through the work of Jesus the Messiah (see 3:2; 4:17, 23), so the disciples are thus encouraged to pray that what has begun in the ministry of Jesus, what they have now begun to participate in, may be experienced in all fullness (cf. the prayer *Marana tha*, "our Lord come," in 1 Cor 16:22; cf. Rev 22:20). The tension between a realized eschatology and future eschatology comes to expression in the mystery of the kingdom elaborated in the parables of chap. 13.

Third Petition. γενηθήτω τὸ θέλημά σου ὡς ἐν οὐρανῷ καὶ ἐπὶ γῆς, "cause your will to be fulfilled on earth as it is in heaven." This petition is essentially synonymous with the preceding petition (cf. its omission in Luke 11:2). The accomplishment of God's will on earth obviously means the overturning of the present evil order and thus a regeneration of the earth as we know it. God's will is done in the realm of his sovereign transcendence; let that sovereignty now be expressed upon the earth (cf. 1 Macc 3:60). Alternatively, the ὡς . . . καί may be understood as a petition for the will of God to be done both in heaven and on earth (cf. Thompson, 380). All of reality must finally come under his rule.

The first three petitions, although appealing in the first instance to the activity of God in history (all are in the aorist tense), are not without ethical implications for the disciples who are thus taught to pray. The very form of the third person imperatives (tr. "let . . ."), rather than the second person imperative, may point to the involvement of those who pray (thus Gerhardsson). The disciples, after all, already participate in the reign of God brought by Jesus and are therefore representatives of that reign in the present. Although they cannot bring that kingdom into existence by their own efforts, yet they are to reflect the good news of its inauguration in and through Jesus. They are to manifest the reality of the presence of the kingdom (cf. 5:13–16). There is thus a sense in which the first three petitions of the prayer are also a prayer that the disciples will be faithful to their calling, that they will do their part (in obedience), not to bring the kingdom but to manifest its prophetic presence through Jesus and the Spirit. (Cf. Luz, who says of the third petition: "an alternative between divine action and human action would be a false alternative" [1:380]; cf. Davies-Allison.) Realized eschatology is in continuity with the future eschatology it foreshadows.

11 *Fourth Petition.* With the shift to the first person pronouns ("us"; "our") beginning in this petition, it is difficult to decide whether the eschatological perspective of the first three petitions is left behind or is at least significantly modified (thus Vögtle). Some insist that the petitions remain consistently eschatological in perspective (e.g., Jeremias; Brown, "Pater Noster"; Davies-Allison). The issue is raised sharply by the question of the meaning of the fourth petition. The position taken here is that the "we petitions" are primarily eschatological but include present aspects that may be understood as anticipating the end time. (Indeed, even the first three petitions have relevance to the actions of those who pray [see Brown, "Pater Noster," 292, n. 53; 300, n. 79].)

τὸν ἄρτον ἡμῶν τὸν ἐπιούσιον δὸς ἡμῖν σήμερον, "give to us today the eschatological bread that will be ours in the future." In this petition, with the use of the first person plural pronoun, the prayer turns to the more specific needs of the disciples. Petitions of cosmic scope thus give way to the meeting of personal needs with the former as the basis of the latter. The much-debated interpretation of this passage depends on the difficult question of the meaning of the adjective ἐπιούσιον.

The following main proposals have been suggested. (1) ἐπιούσιον = ἐπὶ τὴν οὖσαν [from ἐπεῖναι] ἡμέραν, "for the present day." In this interpretation, the petition is for the provision of the disciples' daily needs for food. But this interpretation makes the petition unnecessarily redundant: "Give us our bread for the present day today." Why are *both* ἐπιούσιον and σήμερον in the same sentence? (The question is even more difficult for Luke 11:3 with its τὸ καθ' ἡμέραν, "for each day," and the present δίδου, "keep giving." Luke, however, seems to have understood ἐπιούσιον in a non-eschatological way, despite the degree of redundancy involved.) (2) ἐπιούσιον = (a) ἐπί plus οὐσία, "for existence." The meaning in this case is clear enough: "give us today the bread necessary for our existence." That is, give us today only the bread we need to survive. But again, the reason for the prayer is less than clear. Most important, the reason for the (on this view) redundant σήμερον, "today"—which is, moreover, in an emphatic position at the end of the sentence—is hardly apparent. (b) The combination of ἐπί and οὐσία, interpreted as *supersubstantialis* (as in the Vulgate; thus, lit., "the bread above the substance"), enabled many in the early Church (e.g., Jerome) to see the petition as a reference to the Eucharist. But this interpretation imports later concepts into the passage and does not fit the context well. (3) ἐπιούσιον = ἡ ἐπιοῦσα [from ἐπιέναι] ἡμέρα, for "the following day," or "the coming day." Here what is in view is either tomorrow's ration of food and, in this case, the petition is "give us tomorrow's ration of food today," or today's ration of bread prayed for the night before or early the same morning (thus Hemer, who shows that Matthew's word can be related to the meaning of the commonly used substantive ἡ ἐπιοῦσα < ἐπιέναι). In this case the petition would amount to: "Give us bread for the day that is beginning." Asking for tomorrow's bread today, taken in the ordinary sense, stands in some tension with the exhortation not to be anxious about tomorrow (6:34, with reference to what there will be to eat!). To pray for bread for the day that is beginning makes good sense in itself, but on this view the emphatic σήμερον, "today," again seems both unnecessary and difficult to explain. (4) ἐπιούσιον is derived from ἐπιέναι, "to come." Bread for "the coming day" could be interpreted as bread for tomorrow (or the future), i.e., the equivalent of the preceding option (and, according to Luz, etymologically the most probable; cf. Hultgren, who accepts this etymology but proposes that the adjective modifies "bread" rather than "day"—hence τὸν ἐπιούσιον ἄρτον, the meaning of which he paraphrases "our bread which comes upon us from you"). As some have argued who accept this view (esp. Jeremias; so too Brown, "Pater Noster"), the coming day in view could well be the day of the eschatological banquet (see on 8:11). Brown ("Pater Noster," 306) also sees an allusion to the (messianic) miracle of manna on "the morrow" (Exod 16:4). The petition thus reflects an imminent eschatological expectation (cf. Harner, 84). Such an interpretation is in keeping with the content of the first three petitions, but what is more important, it is the only one to give an adequate understanding of the emphatic σήμερον, "today," at the climactic end of the sentence. The disciples should pray for the experience of the eschatological blessing today, of the bread that brings the time of the eschaton, the messianic banquet.

The prayer thus asks for the present realization of the blessing of the eschaton. The prayer *is* nevertheless a prayer for bread. And there is a sense in which the bread (by synecdoche, "food") we partake of daily is an anticipation of the eschatological banquet. This fourth petition, in moving from the cosmic to the particular, does not leave behind eschatological concerns. On the contrary, it looks for eschatological benefits in the present, and in this sense it is perhaps the most significant type of petition that the disciples can pray. At the same time, however, the fulfillment of present needs—even in so ordinary a thing as bread—is for the disciples anticipatory of the eschatological fulfillment of needs.

12   *Fifth Petition.* καὶ ἄφες ἡμῖν τὰ ὀφειλήματα ἡμῶν, ὡς καὶ ἡμεῖς ἀφήκαμεν τοῖς ὀφειλέταις ἡμῶν, "and forgive us our offenses as we ourselves forgive those who offend us." The exegesis of this verse is facilitated by the appended emphases in vv 14–15. Thus, ὀφειλήματα, "shortcomings" (lit., "debts"), finds its parallel in παραπτώματα, "sins" or "transgressions." This is also clear from the Lukan parallel to the present verse (Luke 11:4), which uses the word ἁμαρτίαι, "sins." Here probably Luke has avoided the more archaic ὀφειλήματα, which may not have been as easily understood by his gentile readers (but he has kept the root in the participial form at the end of v 4). The concept of sin as a "debt" owed to God has an Aramaic background (in the rabbinic literature, חוֹבָא, *hôbā*ʾ, is sin construed as a debt). ἀφήκαμεν is in the aorist tense, conveying the sense of having already forgiven others in the past and thus to a degree anticipating the point of vv 14–15. On the other hand, ἀφήκαμεν could be a Greek rendering of the Aramaic *perfectum praesens* and thus be translated with a present tense, "as we forgive" (Jeremias; Hill). It seems probable here that our being forgiven at the future judgment is in view (cf. the future tenses of vv 14–15 referring to God's forgiveness), so that again the petition is eschatological in reference. And yet again here a present aspect is also implicit since divine forgiveness is also experienced in the present in advance of eschatological forgiveness (cf. Davies-Allison). The great importance placed upon forgiveness by Jesus is also to be seen later in the Gospel in 18:21–22 and especially in the following parable concerning the unforgiving servant (18:23–35). The connection that is presupposed between our forgiving of others and God's forgiving of us (ὡς καὶ ἡμεῖς, "as also we," where the "we" is emphatic) is made more explicit in vv 14–15 (see *Comment*). τοῖς ὀφειλέταις ἡμῶν is literally "our debtors," a cognate noun to ὀφειλήματα.

13 *Sixth Petition.* καὶ μὴ εἰσενέγκῃς ἡμᾶς εἰς πειρασμόν, "and do not bring us into testing." πειρασμός, depending on the context, can be translated "temptation" or "testing." Here the latter is to be preferred because God does not lead into temptation (cf. Jas 1:13); he does, however, allow his people to be tested. "To be tempted" is to be enticed to sin; "to be tested" is to be brought into difficult circumstances that try one's faithfulness. The two are similar, since sin can result in either case; yet they are also to be differentiated, since the former has a negative purpose, the latter a positive one. The petition in this instance concerns severe testing (see Sykes, who notes Sir 2:1; 33:1) that could eventuate in apostasy. Again the question arises concerning whether the testing in view is eschatological, i.e., in connection with the coming of the eschaton (thus Jeremias, Brown), or whether it refers to the testing of everyday life (thus Luz), or perhaps both (Davies-Allison). Favoring the eschatological understanding are the aorist tenses of this and the next petition and the tenor of the whole prayer. Against it is the fact that πειρασμόν lacks the definite article (cf. Rev 3:10). Perhaps again the future is primarily in view, but the petition is expressed in such a way as to leave open application to "ordinary" testing in the present age. Such testing again anticipates the great final test. The disciple thus prays not to be led into such a situation, i.e., not to be led into a testing in which his or her faith will not be able to survive. This interpretation is allowable because of the next petition, which is connected with the present petition and which implies that some testing is inevitable and therefore asks for preservation in it. (In this Jeremias is correct [*Prayers*, 104–5].) It was indeed a common expectation that a time of severe testing would necessarily precede the dawning of the messianic age. This much testing could not be avoided. The disciple thus prays to be kept from testing that, anticipating the eschatological testing, will bring a genuine crisis of faith (cf. 2 Pet 2:9).

Seventh Petition. ἀλλὰ ῥῦσαι ἡμᾶς ἀπὸ τοῦ πονηροῦ, "but deliver us from the Evil One." This petition is connected to the preceding by the adversative "but"; i.e., it is assumed that some testing is inevitable. Thus, when testing comes, the disciple prays for deliverance (for the promise of deliverance, see Sir 33:1 and 2 Pet 2:9). τοῦ πονηροῦ (lit. "the evil") here may be either masculine or neuter. The definite article can be used in referring either to evil (so Harner) or to the Evil One, and the context provides little help in deciding which is intended at this point. If, however, one interprets the testing of the preceding petition to be eschatological in nature, one will naturally favor the latter view. The same ambiguity may be seen in the similar references in 2 Thess 3:3 and John 17:15. In at least three places in Matthew the articular πονηρός probably refers to the Evil One or Satan (5:37; 13:19, 38; cf. 1 John 5:18), but in one instance it seems certainly to refer to evil rather than the Devil (5:39; elsewhere in the NT, Christians *are* to resist the Devil, e.g., Jas 4:7; 1 Pet 5:9). The difference between Satan and evil is small in the present petition: to pray to be free from one is to pray to be free from the other. But the more vivid, personal interpretation may be slightly preferable here; Satan desires to use any severe testing of the Christian to his advantage. The sixth and seventh petitions together may be paraphrased in the following words: Do not lead us into a testing of our faith that is beyond our endurance, but when testing does come, deliver us from the Evil One and his purposes.

14–15   This appended statement, not a part of the prayer itself, emphasizes the point of the fifth petition, in which human involvement is most evident (Luz, 1:389). Since it is apparently of great importance to the evangelist and interrupts the flow of 6:1–18, it may point to the existence of tensions in his community. It is not found in Luke; however, Mark 11:25 is a close parallel (11:26 is not in the best manuscripts but has apparently been inserted by later copyists from the passage before us). V 15 simply repeats v 14 in negative form, showing how important the point is considered to be. The basic symmetry of the parallelism is broken by the chiasm, wherein according to v 14 παραπτώματα is the object of the protasis while in v 15 it is object of the apodosis, thus creating an effect of emphasis. These verses need not be taken to mean that the forgiveness we enjoy from God stands in a causal relation to our forgiveness of others, or that God's forgiveness of us is the result of our forgiveness of others (see the useful discussion in Harner, 100–106; cf. Moule, "'As we forgive'"). It is clear from these verses that a direct connection exists between God's forgiveness and our forgiveness. But it is a given that God's forgiveness is always prior (cf. 18:23–35). These verses are a forceful way of making the significant point that it is unthinkable—impossible—that we can enjoy God's forgiveness without in turn extending our forgiveness toward others. Paul makes use of this logion in Col 3:13.

Explanation

Prayer is straightforward and simple for those who have experienced the grace of the kingdom in Christ. In prayer the disciple does not try to coerce or manipulate God. There are no magical words or formulae, nor does an abundance of words count with God. Short, direct, and sincere prayers are adequate. Prayer, furthermore, is not made to inform God of our needs and desires. Nevertheless, the Christian should pray. And when Jesus teaches his disciples to pray, he follows the pattern of the synagogue prayers of his day. The Lord's Prayer thus centers on the large issues of God's redemptive program rather than on more mundane matters. The disciples are to pray above all for the realization of God's eschatological program on earth. Most of the petitions in the prayer are dominated by this concern for the end time. Yet, at the same time, the petitions have implications for the present. The first three petitions at least imply the present importance of discipleship in the words "on earth as in heaven." The fourth petition, for daily bread, also has to do with present sustenance of the disciples as a sign of imminent eschatological blessing. But the present dimension of the Lord's Prayer is seen most clearly and most forcefully in the fifth petition (and the added words of vv 14–15), with its reference to our forgiveness of others in the manner of God's forgiveness of us. The closing petitions reflect a confidence in the sovereign love of God that will preserve us in the testing of our faith now and in time of tribulation.

The one who prays the Lord's Prayer prays thus from a perspective of one who is involved in the great redemptive drama that is beginning to unfold in the Gospel narrative itself. The measure of eschatological fulfillment already realized focuses one's thoughts and desires upon the consummation of God's purposes as well as upon the consciousness and importance of present discipleship.

Fasting (6:16–18)

Bibliography

Banks, R. "Fasting." *DJG* 233–34. **Gerhardsson, B.** "Geistiger Opferdienst nach Matth 6,1–6. 16–21." In *Neues Testament und Geschichte.* FS O. Cullmann, ed. H. Baltensweiler and B. Reicke. Zürich/Tübingen: Theologischer/Mohr, 1972. 69–77. **George, A.** "La justice à faire dans le secret (Mat. 6,1–6. 16–18)." *Bib* 40 (1959) 590–98. **O'Hara, J.** "The Christian Fasting (Mt. 6.16–18)." *SCR* 19 (1967) 3–18, 82–95. **Str-B.** "Vom altjüdisches Fasten." 4:77–114.

Translation

^{16} *"And whenever you fast, do not look sullen as the hypocrites do. For they distort their faces so that they will be seen by others to be fasting. I tell you surely, they are receiving their reward at that moment.* ^{17} *By contrast, whenever you are fasting, anoint your head and wash your face,* ^{18} *so that it is not obvious to others that you are fasting, but only to your Father who is in secret.*[a] *And your Father who sees in secret*[a] *will reward you."*[b]

Notes

[a] In the older MSS (א B D^c *f* ^{1}), κρυφαίῳ, "in secret," is found twice in this verse, against the previous occurrences of the synonymous κρυπτῷ in the parallel sentences in vv 4 and 6. Later MSS, including *f* ^{13} L W Θ, harmonize by substituting κρυπτῷ.

[b] A few MSS (Δ 0233 1241 it) add the words ἐν τῷ φανερῷ, "in the open," as a contrast to the unseen "reward" received by the hypocrites. For the same antithetic parallelism with ἐν τῷ κρυπτῷ, see the similar textual variants of vv 4 and 6.

Form/Structure/Setting

See *Form/Structure/Setting* for 6:1–4.

Structurally this pericope is very similar to the form of the first two contrasts concerning the practice of piety (vv 2–4; 5–6). V 17 is chiastic in structure: σου τὴν κεφαλήν follows its verb, while τὸ πρόσωπόν σου precedes its verb. The final sentence that concludes each of the three contrasts (vv 4, 6) is here found verbatim except for the variant κρυφαίῳ for κρυπτῷ, which could stem from a slightly different oral tradition of the material.

Comment

16 Again here, as in the preceding two examples of piety, "the hypocrites" (cf. v 2) are characterized by their desire "to be seen by others" (cf. 23:5). In this instance they desire to make it plain to all that they are engaging in the righteous activity of fasting and that they are thus holy men. Accordingly, they go out of their way to make themselves conspicuous when they fast. In view here is the voluntary practice of private fasting (cf. Luke 18:12; *Did.* 8:1) and not the prescribed fasting associated with the great festivals of the Day of Atonement and New Year. This is the only place in the NT where fasting is actually taught. In the only other major reference to fasting in the Gospels, fasting is regarded as temporarily inappropriate (see Matt 9:14–15). The reference in the Pharisee's prayer (Luke 18:12) is more negative than positive in its impact. In Luke-Acts, however, we generally see more positive references (Luke 2:37; Acts 13:2–3; 14:23, where we have the common link of prayer with fasting). No NT epistle encourages its readers to fast. It is at least clear that the fasting of a disciple, who has already in some measure experienced the joy of fulfillment, must be quite different from the fasting of a Jew who grieves over the apparent failure of God to act on behalf of his people. (See below on 9:14.) Elsewhere in the NT the word σκυθρωποί, "sullen," "gloomy," occurs only in Luke 24:17; it occurs only infrequently in the LXX (e.g., Gen 40:7), where it refers to a sad countenance. The verb ἀφανίζουσιν literally means "to make invisible" (cf. Jas 4:14), but here in reference to the face, it must mean to make unrecognizable. This refers not simply to the gloominess of the facial expression but probably to a face made dirty with ashes (cf. "sackcloth and ashes") and a generally disheveled appearance. A wordplay exists in ἀφανίζουσιν and φανῶσιν: they hide their faces in order to be seen. Again, as in the previous two examples of ostentatious piety (see vv 2, 4), the present tense of ἀπέχουσιν, "they are having," is emphatic and ironic. They are at that moment receiving the only reward they will get.

17–18 σὺ δέ is emphatic, as also in vv 3 and 6. ἀλείφειν is strictly used in ordinary references to anointing, in contrast with the religious anointing for special office, for which χρίειν is reserved. In view here is a special instance of grooming (cf. 2 Sam 12:20; Eccl 9:8) and personal enjoyment, a sign of happiness that was forbidden on fast days. Jesus thus exhorts even an extra measure of care to one's appearance, so that it could not give the slightest hint that one was fasting. One's fasting, on the contrary, is to be known only to the Father, τῷ ἐν τῷ κρυφαίῳ, "who is in secret." Here, as in the preceding instances, the Father, who exists "in secret" and thus cannot be seen, is ὁ βλέπων ἐν τῷ κρυφαίῳ, the one who "sees" everything done "in secret." Only this kind of conduct will receive a true reward. For OT background concerning fasting that is pleasing to God, cf. Isa 58:3–12, which may to some extent serve as the background to the teaching of Jesus.

Explanation

In the first century, fasting apparently provided an exceptional opportunity for impressing others with the extent of one's piety. Here, as in the previous two species of piety, the activity was carefully designed so as to inflate personal pride (cf. Luke 18:12). Jesus tolerates no such conduct. Our righteousness is a matter of service to God and is to be directed to him. True righteousness is, in the last analysis, seen in secret. Only this kind of righteousness will be truly rewarded in any lasting way.

Dependence upon God   (6:19–34)

Serving God Rather Than Wealth   (6:19–24)

Bibliography

Allison, D. C. "The Eye Is the Lamp of the Body (Matthew 6:22–23=Luke 11:34–36)." *NTS* 33 (1987) 61–83. **Amstutz, J.** *ΑΠΛΟΤΗΣ: Eine begriffsgeschichtliche Studie zum jüdisch-christlichen Griechisch.* Bonn: Hanstein, 1968. 96–103. **Betz, H. D.** "Matt. 6:22–23 and Ancient Greek Theories of Vision." In *Essays on the Sermon on the Mount.* 71–87. **Cadbury, H. J.** "The Single Eye." *HTR* 47 (1954) 69–74. **Edlund, C.** "Das Auge der Einfalt." *ASNU* 19 (1952) 51–122. **Fensham, F. C.** "The Good and Evil Eye in the Sermon on the Mount." *Neot* 1 (1967) 51–58. **France, R. T.** "God and Mammon." *EvQ* 51 (1979) 3–21. **Groenewald, E. P.** "God and Mammon." *Neot* 1 (1967) 59–66. **Hengel, M.** *Property and Riches in the Early Church.* London: SCM, 1974. **Honeyman, A. M.** "The Etymology of Mammon." *Archivum Linguisticum* 4.1 (1952) 60–65. **Koch, K.** "Der Schatz im Himmel." In *Leben angesichts des Todes,* ed. B. Lohse and H. P. Schmidt. Tübingen: Mohr, 1968. 47–60. **Pesch, W.** "Zur Exegese von Mt 6, 19–21 und Lk 12,33–34." *Bib* 41 (1960) 356–78. **Riesenfeld, H.** "Vom Schätzensammeln und Sorge—ein Thema urchristlichen Paränese: Zu Mt vi 19–34." In *Neotestamentica et Patristica.* FS O. Cullmann, ed. W. C. van Unnik. Leiden: Brill, 1962. 47–58. **Roberts, R. L.** "An Evil Eye (Matthew 6:23)." *ResQ* 7 (1963) 143–47. **Rüger, H. P.** "Μαμωνᾶς." *ZNW* 64 (1973) 127–31. **Safrai, S.,** and **Flusser, D.** "The Slave of Two Masters." *Immanuel* 6 (1976) 30–33. **Sjöberg, E.** "Das Licht in dir: Zur Deutung von Matth. 6,22f Par." *ST* 5 (1952) 89–105. **Thienemann, T.** "A Comment on an Interpretation by Prof. Cadbury." *Gordon Review* 1 (1955) 9–22.

Translation

[19] *"Do not store up for yourselves treasures in this world[a] where they are subject to the ravage of such things as[b] moth and corrosion and where thieves can[c] break in and steal.* [20] *But store up your treasures in heaven where moth and corrosion do not destroy and where thieves cannot[d] break in or steal.* [21] *For wherever your[e] treasure is, there too will be your[f] heart.*

[22] *"The eye enables a person to see light.[g] If therefore your eye is generous,[h] your whole person[i] will be full of[j] light.* [23] *But if your eye is covetous,[k] your whole person[l] will be full of[m] darkness. If therefore the very organ that should bring you light is the source of darkness in you,[n] how great is your[o] darkness.*

[24] *"It is impossible for anyone[p] to be the slave of two masters. For a person will either neglect[q] one master and prefer[r] the other, or will pay attention to the one and will disregard the other. You cannot be a slave to God and to money at the same time."[s]*

Notes

[a] ἐπὶ τῆς γῆς, lit. "on the earth."
[b] "Such things as" added to translation.
[c] "Can" added to translation.

^d Lit. "do not."

^e The majority of MSS have the pl. ὑμῶν here in order to make the number of the second person pronoun agree with the pl. of vv 19–20, as well as with the parallel in Luke 12:34. The harder reading σου (sing.) is found in ℵ B lat co and a few other witnesses.

^f Here too the pl. is found in some MSS. See preceding *Note.*

^g ὁ λύχνος τοῦ σώματός ἐστιν ὁ ὀφθαλμός, lit. "the eye is the light of the body."

^h ἁπλοῦς, lit. "single."

ⁱ σῶμα, lit. "body."

^j "Full of" added to translation.

^k πονηρός, lit. "evil."

^l σῶμα, lit. "body."

^m "Full of" added to translation.

ⁿ This is a paraphrase for εἰ οὖν τὸ φῶς τὸ ἐν σοὶ σκότος ἐστίν, translated literally: "If therefore the light that is in you is darkness."

^o "Your" added to translation.

^p L 1241 insert οἰκέτης, "slave," probably through the influence of the parallel in Luke 16:13.

^q μισήσει, lit. "will hate."

^r ἀγαπήσει, lit. "will love."

^s "At the same time" added to translation to complete the sense of the statement.

Form/Structure/Setting

A. In a new section of the sermon, the evangelist now presents three short pericopes that contrast the pursuit of the wealth of this world with the single-hearted desire of the disciple to do the will of the Father, wherein alone lies true wealth. These pericopes are in line with and extend the emphasis of the sermon on right-eousness and discipleship.

B. Each of these three pericopae finds a parallel in Luke: the first (vv 19–21) only a partial one (Luke 12:33–34); the third (v 24) a verbatim one, except for Luke's added οἰκέτης (Luke 16:13); the second (vv 22–23) is closely paralleled in Luke 11:34–36. The distribution of the common material in Luke implies that, as elsewhere in the sermon, Matthew has collected these sayings together in pro-ducing the first major discourse. The first pericope with its skillfully constructed parallelism, ideal for memorization, was probably drawn from an oral tradition independent of Luke's source, but overlapping it to a considerable extent in the last sentence, "where your treasure is there also will be your heart" (Luke 12:34). In the second pericope, where Luke argues very closely with Matthew, we per-haps should suppose common dependence on Q, although here too dependence upon similar oral tradition, given the mnemonic parallelism, is also a possibility. In the third pericope we probably have mutual dependence on Q, with Matthew omitting the unnecessary οἰκέτης. But even the Q material shows the marks of oral transmission in the studied parallelism.

C. The three related, but independent, pericopes are: (1) the storing up of treasures, vv 19–21; (2) the uncovetous eye, vv 22–23; and (3) the impossibility of serving two masters, v 24. Each of the pericopes reflects a wisdom genre and is set forth in striking parallelism of form. The first and longest contains the most striking symmetry. Thus v 20 is a verbatim repetition of v 19 except for the initial μή, the contrasting ἐν οὐρανῷ for ἐπὶ τῆς γῆς, the necessary negatives before the nouns σής and βρῶσις, and the verbs διορύσσουσιν and κλέπτουσιν. V 21, con-taining the punch line, is itself exactly parallel in form except for the change of tense in the second verb and the substitution of ἐκεῖ for ὅπου. Within the second pericope we also encounter exactly symmetrical parallelism. After the opening sentence (v 22a) and before the concluding sentence (v 23b) are two verbatim conditional sentences except for the contrasting pairs of rhyming predicate nominatives: φωτεινόν/σκοτεινόν and ἁπλοῦς/πονηρός. In the third pericope (v 24), there is a degree of parallelism between the opening and closing sentences, but between these is a symmetrical "either . . . or" contrast, involving two parallel elements with contrasting verbs (all in the future tense) and the alternation of "the one . . . the other." A chiastic pattern is also evident: *a, a′* = serving two masters; *b, b′* = disregarding the one; *c, c′* = preferring the one.

D. Each of these pericopes finds a parallel in the *Gospel of Thomas* (respectively logia 76, 24, and 47). If the *Gospel of Thomas* is not dependent on the synoptic Gospels, then we have further evidence of the widespread influence of these passages in oral tradition.

Comment

19–20 The clause ὅπου σὴς καὶ βρῶσις ἀφανίζει, "where moth and rust consume," expresses the truth that treasures stored up on the earth are at best insecure. They are subject to the destruction caused by nature in a variety of forms, of which moth and decay are only two examples. ἀφανίζειν is a strong word in this context, connoting ruin or destruction. The moth (σής) was a well-known destroyer in the ancient world and, hence, frequently came to be used as a symbol of destruction (cf. Isa 50:9; 51:8; and esp. Job 4:19, "those who dwell in houses of clay, whose foundation is in the dust, who are crushed before the moth"). The meaning of βρῶσις is much more difficult to ascertain. The literal meaning of the word is "eating," and the linking with moth has inclined some to understand here some other living organism such as a locust or a worm (cf. *Gos. Thom.* 76; "worm" is parallel to "moth" in Isa 51:8; cf. NJB's translation here in Matthew: "woodworm"). βρῶσις is used in Mal 3:11, apparently to refer to the devouring locust. In classical Greek, however, the word was used for "decay" of teeth (BAGD, 148). In two OT passages (Job 13:28; Hos 5:12), furthermore, the moth is parallel to "rot" or "dry-rot." The same parallel is found in Jas 5:2, which is undoubtedly dependent on the Jesus tradition here recorded in the Sermon on the Mount ("Your riches have rotted and your garments are moth-eaten" [σητόβρωτα, a combination of Matthew's two words]). The next verse in James, to be sure, does go on to talk about rust. But since Greek has a specific word for rust (ἰός), used in Jas 5:3, it seems better to translate βρῶσις here more broadly as "rot," "decay," or "corrosion" (contra Luz, who opts for an insect such as "the death-watch beetle" that would eat wooden storage boxes). The statement ὅπου κλέπται διορύσσουσιν καὶ κλέπτουσιν, "where thieves break in and steal," refers to the other constant danger to earthly treasures. Burglary was not uncommon in the ancient world. It was not difficult for thieves to burrow their way through the mud-brick walls of the typical Palestinian house (cf. Job 24:16). Treasures in the ancient world were often buried under house floors, as archeologists have repeatedly discovered. Hence the verb διορύσσειν, "dig through," may be used here quite literally. Earthly wealth is thus always precarious and may easily be lost.

The disciples are exhorted instead to "treasure up for yourselves treasures in heaven," θησαυρίζετε δὲ ὑμῖν θησαυροὺς ἐν οὐρανῷ. The concept of treasures in heaven as good works stored up before God is a common one in Jewish tradition (see Tob 4:9; 4 Ezra 6:5; Sir 29:10–13; *Pss. Sol.* 9:5; for rabbinic references cf. *m. Peʾa* 1:1; further references in Str-B 1:430). The folly of the person who looks for security by storing up treasures in this world is illustrated in the parable in Luke 12:16–21, which is prefaced by the saying "Take care! Be on your guard against all kinds of greed; for one's life does not consist in the abundance of possessions." "Treasure in heaven" is promised by Jesus to the rich man if he gives away his wealth to the poor (Matt 19:21; cf. 1 Tim 6:18–19).

21 Where a person's treasures are, ἐκεῖ ἔσται καὶ ἡ καρδία σου, "there also will be your heart." This is the main point of these verses (vv 19–21). The main and central organ of the body is a well-known metaphor for the center of a person's inner being (J. Behm, *TDNT* 3:605–14) and thus the center of a person's attention and commitment. With this compare the earlier uses of καρδία in the sermon (5:8, 28). Truly, the one who piles up treasures on earth will have his or her attention and commitment necessarily turned to earthly matters rather than to the will of the Father in heaven (cf. Luke 12:21).

22–23 These difficult verses can only be understood correctly by noting the context in which they stand, i.e., the pericopes on either side, both of which refer to concern with wealth. The ἁπλοῦς eye and the πονηρός eye are not to be understood physically as a healthy and a diseased eye (contra Guelich, *Sermon*). The eye is referred to metaphorically in this passage. The πονηρός eye is the "evil eye" of Near Eastern cultures—an eye that enviously covets what belongs to another, a greedy or avaricious eye (see G. Harder, *TDNT* 6:555–56). For the Jewish use of the expression in this sense, see *m. ʾAbot* 2:12, 15; 5:16, 22 (= Danby, 2:9, 11; 5:13, 19). Other references to an evil eye in this sense are found in Matt 20:15 and Mark 7:22 (cf. Sir 14:8–10; Tob 4:7). The ἁπλοῦς eye, given the symmetrical structure of the passage, is probably the opposite of the evil eye, namely, a generous eye, as in the cognate adverb ἁπλῶς, "generously," in Jas 1:5 (cf. Rom 12:8; 2 Cor 8:2; 9:11, 13)—an eye that is not attached to wealth but is ready to part with it. It is easier to understand ἁπλοῦς as a synonym for the expected ἀγαθός, "good," in the ethical sense argued above, than to understand πονηρός in the physiological sense of "unusual" (as does Guelich, *Sermon*, following Sjöberg). On the other hand, ἁπλοῦς can also mean "single" (BAGD, 86a) in the sense of devotion to one purpose, a meaning consonant with the point made by the following verse (v 24). Cf. too "singleness [ἁπλότης] of heart" in Eph 6:5.

The statement ὁ λύχνος τοῦ σώματός ἐστιν ὁ ὀφθαλμός, "the eye is the light of the body," expresses the common affirmation of the importance of the eye in the Hellenistic world (cf. Philo, *Opif.* 5, 17). What seems to be meant is that the eye is what makes sight possible. When ancient writers said that the eye itself contained fire or light (Allison, "Eye"; for background, cf. Prov 15:30; Sir 23:19), it is doubtful that they meant this literally or meant to imply anything about their theory of sight (contra Allison). It is only a way of speaking about the phenomenon of sight (so too references to the dimming or darkening of the eyes as in, e.g., Gen 27:1; 48:10; Lam 5:17). In v 23b εἰ οὖν τὸ φῶς τὸ ἐν σοὶ σκότος ἐστίν, τὸ σκότος πόσον, "if the light in you is darkness, how great is the darkness," could easily follow this statement in v 22a directly. Here it is a mistake to take "light" literally (as Davies-Allison do). In all probability "light" is an example of simple metonymy for the eye itself. It seems highly improbable that the evangelist here deliberately opposes the Platonic-Stoic anthropology concerning the *lumen internum* (as Betz contends). What interests the evangelist is the eye/light metaphor as a vehicle for his argument concerning the disciple and material wealth. The point is that the eye is what brings light to the body; if instead the eye itself becomes only a source of darkness, how great one's personal darkness is. The nature of the eye problem is specified in the two conditional sentences contained in vv 22b–23a. Metaphorically speaking, a generous eye or the single eye of discipleship is the source of light; an evil, covetous eye is the source of darkness.

24 The situation of a slave having two masters, though unusual, was actually possible, as for example when a slave was owned by two brothers. (The Talmud contains discussion of cases where such a slave gained half his freedom but remained a "half-slave." See Str-B 1:433 for references; see too Acts 16:16,19.) The point here, however, is that a slave with two masters can do justice to neither. Truly to serve a master demands total and undivided commitment. This is why serving two masters is impossible.

The literal translation of ἢ γὰρ τὸν ἕνα μισήσει καὶ τὸν ἕτερον ἀγαπήσει, "for he will hate the one and love the other," is misleading since this Jewish idiom of loving and hating intends to express a matter of absolute versus partial commitment. In view is the degree of commitment of the slave to his duty (thus rightly Gundry), as can also be seen from the clause that follows. This use of "hate" is clear from a passage such as Luke 14:26, where Jesus says, "If anyone comes to me and does not hate his own father and mother and wife and children and brothers and sisters, yes, even his own life, he cannot be my disciple." This does not refer to hatred as we understand the word but is only an emphatic way of referring to the absolute commitment required in discipleship. "Hate" thus equals "love less than," as can be clearly seen from the parallel in Matt 10:37. This idiom is found already in the OT (compare Gen 29:31, 33 with 29:30; in Deut 21:15 the NRSV's "disliked" is lit. "hated").

The next pair of verbs, ἀνθέξεται and καταφρονήσει, should be understood similarly. καταφρονεῖν need not be taken as "despise" but can have the more mild sense of "disregard" (see BAGD, 420); ἀντέχειν in a similar way may be understood as simply "pay attention to" (see BAGD, 73). The point of this verse is that by nature slavery requires absolute loyalty and commitment and, therefore, an exclusive commitment to a single master. In a similar way discipleship requires undivided and absolute commitment.

The potential for divided loyalty expressed in the present passage is emphasized in the concluding sentence: One cannot serve both God and money. (For a sensible examination of the practical issues here, see France, "God and Mammon.") The word μαμωνᾶς, "mammon," is translated from the Aramaic noun מָמוֹן, *mamôn* (emphatic state, מָמוֹנָא, *mamônā'*), meaning "wealth" (in the broad sense of the word) or, more basically, "property," and is here personified and regarded as a potential master. In addition to its occurrence in the Lukan parallel (16:13), the word is found elsewhere in the NT only in Luke 16:9 and 11 where both times it is modified by the ἀδικία stem ("unrighteous"). The word also occurs in 2 *Clem.* 6:1 (in dependence upon Matthew) as well as in *m. Sanh.* 1:1; *b. 'Abot* 2:7, where Hillel is reported as saying "the more possessions, the more care." (See C. Brown, *NIDNTT* 2:836–38.)

Explanation

The issue in view in these passages is not wealth primarily, but an absolute and unqualified discipleship. Wealth, it happens, is only the most conspicuous example of that which can distract from true discipleship. Only the rarest of individuals can possess much of this world's wealth without becoming enslaved to it and without letting it cut the nerve of true discipleship. For this reason, the NT contains a very strong polemic against wealth (e.g., 1 Tim 6:6–10; Heb 13:5). Most important is where one's heart lies, i.e., what controls one's interests, energy, and commitment. There is no absolute requirement here for poverty. But the individual disciple must be sensitive to that point at which wealth and possessions are not compatible with authentic discipleship. Jesus asks for uncompromising commitment to God's will and purposes. This is what it means to store up treasures in heaven. The person who stores up treasures on earth "is not rich toward God" (Luke 12:21) and is in the end "a fool." The person who is distracted from unqualified discipleship because of a covetous eye exists in a deep darkness and is to be pitied. The nature of discipleship is such that it allows no such divided loyalties. If one chooses to follow Jesus, the commitment and service entailed are absolute. It is impossible to be a partially committed or part-time disciple; it is impossible to serve two masters, whether one of them be wealth or anything else, when the other master is meant to be God. This view of the rigorously single-minded nature of discipleship is in keeping with the view of discipleship elsewhere in the Gospel (e.g., 10:34–39; 16:24–26).

The Disciple and Anxiety   (6:25–34)

Bibliography

Glasson T. F. "Carding und Spinning: Oxyrhynchus Papyrus No. 655." *JTS* 13 (1962) 331–32. **Katz P.** "ΠΩΣ ΑΥΞΑΝΟΥΣΙΝ." *JTS* 5 (1954) 207–9. **Olsthoorn, M. F.** *The Jewish Background and the Synoptic Setting of Mt 6,25–33 and Lk 12,22–31.* SBF 10. Jerusalem: Franciscan Press, 1975. **Powell, J. E.** "Those 'Lilies of the Field' Again." *JTS* 33 (1982) 490–92. **Riesenfeld, H.** "Vom Schätzensammeln und Sorge—ein Thema urchristlicher Paränese: Zu Mt 6.19–34." In *Neotestamentica et Patristica.* FS O. Cullmann, ed. W. C. van Unnik. Leiden: Brill, 1962. 47–58. **Schottroff, L.,** and **Stegemann, W.** *Jesus and the Hope of the Poor.* Maryknoll: Orbis, 1986. **Schwarz, G.** "προσθεῖναι ἐπὶ τὴν ἡλικίαν αὐτοῦ πῆχυν ἕνα." *ZNW* 71 (1980) 244–47.

Translation

25 "*With this in view, then, I say to you: Do not be filled with anxiety about your life, concerning, for example,*[a] *what you will eat [or drink],*[b] *or how you will clothe your body. Is not life more significant than nourishment and the body more significant than clothing?* 26 *Consider well the birds of the sky: they neither sow, nor reap, nor gather crops*[c] *into a storehouse, yet your heavenly Father provides them with food. Are you not worth*

much more than they? [27] *Besides, who of you, by being anxious about it, can add to his or her life even one hour?* [d] [28] *And why are you anxious about clothing? Learn a lesson*[e] *from how the flowers of the field grow: they neither labor nor toil,*[f] [29] *but I tell you not even Solomon in all his splendor could match such clothing!* [30] *Now since God clothes the grass of the field like this—grass which is alive one day, but on the next is used as fuel for the oven—will he not much more clothe you, you who have so little faith?* [31] *Therefore do not be full of anxiety, saying: What are we to eat? or What are we to drink? or What are we to wear?* [32] *For the Gentiles are the ones who earnestly seek after precisely*[g] *all*[h] *these things. But your heavenly Father is well aware that you need all of these things.* [33] *So keep seeking above all else the kingdom [of God]*[i] *and the righteousness he demands, and all of these things will also be yours.* [34] *Do not then be filled with anxiety about tomorrow, for tomorrow will have its own share of anxiety. For each day has its own quite sufficient supply of evil.*"

Notes

[a] "For example" added to translation.

[b] The words ἢ τί πίητε, "or what you drink," are lacking in, among other witnesses, א *f*[1] vg sy[c] sa[mss] and many church fathers. They may have been inserted by influence of v 31. On the other hand, they may have been omitted by homoioteleuton (cf. φάγητε) or possibly by influence of Luke 12:22. The Gr. text thus has the words in brackets. See *TCGNT*, 17.

[c] "Crops" added to translation, supplying the object for the verb.

[d] ἐπὶ τὴν ἡλικίαν αὐτοῦ πῆχυν ἕνα can alternately be translated "one cubit to his (or her) stature." See *Comment*.

[e] "A lesson" added to translation.

[f] When read under ultraviolet light, א reveals a third verb (but first in actual order), οὐ ξαίνουσιν, "they do not card" (i.e., disentangle and collect fibers of wool before spinning). This isolated reading is an addition apparently designed to provide a third negated verb to correspond to the three verbs used in reference to the birds in v 26. See BAGD, 547 (ξαίνειν), and T. F. Glasson.

[g] "Precisely" here reflects the emphatic position of πάντα at the beginning of the sentence. But see next *Note*.

[h] א N Δ Θ *f*[13] lat sy[c] have the word order ταῦτα γὰρ πάντα (as in Luke 12:30), in which case πάντα modifies the following τὰ ἔθνη; hence, "all the Gentiles seek these things." But the MS evidence is overwhelmingly in favor of πάντα γὰρ ταῦτα, "all these things."

[i] The critical text has τοῦ θεοῦ in brackets. The words are lacking in two major witnesses (א and B) and can be explained as a natural scribal addition. On the other hand, Matthew only rarely uses βασιλεία without modifiers, and these instances are easy to regard as exceptions (e.g., 8:12; 24:7). Thus the words were possibly omitted accidentally. The αὐτοῦ following δικαιοσύνην also is easier with the presence of the expressed antecedent θεοῦ. βασιλεία is modified by the simple αὐτοῦ ("his kingdom") in the parallel in Luke 12:31. See *TCGNT*, 18–19.

Form/Structure/Setting

A. The discourse now turns naturally from the negative references concerning wealth to the impropriety of anxiety in the true disciple. If the disciples are not to be preoccupied with treasures on earth, if they are not to compromise the singlemindedness of their commitment, it would seem worth asking how their basic needs are to be met. Jesus teaches them not to be anxious about their daily needs but to trust their heavenly Father. Again the teaching of Jesus centers on the importance of getting priorities right (v 33). The reference to ordinary needs, and specifically to food, makes it possible to relate this pericope to the fourth petition of the Lord's Prayer. See discussion above (*Introduction* to the Sermon on the Mount).

B. This passage, except for the last verse (v 34), is paralleled fairly closely in Luke 12:22–31. Apart from very minor differences, the following may be noted: Matthew prefers the probably original rhetorical questions in vv 25 and 30, whereas Luke recasts the material into indicative statements (12:23, 28); Matthew has added the reference to "what you drink" (although some MSS lack this); Luke's question in 12:26, "If then you are not able to do as small a thing as that [add a cubit to one's life-span], why are you anxious about the rest?" is lacking in Matthew, in which the question at this point refers to what follows ("Why are you anxious about clothing?") rather than to what precedes; for Luke's κόρακας, "ravens," Matthew has the more inclusive πετεινά, "birds" (v 26); Luke has ὁ θεός for Matthew's characteristic ὁ πατὴρ ὑμῶν ὁ οὐράνιος, "your heavenly Father" (cf. v 32, where Luke has simply "your Father," 12:30); Matthew alone has the summarizing μὴ οὖν μεριμνήσητε λέγοντες, "Do not therefore be anxious, saying" (v 31); Luke has τοῦ κόσμου, "of the world" (12:30) modifying "the Gentiles," words not found in Matt 6:32; only Matthew uses ἁπάντων and πάντα, "all," to modify "these things" in vv 32 and 33; finally, in v 33 only Matthew has πρῶτον, "first," modifying "seek" and the words καὶ τὴν δικαιοσύνην αὐτοῦ, "and his righteousness." In many of these changes, especially the last, we can see Matthew's redactional activity, reflecting his special interests and characteristic terminology. It may be, however, that at points Matthew reflects a more primitive form, e.g., in the strong parallelism, which is not so apparent in Luke, and in the rhetorical questions. Without question, this passage in Matthew and Luke derives ultimately from the same source, that is, Q. But a number of the many smaller differences appear to be just what might occur through the influence of particular separate, though similar, oral traditions.

C. This lengthy passage finds its unity in the common subject matter and particularly in the verb μεριμνᾶν ("be anxious"), which occurs six times in these verses (the only other occurrence in Matthew is in 10:19). Also to be noted are the repeated imperative verbs in this pericope (vv 25, 26, 28, 31, 33, 34). Except for v 27, which broadens the teaching (as does v 34), vv 25–31 concern the two basic needs of (1) nourishment and (2) clothing. (1) In an introductory way, v 25 exhorts the hearers not to be anxious for 1 or 2 and then rhetorically asks whether life is not more than 1 and the body more than 2. Both the exhortations and the questions are in strikingly parallel forms. (2) V 26 then focuses on 1, while (3) vv 28–30 focus on 2. Considerable parallelism of form is found here too, especially between v 26 and v 28, where τὰ κρίνα τοῦ ἀγροῦ, "the flowers of the field," parallels τὰ πετεινὰ τοῦ οὐρανοῦ, "the birds of the sky," and where three verbs occur in both verses (even though the first in v 28 is not negated). The rhetorical question at the end of v 26 finds its parallel in the expanded rhetorical question of v 30. V 29 alone breaks the parallelism with its illustration from Solomon. (4) V 31 again in a summarizing way combines 1 and 2 in an exhortation that forms an inclusio with v 25. (5) Vv 32–33 draw the conclusion that impinges on discipleship by contrasting the favorable situation of the disciples when compared to the Gentiles. (6) V 34 broadens the discussion even more by referring to anxiety concerning the future, again in parallel form and with a concluding proverb. For the possible chiastic structure of vv 25–33 (a: v 25; b: v 26; c: vv 27–29, [c']; b': v 30; c': vv 31–33), see Olsthoorn, who regards the outer sayings as of determinative importance for the evangelist.

D. The brilliant use of parabolic imagery in illustrating the main points of this passage conforms with Jesus' use of parables elsewhere in the Gospel tradition and thus lends confidence to the conclusion that these are words of the historical Jesus. But the context too, with its stress on dependence upon God and the priority of the kingdom, is consonant with what has hitherto been encountered in the Gospel. The parallel to our passage in Justin, *Apol.* 1.15.14–16, is certainly, and that in POxy 655 possibly, dependent on Matthew.

Comment

25 Διὰ τοῦτο, lit. "on account of this," refers at least to v 24, but probably to the whole preceding section, vv 19–24. If one's allegiance to God is to be absolute, then what about one's material needs? The λέγω ὑμῖν, "I say to you," echoes the authority of Jesus found, for example, in the antitheses of 5:21–48.

μὴ μεριμνᾶτε, "do not be anxious," is emphatic in this context. μεριμνᾶν here means "to be anxious" in the sense of being fearful. The cognate noun μέριμνα occurs in 1 Macc 6:10 and Sir 42:9, where it is associated with sleeplessness. In Sir 30:24 the noun occurs in this sentence: "Jealousy and anger shorten life, and anxiety brings on old age too soon." (In Matt 13:22 the noun has the more neutral sense of "cares.") The verb, which occurs more here than anywhere else in the NT (three imperatives in this passage [vv 25, 31, 54]), is used also in the LXX to mean "to be anxious" (= NRSV's "disturb" in 2 Sam 7:10; 1 Chr 17:9). In the present passage, the meaning is defined by the vitally important items in view. To be anxious for such things as our passage enumerates is to be anxious about survival itself. This is thus a paralyzing anxiety that can only enervate discipleship. τῇ ψυχῇ is lit. "for your soul" (dative of advantage), but ψυχή is regularly used for life in the NT (cf. John 12:25; see BAGD, 893–34). Food and drink are essential to life; thus the questions, which are only loosely connected syntactically, define the anxiety by showing how it is expressed. Similarly, anxiety about τῷ σώματι, "the body" (dative of advantage), is reflected in the question about clothing. These items, sustenance and clothing, are only examples of the anxiety about this life that can hinder a person's undistracted and absolute discipleship.

Through his rhetorical question, Jesus makes the statement that existence (the life, the body) is more than food and clothing, as necessary as they may be. If God is the source of the former (the greater), will he not also provide the latter (the lesser)? Accordingly, a life dominated by concern for such matters is misdirected and will of necessity lack full commitment to what is really important. The teaching of Jesus in this passage is reflected in NT parenesis, esp. in Phil 4:6 and 1 Pet 5:7. The absurdity of being anxious is illustrated beautifully in the following verses (see *Form/Structure/Setting* §C).

26 τὰ πετεινὰ τοῦ οὐρανοῦ, "the birds of the sky" (Luke: "the ravens"; cf. Job 38:41), is probably a broadening by the evangelist (possibly by the influence of a passage such as Job 12:7, but cf. Matt 8:20; 13:32). That God provides food for the birds was apparently a common Jewish thought (see *Pss. Sol.* 5:9–10, where fish too are mentioned; cf. Pss 104:14; 147:9). The three parallel verbs σπείρουσιν, θερίζουσιν, and συνάγουσιν, "sow," "reap," and "gather," point to human preoccupation with financial security (cf. Luke 12:16–21). Luz points out that these types of labor are traditionally those of men, in contrast to those of women mentioned in v 28. The birds, by contrast, are carefree, and God supplies their needs. The evangelist uses his favorite and distinctive title for God, ὁ πατὴρ ὑμῶν ὁ οὐράνιος, "your heavenly Father," which occurs again in v 32 (see on 5:48).

The rhetorical question here, οὐχ ὑμεῖς μᾶλλον διαφέρετε αὐτῶν, "Are you not worth much more than they?" becomes an assertion in 10:31, in a context that similarly stresses God's sovereign care even for sparrows: "Fear not, therefore; you are of more value than many sparrows" (cf. 12:12). The μᾶλλον heightens the comparison (BDF §246). If disciples are worth more than birds, then they may be assured of God's providential care for their needs just as certainly as the birds depend upon God for theirs (for a similar argument, cf. m. Qidd. 4:14). They need not be distracted from their discipleship by an inordinate attention to their ongoing need of physical sustenance. For a similar statement about distraction from study of the Torah by concern with food, drink, and clothing, see Mek. Exod. 16:14.

27 From the immediate context it is clear that μεριμνῶν is to be understood as an instrumental participle (or less probably conditional), hence, "by being anxious." The key difficulty of this verse concerns the meaning of ἡλικίαν (is it "length of life" or "physical stature"?) and πῆχυν ("cubit" or something like "hour"?). ἡλικίαν in classical Greek means primarily "age," but then also in a related way "height," as a sign of age. In the papyri, LXX, and Philo, the predominant meaning is again "age." (See J. Schneider, TDNT 2:941–43.) In other NT occurrences, the word means "stature" (Luke 2:52; 19:3; but in Eph 4:13 it is used metaphorically for "maturity"), but also "age" (John 9:21, 23; Heb 11:11). Those who argue in favor of "stature" here depend on the ordinary use of πῆχυν, "cubit," as a spatial measure, namely, the length of the forearm to the tip of the middle finger (approx. eighteen inches). It is commonly used this way in the LXX and twice in the NT (John 21:8; Rev 21:17). It is a mistake, however, to conclude from this that ἡλικία should here be taken to mean stature (with Davies-Allison; contra Luz). The addition of a cubit, or eighteen inches, to one's stature does not make good sense, especially given the Lukan words that follow this question: "If you cannot do the least [ἐλάχιστον] of these things, why are you anxious about the others?" (Luke 12:26). In the context, it makes the best sense to take ἡλικία as length of life and then to take πῆχυς as a fraction of time. The Hebraic use of a spatial measure for a portion of time can be seen in Ps 39:5 ("thou hast made my days a few handbreadths"); "cubit" only seldom refers to time, but there is at least one such reference extant in the sixth century B.C. Greek writer Mimnermus (see BAGD, 657). Therefore, the rhetorical question elicits the answer that by being anxious one cannot extend one's life even by a small amount of time. Behind this view lies the Hebraic concept of the sovereignty of God in life and death, including the predetermined hour of one's death.

28–30 These three verses address the matter of clothing by another example from the natural world created by God. The opening question of v 28, not found in the Lukan parallel, focuses attention on the foolishness of anxiety for clothing. The parallelism in form with v 26 is striking, if nevertheless incomplete. Thus there are three parallel verbs in v 28 (as in v 26), although the first, αὐξάνουσιν, "they grow," is preceded by πῶς, "how," rather than the negative.

It is not necessary for us to be able to identify what, if any, specific flower τὰ κρίνα refers to. τοῦ ἀγροῦ, "the field," has a generalizing effect, and in any case many beautiful flowers were to be seen in the Galilean fields (see BAGD, 451). οὐδὲ νήθουσιν, "nor do they spin," means they do not do the labor of drawing out some fiber and twisting it together to make thread—labor necessary for the making of clothes (the labor of women; contrast v 26).

The beginning λέγω δὲ ὑμῖν, "but I tell you," recalls the formula at the beginning of v 25 (see *Comment* there). Σολομὼν ἐν πάσῃ τῇ δόξῃ αὐτοῦ, "Solomon in all his glory," could not match the splendor of the wild flowers. The glory of Solomon with all of his wealth had of course become proverbial because of such OT passages as 1 Kgs 3:13; 10:14–27 (= 2 Chr 9:13–28). In v 30 εἰ plus the indicative constitute a true-to-fact condition that may appropriately be translated "since." Whereas in vv 28–29 the flowers are regarded as "clothed" by God, in v 30 τὸν χόρτον, "the grass," is said to be clothed, viz., with the beauty of the flowers. This slight shift is, however, of no consequence. It is made presumably because of the reference to fuel cast into the oven. This emphasizes both the short life (cf. "today . . . tomorrow") and the little worth of what is so beautifully clothed. The "flower of the field" and grass are linked together in precisely this connection in Ps 103:15–16 and Isa 40:6–8 (cf. Jas 1:10–11). Grass was then, as even today in the Middle East, common fuel for ovens. The conclusion to be drawn is readily apparent: since God so wonderfully "clothes" what is so transitory and worthless, how much more true it must be that God will provide clothing for the disciples, quite apart from any anxiety on their part. And those to whom such a remark must be addressed, i.e., those prone to anxiety, must be characterized as ὀλιγόπιστοι, lit. "little faiths," a favorite word of Matthew (see also 8:26; 14:31; 16:8; 17:20; elsewhere in the NT only in the parallel to our passage, Luke 12:28; for rabbinic parallels to the expression "those of little faith," cf. Str-B 1:438–39; in the NT, the word is applied only to the disciples in reference to their failure to trust God completely).

31 This verse is a summarizing recapitulation of the passage (vv 25–30) that tersely repeats the imperative (but now in the aorist tense) and the three questions of v 25, but using the synonym περιβαλώμεθα, "wear" (as in v 29), instead of ἐνδύειν. The participle λέγοντες, "saying," and the first person plural verbs make the syntax smoother than that of v 25.

32–33 τὰ ἔθνη, "the Gentiles," here is a negative word, referring to those outside the family of faith, i.e., the pagans (cf. v 7 for the same use of the word). The pagans are taken up with the pursuit of these mundane needs. But the disciples can be free of such concerns because their "heavenly Father" (see *Comment* on v 26 for this expression) knows that all these things are legitimate needs that must be met. This same point is made in very similar language earlier in the sermon (6:8; cf. 7:11). τούτων ἁπάντων, "all these things," in 32b matches the preceding πάντα ταῦτα. The disciple is to be concerned with one thing, to have one priority, namely, the kingdom of God, and all (note the third use of ταῦτα πάντα, "all these things," in these two verses) the other things will be supplied.

V 33 concisely states the climactic point of the entire pericope. The kingdom, and the kingdom alone, is to be the sole priority of the disciple and that toward which the disciple devotes his or her energy. ζητεῖτε, "seek," here does not necessarily mean to look for something not yet present and, given the context of the Gospel, certainly cannot mean one should seek to bring in the kingdom. This imperative means rather that one should make the kingdom the center of one's existence and thus experience the rule of God fully in one's heart, hence the present tense, "keep seeking." To pursue the kingdom in this way is also to seek τὴν δικαιοσύνην αὐτοῦ, "his [viz., God's] righteousness," i.e., true righteousness or that which is truly the will of God as it is defined by the teaching of Jesus (so too Olsthoorn, 84). Participation in the kingdom, as Matthew has already informed us (see 5:20), necessitates righteousness of a qualitatively new kind. The gift of the kingdom and the demand of this new righteousness are inseparable. Thus gift, and not merely demand, is implied in this text (thus rightly, Guelich, *Sermon;* Reumann, *Righteousness;* contra Davies-Allison). καὶ τὴν δικαιοσύνην αὐτοῦ, "and his righteousness," is thus practically epexegetical of the preceding phrase (cf. Rom 14:17). The emphatic πρῶτον, "first" or "above all," means to make the kingdom and righteousness one's clear priority in life. The passive voice of προστεθήσεται, "will be added," is, with v 32 in mind, a divine passive (it is God who will add these things). ταῦτα πάντα, "all these things," indicates the fullness of God's provision (cf. v 32 and see especially 7:7–11). See *Comment* on 3:15 for discussion of "righteousness" in Matthew. For numerous parallel references in the rabbinic literature referring to the supreme and prior importance of studying Torah, see Str-B 1:439–40. In the wisdom tradition, cf. Wis 7:11; Ps 37:3–4, 25.

34 In these final words against being anxious, Jesus broadens the exhortation to include anything that might make people fearful of tomorrow. As the present is fully under God's control, so also is the future. Anxious worry is out of place for the disciple, whether with respect to today or tomorrow. The universal application of this saying of Jesus is reflected in the teachings of the early Church in Phil 4:6 and 1 Pet 5:7, which probably depend upon the logia of the present passage.

ἡ γὰρ αὔριον μεριμνήσει ἑαυτῆς, "tomorrow will be anxious for itself," is probably to be understood as meaning what the following statement asserts directly. That is, since each day has its own share of trouble and anxiety, let tomorrow (and all future days), so to speak, worry about itself. The disciple should live in the present, not in the future (nor for that matter, the past either).

ἀρκετὸν τῇ ἡμέρᾳ ἡ κακία αὐτῆς, lit. "sufficient to the day is its evil." By its position, the first word is emphatic. The predicate adjective ἀρκετόν is neuter singular because the subject is an abstract class (BDF §131). The saying has a proverbial ring to it. It is placed here to show the stupidity of being anxious about tomorrow or the future. It provides no warrant for being anxious even about the present day. Each day contains its share of evil, but God's faithfulness can be counted upon on a daily basis. No exact parallels to these logia have been found (but cf. Prov 27:1; and for the similar rabbinic perspective, cf. *b. Sanh.* 100b; *b. Ber.* 9a). For a similar idea in early Christian parenesis probably dependent on the Jesus tradition reflected in this passage, cf. Jas 4:13–15.

Explanation

This passage, like the preceding one, stresses the importance of undistracted, absolute discipleship. The key to avoiding anxiety is to make the kingdom one's priority (v 33). The disciples have a "heavenly Father" who knows of their ongoing needs and who will supply them. If he takes care of his creation, he will surely take care of those who participate in his kingdom. The passage does not mean, however, that food, drink, clothing, and other such necessities will come to the disciple automatically without work or foresight. It addresses only the problem of anxiety about these things. The answer to this anxiety and all such debilitating anxiety is to be found in an absolute allegiance to the kingdom and the right-eousness that is the natural expression of that kingdom. Thus it is not simply God's sovereign care that can be trusted but more importantly his special fatherly love and grace, which are the basis of the kingdom. The teaching of Jesus on this subject probably had in mind the itinerant ministry of the disciples who first widely proclaimed the kingdom of God. To them, it would have had special relevance. And with some modification it has ongoing relevance to the established Church. For Christians of every age, anxiety is incompatible with a lifestyle focused on God's kingdom. Indeed, anxiety and worry need not govern the disciple who has known the grace of the kingdom.

Various Teachings and the Golden Rule   (7:1–12)

On Not Judging Others   (7:1–5)

Bibliography

Bretscher, P. M. "Log in Your Own Eye (Matt. 7:1–5)." *CTM* 43 (1972) 645–86. **Couroyer, B.** "'De la mesure dont vous mesurez il vous sera mesuré.'" *RB* 77 (1970) 366–70. **Derrett, J. D. M.** "Christ and Reproof (Matthew 7.1–5/Luke 6.37–42)." *NTS* 34 (1988) 271–81. **Hedley, P. L.** "'The Mote and the Beam' and 'The Gates of Hades.'" *ExpTim* 39 (1927–28) 427–28. **Hendry, G. S.** "Judge Not: A Critical Test of Faith." *TToday* 40 (1983) 113–29. **King, G. B.** "A Further Note on the Mote and the Beam (Matt VII.3–5; Luke VI.41–42)." *HTR* 26 (1933) 73–76. ————. "The Mote and the Beam." *HTR* 17 (1924) 393–404. **Rüger, H. P.** "'Mit welchem Mass ihr messt, wird euch gemessen werden.'" *ZNW* 60 (1969) 174–82. **Webster, C. A.** "The Mote and the Beam (Lk vi. 41, 42 = Matt vii. 3–5)." *ExpTim* 39 (1928) 91–92.

Translation

[1] *"Do not judge unfairly,*[a] *lest you be judged in a similar way.*[b] [2] *For by the kind of judgment with which you judge others, you will be judged; and with whatever measure you measure to others, it will also be measured*[c] *to you.* [3] *Why do you see so well*[d] *the speck in the eye of your brother or sister,*[e] *but fail to regard the log in your own eye?* [4] *Or how will you*[f] *say to your brother or sister:*[g] *'Let me take the speck out of your eye,' while behold there is a log in your own eye?* [5] *Hypocrite! First take out the log from your own eye, and then you will see clearly enough to take the speck out of your brother's or sister's*[h] *eye."*

Notes

a "Unfairly" added to translation.

b "In a similar way" added to translation.

c For μετρηθήσεται, some MSS (Θ f^{13} it vg^{cl}) read ἀντιμετρηθήσεται, "it shall be measured to you in return," probably by the influence of the Lukan parallel (Luke 6:38).

d "So well" added to translation.

e τοῦ ἀδελφοῦ σου, lit. "your brother."

f Some MSS (א* Θ lat mae) have the present tense λέγεις for the future ἐρεῖς, a natural scribal alteration.

g τῷ ἀδελφῷ σου, lit. "your brother."

h τοῦ ἀδελφοῦ σου, lit. "your brother's."

Form/Structure/Setting

A. The sermon turns to the importance of avoiding a judgmental attitude toward others. We encounter a relatively abrupt break with the preceding material as this new subject is addressed. Nevertheless, earlier material in the sermon may be regarded as related generally to the present passage (viz., 5:7, 9, 22, 44; 6:14–15). Possibly this pericope corresponds to the fifth petition (6:12) of the Lord's Prayer (thus, e.g., Bornkamm, *NTS* 24 [1978]), which concerns forgiving and being forgiven (see discussion of structure in the *Introduction* to the Sermon on the Mount).

B. The fact that vv 3–5 shift from the second person singular to the plural points very probably to the evangelist's combination of logia derived from different strata of oral tradition. To be sure, the same shift is found in the Lukan parallel (Luke 6:41–42), but there the sayings are preceded by other material that softens the transition. Some of the material of this passage can be said to derive from Q: e.g., v 1 = Luke 6:37; v 2b = Luke 6:38c; and especially vv 3–5, which, apart from word order, are closely paralleled in Luke 6:41–42. Matthew appears to have dropped the inappropriate vocative ἀδελφέ, "brother," at the beginning of the statement in v 4 (cf. Luke 6:42). V 2a, however, is altogether lacking in Luke and probably derives directly from oral tradition. The only verse of the passage found in Mark (4:24) is 2b, where Mark's μετρηθήσεται agrees with Matthew, against Luke's ἀντιμετρηθήσεται, and where Mark alone adds καὶ προστεθήσεται ὑμῖν, "and it shall be added to you."

C. Once again we encounter extensive use of parallelism. Each of the first three verses contains its own parallelism, and vv 4–5 also contain some parallelism. V 1 is tersely parallel with μὴ . . . ἵνα μή and serves as the basic proposition of the passage. The two halves of v 2 are exactly parallel, both beginning with ἐν ᾧ, except for the insertion of the final ὑμῖν with the preceding verb. The sayings of this verse seem to have become a standard part of the oral, memorized catechetical tradition of the early Church, as the successive words κρίματι, κρίνετε, κριθήσεσθε and μέτρῳ, μετρεῖτε, μετρηθήσεται show. The logia of v 2 are found in *1 Clem.* 13:2 and Polycarp, *Phil.* 2:3, but in both cases oral tradition is reflected rather than dependence on Matthew (see Hagner, *Use*, 135–51). The two halves of v 3 are chiastically constructed (*a b b a*; verb, noun, noun, verb) and are closely, though not exactly, parallel. This enhances the contrast being set forth. Vv 4–5 are again chiastic in structure (speck, log, log, speck) with some parallelism in the log sayings and more in the speck sayings. A partial parallel to vv 3–5 is found in *Gos. Thom.* 26b.

Comment

1-2 The command μὴ κρίνετε, lit. "do not judge," should not be taken as a prohibition of all judging or discerning of right and wrong, since elsewhere in Matthew's record of the teaching of Jesus—indeed, already in v 6—the making of such judgments by disciples is presupposed (see 7:15–20; 10:11–15; 16:6, 12; 18:17–18). Furthermore, v 2a assumes the making of fair or charitable judgments and does not entail the avoidance of judgments altogether. The meaning here, accordingly, is that unfair or uncharitable judgments should be avoided. A note of humility is suggested too by the immediate context (vv 3–5): one should not judge others more harshly or by a different standard than one judges oneself.

Similarly, the warning ἵνα μὴ κριθῆτε, "lest you be judged," does not imply that one can avoid judgment by God at the eschatological judgment (this judgment is presupposed in the following words) but merely that the way in which one judges others will be the way one is judged by God at the eschatological judgment (for a parallel principle, see 6:14–15; 18:32–35). The viewpoint expressed in these verses finds strong Jewish parallels in Sir 18:20 and *m. ʾAbot* 1:6; 2:5; *m. Soṭa* 1:7. See Str-B 1:441–42, 444–46. Paul seems clearly dependent on these sayings of Jesus when he writes in Rom 2:1 (NRSV), "Therefore you have no excuse, whoever you are, when you judge others; for in passing judgment on another you condemn yourself, because you, the judge, are doing the very same things" (cf. 14:4; 1 Cor 4:5; and 5:12, reflecting a tension similar to that of the present passage). See too Jas 4:11–12 and 5:9 for dependence on these logia of Jesus.

κριθήσεσθε is a divine passive: God is the acting subject who will judge. Judgment is God's prerogative alone. The formal parallelism between v 2a and v 2b leads naturally to the conclusion that the latter constitutes a synonymous parallelism in the manner of the Psalms. The "measuring" then has to do with charitable judging. If there is a wider connotation here, it is not as clear as it is in both Mark 4:24 (with the added προστεθήσεται, "it will be added") and Luke 6:38 (in a context explicitly referring to giving). With v 2b, cf. *m. Soṭa* 1:7.

3-5 κάρφος refers to a small speck of anything (perhaps here "sawdust," given the meaning of δοκός) that may get in a person's eye; here it is used metaphorically to indicate some slight or insignificant shortcoming. The repeated reference in these verses to "your brother" indicates that it is primarily the Christian community that is in view. δοκός, "log," is an intentionally ludicrous exaggeration in its contrast to the speck of sawdust. What is a tiny flaw in another is seen so clearly by a censorious person, while ironically what is an outrageously huge failure in the latter is conveniently overlooked altogether. It is the self-righteous, censorious person who is particularly eager to correct the faults of others. The logic of v 4 is clear: with a log in one's own eye (καὶ ἰδού, "and behold," makes the point an emphatic one), it is impossible to see well enough to take out the speck in the eye of another. The hyperbolic speck and log contrast is found also in *b. ʿArak.* 16b *Bar.; b. B. Bat.* 15b (see Str-B 1:446). Also to be kept in mind in this analogy, however, is the familiarity of Jesus with the carpenter's shop (cf. Matt 13:55, "the carpenter's son"; Mark 6:3, "the carpenter"). The vocative address ὑποκριτά, "hypocrite," at the beginning of v 5 indicates that some form of deception is involved (whether only of self or deliberately of others). For "hypocrite," see *Comment* on 6:2. The solution indicated by v 5 indicates the responsibility that is prior: one's own faults are to be remedied first. Then, and only then, may one turn to help with the shortcomings of another. διαβλέψεις in v 5, "see clearly," intensifies the βλέπεις, "see," of v 3. Behind the exhortation of v 5 is the obvious implication that an awareness of one's own faults (it is assumed that all have such) will make more charitable one's judgment of others. Thus in this way we are reminded of vv 1–2. There is no need to conclude from this passage that one is not to judge at all (contra Hill; Schweizer; Guelich, *Sermon*; Davies-Allison understand Jesus to have meant no judging at all, but not the evangelist [673–74]).

Explanation

This passage concerns relationships in the community of faith and may be regarded as one expression of the ethic of love that is the summary of the law and the prophets (see 7:12; 22:39–40). Although the disciples cannot avoid making judgments (cf. 18:15–18), their judgments are to be made charitably and not censoriously. Judgment of faults is to begin with oneself, and one is to be as scrupulous in this self-judgment as one is generous and tolerant in this judgment of others. For the same standard of judgment that we apply to others will in turn be applied to us. The hypocrite ignores the significant failures in his or her own life while becoming preoccupied with the slighter failures of others. Such a person violates the love commandment.

Discernment in Proclaiming the Gospel   (7:6)

Bibliography

Bennett, T. J. "Matthew 7:6—A New Interpretation." *WTJ* 49 (1987) 371–86. **Jeremias, J.** "Matthäus 7,6a." In *Abba.* 83–87. **Lips, H. von.** "Schweine füttert man, Hunde nicht—ein Versuch, das Rätsel von Matthäus 7:6 zu lösen." *ZNW* 79 (1988) 165–86. **Llewelyn, S.** "Mt 7:6a: Mistranslation or Interpretation?" *NovT* 31 (1989) 97–103. **Maxwell-Stuart, P. G.** "Do not give what is holy to the dogs (Mt 7.6)." *ExpTim* 90 (1979) 341. **Perles, F.** "Zur Erklärung von Mt 7:6." *ZNW* 25 (1926) 163–64. **Perry, A. M.** "Pearls before Swine." *ExpTim* 46 (1934–35) 381–82. **Schwarz, G.** "Matthäus vii 6a: Emendation und Rückübersetzung." *NovT* 14 (1972) 18–25.

Translation

> [6] *"Do not give what is holy to dogs and do not set your pearls before pigs, lest they trample them down*[a] *with their hoofs and then turn to slash you with their teeth."*[b]

Notes

[a] The critical text, following B C L N W Θ f^{13} 33, prints the future indicative καταπατήσουσιν, which is grammatically allowable following μήποτε in contexts of fearing (see Turner, 3:99). ℵ f^1 and the majority text have the subjunctive καταπατήσωσιν, probably by influence from the other subjunctive verbs in the verse.

b "Slash with their teeth" is an interpretive paraphrase of the verb ῥήξωσιν, "tear in pieces" (see BAGD, 735).

Form/Structure/Setting

A. This verse appears to be a detached independent logion apparently unrelated to the preceding (*pace* Guelich, *Sermon*; Davies-Allison) or following context, inserted here for no special reason but only as another saying of Jesus. It has the character of a proverb, which may have had a range of application. Although it is very obscure as it presently stands in Matthew, when Jesus first uttered these words he quite probably made clear what he meant by them. That explanatory material has not come down to us.

B. This verse is from Matthew's special source and is not found in any other canonical Gospel. The first half of the verse is found in the "Gospel according to Basilides" as reported by Epiphanius (*Pan. haer.* 24.5.2). It is also found, slightly modified and incomplete, in the *Gos. Thom.* 93. The first clause of the verse is found in the *Didache* (9:5), where "the holy thing" is understood to be the Eucharist. All of these instances are probably to be explained through dependence on Matthew.

C. The structure of the logion is balanced, with the two halves of the verse each having parallel clauses. The first two clauses constitute a synthetic parallelism and make essentially the same point. The second two parallel clauses describe the results of the foolhardy action described in the first half of the verse. Possibly this second half of the verse forms a chiasm with the first half of the verse. That is, the first verb (καταπατήσουσιν) obviously refers to the second element of the first half (the pigs), while the second verb (ῥήξωσιν) may refer to the first element of the first half (the dogs), thus giving an *a b b a* pattern.

Comment

6 The key question of this difficult verse concerns, of course, the meaning of the metaphorical terms in the first half of the verse. To whom do these words refer, these words that are among the most derogatory in the Jewish vocabulary—the dogs and the swine? And what is depicted by "the holy thing" and "the pearls"? Some (e.g., with variations: Perles, Jeremias, Schwarz) have speculated that τὸ ἅγιον is a mistranslation of the underlying Aramaic word "the ring" (קְדָשָׁא, *qědāšāʾ*, the same consonants as for the word "holy") and that the logion alludes to Prov 11:22, which refers to "a gold ring in a pig's snout." Little is gained from this, however, in understanding the intended meaning. By the time of the *Didache* (early second century?), the saying was applied to the exclusive access of believers to the eucharist. The "dogs" and "swine" in this instance were the unbelievers. It is unclear, however, why witnessing or participating in the Eucharist would cause unbelievers to turn upon believers. It is also improbable that esoteric teachings are in view (contra Davies-Allison), since Matthew never hints at such things elsewhere. More likely, "what is holy" and "pearls" (cf. 13:45–46) refer to the gospel of the kingdom. Since for the Jews "swine" are unclean animals and the term "dogs" was often used for "Gentiles" (cf. 15:26), it is possible that this logion prohibits the preaching of the gospel to the Gentiles (thus reinforcing the teaching of 10:5 and 15:24; cf. Manson, *Sayings,* 174). In the Torah, the "outsider" was not allowed to eat the food of the offerings because they were "holy" (Exod 29:33; Lev 22:10). Still, Matthew believes the gospel *will* go to the Gentiles. And while Jews, for whom the gospel was clearly a stumbling block (1 Cor 1:23), might be expected to react violently to the proclamation of the gospel (as, for example, repeatedly in Acts), it is uncertain that Gentiles, for whom the gospel was only a kind of foolishness, would react this way. It seems best not to limit this verse unnecessarily but to regard it as applicable to both Gentiles and Jews, i.e., to all who are unreceptive. (Cf. the similar attitude, clearly pertaining to Jews, in 10:11–14.) The imagery of trampling down in the sense of spurning and profaning what is holy is found also in Heb 10:29, where, however, it refers to apostate Christians. It is unlikely that our passage specifically has apostates in view (contra Guelich, *Sermon*) or that it corresponds to the final petitions of the Lord's Prayer. Insofar as apostates become and continue to be unreceptive of the gospel, however, they could well be included in the application of this proverb.

Explanation

The mission to proclaim the gospel of the kingdom is an urgent one, and at least by the end of Matthew it is a universal one (28:19; cf. 24:14). In this mission everything depends on the receptivity of those who hear the message. Although it cannot be known in advance what the response will be, when the disciples encounter resistance or hostility they are not to persist, but as emphasized in 10:13–14, they are to proceed on their way in order to reach others with the message. The issue here thus focuses on the lack of receptivity rather than on any intrinsic unworthiness of any individuals or group.

The Answering Father   (7:7–11)

Bibliography

Brox, N. "Suchen und Finden: Zur Nachgeschichte von Mt 7,7b, Lk 11,9b." In *Orientierung an Jesus.* FS J. Schmid, ed. P. Hoffmann et al. Freiburg im Breisgau: Herder, 1973. 17–36. **Goldsmith, D.** "'Ask, and it will be given . . .': Toward Writing the History of a Logion." *NTS* 35 (1989) 254–65. **Greeven, H.** "'Wer unter euch . . .?'" *WD* 3 (1952) 86–101. **Kraeling, C. H.** "Seek and You Will Find." In *Early Christian Origins.* FS H. R. Willoughby, ed. A. Wikgren. Chicago: Quadrangle, 1961. 24–34. **Piper, R. A.** "Matthew 7,7–11 par. Lk 11,9–13: Evidence of Design and Argument in the Collection of Jesus' Sayings." In *Logia: Les Paroles de Jésus—The Sayings of Jesus.* FS J. Coppens, ed. J. Delobel. BETL 59. Leuven: Leuven University, 1982. 411–18. **Theunissen, M.** " Ὁ αἰτῶν λαμβάνει: Der Gebetsglaube Jesu und die Zeitlichkeit des Christlichen." In *Jesus: Ort der Erfahrung Gottes,* ed. B. Casper. 2nd ed. Freiburg im Breisgau: Herder, 1976. 13–68.

Translation

[7] *"Ask*[a] *and it will be given to you; seek and you will find what you want,*[b] *knock and the door will be opened for you.* [8]*For everyone asking*[c] *receives; the one seeking finds; and for*

the one knocking the door will be opened. [9] *There is no one among you who when a son or daughter asks for bread will give a stone, is there?* [10] *And there is no one who will give a snake to the child who asks for a fish, is there?* [11] *Well, then, if even you who are sinful know how to give good gifts to your children, how much more is it true that your heavenly Father will give good things to those who ask him?"*

Notes

[a] The three imperatives in this verse are in the present tense and could also be translated "keep asking," etc.

[b] "What you want" added to translation, supplying a direct object for the verb.

[c] The three participles are in the present tense and could also be translated "who keeps asking," etc.

Form/Structure/Setting

A. This is another self-contained unit having no real connection with the material that precedes or follows it. In Luke, this pericope occurs together with other passages on prayer, viz., after the Lord's Prayer and the parable of the importunate friend (Luke 11:1–8). Bornkamm (*NTS* 24 [1978] 419–32, followed by Guelich, *Sermon*) relates this pericope also to the Lord's Prayer in Matthew (cf. 6:8–9, 11).

B. This pericope is found also in Luke 11:9–13. Except for Luke's introductory "and I say to you," vv 7–8 are in verbatim agreement with Luke 11:9–10. The questions of vv 9–10 are also represented in Luke 11:11–12, except that the fish/snake question comes first in Luke and is followed by an egg/scorpion question rather than the bread/stone question found in Matthew. The explanation of this difference can now only be speculative. If Matthew and Luke are using the same form of Q, the bread/stone question could have been added by Matthew (cf. the same contrast in 4:3), bread being a staple food, and the egg/scorpion question omitted because of difficulty in seeing a connection between these last two items. On the other hand, the two forms could represent two independent oral traditions (tracing back perhaps to the same original logion). Apart from minor differences, v 11 agrees verbatim with Luke 11:13, with the single important difference of Matthew's ἀγαθά, "good things," for Luke's πνεῦμα ἅγιον, "Holy Spirit." Probably Luke wants here to make more of a contrast between what God gives and what humans give, and so he avoids repeating ἀγαθά, heightening it and making it more specific by substituting "Holy Spirit." This explanation is supported by Luke's obvious interest in the Holy Spirit in his second volume (cf. esp. Acts 2:1–4).

C. The passage readily divides into two major sections: (1) three exhortations and complementary assertions of God's faithfulness, vv 7–8; (2) two examples of human faithfulness, followed by an *a minori ad maius* argument concerning the faithfulness of God to those who call upon him, vv 9–11. Both sections involve considerable parallelism. Each of the three imperatives in v 7 is immediately followed by the result expressed in the future tense; v 8 reflects the same sequence of verbs (except for λαμβάνει, "receives," which actively expresses the meaning of the passive δοθήσεται, "shall be given"). Furthermore, the rhetorical questions in vv 9 and 10 are almost exactly parallel in form. V 11 ends with a reference to the giving of what is asked for and thus forms an inclusio with the beginning of v 7.

Comment

7–8 The three imperatives in v 7 and three participles in v 8 refer to the same activity. No object is specified. One is not told what to request, what to seek, or that for which one knocks. The invitation is apparently as broad as the questions of vv 9–10 imply and the object thus as general as the ἀγαθά, "good things," of v 11. These "good things" can be thought of as the eschatological blessings that accompany the presence of the kingdom (cf. Luke's "Holy Spirit"), so that the work of the disciples in proclaiming the kingdom is primarily in view, or alternatively the more ordinary and ongoing needs of the disciples (cf. 6:32–33). Less likely is the suggestion (e.g., Carson) that the qualities of character and life demanded by the sermon (i.e., righteousness, humility, purity, love) are intended. In the present passage we do not have the seemingly unlimited "whatsoever you ask," including even the miraculous, found in 21:22 (cf. 18:19; John 14:13–14; 15:7). The passage does not emphasize the "good things" themselves but the faithfulness of God as the provider of his people's needs. Thus the passive verbs δοθήσεται, "it will be given," and ἀνοιγήσεται, "it will be opened," are so-called divine passives: God is the one who will give (cf. v 11) and open the door. The three imperatives of v 7 as well as the three participles of v 8 are all in the present tense, conveying the idea of a continual asking, seeking, and knocking. This implied notion of persistence in asking is found in the teaching of Jesus (Luke 18:1–8; 11:5–8; both passages lacking in Matthew) and is made explicit in the early Church's transmission of this logion: "Let the one who seeks not cease until he finds" (Clement, *Strom.* 5.14.96.3; cf. POxy 654.1; *Gos. Thom.* 2). The πᾶς, "everyone," of v 8 means, of course, everyone participating in (viz., receiving) the kingdom reality brought by Jesus. Whereas in v 7 the promises are all in the future tense, v 8 contains two present tenses, λαμβάνει, "receives," and εὑρίσκει, "finds," which emphasize the reality of the promises for the present. It is interesting to note that the promises here are not conditional as in 21:22, "if you have faith" (cf. Mark 11:24). The faithfulness of God in answering prayer has a rich OT (cf. Jer 29:13; Prov 8:17 for strikingly parallel language) and rabbinic background (references in Montefiore, *Rabbinic Teaching*, 146–49). Nevertheless, the statements of the present passage have a unique quality about them when considered in the total context of Jesus' teaching and his announcement of the kingdom.

9–10 The rhetorical questions together with the negative constructions beginning with μή amount to affirmations. When a child asks for bread or a fish, no parent would respond with a stone or a snake. The requests here involve food (as also in Luke's "egg"), and this enables us to conclude that the requests in this passage are not requests for the miraculous (usually explicitly conditioned by the necessity of faith, as in 21:22) but requests for the necessities of life (cf. 6:25–34). Round stones look like loaves of bread; a snake can resemble a fish (and some scorpions can apparently be egg-like in shape). The point is not in these specific items, however, but in the faithful provision made by human parents.

11 It must be conceded that human parents give δόματα ἀγαθά, "good gifts," to their children. They know how to do this even though (ὄντες, taken as a concessive participle; Robertson, *Grammar*, 1129) they are πονηροί, "sinful." This word, which occurs far more often (twenty-six times) in Matthew than in any other NT writing, presupposes the moral degradation of all members of the human family, especially when compared, as here, with the righteousness and goodness of the Father who is in heaven (this last phrase alone suggests the same contrast). The ἀγαθά, "good things," that God gives correspond to the δόματα ἀγαθά, "good gifts," given by human parents. Instead of preserving the parallelism by having the Father give τοῖς τέκνοις, "to his children," he has the Father give τοῖς αἰτοῦσιν αὐτόν, "to those who ask him," thus forming an inclusio, reminding the reader of the initial imperative "Ask." Similarly, the δώσει, "will give," echoes the δοθήσεται of v 7.

Explanation

Jesus here invites his disciples to rely upon the faithfulness of their heavenly Father. The threefold invitation and promise of v 7, emphasized in v 8, have as their main point that the disciples may confidently trust God. Much more than parents, who reliably provide their children with what they need, will their heavenly Father provide the disciples with that for which they ask. The unlimited scope of the passage need not entail the expectation that every request will be answered positively; it points rather to the basic principle of God's comprehensive and faithful care of the disciple. The "good things" cover certainly the ongoing needs of the disciples (cf. 6:25–33, where even the form of the argument is the same), but in the larger context of the Gospel, they suggest also the blessings of the kingdom. This passage focuses on the answering, providing Father. It is he who provides the material blessings of the present age as well as the transcendent blessings connected with the coming kingdom of God.

The Golden Rule (7:12)

Bibliography

Bartsch, H.-W. "Traditionsgeschichtliches zur 'goldenen Regel' und zum Aposteldekret." *ZNW* 75 (1984) 128–32. **Borgen, P.** "The Golden Rule, with Emphasis on Its Usage in the Gospels." In *Paul Preaches Circumcision and Pleases Men.* 99–114. **Dihle, A.** *Die goldene Regel.* Göttingen: Vandenhoeck & Ruprecht, 1962. **King, G. B.** "The 'Negative' Golden Rule." *JR* 8 (1928) 268–79. **Metzger, B. M.** "The Designation 'The Golden Rule.'" *ExpTim* 69 (1958) 304.

Translation

[12] "*Therefore*[a] *everything you would like others to do to you, you yourselves do to them. For this is the essence of*[b] *the law and the prophets.*"

Notes

[a] ℵ* L sy[p] bo[mss] omit οὖν, "therefore."
[b] "The essence of" added to translation.

Form/Structure/Setting

A. This separate logion is probably added here by the evangelist because of the reference in the preceding pericope to the giving and receiving of good things. But the connection is not that clear, and this may explain the omission of οὖν in some MSS. This logion functions as the summarizing and climactic demand of the main body of the sermon. It is followed by a collection of concluding warnings (7:13–27).

B. The first sentence is Q material paralleled in Luke (6:31, where it is inserted into the Q passage found also in Matt 5:38–48). Matthew's form of the logion is more emphatic than Luke's: Matthew adds πάντα . . . ὅσα, lit. "everything . . . whatsoever," as well as the more forceful οὕτως καὶ ὑμεῖς, "thus also *you*." Only Matthew has this summarizing of the "law and the prophets" (cf. 22:40, again unique to Matthew).

C. The golden rule is widely known in different cultures and religions (see Dihle, 8–12, 80–109). At least in its negative form it is known in pre-Christian Jewish sources. Hillel summarized the law to a proselyte in these words: "What is hateful to yourself, do to no other: that is the whole law and the rest is commentary" (*b. Šabb.* 31a). It is found also in Tob 4:15 (cf. Sir 31:15), *Ep. Arist.* 207–8 (with the positive also indicated), and the Jerusalem Targum of Lev 19:18. The negative form is found also in Christian sources: *Did.* 1:2, in the Western text (D and a few other witnesses); Acts 15:20, 28; POxy 654.5; and the Coptic *Gos. Thom.* 6. The negative and positive forms are two ways of saying the same thing, but although the former is original and may be more fundamental, the latter is the superior form (contra Luz, Davies-Allison) and "the fuller expression of practical morality" (Abrahams, *Studies* 1:22). The positive form must include the negative form but not vice versa.

Comment

12   The golden rule is properly regarded as an exegesis of the great positive commandment of Lev 19:18, "You shall love your neighbor as yourself." This is probably true also of the negative form in its various occurrences in Jewish tradition (in addition to the references listed above, cf. Sir 31:15, where the Hebrew text has in the second half of the verse "and keep in mind your own dislikes"). That the golden rule as uttered by Jesus is derived from Lev 19:18 is clear from Matt 22:35–40. There, in the only other "summary" of the law in the gospel tradition, Jesus quotes Deut 6:5 and Lev 19:18 as the two commandments upon which "the whole law and the prophets" depend. To "love your neighbor as yourself" is the equivalent of doing to others what you would have them do to you, and thus the latter can also be described as the essence of "the law and the prophets" (cf. Rom 13:8–10; Gal 5:14). With this reference to the law and the prophets, the evangelist brings the main part of the sermon to a close in the same way he began it in 5:17.

The emphatic πάντα ὅσα, lit. "everything whatsoever," and the present tense of ὑμεῖς ποιεῖτε αὐτοῖς, lit. "*you* be doing to them," presents a high challenge to the Christian in his or her relations to others, involving both unlimited scope and faithful persistence. Moreover, the statement that such activity constitutes the fulfillment of the law and the prophets is not less astonishing because rabbinic contemporaries (e.g., Hillel) were saying the same thing concerning the negative formulation of the golden rule.

Explanation

It is from this saying and that of 22:37–40 that love became the dominant and summarizing theme of the Christian ethic. To act in this manner, in constant deeds of love, is to bring to expression that to which the law and the prophets pointed. That is, a world where only good is done to others involves by definition eschatological fulfillment, a return to the paradise of the Garden of Eden. To do good to others is to mirror the activity of the Father (7:11), which of course finds its supreme manifestation in the eschatological fulfillment brought by the Son. If the ethics of the kingdom of God anticipate the coming future in the present, then this is especially true of the ethic of the golden rule, which is the distillation of kingdom ethics. If this teaching of Jesus were to be lived out in the world, the whole system of evil would be dramatically shaken. Even if it were to be manifested seriously in the Church, its impact would be incalculable. In this sublime command, so simple and yet so deep, we encounter a challenge central to the purposes of God and therefore one that is also eschatological in tone. No other teaching is so readily identified with Jesus; no other teaching is so central to the righteousness of the kingdom and the practice of discipleship.

Conclusion   (7:13–27)

The Two Ways   (7:13–14)

Bibliography

Bergman, J. "Zum Zwei-Wege-Motiv: Religionsgeschichtliche und exegetische Bemerkungen." *SEÅ* 41 (1976) 27–56. **Denaux, A.** "Der Spruch von den zwei Wegen im Rahmen des Epilogs der Bergpredigt." In *Logia: Les Paroles de Jésus—The Sayings of Jesus.* FS J. Coppens, ed. J. Delobel. BETL 59. Leuven: Leuven University, 1982. 305–35. **Derrett, J. D. M.** "The Merits of the Narrow Gate." *JSNT* 15 (1982) 20–29. **Mattill, A. J.** "The Way of Tribulation." *JBL* 98 (1979) 531–46. **Michaelis, W.** "ὁδός." *TDNT* 5:70–75. **Rordorf, W.** "Un chapitre d'éthique judéo-chrétienne: les deux voies." *RSR* 60 (1972) 109–28. **Schwarz, G.** "Matthäus vii 13a: Ein Alarmruf angesichts höchster Gefahr." *NovT* 12 (1970) 229–32. **Suggs, M. J.** "The Christian Two Ways Tradition." In *Studies in the New Testament and Early Christian Literature.* FS A. Wikgren, ed. D. E. Aune. NovTSup 33. Leiden: Brill, 1972. 60–74.

Translation

[13] *"Go in through the narrow gate, for[a] the gate[b] is wide and the path that leads to final ruin is broad, and there are many who go that way.[c]* [14]*But[d] how[e] narrow the gate[f] is and confined the path that leads to life, and there are few who find it."*

Notes

ᵃ A few relatively unimportant MSS (118* a b h l q vgᵐˢˢ) have τί, "how," in imitation of the beginning of v 14.

ᵇ The words ἡ πύλη, "the gate," are lacking in ℵ* 1646 itᵃ,ᵇ,ᶜ,ʰ,ᵏ and many patristic citations of this verse, perhaps because of the unusual use of πλατεῖα, "wide," which usually applies to roads, as a modifier of πύλη, "gate." The MS evidence supporting the reading is very great.

ᶜ δι᾽ αὐτῆς, lit. "through it" (i.e., the wider gate).

ᵈ B (but not consistently) sa add δέ, "but," to give expression to the strong contrast between v 13 and v 14.

ᵉ ℵ* B* have ὅτι, "because," matching the ὅτι of v 13. Although the omicron could inadvertently have dropped out, producing the exclamatory τί, "how," it is more likely that the τί is a Semitism (cf. Ps 139:17) not understood by some copyist who proceeded to add the omicron making ὅτι. See *TCGNT*, 19.

ᶠ The words ἡ πύλη, "the gate," are omitted by some cursives and some patristic witnesses (cf. *Note* a). This omission probably occurred because of the familiarity of the two-ways metaphor, which is the focus of the passage, and the unfamiliarity of the two-gates metaphor.

Form/Structure/Setting

A. These verses stand as a kind of climactic admonition, with the very demanding ethical teaching of the sermon in view, and not least the challenging golden rule of the preceding verse. We are at a major turning point in the sermon; no more ethical teaching is given. What follows are warnings and a concluding parable, all involving, as in the present passage, the use of strong contrasts.

B. Luke 13:24 parallels our passage, but more in thought than in actual wording. In answer to the question, "Will only a few be saved?" Jesus in Luke exhorts: "Strive to enter through the narrow door [θύρας], for I tell you many will seek to enter and will not be able to." The Lukan logion refers only to one door, not two, and not at all to the paths or ways. It may well be that here we see two independent, though similar, logia passed down by oral tradition.

C. These verses again reveal a striking antithetical parallelism in their structure: an opening imperative or apodictic clause ("enter through the narrow gate") is followed by a ὅτι that provides the ground for the imperative. This is expressed by exactly parallel descriptions of the two gates and ways (v 13b and v 14). The word order is exactly parallel in the contrasting predicate adjectives and in the adjectival phrase ἡ ἀπάγουσα, "which leads to," modifying ἡ ὁδός, "the way," in each instance. The final clause of the two parts finds a slight variation in the substitution of εὑρίσκοντες αὐτήν, "find it," for εἰσερχόμενοι δι᾽ αὐτῆς, "enter it," but otherwise the structure is parallel.

D. The metaphor of "the two ways" is common in Jewish, Hellenistic, and early Christian writings. The basic choice between two opposite ways with opposite ends is found in the OT (Deut 30:15,19; Jer 21:8; Ps 1:6), in the intertestamental literature (4 Ezra 7:6–14), at Qumran (1QS 3:20–21), in the rabbinic literature (e.g., *m. ᵓAbot* 2:12–13; *Sipre* 86a; *b. Ber.* 28b), and in the Apostolic Fathers (*Did.* 1–6; *Barn.* 18–20). See Str-B 1:460–64 for further references. It is also not uncommon to describe the path of the wicked as easy (e.g., Sir 21:10) and that of the righteous as difficult (e.g., Ps 34:19).

Comment

13–14 The metaphor of a gate, whether as the entrance to eschatological blessing, as in the heavenly Jerusalem, or as the entrance to the place of judgment, as in hell, is not uncommon in Jewish literature (e.g., 4 Ezra 7:6–9; *Pesiq. R.* 179b; and *b. Sukk.* 32b; *b. ʿErub.* 19a). The sequence of gate and way is not significant; one does not enter the gate to get upon the way or at the end of the way enter the gate (contra Luz). The two metaphors refer together to the same thing (thus rightly, Ridderbos; Guelich, *Sermon;* Gundry; Davies-Allison; cf. W. Michaelis, *TDNT* 5:70–75), namely, the rigors of the discipleship to which Jesus calls his people.

πλατεῖα ἡ πύλη καὶ εὐρύχωρος ἡ ὁδός, "the gate is wide and the path is broad." Although the metaphors here are spatial, they imply an easiness and comfort for those who go this way. There are no significant demands to be met, no discipline to acquire, in order to go through this gate and down this path. εἰς τὴν ἀπώλειαν, "to destruction," refers, as elsewhere in the NT, to the final ruin brought by eschatological judgment. The counterpart in v 14 is ζωήν, "life." Surprisingly, in Matthew this is the only occurrence of the word ἀπώλεια with this meaning, despite Matthew's frequent reference to final, apocalyptic judgment.

τί στενὴ ἡ πύλη καὶ τεθλιμμένη ἡ ὁδός, "how narrow the gate is and confined the path." Again the spatial terminology is metaphorical, pointing to the genuine difficulty of this way (cf. a related metaphor in 19:24). Given the context of the preceding ethical teaching of the sermon, the radical character of discipleship is in view. Because of the word τεθλιμμένη (a cognate of θλῖψις, "tribulation"), the reality of persecution (5:10–12; cf. 10:16–23) may also be in view (cf. Acts 14:22, "through many tribulations we must enter the kingdom of God"). εἰς τὴν ζωήν, "to life," refers here to eternal life (cf. 19:16–17; elsewhere in Matthew only in 18:8–9; 19:29; and 25:46), language that is equivalent to entering the eschatological kingdom of God and is the exact opposite of the ultimate ruin referred to in the preceding verse.

ὀλίγοι εἰσὶν οἱ εὑρίσκοντες αὐτήν, "there are few who find it," is primarily descriptive of the situation confronted by Jesus and his disciples during his ministry (so too, 22:14). Although the "few" is clearly hyperbolic, it remains true that the majority of the people (πολλοί, v 13) do not receive Jesus' message (cf. 11:20–24; 12:41–42); they go down the broad path to destruction. Those who do follow Jesus and his summons to the righteousness of the kingdom are comparatively few (ὀλίγοι). That those who follow Jesus are a minority and that their path is a demanding one should come as no surprise, nor should it be discouraging. For from another perspective it may be said that "the harvest is plentiful" so that many more laborers are needed (9:37–38). The kingdom's beginnings may be small, but the promise for the future is great (cf. 13:31–33). The deliberate choice of οἱ εὑρίσκοντες, "who find," to replace the οἱ εἰσερχόμενοι, "who go in," of the parallel in v 13, has the effect of pointing to the privilege of the disciples. There is an echo of joy and fulfillment in the reference to the finding of this path to life. Again the call to righteousness occurs in the context of the reality of grace.

Explanation

Jesus here invites his disciples to travel upon the way he has outlined in the high ethical teaching of the preceding material. The narrow gate and the confined path of the disciples are quite the opposite of the broad path and wide gate chosen by the masses. The ends of the two ways are also radically opposite, as was already well known from this frequently used metaphor. But the way taught by

Jesus, upon which the disciples are invited to travel, is inestimably superior despite the various demands it puts upon its travelers. If it is a rigorous way, it is unmistakably also a way of grace. The disciples are not to worry that they are the minority, the few over against the many. It is not the point of the passage to speculate over the number who are saved or lost. The concern is the challenge afforded by discipleship. But the disciples are not to worry that their path involves the rigors of discipleship as well as the experience of suffering, sacrifice, and persecution. For they, by the grace of God, have found the way to life; they are the privileged.

The False and the Genuine   (7:15–23)

Warning concerning False Prophets   (7:15–20)

Bibliography

Böcher, O. "Wölfe in Schafspelzen: Zum religionsgeschichtlichen Hintergrund von Mt 7,15." *TZ* 24 (1968) 405–26. **Cothenet, E.** "Les prophètes chrétiennes dans l'Évangile selon saint Matthieu." In *Évangile selon Matthieu*, ed. M. Didier. 281–308. **Daniel, C.** "'Faux prophètes': Surnom des Esséniens dans le sermon sur la montagne." *RevQ* 7 (1969) 45–79. **Hill, D.** "False Prophets and Charismatics: Structure and Interpretation in Matthew 7,15–23." *Bib* 57 (1976) 327–48. **Krämer, M.** "Hütet euch vor den falschen Propheten." *Bib* 57 (1976) 349–77. **Légasse, S.** "Les faux prophètes: Matthieu 7, 15–20." *EF* 18 (1968) 205–18. **Minear, P. S.** "False Prophecy and Hypocrisy in the Gospel of Matthew." In *Neues Testament und Kirche*. FS R. Schnackenburg, ed. J. Gnilka. Freiburg im Breisgau: Herder, 1974. 76–93. **Schweizer E.** "Matthäus 7.14–23." In *Gemeinde*. 126–31.

Translation

[15]"Beware[a] of the false prophets, those who come to you looking like[b] sheep while within they are predatory wolves. [16]You can recognize them by their deeds.[c] One[d] does not pick grapes from thorn bushes, does one? Or figs from thistles? [17]Thus every good tree produces good fruit, but a decayed[e] tree produces bad fruit. [18]A good tree is not able to produce[f] bad fruit, nor can a decayed[g] tree produce[h] good fruit. [19]Every tree that does not produce good fruit will be[i] cut down and thrown into the fire. [20]Clearly, then, you can recognize the false prophets[j] by their deeds."[k]

Notes

[a] C L W Θ *f*[1,13] TR sa[mss] bo include δέ, "but," connecting this pericope more closely with the last verse of the preceding pericope, perhaps by way of contrast. It is lacking in the earliest witnesses, however.

ᵇ ἐν ἐνδύμασι προβάτων, lit. "in sheep's clothing."

ᶜ καρπῶν, lit. "fruit (pl.)," a metaphor for "deeds."

ᵈ Lit. "they" (impersonal).

ᵉ σαπρόν can mean simply "bad," but in reference to trees, "decayed" is the common meaning. BAGD, 742.

ᶠ B Tert Or read ἐνεγκεῖν, "bear," for ποιεῖν, "produce." See *Note* h.

ᵍ See *Note* e.

ʰ ℵ* Tert Or (but the latter not consistently) read ἐνεγκεῖν, "bear," for ποιεῖν, "produce." In this case and in *Note* f the variants probably represent an attempt to bring in some stylistic variation in place of the monotonous use of ποιεῖν. See *TCGNT*, 20.

ⁱ ἐκκόπτεται, lit. "is cut down."

ʲ This pronoun αὐτῶν (lit. "them") refers back to the false prophets of v 15.

ᵏ Lit. "fruit." See *Note* c.

Form/Structure/Setting

A. This distinctive warning about false prophets is somewhat surprising at this juncture in the sermon. Its placement here by the evangelist indicates, as the context and especially the following pericope show, that his interest is more in the importance of good deeds than in the false prophets as such. This pericope is the first of three concluding warnings with which the sermon ends (cf. vv 21–23, 24–27). These warnings focus attention on the seriousness of the sermon's call to the righteousness of the kingdom (cf. 5:20). The connection between the present pericope and the immediately preceding verse is hardly direct, despite the δέ of the TR (see *Note* b). The relation to the pericope that follows is clear, however.

Matt 12:33 parallels the present passage in its reference to good and bad trees and fruit and, more particularly, in the words "the tree is known by its fruit." This is not exactly the same as the statement in vv 16a and 20a, however, where the pronouns in context refer to the false prophets rather than to trees. The same thought underlies these passages, and its special application to the false prophets was made either by Jesus or more probably by the evangelist.

B. Our passage finds a parallel in Luke 6:43–44 (which continues in v 45, paralleling Matt 12:35). Luke 6:43 states the tree/fruit relationship negatively and thus is more like v 18 than v 17. Luke 6:44 parallels v 16. Again, however, Matthew's form of the logion in v 16a is directed to the false prophets (for the logion applied to trees, cf. 12:33c). In this verse, Luke's order, "figs are not gathered from thorns, nor are grapes picked from a bramble bush," differs from Matthew's, as does the vocabulary to some extent. Luke and Matthew here probably depend on Q, with Matthew making slight adjustments of the logion in its application to false prophets.

C. The pericope may be outlined as follows: (1) the warning concerning false prophets (v 15); (2) how they are to be recognized (v 16); (3) the basic principle that good comes from good and bad from bad, stated (a) positively (v 17) and (b) negatively (v 18); (4) the reality of judgment (v 19); and (5) repetition of how false prophets will be recognized (v 20; cf. v 16).

After the introductory warning of v 15, this passage reveals a carefully designed structure, including chiasm. Thus *a*, v 16a, corresponds verbatim to *a´*, v 20, as an inclusio; *b*, v 16b, corresponds to *b´*, v 19 (this is the weakest part of the chiasm, although both elements refer to unfruitfulness); and *c*, v 17, corresponds exactly to c', v 18, which restates the thought negatively in terms of impossibility. Symmetry and parallelism are also to be found within certain elements of the larger structure. This is especially true of vv 17 and 18. V 17 contains two exactly parallel lines except for the very slight alteration in line 2, where the adjective σαπρόν, "decayed," precedes the noun δένδρον, "tree." The two lines of v 18 are exactly parallel except for the omission of the verb δύναται, "is able," in the second line. The parallelism of this passage probably derives from the form the material took in oral tradition, but the chiastic structure here probably derives from the evangelist himself, as does the joining of this material to v 15. This passage is quoted in abbreviated form in Justin, *Dial.* 35. 3 and *Apol.* 1.16.12–13.

D. One of the most disputed problems in Matthew is the identity of the false prophets mentioned in v 15.

From the αὐτούς, "them," of v 16, it is clear that vv 16–20 also refer to the false prophets. But are they also referred to in vv 13–14 and/or 21–23? Depending on how this question is answered and how this group is identified, one may then relate other passages in Matthew to the present one. Some proposals can quickly be dismissed as improbable, for example, that the false prophets were gnostics (Bacon, *Studies*, 348), Essenes (Daniel), or Zealots (Schlatter, Cothenet). A number of scholars understand the false prophets primarily in light of the charismatic activity referred to in v 22. Thus for Käsemann (*New Testament Questions*, 82–107) they are post-Easter Palestinian enthusiasts. Guelich (*Sermon*) argues for the unlikely conclusion that the false prophets were Jewish Christians who were over-zealous for the law (so too Gundry) and opposed to the gentile mission. The majority opinion is that these false prophets were Hellenistic libertinists, i.e., antinomians within the Church, and even more specifically Paulinists or ultra-Paulinists according to some (e.g., J. Weiss [*Earliest Christianity* (NY: Harper & Row, 1959) 2:753]; H. J. Holtzmann [*Lehrbuch der neutestamentlichen Theologie* (Freiburg: Herder, 1911) 1:508]; H.-J. Schoeps [*Theologie und Geschichte des Judenchristentums* (Tübingen: Mohr, 1949) 120, 127]; G. Barth [in G. Bornkamm, *Tradition*, 159–64]; H. D. Betz [*Essays*, 155–56]). This view also assumes that the false prophets are those referred to in vv 21–23 and places much emphasis on the ἀνομίαν, "lawlessness," referred to in v 23. The passage in 24:11–12, which refers both to false prophets and ἀνομία, is taken to confirm this hypothesis, and 5:17–20 is then understood to apply directly to the same group. D. Hill [*Bib* 57 (1976)], however, has argued strongly against this view, contending that vv 15–20 and 21–23 refer to two different groups: the former to the Pharisees (with Lagrange) and the latter to charismatic Christians whose righteousness is insufficient. In neither case, according to Hill, does the passage refer to strict antinomianism. (Earlier, in his NCB commentary, Hill had linked v 15 with vv 21–23 and concluded that the "false prophets" were Christian prophets.)

The designation "false prophets" need not be taken in a narrow, technical sense as referring to a particular group. It is impossible to know what specific group, if any, the evangelist had in mind (cf. Aune, *Prophecy*, 222–24). The term can be applied generically to all who fulfill the description in 7:15–20, who bring forth "bad fruit," whether Pharisees (thus Hill), charismatic enthusiasts, libertinists, or even hypocrites in the Church (Minear). Possibly the warning is general and has no specific group in mind (Strecker, *Sermon*). Matthew has in mind, however, something far more grievous than the itinerant false prophets who are identified in the *Didache* (11:5–6) as those who stay more than two days and ask for money. *Didache*, indeed, knows that the real issue is behavior (11:8, in probable allusion to Matthew). In 7:21–23, however, one specific manifestation of such false prophets does come into focus, namely, charismatic enthusiasts within the community who by Matthew's standard show no evidence of the good fruit of righteousness. It is perhaps this particular group that brings an urgency to the evangelist's warning. Confirmation that these enthusiasts of 7:21–23 can be considered "false prophets" may be found in 24:24, where false prophets are associated with "great signs and wonders," even though that verse is a prophecy of the future (cf. 24:11–12, where false prophets are also guilty of ἀνομία, as in 7:23).

Comment

15 τῶν ψευδοπροφητῶν, "the false prophets," is probably best understood generally rather than specifically (cf. above *Form/Structure/Setting* §D). Defined from the immediate context, "false prophets" are persons who appear on the surface to be something they are not. It is of the essence of false prophets that they pretend to have and proclaim the truth while their lives evidence that they themselves do not follow the truth. According to the prophecy of 24:11, 24, "false prophets" will arise and lead many astray before the end time. ἐν ἐνδύμασι προβάτων, "in sheep's clothing," means appearing to be proper members of the people of God. Sheep is a common OT metaphor for the people of God (cf. Ps 78:52; 100:3); in Matthew it is commonly applied to the Church (cf. 10:16; 25:33; 26:31). Probably here this proverbial metaphor indicates that those concerned are Christians, although it is also possible to understand it in a broader sense of "those who present themselves as holding to the truth" (and thus, as Hill, "the Pharisees").

ἔσωθεν δέ εἰσιν λύκοι ἅρπαγες, "but inwardly they are ravenous wolves." Despite their outward appearance and profession, these persons are in fact the mortal enemies of those who belong to the flock. As the wolf, known for its ferocity (hence "ravenous"), is the natural enemy of the sheep (cf. Isa 11:6; 65:25; Sir 13:17; John 10:12), so these deceivers are natural enemies of the truth and the true people of God. (Cf. the similar metaphor in Acts 20:29; Ign. *Phil.* 2:1–2; *Did.* 16:3.) The disciples must therefore be wary of these false prophets. Following their way will lead only to the destruction of the flock.

16 ἀπὸ τῶν καρπῶν αὐτῶν, "by their deeds," is emphatic by its position at the beginning of the sentence. Thus αὐτῶν, "their," indicates that this logion, which was originally probably more general, is here applied specifically to the false prophets. In this and the following verses are the evangelist's definition and critique of the false prophets. The fundamental concern of Matthew is with the conduct of the false prophets. Fruit (καρπός) is, of course, a natural and common metaphor for righteous deeds (cf. 3:8, 10; 21:43; Gal 5:22; John 15:2–8). The future tense of the verb ἐπιγινώσεσθε, "you will know" (as also in v 20), does not refer to the time of the final judgment (contra Guelich, *Sermon*) but is a timeless or gnomic future referring to Matthew's readers then and there (cf. the present tense of the verb in 12:33). Of what point is the warning of v 15 if the "false prophets" will only be recognized at the final judgment? In the allusion to this verse in the Shepherd of Hermas (*Mand.* 6.2.4), the word ἔργων, "works," replaces καρπῶν, "fruit." ἀπὸ ἀκανθῶν σταφυλὰς ἢ ἀπὸ τριβόλων σῦκα, "grapes from thorn bushes or figs from thistles," reflects in a rhetorical question the truth of the declarative statement of v 17. Good fruit comes only from good trees (cf. Isa 5:2, 4; Sir 27:6); righteous deeds come only from those who follow the teaching of Jesus.

17–18 The parallelism of these verses (see above *Form/Structure/Setting* §C), involves a repetition and clear emphasis. V 18 refers (οὐ δύναται) to the impossibility of the situation being otherwise than it is. δένδρον ἀγαθόν, "good tree," in the context of the sermon and the Gospel, represents the disciples of Jesus, the people of the kingdom, and the καρποὺς καλούς, "good fruit," the righteousness expounded in the teaching of Jesus. σαπρὸν δένδρον καρποὺς πονηρούς, "decayed tree, bad fruit," refers, on the other hand, to those (false prophets) who only give the appearance of belonging to the truth and whose true character is revealed in their unrighteous deeds. The word πονηρούς here means literally "bad" or "spoiled" fruit (Jer 24:8), but it also connotes badness in an ethical sense (cf., for example, 5:45; 7:11; 12:34–34, 39). The word σαπρόν, here "decayed," is also used ethically in the NT (Eph 4:29, where NRSV translates "evil"). V 18 stresses that it is contrary to nature for a good tree to produce bad fruit and a bad tree to produce good fruit (cf. Jas 3:12). This proverbial metaphor applied to righteous and unrighteous deeds underlines the absolute essentiality of righteousness for those who follow Jesus, as well as its impossibility for those who do not.

19–20   ἐκκόπτεται καὶ εἰς πῦρ βάλλεται, "is cut down and cast into the fire," is the common metaphorical language of eschatological judgment already encountered in Matt 3:10, 12 (cf. 13:40, 42, 50; 18:8–9; 25:41; Luke 13:6–9; John 15:6). The lack of righteousness will mean condemnation at the end. The present tense of ἐκκόπτεται is either futuristic or gnomic (like the present tenses of vv 17–18), and the passive implies God as the acting subject. ἄρα γε, "therefore," introduces a strong inferential conclusion. V 20 serves as a kind of inclusio (cf. the chiastic structure noted in *Form/Structure/Setting* §C), the verbatim counterpart of v 16a. The pronouns αὐτῶν and αὐτούς, without an immediate antecedent, refer (as do those of v 16a) to the false prophets of v 15.

Explanation

As the sermon draws closer to its conclusion, we are presented with a stern warning against hypocrites and hypocrisy (although neither of these words is used). Some people pretend to be and appear to be something they really are not. These false prophets, as they are here called, can undermine the true flock if they are followed. The ultimate test of truth is in what these people do, not what they say. For what they do inescapably betrays their character and points to the judgment that awaits them. This passage thus points very vividly to the absolute importance of true righteousness—indeed its inevitability for the followers of Jesus and its impossibility for those who propose another way. The ultimate test of the truth is in deeds, not claims or pretensions. The Church must be ever vigilant against appearances and empty words and press the criterion of good works in discerning the true from the false.

The Insufficiency of the Charismata   (7:21–23)

Bibliography

Betz, H. D. "An Episode in the Last Judgment (Matt. 7:21–23)." In *Essays on the Sermon on the Mount.* 125–57. **Flusser, D.** "Two Anti-Jewish Montages in Matthew." *Immanuel* 5 (1975)

37–45. **Mees, M.** "Ausserkanonische Parallelstellen zu den Gerichtsworten Mt 7,21–23; Lk 6,46; 13,26–28 und ihre Bedeutung für die Formung der Jesusworte." *VChr* 10 (1973) 79–102. **Schneider, G.** "Christusbekenntnis und christliches Handeln: Lk 6,46 und Mt 7,21 im Kontext der Evangelien." In *Die Kirche des Anfangs*. FS H. Schürmann, ed. R. Schnackenburg et al. Freiburg/Basel/Vienna: Herder, 1978. 9–24.

See also the *Bibliography* for 7:15–20.

Translation

[21] *"Not everyone who acknowledges me with the words* [a] *'Lord, Lord' will enter the kingdom of heaven, but only the one who actually does the will of my heavenly* [b] *Father.* [c] [22] *There will be many who will say to me on the day of judgment, 'Lord, Lord, in your name did we not prophesy,* [d] *and in your name did we not cast out demons,* [e] *and in your name did we not perform many miracles?'* [23] *And then I will declare to them plainly: 'I have never acknowledged you. Depart from me you* [f] *doers of iniquity.'"*

Notes

[a] ὁ λέγων μοι, lit. "says to me."

[b] τοῦ ἐν τοῖς οὐρανοῖς, lit. "who is in the heavens." The TR omits the definite article, but this involves no change in meaning.

[c] C² W Θ 33 1241 and some other witnesses add the words αὐτὸς [οὗτος C² 33] εἰσελεύσεται εἰς τὴν βασιλείαν τῶν οὐρανῶν, "he [or 'this one'] will enter the kingdom of heaven," described by Metzger as "a clear example of a typical supplementary gloss." *TCGNT*, 20.

[d] sy^c Ju Or (but not consistently) add as the first claim οὐ τῷ ὀνόματί σου ἐφάγομεν καὶ ἐπίομεν καί, "in your name did we not eat and drink," drawn obviously from Luke 13:26.

[e] The first hand of ℵ adds the word πολλά, "many."

[f] L Θ *f* [13] and others add πάντες, "all," agreeing with the LXX (Ps 6:9a) and Luke 13:27.

Form/Structure/Setting

A. We come now to an example of a specific group of people who could be described as one kind of false prophets—people who were able to make claims of an impressive kind but whose lives did not bear the fruit of righteousness. Thus, this pericope represents a striking illustration of the lesson given in vv 15–20. It provides a very serious warning at the end of the sermon, just prior to the final parable concerning the eschatological judgment.

B. The Lukan parallels to this pericope are similar in substance but not very close in wording.

V 21 finds its parallel in Luke 6:46, "Why do you call me 'Lord, Lord,' and do not do the things I say?" (cf. Matthew: "the will of my Father in heaven"), which in Luke also directly precedes the final parable of the sermon, concerning the house built upon rock. The Lukan parallels to vv 22–23, however, are found in another context, i.e., Luke 13:25–27. There we encounter a parable concerning an οἰκοδεσπότης, the master of a house, who says to those who knock (addressed in the second person, "you," and who address him as κύριε, "Lord," but not the repeated "Lord, Lord" of Matt 7:22), "I do not know where you come from." They appeal in turn not to various charismatic deeds they had performed but rather to the fact that they had eaten and drunk in his presence and that he had taught in their streets. His reply is again "I do not know where

you come from," and then, as at the end of the Matthean pericope, Ps 6:9a is quoted.
Here Luke's initial verb ἀπόστητε agrees exactly with the LXX, against Matthew's
ἀποχωρεῖτε (both verbs meaning "depart"), as does πάντες ("all" workers of
unrighteousness), which is lacking in Matthew's citation. But in the remainder of the
quotation Matthew's οἱ ἐργαζόμενοι τὴν ἀνομίαν, "workers of iniquity," agrees exactly
with the LXX against Luke's ἐργάται ἀδικίας, "workers of unrighteousness." It is difficult to know the relationship between the material as represented in Matthew and Luke.
The differences are probably too great to think of both passages as deriving from a
common Q (although Matthew may have inserted vv 22–23 into Q as it is seen in Luke
6:46–49), yet that they ultimately trace back to a common source is difficult to deny.
This could be an instance (esp. given the parabolic form of the Lukan version) in which
Jesus said similar, but slightly different, things on separate occasions and both made
their way independently into the Gospels.

Further partial parallels to the present material are to be seen in Matt 25:10–
12, where in the parable of the wise maidens when the door is shut (as also in
Luke's parable) the foolish maidens, with the repeated κύριε, κύριε ("Lord, Lord")
say ἄνοιξον ἡμῖν, "open for us" (again as in Luke 13:25), and this is in turn followed by the words οὐκ οἶδα ὑμᾶς ("I do not know you").

C. There are some parallelisms in the structure of the passage, even if they
are not as notable as others in the sermon. In v 21 ὁ λέγων, "the one who says,"
stands in contrast to ὁ ποιῶν, "the one who does"; the formula κύριε, κύριε in v 21
is repeated in v 22; the plural "the heavens" occurs at the end of both main clauses
in v 21; the future ἐροῦσίν μοι, "they will say to me," in v 22 is matched by the
future ὁμολογήσω αὐτοῖς, "I will say to them," of v 23; the three main verbs of v 22
linked by καί, "and," are all in the aorist tense; note also the significant thrice-
repeated phrase τῷ σῷ ὀνόματι, "in your name."

The passage consists of: (1) the general assertion of the importance of deeds
and not simply words, v 21, followed by a specific illustration, consisting of (2)
the claim of the enthusiasts, v 22, and (3) the Lord's response, in the form of a
judgment and the citation of Ps 6:9a, v 23.

D. This passage is cited in 2 Clem. 4:1–2, where, however, for Matthew's "enter
into the kingdom of heaven" 2 Clem. reads σωθήσεται, "will be saved," and for
Matthew's "the will of my Father in heaven," τὴν δικαιοσύνην, "righteousness." In
the same context, 2 Clem. 4:5 also contains the Ps 6:9 citation. Justin contains a
more exact quotation of v 21 (Apol. 1.16.9). Apol. 1.16.11 quotes the Lukan version of this material, i.e., Luke 13:26 (but with the repeated κύριε), while Dial.
76.5 contains a conflation of Matthew and Luke, including reference to prophesying and casting out demons.

Comment

21 In the clause εἰσελεύσεται εἰς τὴν βασιλείαν τῶν οὐρανῶν, "will enter into
the kingdom of heaven," the future tense of the verb points to eschatological
salvation at the last judgment (see too the future tense of the verb at the beginning of v 22 and especially the phrase ἐν ἐκείνῃ τῇ ἡμέρᾳ, "in that day"). For the
phrase "kingdom of heaven," see Comment on 3:2. In the final reckoning, words
by themselves will not be sufficient—not even the important words κύριε, κύριε,
"Lord, Lord." The repeated formula "Lord, Lord" here and in v 22 occurs only

once again in the NT (except for the parallel to this verse in Luke 6:46, where the present tense "why do you call me" is used), namely, in 25:11, where it is also used in connection with eschatological judgment. Matthew's community can hardly have failed to think here of the primary Christian confession, that Jesus is Lord (cf. Rom 10:9; Phil 2:11; 1 Cor 12:3), and of the futility of empty profession (cf. the emphasis on "doing" what is righteous in Rom 2:13; Jas 1:22, 25; 2:14; 1 John 2:17). Matthew's constant stress on righteousness in the sermon (as elsewhere) has already been noted (see 5:16, 20, 48; 7:12, 20).

In the contrastive clause ἀλλ' ὁ ποιῶν τὸ θέλημα τοῦ πατρός μου τοῦ ἐν τοῖς οὐρανοῖς, "but the one who does the will of my Father in heaven," we return to the main burden of the sermon. What finally matters is obedience to God, and here at the end of the sermon the focus is upon the will of God as it has been spelled out in the preceding lengthy summary of the teaching of Jesus. In the Gospel, other explicit references to doing the will of the Father are 12:50 and 21:31 (cf. 6:10; 26:42). Mere lip service (λέγων, "saying") to the lordship of Jesus is of no consequence. What *is* important is "doing" (ποιῶν) the Father's will. For the expression τοῦ πατρὸς . . . τοῦ ἐν τοῖς οὐρανοῖς, see *Comment* on 5:16.

22 ἐν ἐκείνῃ τῇ ἡμέρᾳ, "on that day" (i.e., the day of the Lord), is common language for the final judgment (cf. Amos 8:9; 9:11; Isa 2:20; Zeph 1:10, 14; Zech 14:4; 2 Thess 1:10; 2 Tim 4:8). The double κύριε, κύριε, "Lord, Lord," is repeated from v 21. Now, however, the words are backed up with an appeal to an impressive array of deeds accomplished, as the thrice-repeated τῷ σῷ ὀνόματι, "in your name," which moreover stands emphatically before each verb, stresses—in the name (and hence, the power) of Jesus. The deeds cited are recognizably the same as those performed by Jesus and the twelve and were known in the post-resurrection Church of Matthew's day. With the πολλοί, "many," referred to here, cf. the "many" referred to in 24:11, also in an eschatological context.

ἐπροφητεύσαμεν, "prophesy," here means not simply nor even primarily predicting the future, although that can be included (cf. Acts 11:27–28; 21:10–11), but also proclamation of truth in the broadest sense and even the possession of power. In Matthew, both John the Baptist (11:9; 21:26) and Jesus (14:5; 21:11, 46, and a self-designation in 13:57) are described as prophets. In the sending out of the twelve (10:5–15), although the other two items of our passage (exorcisms and deeds of power) are mentioned, there is no explicit command to "prophesy." Their proclamation of the gospel, the truth of God (10:7), however, could be understood as prophesying (cf. 10:41; 23:34; and the implication in 5:12). This may well be the connotation of "prophets" in Eph 2:20 and 3:5 (cf. Rev 19:10). In the early Church, prophecy was an important gift: a universal Christian gift (connected with the Holy Spirit in Acts 2:17–18) and a special gift, according to Rom 12:6 and 1 Cor 12:10, but with wide availability (1 Cor 14:1, 5, 31; see esp. Aune, *Prophecy;* Hill, *New Testament Prophecy*). In the context of the present passage, the claim to have prophesied would appear to be understood in the more spectacular sense of prediction or oracular utterance. Quite probably the reference to prophesying here deliberately echoes the warning concerning false prophets in v 15. Clearly these charismatic enthusiasts are also false prophets, i.e., workers of iniquity (v 23).

The casting out of demons (δαιμόνια ἐξεβάλομεν) is familiar enough from the ministry of Jesus (cf. 4:24; 8:16, 31; 9:33–34; 12:24–29; 17:18) and that of the twelve

(10:1, 8; implicitly 17:19); it was also known in the early Church (e.g., Acts 5:16; 16:18; 19:12). For Jewish background, see excursus in Str-B 4.1:501–35.

δυνάμεις, "mighty deeds," although a general term, probably in this context is to be understood primarily as miraculous healings. Again, these are common in the ministry of Jesus (e.g., 4:24; 8:3, 13; 9:6, 22; 11:4–5), are a part of the commissioning of the twelve (cf. 10:1, 8), and are experienced in the early Church (Acts 3:6; 5:15–16; 9:34; 14:10; 19:11–12; cf. δυνάμεις, the same word used here, in 1 Cor 12:10; Gal 3:5).

Hill is correct, then, in characterizing the activities of these persons as "a continuation of that of Jesus himself . . . in fulfillment of the apostolic commissioning" and as "in no way abnormal in the life of the early church" (*Bib* 57 [1976] 340). These persons are thus not criticized for their charismatic activities but for their dependence upon them as a substitute for the righteousness taught by Jesus. We may conclude that charismatic activities, done apart from this righteousness, have no self-contained importance and are in themselves insufficient for entry into the kingdom of heaven.

23 τότε, "then," refers to the time of "that day" (v 22), the day of eschatological judgment. In response to the claims made in the preceding verse, Jesus himself, in the role of eschatological Judge, will respond with the words οὐδέποτε ἔγνων ὑμᾶς, lit. "I never have known you." Their failure to do the will of the Father (v 21) shows that they have never in fact participated in the kingdom of God (cf. John 10:14; 1 Cor 8:3). At the same time, from a Semitic perspective, Jesus as sovereign Lord and Judge "knows," not merely in the sense of possession of knowledge but in the sense of election (cf. Jer 1:5; Amos 3:2). Behind the free and responsible deeds of human beings lies always the sovereign will of God (cf. 11:27; 13:11). These have shown by their conduct that they have not been chosen by Jesus (cf. John 13:18; 15:16). A similar statement containing the words "I do not know you" is found in 25:12 (cf. 26:74). The quotation from Ps 6:9a is used to portray the lot of the wicked in the final judgment (cf. the statement in 25:41). The LXX's ἀνομίαν, lit. "lawlessness," is a particularly appropriate word for Matthew's view of sin as the violation of the will of the Father (cf. 13:41). Davies-Allison are right in their comment that much Matthean scholarship has overemphasized this word in the argument that the evangelist mainly opposes a Christian (Paulinizing) antinomianism.

Explanation

Perhaps no passage in the NT expresses more concisely and more sharply that the essence of discipleship, and hence of participation in the kingdom, is found not in words, nor in religiosity, nor even in the performance of spectacular deeds in the name of Jesus, but only in the manifestation of true righteousness—i.e., the doing of the will of the Father as now interpreted through the teaching of Jesus. Relationship with Jesus is thus impossible apart from doing the will of God. For Matthew all is narrowed down to this one necessity. Neither good, important words ("Lord, Lord") nor good, random deeds of mercy (e.g., casting out demons) can substitute for the full picture of righteousness the evangelist has given in the sermon. Religion can never take the place of actual obedience to the teaching of Jesus. Matthew will return to this uncompromising view in chap. 25, again in connection with the coming day of judgment. At the same time, the larger framework of grace should not be forgotten, nor the reality of forgiveness available to the disciples (cf. 6:12). The seriousness of the ethical demand upon the disciples does not cancel out the priority or significance of grace manifested in Jesus and the kingdom.

The Parable of the Two Builders   (7:24–27)

Bibliography

Pesch, R., and **Kratz, R.** "Auf Fels oder auf Sand gebaut?" In *So liest man synoptisch: Anleitung und Kommentar zum Studien der synoptischen Evangelien.* Vol. 5. Frankfurt am Main: Knecht, 1978. 25–37.

Translation

[24] *"Everyone, therefore, who hears these[a] words of mine and does them, will be like[b] the wise person who built a[c] house on a foundation of rock.[d]* [25] *When the rain fell and the rivers overflowed,[e] and when the gales blew and these together assailed[f] that house, it did not fall, because it was founded upon rock.* [26] *And everyone who hears these words of mine and does not do them will be like the foolish person who built a[g] house on the sand.* [27] *When the rain fell and the rivers overflowed,[h] and when the gales blew[i] and together assailed[j] that house, it collapsed, and the damage[k] was great."[l]*

Notes

[a] B* 1424 mae bo^ms omit τούτους, "these," smoothing out the roughness of the Gr. text, with the resultant reading "my words."

[b] C L W TR have ὁμοιώσω αὐτόν, "I will liken him to," perhaps by influence of the active verb in the parallel passage of Luke 6:47. *TCGNT* opts for the passive because of "the quality and diversity" of the MS evidence in favor of it.

[c] αὐτοῦ τὴν οἰκίαν, "his house," going with the preceding ἀνδρὶ φρονίμῳ, "a wise man."

[d] ἐπὶ τὴν πέτραν, lit. "on the rock."

[e] ἦλθον, lit. "came."

[f] W reads προσέκρουσαν, "struck against"; Θ Σ have προσέρρηξαν, "shattered," probably by the influence of the parallel in Luke 6:48; 33 and 1424 have προσέκοψαν, "beat against." See *Note* j.

[g] See *Note* c.

[h] See *Note* e.

[i] ℵ* and 33 inadvertently omit ἔπνευσαν οἱ ἄνεμοι καί, "the winds blew and," by homoioteleuton.

[j] The majority of Gr. MSS have a slightly different Gr. verb here (προσέκοψαν) than in v 25 (προσέπεσαν), but with the same meaning.

[k] ἡ πτῶσις, lit. "the fall."

[l] A number of MSS (Θ *f*[13] 33 1241 mae) add the intensifying σφόδρα, "exceedingly."

Form/Structure/Setting

A.   Matthew brings his impressive collection of the teaching of Jesus to an end with this simple, yet very powerful, concluding parable. This parable of eschatological judgment sets before the readers a choice between two opposite outcomes (cf. Lev 26; Deut 28; 30:15–20). It repeats and strengthens the immediately preceding warnings and thus effectively rounds out the entire "sermon" by its emphasis on the ultimate importance of obeying the ethical teaching of Jesus. The parable is in rabbinic idiom (cf. the similar story in ʾAbot R. Nat. 24). It ends, as do all of Matthew's five major discourses, with reference to eschatological reckoning.

B.   Luke's Sermon on the Plain ends with the same parable (6:47–49), but the agreement with Matthew is more in substance than in wording. Luke's briefer version, which lacks the near-perfect symmetry of Matthew's, seems to be a free reformulation of Matthew's more primitive version. While according to Matthew's version the storm is described somewhat generally in terms of rain, swollen rivers, and strong winds, Luke refers only, and more specifically, to a flooding river as the destroying agent that strikes the house. In Luke, furthermore, the one who does the words of Jesus is likened to one who not only built a house on the rock but who literally "dug, and deepened, and laid a foundation" (6:48), this being quite possibly an accommodation to the custom of building Hellenistic houses with basements. Luke accordingly lacks the reference to sand in the second example—a person simply builds "upon the ground, without foundation" (6:49). Luke's version of the parable also lacks the "wise—foolish" contrast; this contrast may well be related to the general favoring of symmetry in Matthew's version.

C.   The parable in Matthew is almost exactly symmetrical in the parallelism of the two parts: (1) the wise person's house, built on rock, vv 24–25; (2) the foolish person's house, built on sand, vv 26–27. The only slight differences are the lack of ὅστις and the replacement of the indicative with participles at the beginning of the second part, slightly different verbs for "beat upon" (προσέπεσαν/ προσέκοψαν), and of course the concluding lines of each section, (a) providing the reason the house did not fall, and (b) recounting the seriousness of the damage of the house that did fall. Otherwise the two parts of the parable are exactly parallel and well-suited for memorization and oral transmission. Each part thus consists of a parallel description of (a) how the house was built, (b) how the storm raged against it, and (c) the effect.

Comment

24   Πᾶς . . . ὅστις, lit. "everyone . . . whoever," gives the beginning of this parable of warning an echo of invitation. The reader is in effect invited to be like the wise man, to do and not simply to hear. The determinative words are clearly ποιεῖ αὐτούς, "does them" (cf. the negative "does not do them" in v 26). The emphasis upon hearing *and* doing is found elsewhere in the NT in reference to the word/will of God (Luke 8:21; cf. Matt 12:50; Jas 1:22–25). The word φρόνιμος, "wise," is a favorite of Matthew (seven occurrences, all in parables or figurative passages; in the other Gospels, only two occurrences in Luke). It refers to the prudent, wise, or discerning person, the person who not only knows the truth but acts upon it (cf. 25:45). The φρόνιμος person is contrasted with the μωρός, "foolish," person, not only here but also especially in the parable of the wise and foolish maidens in 25:1–13 (cf. 1 Cor 4:10 for the same contrast). It is clear that for Matthew the wise person is the obedient one. The focus of the parable is upon the teaching of Jesus: μου τοὺς λόγους τούτους, "these my words," with emphasis on "my," placed first. The standard of orthopraxy, of righteousness, is the words of Jesus, not those of the Torah. τὴν πέτραν, "the rock," here connotes a solid foundation, as it also does in 16:18, but apart from that similarity there is no connection between the two passages, and here no specific rock is meant.

25 Matthew describes typical storms in the hot, dry climate of the Near Eastern lands: blasting winds and torrential rains that produce sudden rivers where formerly there were dry wadis (ἦλθον οἱ ποταμοί, lit. "the rivers came," i.e., with resultant flooding). It is not unusual in the OT for eschatological judgment to be portrayed with this sort of imagery (cf. esp. Ezek 13:10–15, which has some similarities to the present passage; see also Isa 28:17). All three nouns—rain, rivers, and winds—are to be taken as the subject of the verb προσέπεσαν, "beat upon" (as also in v 27, with the verb προσέκοψαν, "beat against"). καὶ οὐκ ἔπεσεν, "and it did not fall," means that the wise person by having built upon rock, i.e., by obedience to the words of Jesus, was not brought to ruin in the eschatological judgment.

26–27 ἀνδρὶ μωρῷ, "a foolish person." μωρός is again Matthean vocabulary (six occurrences; none in the other Gospels). In addition to the occurrences in 25:2–8, where it is the opposite of φρόνιμος, "wise," Matthew links the word with τυφλοί, "blind" (23:17), where it thus points to lack of discernment (μωρός is contrasted with σοφός, "wise," in 1 Cor 3:18). The foolishness of this person in the parable lies in hearing but μὴ ποιῶν, "not doing," the words of Jesus. ἄμμον, "sand," has no other significance in the passage than the mere fact of its unsuitability as a foundation. καὶ ἔπεσεν, "and it fell," refers to disaster, again metaphorically, the full effect of eschatological judgment. This last point receives great emphasis with the deliberate breaking of the symmetrical parallelism of the passage in the brief, ominous concluding words: καὶ ἦν ἡ πτῶσις αὐτῆς μεγάλη, "and its fall was great," the last word receiving an additional emphasis. This conclusion is analogous to that of v 23.

Explanation

The Sermon on the Mount comes to an end with exhortations in the form of warnings. A lengthy discourse containing the ethical teaching of Jesus has been presented, a description of righteousness explicitly said to be the fulfillment of— the exposition of the true meaning of—the law and the prophets. This teaching is to be taken with all seriousness: the words of Jesus are not only to be heard but done. Everything depends on faithfulness to what Jesus has taught. This point is made climactically in the polarities of the concluding parable: wisdom or foolishness, manifested by doing or not doing the words of Jesus, resulting in not falling or in falling in the storm of eschatological wrath. It is easy to make this discourse, with its uncompromising concluding admonitions, into a new nomism, i.e., the pursuit of righteousness through the obeying of commandments (those of Jesus replacing those of Moses). But this conclusion, as plausible as it seems at first glance, makes the mistake of ignoring the larger context, not only of the sermon itself, with the opening, kerygmatic beatitudes, but also and more importantly of the whole Gospel within which this discourse takes its place. There the announcement of the good news of the dawning kingdom has priority. This means above all a new era with a new experience of the grace of God. Any nomism, or law-centeredness, must take account of this new era. Nevertheless, the teaching of Jesus is to be taken in all seriousness, as even Paul would have insisted. And the Sermon on the Mount stands within the canon of the Church as a proper antidote to a Paulinism that (unlike Paul himself) champions a gospel of cheap grace. The gospel of the NT has room for the stern ethic of Jesus, without ceasing to be gospel. The Sermon on the Mount represents an emphasis not simply for Jewish Christians, who may have some lingering interest in satisfying the strictures of Moses, but also for all Christians, who cannot claim that name without interest in the righteousness of the kingdom.

The Astonishment of the Crowds (7:28–29)

Bibliography

Lohfink, G. "Wem gilt die Bergpredigt? Eine redaktionskritische Untersuchung von Mt 4,23–5,2 und 7,28f." *TQ* 163 (1963) 264–84.

Translation

[28]*It happened that when Jesus finished speaking these words, the crowds*[a] *were astonished at his teaching.* [29]*For he was teaching them as one having authority himself,*[b] *and not as their*[c] *professional Torah scholars.*[d]

Notes

[a] A number of MSS (A Θ *f*[1] vg[ms]) insert πάντες, "all."

[b] "Himself" is added in the translation because of the contrast with the scribes.

[c] C* L TR omit αὐτῶν, "their," against the better MSS.

[d] οἱ γραμματεῖς, lit. "the scribes," i.e., those who were professional scholars of the Torah. Some MSS (e.g., C* W 33 lat sy) add καὶ οἱ Φαρισαῖοι, "and the Pharisees," probably because of the influence of this common Matthean combination elsewhere.

Form/Structure/Setting

A. Matthew points only briefly, but effectively, to the popular response to the sermon (and in effect to the ethical teaching of Jesus in his ministry generally). This brief passage serves thus as a rounding out of the first major presentation of the teaching of Jesus by a reference to its effect, before Matthew turns to the series of miraculous deeds that follow in the next two chapters. These verses together with 8:1 correspond to 4:25–5:1 as an inclusio (cf. in both passages ἠκολούθησαν αὐτῷ ὄχλοι πολλοί, "large crowds followed him"; ἀνέβη εἰς τὸ ὄρος/ καταβάντος δὲ αὐτοῦ ἀπὸ τοῦ ὄρους, "he went up to the mountain"/"when he came down from the mountain"; and of course the reference to Jesus beginning to teach and finishing his words.

B. Except for the special concluding formula, "when Jesus had finished speaking these words," these verses are in nearly verbatim agreement with Mark 1:22. Indeed, all three Synoptics have this reference to Jesus' hearers being "astonished"

($\dot{\epsilon}\xi\epsilon\pi\lambda\eta\sigma\sigma o\nu\tau o$) "at his teaching" ($\dot{\epsilon}\pi\grave{\iota}\ \tau\hat{\eta}\ \delta\iota\delta\alpha\chi\hat{\eta}\ \alpha\dot{\upsilon}\tau o\hat{\upsilon}$), because of his "authority" ($\dot{\epsilon}\xi o\upsilon\sigma\acute{\iota}\alpha$). In Mark and Luke (4:32), this statement comes early and is not
connected with any specific portion of teaching as in Matthew (although in Luke
it does come after the sermon in the synagogue at Nazareth). Matthew (begin-
ning with $\dot{\epsilon}\xi\epsilon\pi\lambda\eta\sigma\sigma o\nu\tau o$) agrees exactly with Mark except for the addition of the
words $o\acute{\iota}\ \check{o}\chi\lambda o\iota$, "the crowds," and $\alpha\dot{\upsilon}\tau\hat{\omega}\nu$, "their" (scribes).
    C. A key structural element is found (1) in the formula, $\kappa\alpha\grave{\iota}\ \dot{\epsilon}\gamma\acute{\epsilon}\nu\epsilon\tau o\ \check{o}\tau\epsilon\ \dot{\epsilon}\tau\acute{\epsilon}\lambda\epsilon\sigma\epsilon\nu$
$\acute{o}\ \mathit{I}\eta\sigma o\hat{\upsilon}\varsigma\ \tau o\grave{\upsilon}\varsigma\ \lambda\acute{o}\gamma o\upsilon\varsigma\ \tau o\acute{\upsilon}\tau o\upsilon\varsigma$, "And it happened that when Jesus finished speaking these words," which in moderately variant form concludes each of Matthew's
five teaching discourses (see *Introduction*). Two further elements of this pericope
are (2) the impact on the hearers (v 28b) and (3) the reason for the impact (v 29).

Comment

28   Although the concluding formula at the beginning of this verse occurs at
the end of each of the major teaching discourses in Matthew, only here is it followed with a reference to the impact of the teaching upon the hearers.
$\dot{\epsilon}\xi\epsilon\pi\lambda\eta\sigma\sigma o\nu\tau o$ is a strong verb meaning "to be amazed or overwhelmed," with the
imperfect tense suggesting an ongoing effect. Matthew uses the same verb else-
where only with reference to the impact of Jesus' teaching: generally in 13:54
and making reference to specific elements of his teaching in 19:25 (the difficulty
of the rich entering the kingdom) and 22:33 (teaching about the resurrection).
The last reference is a particularly close parallel to the present passage, with reference to the crowds, the astonishment, and Jesus' $\delta\iota\delta\alpha\chi\hat{\eta}$, "teaching" (a word
used only once further in the Gospel in reference to the teaching of the Phari-
sees and Sadducees, 16:12). $\check{o}\chi\lambda o\iota$, "crowds," needlessly has caused trouble for
some commentators, since at the beginning of the sermon Jesus seems to escape
the crowds in order to teach "his disciples" specifically and privately (though this
latter point is not asserted in the text). As far as the story line in Matthew goes,
nothing excludes the possibility that the crowds nevertheless followed Jesus and
his disciples up the mountain and thus became a secondary audience. This does
not deny, however, that Matthew here adjoins to the sermon a piece of tradition
that refers generally to the widespread astonishment of the crowds wherever Jesus
taught. Matthew finds this record of the response to Jesus' teaching particularly
suitable for the preceding discourse.
29   The periphrastic construction $\mathring{\eta}\nu\ \delta\iota\delta\acute{\alpha}\sigma\kappa\omega\nu$, "he was teaching," draws attention to the repeated teaching that so astonished the listeners. The consistent
element in this teaching that caused the astonishment was the $\dot{\epsilon}\xi o\upsilon\sigma\acute{\iota}\alpha$, "author-
ity," it presupposed. Unlike $o\acute{\iota}\ \gamma\rho\alpha\mu\mu\alpha\tau\epsilon\hat{\iota}\varsigma\ \alpha\dot{\upsilon}\tau\hat{\omega}\nu$, "their scribes," who taught not
with a sense of their own authority but in heavy dependence upon the traditions
of earlier teachers and somewhat diffidently, Jesus set forth his teaching with
unique conviction and authority (cf. "But I say to you": 5:22, 28, 32, 39, 44; "these
my words": 7:24, 26). Nor does his teaching consist mainly of the exegesis of the
text of Torah; it is preeminently *his* own words that are authoritative. This unique
$\dot{\epsilon}\xi o\upsilon\sigma\acute{\iota}\alpha$ is, as the reader of Matthew knows, the result of the true identity of Jesus.
It emerges repeatedly in Matthew (as in the other Synoptics) in relation to Jesus'
deeds (9:6, 8; 21:33), is given in turn to the disciples (10:1), and given by implication to the Church of every age (28:18), where the risen Lord commissions his

disciples to make disciples of all nations. Matthew's addition of "their" ($αὐτῶν$) to "scribes" indicates a distance between the Jewish Christians of Matthew's community and the rabbinic authorities of the synagogue. It thus has an unmistakable polemical tone reflecting the growing hostility between the synagogue and the church.

Explanation

The teaching of the Sermon on the Mount was radical both in content and in the unique authority that undergirded its forthright, confident delivery. Matthew will not miss the opportunity here at the end of a masterful distillation of the teaching of Jesus to call his readers' attention to the supreme authority of this Teacher. Jesus is not one among other rabbinic teachers; his authority centers not on the tradition of the Fathers, nor even on the Torah, but somehow, mysteriously and remarkably, it centers in himself. As the final and authoritative exposition of the meaning of the righteousness of the Torah, this teaching has an incomparable authority that can be accounted for by only one fact: the unique person of Jesus, the one teacher, the one master, the Christ (23:8–10). Only such personal authority can support the radical and surprising teaching and its exclusive claims (cf. John 7:46). This authority is in fact inseparable from the newness of the gospel and the presence of the Agent of that gospel.

The Authoritative Deeds of the Messiah   (8:1–9:38)

General Bibliography

Burger, C. "Jesu Taten nach Matthäus 8 und 9." *ZTK* 70 (1973) 272–87. **Gatzweiler, K.** "Les récits de miracles dans L'Évangile selon saint Matthieu." In *L'Évangile selon Matthieu,* ed. M. Didier. BETL 29. Gembloux: Duculot, 1972. 209–20. **Gerhardsson, B.** *The Mighty Acts of Jesus according to Matthew.* Lund: Gleerup, 1979. **Hawkins, J. C.** "The Arrangement of Materials in St. Matthew viii–ix." *ExpTim* 12 (1900–1901) 471–74; 13 (1901–2) 20–25. **Heil, J. P.** "Significant Aspects of the Healing Miracles in Matthew." *CBQ* 41 (1979) 274–87. **Held, H. J.** "Matthew as Interpreter of the Miracle Stories." In *Tradition and Interpretation in Matthew,* G. Bornkamm, G. Barth, and H. J. Held. Philadelphia: Westminster, 1963. 165–299. **Hull, J. M.** *Hellenistic Magic and the Synoptic Tradition.* SBT 2.28. London: SCM, 1974. 116–41. **Kingsbury, J. D.** "Observations on the 'Miracle Chapters' of Matthew 8–9." *CBQ* 40 (1978) 559–73. **Légasse, S.** "Les Miracles de Jésus selon Matthieu." In *Les Miracles de Jésus selon le Nouveau Testament,* ed. X. Léon-Dufour. Paris: Seuil, 1977. 227–49. **Loos, H. van der.** *The Miracles of Jesus.* NovTSup 9. Leiden: Brill, 1965. **Luz, U.** "Die Wundergeschichten von Mt 8–9." In *Tradition and Interpretation in the New Testament.* FS E. E. Ellis, ed. G. F. Hawthorne and O. Betz. Grand Rapids/Tübingen: Eerdmans/Mohr, 1987. 149–65. **Theissen, G.** *The Miracle Stories of the Early Christian Tradition.* Edinburgh/Philadelphia: T. & T. Clark/Fortress, 1983. **Thompson, W. G.** "Reflections on the Composition of Mt 8,1–9,34." *CBQ* 33 (1971) 365–88.

Introduction to Chapters 8–9

Chaps. 8–9 constitute a major section of the Gospel, focusing on the miraculous deeds of the Messiah. The section ends with a summarizing statement (9:35) that refers to both the teaching and the acts of healing performed by Jesus and functions as an inclusio with the similar summary in 4:23–25. In between the framework of these two summaries the evangelist has presented two major blocks of material, the first concerning the teaching of Jesus (the Sermon on the Mount, chaps. 5–7) and the present section concerning mainly the deeds of Jesus (but also some words), who is thus presented as the Messiah of both word and deed (Schniewind, 36, 103). Clearly the evangelist intends this material as a presentation of a representative collection of Jesus' miraculous deeds in preparation for the answer to the Baptist's question in 11:3–5.

The organization of the material contained in these chapters is not altogether clear. Ten miracles of Jesus are narrated (Klostermann draws an analogy with the ten wonders referred to in *m. ʾAbot* 5:5, 8). Nine of the miracles are healings and one is a so-called nature miracle (the stilling of the storm in 8:23–27). Davies-Allison divide the miracles into three groups of three (8:1–22; 8:23–9:17; 9:18–38; each ending with various words of Jesus), arguing that the two miracles of 9:18–26 are part of one indivisible unit. The chapters have also been subdivided either into three sections (thus Held, Thompson) with thematic emphases: 8:1–17 (Christology); 8:18–9:17 (discipleship); and 9:18–34 (faith); or four sections (thus Burger, Kingsbury): 8:1–17 (Christology); 8:18–34 (discipleship); 9:1–17 (separation from Israel); and 9:18–34 (faith). This thematic approach is only of limited usefulness, however, since the material is really of a mixed character (Gerhardsson) and the various themes are intertwined (Luz).

A key aspect of these chapters is the way in which Jesus confronts various groups who accept or reject him. Important markers of the division are found in such places as the reference to the faith of the centurion in contrast to Israel (8:10), the amazement of the disciples (8:27), the response of the crowds to the healing of the paralytic (9:8), the criticism of the scribes and Pharisees (9:3, 11), and esp. 9:33–34, where the crowds respond appropriately in wonder at the deeds of Jesus but the Pharisees attribute them to an alliance with "the ruler of demons."

It is clear that this section of Matthew focuses on matters such as Christology, discipleship, and faith as it narrates the mighty deeds of Jesus. In these narratives we encounter the story of the founding of the Church (thus Burger, followed by Luz). The stories told here, therefore, have a fundamentally important significance for Matthew's community, not as mere history (of the separation of the Jewish church from Israel) but for the present experience of that church. The stories of these chapters thus have a transparency (Luz) or a paradigmatic function (Kingsbury) that makes them directly applicable to the life and discipleship of Matthew's community.

The Healing of a Leper   (8:1–4)

Bibliography

Elliott, J. K. "The Healing of the Leper in the Synoptic Parallels." *TZ* 34 (1978) 175–76. **Kingsbury, J. D.** "Retelling the 'Old, Old Story': The Miracle of the Cleansing of the Leper as an Approach to the Theology of Matthew." *CurTM* 4 (1977) 342–49. **Pesch, R.** "Die matthäische Fassung der Erzählung Mt 8,2–4." In *Jesu ureigene Taten? Ein Beitrag zur Wunderfrage.* Freiburg: Herder, 1970. 87–98.

Translation

[1] *When he had come down from the mountain, large*[a] *crowds followed him.* [2] *And look, a leper came to him and knelt down before*[b] *him, saying: "Lord,*[c] *if you want to, you are able to cure me."* [3] *And Jesus*[d] *extended his hand and touched him, saying: "I do want to. Be whole." And he was immediately cleansed of his leprosy.* [4] *And Jesus said to him: "Be careful not to tell anyone of this. But go and show yourself to the priest and bring as an offering the gift commanded by Moses, as a witness to the people."*[e]

Notes

[a] πολλοί, lit. "many."

[b] προσεκύνει here can also be translated "worshiped."

[c] κύριε can also be translated "sir," but this seems to be too weak in the context.

d Although not in the best MSS, "Jesus" is added for clarity (ὁ Ἰησοῦς does occur here in C² L W Θ TR lat sy sa^ms mae).

e αὐτοῖς, lit. "to them." See *Comment.*

Form/Structure/Setting

A. Matthew moves immediately from the sermon and its effect to the first specific healing narrative of the Gospel, the first of ten specific miracles in chaps. 8–9 (a summary of the miracles performed by Jesus had been given earlier in 4:23–25). It is no accident that the first specific instance of a healing concerns a Jew rather than a Gentile (as in the next pericope). Jesus' priority in his ministry is the mission to Israel (cf. 10:5–6; 15:24). The story is brief and direct, but at the same time a powerful narrative. No specific setting or location of the miracle is given. We are abruptly moved into a collection of stories concerning some particularly impressive miracles performed by Jesus.

B. In this triple tradition passage (Matt 8:1–4//Mark 1:40–45//Luke 5:12–16), Matthew, like Luke, depends upon and abbreviates Mark's somewhat longer account. Matthew (like Luke) omits Mark's σπλαγχνισθείς, "being moved with compassion" (Mark 1:41), perhaps shying away from human emotion in Jesus. Similarly, Matthew (and Luke) omits ἐμβριμησάμενος αὐτῷ, "very sternly warning him" (Mark 1:43), for perhaps a similar reason. Matthew further omits Mark's note that the offering in view was περὶ τοῦ καθαρισμοῦ σου, "for your purification" (Mark 1:44), probably to emphasize that it was Jesus who had cleansed the leper; the priests could only certify the cleansing. Finally, Matthew omits the Markan sequel to the healing, which tells how as a result of the man's failure to keep silence about his cure, Jesus was no longer able to be seen in public because of the throngs clamoring to be healed (Mark 1:45). Matthew has no interest in recording this example of disobedience to the command of Jesus. Solidly fixed in the triple Synoptic tradition are the words ἐὰν θέλῃς, δύνασαί με καθαρίσαι, "if you want to, you are able to cure me"; the account of Jesus extending his hand and touching the leper; his response, θέλω, καθαρίσθητι, "I do want to. Be whole"; and his admonition to keep quiet about the cleansing and the offering of the gift commanded by Moses εἰς μαρτύριον αὐτοῖς, "as a witness to the people."

C. Apart from the transitional v 1, the passage can be divided into three main parts: (1) the appeal of the leper, v 2; (2) the response of Jesus and the cleansing, v 3; and (3) the subsequent commands (four imperatives) concerning silence and the visit to the priest, v 4. An interesting parallelism is to be found in the first two parts representing the approach of the man and the response of Jesus: corresponding to προσελθών, "came to him," is ἐκτείνας τὴν χεῖρα, "extended his hand"; corresponding to προσεκύνει, "knelt down," is ἥψατο αὐτοῦ, "touched him"; this is followed by the participle λέγων in each instance and then the suggestive correspondence between the words of the leper (v 2) κύριε, ἐὰν θέλῃς, δύνασαί με καθαρίσαι, "Lord, if you want to, you are able to cure me," and the responding words of Jesus (v 3) θέλω, καθαρίσθητι, "I do want to. Be whole." This rather brief healing pericope thus can be seen to lack the first and last elements of the full form of such pericopes: i.e., no attention is given to the leper's condition (perhaps this needed no elaboration in that age), and no reaction of any observers is reported. (The full form can readily be seen in the healing of the demon-possessed men in 8:28–34.) See Theissen for analysis of the various motifs in miracle stories (*Miracle Stories,* 72–80).

Comment

1 Jesus' popularity because of his amazing teaching is underlined by the reference to the ὄχλοι πολλοί, "large crowds" (i.e., those also referred to in 4:25), that followed him "when he had come down from the mountain" (these last words being possibly an allusion to Moses' descent from the mountain in Exod 34:29). Although it is more often the case than not that ἀκολουθεῖν in Matthew means following in the sense of discipleship (see on 4:20), probably only a fraction of the nameless crowds that followed Jesus (for the linking of the words in Matthew, see *Comment* on 4:25) were followers in the sense of discipleship. The majority followed more out of curiosity than belief.

2 Matthew's ἰδού, "look," is his flag word for something exceptional about to happen (see *Comment* on 1:20). For προσελθών, "came to," see *Comment* on 5:1. When the leper prostrates (προσεκύνει, "knelt down before") himself before Jesus, this is obviously a great act of respect and homage, but the translation "worship" seems too strong for that particular moment. (Grundmann regards Jesus as representing here a new cultic center taking the place of the temple. Davies-Allison, referring to the verbs "came to" and "knelt down before," say of this view that it "could well be correct.") On the other hand, "Sir" as a translation of κύριε hardly seems adequate (so too Luz; Davies-Allison). κύριε, "Lord," introduced by Matthew (and Luke, probably by influence of oral tradition), is a confession of faith in Jesus as God's messianic agent but not necessarily belief in Jesus' deity. (Of course, Matthew's readers understand Jesus as one rightly worshiped as manifesting the very presence of God.) The leper's statement indicates that he had come to the conclusion, probably from having seen or heard of Jesus' other miracles, that Jesus could cure him of his leprosy (according to 11:5, the curing of leprosy could be expected from the Messiah). Thus the question was simply whether he wanted to do it, ἐὰν θέλῃς, "if you want to."

3 No disease was more dreaded in the ancient world than "leprosy." Whether or not the disease of this man was actually the leprosy we know as Hansen's disease or some other skin disease, the social and psychological effects were no less devastating. (On the question of the relation between the leprosy of the Bible and that of today, see van der Loos, *Miracles,* 464–68.) In addition to the horror of the effects of the disease itself and its incurable nature (cf. 2 Kgs 5:7: Naaman was cured by God; cf. Luke 4:27), the sufferer experienced banishment from society. The person who contracted the disease was considered as good as dead (cf. Num 12:12; *b. Ned.* 64b). These living dead were also thought to be under God's judgment (cf. 2 Chr 26:20). As ceremonially unclean and as contagious persons, they were required to keep themselves separate from society and to announce their approach with the words "Unclean, unclean!" (Lev 14:45–46; cf. Luke 17:12), as the leper no doubt did in the present instance. These wretched untouchables were trapped in a hopeless misery. The fact that they would have been avoided by others at all cost for fear of contagion makes the action of Jesus in reaching out and touching the leper all the more astonishing, as the Greek underlines with ἐκτείνας τὴν χεῖρα, "extended his hand." Although Jesus could have cured the leper with just a word, he touched the leper, ἥψατο αὐτοῦ—touching the unclean violates the law (cf. Lev 5:3)—and responded θέλω, καθαρίσθητι, "I do want to. Be whole." At the mere command, εὐθέως, "immediately," the leper was "cleansed" of his leprosy. The threefold repetition of the catchword "make clean," in vv 2–3 (translated here as "cure," "be whole," and "cleansed") is a Matthean literary device (cf. Pesch, *Jesu ureigene Taten?* 94–95). Because of the concerns reflected in the next verse, no attention is given to the astonishment of the man himself or of those who may have witnessed the miracle. The astounding character of the miracle was self-evident in that particular historical context.

4 The command ὅρα μηδενὶ εἴπῃς, "be careful not to tell anyone," is the first instance of the "messianic secret" motif in Matthew (it is found again in the healing of the blind men in 9:30, in 12:16 in a general reference, in 16:20 explicitly regarding Jesus' messianic identity, and in 17:9 regarding the transfiguration). As in Mark, where this motif is more frequent, this emphasis arises not from an attempt to explain the non-messianic character of the tradition received by the evangelists (as Wrede, *The Messianic Secret*, would have it) but is to be understood as historically authentic: Jesus desires simply to avoid inflaming popular, but mistaken, messianic expectations that looked for an immediate national-political deliverance. It is clear, however, that Matthew is less interested in the messianic secret motif than is Mark. In the present instance, the report of the curing of a leper would perhaps have caused the crowds to think of an eschatological prophet (cf. 2 Kgs 5:8). The charge to silence seems strange if the healing was witnessed by the great crowds of v 1. Matthew, however, does not say the crowds witnessed this event, and he records no reaction of the crowd. V 1 is a transitional verse rather than a setting for the event, which only relatively few may have seen. The problem is clearly caused by Matthew's insertion of this pericope at this point (cf. v 10). The command σεαυτὸν δεῖξον τῷ ἱερεῖ, "show yourself to the priest," and the following προσένεγκον τὸ δῶρον ὃ προσέταξεν Μωϋσῆς, "bring as an offering the gift commanded by Moses," correspond to requirements for the cleansing of a leper according to Lev 13–14 (examination and offering, the latter described in great detail in Lev 14:1–32). Provision for cleansing is made there ("the law for leprosy"; Lev 14:57) because virtually any skin eruption, and not merely clinical leprosy (Hansen's bacillus), could be classified as a leprosy, and, of course, other skin diseases could clear up. The same command to cleansed lepers to show themselves to the priests is found in Luke 17:14 (see too Papyrus Egerton 2, frag. 1r, which, however, is almost certainly dependent on our passage).

Jesus is thus shown to be faithful to the stipulations of the Torah in spite of an infraction of the command not to touch. The final words of our pericope, εἰς μαρτύριον αὐτοῖς, lit. "for a witness to them," have been interpreted in several ways depending on the meaning of μαρτύριον and αὐτοῖς.

That is, the cleansed leper is to do these things (1) as a witness *to* the priests or the people (about Jesus' faithfulness to Torah commandments)—thus the majority of commentators; (2) as a witness perhaps *against* the priests or people (that Jesus was indeed the Messiah)—thus France; H. Strathmann, *TDNT* 4:503; van der Loos; or (3) to receive a testimony concerning his cleanness *for* "them," i.e., the people (thus RSV: "for a proof to the people"; even better, NEB: "that will certify the cure"; thus Schniewind; Klostermann; Luz, but also a witness to the priests). But since neither of the first two options receives support from anything in the immediate context, and thus both survive only by appeal to material some distance away, they are not convincing. The plural pronoun αὐτοῖς, "them," is awkward if it is meant to refer to the priests, since then its antecedent (ἱερεῖ, "priest") is singular. The phrase seems particularly cryptic for making either of these rather substantial points. Moreover, since the phrase is drawn from Mark, it need not be taken as reflecting Matthew's special interest in Jesus' faithfulness to the law. The second option, furthermore, conflicts with the command to be silent about the healing. The third option, however, makes perfectly good sense. The man was to go to the priests and make the offering not because of the need to be faithful to the stipulations of Lev 13–14, nor because he yet needed cleansing, but for the pragmatic reason of being able to gain entrée into society, as fully clean and restored. As Theissen points out, he had to "outwardly conform to the Jewish custom which is really superfluous for him." The story fits "the context of a Jewish Christianity which respects Temple, sacrifices and Law but, as a result of its new faith, is no longer inwardly bound by these authorities. The conflict which has been overlaid with this loyalty can emerge at any time" (*Miracle Stories*, 146).

Explanation

The unique authority of Jesus, just previously heard in his exceptional words, is now to be seen in a series of exceptional deeds. The first of them is recounted briefly and directly. There is a sense in which leprosy is an archetypal fruit of the original fall of humanity. It leaves its victims in a most pitiable state: ostracized, helpless, hopeless, despairing. The cursed leper, like fallen humanity, has no options until he encounters the messianic king who will make all things new. His simple confidence in the ability of Jesus to cure his disease is impressive. If only he wills to do it! But this precisely is the work of the Messiah: to restore the created order from its bondage to decay: "I do want to do it!" The very presence of Jesus represents God's "Yes!" to the request of this poor man and to all who suffer. As Jesus reached out to the leper, God in Jesus has reached out to all victims of sin. The leper was cured immediately by only a word from Jesus. This same Jesus cures his people, the Church, from a whole host of maladies stemming from the fall, both spiritual and physical. Indeed it is the ultimate purpose of Jesus, as part of the future eschatological consummation, to heal every malady without exception.

The Curing of the Centurion's Son   (8:5–13)

Bibliography

Allison, D. C. "Who Will Come from East and West? Observations on Matt 8.11–12/Luke 13.28–29." *IBS* 11 (1989) 158–70. **Cadoux, C. J.** "S. Matthew viii. 9." *ExpTim* 32 (1920–21) 474. **France, R. T.** "Exegesis in Practice: Two Samples." In *New Testament Interpretation*, ed. I. H. Marshall. Grand Rapids: Eerdmans, 1977. 253–64. **Frost, M.** "I also am a man under authority." *ExpTim* 45 (1934) 477–78. **Grimm, W.** "Zum Hintergrund von Mt 8.11f./Lk 13.28f." *BZ* 16 (1972) 255–56. **Hooke, S. H.** "Jesus and the Centurion: Matthew viii. 5–10." *ExpTim* 69 (1957) 79–80. **Martin, R. P.** "The Pericope of the Healing of the 'Centurion's' Servant/Son (Matt 8:5–13 par. Luke 7:1–10): Some Exegetical Notes." In *Unity and Diversity in New Testament Theology.* FS G. E. Ladd, ed. R. A. Guelich. Grand Rapids: Eerdmans, 1978. 14–22. **Pilch, J. J.** "Biblical Leprosy and Body Symbolism." *BTB* 11 (1981) 108–13.

Schnider, F., and **Stenger, W.** "Der Hauptmann von Kapharnaum—die Heilung des Sohnes des Königlichen." In *Johannes und die Synoptiker.* Munich: Kösel, 1971. 54–88. **Schwank, B.** "Dort wird Heulen und Zähneknirschen sein." *BZ* 16 (1972) 121–22. **Sparks, H. F. D.** "The Centurion's *pais.*" *JTS* 42 (1941) 179–80. **Wegner, U.** *Der Hauptmann von Kafarnaum.* WUNT 2.14. Tübingen: Mohr, 1985. **Zeller, D.** "Das Logion Mt 8,11f, Lk 13,28f und das Motiv der 'Völkerwallfahrt.'" *BZ* 15 (1971) 222–37; 16 (1972) 84–93. **Zuntz, G.** "The 'Centurion' of Capernaum and His Authority (Matt. viii. 5–13)." *JTS* 46 (1945) 183–90.

Translation

^{5}*When he came into Capernaum,*[a] *a centurion*[b] *came to him, urgently imploring him* ^{6}*and saying: "Lord,*[c] *my son*[d] *lies crippled in bed at home suffering terribly."* ^{7}*And Jesus*[e] *said to him: "I will come and heal him."*[f] ^{8}*The centurion answered:*[g] *"Lord, I am not worthy that you should come under my roof, but only speak a word, and my son*[h,i] *will be healed.* ^{9}*For I too am a man with authority,*[j] *having under me soldiers. And I say to this one, 'Go,' and he goes, and to another, 'Come,' and he comes, and to my slave, 'Do this,' and he does it."* ^{10}*When Jesus heard this, he marveled at the man,*[k] *and said to those who were following him: "I tell you truly, with no one in Israel have I found such faith.*[l] ^{11}*I tell you that many will come from the east and the west and will recline at table with Abraham and Isaac and Jacob in the kingdom of heaven.* ^{12}*But the kingdom's own children*[m] *will be thrown*[n] *into 'the outer darkness,' where there will be weeping and the grinding of teeth."* ^{13}*And Jesus said to the centurion: "Go, it*[o] *will be to you as you have believed." And [his]*[p] *son was healed in that very hour.*[q]

Notes

[a] The MSS k and (sy[s]) have μετὰ δὲ ταῦτα, "after these things," in place of this opening clause.

[b] sy[s,hmg] Cl[hom] Eus describe the man as a higher officer, χιλιάρχης, a "chiliarch," i.e., commander of a thousand soldiers (= military tribune). So too in vv 8 and 13.

[c] ℵ* k sy[s,c] omit κύριε, "Lord."

[d] παῖς can be translated either "servant" or "son." See *Comment.*

[e] Although C L W Θ *f*[1,13] TR lat sy[c,p,h] sa mae bo[mss] have ὁ Ἰησοῦς, "Jesus," it is lacking in the earlier MSS. It is added in the translation for clarity.

[f] Since there was no punctuation in the earliest papyri MSS, it is possible to understand this as a question: "Shall I come and heal him?" See *Comment.*

[g] ἀποκριθεὶς . . . ἔφη, lit. "answered and said."

[h] A few MSS (*f*[1] k sa bo) lack the words ὁ παῖς μου, "my son"; thus, "he will be healed." See too *Note* d above.

[i] ὁ παῖς μου, "my son (servant)," is omitted by *f*[1] k sa mae bo[mss], probably by simple abbreviation.

[j] ὑπὸ ἐξουσίαν, lit. "under authority" (see *Comment*). τασσόμενος is added by ℵ B it vg, resulting in "being put under authority," but the word is almost certainly derived from the parallel in Luke 7:8. See *TCGNT,* 20.

[k] "At the man" is added in the translation, supplying the object assumed by the Gr. verb.

[l] The reading of ℵ C L Θ *f*[13] TR lat sy[h] bo[ms], οὐδὲ ἐν τῷ Ἰσραὴλ τοσαύτην πίστιν εὗρον, "I have not found such faith in Israel," is again derived from the Lukan parallel (Luke 7:9).

[m] οἱ δὲ υἱοὶ τῆς βασιλείας, lit. "the sons of the kingdom," is a technical expression for the covenant people of God.

[n] ℵ* it[k] syr arm have ἐξελεύσονται, "will go out," substituted perhaps to parallel the ἥξουσιν, "will come," of v 11 or to soften ἐκβληθήσονται, "will be cast out."

[o] C L Θ *f*[1,13] TR lat sy[h] bo[ms] insert καὶ, "even," before this clause, with the resultant meaning "even as you have believed."

[p] αὐτοῦ, "his," is in brackets in the critical text because of the disagreement of the textual witnesses. The word is in any event unnecessary since the articular ὁ παῖς can here be translated "his child."

^q Some MSS (W 700 1424) have ἐν τῇ ἡμέρᾳ ἐκείνῃ, "on that day"; others (C N Δ Θ) have ἀπὸ τῆς ὥρας ἐκείνης, "from that hour." But the best MSS favor ἐν τῇ ὥρᾳ ἐκείνῃ, "in that hour." Some MSS (e.g., א*² C Θ f¹ syʰ) have a further concluding sentence, καὶ ὑποστρέψας ὁ ἑκατόνταρχος εἰς τὸν οἶκον αὐτοῦ ἐν αὐτῇ τῇ ὥρᾳ εὗρεν τὸν παῖδα ὑγιαίνοντα, "and when the centurion returned to his house in that hour, he found the servant well" (cf. Luke 7:10).

Form/Structure/Setting

A. If the first miraculous deed recorded in this section was performed for an outcast, the same may be said (from a Jewish perspective) of this second miracle, performed for a gentile centurion. The healing of the leper was by direct touch; now we come to an example of a healing at a distance through a word of Jesus. But most importantly, this healing pericope becomes also a vehicle for teaching, in particular for the first direct statement of the salvation–historical rejection of the Jews (intimated earlier in 3:9). The story is thus primarily a miracle narrative but is transformed by Matthew into a pronouncement story, where the main point becomes the teaching of vv 10–12 (cf. Schulz, Q, 243). The geographical notice that this miracle occurred in Capernaum (found also in Luke) is drawn from Q. Capernaum remains the site for the next two episodes until 8:23, when Jesus and his disciples depart by boat to return to Capernaum in 9:1.

B. Since the passage is parenthetical in Luke 7:1–10, which occurs immediately after Luke's Sermon on the Plain and is not found in Mark (the only miracle story in Matthew not found in Mark), we may assume the source was Q (or something like Q, which contained at least this much narrative material; cf. Schulz). There are nevertheless some very interesting differences between Matthew and Luke, and although there is some verbatim agreement, the wording can differ considerably. In Luke it is clearly the centurion's δοῦλος, "slave" (7:2, 3, 10; but παῖς is used in 7:7), who is not merely suffering but ἤμελλεν τελευτᾶν, "about to die." The most striking difference, however, is that in Luke the centurion never has any direct contact or conversation with Jesus. Rather than coming directly to Jesus himself (as in Matthew), the centurion sends "elders of the Jews" on his behalf, who present his credentials as a God-fearer (ἄξιος, "worthy") who loves the Jews and had built a synagogue for them (7:3–5). Matthew does not mention that the centurion was a friend of the Jews, thus sharpening the grace toward a Gentile as a Gentile. Even in the second part of the Lukan version (7:6–8), the words of the centurion's humility and his authority over others, in very close verbal agreement with Matthew, are delivered by φίλοι, "friends," and not by the centurion himself. Matthew thus appears to have abbreviated Q considerably to emphasize the faith of the centurion and the direct contact and acceptance of the Gentile by Jesus. Matthew's purpose is clearly seen when he inserts vv 11–12 into the pericope, Q material found in another context in Luke (13:28–29, but transposed in Matthew). The effect of this insertion is to turn the story into a judgment oracle against unbelieving Israel (already hinted at in v 10b, found also in Luke 7:9b). Indeed, it would appear that v 10b prompted Matthew to insert vv 11–12. Finally Luke 7:10, which is quite different from Matthew, lacks Matthew's ἐν τῇ ὥρᾳ ἐκείνῃ, "in that hour," probably added by Matthew to stress the immediacy of the remote healing (cf. 8:3c).

C. The presence of a similar story in John 4:46b–54, the second Johannine "sign," raises the question of its relation to the Q pericope represented by Matthew and Luke.

John's story, too, is set in Capernaum, but it concerns a βασιλικός, "royal official," whose υἱός, here clearly "son," was sick (a fever is mentioned in 4:52), indeed ἤμελλεν γὰρ ἀποθνήσκειν, "about to die" (John 4:47, 49; cf. Luke 7:2). This official, in contrast to the one in the Synoptic story, begs Jesus to "come down" to heal his son. Further-more, in the Johannine story it is by Jesus' own initiative that the son is healed at a distance. The conclusion of the Johannine pericope makes much of the fact that the official discovers that it was "in that very hour" (as in Matthew) that his son was healed. The stories are too similar to deny they are variant accounts tracing back to the same original. In independent transmission they have acquired certain differences to be sure, but the common elements are striking. An important official requests help for some-one in his house. Matthew's consistent use of παῖς, with its possible nuance of "son" as well as "servant," can well stand as the middle term between Luke's δοῦλος, "slave," and John's υἱός, "son." That παῖς was the fundamental term in the tradition is indeed indi-cated by its occurrence in Luke 7:9 as well as in John 4:51 (cf. also τὸ παιδίον μου, "my little child" [John 4:49]). When Luke thus took Q's παῖς as a δοῦλος, "slave," in itself a legitimate rendering, he removed the inherent ambiguity of παῖς from the tradition (cf. Zuntz). The closeness to death is shared by the Lukan and Johannine accounts. The ἐλθών of Luke 7:3 (ASV, "asking him to come"), although in some tension with the later demurral (Luke 7:6), is in accord with the Johannine account and the request of the official for Jesus to come. Both in Matthew and in John the request is direct. Fi-nally, the story decribes the actual healing at a distance together with (in Matthew and John) the special notice of the very hour the healing occurred.

D. The basic healing narrative has four parts: (1) the request (vv 5–6); (2) the response of Jesus (v 7); (3) the centurion's demurral, with its parallelism at the end (vv 8–9); and (4) the healing (v 13). This is compact and concise, except for the lengthy demurral, consisting of (a) the profession of unworthiness (v 8) and (b) the authority analogy (v 9). In this narrative, however, there was a saying of Jesus in the Q version complimenting the faith of the centurion while criticizing the lack of faith in Israel (v 10). Matthew is prompted by this to add other Q material along the same line (vv 11–12). This lengthy insertion, with its polarity of πολλοί, "many," and οἱ υἱοὶ τῆς βασιλείας, "the sons of the kingdom," impor-tant in Matthew's theological perspective, turns the healing narrative into a teaching pericope.

Comment

5–6 Capernaum was the center of Jesus' Galilean ministry (cf. 4:13). Being near the border and on a major trade route, the town probably had a contingent of Roman soldiers (despite Green's point that Galilee was under the rule of the tetrarch Herod Antipas and not under Roman rule during the ministry of Jesus). The ἑκατόνταρχος, "centurion," was an officer in charge of a company of such troops (originally one hundred in number, hence the name). It goes without say-ing that such a person was a Gentile and not a Jew (Grundmann speculates he was a Syrian; Davies-Allison that he was a Roman). This centurion nevertheless comes to Jesus (προσῆλθεν; see on 8:2), παρακαλῶν, "urgently imploring," him for the healing of his son. Again the question arises concerning the import of the address κύριε (see *Comment* on v 2). While the centurion may not have shared the high Christology of the Matthean community, he still probably meant more than merely "sir" when he addressed Jesus as κύριε. He at least regarded Jesus as a person uniquely endowed by God with authority, if not sovereignty, over the physical realm.

Matthew's παῖς is probably to be taken as "son" (with Luz; cf. John's υἱός, "son") rather than "servant" (cf. Luke's δοῦλος, "slave"), although the latter is far from impossible (see Davies-Allison, Sparks). παῖς rather than υἱός may well have been used in the original Q tradition because of the young age of the child (cf. John's τὸ παιδίον, "little child"). If the παῖς was a servant and not a son, he was a servant very close to his master (not an uncommon phenomenon in the ancient world). Yet the deep concern is, of course, more natural in the case of a son (the similar concern of a gentile mother for her daughter is found in what could be called a companion passage, Matt 15:21–28). The nature of the illness is left vague. Although there is no reference to it being a life-threatening situation (as in Luke or John), it was clearly a desperate case judging by the centurion's deep concern. Matthew has removed the larger context referred to in Luke about the centurion's interest in Judaism so that no preparation is given for such a person approaching or having such confidence in Jesus. But the centurion seems to know that as a Jew, Jesus must not enter the house of a Gentile (cf. v 8).

7 ἐγὼ ἐλθὼν θεραπεύσω αὐτόν, lit. "I, having come, will heal him." The unusual syntax (esp. ἐγὼ ἐλθών) has caused many to speculate that this sentence should be understood as a question (thus Zahn; Bultmann, *History,* 38; Lohmeyer; Klostermann; Jeremias, *Jesus' Promise;* Held, in Bornkamm et al., *Tradition,* 194; Gnilka; Davies-Allison; Luz): "Shall *I* come and heal him?" The question would express surprise at the request of a Gentile (Gentiles not being in Jesus' purview at this point; cf. 10:5–6; 15:24) and perhaps the objection of a Jew going to the house of an unclean Gentile, even though a God-fearer (cf. the same issue regarding another gentile centurion, Acts 10:28–29). The latter, however, is not an issue in this passage. Matthew is very probably here content to follow Q (reflected in Luke 7:6), where Jesus expresses no hesitancy in going. The unusual syntax is caused by Matthew's terseness together with the need for something to correspond to the centurion's statement (v 8) that he is unworthy for Jesus to come to his house. The participle ἐλθών serves that purpose but by itself is too naked, giving rise to the ἐγώ. The ἐγώ ("I"), furthermore, prepares for the way the story develops. In the case of the centurion's son, no less than that of the leper (v 3), Jesus responds immediately and positively.

8 οὐκ εἰμὶ ἱκανός, "I am not worthy," rather than being a reference to personal unworthiness, very probably reflects the centurion's sensitivity to Jewish mores, which prohibited association with Gentiles (cf. *m. Ohol.* 18:7), e.g., as in the entering of their homes (again cf. Acts 10:28f.); thus ἵνα μου ὑπὸ τὴν στέγην εἰσέλθῃς, "that you should come in under *my* roof," where the μου by its early position is emphatic. The centurion's confidence in Jesus, however, is such that he urges μόνον εἰπὲ λόγῳ, "only speak (by) a word," and the healing can be accomplished. The basis for this view is the centurion's concept of ἐξουσία, "authority" (and the implied belief in the ἐξουσία of Jesus), elaborated in the following verse.

9 ἐγὼ ἄνθρωπός εἰμι ὑπὸ ἐξουσίαν, lit. "I am a man under authority." There is no need to suppose that the Old Syriac version, which reads "a man with authority," better reflects the underlying Aramaic (cf. Black, *Aramaic Approach,* 159; C. J. Cadoux; M. Frost) and is thus to be preferred. The passage as it stands, though the harder reading, makes good sense. "To be under authority" means to have been granted authority by superiors (hence "under authority"), which is in turn to be exercised over others (ἔχων ὑπ' ἐμαυτὸν στρατιώτας, "having under me soldiers"). The emphasis here is clearly upon the authority held by the centurion over his troops and servants, regarded by him as analogous to the authority of Jesus (under the authority of God) over the evil powers responsible for his son's illness (part of the common world view of that age). As the orders of the centurion are obeyed, whatever they may be, so must the orders of Jesus be obeyed—a view that implies belief in the messianic authority and status of Jesus.

10 Jesus is amazed at the profound faith of the gentile centurion (cf. the acclaim of the gentile woman's faith in 15:28) and takes the opportunity to make a point of it "to those who were following him." τοῖς ἀκολουθοῦσιν, "to those following," here is neutral, but among the crowd would have been some, in addition to the disciples, who authentically believed. The weighty statement (and concluding statement in the Q pericope) now given is prefaced by ἀμήν, "truly" (see *Comment* on 5:18), for emphasis. The initial position of παρ' οὐδενί, "from no one," is emphatic. The implicit faith of this Gentile has exceeded anything that Jesus has thus far experienced in his mission to the Jews. The effect of this statement is not only a criticism of the slowness of Israel to believe, a motif that will have increasing prominence as the Gospel proceeds, but also, and more importantly, to call attention to the genuine possibility of gentile faith, and hence participation in the kingdom (cf. 24:14; 28:19). With this first introduction to the word "faith" in the Gospel (but see 6:30), Matthew has reached an important theme that will be referred to often (e.g., 9:2, 22, 29; 15:28; 17:20; 21:21; 23:23).

11–12 It is understandable with this last point in mind—and an example of Matthew's genius—that Matthew inserts another piece of Q material here to draw out further the theological significance of the centurion's faith. Transposing the material as it is found in Luke (13:28–29) to a completely different context, Matthew begins with the statement about "many" (πολλοί) who will come from east and west (Luke in the parallel has apparently added "north and south") to recline at table with the patriarchs (listed with due deference in the repeated καί, "and"; cf. 22:32). The allusion is to the eschatological banquet (J. Behm, *TDNT* 2:34–35; Str-B 4:1154–56), a great festival of rejoicing and feasting in celebration of the victory of God, anticipated in both the OT and NT (see, e.g., Isa 25:6; Matt 22:1–14; 25:10; Rev. 19:9; Luke 14:15–16; *b. Pesaḥ* 119b; *Exod. Rab.* 25, 10). Until this point, such a banquet was thought to be a strictly Jewish affair (cf. Zeller), with the Gentiles at best receiving the overflow from the blessing to the Jews. The Gentiles would indeed make their pilgrimage to Jerusalem at the end (cf. Isa 2:2–3), but mainly as witnesses of God's blessing of Israel, not as direct participants in it. The references concerning the coming of many from east and west (e.g., Ps 107:3; Isa 43:5; Bar 4:37) were understood as referring to the return of diaspora Jews to Israel. The great family of the covenant people of God would gather with the patriarchs, who symbolize Israel, in the new eschatological kingdom and feast together with them—thus manifesting in this table communion their oneness (cf. *Comment* on 9:10–11). But now with the coming of the Messiah, that exclusivism is turned on its head in an apparent reversal of salvation-history. It is the Gentiles who are being called from the ends of the earth (contra Davies-Allison; cf. France, Luz). The centurion represents in effect the beginning of a stream of Gentiles who will come from east and west to join the eschatological banquet, while—and consider the offense of this unparalleled teaching—the Jews, "the sons of the kingdom," will themselves (in large part, i.e., who reject the Messiah) be rejected, although, of course, this does not apply to the OT saints. υἱοὶ τῆς βασιλείας, "sons of the kingdom," means those who belong to the kingdom (cf. "sons of the covenant" at Qumran; 1QM 17:3; cf. Matt 9:15). The true "sons of the kingdom" are now those who respond to the proclamation of Jesus (cf. 13:38; cf. 5:45). The theological point is made in absolute terms (even though hyperbolically; thus Davies-Allison), though of course all of Jesus' followers and the early Church were Jews and hence "children of the kingdom." The expression τὸ σκότος τὸ ἐξώτερον, "the outer darkness," here refers to the greatest possible contrast with the brilliantly illuminated banquet hall (cf. 22:13; 25:30; for darkness as judgment generally, see 2 Esdr 7:93; *1 Enoch* 63:10; *Pss. Sol.* 14:4; 15:10). "Weeping and grinding of teeth" is Matthew's favorite language for referring to the experience of eschatological judgment (cf. 13:42, 50; 22:13; 24:51; 25:30). Schwank argues that the phrase describes anguished self-reproach rather than fear or rage (according to Davies-Allison, it connotes anger).

13 This verse reverts to the request of the centurion and records the happy outcome. ὡς ἐπίστευσας γενηθήτω σοι, lit. "as you have believed, let it be to you." The healing occurs at a distance (Schweizer notes that such remote healings happen only in the case of Gentiles; cf. 15:21–28). This link between faith and healing is found elsewhere in Matt 9:29 and 15:28. The fact that the son was healed ἐν τῇ ὥρᾳ ἐκείνῃ, "in that very hour" (cf. 9:22; 17:18), effectively makes the point that the word of Jesus was responsible for the immediate healing (cf. the more elaborate account making the same point in John 4:50–53).

Explanation

The second miracle performed by Jesus in this section is indeed remarkable in its own right: the healing of a terribly ill child at a distance and by the speaking of a word. The story in itself stresses the sovereign authority and uniqueness of Jesus, though Matthew draws no special attention to the christological significance of the story. Indeed he focuses on the faith of the gentile centurion, faith that put Israel to shame. In Matthew's insertion of vv 11–12, Jesus declares that in the future Israel will be displaced by believing Gentiles, an emphasis that comes to sharp expression later in the parables of 21:33–44 and 22:1–10. The kingdom brought by Jesus is by its nature undeniably universal in scope. The centurion's faith is the first fruit of a ministry that will be designed to "make disciples of all nations" (28:19; cf. 24:14). What is anticipated here and commanded at the end of the Gospel finds its fruition in the course of the events narrated by the Acts of the Apostles. According to Paul's outline of events in Rom 11, the failure of the Jews made possible in God's wisdom the opportunity of the Gentiles. And Israel, not excluded from the great commission (28:19), "if they do not persist in their unbelief" (Rom 11:23), will yet take her proper place at the banquet of the table, together with Abraham, Isaac, and Jacob, and the Gentiles, whose faith (cf. Rom 11:20) is ultimately made possible by Israel herself (cf. Rom 9:5; 11:18).

The Healing of Peter's Mother-in-Law and Others   (8:14–17)

Bibliography

Fuchs, A. "Entwicklungsgeschichtliche Studie zu Mk 1,29–31 par Mt 8,14–15 par Lk 4,38–39." *SNTU* 6 (1981) 21–76. **Lamarche, P.** "La guérison de la belle-mère de Pierre et le genre littéraire des évangiles." *NRT* 87 (1965) 515–26. **Léon-Dufour, X.** "La guérison de la belle-mère de Simon-Pierre." In *Études d'Évangile.* Paris: Editions du Seuil, 1965. 125–48. **Olsson, B.** "Att umgås med texter." *STK* 52 (1976) 49–58. **Pesch, R.** "Die Heilung der Schweigermutter des Simon-Petrus." In *Neuer Exegese: Verlust oder Gewinn?* Freiburg: Herder, 1968. 162–69. **Strange, J. F.,** and **Shanks, H.** "Has the House Where Jesus Stayed in Capernaum Been Found?" *BARev* 8 (1982) 26–37.

Translation

[14]*And when Jesus came into Peter's house, he saw that Peter's mother-in-law was lying ill with a fever.* [15]*And he touched her hand, and the fever left her, and she rose and began*[a] *serving him.*[b] [16]*And when evening had come, they brought to him many possessed by demons, and he cast out the spirits*[c] *with a word, and he healed all those who were sick,* [17]*so that the word spoken through Isaiah the prophet was fulfilled: "He himself took our weaknesses, and he bore our diseases."*

Notes

[a] διηκόνει, lit. "was serving," is taken here as an inceptive impf.

[b] Some MSS (א[1] L Δ *f*[1,13] 33 lat syr bo) have the pl. αὐτοῖς, "to them," probably by influence of the Markan and Lukan parallels.

[c] The demons are here literally called τὰ πνεύματα, "the spirits."

Form/Structure/Setting

A. In this third of the three initial healing pericopes, we come to yet another representative of the disenfranchised: a woman. This independent story, which has clearly the ring of truth to it, involves the healing of one of the family, Peter's mother-in-law, in the household in Capernaum in which Jesus was presumably staying. The story was preserved in the early tradition perhaps just because of this personal element. This short pericope is followed by a miracle summary passage in which the fame of Jesus as a healer becomes obvious. He heals multitudes, delivering the demon possessed and healing the sick. Again the power, authority, and person of Jesus are in focus as the reader is reminded that the specific stories recounted in the Gospel are only representative of a whole host of other healings performed by Jesus.

B. Matthew depends on Mark (1:29–31) for this first part of the material (vv 14–15) and, as usual, abbreviates freely, thereby producing a terser narrative. Matthew omits the opening Markan words "immediately coming from the synagogue," because of his altered setting of the story. Matthew substitutes Πέτρου for Mark's (and Luke's) Σίμωνος, as is consonant with his special interest in "Peter." The names of Andrew, Peter's brother, and James and John, who accompanied them according to Matthew, are omitted (as in Luke) as unnecessary information. The focus then falls on Jesus (cf. Theissen's reference to "compression of compositional structures" and Matthew's reduced "character field" [*The Miracle Stories*, 177]). Matthew also omits the report of the situation (which Luke alters to an inquiry) for the same reason. Indeed, Matthew's account is conspicuous for its total lack of discourse. In addition to other slight changes in wording, there are three further alterations of the Markan account: Matthew describes the healing taking place with the mere touch of her hand in contrast to Mark's "he raised her, taking her hand"; Matthew employs ἠγέρθη, "she rose," suggesting she could do so on her own power; and Matthew changes Mark's final αὐτοῖς, "to them," to αὐτῷ, "to him," lending thereby a distinct christological aspect to the story. Interestingly, and perhaps in some tension with the notion of Luke being a physician, only Luke has personified the fever with his added words "he rebuked the fever."

In the second part (vv 16–17), Matthew follows Mark's opening genitive absolute, "when evening came," and omits Mark's redundant "when the sun had gone down" (Mark 1:32). He omits Mark's vivid, hyperbolic statement: "the whole city was gathered at the door" (Mark 1:33). Then, whereas Mark refers to the people bringing "*all* those sick and demon possessed" (Mark 1:32) and Jesus healing "many" (πολλούς, πολλά; Mark 1:34), Matthew transposes this to the people bringing "many demon possessed" and Jesus casting out the spirits and healing *all* (πάντας) who were sick. This last change, in addition to calling further attention to the power of Jesus, prepares the way for the formula quotation of v 17. Finally, Matthew omits the reference to Jesus prohibiting the demons from speaking because "they knew him" (elaborated upon by Luke), probably because it only distracts from Matthew's main purpose in including the summary passage. Although this miracle summary passage is here probably because such a healing ministry actually took place out of the house of Peter in Capernaum, it does bear obvious similarities with other such passages in the Gospel (e.g., 4:23–24; 9:35; 12:15; see Gerhardsson, *Mighty Acts*, 20–37).

C. In the quotation of Isa 53:4 in v 17 (one of Matthew's special formula quotations; see *Introduction*). Matthew "presents a rendering of the Hebrew almost wholly independent from the LXX" (Gundry, *Use*, 111). The LXX reads: οὗτος τὰς ἁμαρτίας ἡμῶν φέρει καὶ περὶ ἡμῶν ὀδυνᾶται, "this one bears our sins and suffers for us," interpreting these lines in the light of the clear reference to the removal of sin and the vicarious suffering for sin in the following verses of Isa 53. Matthew's version of the quotation is closer to the Hebrew of Isa 53:4: "Surely he has borne our infirmities and carried our diseases" (NRSV). Either Matthew has served as his own targumist (Gundry, *Use;* Stendahl, *School,* 106–7) or is dependent upon a source unknown to us. Matthew's version obviously ties in much better with the emphasis upon the healing of the sick and tormented.

D. The structure of the narrative about the healing of Peter's mother-in-law is that of a striking chiasmus (cf. B. Olsson, 52–53; Gerhardsson, *Mighty Acts*, 40–41):

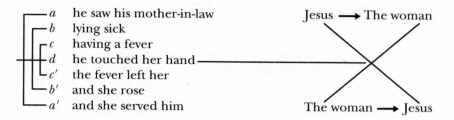

a	he saw his mother-in-law	Jesus → The woman
b	lying sick	
c	having a fever	
d	he touched her hand	
c'	the fever left her	
b'	and she rose	
a'	and she served him	The woman → Jesus

The narration is brief, direct, and without a change of words. Matthew appears to have imposed the carefully contrived structure upon the material in abbreviating the Markan tradition. Hill rightly notes that the special form of the passage "may be evidence of a Christian 'rabbinic' mind in action, making a narrative easily remembered for the community" (160).

Vv 16–17 are again straightforward and without comment except in the climactic quotation in v 17. Parallelism in v 16b can be seen in the main verbs ἐξέβαλεν, "he cast out," and ἐθεράπευσεν, "he healed," representing the two main categories of those healed. The quotation from Isa 53:4 provides a good example of synonymous parallelism, where the second clause repeats the content of the first in different language.

Comment

14–15 Peter's house in Capernaum naturally became a kind of headquarters for the Galilean ministry of Jesus. Archaeologists may well have discovered the foundation of this very house in Capernaum (see J. F. Strange and H. Shanks), not far from the Sea of Galilee (cf. 4:18). Since the extended family usually lived together, it was not unusual that the mother of Peter's wife would have lived there. (That Peter was married is also independently attested by 1 Cor 9:5.) Her condition is described very simply in the participles βεβλημένην and πυρέσσουσαν, "lying ill with a fever." As usual, in the ancient world fever is a disease itself rather than something that accompanies other diseases (Davies-Allison, however, speculate that she may have suffered from malaria). At this point, because of the preceding healing stories, the reader expects a healing and is not disappointed. There is no request for healing in Matthew; here alone in the narrative does Jesus take the initiative himself: he "saw" her. Again, as in the curing of the leper, Jesus "touched" (ἥψατο) his patient (cf. also 9:29, 20:34), nothing more, with the cure recorded directly: "the fever left her." (For other healings of fevers, cf. John 4:52; Acts 28:8.) Touching a person with a fever was forbidden in rabbinic tradition (see Str-B 1:479–80 for references). The fact that she got out of bed (ἠγέρθη) and "served" (διηκόνει) has the effect of confirming the reality of the healing. But it also takes on a certain christological tone, especially in Matthew's alteration of Mark's αὐτοῖς, "them," to αὐτῷ, "him." Thus Jesus remains the sole focus of attention, and the grateful woman's response in service becomes a model for the Christian readers of Matthew (cf. Held, in Bornkamm et al., *Tradition,* 170; Pesch, 166). She ministered to him in grateful response to what he had done for her—a fundamental aspect of discipleship.

16 At the end of the day, when leisure allowed (or perhaps waiting for the end of the Sabbath, when the sick could be carried; cf. "when the sun went down"

[Mark 1:32]), the crowds, having heard of Jesus' healings, brought the sick of their households (προσήνεγκαν, "they brought," like προσέρχεσθαι, "to come to," is a favorite word of Matthew's for those in need; cf. 4:24; 9:2, 32; 12:22; 14:35). Matthew mentions δαιμονιζομένους πολλούς, "many who were demon possessed." No mention is made of those with other maladies, but they *are* referred to in the statement immediately following concerning the healings performed by Jesus (τοὺς κακῶς ἔχοντας, "those who were sick"). Indeed, it was not easy to draw the line between demon possession and other sorts of maladies (cf. Luke 4:39, where in the reference to Jesus rebuking the fever, one senses the notion that it was thought to be caused by a spirit of some kind; see *T. Sol.* 7:6–7). Presumably many diseases we would explain differently today (e.g., epilepsy; cf. 17:15–18) were then classified as cases of demon possession, especially those that left the person in a state of obvious disorientation. But, in any event, apparently not every physical malady was attributed to spirits or demons, as our text shows. Aside from the miracle summary passages (cf. also 4:24; 7:22), Matthew records five specific instances of exorcism (8:28–34; 9:32–34; 12:22; 15:22–28; and 17:18). The absolute use of πνεύματα, "spirits," to refer to demons, without qualifying adjectives such as "unclean" (most common in the Synoptics; cf. Matt 10:1; 12:43–45) or "evil," is unusual in the Synoptics (cf. Mark 9:20; Luke 9:39; 10:20). Mark and Luke in the parallel passages simply have δαιμόνια, "demons." John never uses πνεῦμα, "spirit," in a negative sense, with or without qualifying adjectives. λόγῳ, "with a word," a Matthean addition, is important in referring to Jesus' unique authority and recalls the centurion's statement (8:8–9, "only say the word"). The general reference to healing the sick is found in all the summaries, of course, and in almost every instance it is stressed, as here with Matthew's addition of πάντας, "all," that Jesus healed all who came to him. This inclusiveness suggests (1) that there was no disease Jesus could not heal and (2) the universal scope of the grace of the kingdom announced by Jesus.

17 A fulfillment formula quotation (see *Introduction*) now shows that what is occurring in these healings is the fulfillment of the OT, specifically Isa 53:4. The Greek text of the quotation in Matthew (see above *Form/Structure/Setting* §C) may well be Matthew's own. It both better reflects the meaning of the Hebrew than the LXX translation and better links up with the summary of Jesus' healing ministry that has just preceded. And yet Matthew has not woodenly conformed the wording of the summary to agree with the quotation (e.g., the word νόσους, "diseases," in the quotation occurs in the miracle summaries of 4:23; 9:35; cf. 10:1; but not here; ἀσθενείας, "weaknesses," does not occur elsewhere in Matthew). Nor do the two predictions of the quotation correspond to demon exorcism and healing. They represent instead an example of synonymous parallelism, common in Hebrew poetry, where the second line repeats the thought of the first. Thus no important distinction is to be made between "weaknesses" and "diseases." In this quotation from Isa 53, Matthew reflects his familiarity with the identification of Jesus with the Servant of the Isaiah songs (cf. also his probable allusion to Isa 53 in 26:28; 27:12; and 27:38). It was said of that Servant, as it was believed of the Messiah, that he would take and bear the sicknesses of the people. The Jesus of Matthew's narrative in the three miracles performed and in those to follow (cf. also the miracle summaries) now heals in fulfillment of prophecy. He does not thereby accomplish his mission, however, for his fate is that of the Servant: the bearing of sin through the suffering of death. But that echo of the Isa 53 passage and the notion of vicarious suffering are not yet evident in the Gospel (thus correctly, Luz). See the helpful discussion in Carson, 205–6.

Explanation

A third miracle is reported by Matthew with deliberate brevity. With a touch, Jesus cures the fever of Peter's mother-in-law, and again the incomparable authority of Jesus becomes apparent. The passage thus has a basically christological character. Even the concluding words that suggest the proper response of the disciple point again to Jesus himself. The miracle summary passage has the same effect. With a word, Jesus casts out demons; he heals *all* the sick who come to him. The particular miracle stories chosen by Matthew for his narrative are thus but representatives of the vast healing ministry Jesus had among the people. This is an important part of the story for Matthew and is designated specifically as the fulfillment of OT prophecy. It is a sign of the reality of the presence of the kingdom of God announced by Jesus. Yet it must not be overstressed as by some modern charismatics who misuse v 17 to claim the availability of universal physical healing now. The point of the healings is not so much to be found in the events themselves but in their witness to the person of Jesus; i.e., they are basically christological in character. Given the entire sweep of the Gospel, the healing pericopes become relatively insignificant. As the Isa 53 quotation suggests to the reader who knows the story to its end, the healings are but one aspect of a much more important work to be performed by Jesus. The Gospel, in fact, has something far more important to tell than that Jesus healed (or can heal today). These single stories, these specific healing narratives, are not the heart of the gospel. Disease is not the true enemy that must be overcome: that enemy is sin, for the fallen world produced by sin lies ultimately behind the suffering and sickness of this age. This is the enemy to be conquered by the end of the story (cf. 26:28). Properly perceived, these healings are most important as symbols of the much greater "healing" that is at the heart of the gospel, the healing of the cross. At the same time, they foreshadow the fulfillment of the age to come when all suffering and sickness are finally removed (cf. Rev 21:1–4). During his ministry, the healings performed by Jesus were the fulfillment of prophecy; but Isa 53:4 guarantees no one healing in the present age. What is guaranteed is that Christ's atoning death will in the eschaton provide healing for all without exception. The healings through the ministry of Jesus and those experienced in our day are the first-fruits, the down payment, of the final experience of deliverance.

Two Comments on Discipleship   (8:18–22)

Bibliography

Black, M. "Let the Dead Bury Their Dead." *ExpTim* 61 (1950) 219–20. **Casey, M.** "The Jackals and the Son of Man (Matt. 8.20//Luke 9.58)." *JSNT* 23 (1985) 3–22. **Davies, W. J.,**

and **Ellison, C. S. S.** "Was His Father Lying Dead at Home?" *ExpTim* 62 (1950–51) 92. **Ehrhardt, A. A. T.** "Lass die Toten ihre Toten begraben." *ST* 6 (1953) 128–64. **Hengel, M.** "On the Exegesis of Mt 8.21–22: 'Let the dead bury their dead.'" In *The Charismatic Leader and His Followers*. Tr. J. Greig. New York: Crossroad, 1981. 3–15. **Kingsbury, J. D.** "On Following Jesus: The 'Eager' Scribe and the 'Reluctant' Disciple (Matthew 8.18–22)." *NTS* 34 (1988) 45–59. —————. "The Verb AKOLOUTHEIN ("To Follow") as an Index of Matthew's View of His Community." *JBL* 97 (1978) 56–73. **Klemm, H. G.** "Das Wort von der Selbstbestattung der Toten." *NTS* 16 (1969–70) 60–75. **Nestle, E.** "A Parallel to Matt. viii.20." *ExpTim* 11 (1889–90) 285. **Perles, F.** "Noch einmal Mt 8.22, Lc 9.60 so wie Joh 20.17." *ZNW* 25 (1926) 286. —————. "Zwei Übersetzungsfehler im Text der Evangelien." *ZNW* 19 (1919–20) 96. **Smith, M. H.** "No Place for a Son of Man." *Forum* 4 (1988) 83–107. **Schwarz, G.** "Ἄφες τοὺς νεκροὺς θάψαι τοὺς ἑαυτῶν νεκρούς." *ZNW* 73 (1982) 272–76. **Schweizer, E.** *Lordship and Discipleship*. SBT 28. London: SCM, 1960. 78–79. **Wilkins, M. J.** *The Concept of Disciple in Matthew's Gospel*. NovTSup 59. Leiden: Brill, 1988.

Translation

¹⁸ *When Jesus saw the crowd*[a] *around him, he commanded his disciples*[b] *to go across to the other side of the lake.*[c] ¹⁹ *And a Torah scholar came to him and said: "Teacher, I want to follow you wherever you go."* ²⁰ *And Jesus said to him: "Foxes have their lairs and the birds of the sky their nests, but the Son of Man has no place to lay his head."* ²¹ *And another of [his]*[d] *disciples said to him: "Lord, let me first go and bury my father."* [e] ²² *But Jesus said to him: "Follow me, and let those who are dead look after the dead."* [f]

Notes

[a] Despite slender textual witness (only B and sa^mss), the standard critical text favors the sing. "crowd." א² C L Θ *f*¹³ TR lat sy have πολλοὺς ὄχλους, "many crowds," or "a great crowd," or simply the pl. "crowds," thought to be a heightening introduced into Matthew's text. See *TCGNT*, 21.

[b] The translation supplies this direct object, which the Gr. is lacking.

[c] "Of the lake" implied, but not in the Gr. text.

[d] The standard critical text puts αὐτοῦ, "his," here in brackets because of the difficulty of deciding from the divided MS evidence (א B 33 it sa omit it; C L W Θ *f*¹,¹³ TR lat sy mae bo include it) whether it was in the original text. A majority of the committee thought it possible that αὐτοῦ was deleted by some copyists in order to avoid the impression that the scribe of v 19 was a disciple of Jesus. See *TCGNT*, 22.

[e] Or possibly "Let me first look after my father until he dies." See *Comment*.

[f] Possibly to be understood as "let the grave-diggers look after the dead." See *Comment*.

Form/Structure/Setting

A. V 18 is clearly a preparation for the narrative that begins in v 23. It is followed, however, by material relating to discipleship, which appears to be inserted into the flow of the text somewhat arbitrarily at this point. There are two factors that may help explain why vv 19–22 occur just here: (1) v 18 refers to the command of Jesus to cross the sea to the other side, which prompts the recollection of the Gospel tradition of the saying of one who promised to follow Jesus wherever he went; (2) healing, faith, and discipleship are linked together in the preceding material, and the last, as we have seen, is especially evident in v 15. Here the following that is the appropriate response of discipleship comes into focus. The second discipleship saying was apparently already attached to the first in the tradition (cf. Luke 9:57–62; Luke adds a third saying on the rigorous demands of discipleship) and thus automatically follows. The discipleship sayings in this pericope have an exemplary or paradigmatic character (Hengel). Bultmann describes the whole situation as "imaginary" (*History*, 29).

B. Vv 19–22 are paralleled in Luke 9:57–60 and are thus derived from Q. Luke's third saying on discipleship (9:61–62, about another would-be disciple who wants first to take leave of his family) is not found in Matthew. More probably this has been added by Luke from his other sources rather than having been omitted by Matthew from his Q source. As for the Q material, Matthew differs from Luke in describing the first man as a γραμματεύς, "scribe, Torah scholar" (Luke, merely τις, "someone"), and in his addressing Jesus as διδάσκαλε, "teacher" (lacking in Luke). The subsequent saying of Jesus (v 20) is in verbatim agreement in Matthew and Luke (except for the inversion of the final two words). In the second instance, Luke has Jesus taking the initiative with the invitation "follow me" (Luke 9:59). Matthew puts this invitation into Jesus' response (v 22). Matthew describes this person as "another of [his] disciples" (v 21); Luke simply as ἕτερον, "another" (9:59). Matthew inserts ὁ Ἰησοῦς, "Jesus," in v 22 (lacking in Luke). Again the actual saying of Jesus in response, apart from the initial "follow me," is in verbatim agreement with Luke (9:60). Typically, then, the actual sayings of Jesus are seen to be the most stable element in the tradition, while the framework is subject to a variety of changes.

C. Apart from the introductory and transitory verse that begins this passage (v 18, which is connected with vv 23–27), the passage is symmetrically structured in two major parts, each representing an interchange with Jesus: (1) the Torah scholar who wanted to follow Jesus (vv 19–20) and (2) the disciple with an apparently legitimate excuse (vv 20–22). Each of these parts can be further subdivided into (a) a statement of a disciple or would-be disciple (vv 19 and 21) and (b) a slightly cryptic response of Jesus in words about the nature of discipleship (vv 20 and 22). Each major part contains the key words ἀκολουθεῖν, "follow," and ἀπέρχεσθαι, "go," with the latter being found also in v 18 in the command to the disciples. The dominical saying of v 20 is found almost exactly in the *Gospel of Thomas* (logion 86), where to the words "and has no place to lay his head" is added "and to rest."

D. In this passage (v 20) we encounter for the first time in Matthew the very problematic title "Son of Man."

Excursus: Son of Man

Bibliography

Bauckham, R. J. "The Son of Man: 'A Man in My Position' or 'Someone.'" *JSNT* 23 (1985) 23–33. **Bruce, F. F.** "The Background to the Son of Man Sayings." In *Christ the Lord*. FS D. Guthrie, ed. H. Rowdon. Downers Grove, IL: InterVarsity, 1982. **Caragounis, C. C.** *The Son of Man: Vision and Interpretation*. WUNT 38. Tübingen: J. C. B. Mohr, 1986. **Casey, M.** "General, Generic and Indefinite: The Use of the Term 'Son of Man' in Aramaic Sources and in the Teaching of Jesus." *JSNT* 29 (1987) 21–56. ———. *Son of Man*. London: SPCK, 1979. **Collins, A. Y.** "The Origin of the Designation of Jesus as 'Son of Man.'" *HTR* 80 (1987) 391–407. **Donahue, J. R.** "Recent Studies on the Origin of 'Son of Man' in the Gospels." *CBQ* 48 (1986) 484–98. **Dunn, J. D. G.** *Christology in the Making.* Philadelphia: Westminster, 1980. 65–97. **Fitzmyer, J.** "The NT Title 'Son of Man' Philologically Considered." In *A Wandering Aramaean: Collected Aramaic Essays.* Missoula, MT: Scholars Press, 1979. **Fuller, R. H.** "The Son of Man: A Reconsideration." In *The Living Text.* FS E. Saunders, ed. I. Groh and R. Jewett. Lanham, MD: University Press of America, 1985. 207–17. **Gese, H.** "Wisdom, Son of Man, and the Origins of Christology: The Consistent Development of Biblical Theology." *HBT* 3 (1981) 23–57. **Hare, D. R. A.** *The Son of Man Tradition.* Minneapolis: Fortress, 1990. **Higgins, A. J. B.** *The Son of Man in the Teaching of Jesus.* SNTSMS 39. Cambridge: Cambridge University, 1980. **Hooker, M.** "Is the Son of Man Problem Really Insoluble?" In *Text and Interpretation.* FS M. Black, ed. E. Best and R. McL. Wilson. Cambridge: Cambridge University, 1979. 155–68. **Horbury, W.** "Messianic Associations of 'The Son of Man.'" *JTS* 36 (1985) 34–55. **Kim, S.** *"The Son of Man" as the Son of God.* Grand Rapids: Eerdmans, 1983. **Leivestad, R.** "Exit the Apocalyptic Son of Man." *NTS* 18 (1972) 243–67. **Lindars, B.** *Jesus Son of Man: A Fresh Examination of the Son of Man Sayings in the Gospels in the Light of Recent Research.* London: SPCK, 1983. ————. "Re-enter the Apocalyptic Son of Man." *NTS* 22 (1975) 52–72. **Marshall, I. H.** *The Origins of New Testament Christology.* Rev. ed. Downers Grove, IL: InterVarsity, 1990. ————. "The Son of Man and the Incarnation." *Ex Auditu* 7 (1991) 29–43. **Tödt, H. E.** *The Son of Man in the Synoptic Tradition.* Philadelphia: Westminster, 1965. **Tuckett, C.** "The Present Son of Man." *JSNT* 14 (1982) 58–81. **Vermes, G.** "The Present State of the 'Son of Man' Debate." *JJS* 29 (1978) 123–34.

"Son of Man" has been a *crux interpretum* in twentieth-century NT scholarship for basically two reasons: (1) the great variety of the Son of Man sayings, which include those referring to (a) the glorious coming of the apocalyptic Son of Man (this is the primary connotation of the phrase in the majority of its occurrences, from its basic dependence on Dan 7:13–14; cf. Matt 24:30 and 26:64), (b) the suffering and dying Son of Man, and (c) the earthly ministry of Jesus (see G. E. Ladd, *A Theology of the New Testament,* 3rd ed. [Grand Rapids: Eerdmans, 1993] 147–57); and (2) the disputed authenticity of some of these sayings, of one or more of the three groups or of all of them together. The sheer variety of the Son of Man sayings has itself given rise to questions about their authenticity. Modern radical criticism has been unable to accept that Jesus could have used the title in such different statements and predications concerning himself. It furthermore finds the content of the apocalyptic Son of Man sayings and the suffering/dying sayings unacceptable: the first imply too much self-consciousness of his messianic identity (and if authentic, must therefore refer to the coming of someone else); the second imply knowledge of the future and find no parallel in Son of Man references in ancient literature. In the case of the sayings referring to Jesus' ministry, the phrase "Son of Man" in a non-titular sense (cf. "son of man" as "man" in Ps 8 and Ezekiel *passim*) is often accepted as a circumlocution for "I." Recently G. Vermes has argued, rather implausibly, that *all* of the authentic Son of Man references in the mouth of Jesus (except in OT quotations of Dan 7) are of the circumlocutory type and not titular. His arguments have been contested by J. Fitzmyer. Radical critical scholarship further defends its skepticism about the authenticity of the Son of Man sayings by showing that none of them is related to the concrete bedrock of Jesus' proclamation of the kingdom. This statement, however, ignores the possibility of indirect connection between the two, which the evangelists, at least, surely accepted: the kingdom announced by the Messiah who is the Son of Man is possible only through his death and will be finally and fully realized on earth only at his glorious return. This is indeed the heart of the gospel.

The alternative to accepting the Son of Man sayings as authentic is, of course, to attribute them to the creativity of the post-resurrection Church. Yet, as has often been pointed out, Jesus is referred to as the Son of Man outside the Gospels in only a few special instances (Acts 7:56; Rev. 1:13; 14:14). This was not a title (like others) that the early Church used to express its Christology or its faith in Jesus. It is thus very improbable that the early Church was responsible for the wholesale custom of such a wide range of Son of Man sayings and ascription of them to Jesus. If such a saying may on occasion have been created in the early Church, it would have been on the model of those authentic Son of Man sayings contained in the most primitive tradition. It is fully understandable that Jesus would have preferred the ambiguous title of Son of Man in referring to himself (cf. his concern to keep his messiahship secret). Perhaps because of just that ambiguity, the title did not become a part of the Church's language, other than in the presentation of the Gospel tradition. It stands in the Gospel tradition as almost a historical relic, adding to the complexity of Jesus' own expression of his mission. The main background for the title "the Son of Man" is almost certainly the Dan 7:13–14 passage (but cf. too the parallel material in the *Similitudes of Enoch* [*1 Enoch* 37–71; on the currently emerging consensus concerning the first-century dating of these materials, see J. H. Charlesworth in *The Old Testament Pseudepigrapha and the New Testament* (Cambridge: Cambridge University, 1985) 102–10] and 2 Esdr 13). Here we read, to be sure, of a glorious, triumphant figure; but the "saints" represented in the corporate notion of Son of Man also suffer persecution and martyrdom (cf. Dan 8:24; 12).

The concern of this commentary is the meaning intended by Matthew as he wrote it for his readers and those who would follow them. For Matthew and his church, Jesus spoke with full self-consciousness of the ministry of the human Son of Man as one who was at the same time the Son of God. This Son of Man was to die (yet deliberately and majestically) and would return before long as the glorious personage he is. The "Son of Man" is for Matthew's church, though not part of its working vocabulary, perhaps familiar solely through the Gospel tradition about the Jesus of history. Although we cannot further discuss the difficult question of authenticity here, the preceding bibliography offers further reading (see also J. Nolland, "Excursus: Son of Man," in *Luke 9:21–18:34*, WBC 35B [Dallas: Word, 1993] 468–74).

Comment

18   This transitional verse (following Mark 4:35; cf. Luke 8:22) looks very much as though it ought to introduce vv 23–27. Instead, because of the command to the disciples (not yet the twelve but a more nebulous grouping) ἀπελθεῖν εἰς τὸ πέραν, "to go to the other side," it becomes the occasion for Matthew to include two discipleship sayings. Apparently beleaguered by the crowd, Jesus decides to escape to the deserted area across the sea. In Jesus' command Matthew senses a hint of the radical call and demands of discipleship. Was it merely the labor of the boat journey, or perhaps the ominous clouds that may have threatened against such a voyage just then, or just the assumed readiness to be away from the comforts of home for probably at least several nights? In the word "commanded" (cf. 8:9) and in the verb ἀπέρχεσθαι, "to go" (the one common element in vv 18, 19–20, and 21–22), Matthew not only reminds the readers of the authority of Jesus but turns them to the rigors of discipleship, inserting the following material.

19   Again we encounter Matthew's favorite προσέρχεσθαι (see on 5:1). εἷς is used here as an indefinite article, "a" γραμματεύς, "scribe." Either Matthew has access to a tradition that informs him that the man was a scribe, or he speculates that the man was a scribe, perhaps one of the crowd who had been particularly impressed with the amazing teaching of Jesus. He is not yet a disciple (correctly, Kingsbury, *NTS* 34 [1988] 47–48) but believes he would like to become one. Matthew's Jewish-Christian community doubtless included some of its own scribes (cf. Christian scribes in 13:52 and 23:34), rivaling the scribes of the synagogue (see D. Orton, *Understanding Scribe*, 137–63). A scribe was a professional Torah scholar and would have had a very special interest in what Jesus taught. Hence, this scribe addresses Jesus as διδάσκαλος, "teacher." This address is not necessarily to be taken as negative, even by implication or comparison, for example, with κύριος, "Lord" (as, for example, in v 21). To be sure, in the majority of instances it implies a clearly deficient understanding or estimate of Jesus (e.g., when used by the Pharisees in 9:11; 12:38; 22:16, 24, 36). Furthermore, there is a clear tendency in Matthew to avoid having the disciples address Jesus as "teacher," as he is in certain Markan passages (e.g., Mark 4:38; 9:38; 10:35; 13:1). But on occasion the address can be positive, as when used by the potential disciple in 19:16 or, more importantly, by Jesus himself, as in 23:8; 26:18; or especially 10:24–25, where "teacher" is paired in rabbinic fashion with "disciple" (μαθητής). The scribe, according to Matthew's storyline, perhaps overhearing the command to cross the sea, expresses readily (perhaps too readily) his unqualified willingness to follow Jesus wherever he is going at that time and, by implication, also in the future (ὅπου). As Schulz remarks (*Q*, 106), the man wanted to take his permanent place as a *Talmid* (rabbinical student) of Jesus. "Follow" (ἀκολουθεῖν) and "go" (ἀπέρχεσθαι) are, as we have noted, key words in the vocabulary of discipleship. Here the word ἀκολουθήσω, "I want to follow," meaning "following" literally, becomes infused with the notion of discipleship in the broadest sense. Discipleship, as Jesus will suggest, involves more than just willingness to follow in the sense of accompanying someone, or even willingness to listen to and learn from someone and to live with that person as did students with their rabbis; it involves at bottom a total lifestyle. It is important to note (with Kingsbury, *NTS* 34 [1988] 45–59) that although the scribe reflects good Jewish practice in choosing his teacher, in the Gospel narrative it is consistently Jesus who initiates the disciple-master relationship by his sovereign choice of disciples. This perhaps explains the coolness of Jesus' response in the next verse.

20   Because Jesus expands the scribe's concept of following by referring to discipleship in terms of a kind of urgent, wandering, and homeless ministry, his answer may well have surprised the scribe. Jesus means that life for him and the disciples who do follow him will be a matter of rigorous and self-denying living. As he was accustomed to doing, Jesus used the ordinary things of nature (cf. 6:26, 28) to make his point. Even what the foxes and the birds have is denied Jesus and so also the disciples who would follow him (note 10:24: "a disciple is not above his master"; cf. the homelessness of the apostles, 1 Cor 4:11). The response of Jesus is anything but flat prose. It is beautiful, vivid, and memorable. The foxes and the birds (cf. Ps 84:3), simple creatures of God, have their homes, but the Son of Man has not so much as a place to lay his head. There is undeniably a hyperbolic element here (e.g., during the Galilean ministry Jesus used Capernaum as his "home"), but Jesus' mode of life was anything but a "settled" one. Also possibly in view is the opposition and persecution experienced by him (cf. Kingsbury, *NTS* 34 [1988] 45–59; Schweizer, *Lordship*, 78). The attempt to find symbolism in the foxes and birds (cf. T. W. Manson, *Sayings*, 72) seems unjustified and unnecessary.

Perhaps the words were part of a familiar proverb (for a parallel use of the metaphor, E. Nestle points to Plutarch's *Life of Tiberius Graechus,* chap. 9). υἱὸς τοῦ ἀνθρώπου, "Son of Man" (cf. above "Excursus: Son of Man"), here stands in the place of "I." But although it is not a titular instance of "Son of Man" (*pace* Davies-Allison; Luz), that aspect can hardly be altogether absent from the readers' minds. The Son of Man, elsewhere in the Gospel to be described in such exalted language (and mysterious language, too, for the predictions of suffering and death), lives here in fulfillment of this phase of his ministry in abject humility.

21–22 ἕτερος δὲ τῶν μαθητῶν [αὐτοῦ], "another of his disciples," is presumably not one of the twelve but one from the larger circle of sincere disciples who had begun to follow Jesus as a part of the nameless crowd (see Wilkins). ἕτερος, "another," could imply that the scribe of v 19 is also to be considered one of the larger circle of disciples—a possible, but not a necessary, conclusion. Perhaps both are to be regarded as beginning or apprentice disciples who are now being initiated into the radical demands their discipleship will entail if they are true to it (Kingsbury, *NTS* 34 [1988] 45–59, regards the former as a would-be disciple, the latter as a "true disciple"). (The pure speculation of Albright-Mann that δέ should be οὐδέ, "*not*" one of the disciples, is hardly necessary.) This disciple does not make a statement as in the previous instance. Instead he makes a request that seems particularly reasonable, namely, that before he follows Jesus, he be allowed to ἀπελθεῖν (the same verb used in the call *to* discipleship, now used in the call away *from* discipleship) καὶ θάψαι τὸν πατέρα μου, "go and bury my father."

Indeed, this was required of a son by the Torah implicitly in the commandment to honor one's father and mother and hence explicitly in later Jewish tradition (cf. Gen 50:5; Tob 4:3; cf. Sir 38:16; *m. Ber.* 3:1, where burial of the dead supersedes other religious duties; in Lev 21:2 priests are allowed the defilement of touching the dead in the case of close family members); indeed, not to do so would violate the command of God. Yet Jesus in his response denies the legitimacy of such a delay. It is tempting for this reason to understand θάψαι τὸν πατέρα μου, "to bury my father," in the sense of "look after him until he dies" (for evidence that the phrase could have been understood in this sense, see K. E. Bailey, *Through Peasant Eyes* [Grand Rapids: Eerdmans, 1980] 26–27), but this too is required by the Torah. In fact, so important is the commitment to honor one's parents that to fail in any of the following responsibilities is to be untrue to the Torah: to bury a father who has just died, to participate in the six days of official mourning after such a death, to look after one who is sick and perhaps near death, and to provide for an aging parent who may yet live many years. From the standpoint of the call to discipleship, the longer the delay involved the more reasonable Jesus' negative reaction becomes (cf. 15:4). But the call to discipleship is for Jesus an absolute one that need not satisfy any normal canons of responsibility (Luz rightly uses such words as *respektlosradikal; skandalös*): "Follow [for the importance of ἀκολουθεῖν in Matthew, see *Comment* on 4:20] me, and let the dead bury the dead." Jesus' call in this case supersedes even strict obedience to the commandment of the Torah. For a similar exception pertaining to high priests and Nazirites, see Lev 21:11, Num 6:6–7 (for an analysis of its radical character, see E. P. Sanders, *Jesus and Judaism* [Philadelphia: Fortress, 1985] 252–55). Jesus' response to the disciple is "typical of the shock-tactics with which Jesus' radical demand is presented" (France, 161). Hengel finds hardly any logion "which more sharply runs counter to law, piety and custom" (14). Nothing can come before (cf. πρῶτον, "first") discipleship to Jesus in the cause of the kingdom. The same type of radical call demanding immediate response is found in Luke's added response to a disciple who wanted merely to say farewell to his family, where there is little uncertainty about the brevity of time involved (Luke 9:61–62). In a passage with some interesting ties to these discipleship sayings of Jesus as well as a remarkable contrast, Elisha was in fact allowed to return home just in order to take proper leave of his parents before assuming his new role as the follower of Elijah (1 Kgs 19:19–21). The concluding words of Jesus as they stand in the Greek text, ἄφες τοὺς νεκροὺς θάψαι τοὺς ἑαυτῶν νεκρούς, mean "let the dead bury their own dead" and are perhaps to be understood as "let the spiritually dead bury their own physically dead." The notion of being "spiritually dead" was not unknown to the Jews (cf. Str-B 1:489; 3:165). On the other hand, it may well be that the Greek has misunderstood this underlying Aramaic, reading lĕmiqbar, "to bury," for limqabber, "to the burier, to the undertaker" (see Perles; Montefiore, *Synoptic Gospels* 2:134), which may have run "let the grave-diggers bury the dead." (Cf. M. Black's suggestion [*Aramaic Approach*, 207–8] that mîtîn, "dead," has been mistakenly read for mĕtînîn, "waverers" ["Let the waverers bury the dead"].) T. W. Manson may be closest to the truth, however, when he speculates that the statement means something like "that business can take care of itself" (*Sayings*, 73). The reading of the text as it now stands and the interpretation of the first νεκρούς as the spiritually dead would have been aided by the later theology of the Church (cf. for example, Rom 6:3; Eph 2:1). Be that as it may, the clarity of the point remains that the disciple is not to let himself or herself be distracted by anything, however legitimate in itself.

Explanation

This pericope is about disciples and discipleship. Well-meaning disciples suggest their willingness to follow Jesus but are shown to be in need of further instruction regarding the full demands of discipleship. Discipleship means not only an initial decision but also the constantly renewed decisions that attachment to Jesus involves (Grundmann). Jesus, having expressed in the Gospel his sovereign lordship in word and now in deed, calls individuals to discipleship in an equally sovereign and absolute manner. Discipleship for Jesus, like the related call to righteousness (cf. the Sermon on the Mount), is an all or nothing matter. Discipleship, as will emerge even more clearly as Matthew proceeds (cf. 10:34–39; 16:24–25; 19:29; 20:26–27), involves self-denial, service, suffering, persecution, and perhaps even death. There is furthermore in several of these passages mention of the possible impact of discipleship upon family relationships. Disciples are therefore in a sense always learners who are discovering more about discipleship as they attempt to live in obedience to Jesus. But the key point is that the call is radical; so too must the responding commitment be radical. It would be as much a mistake to take the statement of v 22 quite literally (unless in fact the proposed delay was to be a long one) as it would be to dismember oneself for the sake of righteousness (thus Carson rightly). But, despite the hyperbole, there is a fundamental principle here about the radical character, urgency, and uncompromising nature of discipleship that is to be heard with every invitation to, or volunteering of, discipleship to Jesus and the cause of the kingdom.

The Stilling of the Sea   (8:23–27)

Bibliography

Bornkamm, G. "The Stilling of the Storm in Matthew." In *Tradition and Interpretation in Matthew*, G. Bornkamm, G. Barth, and H. J. Held. 52–57. **Duplacy, J.** "Et il y eut un grande calme. . . . La tempête apaisée (Matthieu 8.23–27)." *BVC* 74 (1976) 15–28. **Feiler, P. F.** "The Stilling of the Storm in Matthew: A Response to Günther Bornkamm." *JETS* 26 (1983) 399–406. **Goldammer, K.** "Navis Ecclesiae." *ZNW* 40 (1941) 76–86. **Hilgert, E.** "Symbolismus und Heilsgeschichte in den Evangelien: Ein Beitrag zu den Seesturm- und Gerasener-erzählungen." In *Oikonomia*. FS O. Cullmann, ed. F. Christ. Hamburg: Reich, 1967. 51–56. **Iersel, B. M. F. van,** and **Linmans, A. J. M.** "The Storm on the Lake, Mk 4.35–41 and Mt 8:18–27 in the Light of Form Criticism." In *Miscellanea Neotestamentica*, ed. T. Baarda et al. NovTSup 48. Leiden: Brill, 1978. 17–48. **Peterson, E.** "Das Schiff als Symbol der Kirche." *TZ* 6 (1950) 77–79. **Pittenger, N.** "Great Calm." *ExpTim* 85 (1974) 209–10.

Translation

[23]*And when he got into the*[a] *boat, his disciples followed him.* [24]*And look, there was a great earthquake under*[b] *the sea, so that the boat was covered by the waves. But he himself continued sleeping.*[c] [25]*And they*[d] *came to him and woke him, saying: "Lord, save us!*[e] *We are perishing!"* [26]*And he said to them: "Why are you so fearful, you who have such little faith?"*[f] *Then when he got up, he rebuked the winds and the sea, and there was a great calm.* [27]*But the men marveled at all this,*[g] *saying: "What sort of a person is this that even the winds and the sea obey him?"*

Notes

[a] Substantial MS evidence (e.g., אᵇ B C *f*[1.13] 33) supports the omission of the definite article (thus, "a boat"). Yet Matthew's usage elsewhere favors the article here, and its omission may be due to influence of the parallel text in Luke 8:22.

[b] Lit. "in" (ἐν) the sea. See *Comment.*

[c] The impf. tense signifying ongoing action warrants this translation.

[d] C² L *f*[13] and TR have οἱ μαθηταί, "the disciples"; other witnesses (e.g., C* W Θ *f*[1]) have οἱ μετ' αὐτοῦ, "those with him." But the shorter text with no specified subject is contained in א B 33 and the Western witnesses (it vg Jer). It would be natural for scribes to add a subject. See *TCGNT*, 22.

[e] σῶσον, lit. "save." Although L W Θ TR lat sy include ἡμᾶς, "us," the best witnesses (א B C *f*[1.13] 33) omit it. The direct object is included in the translation since English transitive verbs require direct objects, whereas Gr. verbs survive easily without direct objects.

[f] It would be possible to punctuate the text so that two questions, rather than one, are asked: i.e., "What? Are you afraid?"

[g] "At all this" is only assumed in the Gr. text and supplied in the translation.

Form/Structure/Setting

A. Following the sayings on discipleship comes a narrative that involves both testing for the disciples of Jesus and a further demonstration of the authority of Jesus in deeds of power—in this instance, power over the forces of nature. V 23 could easily follow immediately after v 18; but the effect of the inserted sayings on discipleship is to focus attention on the disciples and their little faith, as well as on the unique authority of Jesus. The passage is thus as much a lesson on discipleship (Bornkamm calls it "a kerygmatic paradigm of the danger and glory of discipleship" [*Tradition*, 57]) as it is a record of a further mighty deed done by Jesus, the first of the second group in the series of ten in chaps. 8–9. A sovereign call to an absolute discipleship is balanced by the powerful authority and person of the one who issues that call. The passage thus concerns both discipleship and Christology (the latter is rightly emphasized by Feiler).

B. Matthew depends on Mark (4:36–41) as does the Lukan parallel (Luke 8:22–25). As usual, Matthew abbreviates Mark's narrative considerably. Among the more substantial and significant changes, the following must be mentioned. Whereas in Mark the disciples "took him" with them in the boat, Matthew, in keeping with his discipleship theme, has Jesus get into the boat first and then adds ἠκολούθησαν αὐτῷ οἱ μαθηταὶ αὐτοῦ, "his disciples followed him." After the added ἰδού of v 24, Matthew substitutes σεισμός . . . ἐν τῇ θαλάσσῃ, "an earthquake . . . in the sea," for Mark's (followed by Luke's) λαῖλαψ . . . ἀνέμου, "a fierce whirlwind." Matthew omits Mark's vivid statement that "the boat was already filling" and the reference to Jesus being "in the stern . . . on the cushion" as unnecessary to the story. Matthew inserts his favorite προσελθόντες, "coming to him," at the beginning of v 25 (so too Luke). For Mark's διδάσκαλε, "teacher," Matthew substitutes κύριε, "Lord" (Luke has the repeated ἐπιστάτα, ἐπιστάτα, "master, master," a Lukan favorite, and used only by Luke). Matthew inserts the key word σῶσον, "save (us)," and omits Mark's "do you not care that," perhaps to avoid the implied reproach. V 26a is transposed from its later position in the Markan narrative (4:40), and Matthew employs his favorite ὀλιγόπιστοι, "you of little faith," thus softening considerably the separate Markan question: "Do you not have faith?" Matthew (like Luke) omits the words spoken by Jesus to the elements, σιώπα πεφίμωσο, "peace, be still." For Mark's ἐφοβήθησαν φόβον μέγαν, lit. "they were afraid with a great fear," Matthew has simply ἐθαύμασαν, "they marveled" (v 27). But Matthew alone has οἱ ἄνθρωποι, "the men," as the subject of that verb. Finally, Matthew omits "to one another," having simply λέγοντες, "saying," and uses the word ποταπός, "what sort of person," for Mark's (and Luke's) "Who then is this?"

C. The structure of the passage is simple and direct, despite the mixing of the two concerns of discipleship and Christology: (1) the occasion (v 23; cf. v 18); (2) the dire need of the disciples with the added note about Jesus sleeping (v 24); (3) the appeal for help (v 25), which stands at the center of the passage; (4) the response of Jesus in word and deed (v 26); and (5) the disciples' amazement expressed in a question (v 27). See Davies-Allison for the possibly chiastic structure of this pericope.

D. There are some similarities between this passage and the otherwise quite different story in 14:22–33. In the latter, the disciples are also told to cross over to the other side in a boat (14:22), the boat is tossed by the waves (14:24), and Peter's cry when he begins to sink, κύριε σῶσόν με, "Lord, save me" (14:30), is particularly like the cry of 8:25. Peter is addressed as ὀλιγόπιστε, "you of little faith" (14:31; cf. 8:26); he is asked why he doubted (14:31); the storm ceases; and a christological point is made, not by a question but in the outright affirmation: "Truly you are the Son of God" (14:33). Although it is possible that there has been some crossover influence of the vocabulary of the one story upon the other, these are truly independent episodes, and the similarities are completely natural and to be expected. Matthew's story also is similar in some ways to the story of Jonah in Jon 1:4–16: while a great sea storm threatens the ship, Jonah lies asleep (Jon 1:5); he is awakened and told to call upon his god that they may not perish (1:6); the storm stops when Jonah is thrown overboard (1:15); and the men feared the Lord (1:16). Cf. too Ps 107:23–32.

Comment

23 From the way Matthew has structured this passage, with the inserted material of vv 19–22, the focus of this passage falls naturally on the disciples and discipleship. Thus it is reported that "his disciples," οἱ μαθηταὶ αὐτοῦ, in fact ἠκολούθησαν αὐτῷ, "followed him." Again, according to the story line, these are not quite yet the twelve (cf. 9:9 and 10:2, where the twelve are first mentioned in Matthew). Matthew deliberately alters Mark's wording to make this point. This example of obedience stands in stark contrast to the hesitance of the disciple of v 21, if not also the would-be disciple of v 19. But this faithful discipleship in following Jesus is about to be tested in what now happens.

24 Again we encounter Matthew's favorite signaling word ἰδού, "look," indicating that something special is about to happen. Matthew's peculiar reference to σεισμὸς μέγας, "a great earthquake" (or "shaking"), reflects his special interest in earthquakes (four references, while only one each in the other Synoptics). In two other instances, the earthquakes are at key points, one may even say revelatory points, in the narrative (27:51–54 and 28:2, where the language is practically verbatim). The one remaining instance has an eschatological and threatening character, referring to the earthquakes that will accompany the signs of the end of the age (24:7). While earthquakes are in fact the cause of enormous "tidal waves," the introduction of an earthquake here stands in some tension with the later reference, borrowed from Mark, to "the wind," usually associated with storms rather than earthquakes. Evidence exists in Greek literature, however, that earthquakes were at times associated with winds and heavy seas (cf. BAGD, 746). The result, regardless of the technical cause, was such a rough sea that the boat was literally "covered by the waves." Although this clearly appeared to be a life-threatening situation, Jesus continued to sleep (ἐκάθευδεν, imperfect tense). There is an obvious intentional, christological aspect here. The one who has nowhere to lay his head (v 20) is yet paradoxically at home everywhere, apparently untroubled by normal anxieties. In the OT such sleep is evidence of a trust in God's protection (cf. Job 11:18–19; Pss 3:5–6; 4:8; Prov 3:24–26). Jesus' sleeping under such circumstances can itself easily give rise to the question with which the pericope ends: "What sort of man is this?" (The similarity with Jonah [1:5] is interesting, but Jonah was traveling in a much larger vessel and probably exhausted with fleeing from the presence of the Lord. A little later [12:41] Matthew describes Jesus as "one greater than Jonah.")

25 The disciples προσελθόντες, "came," to Jesus (again Matthew's favorite vocabulary; cf. on 5:1) and woke him, saying: κύριε, σῶσον, ἀπολλύμεθα, "Lord, save (us)! We are perishing!" Matthew finds κύριε more appropriate than Mark's διδάσκαλος, "teacher," as he usually does, here because of the discipleship theme but perhaps even more so because of the sovereign power displayed by Jesus over the elements and the focus on the christological question at the conclusion of the passage (for "Lord," see *Comment* on 7:21). The insertion of the word σῶσον, "save," so important in the vocabulary of the Church after the middle of the first century, is particularly suggestive. Possibly in this language we even hear an echo of the liturgical language of Matthew's church (Bonnard). The Lord who saves his disciples (cf. 14:30) is the Lord who saves his Church (cf. 1:21; 18:11; 19:25). ἀπολλύμεθα, "we are perishing," thus also connotes more than just the peril of the disciples; it, like σῶσον, has a timeless application.

26   The question τί δειλοί ἐστε, "Why are you so fearful?" together with the address ὀλιγόπιστοι, "you who have such little faith" (see *Comment* on 6:30), is a rebuke to the disciples for not trusting and not fully appreciating their master. This question comes in Matthew before the stilling of the sea (unlike in Mark and Luke, where it follows the miracle) in keeping with the discipleship theme and thus heightening its impact. If the disciples respond to an absolute call to discipleship and hence leave all and risk their lives, they must also understand that the one who calls them will also preserve them in whatever circumstances they may find themselves. Then, in a majestic way, ἐγερθεὶς ἐπετίμησεν, "he got up and rebuked," the elements. Matthew is content simply to report this and does not retain the Markan words spoken by Jesus to the sea. The idea of "rebuking" (the same language used in exorcism [e.g., 17:18] but much more often in Mark and Luke) may presuppose evil spirits as expressing themselves in the storm. καὶ ἐγένετο γαλήνη μεγάλη, "and there came a great calm," refers to more than simply the cessation of the storm. It instead means there was a mysterious, supernatural calm that testified to the sovereign power of Jesus but that also symbolized the deep peace and security that belong to those who follow Jesus (cf. the strong contrast with the "great [μέγας] earthquake").

27   It is tempting to suppose that Matthew inserts οἱ ἄνθρωποι as the subject of "they marveled" in order to avoid having the disciples so ignorant as to need to ask the question: "What sort of person is this?" More likely, however, since the men of v 27 must be the disciples of v 23, this is not the issue. Mark's reference to "other boats" (4:36) is omitted by Matthew, and thus there are no other observers available who could be described as "the men." (It is even more unlikely that the men are those who heard the story, as some have argued [e.g., Bornkamm, *Tradition,* 56; so too Luz].) Perhaps ἄνθρωποι here simply reminds us that in Matthew's narrative "the disciples" had apparently not yet been constituted as "the twelve." The verb θαυμάζειν, "to marvel," is very common in the miracle narratives of the Synoptics (for Matthew, cf. 9:33; 15:31; 21:20). Matthew's ποταπός, "what sort of person," rather than the simple "who," adds emphasis to the christological implication of the final question. It strengthens the assumption that it can be no ordinary person to whom even the elements of nature, the wind and the sea, are obedient. Power over the sea, which is often symbolic of evil or the dwelling place of evil, was regarded as especially impressive. "Who is as mighty as you, O LORD?" asks the Psalmist, who then continues, "You rule the raging of the sea; when its waves rise, you still them" (Ps 89:8–9, NRSV; cf. Pss 65:7; 107:29). If we press the symbolism of evil, then Jesus' power over the sea is of the same kind as his healings and exorcisms, and hence truly representative of the dawning of the eschatological kingdom. No conclusions were yet drawn by these disciples, but they knew beyond a shadow of doubt that Jesus was an extraordinary person with incomparable power and authority. And, as Duplacy points out, Matthew's readers knew the answer to this question raised by the disciples (26–27).

Explanation

This passage, involving a deep symbolism that makes it live for the Church, was meant to be read at more than one level. The story is basically about a miraculous quieting of the sea by Jesus in which the disciples learn about the power of Jesus and the meaning of discipleship. In the combination of the sovereign power of the Church's Lord and the challenge of discipleship, however, the passage contains a vitally relevant message for Matthew's church and the Church of every era. For early Christian interpreters (e.g., Tertullian, *On Baptism* 12; cf. Goldammer), the boat symbolizes the Church, and the storm, whatever evil threatens the Church (cf. 16:18). The call to discipleship involves an absolute demand that can often involve risks. But in the living out of discipleship, faith enables the disciple to know that he or she can count upon the provision of the Master (cf. Jas 1:6), whatever storms may be encountered. It is, after all, the sovereign Lord who has called them to that discipleship, who looks after his own, and who has promised to be with them to the end of the age (18:20; 28:20).

Exorcism of the Gadarene Demoniacs   (8:28–34)

Bibliography

Baarda, T. "Gadarenes, Gerasenes, Gergesenes and the 'Diatessaron' Tradition." In *Neotestamentica et Semitica.* FS M. Black, ed. E. E. Ellis. Edinburgh: T. & T. Clark, 1969. 181–97. **Bligh, J.** "The Gerasene Demoniac and the Resurrection of Christ." *CBQ* 31 (1969) 383–90. **Braumann, G.** "Die Zweizahl und Verdoppelungen im Matthäusevangelium." *TZ* 24 (1968) 255–66. **Cave, C. H.** "The Obedience of Unclean Spirits." *NTS* 11 (1964–65) 93–97. **Craghan, J.** "The Gerasene Demoniac." *CBQ* 30 (1968) 522–36. **Derrett, J. D. M.** "Contributions to the Study of the Gerasene Demoniac." *JSNT* 3 (1979) 2–17. ————. "Legend and Event: The Gerasene Demoniac: An Inquest into History and Liturgical Projection." In *Studia Biblica 1978. II. Papers on the Gospels*, ed. E. A. Livingstone. Sheffield: JSOT, 1980. 63–73. **Gibbs, J. M.** "Purpose and Pattern in Matthew's Use of the Title 'Son of God.'" *NTS* 10 (1963–64) 446–64. **Hull, J. M.** *Hellenistic Magic and the Synoptic Tradition.* SBT 2.28. London: SCM, 1974. 116–41. **Kleist, J. A.** "The Gadarene Demoniacs." *CBQ* 9 (1947) 101–5. **Lamarche, P.** "Le possédé de Gérasa (Mt 8,28–34; Mc 5,1–20; Lc 8,26–39)." *NRT* 90 (1968) 581–97. **Loader, W. R. G.** "Son of David, Blindness, Possession, and Duality in Matthew." *CBQ* 44 (1982) 570–85. **Maynard, A. H.** "TI EMOI KAI SOI." *NTS* 31 (1985) 582–86. **Pesch, R.** *Der Besessene von Gerasa.* SBS 56. Stuttgart: Katholisches Bibelwerk, 1972. **Vögtle, A.** "Die historische und theologische Tragweite der heutigen Evangelienforschung." *ZKT* 86 (1964) 385–417.

Translation

[28]*And when he*[a] *had come across to the other side into the country of the Gadarenes,*[b] *two demoniacs who had come out of the tombs encountered him. They were extremely*

violent, so that no one was able to pass by on that particular road. [29] *And look, they cried out and said: "What have we to do with each other,*[c] *Son of God?*[d] *Have you come here to torment*[e] *us before the appointed time?"*[f] [30] *And some distance*[g] *from them there was a herd of many swine, feeding.* [31] *And the demons began to implore him,*[h] *saying, "If you are going to cast us out, send us*[i] *into the herd of swine."* [32] *And he said to them, "Go." And they departed and went into the swine.*[j] *And behold, the entire herd*[k] *rushed down the steep bank into the sea and died in the water.* [33] *But those tending the herd fled, and when they came to the city, they reported everything including the curing*[l] *of the demoniacs.* [34] *And look, the whole city came out to meet Jesus, and when they saw him, they begged that he would leave their territory.*

Notes

[a] א* and (vg^{mss}) have the pl. gen. absolute, hence "they."

[b] The well-known textual problem here, as to whether the name is Γαδαρηνῶν, Γερασηνῶν, or Γεργεσηνῶν (Gadarenes, Gerasenes, or Gergesenes), is caused by the fact that all three readings are found in the MS tradition lying behind each of the three Synoptic occurrences (cf. Mark 5:1; Luke 8:26). For the other Synoptic occurrences, the MS evidence favors Gerasene. Here the evidence favors Gadarenes ([א*] B C [Δ] Θ syr^{s,p,h}). Gadara may well be more correct historically since Gerasa was more than thirty miles southeast of the Sea of Galilee. See *TCGNT*, 23.

[c] τί ἡμῖν καὶ σοί, lit. "What to us and to you?" Cf. *Comment.*

[d] C³ W Θ *f*¹³ TR it vg^c sy^{p,h} sa bo^{pt} add Ἰησοῦ, hence "Jesus, Son of God," probably by influence of the parallel passage in Mark and Luke.

[e] א* (W) vg^{mss} bo^{pt} read ἀπολέσαι, "destroy," perhaps through influence of the narrative that follows.

[f] Possibly a statement rather than a question: "You have come to destroy us before the time."

[g] The Latin version inserts the negative, "not" far away, as seemingly more logical.

[h] Taking the impf. παρεκάλουν as an inceptive.

[i] C L W *f*¹³ TR sy^{p,h} here ἐπίστρεψον ἡμῖν ἀπελθεῖν, "permit us to go," probably by influence of the parallel in Luke 8:32 (cf. Mark 5:13).

[j] Many MSS (C³ L W Θ *f*¹³ TR sy^h) read τὴν ἀγέλην τῶν χοίρων, "the herd of swine," in imitation of v 31.

[k] C³ K L TR bo mae insert τῶν χοίρων, "of swine," thus keeping the phrase uniform.

[l] τὰ τῶν δαιμονιζομένων, lit. "the things concerning the demoniacs."

Form/Structure/Setting

A. This fifth miracle narrative, the middle one in the second group of three, concerns the direct confrontation of demonic forces by Jesus on the other side of the Sea of Galilee. We now arrive in Matthew at the story toward which v 18 already pointed. Matthew follows Mark in placing this narrative after that of the calming of the storm. Again the sovereign power of Jesus is in view. The christological aspects of that power find explicit articulation from the demons (v 29) and are implicit in the concluding verse of the pericope. The mysterious character of the story is conspicuous at several points.

B. The most striking difference between Matthew and the other Synoptics is, of course, that whereas their story involves one demon-possessed man, Matthew has two (see below, §C). Matthew's account of this story is only half as long as Mark's (5:1–20); Luke (8:26–39) follows Mark much more closely and is slightly shorter than Mark. The large chunks of material omitted by Matthew are the following: (1) the detailed description of the man as one often bound with chains, crying out, and bruising himself (Mark 5:3–5), while Matthew simply characterizes the men as "extremely violent, so that no one was able to pass by on that particular road"; (2) the dialogue between Jesus and the man (Mark 5:8–10); (3) the description of the crowd's fear when they see what had been done (Mark 5:15–16); and (4) the final conversation between the cured man and Jesus in which he is told that he may not accompany Jesus but is to bear witness in that region (Mark 5:18–20). Despite these lengthy omissions, Matthew has preserved the central elements of the story in a coherent manner. For the most part, the economy of Matthew here is probably to gain needed space for the great amount of teaching material included in his Gospel. Hull (131) has noted Matthew's suppression of Mark's information concerning the technique of exorcism, thus reflecting Matthew's anti-magic emphasis. In the last omission (i.e., of Mark 5:18–20), it may well be that this material was not in keeping with Matthew's emphasis on following Jesus as a disciple, with his general emphasis on discipleship, or with his restriction upon a mission to the Gentiles at this particular period (see *Comment* on 10:5–6). Although it is possible that Matthew here depends upon an independent tradition (thus Grundmann) rather than on Mark, such a conclusion is by no means necessary. And in the omission of Mark 5:8–10, Matthew probably disliked the implication that the demon did not come out at once. The effect of Matthew's shortening of Mark is to focus attention on Jesus (and hence away from the two demoniacs, whose healing is assumed rather than stated).

Other differences to be noted are the following: Matthew's omission of Mark's note that the demon-possessed man "ran and worshiped him" (this omission is deliberate, perhaps with an eye to the Beelzebul controversy of 12:22–30); Matthew's simple υἱὲ τοῦ θεοῦ, "Son of God," in the address of the demons to Jesus, which omits Mark's Ἰησοῦ, "Jesus" (perhaps for the overfamiliarity and the unnecessary attention to the humanity of Jesus), and the modifier τοῦ ὑψίστου, "the highest" (perhaps as unnecessary, or as distracting from the emphasis on Jesus). Mark's reference to the demons answering by God's name is also understandably omitted. Matthew (and Luke) also omits Mark's ὡς δισχίλιοι, "about two thousand," an affirmation reflected in Matthew's πολλῶν, "many," in v 30.

C. There can be little doubt that Matthew has introduced two demoniacs into Mark's (and Luke's) story of a single demoniac. It is easier to explain why Matthew would have increased the number than why Mark would have reduced it. The same phenomenon may be observed in Matthew's doubling of the single blind man of Mark 10:46–52 (and Luke 18:35–43) in 20:29–34 (cf. also the two blind men of 9:27–31). A possible reason for Matthew's doubling here may be to compensate for his omission of Mark's first exorcism story (Mark 1:23–28) from his narrative (Gundry, Green, McNeile) as well as an earlier story of the healing of the blind man (Mark 8:22–26). Matthew apparently has a liking for these stories of pairs of healed individuals and may well regard such a practice as justifiable, given the large number of exorcisms and healings that Jesus performed. It is unlikely, however, that the doubling is simply due to such a tendency in the telling of folk stories (cf. Bultmann, *History*, 314–17). It may also be the case, given Matthew's Jewish-Christian readers and their debate with the synagogue, that Matthew is thinking of the importance of more than one witness in Jewish tradition (so too Lamarche; Loader). And as Gibbs notes, in each instance of the pairs produced by Matthew, there is an important christological confession (cf. France). Thus Matthew alone among the evangelists quotes the OT text—granted in another context, but at least showing that Matthew had the verse in mind—which says that every matter is to be "confirmed by the evidence of two or three witnesses" (18:16, quoting Deut 19:15, cf. Matt 26:60). In short, Matthew's doubling of those healed is a way of representing something of the true extent of Jesus' healings. This device is analogous to his frequent miracle summaries (which also indicate a concern with this matter) and lessens the need to record further individual stories and thus lengthen the work excessively. (Cf. Matthew's mute *and* blind demoniac in 12:22–24, for Luke's [and Q's] mute demoniac.) The suggestion (e.g., J. Wellhausen, *Das Evangelium Matthaei*, 2nd ed. [Berlin: Georg Reimer, 1914]) that Matthew's reference to two demoniacs in the present passage is caused by Mark's "My name is Legion [λεγιών]; for we are many" (Mark 5:9) is not warranted, since "two" hardly corresponds to "many." It is fair to say, however, that the name Legion was consonant with Matthew's inclination to double the number of demoniacs.

D. The structure of this exorcism narrative is as unusual as the story itself. It may be outlined as follows: (1) description of the situation (v 28); (2) the confrontation of Jesus by the demons (v 29); (3) the special request of the demons (vv 30–31); (4) the exorcism and death of the herd of swine (v 32); and (5) the report to and reaction of the people of the town (vv 33–34). The person of Jesus is at the core of the narrative, as can be seen from the following: he is encountered (v 28); confessed as Son of God (v 29); implored by the demons (v 31); portrayed as the sovereign Lord who commands (v 32); and again encountered and implored, this time by the crowds (v 34). In the last point there is an interesting parallel between the people from the city and the demons: both meet Jesus and implore him (see *Comment*).

Comment

28 If Gadarenes is the best textual reading (see *Note* b above; cf. Zahn and Baarda's evidence from the Diatessaron, which indirectly supports this reading), it should be noted that the city of Gadara (= modern Um Qeis) was approximately five miles southeast of the Sea of Galilee. As Metzger points out (*TCGNT*, 23), Josephus (*Life* 9.42) speaks of the territory of Gadara as reaching Tiberias (the Lake of Tiberias or the Sea of Galilee). Metzger also notes that coins from Gadara often have the image of a ship. Matthew's inserted μακράν, "far from" (v 30), may hint at the problem of the distance of Gadara from the lake. Gerasa (= modern Jerash) is too far away (thirty miles) from the lake. Gergasa, on the other hand, preferred by Origen (see Metzger), refers to a site named Khersa (or Kursi) among the cliffs overlooking the lake—the "traditional" site, but with little to argue in its favor. When Jesus had come across the lake to the other side (cf. v 18), he was met by two demoniacs whose possession was particularly grievous and frightening. (For "two," see *Form/Structure/Setting* §C.) Matthew's δαιμονιζόμενοι, "demon possessed" (cf. Luke's ἔχων δαιμόνια, "having demons"), is stronger in tone than Mark's ἐν πνεύματι ἀκαθάρτῳ, "with an unclean spirit." On demon possession, see *Comment* on 4:24. Matthew's very brief descriptive words χαλεποὶ λίαν, "extremely violent," together with the note that "none could pass that way," effectively describe the seriousness of the situation. ἐκ τῶν μνημείων ἐξερχόμενοι, "coming out of the tombs," suggests not merely the ritually unclean place where the demoniacs lived but the close association of such possession with death and the powers of evil (cf. Isa 65:4; Matt 23:27). The cavelike tombs provided convenient shelter.

29 Matthew's inserted ἰδού, "look," calls attention to the exceptional thing that happens at this point. There is an immediate perception of the true identity of Jesus on the part of the demons: they address him as υἱὲ τοῦ θεοῦ, "Son of God." This title has already appeared earlier in the Gospel (cf. 1:23; 2:15; and 3:17) but interestingly has been explicitly used hitherto only by the devil, the Tempter, in 4:3, 6. The title will become extremely important, not least as a confession of the disciples as the Gospel proceeds (cf., for example, 14:33; 16:16; 17:5; 27:54). The demons here, as elsewhere in the gospel tradition (Mark 1:24; 3:11; cf. Mark 1:34b), sense immediately the identity of Jesus, veiled though it is to human eyes, and know at once that their realm is fundamentally threatened by his presence. This is all suggested even by the question τί ἡμῖν καὶ σοί, lit. "what to us and to you?" meaning something like "what do we have in common?" or "whatever do you want of us?" Rather than a real question, it is a rhetorical question that makes a statement. The question occurs in John 2:4 in a very different context but with a similar meaning. The demons' subsequent question, "Have you come here to torment us before the time?" (πρὸ καιροῦ), is interesting from at least two aspects: first, in it the demons recognize that at the eschatological judgment they will experience God's judgment and the end of their power (cf. *1 Enoch* 15–16; *Jub.* 10:8–9; *T. Levi* 18:12); and second, they recognize that that καιρός, "time," has not yet come; Jesus has in effect come too early and threatens their realm too soon (for the eschatological judgment of demons, cf. *1 Enoch* 55:4; *T. Levi* 18). This, of course, fits in with Matthew's perspective of realized eschatology: the kingdom has come, but in advance of its fullest and final coming (cf. 12:28; 13:30). ὧδε, "here," has no special significance, such as pointing to gentile territory (*pace* Hill).

30–31 At this point the reader will undoubtedly bring to the text questions that the commentator is ill-equipped to answer, questions such as, Why do the demons make this request (v 31)? Why does Jesus heed their request (v 32)? And what was the fate of the demons when the herd of swine drowned (v 32)? In these and other such questions, without a knowledge of the mental and metaphysical worlds of demons, speculation is the only recourse. Matthew's μακράν, "at some distance," is possibly a way of saying "in the neighborhood of the lake" (cf. *Comment* on v 28). That it was an ἀγέλη χοίρων, "herd of swine," is significant, since swine were unclean animals according to the OT (e.g., Lev. 11:7; Deut 14:8); their presence also indicates that the swine-herders and the population of that area were non-Jewish (cf. the prohibition in *m. B. Qam.* 7:7). Whether the demoniacs themselves were Jews or Gentiles remains unclear. The demons, probably not two but a multitude (corresponding to πολλοί, "many," swine) as in the case of Mark's "Legion," began imploring Jesus to send them εἰς, "into," the herd of pigs. εἰ ἐκβάλλεις, a construction assuming the truth of the condition, can also be translated "since you are going to cast us out"; no uncertainty on the part of the demons is meant. This strange request to be sent into swine or any other form of life is unparalleled in the biblical literature. The parable of 12:43–45, if it contains information that can be taken with some literalness, suggests that although unclean spirits (= demons) are to be found in desert places (cf. Isa 13:21–22; 34:14), their preference is to reside in some form of body. In their desire not to return to the desert places, the demons are apparently content at this point to inhabit even the bodies of the unclean swine (cf. Luke 8:31, "not to command them to depart into the abyss").

32 The yielding of Jesus to the demons' request almost certainly has a pedagogical purpose. If the narrative perhaps shows the resourcefulness of the demons, more significantly it makes the point that not even the unclean swine were prepared to contain the demons, and the demons end up destroying the swine. The suggestion that the purpose of sending the demons into the swine was that the men might be convinced that they had been exorcised seems less plausible. The entire herd of swine accordingly plunges to its death, drowning in the sea. The report of this is preceded by Matthew's ἰδού, "behold," pointing to the remarkable event. (There is a superficial similarity in the experience of this "sign" of the exorcism with similar reports in Jos. *Ant.* 8.48, and Philostratus, *Life of Apollonius* 4.20.)

The argument of a number of commentators (e.g., Grundmann, Schweizer, Bonnard, Held [in Bornhamm et al., *Tradition*], Gundry, Patte, Luz) that the subject of ἀπέθανον, "they died," is the demons and that thus it is they who died when the swine rushed into the sea is dubious. The switch from a singular verb with a collective subject ("herd") to a plural verb without a change of subject is not at all unusual. The plural ἀπέθανον is caused rather by Mark's plural ἐπνίγοντο, "they drowned"; thus in Mark the same shift occurs from a singular to a plural verb (with Carson, contra Gundry). The Greek, in fact, is far from clear that a change of subject is envisioned (contra Green, Mounce). Had Matthew wanted to make the important theological point seen by some in this matter, the simple insertion of οἱ δαίμονες, "the demons," before ἀπέθανον would have been natural. (Furthermore, in Gundry's hypothesis what does it mean for demons to "die," if, as he argues, they then go to the torments of hell?) The sovereignty of the one-word command, ὑπάγετε, "go," spoken by Jesus is striking; it is Matthew's major emphasis here. The feat performed by Jesus is in itself unparalleled and astonishing. The end result, however, is much the same as if Jesus had not first sent the demons into the swine; viz., they are dispersed and rendered powerless. They were not accommodated by Jesus. They gained nothing by their delaying tactics but were cast out—and not into some temporary lodging from which they might be able to do further harm. Beyond this Matthew gives us no information.

33–34 The herders fled, probably in fear of the events they had seen. They went into the city, which was several miles from the sea, and reported what had occurred. καὶ τὰ τῶν δαιμονιζομένων, "and the things concerning the demon possessed," represents the Markan report concerning the well-being and soundness of mind of the cured demoniacs. Matthew's interest lies not in the cured demoniacs but in the one who accomplished the feat. The response, indicated by Matthew's ἰδού, "look" (the third of this pericope), was that πᾶσα ἡ πόλις, "the whole city," came out to meet (ὑπαντᾶν, as in v 28) Jesus. What happens at this point, however, is unexpected. On the basis of what had been reported to them, these non-Jews, lacking the theological framework of the OT, can only regard Jesus as a strange and dangerous magician without whom their region would be better off (contrast this with the response to Jesus in Luke 4:42, where the people "would have kept him from leaving them"). They implore (παρακαλεῖν, the same verb used by the demons in v 31) Jesus to depart. But even with this note of fear (cf. Luke 8:37, who makes this point explicit), Matthew's argument concerning the unique power and authority of Jesus is brought home to the reader.

Explanation

The sort of demon possession referred to in this passage gives our human, and thus limited, sight a vivid representation of the mysterious and cruel reality of evil. The demons and the one they serve are the very antithesis of Jesus and the One he serves. The essence of evil is confronted by Jesus, the essence of good. The demons with their supernatural knowledge know immediately who now stands before them, and they cry out almost unwillingly "Son of God" (cf. Jas 2:19). This christological conclusion is at the very heart of the passage. Though from the mouths of demons, its truth remains. The sending of the demons into the swine by the powerful word of Jesus confirms their acknowledgment of his unique identity. The story reveals the sovereignty of Jesus in the miraculous healing of the two men; it does not address the effect of the evil upon the swine or the destruction of the latter and its possible moral implications. Nor does it address the issue of the inhabitants of that region who strangely ask Jesus to leave. This final element too witnesses to the power, authority, and person of Jesus: the Christ has come revealing the advent of the kingdom.

In the modern, scientific world of the West, few take the existence of demons (or the devil) seriously. This hardly means, however, that we have a shortage of evil. We have merely demythologized it and given it new names. This is far from an unhappy development. But the mystery of evil and the web of malevolent causation behind it remain. We are unduly confident, therefore, if we assert that demons cannot exist and demon possession cannot occur. If we today have more rational explanations for much that in earlier eras would have been attributed to demon possession, that does not mean that we can rule out the phenomenon altogether. The Gospel presents Jesus as the answer to every manifestation of evil— that which can be explained "naturalistically" and that which may find its causation in a realm inaccessible to our scientific instruments.

The Healing of a Paralytic   (9:1–8)

Bibliography

Duplacy, J. "Marc II, 10: Note de syntaxe." In *Mélanges bibliques rédigés en l'honneur de André Robert.* Paris: Bloud et Gay, 1956. 420–27. **Dupont, J.** "Le paralytique pardonné (Mt 9,1–8)." *NRT* 82 (1960) 940–58. **Greeven, H.** "Die Heilung des Gelähmten nach Matthäus." *WD* 4 (1955) 65–78. **Klauck, H.-J.** "Die Frage der Sündenvergebung in der Perikope von der Heilung des Gelähmten (Mk 2.1–12 parr)." *BZ* 25 (1981) 223–48. **Leroy, H.** *Zur Vergebung der Sünden.* SBS 73. Stuttgart: Katholisches Bibelwerk, 1974. **Reicke, B.** "The Synoptic Reports on the Healing of the Paralytic: Matthew 9,1–8 with parallels." In *Studies in New Testament Language and Text.* FS G. D. Kilpatrick, ed. J. K. Elliott. Leiden: Brill, 1976. 319–29. **Schenk, W.** "'Den Menschen' Mt 9.8." *ZNW* 54 (1963) 272–75. **Vargas-Machuca, A.** "El paralitico perdonado en la redación de Mateo (Mt 9,1–8)." *EstBib* 44 (1969) 15–43.

Translation

¹*And he*ᵃ *got into a boat*ᵇ *and crossed over to the other side of the sea*ᶜ *and came to his own city.* ²*And look, they brought to him a paralytic lying upon a bed. And when Jesus saw their faith, he said to the paralytic: "Have courage,*ᵈ *my child,*ᵉ *your sins are forgiven."*ᶠ ³*And look, some of the scribes said to themselves: "This man is blaspheming."* ⁴ *And when Jesus discerned*ᵍ *their thoughts, he said,*ʰ *"Why do you think evil things in your hearts?* ⁵*For what is easier? To say, 'Your sins are forgiven,'*ᵃ *or to say, 'Rise and walk'?* ⁶*But so that you may know that the Son of Man has authority on earth to forgive sins . . ."*ⁱ *then he said to the paralytic: "Rise, take your bed and go to your house."* ⁷*And he rose and went to his house.* ⁸*But when the crowds saw this they were awe-struck,*ʲ *and they glorified God who had given such authority to human beings.*

Notes

ᵃ C*³ F Θᶜ *f*¹³ vgˢ add ὁ Ἰησοῦς, "Jesus."
ᵇ C* W TR have the definite article τὸ πλοῖον, "the boat"; without the article are ℵ B C³ L Θ *f*¹·¹³ 33.
ᶜ The phrase "to the other side of the sea" is added in the translation for clarity.
ᵈ θάρσει can also be translated "don't be afraid," or even "be cheerful" (see BAGD, 352a).
ᵉ τέκνον may also be translated "my son." For the "my" (not actually in the Gr. text), see BAGD, 808.
ᶠ C L W Θ *f*¹·¹³ TR it have the subjunctive ἀφέωνται, "let your sins be forgiven" (cf. KJV: "thy sins be forgiven thee"); ℵ B (D) lat have the indicative. D (C³) L Θ *f*¹³ TR lat vgᵐˢ sy have σοί, "to you," before "your sins."
ᵍ καὶ ἰδών, lit. "and seeing"; but a few MSS (B [Θ] *f*¹ syrᵖ·ʰ sa mae) have εἰδώς, "knowing," perhaps through the influence of ἐπιγνούς in the parallel passages (Mark 2:8 and Luke 5:22). See TCGNT, 24.
ʰ Many MSS again have the subjunctive, "Your sins be forgiven." See Note f.
ⁱ The sentence is incomplete in the Gr. text, and the editors have added a dash to indicate the break.
ʲ Lit. "were afraid." C L Θ *f*¹³ TR syʰ substitute ἐθαύμασαν, "they marveled," as seemingly more appropriate and perhaps by influence of other passages where the word occurs.

Form/Structure/Setting

A. The sixth miracle story, and the last of the second group in this major section of Matthew devoted to the powerful deeds of the Messiah, concerns the dramatic healing of a paralytic. We have seen how in previous instances Matthew has dealt with themes of faith and discipleship in connection with the wonder narratives of chap. 8. Now for the first time the theme of forgiveness of sins is introduced into a healing narrative. So important is this theme that it dominates the pericope: the actual healing of the paralytic is nearly eclipsed by it, being performed mainly to demonstrate the reality of the forgiveness of sins. Nevertheless, Held's (in Bornkamm et al., *Tradition*) contention that Matthew has transformed the original healing narrative into a controversy story is an exaggeration (cf. Heil's just criticism, *CBQ* 41 [1979] 277–78). Again the focus remains on Jesus, who now not only heals but also forgives sins. Observing that the pericope is placed at the center of chaps. 8–9, which are focused on the deeds of Jesus, Grundmann notes the emphasis upon Jesus' authority to forgive sins.

B. In the usual fashion, Matthew abbreviates his Markan source (Mark 2:1–12; followed closely by Luke 5:17–26) quite freely. The larger omissions are at the beginning: (1) the setting, with its reference to speaking the word (Mark 2:1–2), and (2) the part of the story about letting the paralytic down through the roof (Mark 2:4). The only other significant omission, probably for theological reasons, is Mark's τίς δύναται ἀφιέναι ἁμαρτίας εἰ μὴ εἷς ὁ θεός, "Who is able to forgive sins, except one, God?" (Mark 2:7b). Matthew omits this question, not so much because it could be taken to conflict with his view of Jesus (but could he not, with Mark and Luke, have seen the question as a *confirming* element in his Christology?) but because as his concluding sentence shows (9:8), he regards the question as wrongly based. For Matthew, human beings can forgive sins (cf. 16:19; 18:18). The remaining omissions in Matthew are insignificant shortenings of Mark and need not be listed here. Matthew does make a few *additions:* the favorite ἰδού, "look," twice (vv 2, 3); the word θάρσει, "have courage," as the first word to the paralytic (v 2); the word πονηρά, "evil things," in regard to the thoughts of the scribes (v 4); and finally, and most importantly, the substitution of the concluding words of the pericope: τὸν δόντα ἐξουσίαν τοιαύτην τοῖς ἀνθρώποις, "the one who had given such authority to human beings" (v 8), for Mark's "saying that never have we seen such a thing" (Mark 2:12). There are few agreements in this pericope between Matthew and Luke against Mark. The command to take up one's bed and walk is paralleled in the Johannine narrative of the lame man at the pool of Bethzatha (John 5:2–9), but that is the extent of similarity between the Synoptic and Johannine narratives.

C. The issue of the forgiveness of sins complicates the structure of the narrative, which after the transitional v 1 may be divided as follows: (1) the bearing in of the paralytic (v 2a); (2) the announcement of Jesus about the forgiveness of the paralytic's sins (v 2b); (3) the exchange between the scribes and Jesus (vv 3–5); (4) the healing of the paralytic (vv 6–7), with the direct command of v 6b and the corresponding response in v 7; and (5) the response of the crowds (v 8). From the amount of space given to the issue concerning the forgiveness of sins and the demurral of the scribes, it is apparent how the healing narrative has become the vehicle for a more important theme. This is of course the situation with Mark (and Luke) too, but Matthew's abbreviations have the effect of making the point even sharper. Matthew's form thus has the primary characteristic not of a healing narrative so much as a controversy story plus apophthegm (cf. v 6). But this hardly necessitates the conclusion that the passage is the result of the conflation of what were originally two independent stories (so, e.g., Bultmann, *History*).

Comment

1 This transitional verse refers to the return journey of the trip begun in 8:23, where Jesus also gets into a boat (cf. 8:18). τὴν ἰδίαν πόλιν, "his own city," is Capernaum (cf. 4:13; 8:5), and this corresponds with the explicit reference to Capernaum at the beginning of the Markan passage (Mark 2:1; cf. 5:18) that is Matthew's source.

2 Matthew's ἰδού, "look," points to a new, remarkable happening: a paralytic is brought to Jesus, and Jesus without delay announces that the man's sins are forgiven. The omission of Mark's reference to the four men letting down the paralytic through the roof because of the crowd (Mark 2:3–4) focuses the readers' attention on the forgiveness of sins but leaves the phrase τὴν πίστιν αὐτῶν, "their faith" (taken from Mark), with little foundation, other than the mention that "they" brought the man to Jesus. Matthew here almost presupposes a knowledge of Mark (so too Davies-Allison, 2:88). The αὐτῶν here includes the faith of the paralytic as well as those who carried him: they had complete confidence in Jesus' ability to heal (cf. Acts 14:9). παραλυτικός means simply "lame," or "unable to walk" (the word occurs elsewhere in Matt 4:24 and 8:6). The man lay in his bed (κλίνη, in this case a kind of mat or pallet, as Mark's κράβαττος indicates; cf. Luke's use of κλινίδιον in 5:24), which the man himself would later carry away. The faith of the paralytic and those who carried him is rewarded not at first by the healing of the man but by the quite unexpected announcement that his sins are forgiven. It is important to note that this actually refers to the forgiving of sins then and there (present tense, "your sins *are* forgiven"; note v 6) and not merely a declaration that God had forgiven the man's sins and that this was now being announced (something that was performed regularly by priests). Until the fundamental connection between sin and sickness (and thus sin and healing) is appreciated, the reason for this statement does not seem apparent.

Although we have encountered no reference to the matter of sin and its forgiveness in the preceding healing narratives, its mention here necessitates a brief comment about the relation between sin and sickness. Although it is nearly a universal belief that suffering and sickness are the result somehow of having offended the gods or God, this is not the biblical view. To be sure, that perspective is sometimes encountered among the people of the Bible (e.g., John 9:2; notoriously in Job's "comforters"), but it is never upheld as a correct or appropriate view (note John 9:3; the story of Job and the *if* in Jas 5:15). The fundamental premise is, of course, fixed: in the biblical view (Gen 3), all sickness and suffering, like death itself, trace back to the entry of sin into the world. In this sense all sickness is caused by sin. But apart from the immediate cause–effect connection between some sin and some sickness (e.g., abuse of the body), there is no direct or immediate correlation between an individual's sin and his or her sickness or suffering. This is only to say that most sinning does not receive its due punishment in the present time. In this age there is nothing unusual about the righteous suffering and the wicked prospering. The present pericope suggests neither that the man's sickness was caused by his sin nor that his sin had to be forgiven before he could be healed. The point of this narrative is that the problem of sin, though not as apparent to the eye as paralysis, is a fundamental—indeed, as becomes obvious as the Gospel proceeds, *the* fundamental—problem of humanity that Jesus has come to counteract. Compared to the healings, the forgiveness of sins is by far the greater gift Jesus has brought in his ministry.

If the healings done by Jesus presuppose the invasion of the kingdom of God into the realm of suffering caused by evil (as can most graphically be seen in the demon exorcism of the preceding passage), then the healing of diseases is only a part of a much larger picture, wherein sin itself, and not just its symptoms, is dealt a final blow. The primary mission of Jesus is the overcoming of sin through the cross (cf. 1:21; 20:28; 26:28); the healings are only a secondary indication of that fact. This connection, indeed, has already been seen in the citation of Isa 53:4 in 8:17. In Isa 53 the sin-bearer is also the disease-curer; and the same connection is made quite explicit in Ps 103:3, "who forgives all your iniquity, who heals all your diseases" (cf. Pss 25:18; 32:1–2; 41:5; 79:9). The effect then of Matthew's θάρσει, τέκνον, "have courage, child" (cf. v 22; 14:27), is to say that the optimism reflected in your faith is well warranted because in fact your sins have been forgiven. The man's sins can be forgiven because sin itself is going to be dealt a final blow. Where sin is fundamentally overcome, the way is made clear for any and every healing. τέκνον here means "my child" or "my son," an intimate term that can be used in certain circumstances to address grown persons.

3–5 Matthew's ἰδού, "look," points now to the next development in the story. Having heard this statement forgiving the paralytic of his sins, some of the scribes said οὗτος βλασφημεῖ, "this man is blaspheming." The basic meaning of blasphemy in Judaism is to revile the very name of God (Str-B 1:1019–20). By extension this comes to refer to any pretense to be or do what only God can be or do, as in the present passage (cf. 26:65; John 10:33). The rabbis believed that only God could forgive sins (Str-B on 9:2). The rhetorical question that follows in Mark (2:7b) defines the sense in which blasphemy is understood here: "Who is able to forgive sins but God alone?" Although Matthew omits this statement, his simple statement "this man is blaspheming" contains the same unavoidable implication. The scribes, as professional Torah scholars, would have been especially sensitive to the assumption of God's prerogative. Although the scribes said this ἐν ἑαυτοῖς, "to themselves," perhaps not yet feeling prepared to launch a public attack against Jesus, he supernaturally discerns their thinking ("seeing their thoughts"; cf. 12:25; 22:18) and in his rhetorical questions (v 4) faults them for thinking "evil things" (πονηρά) in their hearts. Matthew's insertion of πονηρά here implies a malice toward Jesus not hinted at in Mark or Luke. The scribes would surely have argued it was a good thing to desire to protect the name and honor of God. Yet from Matthew's perspective, to oppose Jesus is to oppose God, and the resistance to Jesus that begins here will lead only to his death. Since any charlatan can claim to forgive the sins of another, Jesus decides to demonstrate the unseen by means of the seen. It is, of course, easier to say "your sins are forgiven," something that cannot be seen, than to say "rise and walk," which would entail a miraculous healing plain for all either to see or not to see.

6–7 The opening words of v 6 constitute a subordinate clause that lacks a main clause. This ellipsis (technically "brachylogy"; BDF §483), marked with a dash in the Greek text, interestingly occurs in all three Synoptics, uncorrected by either Matthew or Luke, and thus is a fixed feature of the common Gospel tradition. What is assumed is a clause saying, "I do this." In its place (natural in the process of thinking, but awkward syntactically) is the actual performance of the healing: "then he said to the paralytic, 'Rise, take your bed and go to your house.'" The purpose of the miracle is unambiguously stated in the purpose clause: ἵνα δὲ εἰδῆτε, "but so that you may know," ὅτι ἐξουσίαν ἔχει ὁ υἱὸς τοῦ ἀνθρώπου ἐπὶ τῆς γῆς ἀφιέναι ἁμαρτίας, "that the Son of Man has authority on earth to forgive sins." ἐξουσία, "authority," as the first word of the ὅτι clause, receives special emphasis. Possibly the initial ἵνα is imperatival (Duplacy): "Know that the Son of Man has authority on earth to forgive sins." The authority of Jesus has been a special concern of the Gospel since the end of the Sermon on the Mount (see on 7:29), where it was seen in word, and in the healing narratives, where it is seen in deed (cf. 8:9). It remains an important theme right to the end of the Gospel (cf. 10:1; 21:23–27; 28:18). ἐπὶ τῆς γῆς, "on the earth," means now, in advance of the coming of the eschaton. For ὁ υἱὸς τοῦ ἀνθρώπου, "the Son of Man," the title that occurs in all three Synoptics at this point, see *Comment* on 8:20. Although Jesus refers to himself in using the title (Davies-Allison do not think Jesus spoke v 6a), it does remain a title and cannot adequately be translated with the simple "I." In the response of the crowds (v 8), the title is obviously not understood, but the readers of Matthew's Gospel would not have missed its significance. If the Son of Man is the person of Dan 7:13–14 and he begins through his presence to bring the blessings of the eschaton (one of which was the forgiveness of iniquity [cf. Isa 33:24; Jer 31:34; at Qumran, CD 14:19; 11Q Melch 4–9]), then it is no surprise that he has the authority to forgive sins on the earth as an intrinsic part of his ministry. In order to demonstrate the reality of the forgiveness of sins, Jesus directly and authoritatively commands the man to rise, take his bed, and go home. The response of the paralytic is reported with equal directness (v 7) and corresponds (except for the incidental omission of taking up his bed) exactly to the command, perhaps as a model of the obedience of discipleship.

8 οἱ ὄχλοι, "the crowds" (to this point only the presence of scribes had been mentioned, v 3), responded with predictable awe (ἐφοβήθησαν) and astonishment. It is rather remarkable at this point, however, that Matthew concludes the pericope with words that detract somewhat from the christological emphasis of the passage. One expects a conclusion like that of Luke 7:49, "Who is this, who even forgives sins?" But Matthew's ending is particularly unusual, especially considering the pattern we have seen in other of the evangelist's healing narratives. The report that the crowds ἐδόξασαν τὸν θεόν, "glorified God," is drawn from Mark, but to that Matthew uniquely appends the words τὸν δόντα ἐξουσίαν τοιαύτην τοῖς ἀνθρώποις, "the One who had given such authority to human beings." This response is, of course, partially correct: Jesus has forgiven sin and performed a miracle; he is a human being, and therefore surely God has given this authority to human beings. The question is, Why did Matthew not write "who had given such authority to *the Son of Man*"? Is this his deliberate attempt to show the failure of the crowd to understand the title and thus to indicate their inadequate understanding of Jesus despite the logic of the narrative? In light of the surprise of the conclusion of the passage, this analysis seems reasonable, but there is perhaps another point to be made concerning Matthew's decision to end the passage with these words. If τοῖς ἀνθρώποις, "to human beings," is inadequate for Matthew's Christology, it may reflect an ecclesiastical concern of his (cf. Leroy) about the ability of Christ's representatives to forgive sins in the sense of declaring God's forgiveness or non-forgiveness, as reflected especially in 18:18 (cf. 16:19; Dupont, Greeven; and contra Schenk, who attempts to explain the dative "to human beings" as a dative of advantage). Despite the unusual ending, however, the passage has an unmistakable christological dimension. The ἐξουσία, "authority," probably includes that of forgiving sins (cf. v 6), but given the pattern pursued by Matthew in these chapters, it may also indicate the healing of the paralytic. Indeed here the two go together and cannot be separated. It is clear that Matthew's readers were able to penetrate to the christological (and ecclesiastical) significance of the events much more readily than those who first experienced them. It is unlikely (contra Gundry) that Matthew or his readers understand Jesus as the God glorified by the crowd. The unmistakable divine character of Jesus in the Gospel does not yet entail the direct equation of Jesus and God (as in John, for example).

Explanation

Here again the authority of Jesus stands at the center of the passage. The one who can heal has also the power to attack the very root of all sickness and suffering, namely, sin. There can indeed be no ultimate healing, well-being, or *shalom* unless the evil power opposed to these things is defeated. The healings performed by Jesus are signs of the imminent defeat of sin and the power of evil. This is the true work of Jesus, and any attempt to put the healings at the center of his purpose is to misunderstand the centrality of the cross in Jesus' ministry. When this passage is seen within the context of the whole book, it is clear that for Matthew there can be no forgiveness of sins without the cross, just as there can be no healing without the cross. This theological connection cannot be broken. But the healing of sickness and suffering, like death, the fruit of sin, depends on the prior and greater work of Jesus. So in this narrative with the forgiveness of sins we are, as at many key junctures in the Gospel, brought to the central necessity of the cross. It is from the cross that the Son of Man ultimately derives his authority in word and deed, and with it the possibility of the proclamation of the dawning of the kingdom of God.

The Call of Matthew and a Dinner Party with Tax Collectors and Sinners   (9:9–13)

Bibliography

Hill, D. "The Use and Meaning of Hosea 6,6 in Matthew's Gospel." *NTS* 24 (1977–78) 107–19. **Iersel, B. M. F. van.** "La vocation de Lévi (Mc 2.13–17; Mt 9.9–13; Lc 5.27–32): Traditions et rédactions." In *De Jésus aux Évangiles,* ed. I. de la Potterie. BETL 25. Gembloux: Duculot, 1967. 212–32. **Kiley, M.** "Why 'Matthew' in Matt 9,9–13?" *Bib* 65 (1984) 347–51. **Lee, G. M.** "'They that are whole need not a physician.'" *ExpTim* 76 (1965) 254. **Pesch, R.** "Levi-Matthäus (Mc 2,14/Mt 9,9; 10:3): Ein Beitrag zur Lösung eines alten Problems." *ZNW* 59 (1968) 40–56. **Sheehan, G. D.** "Publicani." *BT* 19 (1968) 99–100. **Theobald, M.** "Der Primat der Synchronie vor der Diachronie als Grundaxiom der Literarkritik: Methodische Erwägungen an Hand von Mk 2.13–17/Mt 9.9–13." *BZ* 22 (1978) 161–86. **Wibbing, S.** "Das Zöllnergastmahl (Mk 2.13–17; vgl. Mt 9.9–13; Lk 5.27–32)." In *Streitgespräche,* ed. H. Stock, K. Wegenast, and S. Wibbing. Gütersloh: Mohn, 1968. 84–107.

Translation

⁹*And as Jesus was leaving there, he saw a man sitting at the tax collection,*ᵃ *named Matthew, and said to him: "Follow me." And he rose and followed him.*
¹⁰*And it happened that when Jesus was reclining at table in Matthew's*ᵇ *house, look,*ᶜ *many tax collectors and sinners came and reclined at the table with Jesus and his disciples.* ¹¹*And when the Pharisees saw this, they (later) were saying*ᵈ *to his disciples: "Why does your teacher eat*ᵉ *with tax collectors and sinners?"* ¹²*But when he*ᶠ *heard this, he*

said to them:[g] *"The healthy*[h] *have no need of a physician, but rather those who are sick.*
¹³*But go and learn what this means: 'I desire mercy and not sacrifice.' For I did not
come to call the righteous but sinners."*[i]

Notes

ᵃ Or, "in the tax collector's office."

ᵇ Lit. "in the house," but implying Matthew's house (see *Comment* on vv 10–11).

ᶜ The Gr. text includes an apparently extra καί, "and," before ἰδού, "look," perhaps because this is
such a common pairing. Hence a few MSS omit it (e.g., א D 892 lat co).

ᵈ ἔλεγον, impf. tense, suggesting repetition, or perhaps inceptive impf., hence "began to say." But
D Θ f¹³ TR have the aorist εἶπον here.

ᵉ M 565 add καὶ πίνει, "and drink"; syˢ has ἐσθίετε καὶ πίνετε, "do you eat and drink," probably by
the influence of the parallel in Luke 5:30.

ᶠ Many MSS (C L W Θ f¹·¹³ TR lat syᵖ·ʰ bo) insert Ἰησοῦς, "Jesus," here, probably from the influence of the parallel passage in Mark and Luke.

ᵍ "To them" is supplied here to complete the sense of the passage. This word, i.e., αὐτοῖς, appears
in some MSS (e.g., C³ L W Θ f¹·¹³ TR vgᵐˢˢ syᵖ·ʰ mae boᵖᵗ), again however probably by the influence of
the Markan parallel.

ʰ οἱ ἰσχύοντες, lit. "the strong."

ⁱ Many MSS (C L Θ f¹³ TR syˢ·ʰᵐᵍ sa mae boᵖᵗ) include the words εἰς μετάνοιαν, "to repentance,"
which are borrowed from the Lukan parallel (Luke 5:32).

Form/Structure/Setting

A. Here and in the next pericope Matthew follows the order of Mark, although
he omits Mark's summary verse about Jesus teaching the crowd (Mark 2:13). The
subject of the forgiveness of sins in the previous narrative now raises the further
issue of Jesus' free association with sinners. Again the important theme of discipleship and the central purpose of Jesus, namely, the forgiveness of sins, are
highlighted. Here the two come naturally together in the scandal of the invitation of a tax collector to discipleship.

B. Matthew follows Mark, but with some freedom. Matthew supplies Ἰησοῦς,
"Jesus," as the subject of the verb εἶδεν, "saw" (v 9), and substitutes Μαθθαῖον
λεγόμενον, "named Matthew," for Mark's Λευὶν τὸν τοῦ Ἀλφαίου, "Levi the son of
Alpheus" (Luke has the simple "Levi"). The latter change, together with the reference to "Matthew the tax collector" in 10:3 ("the tax collector" being unique to
Matthew at this point), is sometimes taken to be tied in with the attribution of
the Gospel to Matthew (see *Introduction*). Matthew omits αὐτοῦ, "his," after οἰκία,
"house" (v 10), but this causes no different meaning since the τῇ before "house"
can carry this nuance. Matthew inserts ἰδού, "look," before the notice that many
tax collectors and sinners joined the banquet (v 10). Matthew's lengthiest omission is of Mark's slightly awkward and difficult ἦσαν γὰρ πολλοὶ καὶ ἠκολούθουν
αὐτῷ, "for they were many and they were following him" (v 10; Mark 2:15c). Matthew has by this time, unlike Mark, already referred more than once to the disciples
and those who followed Jesus (e.g., 5:1; 8:1, 23). He omits γραμματεῖς, "scribes"
(v 11), for no other discernible reason than to abbreviate. And the same is true
of his omission of Mark's ἰδόντες ὅτι ἐσθίει μετὰ τῶν ἁμαρτωλῶν καὶ τελωνῶν,
"seeing that he was eating with the sinners and tax collectors" (v 11), since that
exact point is contained in the question that follows. Matthew's insertion of ὁ
διδάσκαλος ὑμῶν, "your teacher" (v 11), is intentionally descriptive of the Pharisees'

perception of Jesus and the inadequacy of that perception. Finally, Matthew's insertion of πορευθέντες δὲ μάθετε τί ἐστιν ἔλεος θέλω καὶ οὐ θυσίαν, "but go and learn what this means: 'I desire mercy and not sacrifice'" (v 12), has no parallel in either Mark or Luke. Matthew almost certainly has added this to make a special point for his readers (see *Comment*).

C. This passage consists of two major parts: (1) the calling of Matthew (v 9) and (2) the controversial banquet with tax collectors and sinners (vv 10–13). The former, which serves as a kind of introduction to the latter, consists of (a) Jesus encountering Matthew and (b) the call to discipleship and the immediate response (ἀκολούθει μοι, "follow me"—ἠκολούθησεν αὐτῷ, "he followed him"). There is also the contrast of Matthew's καθήμενον, "sitting," at the tax collection and ἀναστάς, "having stood up," to follow Jesus. The second major part, basically a controversy dialogue, can be outlined as follows: (a) the description of the banquet and those attending (v 10); (b) the question of the Pharisees (v 11); and (c) the penetrating response of Jesus (vv 12–13) containing the "pronouncement" or the heart of the teaching of the passage, which can further be broken down into three parts: (i) a proverbial saying (v 12); (ii) a Scripture passage (Hos 6:6; v 13a); and (iii) a summary of the purpose of Jesus (v 13b). Each of these final three subsections contains pairs of opposites (ἰσχύοντες–κακῶς ἔχοντες, "the healthy—the sick"; ἔλεος–θυσίαν, "mercy–sacrifice"; δικαίους–ἁμαρτωλούς, "righteous–sinners").

D. The last saying of the pericope, "I did not come to call the righteous but sinners," is quoted verbatim in writings of the early Church. Thus *2 Clem.* 2:4 quotes it, introducing it as γραφή, "scripture," in dependence upon either Matthew or Mark; *Barn.* 5:9 quotes it either from oral tradition or from Matthew or Mark; and Justin Martyr (*Apol.* 1.15.8) quotes the Lukan version with the final additional words εἰς μετάνοιαν, "to repentance."

Comment

9 The opening words παράγων ὁ Ἰησοῦς ἐκεῖθεν, "as Jesus was leaving there," are general and transitional (cf. v 27; and contrast v 35). Walking from Capernaum, Jesus came upon the tax collecting station (τὸ τελώνιον) where Matthew worked. Sheehan suggests that this was in fact an open-air tax market where tax farmers such as Matthew would have been selling tax collecting privileges, tax lots, to others. The name Matthew is of course important for this Gospel (cf. 10:3 where Matthew is also called a tax collector). We are clearly meant by our passage to know that the tax collector named Levi in the remainder of the Gospel tradition is to be understood to be Matthew (the name that regularly occurs in the listings of the twelve).

A number of suggestions have been made concerning the change of the name Levi to Matthew. Pesch argues that for the evangelist this call of a disciple (μαθητής) must be the call of one of the twelve, and thus the evangelist picks a name from the list available to him (e.g., in Mark 3:14–19). Yet it is not at all clear that the evangelist restricts μαθηταί to the twelve (cf. the ambiguity of 5:1; 8:21; 9:10) and that he thus had to make the shift for that reason. Kiley's suggestion that the name Matthew was picked because it served as a symbol for learning-discipleship remains, without indication from the evangelist, ingenious speculation. The similarity between Μαθθαῖος and μαθητής is probably only coincidental. The most natural explanation is that Levi and Matthew were in fact the same person (with Gundry; *pace* Luz). It is very improbable that the evangelist could have gotten away with the substitution of Matthew for Levi were they not in reality the same person. It is, of course, not unusual for individuals in the NT to have more than one name. Matthew (abbreviated form of "gift of Yahweh") may have been the Christian name taken by Levi after his conversion to indicate his new life (cf. Saul-Paul).

Tax collectors, or tax farmers, in that culture were despised as greedy, self-serving, and parasitic. They grew rich at the expense of the poor by extorting from them more than was required by their superiors in order to fill their own pockets. They furthermore often compromised regulations for purity in their handling of pagan money and their dealings with Gentiles. That Jesus should call a tax collector to be his disciple must have been in itself scandalous. We hear no objection to that here, but when in the following narrative Jesus fraternizes with tax collectors and sinners (the "lower" end of society), we do encounter a protest. The call and response of Matthew are recorded in especially brief and matter-of-fact fashion: the direct ἀκολούθει μοι, "follow me," and the simple words ἀναστάς ("having stood up," which at least suggests the break from "sitting" at the tax collection; cf. Luke 5:28; καταλιπὼν πάντα, "leaving everything") and ἠκολούθησεν αὐτῷ, "he followed him." This is paradigmatic discipleship for Matthew: the command followed by immediate obedience (cf. 8:22).

10–11 Luke (5:29) makes clearest what we are left to infer in Matthew, viz., that Levi-Matthew threw a δοχὴν μεγάλην, "great banquet," in honor of Jesus, who had first invited the unworthy tax collector to be with him. ἐν τῇ οἰκίᾳ, lit. "in the house," although unspecified by Matthew, refers probably to Matthew's own house (only Luke 5:29 makes this absolutely clear) in keeping with the tax collector's financial well-being (*pace* Davies-Allison, who argue for either Jesus' house or, more probably, Peter's). The genitive absolute αὐτοῦ ἀνακειμένου, "when he was reclining at table," refers to Jesus and suggests that he was the guest of honor. The "reclining at table" in itself points to a special meal rather than an ordinary one (see Jeremias, *Eucharistic Words*, 48–49). With the characteristic ἰδού, "look," Matthew calls his reader's attention to the strange combination of guests around this banquet table: together with "Jesus and his disciples" (τοῖς μαθηταῖς αὐτοῦ) were πολλοὶ τελῶναι καὶ ἁμαρτωλοί, "many tax collectors and sinners." The tax collectors were probably Matthew's own (and now former) colleagues who were now given the chance to meet this Jesus, Matthew's new master. The "sinners," presumably friends of the same crowd, were contaminated by association but probably also disreputable figures in their own right who had abandoned the law (so Davies-Allison). Clearly righteousness was the last concern of this crowd, and yet here they were sitting at the same table with Jesus and his disciples. It must be noted here that table fellowship in that culture was regarded as a very important symbol of the closeness, indeed the oneness, of those participating. This is one reason, for example, that Jews were not allowed to sit at the same table with Gentiles. For Jesus and his disciples to be at the same table with tax collectors and sinners implied a full acceptance of them. (With this background, the symbolism of the messianic banquet in 8:11 becomes all the more remarkable.) Thus the question of the Pharisees, who were guardians of such separation in the cause of righteousness, comes as no surprise. For Jesus' association with tax collectors and sinners challenges a basic principle of the Pharisees and from their perspective calls into question his real commitment to doing God's will. "Why does your teacher [ὁ διδάσκαλος ὑμῶν] eat with tax collectors and sinners?" they ask the disciples. The word order of the question puts "tax collectors and sinners" first for emphasis. διδάσκαλος is used here again in the mouth of Jesus' opponents (cf. on 8:19). Parallel to the present story in many respects is that concerning another tax collector, in this instance a "chief tax collector," Zacchaeus in Luke 19 (see the specific charge in Luke 19:7; cf. 15:2).

12 Although the question was addressed to the disciples, it inquired about the reason not for *their* conduct but for their teacher's conduct. In rabbinic tradition the closeness between a rabbi and his disciples is such that a rabbi is responsible for the conduct of his disciples and vice versa. In this instance, Jesus himself takes the initiative to answer the question. οὐ χρείαν ἔχουσιν οἱ ἰσχύοντες ἰατροῦ ἀλλ᾽ οἱ κακῶς ἔχοντες, "the healthy have no need of a physician, but rather those who are sick," may well be or allude to a proverbial saying. The parable from Diogenes (fourth century B.C.) points to such a conclusion: "neither does a physician . . . who is capable of giving health practice among those who are well" (Stobaeus, *Eclogues* 3.462.14). The sense in which Jesus means the words to be understood is conveyed in the parallel final sentence of the pericope (which in Mark [and Luke] follows this proverb directly): "I did not come to call the righteous, but sinners" (v 13b). In this context the symbolism of the proverb is transparent: the healthy are the righteous; the ill are the sinners. (For the connection between sin and illness that may have suggested the proverb, see the commentary on the preceding pericope.) The ill need to be made healthy; the sinners need to be made righteous. But in between these companion sentences, Matthew inserts a third sentence containing an OT quotation.

13 If the Pharisees refer to Jesus as "teacher," Jesus will give them something to learn. μάθετε, "learn," has the same root as μαθητής, "disciple" or "learner." In the formulaic school language of the Pharisees themselves (the Aramaic formula is צֵא וּלְמַד, sēʾ ûlmōd, "go and learn"; cf. W. Bacher, *Die Agada der Tannaiten*, 2nd ed. [Strassburg, 1903] 1:75; Schlatter; Grundmann; Str-B 1:499), Jesus the teacher tells them: Go and learn the meaning of a particular text of Scripture (Hosea 6:6), which he now quotes: ἔλεος θέλω καὶ οὐ θυσίαν, "I desire mercy and not sacrifice." The quotation is perhaps from the LXX (which has ἤ, "more than," instead of καὶ οὐ, "and not"), but modified by Matthew to agree more closely with the Hebrew. Although Hos 6:6 was used after the destruction of the temple to indicate that the sacrifices were unnecessary, this was not the point of Jesus: "and not" here can mean "more than." θυσία, "sacrifice," here stands for strict obedience to the commandments of God. From the logic of the Pharisees' position, the verse should read "I desire sacrifice and not mercy," or at least substantiate the conclusion that sacrifice (obedience) is *more* important than mercy. Yet Hosea, speaking for Yahweh, put the emphasis upon mercy (Hebrew *hesed*, "steadfast love") even to the extent of denying the absolute importance of sacrifice. Mercy is a better way of obedience. The same verse, which is obviously important to Matthew, is quoted by Jesus to the Pharisees in 12:7 in the context of the question of Sabbath observance. There too he makes the point that some things are more important than strict obedience to the letter of the law. At its heart, Jesus' healing ministry is about mercy—the granting of unmerited favor to the unworthy. Thus he can now summarize the purpose of his coming, the central work of his ministry, in the words οὐ γὰρ ἦλθον καλέσαι δικαίους ἀλλὰ ἁμαρτωλούς, "I did not come to call [i.e., to invite to discipleship] the righteous but sinners." And for this reason Jesus can be described as τελωνῶν φίλος καὶ ἁμαρτωλῶν, "friend of tax collectors and sinners" (11:19). Again, therefore, as in the preceding pericope (cf. vv. 6, 8), we are brought to the centrality of the forgiveness of sin in the ministry of Jesus. It is for this reason that he comes to call sinners (cf. Luke 19:10) and that sinners are often the quickest to respond to him. In 21:31 Jesus will say, "Truly, I say to you, the tax collectors and harlots go into the kingdom of God before you." It would be a mistake on the basis of vv 12–13 to conclude that the references to the "healthy" and the "righteous" imply, either for Jesus or for Matthew, that there are some who do not need Jesus or for whom he has not come. On the contrary, it is clear that those who perhaps had the most reason to be included in that category, the Pharisees, are paradoxically among those who need Jesus the most. From the standpoint of the kingdom and the ministry of Jesus, culminating in his death, all are unworthy and in need of forgiveness—the "righteous," the Pharisees included.

Explanation

When Jesus calls Matthew the tax collector to be among his twelve disciples, he shows the universal scope of his compassion. Since Jesus' mission is predicated upon mercy and not merit, no one is despicable enough by the standards of society to be outside his concern and invitation. Matthew's life would change dramatically without question; but Jesus had reached out to him just as he was. If that had happened, then Jesus could reach out to others like Matthew, his former co-workers, and other people among the dregs of society. So Matthew's wonderful evangelistic banquet becomes in a very real sense a paradigm of the gospel itself. The totally unworthy are graced by the presence of Jesus himself; for he has come to call such persons to be a part of the kingdom (cf. 1 Tim 1:15). No mistaken sense of the righteous demands of separation from sinners can be allowed to hinder this mission. Nomistic scrupulosity must give way to the gracious announcement to all of mercy and forgiveness. For the evangelist and his community, Jesus again stands *with* the OT, not against it, in his authoritative interpretation of it (cf. Mic 6:6–8).

Combining New and Old   (9:14–17)

Bibliography

Beckwith, R. T. "The Feast of New Wine and the Question of Fasting." *ExpTim* 95 (1984) 334–35. **Brooke, G.** "The Feast of New Wine and the Question of Fasting." *ExpTim* 95 (1984) 175–76. **Cremer, F. G.** *Die Fastenansage Jesu.* BBB 23. Bonn: Hanstein, 1965. **Feuillet, A.** "La controverse sur le jeûne (Mc 2,18–20; Mt 9,14–15; Lc 5,33–35)." *NRT* 90 (1968) 113–36; 252–77. **Gnilka, J.** "'Bräutigam'—spätjüdisches Messiasprädikat?" *TTZ* 69 (1960) 298–301.

Hahn, F. "Die Bildworte vom neuen Flicken und vom jungen Wein (Mk 2,21f. parr)." *EvT* 31 (1971) 357–75. **Kee, A.** "The Old Coat and the New Wine." *NovT* 12 (1970) 13–21. ————. "The Question about Fasting." *NovT* 11 (1969) 161–73. **Muddiman, J. B.** "Jesus and Fasting." In *Jésus aux origenes de la christologie*, ed. J. Dupont. BETL 40. Gembloux: Duculot, 1975. 283–301. **Nagel, W.** "Neuer Wein in alten Schläuchen." *VC* 14 (1960) 1–8. **O'Neill, J. C.** "The Source of the Parables of the Bridegroom and the Wicked Husbandmen." *JTS* 39 (1988) 485–89. **Steinhauser, M. G.** "Neuer Wein braucht neue Schläuche." In *Biblische Randbemerkungen*. FS R. Schnackenburg, ed. H. Merklein and J. Lange. Würzburg: Echter, 1974. 113–23. ————. "The Patch of Unshrunk Cloth." *ExpTim* 87 (1976) 312–13. **Ziesler, J.** "The Removal of the Bridegroom: A Note on Mark 2,18–22 and Parallels." *NTS* 19 (1972–73) 190–94.

Translation

[14] *Then the disciples of John came to him, saying: "Why do we and the Pharisees fast [often],[a] but your disciples do not fast?"* [15] *And Jesus said to them: "Those who are at the side of[b] the bridegroom[c] are not able to grieve[d] as long as the bridegroom is with them, are they? But the days will come when the bridegroom is taken from them, and then they will fast.[e]* [16] *But no one sews a patch of unshrunk cloth on an old garment, for then the repair[f] rips away from the garment and the tear becomes worse.* [17] *Neither do people put new wine into old wineskins: otherwise the skins tear,[g] and the wine pours out,[h] and the skins are destroyed. Instead, they put new wine into new skins and both are preserved."*

Notes

[a] The critical Gr. text puts πολλά, "often," in brackets because a few important MSS omit the word (א* B sa^ms). But the word could have been omitted by way of harmonization with the Synoptic parallel passages, where it is not found. See *TCGNT*, 25. א¹ lat? sy^s? have πυκνά, "frequently," probably by the influence of the parallel in Luke 5:33.

[b] οἱ υἱοὶ τοῦ, lit. "the sons of." See *Comment*.

[c] νυμφῶνος, lit. "of the bridal chamber."

[d] A few MSS (D W it sy^p.hmg sa mae bo^mss) have νηστεύειν, "fast," probably by influence of the parallel passages (Mark 2:19; Luke 5:34).

[e] A few MSS (e.g., D it sy^hmg) add ἐν ἐκείναις ταῖς ἡμέραις, "in those days," again by the influence of the parallel passages.

[f] τὸ πλήρωμα αὐτοῦ, lit. "its fullness," probably the subject of the verb.

[g] D sy^s have ῥήσσει ὁ οἶνος ὁ νέος τοὺς ἀσκούς, "the new wine tears the skins," probably by the influence of the parallels (esp. Luke 5:37).

[h] D (a) k have ἀπόλλυται, "is destroyed," by influence of the Markan parallel.

Form/Structure/Setting

A. The refusal of Jesus and his disciples in the previous pericope to abide by the regulations concerning separation from sinners probably accounts for Mark's conjoining of the present passage to the preceding. Matthew (and Luke) here again follows the Markan order for the third consecutive passage. It is becoming clear in the progress of the narrative that despite the emphasis found in Matt 5:17–20, Jesus possesses a rather different concept of righteousness than do the Pharisees. He associates with tax collectors and sinners, even banqueting together with them, and now as the disciples of John point out, he and his disciples do not fast. What in fact is the position of Jesus concerning the accepted standards of righteousness? In this pericope that subject is addressed directly, and a very important summary of the situation is given by Jesus.

B. As customary, Matthew abbreviates while otherwise following Mark quite closely (Mark 2:18–22; cf. Luke 5:33–39). Matthew (and Luke) omits Mark's opening verse (Mark 2:18) because the point is made adequately in the dialogue that follows. Matthew further omits the reference to οἱ μαθηταί, "the disciples," referring simply to the Pharisees (v 14). Matthew probably has added πολλά, "often," in the reference to the Pharisees' fasting (v 14). In v 15 Matthew has substituted πενθεῖν, "grieve," for Mark's νηστεύειν, "fast," thus calling attention to the essential nature of fasting. Mark 2:19b is omitted because of its obvious redundancy. Matthew (v 15) omits the Markan phrase ἐν ἐκείνῃ τῇ ἡμέρᾳ, "in that day," after the clause "and then they will fast," probably to keep open the possibility of further fasting in the Church. In v 17 Matthew replaces the Markan statement that "the wine perishes" (ἀπόλλυται) with "the wine is poured out" (ἐκχεῖται), so that emphasis falls on the destruction of the skins. Finally, Matthew adds at the very end the revealing phrase καὶ ἀμφότεροι συντηροῦνται, "and both are preserved" (see *Comment*).

C. The pericope, again a controversy passage, has two main parts: (1) the question about fasting (vv 14–15), which in turn gives rise to (2) the statement about combining new and old (vv 16–17). Part 1 consists of (a) the question of John's disciples (v 14) and (b) the answer of Jesus (v 15). The latter consists of a chiasm: *a*–the non-fasting of Jesus' disciples; *b*–while the bridegroom is present; *b'*–the bridegroom will be taken away; *a'*–the disciples will fast. Part 2 consists of two analogies: (a) the piece of cloth (v 16) and (b) the wineskins (v 17). Both analogies consist of (i) the statement that no one combines new and old, for if they do, (ii) certain undesirable consequences will follow. The second analogy alone, however, contains a third part (iii), which for the first time describes what one does with the new—in this case—wine, to which Matthew has appended a short clarifying addition (καὶ ἀμφότεροι συντηροῦνται, "and both are preserved"). On the formal parallelism of v 17, cf. Nagel.

D. In the Coptic *Gospel of Thomas* (logion 104) in response to the invitation to fast, Jesus says, "What sin, then, have I committed, or in what have I been overcome? But when the bridegroom comes out of the bride-chamber, then let them fast and pray." This passage is probably derived from the Synoptic tradition, as is the allusion to the analogies of the piece of cloth and the wineskins in logion 47.

Comment

14 For Matthew's very common τότε, "then," see *Comment* on 2:7. Whereas often it implies no connection with what precedes, in this case it does show the logical link with the preceding pericope. οἱ μαθηταὶ Ἰωάννου, "the disciples of John," indicates the somewhat surprising fact that John the Baptist, now in prison (cf. 4:12), continued to have a group of followers, a point not made much of in the Synoptic tradition (but cf. John 1:40; 3:23, 25–30; 4:1; and Acts 19:1–7). They appear again in Matt 11:2–6 (cf. 21:32). John's way was that of asceticism (cf. 3:4; 11:18) in preparation for imminent eschatological judgment, and it stood in remarkable contrast to the demeanor of Jesus, who was controlled by the joy of the appearing kingdom (see the expression of this contrast esp. in 11:18–19). Matthew's abbreviation of Mark results in the peculiar, almost humorous, "Why do *we* [ἡμεῖς] fast?" The point, however, is not that they did not know why they fasted but that they wondered why Jesus and his disciples did not fast. Any claim to righteousness could hardly neglect the important practice of fasting (cf. Luke 18:12, where the Pharisee refers to his fasting twice a week; cf. *Did.* 8:1, which mentions the fasting of "the hypocrites" on Mondays and Thursdays). The Pharisees and the disciples of John fasted, indeed πολλά, "often," as Matthew emphasizes. These fasts refer to private works of supererogation that went far beyond, for example, the required fast on the Day of Atonement (cf. Lev 16:29–31) or on anniversaries of the several destructions of Jerusalem. The question thus concerns the fundamentally important matter of the practice of righteousness. And the disciples of John, more than the Pharisees, would have worried over the issue perhaps because they saw themselves as related to the mission of Jesus (cf. 21:32).

15 In his answer Jesus turns to the idea of messianic jubilation expressed specifically in the imagery of the bridegroom and his attendants. The announcement of the presence of the messianic kingdom is similar to being present at a great wedding banquet (cf. Feuillet). This imagery is elsewhere particularly appealing to Matthew (cf. 22:1–14; 25:1–13). The phrase οἱ υἱοὶ τοῦ νυμφῶνος, "the sons of the bridal chamber," means those in relation to, belonging to (cf. BAGD, 834, s.v. υἱός 1δ; 545), or hence, attending to, the bridegroom (cf. 8:12, "sons of the kingdom"). Whereas the bridegroom image in the OT refers to God (cf. Isa 62:4–5; "husband": Isa 54:5–6; Hos 2:16–20), in the NT it is applied to Christ (2 Cor 11:2; cf. Eph 5:22–27; Rev 19:7). The question asked by Jesus at the beginning of this verse in response to the question of John's disciples is a kind of statement; it begins with μή and hence presupposes a negative answer: "They cannot grieve while the groom is with them, can they?" Matthew's substitution of πενθεῖν, "grieve," for Mark's νηστεύειν, "fast," has the effect of showing further the incongruity of fasting with the time of celebration and fulfillment signified by the presence of the bridegroom (cf. Zech 8:19; and the note of joy in John 3:29; cf. Str-B 1:500–18). But already in the question ("as long as the bridegroom is with them"), as well as in the clear statement that follows, a time is envisioned by Jesus when the bridegroom will no longer be with his disciples. Feuillet (252–56) sees an allusion to the suffering servant of Isa 53 in the reference to the bridegroom being "taken away" (cf. αἴρεται in Isa 53:8b): ἐλεύσονται δὲ ἡμέραι ὅταν ἀπαρθῇ ἀπ' αὐτῶν ὁ νυμφίος, "the days are coming when the bridegroom will be taken away from them." In this time fasting will be justifiable (but it will only be temporary, cf. John 16:20). Though not quite a passion prediction (cf. 16:21), this is the first clear allusion to the future and unexpected death of Jesus (cf. 26:11; Luke 17:22). Neither the disciples nor uninformed readers of Matthew can yet make sense of the remark, but in retrospect it will make sense. καὶ τότε νηστεύσουσιν, "and then they will fast." Unlike Mark ("in that day") and Luke ("in those days"), Matthew gives no time limitation. Matthew thus finds a place in his church for the good Jewish practice of fasting (cf. 6:16–18; cf. *Did.* 8:1, which encourages Christians to fast on Wednesdays and Fridays, rather than Mondays and Thursdays, as do the Jews). But any such fasting done by Christians who know the reality of the kingdom must, even for Matthew, be distinguished carefully from that of the Jewish communities, who yet wait for some sign of fulfillment. That the wrong kind of fasting can often have little virtue attached to it is a point made clearly in Isa 58:3–9, which contains important contrasts with the ethical priorities of the gospel (cf. the similar tone of "I desire mercy and not sacrifice" [v 13]).

16–17 If fasting has lost its fixed place in the fabric of righteousness because of a new reality now present in and through the ministry of Jesus, then a question mark can be raised over the whole body of inherited practice, and even that stipulated in Torah. How, in fact, is the newness represented by the presence and message of Jesus to be combined with previous conventional modes of conduct? And Jesus replies with two analogies (Luke alone introduces them with the word παραβολή, "parable" [5:36]) that illustrate vividly that the new cannot simply be superimposed upon or contained within the framework of the old. The first analogy (v 16) makes the point by noting the foolishness of putting a new patch of unshrunk cloth upon an old garment. When the new patch becomes wet, it will naturally shrink and thus tear the garment, doing more damage than that which was originally repaired. It would be a mistake to allegorize the details of this analogy, but the main symbolism is clear: the new and the old are not mutually compatible. τὸ πλήρωμα αὐτοῦ, lit. "its fullness," refers to the patch as a kind of supplement or complement (see BAGD, s.v. 1b; Steinhauser: "the 'fill' of the unshrunk cloth that is the material and the thread with which the unshrunk cloth is sewn to the old cloth" [313]). The second analogy (v 17) is parallel and makes the same point. οἶνον νέον, "new wine," is grape juice in an early stage of fermentation (perhaps the illustration was prompted by the Feast of New Wine; cf. Brooke). This would require that the skin bags that hold it be more pliable than old skins (cf. Job 32:19). If ἀσκοὺς παλαιούς, "old skins," are used, three things are sure to happen: (a) the skins will tear, (b) the wine will pour out, and (c) the skins will be ruined (ἀπόλλυνται, lit. "destroyed"). Everything will be lost, both the wine and the skins. On the other hand, new wine is to be put into ἀσκοὺς καινούς, "new skins," and when that happens, Matthew now uniquely points out, ἀμφότεροι συντηροῦνται, "both are preserved." It is not unwarranted allegorizing to draw out the following symbolism, which is inherent in the passage. The new wine is the newness of the gospel (cf. John 2:1–11), personified in Jesus; the old wine skins are the established patterns of conduct regarded as exemplifying the righteousness of the Torah. The former is too dynamic to be contained by the traditional framework of obedience. The proposal to combine the two may well have been a temptation to Matthew's Jewish-Christian readers. But the new reality of the gospel requires instead "new skins," i.e., new patterns of conduct based on the ethical teaching of Jesus as the true exposition of the meaning and intent of the Torah. Here Matthew's special interests and viewpoint (and conservatism too, compared to Mark) become obvious: "both are preserved," that is, the new wine of the reality of the kingdom *and* the new skins (not the *old* skins!) of faithful obedience to the law, but as expounded by Jesus. For Matthew, gospel and law (not Christianity and Judaism; contra Fenton, A. Kee) are held together in the Church, but the standard of interpretation of and obedience to the latter is always solely the authoritative teaching of Jesus.

Explanation

The proper understanding of what constitutes righteous conduct depends in the first instance on an appreciation of the centrality of Jesus (the bridegroom) and the good news he proclaims (the time of rejoicing, the new wine). All conduct is to be judged on the basis of him and his teaching. There is accordingly something fundamentally incompatible between fasting and the joy of the kingdom. If fasting is conceived of as a lamenting or grieving over God's failure to act, if it is thought of as a way to hasten the coming of the Messiah, if it is thought of as a way of gaining God's favor, it is contradictory to what the gospel signifies. The Christian is not a person characterized by sorrow, sackcloth and ashes, laments and fastings, but a person of joy who has experienced grace and fulfillment (cf. 6:16–18). Even the suffering and persecuted Church is characterized by unquenchable joy. If Jesus has been taken away from his disciples, the grief of that separation did not have to last long, for as Matthew knows better than others, Jesus has returned to be with his Church always (28:20; contra Gundry). So if Matthew keeps the door open for the further practice of fasting in the Church, which he probably does (cf. Acts 13:2–3; 14:23; 27:9), that fasting must not be incompatible with the deep joy of the Christian reality. There is a place for such fasting, but it would be very different in nature from that practiced by the disciples of John and the Pharisees. It must be fasting within the larger framework of the fulfillment and joy of the kingdom already present in the Church. Fasting in this case will be a spiritual discipline practiced with prayer, for such purposes as sharpening one's focus or deepening one's experience.

It must be affirmed from the start that the presence of Jesus necessarily means an alteration of previous definitions of the path of righteousness (cf. Rom 7:6). The gospel cannot be added to Judaism. It is not a matter of loyalty to Torah or God's righteousness that is in question. It is rather a matter of the *interpretation* of God's will. And it is exactly in this that Jesus, as God's Messiah, the one Teacher (cf. 23:8–12), excels, as will the Christian scribe (cf. 13:52). Because of the new era represented by the fulfillment brought by Jesus, a new possibility of understanding and obeying God's will becomes available. The disciples' new obedience turns on the unique person and mission of Jesus.

The Healing of the Hemorrhaging Woman and the Raising of the Ruler's Daughter   (9:18–26)

Bibliography

Cummings, J. T. "The Tassel of His Cloak: Mark, Luke, Matthew and Zechariah." In *Studia Biblica 1978: II. Papers on the Gospels*, ed. E. A. Livingstone. JSNTSup 2. Sheffield: JSOT, 1980. 47–61. **Harris, M. J.** "'The dead are restored to life': Miracles of Revivification in the Gospels." In *Gospel Perspectives 6: The Miracles of Jesus*, ed. D. Wenham and C. Blomberg. Sheffield: JSOT, 1986. 295–326. **Hutter, M.** "Ein altorientischer Bittgestus in Mt 9,20–22." *ZNW* 75 (1984) 133–35. **Kalin, E. R.** "Matthew 9:18–26: An Exercise in Redaction Criticism." *CurTM* 15 (1988) 39–47. **Marxsen, W.** "Bibelarbeit über Mk 5.21–43/Mt 9.18–26." In *Der Exeget als Theologe*. Gütersloh: Mohn, 1968. 171–82. **Robbins, V.** "The Woman Who Touched Jesus' Garment: Socio-rhetorical Analysis of the Synoptic Accounts." *NTS* 33 (1987) 502–15. **Rochais, G.** *Les récits de résurrection des morts dans le Nouveau Testament*. SNTSMS 40. Cambridge: Cambridge University, 1981.

Translation

[18]*While he was saying these things to them, look, a ruler came*[a] *and bowed down before*[b] *him, saying: "My daughter has just now died. But come and lay your hand upon her, and she will live."* [19]*And Jesus rose and with his disciples followed him.*

[20]*And look, a woman who had suffered from a hemorrhage for twelve years*[c] *came behind him and touched the fringe of his garment.* [21]*For she was saying to herself, "If only I may touch his garment, I will be healed."*[d] [22]*But Jesus turned,*[e] *and when he saw her, he said, "Have courage, daughter. Your faith has healed you." And the woman was healed from that very hour.*

[23]*And Jesus came into the house of the ruler, and when he saw the flute players*[f] *and the crowd wailing,* [24]*he said,*[g] *"Go away, for the girl has not died: she is only sleeping." And they laughed at him.* [25]*But when the crowd was driven out, he came in and took her hand, and the girl arose.* [26]*And this report*[h] *went out into that whole region.*

Notes

[a] A few important witnesses (ℵ[b] B it vg) read εἷς προσελθών (thus "one [ruler] coming to"), but this is probably an attempt to make clear that εἷς is to be understood as separate from, rather than a part of, the participle ἐλθών. See *TCGNT*, 25.

[b] προσεκύνει, possibly "worshiped," but this may read too much into the man's knowledge of Jesus.

[c] L and a few other witnesses add ἔχουσα ἐν τῇ ἀσθενείᾳ, "being [lit. 'having'] in the weakness [twelve years]." Cf. John 5:5 and Luke 13:11 for the same idiom.

[d] σωθήσομαι, lit. "will be saved," as also both times in v 22.

[e] C L W Θ *f*[1] TR have ἐπιστραφείς, "turned to," for στραφείς.

[f] I.e., professional musicians for mourning.

[g] C L W Θ TR sy have λέγει αὐτοῖς, lit. "he says to them," for ἔλεγεν, "he said," probably by influence of the parallel passage in Mark 5:39.

[h] ἡ φήμη αὕτη, "this report," is the more awkward reading and is thus preferred over ἡ φήμη αὐτῆς, "this report about her" (ℵ C N[vid] Θ *f*[1] 33 mae bo) or ἡ φήμη αὐτοῦ, "his fame" (D sa bo[ms]). See *TCGNT*, 25.

Form/Structure/Setting

A. As Matthew again departs from the order of Mark, we now come to the beginning of the last cluster of miracle narratives (four in number) in this major section of the Gospel (chaps. 8–9). The present double pericope, as it does in all three Synoptics, consists of one healing narrative within the framework of another. Thus the story of the raising of the dead girl (vv 18–19; 23–26) is interrupted by the inserted story of the healing of the hemorrhaging woman (vv 20–22). These stories make clear the point of the preceding pericope that the present is a unique era of incomparable joy, the anticipation of the very blessings of the eschaton.

B. Matthew's characteristic abbreviation of Mark is even more evident here than usual. Matthew seems impatient of Mark's asides and details and gives only the bare essentials of the story. Thus he reduces the length of the first part of the story of the ruler's daughter by one-third and the next two parts (the hemorrhaging woman and the raising of the girl) by no less than two-thirds each.

The major omissions can be tabulated as follows: the name Jairus and that he was a ruler of a synagogue (Mark 5:22); the reference to his insistent pleading (Mark 5:23); the request for her to be healed (Mark 5:23); all reference to the crowds, a central element in the following story according to Mark (Mark 5:24, 27); the extent to which the woman suffered (Mark 5:26); the reference to her healing (Mark 5:29); the knowledge of Jesus that power had gone out of him and his question, "Who touched me?" the latter perhaps being omitted for christological reasons (Mark 5:30–31); the woman's response at being discovered (Mark 5:33); the report of the death of the girl and Jesus' encouragement of the ruler (Mark 5:35–36); the taking of only the inner circle of three disciples and the parents (Mark 5:37, 40); the words pronounced by Jesus, regarded as unnecessary and open to a magical misinterpretation (Mark 5:41); the reference to her walking and the instruction for her to be given something to eat (Mark 5:42–43); and finally, the reference to the astonishment of the crowd (Mark 5:42). The stories are thus nearly transformed into brief summaries of the essentials. This extensive abbreviation does necessitate one important change: according to Matthew the ruler reports initially that his daughter has died (9:19), unlike Mark's ἐσχάτως ἔχει, "near death" (Mark 5:23). Matthew's passage is thus from the start emphatically concerned with the raising of the dead (cf. 11:5) rather than the healing of the sick. Another significant change is Matthew's reference to οἱ μαθηταί, "the disciples" (v 19), accompanying Jesus, which stands in tension with Mark's reference to the three disciples (Mark 5:37). Matthew alone refers specifically to the "flute players" (v 23). In the whole narrative Matthew adds only a few words: κρασπέδου, "fringe" (9:20; so too Luke, but cf. Mark 6:56); that the woman spoke ἐν ἑαυτῇ, "to herself" (9:21); θάρσει, "have courage" (9:22); and the final words about the report spreading in that region (9:26). Matthew's economy here suggests again that Matthew has a special agenda that will not permit him to luxuriate in the details of a story, however attractive. Matthew is interested above all in teaching about Jesus and thus in teaching the Church, rather than in telling stories for their own sake. Rochais describes the pericope of the raising of the dead girl as more of an illustration of the power of faith in Jesus (cf. 21:22) than the recitation of a miracle (96–97). Some commentators (e.g., Lohmeyer, Schniewind, Grundmann), given the great difference between Matthew and Mark, argue for Matthew's use of a special source parallel to Mark but independent of it.

C. The major structural feature of this pericope is of course the insertion of the story of the hemorrhaging woman (vv 20–22) into the story of the raising of the dead girl. It is particularly interesting that both Matthew and Luke preserve the two stories in this form, rather than separating them. This suggests that the conjoining of the two stories was a familiar part of the fixed Gospel tradition from an early time. It is difficult to find a special reason for this connection of the two stories, which are otherwise quite different. Perhaps Mark and Luke tried to do this in their note (Mark 5:42; Luke 8:42), omitted by Matthew, that the dying girl was twelve years old (corresponding to the twelve years the woman had suffered from her disease). Faith is common to both stories in Mark (cf. Mark 5:34, 36); in Matthew it is only stressed in one (v 22). It may be that the two stories were handed on as they are for no other reason than because the healing of the woman actually did happen on the way to the dead girl's house. This is not to deny, however, the dramatic building of tension that occurs through the delay caused by the parenthetical, new story.

D. Each story could stand independently as is; vv 20–22 could be removed and not otherwise be missed. The story of the dead girl has the following structure: (1) the presentation of the need (v 18a); (2) the father's request (v 18b); (3) the departure of Jesus and his disciples (v 19)—the inserted story—(4) the arrival of Jesus (v 23); (5) the sending away of the mourners (v 24); (6) the raising of the dead girl (v 25), with v 25b corresponding closely to the request of v 18b;

and (7) the spread of the story (v 26). Rochais (89) points out that a form of the
verb ἔρχεσθαι is used to introduce the main elements of the story (cf. vv 18, 23,
25b, 26). The story of the woman with the hemorrhage, which is quite different
in structure from other healing narratives, has these elements: (1) the initiative
of the woman (v 20); (2) her reasoning (v 21); (3) the pronouncement of Jesus
(v 21a); and (4) the healing of the woman (v 21b).

Comment

18–19   The genitive absolute ταῦτα αὐτοῦ λαλοῦντος αὐτοῖς, "while he was
saying these things to them," is Matthew's transition to the new story and is not to
be understood as a particular time indicator (the order in Mark and Luke is very
different). Matthew's ἰδού, "behold," again signifies a new, remarkable story. For
Matthew the simple ἄρχων, "ruler," a Jewish ruler, is understood to be a synagogue official (as in Mark 5:22 and Luke 8:41). This man falls down before Jesus
(προσεκύνει αὐτῷ) in order to make his desperate request. His estimate of Jesus
is not clear, no title being used, but he clearly had heard of Jesus' powerful deeds
of healing and had at least a shred of hope that Jesus could do something in his
dire circumstances. The raising of the dead by special representatives of God was
of course known from the OT (cf. Elijah [1 Kgs 17:17–24] and Elisha [2 Kgs 4:32–
37]). The report that his daughter had "just died" (ἄρτι ἐτελεύτησεν) in contrast
with Mark's "close to death" is the result of Matthew's extensive shortening of the
pericope (see *Form/Structure/Setting* §B). The effect of this alteration on the following words is dramatic, since the father requests now the raising of the dead,
not simply the saving of the dying (note Matthew's omission of Mark's σωθῇ, "she
will be healed" [5:23]). The simple faith of the ruler, reminiscent of that of the
centurion (8:5–13), is impressive: ἐπίθες τὴν χεῖρά σου ἐπ' αὐτήν, καὶ ζήσεται,
"lay your hand upon her, and she will live," Matthew's future tense heightening
the faith of the father (cf. Mark's subjunctive). This is the only reference in Matthew to healing by the laying on of hands (but cf. Mark 6:5; 7:32; 8:23, 25; Luke
4:40; 13:13). The response of Jesus is immediate: ἐγερθεὶς ὁ Ἰησοῦς ἠκολούθησεν
αὐτῷ, "Jesus rose [from the table] and followed him." The final Matthean insertion, καὶ οἱ μαθηταὶ αὐτοῦ, "and with his disciples," is tacked on to the end of the
sentence, indicating that they were to witness the event (cf. Mark 5:37).
20–21   Matthew's καὶ ἰδού, "and look," marks the intrusion of the new story
(cf. v 18). A woman who for twelve years had suffered from some unspecified
hemorrhaging, probably (though not necessarily) from the womb, touched the
fringe of Jesus' garment from behind him in order to be healed. This woman not
only faced the inconvenience and physical danger of such regular loss of blood
but also suffered the stigma of ritual uncleanness in that culture and consequent
ostracism (see esp. Lev 15:25–30). She "comes to" (προσελθοῦσα, Matthew's favorite verb in this connection) Jesus to be healed, but rather than approaching
him directly, which her uncleanness would have prevented her from doing, she
devises a plan of secretly touching his garment. Her reasoning and simple faith
find articulation in v 21. It will suffice to touch the garment of this very special
person. This strategy may well have been dictated by her ritual uncleanness and
her sense of the holiness of Jesus as a divinely empowered healer. τοῦ κρασπέδου
τοῦ ἱματίου αὐτοῦ, "the fringe of his garment," probably refers not simply to the

edge of Jesus' garment but to the tassels (Hebrew צִיצִת, *ṣîṣit*) required by Num 15:38–41 and Deut 22:12 for the four corners of one's outer garment (cf. 23:5). Jesus is thus faithful to the Torah in his dress. The idea of being healed through even the garments worn by a holy person was not so unusual in that culture (cf. 14:36; Mark 6:56; Acts 19:12). It should not be thought of as quasi-magical. If healing power could be experienced by touching a special person directly (e.g., Mark 3:10; Luke 6:19), then it could also extend to touching what had touched that person. If there is a slight hint of magic in this, the woman's strategy is at least commendable as a sign of deep faith in the power of Jesus. Cummings relates the touching of the tassel to Zech 8:23 and thus finds messianic significance in Matthew's specific mention of it (51–52). The secrecy in Mark is not possible in Matthew, who has not recorded the presence of a large crowd pressing upon Jesus (Mark 5:24). σωθήσομαι, lit. "I will be saved," refers here to being freed from her malaise. But its threefold use here (compared to two occurrences each in Mark and Luke) shows Matthew's special interest in the word and suggests a further nuance to it. Elsewhere in Matthew the same verb has the meaning of salvation (e.g., 1:21; 10:22; 16:25; 18:11; 19:25). Whether his readers were to hear an echo of the latter even in the present passage is uncertain but not unreasonable.

22 Without the crowd found in Mark, Matthew's στραφείς, "having turned," lacks the drama of Mark's ἐπιστραφείς (5:30). In Matthew, accordingly, the woman seems almost to be caught in the act. There is no need for a confession on her part (cf. Mark 5:33). Without a word from her, Jesus knows both her plight and her faith, and he responds without hesitation: θάρσει, θύγατερ· ἡ πίστις σου σέσωκέν σε, "Have courage, daughter. Your faith has healed you." θάρσει, "have courage," was used in Jesus' words to the paralytic earlier in this chapter (9:2) and will be used again in 14:27, addressed to the disciples. The woman is addressed tenderly as θύγατερ, "daughter," which is analogous to the use of τέκνον, "son," in 9:2. The important subject of faith is first mentioned in the Gospel in 8:10 (see *Comment*). Only here in Matthew is the significance of faith for healing stressed by making πίστις, "faith," the subject of the verb σῷζω, "make whole" (this is also found beyond parallels to the present passage in Mark 10:52; Luke 7:50; 17:19; 18:42), but the semantic equivalent is found in the expression "let it be to you according to your faith" (see 8:13; 9:29). It is clear that from Matthew's perspective, it was Jesus who had made the woman whole again. But it was her faith, exemplified in her desire to touch Jesus' garment, that appropriated the healing power of Jesus. In this sense her faith had made her whole, had "saved" her. Matthew stresses the immediate occurrence of the healing, after or by the word of Jesus (so Kalin, 44–45), in his added phrase, ἀπὸ τῆς ὥρας ἐκείνης, "from that very hour" (cf. 8:13; 15:28; 17:18). Thus Jesus sovereignly announces that the woman has been healed, and from that hour she is healed.

23–24 With the report of the healing of the woman and the end of the brief, inserted story, the first story resumes. When Jesus comes to the ruler's house, he encounters a gathering of people readying themselves for the funeral that would take place the same day, as was the custom in that culture. τοὺς αὐλητάς, "the flute players," were professional musicians (cf. for festive occasions, 11:17; Rev 18:22) who were apparently hired to play at funerals. Matthew's ὄχλον θορυβούμενον, lit. "crowd in an uproar," represents the loud wailing, typical in that culture, of those mourning the death of the girl (cf. Jer 48:36; Mark 5:38; Jos. *J.W.* 3.9.5 §437 and Str-B 1:521–23 [*m. Ketub.* 4.4; *m. Šabb.* 23.4]). All of this indicated that the girl had died. For Jesus, who is about to bring the girl back to life, the lamenting is inappropriate, and so the mourners are told to "go away." They are not needed because the girl ἀλλὰ καθεύδει, "is but sleeping." Death for Jesus is not the final word; the dead can be brought back to life. This expectation causes the Church ultimately to use the same verb, καθεύδω, for those who have died: they are but "asleep" (1 Thess 5:10; Eph 5:14; cf. κοιμᾶσθαι: 27:52; John 11:11–14; 1 Cor 15:6, 20; 1 Thess 4:13–18; for OT background, see Dan 12:2). Jesus does not deny the girl's death but rather the finality of that death. In Mark and Luke the messianic secret motif may be the main reason Jesus says the girl is only sleeping (cf. Mark 5:43; Luke 8:56); it must not be made public that Jesus has raised the dead. But Matthew lacks any concern here for the messianic secret (cf. v 26). The crowd ridicules Jesus (κατέγελων αὐτοῦ, "laughed at him") for any suggestion that the girl was not truly dead. This note, which is common to the Synoptic tradition, serves as an indirect confirmation of the actuality of the girl's death.

25   After the crowd had been removed, Jesus entered (εἰσελθών) the room where the girl lay. Matthew mentions neither the four disciples nor the girl's parents, thus heightening the special and private character of the miracle. ἐκράτησεν τῆς χειρὸς αὐτῆς, "he took her hand," as in all the Synoptics (cf. the healing of Peter's mother-in-law by touching her hand; 8:15). Without any further note about Jesus' words or actions, Matthew records simply ἠγέρθη τὸ κοράσιον, "the girl arose." τὸ κοράσιον is the subject of the passive intransitive verb ἠγέρθη (cf. ἀνέστη in Mark and Luke). In this extremely economical statement, Matthew records one of the most impressive miracles of Jesus in the whole of his narrative.

26   No attention is called to the great faith of the ruler so evident in the first part of the narrative. Similarly, no report is given of the astonishment of those who saw the girl emerge from the room alive (cf. Mark 5:42). The actual miracle is simply reported by Matthew, and this is followed only by the comment that the report of the event spread throughout that region (i.e., Galilee). Although only here and in Luke 4:14 is the word φήμη, "report, fame," found in the NT, the point is made several times, especially in the miracle summaries (cf. 4:24; 9:31). Matthew does not say, as do Mark and Luke, that Jesus had encouraged silence upon anyone concerning the miracle. Matthew is concerned only with the deed itself and what it says about Jesus, although in this instance the deed is so remarkable that it is left to speak for itself.

Explanation

In a real way these miracle narratives point beyond themselves to realities at the heart of the Church's confession and experience. The raising of the dead to life is a basic symbolism of the gospel (e.g., Rom 4:17; Eph 2:1, 5; Col 2:13). What Jesus did for the dead girl he has done for all in the Church who have experienced new life. There is too, beyond this life, the Church's confidence that Jesus will literally raise the dead (cf. 1 Thess 4:16; 1 Cor 15:22–23). In a similar way in the healing of the hemorrhaging woman, the repeated use of σῴζειν (lit. "save") for her healing points beyond itself to the greatest healing experienced by the Church, the "healing" of salvation. For the Church is saved primarily not from the experience of limited ills here and now but from the deadliest enemy of all, the curse of sin. Thus while enjoying the stories of what Jesus did in his ministry and rejoicing in the power and authority of Jesus displayed in these miraculous deeds, the Church at the same time—Matthew's readers together with Christians from every era—sees in these narratives something of its own personal history and hopes, something of the power of the risen Jesus in their lives here and now. Thus these narratives concern not simply past history but present experience. The present faith of the Church thus receives considerable encouragement in this passage.

The Healing of Two Blind Men (9:27–31)

Bibliography

Berger, K. "Die königlichen Messiastraditionen des Neuen Testaments." *NTS* 20 (1973) 1–44. **Chilton, B. D.** "Jesus *ben David*: Reflections on the *Davidssohnfrage.*" *JSNT* 14 (1982) 88–112. **Duling, D. C.** "The Therapeutic Son of David: An Element in Matthew's Christological Apologetic." *NTS* 24 (1977–78) 392–410. **Fuchs, A.** *Sprachliche Untersuchungen zu Matthäus und Lukas.* AnBib 49. Rome: Pontifical Biblical Institute, 1971. **Gibbs, J. M.** "Purpose and Pattern in Matthew's Use of the Title 'Son of David.'" *NTS* 10 (1963–64) 446–64. **Kingsbury, J. D.** "The Title 'Son of David' in Matthew's Gospel." *JBL* 95 (1976) 591–602. **Loader, W. R. G.** "Son of David, Blindness and Duality in Matthew." *CBQ* 44 (1982) 570–85. **Suhl, A.** "Der Davidssohn im Matthäus-Evangelium." *ZNW* 59 (1968) 67–81.

Translation

[27] *And as Jesus was leaving there, two blind men followed [him],[a] crying out and saying: "Have mercy on us, Son of David!"* [28] *And when he had come into the house, the blind men[b] came to him, and Jesus said to them: "Do you believe that I am able to do this?" They said to him: "Yes, Lord!"* [29] *Then he touched their eyes, saying: "Let it be to you according to your faith."* [30] *And their eyes were opened. And Jesus sternly warned[c] them, saying: "See to it that no one knows of this."* [31] *But they went out and spread his fame in that whole[d] region.*

Notes

[a] A few important MSS (B D) omit αὐτῷ, "him," and thus the critical text has the words in brackets. The omission does not affect the sense.

[b] ℵ* D vg insert δύο, "two," before "blind men."

[c] The critical text prefers ἐνεβριμήθη, the passive and harder reading (ℵ B* *f*[1]), to ἐνεβριμήσατο, which is found in B[2] C D L W Θ *f*[13] TR. The passive would ordinarily have the literal meaning "Jesus was angry at them."

[d] ℵ* sy[s] omit ὅλη, "whole."

Form/Structure/Setting

A. Matthew now moves to the ninth miracle narrative of chaps. 8–9. By turning from the raising of the dead to the healing of the blind, Matthew continues to document the sovereign power of Jesus in terms of a full range of miracles, corresponding closely to those expected with the coming of the messianic age. The latter comes clearly into view by the reference of the blind men to Jesus as the Son of David. Thus, in addition to outlining the unique power and authority of Jesus, the present passage involves another important theme in Matthew, that of fulfillment. The healing of the blind ($\tau\upsilon\phi\lambda o\acute{\iota}$) is mentioned first in the list that provides the answer to John the Baptist's question about whether Jesus is the promised one, the Messiah (11:5).

B. Matthew has two narratives about the healing of two blind men (see also 20:29–34). The relationship between these two narratives remains unclear (for a full survey of possibilities, see Fuchs, 18–37). The second of them is by far the most closely related to the healing of the blind man in Mark 10:46–52. (Mark also has a second such narrative [8:22–26], but interestingly it is omitted by both Matthew and Luke.) The contacts between the present passage and Mark 10:46–52 are so few that any dependence here seems unlikely. The following are all that can be listed: the plea $\acute{\epsilon}\lambda\acute{\epsilon}\eta\sigma o\nu$, "have mercy," together with the address $\upsilon\acute{\iota}o\varsigma$ (Mark: $\upsilon\acute{\iota}\grave{\epsilon}$) $\Delta\alpha\upsilon\acute{\iota}\delta$, "Son of David" (v 27; cf. Mark 10:48); the fact that in both passages the person(s) to be healed comes to Jesus (v 28; cf. Mark 10:50); and the reference to $\pi\acute{\iota}\sigma\tau\iota\varsigma$, "faith," in connection with both healings (v 29; cf. Mark 10:52). Matthew's passage indeed finds no other true parallel in the Gospels (Luke 18:35–43 follows Mark 10:46–52).

C. There are a few interesting parallels between the two Matthean passages: strikingly there are two blind men in each passage (v 27; 20:30); in both they cry out and say: "Have mercy on me, Son of David" (v 28; 20:30, but with the possible addition of $\kappa\acute{\upsilon}\rho\iota\epsilon$, "Lord"); and in both Jesus "touched" ($\mathring{\eta}\psi\alpha\tau o$) their eyes (v 29; 20:34, but with a different word for "eyes"). Some of these common elements may result from crossover in language between the passages, perhaps during the transmission of the separate stories in oral tradition. Thus the language of one passage may have to some extent influenced the language of the other, producing some of the agreements noted. It is possible, though by no means certain (contra Fuchs; Gibbs), that Matthew has generated this story on the model of the Markan story he uses in 20:29–34 in order to represent the many instances of the blind being healed by Jesus (cf. 15:30–31) and in order to have an example of this prior to the sending out of the twelve (chap. 10) and prior especially to the response to the disciples of John the Baptist (11:5). Matthew's $\epsilon\mathring{\iota}\varsigma$ $\tau\grave{\eta}\nu$ $o\mathring{\iota}\kappa\acute{\iota}\alpha\nu$, "into the house," on the other hand, is an unnecessary detail (going against Matthew's economy of words) that finds no parallel in any of the other healing-of-the-blind narratives and may well indicate a specific and independent story that Matthew gleaned from oral tradition available to him (see Roloff, *Kerygma*, 132, for other un-Matthean elements). Matthew's creativity, at least in selecting and rendering, if not creating, a story, can be seen in the next pericope, the healing of the mute demoniac in 9:32–34 (cf. the parallel passage in 12:22–24; and again the requirements of 10:1 and 11:5). The story of the healing of the blind man in Mark 8:22–26 (like that of John 9:1–7, if it was known to Matthew) was not taken up by Matthew, probably because of its reference to stages of healing, a point of view not in keeping with the immediate healings and the sovereign power of Jesus as Matthew desires to present them. On Matthew's tendency to double, see the discussion above (on 8:28–34, see *Form/Structure/Setting* §C).

D. The form of the pericope is typical of healing narratives. The structure is simple: (1) the blind men's plea for mercy (v 27); (2) the testing of the blind men's faith, with (a) the question of Jesus and (b) their answer (v 28); (3) the healing of the blind men (v 28–30a); and (4) the aftermath in (a) Jesus' warning and (b) the telling of the story by the blind men (v 30b–31). Matthew's economy is again evident, as well as his special interest in faith (vv 28–29) and in the impact of the person of Jesus (v 31).

Comment

27 Matthew's καὶ παράγοντι ἐκεῖθεν, "and passing on from there," is transitional, preparing the way for the present pericope (rather than the typical opening genitive absolute, the dative participle, agreeing with τῷ Ἰησοῦ, is used). ἠκολούθησαν [αὐτῷ] δύο τυφλοί, "two blind men followed [him]," not in the sense of discipleship here (contra Gibbs, 454–55) but in order to be healed of their blindness. κράζοντες, "crying out," suggests the strength of their entreaty. To be blind in that culture was to be a social outcast. Blindness was frequently regarded as the judgment of God (Gen 19:11; Exod 4:11; Deut 28:28f.; *b. Sabb.* 108b–9a; cf. John 9:2), and it put serious religious limitations upon the blind (Lev 21:20; 2 Sam 5:8b; cf. 1 QM 7:4–5). The appeal for mercy, ἐλέησον ἡμᾶς, υἱὸς Δαυίδ, "Have mercy on us, Son of David," refers naturally to their being healed of their blindness (the request is also assumed, but not stated, in v 28). The title "Son of David" refers to the royal figure of 2 Sam 7:12–16 whose kingdom would have no end, i.e., the Messiah. For the essential equivalence of Son of David and Messiah, see 22:42 (cf. *Pss. Sol.* 17:23). It is very unlikely (*pace* Davies-Allison, who follow Berger and Chilton) that in his use of the title Matthew has in mind a similarity between Jesus and Solomon, who according to late Jewish tradition performed exorcisms and healings (for arguments against this conclusion, see Luz's excursus on the Son of David, 2:59–61). In using just this title, the blind men indicate their hope that Jesus is this messianic figure and that therefore they can expect the possibility of such a messianic gift as the giving of sight to the blind. Thus in response to John the Baptist's question, which centers on the identity and purpose of Jesus, reference is made to the miracles being performed by Jesus (11:2–6), which are regarded as signs of the presence of the messianic age (with regard specifically to the blind, see Isa 29:18; 35:5; 42:7). The cry for mercy from Jesus addressed as the Son of David is found also in 15:22 from the Canaanite woman and in 20:30 from the second pair of blind men, and the title Son of David is again linked with the healing of the blind (and lame) in 21:14–15. The plea for mercy (ἐλέησον) is also found in 17:15, but there it is addressed to κύριε, "Lord." The healing of the blind (and mute) is yet again linked with the title Son of David in 12:23 (cf. 21:9). For the title, which is used far more frequently in Matthew than in the other Gospels, see *Comment* on 1:1 (Str-B 1:525).

28 τὴν οἰκίαν, "the house," is not specified, but it cannot be the house of v 23 (nor probably that of v 10) and probably refers to the house of Peter in Capernaum

(9:14; cf. 9:1). The healing of the blind "in the house" is in keeping with the secrecy motif of v 30b. Jesus does not heal the blind men immediately, in order to provide the opportunity to ask about their faith. The two blind men προσῆλθον αὐτῷ, "came to him," in the unique and familiar Matthean phraseology. Here alone in the Gospel tradition is it reported that Jesus directly asks someone if they believe he has the power to heal them (πιστεύετε, "do you believe?"). Since the blind men had already revealed their faith in their cry for mercy, the question takes on a didactic character (cf. too v 29), calling attention to the importance of faith. In the other healing-of-the-blind narratives (20:32; Mark 10:51; Luke 18:41), Jesus asks instead, "What do you want me to do?" which is another way of eliciting a response of faith. By this emphasis on faith, the present passage is linked directly with the preceding healing narratives where faith is stressed (see 8:2, 10, 13 [26]; 9:2, 18, 21). The answer of the blind men is as direct as was the question of Jesus: ναὶ κύριε, "Yes, Lord." (For the use of κύριε in this connection, see *Comment* on 8:2; cf. 8:6, 8, 21, 25.)

29–30a ἥψατο τῶν ὀφθαλμῶν αὐτῶν, "he touched their eyes." Again Jesus heals directly, by touch (cf. 8:3, 15; cf. 9:25), as will also be the case in 20:34. And again he stresses the relationship between faith and healing, κατὰ τὴν πίστιν ὑμῶν γενηθήτω ὑμῖν, "Let it be to you according to your faith" (cf. 8:13; v 28, especially in the preceding pericope, v 22; and 15:28). The fact of faith is in view here, not the quantity. The miracle is accomplished immediately—καὶ ἠνεῴχθησαν αὐτῶν οἱ ὀφθαλμοί, "and their eyes were opened"—thus testifying to the astonishing power and authority of Jesus.

30b–31 Once again, despite the admonition to silence, the report of the healing spreads almost inevitably. Matthew thus shows that although Jesus wants to avoid stirring up the popular expectations concerning the Messiah, which have no room for his more important work on the cross, the news of such wonderful deeds is simply too good to be kept a secret. The strong verb ἐνεβριμήθη, "warned," is found only here in Matthew (cf. Mark 1:43; 14:5). For the stress on the secrecy motif, see *Comment* on 8:4. As a part of his christological argument in these chapters, Matthew repeatedly indicates the impression of the healings upon the people (see 8:34; 9:8, 26, 33). V 31 is especially close in wording and parallel in substance to v 26. The point in these verses is not the disobedience of those who have been healed (no faulting of them for their disobedience is found) but simply the impossibility of stifling the incredibly good news of the kingdom.

Explanation

It is no coincidence that the blind are the first to call upon Jesus as "Son of David." A number of miracles performed by Jesus in these chapters have messianic associations. The blind in Israel, we can be certain, would have known well that the Scriptures spoke of the time to come when the blind would receive their sight. It would be the age of fulfillment, the age of the kingdom promised to David's Son. Now they heard that this Jesus had been proclaiming the presence of that kingdom and that he was performing miracles of healing. And so they seek out Jesus and cry to him for mercy as the Son of David. They believe in him and they receive their sight. Again Matthew intends not simply a historical report about the past but an illustration of the power and authority of the Lord of the Church. Neither the literally blind of Matthew's church nor the literally blind of our churches receive their sight again from the Jesus in whom they believe (although it would, of course, be a mistake to assert this as an absolute impossibility), despite the present dimension of the kingdom. In those healings, however, they find the assurance that they too will ultimately see again because the literal healing of the blind points beyond itself. The image of the blind receiving their sight expresses at the same time the experience of every believer. It is a powerful symbol of the gospel whereby those who believe receive. Those who walked in darkness have thus now received light (cf. 4:16). And the children of the kingdom are now themselves in turn "the light of this world" (5:14–16).

The Healing of the Mute Demoniac (9:32–34)

Bibliography

Twelftree, G. H. "EI DE . . . EGŌ EKBALLŌ TA DAIMONIA." In *Gospel Perspectives 6: The Miracles of Jesus*, ed. D. Wenham and C. Blomberg. Sheffield: JSOT, 1986. 361–400.

Translation

[32] *And while the blind men[a] were going out, look, they brought to him a mute man[b] who was demon possessed.* [33] *And when the demon had been cast out, the mute spoke. And the crowds marveled, saying: "Never has anything like this been seen in Israel."* [34] *But the Pharisees began to say: "He is casting out demons by the power of[c] the prince of demons."* [d]

Notes

[a] αὐτῶν, lit. "they," by which is understood the blind men of the preceding narrative.

[b] A few important witnesses (א B *f*[13] sy[s.p] co) omit the redundant ἄνθρωπον, "man," but the sense of the passage is not thereby affected.

[c] "The power of" is added to translation to clarify sense.

[d] A few MSS representing the Western text (D it[a.d.k] sy[s]) omit this verse entirely. It is possibly an insertion here from 12:24 (or Luke 11:15), but the MS evidence for its inclusion is overwhelming, and Metzger points out that the verse is needed to make sense of 10:25. See *TCGNT*, 25–26.

Form/Structure/Setting

A. This short healing narrative is the tenth and last of the miracle stories collected by Matthew in chaps. 8 and 9. Since Matthew has already given an exorcism narrative (8:28–34), the emphasis here falls on the gift of speech (and hearing?) to the mute (the exorcism itself is referred to only in a genitive absolute construction). With this miracle Matthew rounds out his representative catalogue of the powerful deeds of Jesus, thus preparing for the charge to the disciples in 10:1, 8 and the response to the disciples of John in 11:5, where the κωφοί, "mute, deaf," are explicitly mentioned.

B. As in the preceding pericope, the present story is also paralleled by a second Matthean passage (12:22–24). In both passages a demon-possessed mute is brought to Jesus, and he is healed; the crowds are astonished and register a conclusion; and finally, the Pharisees charge that Jesus casts out demons by the prince of demons. The differences, on the other hand, are comparatively superficial: in chap. 12, the man is both mute and blind; the healing is described with the verb ἐθεράπευσεν αὐτόν, "he healed him," rather than by reference to the casting out of the demon; the man is accordingly enabled to see as well as speak; the verb ἐξίσταντο, "they were astonished," is used instead of ἐθαύμασαν, "they marveled," in describing the crowd's reaction; the crowd says, "Is not this the Son of David?" instead of "Never has anything like this been seen in Israel"; and finally, the comment by the Pharisees is worded in a slightly different way, employing the name Beelzebul. Probably we have here two originally independent stories of demon exorcism that have taken the same form, concluding with a christologically related conclusion from the crowds. To each story, furthermore, has been added the same accusation of the Pharisees. This is the kind of thing that can easily happen in the process of oral transmission; originally similar stories tend to become even more similar by mutual influence. See further *Comment* on 12:22–24.

C. Except for the statement of the crowd, which is unique to Matthew, the present passage may have been drawn from some form of Q (cf. Luke 11:14–15). The same story at least seems to be recounted in Luke, which, however, lacks any actual comment from the crowd beyond the fact that (as in our pericope) "they marveled." The opening genitive absolute and the words ἰδοὺ προσήνεγκαν αὐτῷ, "look, they brought to him," are Matthew's own. The unique statement of the crowd in Matthew is close to the comment in Mark 2:12 at the conclusion of the healing of the paralytic and the forgiving of his sins: οὕτως οὐδέποτε εἴδομεν, "We have never seen anything like it!" (cf. Matthew's οὐδέποτε ἐφάνη οὕτως ἐν τῷ Ἰσραήλ, "Never has anything like this been seen in Israel!"). The closing words of the passage, τῷ ἄρχοντι τῶν διαμονίων ἐκβάλλει τὰ δαιμόνια, "by the prince of demons he casts out demons," are found in verbatim agreement in all the parallel passages (i.e., Mark 3:22; Luke 11:15), except 12:24 where, however, the wording is similar.

D. This short healing pericope consists typically of the statement of need and the healing but is followed by the unusual record of two opposing responses, one from the crowd and another from the Pharisees: (1) presentation of the need (v 32); (2) the healing of the demoniac and his speaking (v 33a); (3) the positive response of the crowd (v 33b); and (4) the accusation of the Pharisees (v 34). The two responses point to the fact that the same evidence can produce opposite evaluations (indeed as for all of chaps. 8–9). (Matthew pursues this point later in 11:25–27.) By its nature, in this healing pericope there can be no dialogue, and thus there is no testing of faith as in other such narratives. Matthew's terseness is again remarkable.

Comment

32 αὐτῶν δὲ ἐξερχομένων, "while they were going out," found only in Matthew, is Matthew's transition from the preceding story to the present narrative. This has the effect not only of providing a smoother flow but also of pointing to the constant pressure upon Jesus to heal: no sooner are the blind healed and depart than the next candidate for healing is presented. On the possibility that αὐτῶν refers to Jesus and his disciples rather than to the blind men, see *Comment* on the next verse.

Matthew's characteristic ἰδού, "look," introduces the new story illustrating Jesus' power in deeds of healing. προσήνεγκαν αὐτῷ, "they brought to him," is found in connection with healing narratives in 4:24; 8:16; 9:2 (present tense); 12:22; 14:35. It is clear from the following verse that ἄνθρωπον κωφὸν δαιμονιζόμενον, "a mute man who was demon possessed," means that the man's inability to speak was caused by the demon possession. For the connection between disease and demon possession, see *Comment* on 8:28. κωφός can mean either deaf (cf. 11:5, quoted from Isa 35:5) or mute; the context here indicates the latter.

33 Matthew's terseness results in the lack of any actual statement that Jesus cast out the demon or enabled the man to speak. This is, of course, assumed, especially given the pattern of the preceding narratives. The former is described in a genitive absolute, ἐκβληθέντος τοῦ δαιμονίου, "when the demon had been cast out"; the latter is indicated simply in the affirmation ἐλάλησεν ὁ κωφός, "the mute spoke." The sovereign power of Jesus is responsible for both, but the focus falls on the ability of the man to speak. A slight awkwardness results from the mention of οἱ ὄχλοι, "the crowds," at this point since according to the larger flow of Matthew's narrative, Jesus is still in the house (v 28). (It would be possible to take the opening genitive absolute of v 32 as referring to Jesus and his disciples, but this conclusion does not fit well with the following προσήνεγκαν αὐτῷ, "they brought to him.") Probably Matthew at this point is unconcerned with details of this kind. His purpose is to record the astonishment of the crowds—whether they saw the miracle itself or only the results of it afterwards. ἐθαύμασαν, "they marveled," is a nearly formulaic description of the response to the deeds of Jesus (cf. *Comment* on 8:27). The conclusion, "never has anything like this been seen in Israel" (cf. Mark 2:12), must refer not to demon exorcism, which was performed by others (cf. 12:27), but to the miracle of the cure of the man's inability to speak (cf. 15:31). The conclusion to be drawn is that something remarkably new, indeed something eschatological (cf. 12:28), is happening in Israel: the Messiah has come to Israel and with him signs of his messianic kingdom.

34 In contrast to the crowds, the Pharisees had already begun to evaluate Jesus in a hostile manner. They do not deny the power of Jesus but attribute the exorcism to black magic, as a deed performed in the name of the prince of demons. τῷ ἄρχοντι τῶν δαιμονίων, "the prince of demons," is assigned the name Beelzebul in the important cognate passage, 12:24–28, where the accusation is again made and where the argument of the Pharisees is refuted by Jesus. Matthew is content here simply to record the objection since it is dealt with later. This verse presents the first open expression of hostility on the part of the Pharisees (9:3 is still private; 9:14 is only implicit). What begins here will escalate quickly as the Gospel proceeds (cf. 12:2, 10, 14, 24; 22:15) and anticipates what will be the disciples' own experience (cf. 10:24–25).

Explanation

Again Jesus performs a messianic sign that points to his identity and his power and authority. The crowd marvels, for nothing like this had been seen in Israel.

This reaction points to the newness of what Jesus represents. The direct, unmediated healing of the man's inability to speak symbolizes the fulfillment and joy of the kingdom announced by Jesus. The image of the mute being given the gift of speech is itself again suggestive of the gospel. The readers of Matthew know that they participate in the good experienced by the mute demoniac. And those who have been healed in the most fundamental sense of the word—who have experienced salvation—are now themselves liberated to speak the good news of the kingdom. The response to that proclamation will be mixed, as it was to the ministry and message of Jesus. While some will respond positively, others like the Pharisees will be all too ready to find only evil in Jesus and his disciples (cf. 10:25).

A Summary and the Call for Workers   (9:35–38)

Bibliography

Legrand, L. "The Harvest Is Plentiful (Mt 9.37)." *Scr* 17 (1965) 1–9. **Venetz, H.-J.** "Bittet den Herrn der Ernte: Überlegungen zu Lk 10.2/Mt 9.37." *Diak* 11 (1980) 148–61.

Translation

[35] *And Jesus went about all the cities and villages teaching in their synagogues and proclaiming the gospel of the kingdom and healing every sickness and every malady.*[a]
[36] *And as he saw the crowds, he*[b] *was moved with compassion for them because they were harassed*[c] *and confused*[d] *"like sheep who have no shepherd."* [37] *Then he said to his disciples: "The harvest, on the one hand, is large, but the workers, on the other, are few.* [38] *Pray therefore to the Lord of the harvest that he may send out workers into his harvest."*

Notes

[a] A number of MSS have additional words here: C³ K Γ Θ c vg^mss add ἐν τῷ λαῷ, "among the people," by influence from 4:23; a b h add καὶ πολλοὶ ἠκολούθησαν αὐτῷ, "and many followed him"; ℵ* L f¹³ g¹ have a combination of both of these additions (ℵ*, however, lacks πολλοί, "many"). But the MS evidence against these additions is overwhelming.
[b] C N f¹³ g¹ sy^p.h insert ὁ Ἰησοῦς, "Jesus."
[c] L V 1424 have ἐκλελυμένοι, "weary," instead of ἐσκυλμένοι (from σκύλλειν).
[d] The translation of ἐρριμμένοι (from ῥίπτειν) is difficult. The verb literally means "to throw" or "to lie down." A possible connotation of being "thrown" is to be in a state of helplessness or confusion.

Form/Structure/Setting

A. A major section of the Gospel has been completed with the preceding narrative, the tenth miracle of chaps. 8–9. There will be more healing narratives in Matthew (the next is in 12:9–14), but for the time being Matthew turns to other concerns. The present passage together with the opening verses of chap. 10 (10:1–4) is a transition and preparation for the second major teaching discourse (the remainder of chap. 10). Thus, the first part of the present passage (v 35) can be seen to serve as a summarizing inclusio in relation to 4:23–25. In between these two miracle summary passages, Matthew has given examples of the powerful, authoritative words (chaps. 5–7) and deeds (chaps. 8–9) of the Messiah. In chap. 10 he returns again to the words of Jesus. Now they are directed to the disciples as instructions for the missionary work Jesus sends them out to do. The second part of the present pericope (vv 36–38) deals with the sending out of workers (cf. 10:1) to extend the mission work of Jesus. It serves as both transition and introduction to the discourse that follows.

B. Matthew's relation to the Synoptic tradition in this passage is complicated. V 35 is practically a verbatim repetition of 4:23, the only differences being the latter's ἐν ὅλῃ τῇ Γαλιλαίᾳ, "in the whole of Galilee," for τὰς πόλεις πάσας καὶ τὰς κώμας, "all the cities and the villages," and the final three words of 4:23, ἐν τῷ λαῷ, "among the people." The Matthean summary in these two passages has a formulaic ring to it. 4:23 seems dependent to some extent on Mark 1:39, but the verb περιῆγεν, "went about," both in 4:23 and here may depend on Mark 6:6b. V 36 is clearly dependent on Mark 6:34. There Matthew only restructures the opening words (omitting Mark's ἐξελθών, "when he went out," and changing εἶδεν, "he saw," to ἰδών, "seeing"); omits Mark's πολύν, "large," before ὄχλον, "crowd," changing the latter to a plural (cf. 14:14 for more exact agreement here); adds the participles ἐσκυλμένοι, "harassed," and ἐρριμμένοι, "confused"; and deletes Mark's final words, "and he began to teach them many things" (cf. v 35). Matthew's final two verses (37–38) are, on the other hand, drawn from Q, and except for the introductory words (e.g., τοῖς μαθηταῖς, "to the disciples," for Luke's πρὸς αὐτούς, "to them"), the words of Jesus are quoted in verbatim agreement with Luke 10:2 (except for the reversed order of ἐκβάλῃ ἐργάτας).

C. The pericope falls into three parts: (1) the formulaic summary of Jesus' ministry (v 35), expressed by the three parallel participles (διδάσκων, κηρύσσων, θεραπεύων, "teaching, proclaiming, healing"); (2) the statement about the compassion of Jesus for the crowds, together with the quotation of Num 27:17 (v 36); and (3) the harvest and the need of workers, divided into (a) a description of the need in parallel clauses (v 37) and (b) the call for prayer for the meeting of that need (v 38).

D. The saying of Jesus in vv 37–38 is found exactly in the *Gospel of Thomas* (logion 73). The Johannine passage about the time of the harvest (John 4:35) is closely related to the present passage: "I tell you, lift up your eyes, and see how the fields are already white for harvest"—words that are also followed by reference to labor and laborers.

Comment

35 See the *Comment* on 4:23, where this verse is found almost verbatim. The summary occurs again here in order once more to state the essence of the ministry of Jesus. περιῆγεν ὁ Ἰησοῦς τὰς πόλεις πάσας καὶ τὰς κώμας, "Jesus went about all the cities and the villages," shows that Matthew, like the other evangelists, has only given a representative sampling of the words and deeds of Jesus. The word πάσας, "all," here, as in its occurrences at the end of the verse, is again hyperbolic and symbolic. The healing ministry of Jesus (θεραπεύων, "healing") to which Matthew has just devoted so much attention and space in his Gospel is once more considered secondary to the prior references to teaching (διδάσκων) and proclaiming (κηρύσσων). See too 11:1, where διδάσκειν καὶ κηρύσσειν, "teaching and preaching," but not healing, are mentioned. At the heart of all the words and deeds of Jesus is τὸ εὐαγγέλιον τῆς βασιλείας, "the gospel of the kingdom" (the phrase also occurs not only in 4:23 but also in 24:14).

36 At some unspecified moment Jesus, surveying the crowds that now followed him everywhere, ἐσπλαγχνίσθη, "was moved with pity"—a strong word describing deep compassion. The word is used again to describe Jesus' response to need in 14:14; 15:32; 20:34 (cf. 18:27). Whereas in these instances the compassion is caused by quite specific needs, here the cause is expressed only in general terms: ὅτι ἦσαν ἐσκυλμένοι καὶ ἐρριμμένοι, "for they were harassed and confused." σκύλλειν, which occurs in Matthew only here (cf. Mark 5:35; Luke 7:6; 8:49), means "to bother" or "to harass." ῥίπτειν elsewhere in the NT always means "to throw" (cf. 15:30; 27:5) and here is perhaps used metaphorically to mean something like "confused" or "exhausted" (cf. BAGD, 736b, "lying down"; NJB: "dejected"). The reference to "sheep who have no shepherd" is a common OT image that occurs, for example, in Num 27:17; 2 Chr 18:16; and Jdt 11:19. All these passages agree verbatim: ὡς (Num 27:17, ὡσεί) πρόβατα οἷς οὐκ ἔστιν ποιμήν (cf. Zech 10:2); but none agrees exactly with Matthew's ὡσεὶ πρόβατα μὴ ἔχοντα ποιμένα. The 2 Chr 18:16 passage (cf. 1 Kgs 22:17) is suggestive in its reference to those who "have no master." What causes Jesus' deep compassion at this point is not the abundance of sickness he has seen but rather the great spiritual need of the people, whose lives have no center, whose existence seems aimless, whose experience is one of futility. The whole Gospel is a response to just this universal human need. (Cf. the reference to the gospel being sent out to "the lost sheep of the house of Israel" [10:6; 15:24]; cf. 18:12, "the lost sheep"; and 26:31, the "scattering of the sheep"; cf. 1 Pet 2:25.) Jesus, as the promised messianic ruler, is to "shepherd" his people Israel (2:6, a quotation of Mic 5:1; cf. Ezek 34:23; 37:24). In relation to the concern of the following verses with the need of workers, Ezek 34:6 may be in view: "my sheep were scattered over all the face of the earth, with none to search or seek for them" (cf. Isa 53:6). Jesus himself is the shepherd of his people according to many NT references (cf. 25:32; 26:31; John 10:11–16; Heb 13:20; 1 Pet 2:25).

37–38 In the light of the great need of the people and just prior to the sending out of the twelve, Jesus refers to the harvest and the need of workers. The saying has a somewhat rabbinic tone (cf. its counterpart in *m. ʾAbot* 2:15). ὁ θερισμὸς πολύς, "the harvest is large," points distinctly to the present era of fulfillment, the era of the proclamation of the kingdom. "Harvest," like "kingdom of God," has inevitable eschatological associations but cannot mean the eschatological judgment, as it means elsewhere (e.g., Rev 14:15; cf. Matt 13:24–30; esp., 13:39, "the harvest is the close of the age"). But the eschatological tone of the word has an unquestionable urgency about it. There are many yet to be reached with the gospel of the kingdom, and the mission of Jesus must be carried on by his disciples (cf. 10:1), yet few in number, and other workers. The prayer of v 38 is that God himself ("Lord of the harvest") will also raise up others, like those of Matthew's church, to carry on the work of proclaiming the presence of the kingdom. That work is finally τὸν θερισμὸν αὐτοῦ, "his harvest," the work of the Lord of the harvest and not that of human beings.

Explanation

Matthew has concluded his presentation of the first discourse (the Sermon on the Mount) and the collection of stories concerning Jesus' mighty deeds (chaps. 8–9)—the sovereign authority of Jesus in word and deed—and returns to the general characterization of the ministry of Jesus with which he began (4:23). He calls attention once again to the teaching, proclaiming, and healing of Jesus by means of a summary statement. The center of Jesus' activity is "the good news of the kingdom." His words and deeds, indeed his very person, point to and presuppose that reality. The crowds, who think mainly of their physical maladies, have a more serious need of which those maladies are but indicators. The real need of these troubled and bewildered people, who have no master to lead them out of their plight, is met by the fundamental reality Jesus has come to bring. But a universal need of this kind, a harvest this great, requires workers to extend the proclamation of the good news. The small band of disciples is about to be sent out to that specific end. But the Christians of Matthew's church are themselves the workers sent by the Lord of the harvest. And so, as we shall see, they along with the disciples are addressed in the discourse of Jesus to be presented in 10:5–42. The prayer for workers is thus directed to and answered by the Church of every generation. As the harvest continues, so too does the need for workers.

The Second Discourse:
The Missionary Discourse   (10:1–11:1)

General Bibliography

Beare, F. W. "The Mission of the Disciples and the Mission Charge: Matthew 10 and Parallels." *JBL* 89 (1970) 1–13. **Brown, S.** "The Mission to Israel in Matthew's Central Section." *ZNW* 69 (1978) 73–90. **Combrink, H. J. B.** "Structural Analysis of Mt 9,35–11,1." *Neot* 11 (1977) 98–114. **Grassi, J. A.** "The Last Testament-Succession Literary Background of Matthew 9.35–11.1 and Its Significance." *BTB* 7 (1977) 172–76. **Mangatt, G.** "Reflections on the Apostolic Discourse (Mt 10)." *BibLeb* 6 (1980) 196–206. **McKnight, S.** "New Shepherds for Israel: An Historical and Critical Study of Matthew 9.35–11.1." Diss., Nottingham, 1986. **Morosco, R. E.** "Matthew's Formation of a Commissioning Type-Scene." *JBL* 103 (1984) 539–56. ———. "Redaction Criticism and the Evangelical: Matthew 10 as a Test Case." *JETS* 22 (1979) 323–32. **Rademakers, J.** "La Mission, engagement radical: Une lecture de Mt 10." *NRT* 93 (1971) 1072–85. **Uro, R.** *Sheep among the Wolves: A Study on the Mission Instructions of Q.* Annales Academiae Scientiarum Fennicae, Dissertationes Humanarum Litterarum 47. Helsinki: Suomalainen Tiedeakatemia, 1987. **Weaver, D. J.** *The Missionary Discourse in the Gospel of Matthew: A Literary Critical Analysis.* JSNTSup 38. Sheffield: JSOT Press, 1990.

Matthew's second major discourse presents instructions concerning the missionary work of his disciples. In the flow of Matthew's narrative, the instructions are given in the first instance to the twelve, and some material of the discourse—especially in the earlier part (e.g., vv 5–15, 23)—applies directly to the mission they are to undertake in Israel. The evangelist, however, widens the discourse to include material concerning the later, ongoing mission of the Church (cf. esp. v 18, with its reference to the gentile mission, and the eschatological aspects of the discourse, as in vv 22, 26, etc.). The discourse thus has relevance both for the sending out of the twelve and for the Church of Matthew's day and later. The mission of the Church is the mission of Jesus, for the Church too proclaims the dawning of the kingdom of God. But to engage in the mission of Jesus means also to follow him in the experience of rejection and hostility. Thus Jesus prepares his disciples for the persecution that they will experience. The disciples will be treated as was their Master, but they are not to be afraid. Nothing is more important than what they are assigned to do (cf. vv 32–33; 40–42).

Although 9:36–38 is often included in the structural analysis of the missionary discourse, since it can be regarded as a narrative introduction to the discourse proper, our analysis is limited to the discourse itself. Because of the nature of its contents, there is no consensus on its structure. Some see two major sections: vv 5b–23 and 24–42 (thus Luz); some three: vv 5b–15, 16–23, and 24–42, each of which ends with a saying introduced with the formula "truly I say to you" (thus Weaver). Davies-Allison labor very hard to find a chiasm in the seven discrete sections. The following outline follows the natural breaks in the material and simply lists the sections in their order.

   I.   Mission Instructions (vv 5–15)
   II.   The Experience of Persecution (vv 16–23)
   III. The Maligning of Both Teacher and Disciples (vv 24–25)
   IV.   Have No Fear of Your Persecutors (vv 26–31)
   V.   Confession and Denial (vv 32–33)
   VI.   Division and Discipleship (vv 34–39)
   VII. A Concluding Note on Receiving the Servants of Christ (vv 40–42)

The Empowering of the Twelve Apostles   (10:1–4)

Bibliography

Cullmann, O. "Le douzième apôtre." *RHPR* 42 (1962) 133–40. **Horbury W.** "The Twelve and the Phylarchs." *NTS* 32 (1986) 503–27. **Luz, U.** "Die Jünger im Matthäusevangelium." *ZNW* 62 (1971) 141–71 = "The Disciples in the Gospel according to Matthew." In *Interpretation*, ed. G. N. Stanton. 98–128. **Pesch, R.** "Levi-Matthäus (Mc 2.14/Mt 9.9; 10.3): Ein Beitrag zum Lösung eines alten Problems." *ZNW* 59 (1968) 40–56. **Rigaux, B.** "Die 'Zwölf' in Geschichte und Kerygma." In *Der historische Jesus und der kerygmatische Christus*, ed. H. Ristow and K. Matthiae. Berlin: Evangelische Verlagsanstalt, 1963. 468–86. **Trilling. W.** "Zur Entstehung des Zwölferkreises." In *Kirche*, ed. R. Schnackenburg et al. 201–22.

Translation

> [1] *And when he had called his twelve disciples together, he gave them authority over unclean spirits so that they could cast them out and heal every sickness and every malady.*[a]
> [2] *Now*[b] *the names of the twelve apostles are these: first Simon, who is called Peter, and Andrew, his brother, and*[c] *James the son of Zebedee and John, his brother,* [3]*Philip and Bartholemew, Thomas and Matthew, the tax collector, James the son of Alphaeus and Thaddeus,*[d] [4]*Simon the Cananean*[e] *and Judas the Iscariot,*[f] *the one who also betrayed him.*

Notes

[a] L b g[1] include ἐν τῷ λαῷ, "among the people," probably from the influence of 4:23 (cf. 9:35).

[b] δέ, "but," here translated "now," is omitted by D* Θ *f*[13] 1010.

[c] καί, "and," is omitted by ℵ* C D L W Θ *f*[1,13] TR, probably by the influence of the succeeding pairs of names.

[d] Some MSS read Λεββαῖος, "Lebbaeus" (D k μ), and some a combination of "Thaddeus called Lebbaeus" or vice versa (C* C² L W Θ *f*[1] TR). Supporting the simple "Thaddeus," however, is the strong combination of ℵ B *f*[13] lat co (thus Alexandrian, Western, Caesarean, and Egyptian witnesses). See *TCGNT*, 26.

[e] Καναναῖος, lit. "Cananean" (i.e., Zealot), found in B C (D) L N *f*[1] 33, is preferred to κανανίτης, "Cananite" (i.e., from Cana), of ℵ W Θ *f*[13] TR.

[f] Ἰσκαριώτης, "Iscariot," is the best attested reading; variant readings: Ἰσκαριώθ, "Iscarioth" (c 1424); Σκαριώτης, "Scariotēs" (D lat).

Form/Structure/Setting

A. The focus of attention now moves from the ministry of Jesus to that of the disciples. The initial response to the need for workers in the great harvest, mentioned in the preceding passage, is now seen in the empowering of the twelve to extend the ministry of Jesus (cf. vv 7–8). The twelve are the beginning of a stream of workers in the Church who will continue the work of proclaiming the presence and displaying the power of the kingdom. Matthew's first mention of "the twelve" leads parenthetically to the listing of their names prior to the instructions that are to follow.

B. Matthew as usual is dependent on Mark. V 1 is close in wording to Mark 6:7, except for Matthew's omission of the words "and he began to send them out two by two" and the addition of the words "so that they could cast them out and heal every sickness and every malady" (cf. Mark 3:15). The remaining verses are probably dependent on Mark 3:14–19. Matthew's list of the twelve (cf. too Luke 6:14–16; Acts 1:13) agrees with the order of Mark's except for two changes: Andrew, the brother of Peter, is moved from Mark's fourth position and listed immediately after Peter, thereby moving the brothers James and John to the third and fourth positions (the list of the first six names in Luke 6:14–16 agrees with Matthew's list); and Matthew reverses the order of Mark's seventh and eighth names, putting Thomas before, rather than after, Matthew (only the list in Acts agrees in putting Matthew in the eighth position, although the order differs from both Matthew and Mark). The first of these changes is due to the desire to keep the pairs of brothers together, and Matthew and Luke here probably follow an ancient alternative list. The second change is harder to explain, but it may result from the desire to make Matthew the second rather than the first member of a pair and is probably related to the special description of Matthew as "the tax collector." Beyond these changes in the order of the twelve names, a few other changes from Mark are to be noted: Matthew (with Luke) describes Andrew as "his [i.e., Peter's] brother"; Matthew omits (as do the other NT lists) the description of James and John as "Boanerges," or "sons of thunder"; Matthew (alone among the NT lists) adds the description of Matthew as "the tax collector"; and finally Matthew writes Ἰσκαριώτης for Mark's Ἰσκαριώθ (see *Comment*).

> In the four NT lists of the twelve, the only fixed positions in the order of names are at the beginning of each group of four: Peter (always first), Philip (always fifth), James the son of Alphaeus (always ninth); Judas Iscariot (always last, but omitted in Acts 1:13). In the variations of the order of the other names, it is worth noting that there is never a shift of more than three places, and thus the three groups of four always remain intact. The only serious problems concerning the names (leaving the Nathaniel of John 1:45–51 out of the consideration here) are the presence of Thaddaeus in Matthew and Mark but not in Luke or Acts and the presence of Judas son of James in Luke and Acts but not in Matthew or Mark. The implication is that the two names refer to the same person (see *Comment*).

C. This passage has two obvious parts: (1) the bestowal of power upon the twelve (v 1) and (2) the listing of the names of the twelve (vv 2–4). The second part functions as a parenthesis before the giving of the instructions that follow. V 1 has parallelism in its structure with the two infinitives (ἐκβάλλειν, "cast out," and θεραπεύειν, "heal") and in the two direct objects of the second infinitive (πᾶσαν νόσον, "every sickness," and πᾶσαν μαλακίαν, "every malady"). In the listing of the twelve, particularly common names are given further designations (two Simons, two Jameses), brothers are indicated (Andrew, John), Matthew is specified as "the tax collector," and Judas is not only "Iscariot" but "the one who betrayed him."

Comment

1 Matthew puts the list of the twelve relatively late in his Gospel (cf. Mark 3:13–19) because of his desire to have the names just before the discourse concerning their mission. This delay causes some ambiguity about earlier references to μαθηταί, "disciples," where a larger circle may be in view. The first four of the twelve are introduced in 4:18–22. Matthew refers to "the twelve" again in 10:5; 11:1; 20:17; 26:14, 20, 47 (cf. 19:28). But Matthew continues to use the word μαθηταί, "disciples," frequently in his narrative, and from now on there is a natural presumption that the twelve are meant, unless the context supports a wider interpretation of the word. The choice of twelve disciples is full of symbolic meaning since the number corresponds to the twelve tribes of Israel (cf. 19:28) and in itself suggests the fulfillment of the hope of Israel (cf. Acts 28:20); it also establishes the identity of Jesus' disciples and the Church as the true Israel (cf. 1QS 8:1–19). Indeed, in the post-resurrection Church the apostles assume great importance as the locus of authority and the guarantors of the tradition. Jesus calls his disciples to himself for the purpose of equipping them for the ministry they are now to perform in his footsteps. He gives them ἐξουσία, "authority," the very thing he demonstrated about himself in the five preceding chapters (cf. 7:29; 9:6, 8). At the very end of the Gospel, when Jesus commissions the eleven to continue his work, he announces that πᾶσα ἐξουσία, "all authority," has been given to him and hence to them because he will be with them to the end of the age (28:18–20). The ἐξουσία, "authority," here is defined specifically as πνευμάτων ἀκαθάρτων, "over unclean spirits" (cf. 12:43; cf. 8:16). The result clause, ὥστε, "so that," refers accordingly not only to the casting out of the demons but also to the healing of all sicknesses and maladies (cf. v 8). This may mean that the authority over demons is linked with the healing of sickness, presupposing the popular view that most, if not all, sickness was caused by demons (see the *Comment* on 8:5–13). On the other hand, the expression θεραπεύειν πᾶσαν νόσον καὶ πᾶσαν μαλακίαν, "heal every sickness and every malady," is clearly formulaic (cf. 4:23; 9:35) and may be added here to describe further the work of the disciples and the authority Jesus gave them to perform it.

2 The word ἀπόστολος, "apostle" (Greek for the Hebrew שָׁלִיחַ, šālîaḥ), means someone who is "sent" (ἀποστέλλειν) and who shares the authority of the one who sends, as his representative. It appropriately appears only here in Matthew and is thus used exclusively in reference to "the twelve." It is a formal title of the office for the formal list of names. The initial calling of the four disciples in this verse is found in 4:18–22. The only other initial call recorded is that of Matthew, the tax collector (9:9). The names of "the twelve" (note the repetition; cf. v 5) are paired in Matthew, perhaps reflecting Mark's "two by two" (Mark 6:7). The πρῶτος before "Simon, who is called Peter" implies not just the first called but the first in rank (cf. 16:18). Peter plays a most prominent role in the Gospel as the spokesman for the apostles but most importantly as the rock (hence, "Peter") upon which Jesus promises to build his Church (twenty-three occurrences; see esp. 14:28–29; 16:16–19; 18:21; 19:27; 26:33–35). Andrew, Peter's brother, is not referred to again in the Gospel. James and John, who with Peter make up a kind of inner circle of the disciples, appear only twice again in Matthew: in the story of the transfiguration of Jesus (17:1; cf. 27:56) and in connection with their mother's special request on their behalf (20:20–28).

3 The names Philip, Bartholomew (perhaps = the Nathaniel of John 1:45–51) and Thomas occur only here in Matthew. Matthew, ὁ τελώνης, "the tax collector," is referred to only here and in the narrative of his call (9:9). James, the son of Alphaeus, and Thaddaeus are names found only here in the Gospel. Thaddaeus (also in Mark 3:18), not found in Luke 6:14–16 or Acts 1:13, is probably to be equated with Judas the son of James in Luke and Acts, who is listed after Simon rather than before Simon. The name Judas may well have been supplanted by a new one, Thaddaeus, in order for there to be only one Judas among the twelve.

4 The Simon of this verse is described as ὁ Καναναῖος, "the Cananean," derived neither from Canaan nor Cana but from the Aramaic קַנְאָן, qanʾān, meaning "zealot" or "enthusiast." The name is thus the equivalent of the label ζηλωτής, "zealot," given to Simon in the lists in Luke and Acts and may well refer to his intense nationalism and hatred of Rome. This Simon is mentioned only here in Matthew. Judas Iscariot is referred to more often than any of the other disciples in Matthew except for Peter. The name Ἰσκαριώτης, "Iscariotēs," is the Greek equivalent of the transliterated Aramaic of Mark's Ἰσκαριώθ, "Iscarioth," אִישׁ קְרִיּוֹת, ʾîš qĕrîyyôt, "man from Kerioth" (located in southern Judea, twelve miles south of Hebron [cf. Josh. 15:25]; cf. ἀπὸ Καρυώτου, "from Karuotos," in John 6:71 [א* Θ ƒ¹³]; and the D text of 12:4; 13:2; 14:22). The reading of D in the present passage is Σκαριώτης, "Scariotēs," which stimulated some scholars to understand the word as a variant of σικάριος, "dagger man," or "assassin," i.e., a militant revolutionary. There are other perhaps less plausible theories about Iscariot that depend on speculations about the underlying Aramaic (e.g., leading to such conclusions as "false, hypocrite" hence "betrayer" [ʾ îš qaryāʾ; thus C. C. Torrey], "red [ruddy]," "redhead" or "[red] dyer," "[leather] bag carrier"). The words ὁ καὶ παραδοὺς αὐτόν, "the one who also betrayed him," are added to make it quite clear which Judas this is. The epithet is found also in 26:25 and 27:3. Here it also alludes to Jesus' suffering and death, which constitute the climax of Matthew's narrative. Elsewhere Judas is deliberately identified as "one of the twelve" (26:14, 47). It is worth calling attention to the diverse and unusual character of the twelve, who include fishermen (cf. 4:18–22), a tax collector, a zealot, and a traitor.

Explanation

The disciples of Jesus are about to be sent on a mission in which they will extend the message and ministry of Jesus. To equip them to accomplish this mission, Jesus bestows upon them the ἐξουσία, "authority," they need. Without that authority there could be no such mission. The context of this mission will be spelled out in the next section (vv 5–8). The Lord is sending out workers into the harvest (9:38). The twelve are the core of the new movement representing the new era and the new activity of God. But more must go, and Matthew's readers know themselves to be in continuity with those who are sent in this pericope. Strangely, we know next to nothing about ten of the twelve. Yet they faithfully carried on with the mission Jesus assigned them. In a similar way, we know nothing about the individual members of Matthew's church—only that they, as a part of the Church throughout the ages, were called like the twelve to carry out the mission their Lord had given them. Instructions regarding their mission will follow.

Mission Instructions (10:5–15)

Bibliography

Ahern, B. "Staff or No Staff?" *CBQ* 5 (1943) 332–37. **Bartnicki, R.** "Der Bereich der Tätigkeit der Jünger nach Mt 5b–6." *BZ* 31 (1987) 250–56. **Brown, S.** "The Matthean Community and the Gentile Mission." *NovT* 22 (1980) 193–221. ————. "The Two-fold Representation of the Mission in Matthew's Gospel." *ST* 31 (1977) 21–32. **Caird, G. B.** "Uncomfortable Words: II. 'Shake off the dust from your feet.'" *ExpTim* 81 (1969) 40–43. **Cerfaux, L.** "La mission apostolique des Douze et sa portée eschatologique." In *Mélanges Eugène Tisserant.* Rome: Città del Vaticano, 1964. 1:43–66. **Fenton, J. C.** "Raise the Dead." *ExpTim* 80 (1968) 50–51. **Frankemölle, H.** "Zur Theologie der Mission im Matthäusevangelium." In *Mission im Neuen Testament,* ed. K. Kertelge. QD 93. Freiburg: Herder, 1982. 93–129. **Harvey, A. E.** "'The Workman Is Worthy of His Hire': Fortunes of a Proverb in the Early Church." *NovT* 24 (1982) 209–21. **Hooker, M. D.** "Uncomfortable Words: X. The Prohibition of Foreign Missions (Mt 10.5–6)." *ExpTim* 82 (1971) 361–65. **Jeremias, J.** *Jesus' Promise.* **Manson, T. W.** *Only to the House of Israel? Jesus and the Non-Jews.* Philadelphia: Fortress, 1964. **Schürmann, H.** "Mt 10,5b–6 und die Vorgeschichte des synoptischen Aussendungsberichtes." In *Traditionsgeschichtliche Untersuchungen.* 137–49. **Schulz, S.** "Die Gottesherrschaft is nahe herbeigekommen (Mt 10.7/Lk 10.9)." In *Die Wort und die Wörter.* FS G. Friedrich, ed. H. Balz and S. Schulz. Stuttgart: Kohlhammer, 1973. 57–67. **Scott, J. J.** "Gentiles and the Ministry of Jesus: Further Observations on Matt 10:5–6; 15:21–28." *JETS* 33 (1990) 161–69. **Wilkinson, J.** "The Mission Charge to the Twelve and Modern Medical Missions." *SJT* 27 (1974) 313–28.

Translation

[5]*Jesus sent out these twelve when he had instructed them, saying: "Go neither to the Gentiles*[a] *nor among the Samaritans.*[b] [6]*But go instead to the lost sheep of the house of Israel.* [7]*And as you go, proclaim the gospel,*[c] *saying that*[d] *the kingdom of heaven has drawn near.* [8]*Heal the sick,*[e] *raise the dead,*[f] *cleanse the lepers, cast out demons. You have received freely; give freely.* [9]*Do not acquire gold or silver or copper coins for your money belts,* [10]*nor a knapsack for the road, nor two shirts, nor sandals, nor a staff.*[g] *For the worker is worthy of support.*[h] [11]*When you enter into any city or village, carefully search for someone there who is worthy. And stay with that person*[i] *until you leave.* [12]*When you come into a household, greet it.*[j] [13]*And if the household is worthy, let your peace remain upon it, but if it is not worthy, let your peace return to you.* [14]*And as for*[k]

whoever does not receive you or listen to your words, when you are outside that house or[1] city,[m] shake off its dust from your feet. [15]*For truly I say to you, on the day of judgment it will be more bearable for the land of Sodom and Gomorrah than for that city."*

Notes

[a] εἰς ὁδὸν ἐθνῶν, lit. "in the way of Gentiles."

[b] εἰς πόλιν Σαμαριτῶν, lit. "into a city of the Samaritans."

[c] κηρύσσετε, "preach." The translation adds "the gospel" to supply the assumed object (cf. the following words).

[d] A few unimportant MSS have μετανοεῖτε ὅτι, "repent because," by influence of the parallel in 4:17.

[e] ἀσθενοῦντας, lit. "the weak."

[f] C³ K L Γ Θ TR (sy^p) sa mae omit the words νεκροὺς ἐγείρετε, "raise the dead." A number of other MSS disagree on the position of the clause in the list. Here, although (1) the position varies (as often with interpolations), (2) Matthew often has groups of three, and (3) the shorter reading is usually preferred, the committee producing the standard critical text includes the clause because of wide textual support (Alexandrian, Western, and Caesarean text types). In this case the omission in some MSS is accidental (note the similar endings of clauses). The rhythm of the passage also favors its inclusion. Furthermore, deliberate omission of the command could have been motivated by its virtual impossibility for the generation of Christians following the apostles. See *TCGNT*, 27–28.

[g] C L W f¹³ TR sy^h bo^ms and other MSS have the pl. ῥάβδους, "staffs," perhaps by way of harmonization with Mark's allowance of a (one) staff: εἰ μὴ ῥάβδον μόνον, "except only a staff" (Mark 6:8). The sing. is found in ℵ B D Θ f¹ 33 and other MSS.

[h] τῆς τροφῆς αὐτοῦ, lit. "his food." But the context suggests a somewhat broader sense of provision. K, a few minuscule MSS, it and syr^hmg read τοῦ μισθοῦ, "payment," perhaps through the influence of Luke 10:7 and 1 Tim 5:18.

[i] κἀκεῖ, lit. "there."

[j] ℵ*² D L W Θ f¹ it vg^cl and other witnesses add: λέγοντες· εἰρήνη τῷ οἴκῳ τούτῳ, "saying, 'Peace be to this house,'" words found in Luke 10:5 and implied by v 13.

[k] "As for" added to translation for clarity.

[l] τῆς οἰκίας ἤ, "the house or" is omitted in D.

[m] ℵ f¹³ vg^mss co add ἢ κώμης, "or village" (cf. v 11).

Form/Structure/Setting

A. Matthew's second major teaching discourse concerns instructions to the disciples for the completion of their mission. This section follows immediately upon the transition material of the preceding sections (9:36–10:4). The need of workers has been presented, the twelve have been given the requisite authority for their work, and they have been parenthetically named. In this first and basic section of the longer discourse, Jesus now proceeds to specific instructions to the twelve.

B. This passage apparently consists of material borrowed from Q (similar material exists in both Luke 9:2–5 and 10:4–7) and Mark (6:8–11) combined together with some material unique to Matthew, probably derived from oral tradition.

The only absolutely clear Markan influence (i.e., material not found also in Luke) is limited to the reference to μηδὲ χαλκὸν εἰς τὰς ζώνας ὑμῶν, "nor copper for your money belts" (v 9; cf. Mark 6:8, but with the singular ζώνην, "money belt"; Luke [9:3] refers only to ἀργύριον, "silver," and not to money belts), and καὶ ὃς ἂν μὴ δέξηται ὑμᾶς μηδὲ ἀκούσῃ τοὺς λόγους ὑμῶν, "and whoever does not receive you or listen to your words" (v 14; cf. Mark 6:11, with a few minor differences; Luke's wording [9:5; 10:10] is not nearly as close and lacks any reference to not listening).

Vv 5–6 are unique to Matthew (on the possible pre-Matthean function of vv 5b–6, see Schürmann). The core of v 7 is from Q (cf. Luke 9:2, which, however, has simply "preach the kingdom of God and heal the sick"). V 8, which expands the commission to the twelve and refers to giving freely as they received, is again unique to Matthew. Beginning in v 9 and through v 14 Matthew parallels Mark but is probably mainly dependent on Q. The unique Matthean material in vv 9–14 is limited to the following: the use of κτήσησθε, "acquire, get" (v 9), for Mark's and Luke's αἴρειν, "take"; the reference to χρυσόν, "gold" (v 9); the words εἰς ὁδόν, "for the road," after "knapsack" (v 10); the reference to πόλιν ἢ κώμην, "city or village" (v 11; contrast "house" in Mark and Luke); the command ἐξετάσατε τίς ἐν αὐτῇ ἄξιός ἐστιν, "search out for someone in it who is worthy" (v 11); the command ἀσπάσασθε αὐτήν, "greet it" (v 12; Luke 10:5 supplies the greeting); and the reference to Gomorrah in v 15 (cf. Luke 10:12). Finally, Matthew omits the words "for a witness against them" (Mark 6:11; Luke 9:5) in relation to the shaking of the dust (κονιορτόν with Luke, against Mark's χοῦν) off the feet (v 14), probably as redundant in the context that follows (v 15).

C. The differences between the four lists of what to take on the missionary journey are not significant since essentially the same point is being made by all: one is not to be encumbered by the usual equipment taken on journeys. There is clearly a tendency in the lists for the later ones to become more stringent in their stipulations. Thus, whereas Mark (6:8–11) allows a staff and sandals, Matthew (v 10) and Luke (9:3 prohibiting a staff; 10:4 prohibiting sandals) disallow both. Luke has the further command not to greet those on the road (10:4). Since it is practically unthinkable that Jesus would have prohibited sandals or a staff (moreover, as France points out, v 14 presupposes sandals), both extremely practical for travel at that time, the restrictions against these in Matthew and Luke must either be understood as directed against extra sandals (cf. Luke 10:4, βαστάζετε, "carry," i.e., in addition to wearing) and staff or, more likely, as an idealization of the urgency of the mission and the total dependence upon the Lord (cf. Luke 22:35). Also, Luke 22:36 suggests that the restrictions were temporary rather than binding in the new (and increasingly hostile) era of the post-resurrection Church. Hospitality in Jewish towns and villages would not be difficult for the disciples to obtain; the closeness and solidarity of the Jewish people in Israel and the proximity of such communities would make this mission possible. Travel outside Israel in gentile lands would not be possible in this same way.

D. As in the first discourse, the present discourse is full of parallel structures, involving repetition and symmetry of the type one would expect in material designed for memory and oral transmission. Some of these aspects can be pointed out in connection with the following outline of this section of the discourse: (1) the direction away from the Gentiles and Samaritans (in parallel sentences, v 5b) and to the "house of Israel" (v 6); (2) the message to be proclaimed (in the formula of 3:2 and 4:17, v 7) and the deeds to be performed (four parallel clauses, v 8a–d); (3) the question of daily needs: (a) the gospel to be given freely (parallel clauses, v 8e), (b) the disciples to travel light (a list of seven items, vv 9–10a), (c) the provision to be expected (v 10b); (4) the procedure for finding lodging (parallelism in verbs, v 11); (5) the giving or non-giving of peace to a household (symmetrical parallelism in syntax, vv 12–13); (6) the procedure in the case of rejection (parallelism at the beginning, but broken syntax, v 14); and (7) an oracle of warning (parallelism, v 15). The artistic structure exists at the level of verses and half verses. There is little to note in terms of the macrostructure of this pericope, other than the implied invitation at its beginning and the corresponding judgment motif pertinent to those who refuse the gospel at its end. The joining together of the material as it stands also reveals certain substructures (e.g., the movement from city/village to house in vv 11–12 and the dividing point in the middle of v 13, where 13a stands together with the preceding, hospitable reception and 13b goes with the following material, i.e., the hostile rejection).

E. A number of parallel passages are found in the NT and in early Christian literature. Luke 22:35–38 is an important passage that suggests the temporary character of the details of the missionary instruction, indicating that the specific instructions are to be understood not as permanent commands but as an indication of the style of ministry (e.g., urgency, economy, single-mindedness) and the legitimacy of receiving support. On this last, rather sensitive point, Paul depends on the teaching of Jesus for the right of support, while not himself taking advantage of it (1 Cor 9:4–18, esp. v 14; 2 Cor 11:7). The same point is stressed in 1 Tim 5:18 (cf. 2 Thess 3:9), where the logion of v 10b is quoted (but with Luke's μισθοῦ, "wages" [Luke 10:7], for Matthew's τροφῆς, "food"). The importance of the whole issue of support for Christian workers ("apostles and prophets") is again raised in *Did.* 11:3–6, 11–12, and in 13:1–2, where the logion of Matt 10:10b is cited. This right to support explains the emphasis in the NT on the importance of hospitality (cf. Rom 12:13; Heb 13:2; 1 Pet 4:9).

Comment

5–6 When Jesus sent the twelve out on their mission, he first gave them instructions (παραγγείλας, which occurs again in Matthew only in 15:35). These begin with the question of whether the mission is to be directed to Samaritans and Gentiles as well as to Jews. It must have been as surprising for Matthew's first readers, for whom gentile Christianity was an undeniable reality, as it is perhaps for us, to hear that Jesus restricted the ministry of the twelve (as well as his own, too; cf. 15:24) to Israel. The disciples are prohibited from going εἰς ὁδὸν ἐθνῶν, lit. "in the way of the Gentiles," probably a Semitism meaning "toward the Gentiles" (see BAGD, 554a), and from entering πόλιν Σαμαριτῶν, lit. "a city of the Samaritans," denoting the inhabitants of a region, i.e., "among or to the Samaritans" (see BAGD, 685b). If the Aramaic word underlying πόλιν was mĕdînāʾ, which can mean "city" or "province," probably "province" is meant. The exclusion of the Gentiles and Samaritans is made clear by v 6: μᾶλλον πρὸς τὰ πρόβατα τὰ ἀπολωλότα οἴκου Ἰσραήλ, "instead to the lost sheep of the house of Israel." The same phrase is used again in Jesus' characterization of his own ministry (15:24) and recalls the reference to "sheep without a shepherd" in 9:36 (cf. Jer 50:6; Ezek 34:11, 16; for "house of Israel" cf. Ezek 34:30). "Lost sheep" here refers not to a portion of Israel (thus Stendahl, who unnecessarily identifies the phrase with the ʿammê hāʾāreṣ, "the people of the land") but to all of Israel (hence the genitive is epexegetical). The particularism of the present passage and that in 15:24 is found only in Matthew among the Gospels. It reflects accurately the perspective of first-century Judaism. The Samaritans were despised as racially intermixed and disloyal to the law, and the Gentiles were viewed as outright pagans. Both groups were outside the scope of God's promises to Israel and would only receive a portion of the overflow of blessings to Israel in the eschaton. Thus this restriction would have come as no surprise to the apostles. (Cf. the controversial character of missions to the Samaritans and Gentiles even after the resurrection of Jesus in Acts 8:14–15; 11:1–18.) For Gentiles and Jews, see also above on 8:5–13.

It is clear in Matthew that this particularism is temporary (contra S. Brown, *ST* 31 [1977] 29; cf. Hooker). In addition to repeated allusions to the acceptability of Gentiles (e.g., 2:1–12; 3:9; 8:10–11; 15:21–28), there are allusions (e.g., 22:1–10) as well as clear statements about the future situation when the gospel *will* go to the Gentiles (e.g., 21:43; 24:14; cf. already 10:18). Moreover, the great commission of 28:19 clearly countermands the present restriction. We thus encounter in Matthew what may be called a salvation-history perspective, which sees a clear distinction between the time of Jesus' earthly ministry and the time following the resurrection and thus a movement from particularism to universalism: in the former only Israel is in view; in the latter the Gentiles are also in view. (But in Matthew's view the ongoing existence of Jewish Christians and the continued evangelization of Jews remains important; cf. *Comment* on 28:19.) Why has Matthew (and he alone) preserved this obviously anachronistic material with its particularistic emphasis? Not merely for "historical" reasons, or only because it was in the tradition available to him, but rather because of the special significance of this emphasis to his Jewish-Christian readers. The fact that Jesus came initially to Israel and only to Israel underlined the faithfulness of God to his covenant promises, the continuity of his purposes, and also the truth that the church, and not the synagogue, was to be understood as the true Israel. That is, in Jesus God was being preeminently faithful to Israel; and Jewish Christians, although they are united by faith with gentile believers, have in no way believed in or become part of something alien to Israel's hope. Jesus is first and foremost Israel's savior; Israel is saved in and through the church.

7–8a With the specification of those to be reached by the mission, the purpose of the mission is now spelled out. The fundamental object of the mission is the proclamation of the dawning of the kingdom of heaven. The disciples are to go and κηρύσσετε, "preach," a verb that has thus far been used only in connection with the kingdom (see 3:1–2; 4:17, 23; 9:35; cf. 24:14). For the content of the proclamation, see 3:2 and 4:17, where the same words, ἤγγικεν ἡ βασιλεία τῶν οὐρανῶν, "the kingdom of the heavens is at hand," are found verbatim. Thus John the Baptist, Jesus, and now the disciples all proclaim the same message. For further exegetical comments, see *Comment* on 3:2. The four imperatives of v 8 are subordinate to the proclamation of the kingdom. Healing of the sick, raising of the dead, cleansing of lepers (these middle two not mentioned in v 1), and casting out of demons are not of importance in themselves but only as a part of the good news of the kingdom—indeed, it is that which they exemplify and symbolize. Matthew has given examples of each of these from the ministry of Jesus himself (cf. in order: 8:15; 9:25; 8:3; 8:32). The omission in the instructions to the disciples to heal the blind and mute, miracles performed by Jesus in 9:29, 33, is not significant, for they can be included either under healing the sick or under casting out demons. It is unlikely that the commands were intended or originally understood in any other way than literally (cf. the raising of the dead in Acts 9:36–43; 20:7–12), although by the time of Matthew's readers, when the commandments were taken as applying to them, they may have been understood in a spiritual sense, i.e., as referring to what happens in the reception of the good news of the kingdom (cf. Fenton, *ExpTim* 80 [1968] 50–51). The commission in its literal terms applied fully only to the apostolic age (cf. Wilkinson, 320).

8b–10 There is to be no charge for the proclamation or the accompanying healings. As the disciples received δωρεάν, "freely," so they are to give freely (in both cases the word is emphatic because of its position). A parallel statement concerning the Torah is found in *b. Bek.* 29a: "Just as you received it [Torah] without payment, so teach it without payment" (cf. *m. ʾAbot* 1:3, 13; *m. Ned.* 4:3). But while there can be no question of "selling" the gospel (cf. Acts 8:20), it is at the same time true, on the other hand, that the disciples are to receive their subsistence from those to whom they go: thus, the worker is worthy of his τροφῆς, "food" (v 10b). Matthew's τροφῆς here is probably more original than the broader μισθοῦ, "wages," of Luke 10:7, but given the stipulations of the context, Matthew's τροφῆς too is probably to be understood in the somewhat broader sense of subsistence. The disciples are not to profit from the gospel, but their basic needs are to be met. Accordingly, they are not to take with them money (silver, gold, or copper) for their belts nor even to bother with the ordinary things a traveler considers, a knapsack, an extra shirt, a pair of sandals, or a staff (used both as an aid to walking and as a means of defense). They are, in fact, to be totally committed to the cause and its urgency and, in that total, unrestricted commitment, to rely exclusively (cf. 6:25–34) on the provision the Lord will make through those who receive them (cf. above *Form/Structure/Setting* §C). This instruction is in the same vein as that concerning the demands of discipleship in 8:20–22.

11 In entering a city or village, the disciples are to "search out" (ἐξετάζειν, elsewhere in Matthew only in 2:8) someone who is ἄξιος, "worthy." The "worthiness" referred to here is demonstrated, according to the following verses (cf. esp. v 14), by the receptivity shown to the disciples and their message. The worthy person is the one who provides hospitality to the disciples, and they are to remain with that person during the time of their ministry in that community (cf. the controls that had to be set upon the length of stay in *Did.* 11:4–5). Matthew refers to cities and villages as well as to houses, probably to parallel the reference to them in the description of the ministry of Jesus (9:35).

12–13 When the disciples enter a house they are to ἀσπάσασθε αὐτήν, "greet it." Presumably something more than a greeting of the household's members is meant. From v 13 it may be concluded that the "salutation" was, as Luke 10:5 has it, some such benediction as "peace be upon this house." If a household is "worthy," i.e., again "receptive" (cf. Luke 10:6, "if a son of peace be there"), the disciples are to let their peace "come" (ἐλθάτω) upon it, or perhaps "remain" upon it in light of v 12. But if the household is unreceptive, "unworthy," the peace or benediction is to return to the disciples (cf. 2 John 10). This εἰρήνη, "peace," is a benediction or blessing (the שָׁלוֹם לָכֶם, *šālôm lākem*), which cannot ultimately be separated from the deeper sense of well-being associated with the gospel and its reception. The peace that the disciples can bestow is not available where the gospel and its messengers are rejected. For the first time in this discourse (cf. 5:10–12), the resistance to the disciples' message is mentioned. This will loom larger as the discourse proceeds.

14 The reference here to those who reject not simply the disciples but also their words (μηδὲ ἀκούσῃ τοὺς λόγους ὑμῶν, "does not listen to your words") calls attention again to the primary importance of the proclamation of the gospel. In a kind of prophetic action the disciples are to shake the dust of that house or city from their feet. The rejection of the gospel entails the rejection of those who will not receive it (cf. Luke 10:10–12). For the practice of this in the early Church, see Acts 13:51 (cf. a similar practice in Acts 18:6). Jews shook the dust off their sandals when they returned from traveling in (unclean) gentile territory (e.g., *b. Sanh.* 12a; *m. Tohar.* 4:5; *m. Ohol.* 18:6; see Str-B 1:571).

15 In a judgment oracle strengthened by ἀμήν, "verily, truly," Jesus asserts that the culpability of those who reject the gospel of the kingdom will be greater on the day of judgment than that of Sodom and Gomorrah. The sins of Sodom and Gomorrah were notorious, and the cities suffered destruction for their sins (Gen 19:24–28). Accordingly they became symbolic of catastrophic judgment (see Rom 9:29; 2 Peter 2:6; Jude 7). ἐν ἡμέρᾳ κρίσεως, "in the day of judgment," refers to the day of eschatological judgment (cf. the same phrase in 11:22, 24; 12:36). The final penalty will be greater for those who have refused the gospel. The same analogy, but mentioning Sodom only, is made later in reference to the unbelief of Capernaum (11:23–24). The gravity of refusing the message and mission of Jesus could hardly be made more emphatic.

Explanation

Matthew is eager to record that Jesus sent his disciples first exclusively to the Jews, thus highlighting the fulfillment of the promises to Israel and confirming that Christianity is not a different "religion" nor one intended primarily for the Gentiles, although Jews were quickly becoming a minority in the Church of Matthew's day. The mission to the Gentiles is, however, clearly anticipated and mandated for the salvation-history time frame following the death and resurrection of Jesus. This pattern is theologically parallel to, though not the same as, the sequence of Jews-Gentiles mentioned elsewhere in the NT (e.g., in the mission work of Paul, cf. Acts 13:46; 28:28; Rom 1:16; 11:11–12, 25–26). Israel has priority because it is through Israel that God brings salvation even to the Gentiles, who, like branches, are grafted onto the olive tree of salvation. To Israel first, then, goes the message of salvation, the dawning of the kingdom of God. This is the message of the twelve, of the members of Matthew's community, and of the Church of every era. It is hard to believe, however, that Matthew's first readers believed that they were called with Jesus and the twelve apostles—whose ministry by its very nature was unique (cf. 2 Cor 12:12)—to perform the miracles listed here. Thus no mention is made of the performing of miracles in the great commission of 28:18–20, which is clearly directed not only to the apostles but to the post-resurrection Church generally. To be sure, the occasional healing miracle was experienced in the community, but this was the exception, not the norm. Thus Matthew's readers almost certainly would have understood these commandments metaphorically or spiritually—as pointing to the glorious character of salvation here and now. Response to the gospel resulted in salvation, i.e., the spiritual raising of the dead in cleansing, healing, and release from the power of evil. This gospel was to be proclaimed with an urgency that had no time for acquiring proper equipment. Although the settled Church was not called to fulfill literally the commandments given to the original itinerant missionaries, it was called to exhibit a similar mindset. Nothing was to be allowed to distract from the call to spread the message of the kingdom. Subsistence, but not profit, was the rightful expectation of those who preached the gospel (cf. 1 Cor 9:18), a point that needs reemphasis for some mass-media evangelists of the late twentieth century for whom preaching the gospel has become a business (cf. 1 Tim 6:6–10; Titus 1:11; 1 Pet 5:2). The disciples, further, were to be prepared for a mixed response to their message. Not all would receive the good news; indeed some would be hostile toward it. Reception and non-reception of the message will occupy much of the remainder of the discourse.

The Experience of Persecution   (10:16–23)

Bibliography

Bammel, E. "Matthäus 10,23." *ST* 15 (1961) 79–92. **Bartnicki, R.** "Das Trostwort an die Jünger in Mt 10.23." *TZ* 43 (1987) 311–19. **Boring, M. E.** "Christian Prophecy and Matthew 10.23—A Test Case." In *SBL 1976 Seminar Papers*, ed. G. MacRae. Missoula, MT: Scholars Press, 1976. 127–33. **Clark, R.** "Eschatology and Matthew 10:23." *ResQ* 7 (1963) 73–81; 8 (1964) 53–68. **Dupont, J.** "'Vous n'aurez pas achevé les villes d'Israël avant que le Fils de l'homme ne vienne' (Mt 10.23)." *NovT* 2 (1958) 228–44. **Feuillet, A.** "Les origines et la signification de Mt 10.23b: Contribution à l'étude du problème eschatologique." *CBQ* 23 (1961) 182–98. **Giblin, C. H.** "Theological Perspective and Matthew 10:23." *TS* 29 (1968) 637–61. **Hampel, V.** "'Ihr werdet mit den Städten Israels nicht zu Ende kommen.'" *TZ* 45 (1989) 1–31. **Kümmel, W. G.** "Die Naherwartung in der Verkündigen Jesu." In *Heilsgeschehen und Geschichte*, ed. E. Grässer, O. Merk, and A. Fritz. Marburger theologische Studien 3. Marburg: Elwert, 1965. 1:457–70. **Künzi, M.** *Das Naherwahrtungslogien Matthäus: Geschichte seiner Auslegung.* BGBE 9. Tübingen: Mohr, 1970. **McDermott, J. M.** "Mt 10:23 in Context." *BZ* 28 (1984) 230–40. **McKnight, S.** "Jesus and the End-Time: Matthew 10:23." In *SBL 1986 Seminar Papers*, ed. K. H. Richards. Atlanta: Scholars Press, 1986. 501–20. **Porter, C.** "'Wise as Serpents: Innocent as Doves': How Shall We Live?" *Encounter* 48 (1987) 15–26. **Robinson, J. A. T.** *Jesus and His Coming.* 2nd ed. Philadelphia: Westminster, 1979. **Sabourin, L.** "'You will not have gone through all the towns of Israel, before the Son of Man comes' (Mt 10:23b)." *BTB* 7 (1977) 5–11. **Schürmann, H.** "Zur Traditions- und Redaktionsgeschichte von Mt 10.23." In *Traditionsgeschichtliche Untersuchungen.* 150–56. **Scott, J. J., Jr.** "Gentiles and the Ministry of Jesus: Further Observations on Matt. 10:5–6; 15:21–28." *JETS* 33 (1990) 161–69. **Strobel, A.** *Untersuchungen zum eschatologischen Verzögerungsproblem.* Leiden: Brill, 1961. 278–86.

Translation

[16] *"Behold, I am sending you as sheep in the midst of wolves. Be as crafty, therefore, as serpents and as innocent* [a] *as doves.*

[17] *"Be wary of people. For some* [b] *will hand you over to sanhedrins, and they will scourge you in their synagogues.* [18] *And for my sake you will be led before governors and kings* [c] *for a witness to them and to the Gentiles.* [19] *But when they hand you over, do not be worried about how or even* [d] *what you should say. For what you should say will be given to you in that hour.* [e] [20] *For you* [f] *will not be the ones speaking, but it will be the Spirit of your Father who speaks through you.*

[21]"*But brother will hand over brother to death, and a father his child, and children will rise up against their parents and have them put to death.* [22]*And you will be hated by everyone because of my name. But it is the one who endures until the end who will be saved.*

[23]"*But when they persecute you in this city, flee to another one.*[g] *For truly I tell you, you will not at all complete your mission*[h] *in the cities of Israel* [i] *before the coming of the Son of Man.*"

Notes

[a] D reads ἁπλούστατοι, "quite simple."

[b] "Some" added in translation for clarity.

[c] D it syˢ have simply ἡγεμόνων σταθήσεσθε, "you will stand before governors" (for the verb, see Mark 13:9).

[d] "Even" added in translation.

[e] D L vgᵐˢˢ and a few other witnesses omit this sentence.

[f] The emphasis is contained in the redundant ὑμεῖς, "you," thus "you yourselves."

[g] C D L Θ TR read ἄλλην for ἑτέραν, with no change in meaning. D L Θ f¹,¹³ it syˢ and other MSS insert a further clause, κᾶν (ἐὰν δὲ) ἐν τῇ ἄλλῃ (ἐκ ταύτης) διώκωσιν ὑμᾶς, φεύγετε εἰς τὴν ἄλλην (ἑτέραν), lit. "and if (but if) in the other (from that) they persecute you, flee into another." The decision of the UBS committee is that the words were added to help explain the following sentence, understanding οὐ μὴ τελέσητε, "you will not have completed," as referring to the cities of refuge. See *TCGNT*, 28.

[h] For this interpretation of τελέσητε, "completed," see *Comment*.

[i] τοῦ Ἰσραήλ, "of Israel," is omitted by B and D.

Form/Structure/Setting

A. The end of the preceding passage makes it clear that some will reject the message of the kingdom. There the focus was on the plight of those who reject the message. Now the discourse moves to the effect of rejection and hostility upon the messengers. Rejection of the message will entail hostility and persecution directed against those who proclaim it. The disciples are sent "as sheep in the midst of wolves" (v 16). Advice is given here to those who find themselves in adverse circumstances. This more somber aspect of instruction to the apostles (and the Church) continues almost until the end of the discourse (i.e., to v 39).

B. The Synoptic parallels to this pericope are mainly from the eschatological discourse, in both Mark (13:9–13) and Luke (21:12). The material has an eschatological ring since it refers to a time of great trouble. Besides Matthew, only Luke (12:11–12) uses some of this material outside the eschatological discourse in connection with the theme of acceptance and rejection of the gospel, or more exactly the confession or denial of Jesus (cf. Matt 10:32–33). Matthew has apparently taken material originally from the eschatological discourse—material that refers to the (distant) future—and includes it in the missionary discourse to the twelve. Thus, Matthew applies the present discourse as much or more to the Church of his day (and onwards) as to the actual sending out of the twelve. V 18, therefore, can refer to witness to the Gentiles, something prohibited to the twelve at the beginning of the discourse (v 5).

Apart from v 16a, which is drawn from Q (cf. Luke 10:3; but ἄρνας, "lambs," for πρόβατα, "sheep"), Matthew follows Mark, although not very exactly in actual wording. Matthew's προσέχετε δὲ ἀπὸ τῶν ἀνθρώπων, "be wary of people" (v 17), is the functional

equivalent of Mark 13:9, βλέπετε δὲ ὑμεῖς ἑαυτούς, "take heed to yourselves." Thereafter Matthew agrees with Mark except for minor details: e.g., the addition of αὐτῶν,
"their," after συναγωγαῖς, "synagogues" (v 17; cf. Mark 13:9); the verb μαστιγώσουσιν,
"scourge" (a more technical term for the punishment meted out by the synagogue),
for Mark's δαρήσεσθε, "beat" (v 17; cf. Mark 13:9); the verb ἀχθήσεσθε, "you will be
led," for Mark's σταθήσεσθε, "you will stand" (v 18; Mark 13:9). Matthew omits Mark
13:10 (it is included in Matthew's eschatological discourse, 24:14). V 19 follows Mark
13:11a fairly closely (the only significant difference is Matthew's inserted πῶς, "how,"
with reference to speaking). V 20 is also very similar to Mark 13:11b, except for
Matthew's alteration of τὸ πνεῦμα τὸ ἅγιον, "the Holy Spirit," to τὸ πνεῦμα τοῦ πατρός,
"the Spirit of the Father." V 21 is the verbatim repetition of Mark 13:12. Matthew's
concluding verses (22–23), on the other hand, find no Synoptic parallels, probably
being drawn from the oral tradition available to Matthew (Schürmann, on the other
hand, regards Q as the source, locating v 23 at the end of Luke 10:1–12). V 22 is paralleled verbatim partly in 24:9 and 13. V 23b with its concern with the mission to Israel
may have been originally an independent logion attached by Matthew to the immediately preceding verses with their wider scope.

C. As usual in the discourses, the form of the material in its smaller components displays a refined structure that makes much use of parallelism. On the
other hand, the structure of the whole reveals a somewhat arbitrary juxtaposition of related material stemming from different contexts but put together here
because of the common theme. The pericope is composed of the following elements: (1) the announcement of the peril of the disciples and an appropriate
proverb with parallelism (v 16); (2) a general warning, followed by three specific
items, indicated by the verbs παραδώσουσιν, "they will hand over," μαστιγώσουσιν,
"they will scourge"—these two clauses being parallel in structure—and ἀχθήσεσθε,
"you will be led" (vv 17–18; cf. the parallel pairs, "sanhedrins" and "synagogues"
[v 17], and "governors and kings" [v 18]; in these verses both Jews and Gentiles
[v 18] are in view); (3) the encouragement not to worry about one's defense
because the Spirit will speak through one, again with much parallelism (vv 19–
20); (4) betrayal, hatred, and death for the cause of Christ (vv 21–22a), with both
parallelism and chiasmus (father-child; children-parents); (5) an encouragement
to endure (v 22b); (6) the command to flee persecution because of a serious
time limitation (v 23). In addition to the common theme of persecution and
trouble, one significant unifying element is christological. Not only does the Shepherd seek the sheep (v 16) and the Son of Man appear at the end (v 23), but the
phrases ἕνεκεν ἐμοῦ, "for my sake" (v 18), and διὰ τὸ ὄνομά μου, "on account of
my name" (v 22), point to Jesus' centrality to the gospel (cf. 5:10–11).

D. The proverbial saying of v 16b is quoted in Ign. *Pol.* 2:2 and is also found in
the *Gos. Thom.* 39 and in POxy 655.

Comment

16 Matthew's familiar ἰδού, "behold," calls attention to the remarkable statement that follows. Jesus sends out (cf. 23:34) the twelve into a hostile and
dangerous world where they will be as vulnerable as πρόβατα, "sheep," in the midst
of λύκων, "wolves." The picture of danger could hardly be sharper. While "sheep"
in Matthew usually refers to those who are lost (e.g., 9:36; 10:6; 15:24; 18:12),

here and in 26:31 it refers to the disciples (cf. 25:32–33). In both places, but especially here, the word is used to refer to the danger that threatens the disciples (Luke's "lambs" [10:3] makes the same point). The nature of this danger will be spelled out in the remainder of the discourse. For the same analogy but with a different frame of reference, see 7:15 (cf. Acts 20:29; John 10:12). In the face of the danger the disciples will encounter, they are instructed to be φρόνιμοι ὡς οἱ ὄφεις, "crafty as serpents," and ἀκέραιοι ὡς αἱ περιστεραί, "innocent as doves." This may well reflect a popular proverb. The idea of the wisdom or craftiness of the serpent goes back to Gen 3:1 where the same word, φρόνιμος, is used (cf. 2 Cor 11:3). The dove, believed by the ancients to be without bile, readily symbolized a variety of virtues (BAGD, 651–52). The instructions are both practical (cf. the command to flee persecution, v 23) and in keeping with the ethical tone of the teaching of Jesus (for ἀκέραιοι, "innocent," cf. Phil 2:15; and for the whole proverb, Rom 16:19, "wise as to what is good and innocent as to what is evil"). Thus when in danger and in persecution, the disciples need practical discernment and at the same time the sort of guilelessness that characterized Jesus.

17–18 In their mission the disciples are to be cautious of others (cf. the need for "wisdom" in the preceding verse), presumably to avoid falling into the hands of those who would do them harm. There are those who will give them over εἰς συνέδρια, "to sanhedrins" (cf. Acts 5:27; 6:12), and those who will beat them ἐν ταῖς συναγωγαῖς αὐτῶν, "in their synagogues" (cf. Acts 22:19; 2 Cor 11:23–25). Matthew's addition of "their" points to a serious cleavage between the synagogue and Matthew's Jewish–Christian community. The "sanhedrins" refers to local judicial bodies within Judaism, not to the Jerusalem sanhedrin specifically (although that sanhedrin is of course not excluded). For "scourging in their synagogues," see the close parallel in 23:34. In v 18 attention shifts suddenly and surprisingly from the strictly Jewish context thus far (cf. vv 5–6) to the mention of ἡγεμόνας, "governors" (probably Roman provincial governors), and βασιλεῖς, "kings" (cf. Acts 25:23, here a Jewish king; 27:24), and the specific reference to witnessing αὐτοῖς, "to them" (i.e., the rulers and kings), and τοῖς ἔθνεσιν, "to the Gentiles" (for similar language, see 24:14). This broadened horizon points to Matthew's combination of disparate material (cf. above *Form/Structure/Setting* §B) and to his intention that the discourse address not just the mission of the twelve but also that of the later Church. ἕνεκεν ἐμοῦ, "on my account," is a significant although indirect christological statement (cf. 5:11; 10:39; 16:25; 19:29).

19–20 When the disciples find themselves handed over (παραδῶσιν, the same verb as in v 17 and v 21) to authorities before whom they must make their defense, they are instructed not to be anxious (μὴ μεριμνήσητε; cf. the commands of 6:25, 31, 34) about what to say. δοθήσεται, "it will be given," is a divine passive wherein God is understood as the acting subject. It is, as Matthew goes on to say, τὸ πνεῦμα τοῦ πατρὸς ὑμῶν, "the Spirit of your Father," who will speak through the disciples (for this concept in the OT, see Exod 4:12). This unusual expression (substituted for Mark's τὸ πνεῦμα τὸ ἅγιον, "the Holy Spirit") is unique in the NT and reflects the Matthean preference for the intimate title "Father" (twenty times in Matthew, once in Mark, and three times in Luke). This intimacy is heightened by the addition of the personal pronoun "your" (5:16, 45, 48, etc.). The notion of Spirit-inspired utterance in special circumstances is not uncommon in the NT (cf. Acts 4:8).

21 Now the picture of persecution becomes even more grim: family members will hand one another over to be put to death. This division among family members emerges again in vv 34–36 (see *Comment* on these verses), where Mic 7:6 is quoted in making the same point. The eschatological tone of this material is obvious (cf. its location in the eschatological discourse in Mark and Luke) and points to the time of messianic woes. The handing over to be killed suggests a time of great persecution and the hostility of the powers of evil just prior to the end of the age (cf. v 22b). This verse stands here as a part of Matthew's collection of logia of Jesus pertaining to persecution. "Brother against brother" is found in Matthew only here; for children against parents (but not the reverse), see v 35.

22 The hyperbolic statement (ὑπὸ πάντων, "by everyone") in the first half of this verse points again to the time of eschatological trouble. There will be widespread hatred of those who follow Jesus and preach his message. διὰ τὸ ὄνομά μου, "because of my name," is again a highly significant christological element in this material (cf. v 18; cf. John 15:21). The words καὶ ἔσεσθε μισούμενοι ὑπὸ πάντων διὰ τὸ ὄνομά μου, "you will be hated by all on account of my name," are found verbatim in 24:9 except that the latter has τῶν ἐθνῶν, "the Gentiles," after πάντων, "all." The situation envisioned here is also anticipated in 5:11 (cf. ἕνεκεν ἐμοῦ, "on my account"), where the persecution is seen paradoxically to be a mark of the blessedness of Jesus' disciples (cf. too the Lukan parallel, 6:22, where the verb μισεῖν, "to hate," is also used [cf. too ἕνεκα τοῦ υἱοῦ τοῦ ἀνθρώπου, "on account of the Son of Man"]; cf. John 15:18; 1 John 3:13). That the persecution and hatred of v 21 and the present verse are a part of the eschatological trouble is indicated by the words ὁ δὲ ὑπομείνας εἰς τέλος οὗτος σωθήσεται, "the one who endures to the end will be saved," words that appear again verbatim in 24:13. The point of the statement is clear: the one who faithfully endures this persecution εἰς τέλος, "to the end" (i.e., the end of the person's life or the end of the persecution and hence the end of the age), will be saved (see 4 Ezra 6:25; 9:7–8; 2 Tim 2:12) and will enter finally into the blessed peace promised to the participants in the kingdom.

23 The disciples are told to flee persecution from one city to the next (cf. ἀπὸ πόλεως εἰς πόλιν, "from city to city," 23:34; cf. 24:16; Acts 8:1; 14:6). The following statement constitutes one of the most difficult challenges to the interpreter of Matthew. (For a history of interpretation of this difficult text, see Künzi; see too Sabourin.) A similar problem emerges in 16:28 and 24:34, which possibly may throw light on the present passage, although each passage must be handled on its own. Much to be preferred is an explanation that makes coherent all three passages (see *Comment* on 16:28 and 24:34). The present verse was most likely a separate logion originally (so, rightly, Kümmel) and was placed here by the evangelist because of its appropriateness. It makes little difference whether οὐ μὴ τελέσητε τὰς πόλεις τοῦ Ἰσραήλ, "you will not at all complete the cities of Israel," is taken to mean "you will not have finished evangelizing" (this can hardly mean Jewish evangelism through the ages [contra Davies-Allison], thus making the point irrelevant for those who first heard these words), or "you will not at all have used up all the cities available for refuge (from persecution)." Either case involves a time limitation (contra A. L. Moore, *Parousia*), i.e., the Son of Man will come and bring that situation to an end, thus bringing comfort and hope to those being persecuted. The crux is what is referred to by the words ἕως ἂν ἔλθῃ ὁ υἱὸς τοῦ ἀνθρώπου, "until the Son of Man comes."

At least three possibilities can be mentioned: (1) the parousia or coming of the Son of Man, i.e., the beginning of the eschaton proper (Künzi, Bonnard, Gundry); (2) the destruction of Jerusalem, i.e., the judgment of the Son of Man upon Israel (Bullinger; Lenski; Lagrange; J. A. T. Robinson, *Coming*, 74–78; Benoit; Feuillet); or (3) some striking experience of the power of the new age, such as the death (R. Clark) or the resurrection of Jesus (Jeremias, *New Testament Theology;* Barth, *Church Dogmatics,* 4.1:295; Stonehouse, *Witness*, 240; Sabourin, *BTB* 7 [1977] 5–11; Albright-Mann; Sabourin, *Matthew*), the pouring out of the Spirit at Pentecost (Calvin, Beza), or even the success of the gentile mission (or a combination of these; cf. Gaechter). The first possibility, which has the advantage of being the most natural understanding of the clause (cf. 24:30, quoting Dan 7:13–14), would normally be preferred. In this case Jesus assumes the parousia will occur in the not too distant future, a view that is theologically justifiable (i.e., the dawning of the kingdom implies the proximity of the newness of the eschaton proper) but, as we know (and perhaps Matthew's readers did too), has proved to be historically wrong. Nevertheless, if the alternative views about to be mentioned should finally be regarded as unsatisfactory, the first possibility may remain the most attractive, taking into account Jesus' full humanity and his own self-confessed ignorance about the time of his parousia (24:36). On the other hand, the other possibilities should not be ruled out too quickly. Künzi, who opts for the eschatological view, still finds value in the non-eschatological interpretations of the phrase. The destruction of Jerusalem (A.D. 70) may possibly have already occurred when the Gospel was written and could easily have been understood as a judgment brought by the Son of Man. This interpretation has the advantage of linking the statement of v 23b closely with the command of v 23a: when the disciples encounter hostility and rejection of the gospel, they are to move on to the next town to complete the mission to Israel before it is too late (cf. 7:6). Perhaps what is in view is the time frame already encountered in 10:5–6; that is, during the time of Jesus the focus of the mission is on the Jews, but after the resurrection of Jesus and the experience of the Spirit at Pentecost, the focus of the mission will quickly move to the Gentiles (cf. Scott). Matthew's church knows that it exists in the time predicted by Jesus, when the Gentiles would hear and respond to the message of the gospel; it probably has not, however, given up on evangelizing the Jews (see on 28:19). If Jesus truly contemplated a time to come when the gospel would go to the Gentiles, it is unlikely that his reference to the coming of the Son of Man meant the parousia, since this event would then occur before the end of the (rather limited) mission to the Jews (McNeile regards this as "impossible"). Carson rightly notes that "'the coming of the Son of Man' bears in Matthew the same rich semantic field as 'the coming of the kingdom'" (253).

In its context, the most natural interpretation of 23b is the following. The γάρ, "for," links this sentence closely with the preceding sentence, providing the ground or reason for fleeing, and thus the two sentences should be understood together (contra Bammel, Green). οὐ μὴ τελέσητε τὰς πόλεις τοῦ Ἰσραήλ, "you will not at all complete the cities of Israel," refers either to exhausting the cities that can be used for refuge from persecution or to the completion of the task of evangelizing, or both (since the former implies the latter). In short, the mission to Israel—the specific mission referred to in v 6 and not an open-ended mission to the Jews in the indeterminate future—will not be concluded before ἔλθῃ ὁ υἱὸς τοῦ ἀνθρώπου, "the Son of Man comes" (i.e., Jesus; for the title "Son of Man," see *Excursus* at 8:18–22). The classical meaning of the coming of the Son of Man, as, for example, found in 16:27–28 and 24:30, relies on Dan 7:13–14 and refers to the end of the present age and the parousia or second coming of Jesus. But we can hardly accept that meaning here since Matthew tells us in several places of a mission to the Gentiles that must take place before the end of the age (cf. 21:43; 24:14). That is, the mission to Israel cannot be interrupted before its conclusion by the parousia without the necessary negation of an important strand of unambiguous material in the Gospel (see too esp. 28:19). Thus the coming of the Son of Man here must refer to something else. Probably we should dismiss the interpretation (e.g., Dupont) of the phrase as meaning "until I [i.e., 'the Son of Man' in a non-titular sense as simply a circumlocution for 'I'] join you," namely, a few weeks or months later (unless such an innocuous statement was somehow misunderstood by the Church). There is furthermore no evidence of persecution of the degree referred to in 23a at this early point. This leaves the possibility of a more dramatic "coming of the Son of Man" in the resurrection of Jesus, in the coming of the Spirit at Pentecost, or in the power and success of the gentile mission. The first two possibilities again seem too early for the experience of persecution, and the last is perhaps too nebulous. A final possibility, and the best one, is that the phrase refers to the coming of the Son of Man in judgment in the destruction of Jerusalem in A.D. 70. Three important points argue in favor of this conclusion: (1) the destruction of Jerusalem foreshadows and is typologically related to the final judgment (see *Comment* on chap. 24) and hence can also be seen as the work of the Son of Man (cf. 24:27–31); (2) the destruction of Jerusalem symbolizes the rejection of the gospel by the Jews and thus the shift of salvation-history from the Jews to the Gentiles, the former losing their priority; and (3) the abundant evidence of Jewish persecution of Christians prior to (as well as after) A.D. 70. According to this interpretation, the meaning of v 23b becomes the following: this exclusive mission of the twelve to Israel, which reflects their salvation-historical priority over the Gentiles, will not reach its completion before it is interrupted by the coming of the Son of Man in judgment upon Jerusalem, thereby symbolizing the time frame shift wherein the Gentiles, rather than the Jews, assume priority in the purpose of God. This mission to the Jews, reflecting their place in salvation-history, thus has a time limitation, the end of which (but not the end of Jewish evangelism) will be marked by the coming of the Son of Man in judgment upon Israel.

Explanation

The strangeness of this new emphasis on the persecution, suffering, and even death of the very ones who proclaim the fulfillment of the promises, the good news of the kingdom, is remarkable. There is a sharp incongruity, which no doubt impressed itself on the disciples. How could a message of such joy and power, if it were true, be compatible with the things the disciples are now told to expect? The disciples, like the Church of every age, had to learn about the present as a kind of interim period, one of fulfillment, yet short of consummation, one in which suffering was being conquered, but still clearly experienced. Yet they are sent by Jesus, and the Spirit of their Father will provide whatever defense they may need. There is, on the one hand, no flashy heroism here, no martyr complexes—they are to be crafty and to flee. Yet, on the other hand, there is a call to endurance. These who endure will finally receive fully and perfectly that eschatological blessing called salvation, that perfect and lasting *shalom* (ultimate well-being). What the disciples experience in their mission work will be the experience of all messengers of the gospel to the end of the age (cf. chap. 24).

The Maligning of Both Teacher and Disciples (10:24–25)

Bibliography

Gaston, L. "Beelzebul." *TZ* 18 (1962) 247–55. **Limbeck, M.** "Beelzebul—eine ursprünglich Selbstbezeichnung Jesu?" In *Wort Gottes in der Zeit.* FS K. H. Schelke, ed. H. Feld and J. Nolte. Düsseldorf: Patmos, 1973. 31–42. **MacLaurin, E. C. B.** "Beelzeboul." *NovT* 20 (1978) 156–60.

Translation

²⁴ "*A disciple is not above the* ᵃ *teacher, nor is a servant above the* ᵇ *master.* ²⁵ *It is enough for the disciple to be like the* ᶜ *teacher and the servant like the* ᵈ *master. If they called* ᵉ *the master of the house 'Beelzeboul,'* ᶠ *how much more will they malign* ᵍ *the members of his household.*"

Notes

ᵃ Some MSS (‫א‬ W *f*¹³ sy) have αὐτοῦ, "his," perhaps through the influence of its presence in v 25, modifying "teacher." Cf. too the αὐτοῦ in the second half of this verse (see following *Note*).

ᵇ αὐτοῦ, lit. "his."

ᶜ αὐτοῦ, lit. "his."

ᵈ αὐτοῦ, lit. "his."

ᵉ D has the present tense καλοῦσιν, "(if) they call"; a few MSS have the aorist middle ἐπεκαλέσαντο (‫א‬* L N), which, however, does not affect the meaning.

ᶠ Some MSS have slightly different spellings: Beezeboul (‫א‬ B and a few others); Beelzebub (c vg syˢ·ᵖ).

ᵍ "Will they malign" added in translation to complete the sense.

Form/Structure/Setting

A. The discussion now proceeds to relate the suffering and rejection to be experienced by the disciples to that which has begun already but which will increase dramatically and be experienced even by Jesus himself. If he is to be treated rudely and rejected, so too must they expect the same. This emphasis will become sharper as the Gospel proceeds, coming to its climax in connection with Jesus' direct predictions of his passion (see 16:24–26).

B. Part of this short passage is borrowed from Q, and part is unique to Matthew; Mark has no parallel to this material. The opening words οὐκ ἔστιν μαθητὴς ὑπὲρ τὸν διδάσκαλον, "a disciple is not above the teacher," are found verbatim in Luke 6:40 but not in a context referring to persecution. The remainder of v 24, the servant/Lord statement, however, is not found in Luke; John has a close, but independent, parallel, which is connected in 15:20 with the expectation of persecution as in Matthew: οὐκ ἔστιν δοῦλος μείζων τοῦ κυρίου αὐτοῦ, "the servant is not greater than his Lord" (cf. too the same words verbatim in 13:16, referring to foot washing, followed by a similar statement concerning an apostle and the one

who sends). V 25 finds only a partial parallel in Luke 6:40b, which says: "everyone who is fully trained will be like his teacher." The reference to Beelzeboul in v
25b anticipates the explicit charge recorded in 12:24 (cf. 9:34).

C. The pericope consists of three parts: (1) the disciple/servant is *not above*
the teacher/master (v 24); (2) the disciple/servant is *to be like* the teacher/mas-
ter (v 25a); and (3) the result: the former can expect to be treated like or worse
than the latter (v 25b). The parallelism especially of v 24, but also of v 25a, is
notable and again suggests a formulation designed for memorization.

Comment

24–25 The thought of vv 24–25a is self-evident and hardly needs articulation
except for the surprise of v 25b. Clearly the disciple is not "greater than" ($\dot{v}\pi\acute{e}\rho$)
the teacher ($\mu\alpha\theta\eta\tau\acute{\eta}s$, "disciple," and $\delta\iota\delta\acute{\alpha}\sigma\kappa\alpha\lambda os$, "teacher," are particularly important words for Matthew; for the latter, cf. 23:8), nor is the servant greater than
the master. "Servant" ($\delta o\hat{v}\lambda os$) and "master" ($\kappa\acute{v}\rho\iota os$, lit. "lord") are different words
for the same relationship. In both cases, one is required to be "like" ($\dot{\omega}s$) the
other, the very point of this relationship in the first place. This was an accepted
viewpoint in Palestinian Jewish culture and may reflect a Jewish proverb (cf. *Gen.
Rab.* 49:2 [30d]; *Midr. Ps.* 27 §5 [113b]; *b. Ber.* 58b). But the disciples and servants
of the messianic king who are sent to proclaim the good news of the kingdom are
not prepared at this point for the fateful rejection their teacher and Lord will
experience or for the fact that they are to experience similar treatment. The relationship between Jesus and his disciples means that they will share rejection,
hostility, and persecution. The same logion, as reflected in John 15:20 (cf. John
13:16), makes the point tersely: "The servant is not greater than his master. If
they persecuted me, they will also persecute you." Here the argument "how much
more" is *a minori ad maius* (Heb. *qal wāḥômer*). Although the name Beelzeboul
has not yet occurred in the Gospel (it will in 12:24, 27), it is implied in 9:34,
where $\tau\hat{\omega}$ ἄρχοντι $\tau\hat{\omega}\nu$ δαιμονίων, "the prince of demons" (i.e., Satan), is mentioned in the very words used to identify Beelzeboul in 12:24. In both passages it
is the Pharisees who use the name for Jesus. The name means "lord [= בַּעַל, *beʿel*,
or *baʿal*] of the house [זְבוּל, *zĕḇûl*, 'height, abode, dwelling']" and thus itself stands
as a play on words opposite Jesus as the "lord of the household" (see Gaston;
MacLaurin). "Lord of dung" is a possible, but less likely, rendering of the name.
The textual variant Beelzebub means "lord of flies" (cf. 2 Kings 1:2). The imagery of
the housemaster and household members refers here to the one who heads and
those who belong to the kingdom. οἰκιακός, "household member," occurs again
in its literal sense in v 36; οἰκοδεσπότης, "master of the house," a favorite term of
Matthew, is often used in the parables and refers almost always to God or Jesus
(e.g., 20:1, 11; 21:33); it also refers twice to the disciples as those given charge of
the kingdom (see 13:52; 24:43). Here the words "housemaster" and "household
members" reflect the same relationship as teacher/disciple and master/servant.

Explanation

Teacher and disciple, master and servant, stand together because of their respective responsibility and allegiance. Jesus and his chosen disciples stand

preeminently together. In the present discourse Jesus is instructing them to extend his ministry to Israel with the same words and deeds that characterized his own ministry, that is, with the good news of the fulfillment and the dawning of the kingdom. But if Jesus suffers hostility and rejection, so must his disciples be prepared for the same. Thus, almost by definition, with discipleship to Jesus and the witness of the gospel comes an unavoidable suffering. A large incongruity exists between the content of the message and the current experience of Jesus and the disciples; no doubt the latter had trouble assimilating the announcement of Jesus at this point, although they probably connected them with the messianic woes preceding the eschatological age itself. Nevertheless, though these words are ominous, the disciples can be comforted that Jesus will have preceded them in the experience of suffering and rejection and in turn can sustain them in the midst of it. This has been the testimony of the Church throughout the ages.

Have No Fear of Your Persecutors (10:26–31)

Bibliography

Allison, D. C. "The hairs of your head are all numbered." *ExpTim* 101 (1990) 334–36. ————. "Matthew 10.26–31 and the Problem of Evil." *St. Vladimir's Theological Quarterly* 32 (1988) 293–308. **Cook, J. G.** "The Sparrow's Fall in Mt 10:29b." *ZNW* 79 (1988) 138–44. **Marshall, I. H.** "Uncomfortable Words: VI. 'Fear him who can destroy both soul and body in hell' (Mt 10.28 RSV)." *ExpTim* 81 (1970) 276–80. **Milikowsky, C.** "Which Gehenna? Retribution and Eschatology in the Synoptic Gospels and in Early Jewish Texts." *NTS* 34 (1988) 238–49. **Pappas, H. S.** "The 'Exhortation to Fearless Confession'—Mt 10:26–33." *GOTR* 25 (1980) 239–48. **Schwarz, G.** "Matthäus 10,28: Emendation und Rückübersetzung." *ZNW* 72 (1981) 277–82.

Translation

[26] *"Therefore do not fear them. For nothing is hidden that will not be revealed and secret that will not be made known.* [27] *What I say to you in the darkness, speak in the light, and what you hear whispered*[a] *in your ear, proclaim*[b] *from the rooftops.* [28] *And do not be afraid*[c] *of those who put the body to death but who are unable to kill the soul. Fear*[d] *rather the one who is able to destroy both soul and body in Gehenna.*[e] [29] *Two sparrows are sold for a penny,*[f] *are they not?*[g] *And not one of them falls to the ground without the consent*[h] *of your Father.* [30] *Even the hairs of your own head are all numbered.* [31] *Do not fear,*[i] *therefore. You are worth more than many sparrows."*

Notes

[a] "Whispered" is not in the Gr. text, but implied by it.

[b] D Θ Origen have κηρύσσεται, "will be proclaimed" (L κηρυχθήσεται; cf. Luke 12:3), probably to maintain parallelism with the future passive tenses of the verbs in v 26. The parallel, however, is with εἴπατε, "speak," in v 27. Perhaps Luke 12:3 has been influential here.

ᶜ A number of important MSS (B D N W Θ *f*¹) have the aorist imperative (φοβηθῆτε) for the present imperative, φοβεῖσθε, perhaps from the influence of the aorist imperative at the beginning of v 26. It is unlikely that any nuance is intended by the shift of tenses, e.g., aorist: "Do not begin to"; present: "Do not keep on." See too the following *Note* and *Note* i.

ᵈ As in the preceding *Note*, some MSS (D L Θ *f*¹,¹³ TR) have the aorist imperative instead of the present.

ᵉ Gehenna is a transliteration of the Gr. γεέννη, which is itself the transliteration of the Heb. (see *Comment*).

ᶠ ἀσσάριον, a small Roman copper coin.

ᵍ This question, beginning with οὐχί, presupposes a positive answer, hence the translation.

ʰ "Consent" is added, but implied by the Gr. ἄνευ, "without" (see BAGD, 65).

ⁱ As in *Notes* c and d, some MSS (C Θ *f*¹³ TR) have the aorist imperative for the present imperative. A few MSS (W *f*¹³ vgᵐˢˢ sa) add αὐτούς, "them," to serve as a direct object for the verb.

Form/Structure/Setting

A. This segment of the discourse addresses the fear that is natural in the face of persecution. The disciples, however, are not to fear those who would do them harm, and several reasons are provided to explain why such fear is unwarranted. This pericope follows the preceding material logically and naturally.

B. Matthew follows Q quite closely here (cf. Luke 12:2–7) but prefaces the passage with an initial μὴ οὖν φοβηθῆτε αὐτούς, "therefore do not fear them" (cf. v 31 and Luke 12:7). The remainder of v 26 agrees closely with Luke 12:2. V 27, however, is rather different from Luke 12:3. The crucial difference is that Luke says that what the disciples say in secret will become known. Thus, in Hebraic synonymous parallelism: "whatever you have said in the dark will be heard in the light, and what you have whispered in private rooms will be proclaimed upon the housetops." Matthew, on the other hand, refers to what *Jesus* says in secret and what the disciples *hear* as that which the disciples are to speak in the light and proclaim from the rooftops. Matthew, whose Greek is more awkward than Luke's, probably preserves the original meaning of the words (cf. Mark 4:22), while Luke has given them a secondary, moral application. Matthew has probably omitted Q's λέγω δὲ ὑμῖν τοῖς φίλοις μου, "But I say to you, my friends" (Luke 12:4), as not fitting well into the context of the discourse (cf. vv 24–25). V 28 agrees with Luke 12:4 in content more than in wording, despite the practically verbatim agreement in μὴ φοβεῖσθε [Luke φοβηθῆτε] ἀπὸ τῶν ἀποκτεννόντων τὸ σῶμα, "do not be afraid of those who put the body to death." Luke appears to have rewritten the more primitive τὸν δυνάμενον καὶ ψυχὴν καὶ σῶμα ἀπολέσαι ἐν γεέννῃ, "the one who is able to destroy both soul and body in Gehenna," as τὸν μετὰ τὸ ἀποκτεῖναι ἔχοντα ἐξουσίαν ἐμβαλεῖν εἰς τὴν γέενναν, "the one who after killing has authority to cast into Gehenna." Matthew probably omits from Q Luke's ναὶ λέγω ὑμῖν, τοῦτον φοβήθητε, "Yes, I tell you, fear this one" (Luke 12:5). Luke's sparrows (12:6), five for two pennies, are worth even less than Matthew's two for one (v 29). Matthew here probably simplifies Q. He alone refers to a sparrow falling "to the ground" (v 29); Luke probably refines Q in saying "none is forgotten before God" (12:6). τοῦ πατρὸς ὑμῶν, "your Father," is Matthew's addition. Vv 30–31 agree essentially in wording with Luke 12:7.

C. Structurally vv 26–31 form a unit marked by the inclusio μὴ οὖν φοβηθῆτε αὐτούς, "therefore do not fear them" (v 26), and μὴ οὖν φοβεῖσθε, "therefore do not fear" (v 31a). V 28a provides yet a third prohibition of fear in this pericope.

The final words πολλῶν στρουθίων διαφέρετε ὑμεῖς, "you are worth more than many sparrows," oddly fall outside the framework: they really belong with v 29 but are placed here apparently in order to strengthen the final exhortation not to fear. Under the main rubric of the passage, "not to fear," are the following specific elements: (1) the proclamation of what was hitherto secret, a point made by (a) a general principle (v 26 with significant parallelism) and (b) the specific application to Jesus and the disciples (v 27, with syntactical parallelism); (2) an exhortation concerning fear, consisting of parallel specification of (a) whom not to fear (v 28a) and (b) whom to fear (v 28b), each with its reference to σῶμα, "body," and ψυχή, "soul"; and (3) two illustrations of the foolishness of fear, (a) concerning sparrows (v 29 and 31b) and (b) concerning hairs of one's head (v 30).

D. The reference to "what you hear in your ear, proclaim" (v 27) is found also in POxy 1.8 and alluded to in *Gos. Thom.* 33. The words about the making known of the hidden are found also in POxy 654.4 and in *Gos. Thom.* 5. V 28 is quoted in *2 Clem.* 5:4 and Justin Martyr, *Apology* 1.19.7 (cf. too *Herm. Man.* 12.6.3).

Comment

26–27 Despite the persecution and trouble that will come their way because of the proclamation of the gospel of the kingdom, the disciples are not to be afraid of αὐτούς, "them" (cf. Jer. 1:8), a general reference, which is to be connected with the unspecific "they" that is the subject of the verbs in the preceding sections (e.g., in vv 19, 23) and with τῶν ἀνθρώπων, "the people," of v 17. The logion of v 26b, "nothing is hidden [κεκαλυμμένον] which will not be revealed [ἀποκαλυφθήσεται] and secret [κρυπτόν] which will not be made known [γνωσθήσεται]," despite the eschatological ring of the words, would seem to have its original meaning in reference to the proclamation of the gospel, esp. in the post-resurrection period as in Mark 4:22. Luke, on the other hand, applies the logion to the words of the disciples (Luke 12:3, contrast Luke 8:17), i.e., as a warning concerning their private conduct, which is thus tied in with the judgment theme in Luke 12:5. The gospel, up till now veiled in a degree of secrecy, is to be made clear and plain through the preaching of the disciples and the Church. There is a kind of inevitability about this making known of the gospel through the disciples, witnessed to by the divine passive verbs ἀποκαλυφθήσεται, "will be revealed," and γνωσθήσεται, "will be made known," where God is understood as the active agent working through the disciples. This full revelation and "making known" in its contrast to the present time must refer to the Church's proclamation in the period following the resurrection (contra Luz). What Jesus speaks then "in the darkness" (ἐν τῇ σκοτίᾳ) and "in the ear" (εἰς τὸ οὖς), privately among the disciples and in sometimes cryptic language, will be spoken ἐν τῷ φωτί, "in the light," and proclaimed ἐπὶ τῶν δωμάτων, "from the rooftops." Thus the time following the resurrection will be a time of proclamation of the gospel in new strength, clarity, and power. The contrast is between the darkness of the pre-Easter period and the light of the post-Easter period (thus Davies-Allison).

28 If the mission is the will and work of God through the disciples, they need not fear. The worst that human persecution can bring, in any event, is the death of the body (σῶμα). But a human being, made in the image of God, is more than a body, being a combination of both body and soul (ψυχή). In this distinction

Matthew may well reflect the influence of Hellenistic Judaism and of contemporary martyrdom theology (cf. Wis 16:13–14; 2 Macc 6:30). The persecutors may kill the body, but only God has power over the soul and thus the whole person. It is thus God, the final judge of all, and not human beings, who alone is to be feared, that is, to be obeyed and trusted (cf. Ps 33:18) in the completion of the mission. This emphasis on freedom from fear of one's persecutors became very important to the early Church in the midst of much suffering (cf. 1 Peter 3:14; Rev 2:10). A Jewish parallel can be seen in 4 Macc 13:14: "Let us not fear him who thinks he kills." The fear of God as judge is referred to in Heb 10:31 and Rev 14:7 (cf. Jas 4:12a). It is not necessary to understand καὶ ψυχὴν καὶ σῶμα ἀπολέσαι ἐν γεέννῃ, "to destroy both soul and body in Gehenna" (a prediction found only here in the NT), as referring to a literal destruction of soul and body. This may be simply a hyperbolic description of the experience of Gehenna (Heb. גֵּי הִנֹּם, gê hinnôm, "valley of Hinnom"; see on 5:22). See I. H. Marshall on this verse.

29–30 Two illustrations of the unrestricted attention of God to even the smallest things of life are now provided: the death of a sparrow and the very number of hairs on one's head (v 29a; see *Comment* on v 31). The implication (cf. v 31a) is not only that these things do not escape the notice of τοῦ πατρὸς ὑμῶν, "your Father," a term of intimacy and endearment, but that they too fall within the scope of his sovereign power and care (ἄνευ, "without the knowledge and consent of"; BAGD, 65). The fact that sparrows were very inexpensive, the cheapest living things used for food (two for an ἀσσάριον, a Roman copper coin worth 1/16 of a denarius), heightens the effect of the logion. The sparrow allusion recalls the illustration in the Sermon of the Mount (6:26, specifically concerning feeding) where another *a fortiori* argument is also found (cf. v 31b). The numbering of the hairs on a head is a variant of the more common idea that when God protects, not even a single hair of a person's head is allowed to perish (e.g., 1 Sam 14:45; 2 Sam 14:11; Luke 21:18; Acts 27:34). Since even the hairs of a person's head are numbered (possibly a proverb), there is no need to fear what one's enemies may do.

31 The conclusion from this reasoning (οὖν, "therefore") is that "you are not to be afraid." God has the knowledge, the power, and the concern to protect the disciples from any *ultimate* harm or injury. This conclusion itself implies the *a fortiori* argument, which is now made explicit in the reference back to the sparrows of v 29. They are actually worth almost nothing, yet they are not outside God's attention and will. The conclusion of this argument comes only now in 31b: "You are worth more than many sparrows" (cf. 12:12, where a sheep is in view). The ὑμεῖς, "you," stands emphatically at the end of the sentence. Still the reader must supply the final point: therefore all the more will he care for you. This is the clear assumption of the exhortation not to fear. Cf. the rabbinic parallel: "Rabbi Simon ben Yohai said: 'No bird perishes without God, how much less man'" (*y. Šeb.* 9, 38d [22]; see Str-B 1:582–85).

Explanation

Wherever the gospel of the kingdom is proclaimed there will be opposition. When that opposition escalates into open hostility, the messengers of the good news are not to be afraid. The message must be proclaimed, and God will surely look after the ultimate welfare of his servants. Even death itself is not to be feared, for the person is more than the body. Life after death is assumed here as a fact, as is the reality of judgment. In short, God, the "Father," who watches over the sparrows and knows the number of hairs on a person's head, will care for his disciples through all that they may have to experience in the service of the gospel. In difficult times the disciples and the witnessing Church of every age have been able to take courage from these words (cf. 8:31).

Confession and Denial   (10:32–33)

Bibliography

Higgins, A. J. B. "'Menschensohn' oder 'ich' in Q: Lk 12,8–9/Mt 10,32–33?" In *Jesus und der Menschensohn.* FS A. Vögtle, ed. R. Pesch and R. Schnackenburg. Freiburg: Herder, 1975. 117–23. **Kümmel, W. G.** "Das Verhalten Jesus gegenüber und das Verhalten des Menschensohns: Markus 8,38 par. und Lukas 12,8f. par. Matthäus 10,32f." In *Jesus und der Menschensohn.* FS A. Vögtle, ed. R. Pesch and R. Schnackenburg. Freiburg: Herder, 1975. 210–24. **Pesch, R.** "Über die Autorität Jesu: Eine Rückfrage anhand des Bekenner- und Verleugnerspruchs Lk 12,8f par." In *Die Kirche des Anfangs.* FS H. Schürmann, ed. R. Schnackenburg et al. Leipzig: St. Benno, 1977. 25–55.

Translation

[32] *"Therefore, everyone who will acknowledge me before others,*[a] *I too will acknowledge that one*[b] *before my Father who is in heaven.*[c] [33] *But whoever will deny me before others,*[d] *I too will deny that one*[e] *before my Father who is in heaven."*[f]

Notes

[a] τῶν ἀνθρώπων, lit. "men."
[b] Lit. "him."
[c] ἐν [τοῖς] οὐρανοῖς, "in (the) heavens." The τοῖς is in brackets in the critical Gr. text because of the seriously divided textual evidence. Omitting the article are P[19] ℵ D L W Θ *f*[1] TR; including it are B C K *f*[13].
[d] See *Note* a.
[e] Lit. "him."
[f] See *Note* c. The textual evidence is approximately the same here, except that here C omits the article.

Form/Structure/Setting

A. The great importance of witness, of carrying the gospel of the kingdom to the world, is now laid out in the strongest of statements. Witness is not optional; it is a requirement. These verses with their combined promise and threat provide further motivational power to the carrying out of the mission, regardless of the experience of hostility and rejection that is encountered.

B. Matthew and Luke (12:8–9) here continue to depend on Q. The agreement between them is close, but the following differences are to be noted: Matthew's omission of Luke's opening words λέγω δὲ ὑμῖν, "But I say to you," which were probably in Q; Luke's ὁ υἱὸς τοῦ ἀνθρώπου ὁμολογήσει, "the Son of Man will acknowledge" (probably a Lukan alteration of Q; so Kümmel) for Matthew's ὁμολογήσω κἀγώ, "I will acknowledge," and Luke's ἔμπροσθεν τῶν ἀγγέλων τοῦ θεοῦ, "before the angels of God," for Matthew's ἔμπροσθεν τοῦ πατρός μου τοῦ ἐν [τοῖς] οὐρανοῖς, "before my Father who is in heaven" (obviously Matthean language, rather than that of Q). In the second verse of this short pericope, the last mentioned change is also found (Luke, however, here uses ἐνώπιον for ἔμπροσθεν) along with the third person passive verb ἀπαρνηθήσεται (but without mention of the Son of Man), "he will be denied."

C. The two verses are a perfectly balanced parallelism: v 33 is the mirror of v 32 (the only slight difference is caused by the Aramaism ἐν αὐτῷ with ὁμολογήσω, not evident in the English translations). Here again is the mark of oral traditions and material designed for catechesis. The two symmetrical parts may simply be titled: (1) the reward of confession (v 32) and (2) the penalty of denial (v 33). The repeated use of ὅστις ("whoever"), plus the ὅς and articular participles of vv 37–42, makes it clear that the present verses have a wider application than just to the twelve (who have been in view from v 16 onwards).

D. The second part (v 33) is reflected in 2 Tim 2:12, "If we deny [ἀρνησόμεθα] him, he also will deny us," and Rom 3:5b. The same logion is quoted (though not exactly) in 2 Clem. 3:2, perhaps from oral tradition rather than from Matthew.

Comment

32   Thus far the discourse has focused on the message of the kingdom, which the disciples must proclaim even in the face of opposition and suffering. We have seen hints of the close connection between this message and the person of Jesus, especially in the "for my sake" of v 18 and "for my name's sake" in v 22. Now it is the person of Jesus that takes center stage (see too vv 37–39). ὁμολογήσει ἐν ἐμοί, lit. "confess in me," is an Aramaism meaning "confess me" (so BAGD, 568). Public acknowledgment of Jesus—in this context perhaps in a court defense—involves acceptance of his message and following him in discipleship (cf. Rom. 10:9). This will result in a corresponding acknowledgment of the disciple in the heavenly court before God (cf. 25:34), referred to here as "my Father," thus underlining the special relationship between Jesus and God, one, however, also shared by his disciples ("your Father"; e.g., vv 20, 29). The passage has an unmistakably eschatological tone. Thus the mission (confession) and the identity of the messenger (as confessed by Jesus) stand closely together. For the same principle expressed in different connections, cf. 6:14–15; 7:1. Davies-Allison find the background to the present pericope in Dan 7.

33   This verse makes the same point, but negatively (cf. 1 Sam 2:30). The verb ἀρνεῖσθαι, "deny," means strongly to repudiate or disown and thus connotes apostasy (BAGD, 107). To reject Jesus is to be rejected by Jesus (cf. 7:23; 25:12) before his Father. The same point is made a little differently in Mark 8:38: "For whoever is ashamed of me and my words in this adulterous and sinful generation, of him will the Son of man also be ashamed, when he comes in the glory of his Father with the holy angels" (RSV; cf. Luke 9:26; the verse is curiously omitted by Matthew in the parallel passage, 16:24–28). See also 1 John 2:22–23; 4:2–3, 15, for similar material.

Explanation

Jesus stands at the center of the message of the kingdom, not only announcing it but bringing it through his ministry of word and deed. In the final analysis, therefore, one's relation to Jesus is all important. Relation to God is only possible through relation to him, and to reject him is in effect to reject God (cf. v 40). The importance of Christology for Matthew is plainly evident in this passage. Jesus is both the object of commitment and the sole mediating subject on behalf of others to the Father. No middle ground or "neutrality" is envisioned here. One is either for Jesus or against him. The boundaries of Judaism are broken here, for no prophet, teacher, or rabbi is capable of such words. Matthew continually keeps before us the uniqueness of Jesus.

Division and Discipleship   (10:34–39)

Bibliography

Barta, K. A. "Mission and Discipleship in Matthew: A Redaction-Critical Study of Mt 10,34." Diss., Marquette, 1979. **Beardslee, W. A.** "Saving One's Life by Losing It." *JAAR* 47 (1979) 57–72. **Black, M.** "Not Peace but a Sword." In *Jesus and the Politics of His Day*, ed. E. Bammel and C. F. D. Moule. Cambridge: Cambridge University, 1984. 287–94. ————. "Uncomfortable Words: III. The Violent Word." *ExpTim* 81 (1969–70) 115–58. **Cope, O. L.** "Mt 10:34–39 and Mic 7:6." In *Matthew: A Scribe.* 77–81. **Dautzenburg, G.** *Sein Leben bewahren: Psychē in den Herrenworten der Evangelien.* SANT 14. Munich: Kösel, 1966. 51–82. **Dinkler, E.** "Jesu Wort vom Kreuztragen." In *Signum crucis.* Tübingen: Mohr, 1967. 77–98. **Fletcher, D. R.** "Condemned to Die: The Logion on Cross–Bearing: What Does It Mean?" *Int* 18 (1964) 156–64. **Fridrichsen, A.** "'Sich selbst verleugnen.'" *ConNT* 2 (1936) 1–8. **George, A.** "Qui veut sauver sa vie la perdra; qui perd sa vie la sauvera." *BVC* 83 (1968) 11–24. **Green, M. P.** "The Meaning of Cross-Bearing." *BSac* 140 (1983) 117–33. **Griffiths, J. G.** "The Disciple's Cross." *NTS* 16 (1970) 358–64. **Schulz, A.** *Nachfolgen und Nachahmen.* SANT 6. Munich: Kösel, 1962. 79–97. **Seccombe, D. P.** "Take Up Your Cross." In *God Who Is Rich in Mercy.* FS D. B. Knox, ed. P. T. O'Brien and D. G. Peterson. Grand Rapids: Baker, 1986. 139–51. **Tannehill, R. C.** "Matthew 10:34–36//Luke 12:49–53: Not Peace but a Sword." In *The Sword of His Mouth.* Philadelphia: Fortress, 1975. 140–47.

Translation

[34] *"Do not imagine that I came to bring peace upon the earth. I came to bring not peace but a sword.* [35] *For I came to divide 'a man[a] against his father,' and 'a daughter against her mother' and 'a daughter-in-law[b] against her mother-in-law,'* [36] *and 'a person's enemies will be members of his or her[c] household.'*

³⁷ *"The person who loves father or mother more than me is not worthy of me, and the person who loves son or daughter more than me is not worthy of me.*^{d 38}*And whoever does not take his or her*^e *cross and follow me is not worthy of me.* ³⁹*The person who 'finds' his or her life will lose it, and the person who loses his or her life for my sake will find it."*

Notes

^a D it sy^{s,c} have υἱόν, "son," rather than ἄνθρωπον, "man," a harmonization with the LXX of Mic 7:6.

^b νύμφην, lit. "bride."

^c "Or her" is added in order to be inclusive, as are the fem. pronouns of vv 38–39.

^d B* (but the original scribe caught his error and includes the words at the foot of the column) D and a few others omit the words καὶ ὁ φιλῶν υἱὸν ἢ θυγατέρα ὑπὲρ ἐμὲ οὐκ ἔστιν μου ἄξιος, "and the person who loves son or daughter more than me is not worthy of me," probably due to homoeoteleuton (skipping from the ἄξιος at the end of the first clause to that at the end of the second clause). P¹⁹ apparently has an even larger omission for the same reason, down to the ἄξιος at the end of v 38.

^e For the fem. pronouns here and in the next verse, cf. *Note* c.

Form/Setting/Structure

A. In this discourse, which focuses on hostility, persecution, and suffering for the sake of the gospel, Matthew now turns to an especially painful reality: the division and hostility within single households. This subject has already been addressed earlier in the discourse in a passing reference (see v 21). Now it returns and with it several important discipleship sayings that have a broader application than the specific orientation of the present context. Matthew thus continues in the universal mode that began in v 32, using the repeated articular participle (translated above, "the person who") or the indefinite relative pronoun ὅς, "whoever."

B. As in the preceding material, Matthew again appears dependent on Q (cf. Luke 12:51–53; 14:25–27; 17:33). The distribution of the material in different parts of Luke points, as in the other discourses, to Matthew as the collector of independent pieces of the tradition, which he weaves together into large discourses.

In the first part of the pericope (vv 34–36) Matthew abbreviates the Q material: Luke's opening question is omitted (Luke 12:51); the division of five into three against two and two against three in Luke 12:52 is omitted altogether, as is the reverse opposition in each of the three cases (i.e., father against son, mother against daughter, and mother-in-law against bride, thus conforming the passage more closely to Mic 7:6). This is typical Matthean abbreviation. Added to this first part, however, is v 36, "a person's enemies will be the members of his or her own household." The second part of the pericope (vv 37–39), which is linked with the preceding verses by the references to father, mother, son, and daughter, again displays abbreviation of Q. Matthew omits the opening εἴ τις ἔρχεται πρός με καί, "if any one comes to me and . . ." (Luke 14:26), and the reference to hating wife, brothers and sisters, and even one's own life (Luke 14:26). In this second part, indeed, Matthew's wording is rather different from Luke's. Thus Matthew has ὁ φιλῶν . . . ὑπὲρ ἐμέ, "whoever loves . . . more than me," for Luke's οὐ μισεῖ, "does not hate" (Luke 14:26), which is the correct understanding and interpretation of the Semitic idiom, and twice the simple οὐκ ἔστιν μου ἄξιος, "is not worthy of me," for Luke's οὐ δύναται εἶναί μου μαθητής, "cannot be my disciple" (Luke 14:26–27). Other differences in wording are minor variations and need not be noted here. Finally, v 39 is quite differently and more simply stated than the parallel in Luke 17:33. Matthew here inserts ἕνεκεν ἐμοῦ, "on my account," before "whoever loses his or her life."

C. The structure of the pericope is complex, with several minor structures and interrelationships within the larger whole. The first part (vv 34–36) concerning division consists of an *a a' b' b* pattern (with considerable syntactical parallelism), wherein the macrostructure is found in (*a*) the mistaken notion (μὴ νομίσητε, "think not") that Jesus came (ἦλθον) to bring peace (εἰρήνην) v 34a, which corresponds to (*b*) the affirmation that Jesus came (ἦλθον) to divide (διχάσαι) members of a household (v 35). Within this larger framework is the same contrast within v 34b, (*a'*) Jesus came not to bring peace (*b'*) but a sword (μάχαιραν). In *b* the subjects of the division are first listed in three parallel categories (v 35) and then in a general statement (v 36). The second part of the pericope (vv 37–39) concerning discipleship is linked at the beginning (v 37) with the first part by the reference to family members. V 37 then serves as a transitional statement from the first main part to the discipleship sayings of vv 38 and 39. Vv 37 and 38 consist of three parallel sentences, each ending with the words οὐκ ἔστιν μου ἄξιος, "is not worthy of me." The two sentences of v 37 are exactly parallel, that of v 38 less exactly so. Vv 38 and 39 turn to discipleship in the broadest way, referring to (1) the taking up of one's cross and (2) the losing of one's life, two centrally important metaphors of discipleship. The two clauses of v 39 are exactly parallel. Almost all of the content of this pericope is set forth in a form that again points to oral transmission and catechesis. Although a simple outline cannot do justice to the structure of the passage, the following may be suggested: (1) the coming of Jesus and the message of the kingdom means division within households (vv 34–36); (2) loyalty to Jesus is more important than family loyalties (v 37); and (3) the importance of dying to self (vv 38–39).

D. A parallel to v 37–38 is found in *Gos. Thom.* 55.

Comment

34 The form of the statement not to expect Jesus to bring peace (μὴ νομίσητε, "do not imagine"; cf. 5:17) suggests that this would have been the natural inclination of the disciples. Was not the gospel a message of peace (cf. 5:9; 10:13)? Would not the age of the kingdom of God bring peace (εἰρήνη) with it (cf. Luke 1:79b; Isa 9:6; 11:9)? The answer must clearly be yes in its final realization and even in some sense in the present (cf. John 14:27). But in the peculiar and unexpected interim period of the proclamation of the kingdom, as has already been shown, strange things may be expected by the disciples and later messengers of the kingdom. The hostility now in view—that between otherwise close family members—is described with the metaphor of a "sword" (μάχαιραν; cf. Luke's διαμερισμόν, "division"). Elsewhere in the Gospels the word is used only in the narrative of the arrest of Jesus (where it is used in its normal sense). Luke 12:49 has a statement similar in structure to the present passage (πῦρ ἦλθον βαλεῖν ἐπὶ τὴν γῆν, "I came to bring fire upon the earth"), but this is probably an allusion to eschatological judgment. For ἦλθον, "I came," which occurs three times in vv 34–35, see *Comment* on 5:17. The sense in which Jesus has not brought peace but a sword is made clear in the following two verses.

35–36 Although ἦλθον διχάσαι, "I came to divide," would ordinarily be taken in the sense of purpose, here it is more a way of describing the effect of the coming of Jesus and the proclamation of the kingdom. Response to the message of Jesus and his disciples will be mixed and hence cause dissension among members of the same household. The potential seriousness of such division was already alluded to in v 21. The words describing the oppositions here are drawn from the LXX of Mic 7:6 with slight differences: Matthew drops the two verbs and substitutes ἄνθρωπον, "man," for υἱόν, "son," employs the preposition κατά for ἐπί (both meaning "against"), and makes a couple of slight changes in the wording of v 36. The Micah passage refers to a time of trouble before eschatological deliverance (cf. the development of this expectation in the intertestamental period; see, e.g., *Jub.* 23:16, 19–20; *1 Enoch* 100:2; 4 Ezra 6:24). The Talmud also regards family dissension as increasing just prior to the messianic age (Montefiore; cf. *m. Soṭa* 9:15). The experience of the disciples and those who come to believe their message will be not only that they will be widely hated (cf. v 22) but that they will be rejected even by their own family members. This is part of the reality of the proclamation of the good news.

37 The division described in the preceding verses must not be allowed to divert a disciple from loyalty to Jesus. Family relationships so important in that culture—even those most honored in the OT and Jewish tradition between father or mother (thus too Jesus; cf. 15:4–6; 19:19) and son or daughter—must not be given precedence over relationship to Jesus (cf., however, the precedent in Deut 33:9 [quoted at Qumran, 4QTestim 16–17]; Exod 32:29). If it is necessary, a break in these relationships, however painful, must be tolerated in the present time frame (there will be future compensations, however; cf. 19:29). The disciples had Jesus' own example here as well (cf. 12:46–50; John 7:3–9). Love (φιλῶν) here refers not to an emotion (though it connotes family intimacy) but to loyalty and commitment, the heart of discipleship. οὐκ ἔστιν μου ἄξιος, "is not worthy of me," means not worthy to be Jesus' disciple (cf. Luke 14:26) or worthy to be a participant in the kingdom. But Matthew's rewording has the effect of again drawing attention to Jesus to make a christological point. To be undeserving of Jesus is to be undeserving of what he brings; the two are inseparable.

38–39 The radical statement of v 37, with its stress on uncompromising loyalty to Jesus, is now exceeded by two remarkable descriptions of the nature of discipleship in absolute terms. The attachment and loyalty to Jesus referred to in the preceding verse are now seen to involve even greater demands: absolute obedience and thus self-denial. To be deserving of Jesus (again the formula, οὐκ ἔστιν μου ἄξιος, "is not worthy of me"), of his call to the kingdom and to discipleship, one most follow (Matthew's favorite ἀκολουθεῖ) in his footsteps (cf. vv 24–25) and take up one's cross (σταυρόν). This reference to taking up one's cross in following Jesus is anachronistic since it becomes understandable only after the initial announcement of Jesus' passion (if then!) (16:21). The exhortation to take up one's cross and follow Jesus is found again, more reasonably, in 16:24, although 20:19 is the first reference to the cross or to crucifixion. The important saying about losing and finding one's life (16:25) is also conjoined to 16:24 (as in the present passage). This anachronism points again to Matthew's redactional activity and to the pertinence of this material to the post-resurrection Church. Taking up one's cross refers not to the personal problems or difficulties of life that one

must bear, as it is sometimes used in common parlance, but to a radical obedience that entails self-denial and, indeed, a dying to self. To take up one's cross is
to follow in the footsteps of Jesus, who is the model of such radical obedience
and self-denial (cf. 4:1–11). Thus in a real sense v 39 is a kind of exegesis of v 38.
"Finding one's life" ($εὑρὼν τὴν ψυχήν$) in v 39a refers obviously to the affirmation
of life on one's own terms within one's self-centered framework apart from allegiance and discipleship to Jesus. "Find" here means "to obtain" or "find for oneself"
(BAGD, 325). This person will in the end lose his or her life, i.e., will not inherit
the life of the future kingdom. On the contrary, the one who loses his or her life
$ἕνεκεν ἐμοῦ$, "for my sake," i.e., in the self-denial entailed in the taking up of
one's cross, which might mean even martyrdom (vv 21, 28; cf. Rev. 12:11), is ultimately the one who will "find" it, i.e., in a degree of fulfillment in the present age
but preeminently in the age to come (cf. John 12:25; for a Jewish parallel, see
ʾAbot R. Nat. II[2], 36a). For the sake of Jesus, and thus the gospel, the disciple is
called to follow after Jesus in unqualified obedience to the will of God, even to
the point of death itself, which becomes for the disciple the entry into life. $ψυχή$
can mean either "soul" (cf. 10:28) or "life" in its more inclusive sense (e.g., 6:25).
Since literal martyrdom is not required to "find life" (though it may be the lot of
some), losing life and finding life are here taken in the extended sense of meaningful existence, fulfillment, purpose, or identity. There is no real life in this sense
apart from relationship to Jesus.

Explanation

Without question, to follow Jesus in discipleship is costly. The proclamation of
the kingdom may well mean the sacrifice of some human relationships, even of
the most intimate kind. There is an absolutism in the call to Jesus and the kingdom that can seem unattractive, if not unendurable. But this is only half the story,
for the rewards are beyond calculation. There is a remarkable paradox in all of
this. The way of the world—well illustrated in the incessant quest for "self-actualization" in contemporary pop psychology—leads only to a shallow and temporary
fulfillment. The seeking of "life" at this level has left many in frustration and dis-
appointment. On the other hand, and strangely, those who give up this useless
quest, who instead yield themselves fully to the service of God and the kingdom—
who willingly follow in the steps of Jesus—these are the ones who paradoxically
find life, i.e., fulfillment and deep, abiding joy. And though the best of this fulfillment awaits the eschaton, it is already experienced proleptically in the present.
Thus those who do not seek self-actualization as understood by the world, who
love Jesus and the kingdom more than themselves (and in that sense alone "hate"
their own life [Luke 14:26]), are alone the ones who realize true and lasting self-
actualization and obtain personal fulfillment and the goal of their existence.

A Concluding Note on Receiving the Servants of Christ   (10:40–11:1)

Bibliography

Hill, D. "DIKAIOI as a Quasi-Technical Term." *NTS* 11 (1964–65) 296–302. **Trilling, W.** "Amt und Amtsverständnis bei Matthäus." In *Mélanges bibliques en hommage au R. P. Béda Rigaux*, ed. A. Descamps and A. de Halleux. Gembloux: Duculot, 1979. 29–44.

Translation

^{40} *"The one who receives you receives me, and the one who receives me receives the one who sent me. ^{41} The one who receives a prophet because that person is^a a prophet will receive the reward of a prophet, and the one who receives a righteous person because that person is^b a righteous person will receive the reward of a righteous person.^{c} ^{42}And who-ever gives one of these little ones^d merely^e a cup of cold water^f because that person is^g a disciple, truly I tell you, that person will by no means^h lose his or her reward."* $^{11:1}$*And it came to pass that when Jesus completed instructing his twelve disciples, he went from there in order to teach and preach in their cities.*

Notes

^{a} "Because that person is" translates εἰς ὄνομα, lit. "in the name of." See *Comment.*

^{b} See above *Note* a.

^{c} The entire second clause concerning the reception of a righteous person is omitted in D and a few other witnesses, almost certainly by homoioteleuton.

^{d} D latt and a few other witnesses have ἐλαχίστων, "least of these," probably by influence of 25:40, 45.

^{e} μόνον, lit. "only," described by *TCGNT*, 28, as "a genuine Matthean touch," is lacking in D sy^{s,c}, probably by the influence of Mark 9:41.

^{f} By influence of Mark 9:41, D lat sy^{s,c} co include the word ὕδατος, "water," a word otherwise to be assumed from ψυχροῦ, "cold."

^{g} See *Note* a.

^{h} "By no means" reflects the emphatic negation οὐ μή.

Form/Structure/Setting

A. From the preceding and more generalized sayings about the demands of discipleship, Matthew returns to the specific sending of the twelve (and the Church) on its mission (cf. vv 5–15). But in this short concluding section of the discourse, attention falls on those who receive the messengers and offer hospital-ity to them. This is important in itself for the practical undertaking of the mission, but it is also significant for what it says indirectly about the importance of the mission and of those who are sent to represent and proclaim the kingdom.

B. V 40b finds Synoptic parallels in Mark 9:37b and Luke 9:48b with slight variations. Both of these parallels, however, occur in connection with the logion about receiving a little child in the name of Jesus (which occurs in 18:5). Luke 10:16a is similar to v 40a: ὁ ἀκούων ὑμῶν ἐμοῦ ἀκούει, "the one who hears you hears me." The same logion as in v 40 is independently found also in John 13:20, the major difference being λαμβάνων for δεχόμενος, both verbs meaning "receive" (cf. John 12:44 for the same statement using πιστεύων, "believe," and 5:23, with τιμῶν, "honor"). All this suggests the ready availability of v 40 with minor variations in the oral tradition. Matthew's version of the logion fits well the conclusion of the discourse, as does the unparalleled v 41 concerning the reception of a prophet and a wise man. V 42 is probably dependent on Mark 9:41 with which it agrees closely except for these changes: the distinctive ἕνα τῶν μικρῶν τούτων, "one of these little ones" (cf. 18:6, 10, 14), for Mark's ὑμᾶς, "you"; the use of ψυχροῦ μόνον, "cold (water) only," for Mark's ὕδατος, "water"; and εἰς ὄνομα μαθητοῦ, "in the name of a disciple" (cf. the pattern of v 41), for Mark's ἐν ὀνόματι ὅτι Χριστοῦ ἐστε, "because you bear the name of Christ." The formulaic ending of the discourse in the words of 11:1 finds no parallel in the Gospels (see on 7:28).

C. The parallelism and symmetry of vv 40 and 41 are striking. Each verse has a double clause with the second clause mirroring the first. Each of the four clauses, moreover, begins with the words ὁ δεχόμενος, "the one who receives." V 42 is independent in form, although in content it is linked with the preceding verse by the word μισθόν, "reward," and the phrase εἰς ὄνομα (μαθητοῦ), "in the name of (a disciple)"; it is introduced with the formula ἀμὴν λέγω ὑμῖν, "truly I tell you" (from Mark). The final verses of the discourse can be outlined as follows: (1) receiving the messengers, Jesus, and the Father (v 40); (2) receiving a prophet and a righteous person (v 41); and (3) the assurance of reward for hospitality given to a disciple (v 42). 11:1 is a transitional verse, closing off the discourse and preparing for the pericope that begins in 11:2. The mission of Jesus is here summarized in the parallel infinitives, διδάσκειν καὶ κηρύσσειν, "to teach and to preach."

D. The logion in v 40 is reflected also in Ign. *Eph.* 6:1 and *Did.* 11:4 (cf. too Justin Martyr, *Apol.* 1.16.10 and 1.63.5).

Comment

40 This verse reveals the close relationship between the disciples and Jesus, on the one hand, and Jesus and God, on the other. δέχεται, "receives," means here not merely to welcome, e.g., into one's home, but to receive in a deeper sense (cf. v 13–14). It is to accept the message of the disciples and thus the message of Jesus and his person, which is inseparable from the disciples' message (cf. 18:5; John 12:44; 13:20; for a negative statement of the same point, see Luke 10:16). This message is in turn the gospel of God (Mark 1:14), so that to receive it is to receive the message of God and thus to accept the grace of God. The key position of Jesus as the middle term, or mediator, between human beings and God is apparent from these astonishing statements. That is why Jesus and the good news are practically identical. To receive one is to receive the other. The Jewish background of the *šālîaḥ* may underlie these statements (cf. "a man's emissary or agent [*šālîaḥ*] is like the man himself" (*m. Ber.* 5.5, cf. *Mek. Exod.* 14:31; 18:12).

41 This verse too concerns the receiving of God's messengers, now described under the title of "prophet" (προφήτης) and "righteous person" (δίκαιος). Although these titles are used of persons in the OT (cf. 13:17 and 23:29 for the same combination referring to OT persons), here they refer to Christian prophets (cf. 23:34) and righteous persons (cf. 13:43, 49; 25:37, 46). For Matthew, all true disciples would qualify for being referred to under the latter title, which is not a "semi-distinct class within the Church" (so Hill). The phrase εἰς ὄνομα προφήτου, "in the name of a prophet" (so too when the phrase is used with "righteous person" and "disciple" [v 42]), is a rabbinic idiom (lĕšēm, "for the sake of") and means something like "just because he is a prophet or bears the name prophet." That is, no further reason is necessary for the offering of hospitality than the identity of the person as a messenger and a Christian. Again, so important is hospitality shown to these persons that one is promised the very reward such persons themselves are to receive in keeping with their callings. Thus to receive such a servant is to put oneself in the position of receiving the same reward as the person received, whether prophet, righteous person, or disciple, just as not to receive such a person means future judgment (v 14–15). Possibly behind this idea of reward to those who show hospitality to prophets are the stories of those who did so to Elijah (1 Kgs 17:9–24) and Elisha (2 Kgs 4:9–37). Against the idea that "prophet" and "righteous person" designate offices in the church (and that the "reward" for those who receive them is what they impart, i.e., the gospel and instruction respectively; so Hill) is the response to the disciple in the parallel in v 42.

42   Given the parallel in the preceding verse, we may take the phrase εἰς ὄνομα μαθητοῦ, "in the name of a disciple," to define ἕνα τῶν μικρῶν τούτων, "one of these little ones," as referring to a disciple—and more specifically, given the context, one who is active in missionary proclamation. εἰς ὄνομα μαθητοῦ refers to the person to whom the kindness is shown, not to the giver (as is clearly the case in the parallel, Mark 9:41). The disciples of Jesus are also referred to as "little ones" (μικροί), perhaps "unexperienced," in 18:6, 10, 14 (cf. Mark 9:42; Luke 17:2; and the reference to "children" in Mark 10:24 and John 21:5) and as "the least [ἐλάχιστος] of these" in 25:40, 45, perhaps as a mark of their humility (cf. 11:25). The giving of a "cup of cold (water)" (ποτήριον ψυχροῦ) is symbolic of a very basic need in the dry climate of Palestine. But merely that degree of hospitality to any Christian messenger (μόνον, "only") is regarded as significant. Here again, μαθητοῦ, "disciple," means not simply one of the twelve but any follower of Jesus.

The close relationship between this passage and 25:35, 40 should be noted. In the latter the giving of drink (among other things) to "one of the least of these my brothers" amounts to having done it for Jesus. This concluding statement of the discourse has the added forcefulness of the ἀμὴν λέγω ὑμῖν, "truly I tell you" (see on 5:18), as well as the strong double negative, οὐ μή, "by no means." Thus the discourse comes to its end with promises to those who not only will be the recipients of the messengers and their message but will make possible the ongoing fulfillment of the charge given to the disciples and the Church.

11:1   The clause with which this verse begins is the formula used by Matthew to mark the end of each of the five major teaching discourses of Jesus in the Gospel (see on 7:28). This is the only instance, however, where the verb διατάσσειν, "command, direct," occurs in the formula (indeed, it is the only occurrence of the word in the whole of Matthew), its participial form complementing ἐτέλεσεν, "finished." Again the "twelve disciples" are mentioned, in a kind of inclusio (cf. v 5; cf. v 1–2), calling attention to the special character of the discourse, which addresses specifically the first messengers of the kingdom. In Matthew, unlike Mark (6:12–13, 30) and Luke (9:6, 10; cf. 10:17–20), there is no report of the fulfillment of the mission of the twelve or of their return from that mission (which would be problematic, given v 23b). The focus thus returns to Jesus and his activity. μετέβη ἐκεῖθεν, "he went from there," is a very general statement made in such transitional summaries (cf. 13:53–54; 19:1–2). The reference to "teaching and preaching" (διδάσκειν καὶ κηρύσσειν) rather than to healing (cf. 13:54) is unusual, considering the importance of Jesus' deeds in the verses that immediately follow (i.e., 11:2–6). For Matthew, however, teaching and preaching are the more fundamental bases of the ministry of Jesus (and of his disciples, cf. 10:7). ἐν ταῖς πόλεσιν αὐτῶν, "in their cities," refers to the cities of Israel (Galilee); i.e., Jesus restricts his mission, like that of the disciples, to Israel. "Their" (αὐτῶν) again reflects the hostility between Matthew's church and the contemporary synagogue (cf. "their synagogues" and "their scribes"; 4:23; 7:29; 9:35; 10:17).

Explanation

The supreme importance of the messengers and their message is made very clear. Reception of the message and the messengers amounts to reception of Jesus and, in turn, the one who sent him, God. For Matthew, this applies not merely to the twelve but to the messengers of the kingdom in his community and thus to those of the Church in every era. Here is the beginning of the NT teaching concerning the mediatorship of Jesus, bridging between humanity and God (1 Tim 2:5; cf. Heb 9:15; 12:24). Thus the reception accorded the messengers of the kingdom is nothing short of the reception accorded God himself! If the messengers are that important, then the hospitality accorded the representatives of the kingdom will not go unrewarded. And one's kind treatment of even a disciple will not be forgotten. Treatment of a disciple will later be described as equivalent to such treatment of Jesus, a point very much in accord with the present passage (cf. 25:40). All of this points finally to the extreme importance of the mission and therefore of the messengers themselves. The gospel must be proclaimed, and those who aid that proclamation, however indirectly, are performing an important, praiseworthy function.

The Negative Response to Jesus (11:2–12:50)

Bibliography

Verseput, D. *The Rejection of the Humble Messianic King: A Study of the Composition of Matthew 11–12.* Europäische Hochschulschriften 23.291. Frankfurt am Main: P. Lang, 1986.

At the heart of this somewhat diverse section of the Gospel are three collections of passages that focus on or allude to the unbelief or opposition of Israel. The first of these, 11:2–24, ends in the dissatisfaction of Israel (11:16–19) and the scathing judgment oracles of 11:20–24. This is followed by a theological explanation in terms of election but also by an invitation to rest (11:25–30). The second, 12:1–21, focuses on the opposition of the Pharisees and ends in the prophetic expectation of the response of the Gentiles (12:15–21). Verseput regards this material as part of a larger interlude (11:25–12:21) that focuses on the nature of the Messiah's mission, but the opposition motif is also very prominent here (cf. 12:2, 10, 14). The third collection of passages is 12:22–45, with the Beelzebub attribution (12:24), the condemnatory words of 12:34, 41–42, and the final reference to "this evil generation" (12:45). The last pericope points to the reality of a new family of Jesus, one commonly oriented to the obedience to the will of the Father, as it is spelled out in relationship to Jesus and his teaching in the Matthean perspective. The disciples of Jesus are his true family and are thus the true family of God.

There is here somewhat of a turning point in the narrative, but it should not be overemphasized as it is by dispensational interpreters of Matthew. The offer of salvation to Israel is not here withdrawn, nor is the new community of the church recognized for the first time. The kingdom of God does not now for the first time become a mystery. There is no turning from an expectation of earthly fulfillment to a heavenly or spiritual one. God's plan is in no way altered by the unbelief of Israel, as if it were a surprise to him. There is therefore no fundamental change in the teaching of Jesus in chap. 13. The key turning point in the teaching of Jesus takes place in chap. 16, when he begins first to talk of his imminent suffering and death.

Jesus' Answer to the Baptist's Question (11:2–6)

Bibliography

Dupont, J. "L'ambassade de Jean Baptiste." *NRT* 83 (1961) 805–21; 943–59. **Kümmel, W. G.** "Jesu Antwort an Johannes den Täufer: Ein Beispiel zum Methodenproblem in der Jesusforschung." In *Heilsgeschehen und Geschichte.* MTS 16. Marburg: Elwert, 1978. 2:177–200. **Lambrecht, J.** "'Are you the one who is to come, or shall we look for another?'" *LS* 8 (1980) 115–28. **Meier, J. P.** "John the Baptist in Matthew's Gospel." *JBL* 99 (1980) 383–405. **Schönle, V.** *Johannes, Jesus und die Juden: Die theologische Position des Matthäus und des Verfassers der Redenquelle im Lichte von Mt. 11.* BBET 17. Frankfurt am Main: P. Lang, 1982.

Trilling, W. "Die Täufertradition bei Matthäus." *BZ* n.s. 3 (1959) 271–89 = *Studien.* 45–65. **Vögtle, A.** "Wunder und Wort in urchristlicher Glaubenswerbung (Mt 11,2–5/Lk 7,18–23)." In *Evangelium.* 219–242. **Wink, W.** *John the Baptist in the Gospel Tradition.* SNTSMS 7. Cambridge: Cambridge University, 1968. 27–41.

Translation

²*And when John in prison heard of the works of the Messiah,*[a] *he sent his disciples and through them*[b] ³*asked*[c] *him: "Are you the one promised to come*[d] *or must we wait for another?"* ⁴*And Jesus answered and said to them: "Go and tell John the things you are hearing and seeing:* ⁵*The blind receive their sight and the lame walk, lepers are cleansed and the deaf hear, and the dead are raised and the poor hear the good news of salvation.*[e] ⁶*And blessed is the person who does not take offense at me."*

Notes

[a] D sy[c] and other witnesses read Ἰησοῦ, "Jesus," probably to make the verse more compatible with the uncertainty reflected in the question of v 3. Furthermore, D has the tendency to substitute Ἰησοῦς for κύριος or αὐτός (fifty-seven times according to Metzger; see *TCGNT*, 29).

[b] πέμψας διὰ τῶν μαθητῶν αὐτοῦ, lit. "having sent through his disciples." C³ L *f*¹ TR vg sy[hmg] bo have δύο, "two," for διά, "through," probably by influence of Luke 7:18 and to make Matthew's Gr. less awkward.

[c] εἶπεν, "said."

[d] ὁ ἐρχόμενος, lit., "the coming one." The first hand of D has ὁ ἐργαζόμενος, "the working one" (cf. v 2).

[e] A few MSS (Θ *f*¹³ sy[c]) exchange the fifth and sixth clauses, thus putting the raising of the dead at the end of the list, apparently regarding it as a more suitable climax, while a few others (k sy[s]) omit the sixth clause, thus achieving the same effect. See *Comment* on v 5.

Form/Setting/Structure

A. Matthew now turns to the question of John the Baptist and Jesus' assessment of the Baptist as a way of casting further light on the reality of the kingdom. The importance of John has the effect of heightening the significance of what he fore-shadowed. In chap. 11, the glorious character of the kingdom of God comes into view and then in turn the reality of judgment for those who reject it, a theme that will become increasingly prominent. John's question enables the summarizing description of Jesus' deeds, which corresponds to the sketch of chaps. 8–9 and to the commission given to the disciples in their missionary activity (cf. 10:8).

B. Matthew is dependent on Q here, agreeing very closely with Luke 7:18–23. The main difference between the two is caused by Matthew's characteristic practice of abbreviation. Matthew shortens the narrative portion by omitting the reference to John calling two of his disciples to him (Luke 7:18) and the report of them going to Jesus, and thus too the repetition of the question (Luke 7:20). Matthew further omits the following insertion (probably Lukan) concerning the healing activity of Jesus (ἐν ἐκείνῃ τῇ ὥρᾳ, "in that hour"), since he has reported this and indeed to some extent shaped his narrative in chaps. 8–9 with John's question in mind. The question of John is verbatim in Matthew (v 3) and Luke (7:19 and 20), except for Matthew's ἕτερον for Luke's ἄλλον; both words mean "another," and there is probably no nuance in Matthew's word such as "another of a different kind." The answer of Jesus, vv 4–6, is in verbatim agreement with Luke 7:22, except for very minor differences. Apart from Matthew's three additional καί's ("and"), the only difference is in his ἀκούετε καὶ βλέπετε, "you are hearing and seeing" (v 4), to emphasize the hearing, for Luke's εἴδετε καὶ ἠκούσατε, "you saw and heard" (Luke 7:22).

C. The only parallelism in the passage is found in the ἀκούετε καὶ βλέπετε of v 4 and the six striking parallel clauses of v 5. The pericope consists of two main parts: (1) John's question (vv 2–3) and (2) Jesus' answer (vv 4–6). The former consists of (a) the occasion and report of the sending (v 2) and (b) the actual question (v 3). The latter has three parts: (a) the general answer (v 4); (b) the specific signs (v 5); and (c) the pronouncement of a blessing on those who are not offended by Jesus (v 6).

Comment

2–3 Matthew's last reference to John the Baptist (4:12) reported his arrest. The Baptist had proclaimed the good news of imminent eschatological fulfillment (3:1–12) and, though under protest, had baptized Jesus as the one destined to bring the promise to fulfillment (3:14–17). He now reappears in Matthew's narrative (the story of his death will be reported finally in 14:1–12), well into the ministry of Jesus, to present his doubt-filled question about the identity of Jesus. John's doubts should not appear unreasonable, since he was obviously expecting an imminent end of the age involving the judgment of the wicked (3:12). And though he had heard rumors of messianic-like deeds performed by Jesus, his wicked captors had not yet been judged and he had not yet experienced the fulfillment of the messianic promise of "liberty to the captives" (Isa 61:1; and even more vividly, Isa 42:7). He continued to sit in the prison of Herod Antipas (in the fortress of Machaerus, east of the Dead Sea, according to Jos. *Ant.* 18.5.2) and thus could only send his disciples (cf. 9:14; 14:12) to Jesus with his question. John had indeed heard of τὰ ἔργα τοῦ Χριστοῦ, "the works of the Messiah" (χριστός, "Christ" = "Messiah," has not been used since 2:4 and is here a Matthean addition to Q in keeping with Matthew's christological emphasis). John had heard of the works but remained unsure that Jesus was the Messiah. The answer of v 5 was thus not news for him; yet it was meant to confirm that Jesus was the Messiah, although it failed to address John's personal difficulty (but see v 6). ὁ ἐρχόμενος, "the coming one," is here clearly a title referring to the Messiah (cf. 3:11; Heb 10:37; Rev 1:4, 8; Acts 19:4; for OT background: Ps 118:26; Dan 7:13; 9:25–27; Mal 3:1). The verb προσδοκᾶν, "expect" or "await," occurs again in Matthew only in 24:50, there in reference to the future parousia of Jesus. Since Jesus had not yet fulfilled John's expectation of apocalyptic judgment of the enemies of God (including Herod), John wonders whether another (ἕτερον) should be expected.

4–5 Jesus' reply to John's disciples is that they report to John ἃ ἀκούετε καὶ βλέπετε, "the things you are hearing and seeing." Jesus points, as Matthew has done in the Gospel, to the words (chaps. 5–7) and deeds (chaps. 8–9) of Jesus, in that order. Matthew presupposes that John's disciples have had ample opportunity to observe the ministry of Jesus (cf. Luke 7:21). A specific list of six types of miracles performed by Jesus is now presented, carefully correlated with the miracles recorded in chaps. 8–9, and at the same time coinciding with OT phraseology that refers to the promised messianic age—thus strengthening the answer to John's question: (1) τυφλοὶ ἀναβλέπουσιν, "the blind receive their sight" (cf. almost the exact language in Isa 29:18; cf. 42:18; 35:5; Matt 9:27–31); (2) χωλοὶ περιπατοῦσιν, "the lame walk" (cf. Isa 35:6; Matt 9:1–8); (3) λεπροὶ καθαρίζονται, "lepers are cleansed" (not a specific OT expectation, but implied in general statements, e.g., Isa 53:4; Matt 8:1–4); (4) κωφοὶ ἀκούουσιν, "the deaf hear" (nearly identical language in Isa 29:18; 35:5; cf. 42:18; Matt 9:32–34, where, however, the κωφός is a mute man enabled to speak); (5) νεκροὶ ἐγείρονται, "the dead are raised" (similar language in Isa 26:19; Matt 9:18–26); and (6) πτωχοὶ εὐαγγελίζονται, "the poor hear the good news of salvation" (Isa 61:1; cf. Matt 9:35). As the last mentioned item, the preaching of the gospel intentionally receives special emphasis, for this is ultimately the meaning of the preceding miracles. The Messiah brings the kingdom: *that* is the gospel. The "poor" (πτωχοί) are the same as those of 5:3, literally poor and hence poor in spirit (see *Comment* on 5:3). These are thus actual miracles, and the clauses are not to be understood spiritually or metaphorically. The only healing miracles of chaps. 8–9 not included in the list are the curing of a fever, a hemorrhage, and more surprisingly, demon exorcism (Matt 8:5–13, 28–34). The latter may not have been included because exorcism was not unique to Jesus (cf. 12:27) and not mentioned in the OT. The OT passages alluded to are remarkably all from Isaiah and noticeably from passages that refer to the anticipated messianic era (Isa 35 is sometimes called the Isaiah apocalypse; Isa 61:1–2 is quoted in Luke 4:18); the reference to judgment contained in the same passages is omitted. V 5 thus is in complete accord with Matthew's stress on Jesus and his ministry as the fulfillment of the OT promises. Since Jesus fulfills these expectations, he is the Messiah awaited by John. A somewhat similar list is found in 15:30–31. For healing as the work of the expected Messiah in the rabbinic tradition, see Str-B 1:593–96.

6 There is in Jesus' concluding words, however, an indirect admission that not everything will work out in accord with John's expectations. If Jesus is the Messiah, he is not the kind of Messiah awaited by John and the populace at large. Although the reason for this has not yet been made clear (as it will for the first time in 16:21–23), the present statement acknowledges that there are those who will be offended by the nature of his messiahship and even of the kingdom (without judgment) he brings in his ministry. But, says Jesus, happy (μακάριος, "blessed," in the same sense as in the beatitudes, 5:3–11) is the person who is "not offended" by me (μὴ σκανδαλισθῇ, used with the same meaning in 13:57; cf. 26:31, 33; John 6:61). In short, John is meant to understand that he was correct in his recognition of Jesus as the promised one but that he must also be prepared to accept the fact that the kingdom Jesus brings does not, for the time being anyway, entail the judgment of the wicked. Indeed, on the contrary, the message of the kingdom goes precisely to the unrighteous (cf. 9:13). The personal consequences for John were to be significant: not only continued imprisonment but eventually a martyr's death. These too were not incompatible with the reality of the kingdom brought by Jesus.

Explanation

There is an important lesson to be learned here for those inclined to a triumphalism of an over-realized eschatology. Without question the kingdom brought by Jesus involves the experience of wonderful things, even if one does not experience the more spectacular miracles mentioned in v 5. Nevertheless, for all the joy and fulfillment available to the recipients of the kingdom in the present, there is at the same time the undeniable reality of the continued experience of the effects of evil in this world. When confronted by the latter, it is possible for Christians to "take offense" at Jesus and the nature of the salvation he has brought. If Jesus has brought the kingdom and if Christians have begun to experience eschatological blessings through the ministry of the Holy Spirit, it is perhaps natural to expect and want the eschaton now. But that is precisely what Jesus does not offer. And thus in the present the disciple of Jesus must be prepared for something less— indeed, for the reality of suffering and death—while even confessing the messianic identity and authority of Jesus (cf. Acts 7:55–56), thereby expressing faith in the good news he has announced. John the Baptist was the first person who had to learn this paradox, and since John, the paradox of existence in an era of fulfillment that is nevertheless short of the consummation has had to be learned by the apostles, by the members of Matthew's church, and by each Christian of every generation.

Jesus' Estimate of John the Baptist   (11:7–15)

Bibliography

Barnett, P. W. "Who Were the 'Biastai' (Mt 11:12–13)?" *RTR* 36 (1977) 65–70. **Braumann, G.** "'Dem Himmelreich wird Gewalt angetan' (Mt 11,12 par)." *ZNW* 52 (1961) 104–9. **Cameron, P. S.** *Violence and the Kingdom: The Interpretation of Matthew 11.12.* ANTJ 5. Frankfurt am Main: P. Lang, 1984. **Catchpole, D. R.** "On Doing Violence to the Kingdom." *IBS* 3 (1981) 77–91. **Daniel, C.** "Les Esséniens et 'Ceux qui sont dans les maisons des rois' (Matthieu 11,7–8 et Luc 7,24–5)." *RevQ* 6 (1967) 261–77. **Moore, W. E.** "*ΒΙΑΖΩ, ΑΡΠΑΖΩ* and Cognates in Josephus." *NTS* 21 (1975) 519–43. ————. "Violence to the Kingdom." *ExpTim* 100 (1989) 174–77. **Pamment, M.** "The Kingdom of Heaven according to the First Gospel." *NTS* 27 (1980–81) 211–32. **Schrenk, G.** "*Βιάζομαι.*" *TDNT* 1:608–13. **Theissen, G.** "Das 'schwankenden Rohr' in Mt 11,7 und die Gründungsmünzen von Tiberias." *ZDPV* 101 (1985) 43–55. **Thiering, B. E.** "Are the 'Violent Men' False Teachers?" *NovT* 21 (1979) 293–97.

Translation

[7]*As these disciples of John[a] were departing, Jesus began to say to the crowds concerning John: "What did you go out into the wilderness to see?[b] A reed blown by the wind? [8]But[c] what did you go out to see?[d] A man clothed in fine apparel?[e] Behold, those wearing fine apparel are in the houses of kings. [9]But what did you go out to see?[f] A prophet? Yes, I tell you, and more than a prophet. [10]This[g] is the one concerning whom it stands written: 'Behold, I send my messenger before you, who will prepare your way before you.'*

[11]*"I tell you, truly, there has not risen among those born of women one greater than John the Baptist. Nevertheless, the least in the kingdom of heaven is greater than he. [12]But from the days of John the Baptist until the present, the kingdom of heaven suffers violence and violent people plunder it. [13]For all the prophets and the law[h] prophesied*

until John. ¹⁴*And if you are willing to accept it, he himself is Elijah, 'the one about to come.'* ¹⁵*Let the one who has ears,ⁱ listen.*"

Notes

ᵃ τούτων δὲ πορευομένων, lit. "as they were departing."

ᵇ Because of the ambiguity of τί, which can mean "what" or "why," and the possibility of alternative punctuation here and in vv 8 and 9, a different translation is possible: "Why did you go out in the wilderness? To see a reed blown by the wind?"

ᶜ ἀλλά, "but," may possibly be rendered "if not" (cf. NIV).

ᵈ Possibly: "Why did you go out? To see a man . . . ." See *Note* b. ℵ* reverses the order of ἰδεῖν ἄνθρωπον, "to see . . . a man," thus making the alternative translation just mentioned a necessary one. See also *Note* f. *Gos. Thom.* 78 supports this alternative translation. See *TCGNT*, 29.

ᵉ C L W Θ *f*¹·¹³ TR insert ἱματίοις, "clothes," probably by influence from Luke 7:25. The word is readily understood from the context.

ᶠ Possibly: "Why did you go out? To see a prophet?" See *Note* b. Here again, as in *Note* d, some MSS (ℵ* B¹ W Z) have the reverse word order, προφήτην ἰδεῖν, "to see a prophet."

ᵍ C L W Θ *f*¹·¹³ TR add γάρ, "for," at the beginning of the sentence.

ʰ syˢ and boᵐˢ delete the words καὶ ὁ νόμος, "and the law."

ⁱ ℵ C L W Z Θ *f*¹·¹³ TR add ἀκούειν, "to hear." B D 700 and others, however, do not have the word. It was probably added because of its presence in the formula elsewhere (e.g., Mark 4:9, 23; 7:16; Luke 8:8; 14:35). See *TCGNT*, 29.

Form/Structure/Setting

A. The question from John the Baptist by means of which he hopes to evaluate Jesus leads naturally to Jesus' own evaluation of John. In the latter the focus is upon John's key role in the transition from the old era (the law and the prophets) to the new era of the kingdom of God. John was thus at the turning point of salvation history, the very forerunner of the promised Messiah. Jesus' testimony concerning John thus inevitably becomes also an implied christological statement about himself.

B. Matthew (except for vv 14–15) and Luke (7:24–28 and 16:16) are dependent on Q for this material. Vv 7–11 agree nearly verbatim with Luke 7:24–28 except at two points. The most substantial differences are in v 8c and v 11. Luke 7:25c, οἱ ἐν ἱματισμῷ ἐνδόξῳ καὶ τρυφῇ ὑπάρχοντες ἐν τοῖς βασιλείοις εἰσίν, "those in glorious raiment and living in luxury are in palaces," which may accurately reflect Q, is apparently abbreviated by Matthew to the simpler οἱ τὰ μαλακὰ φοροῦντες ἐν τοῖς οἴκοις τῶν βασιλέων εἰσίν, "those wearing fine apparel are in the houses of kings" (v 8c), unless Matthew here reflects Q more accurately and thus Luke elaborates Q. In the second instance, v 11a, οὐκ ἐγήγερται ἐν γεννητοῖς γυναικῶν μείζων Ἰωάννου τοῦ βαπτιστοῦ, "there has not risen among those born of women one greater than John the Baptist," seems to be a smoothing out of the more awkward Greek (of Q?) reflected in Luke 7:28a, μείζων ἐν γεννητοῖς γυναικῶν Ἰωάννου οὐδείς ἐστιν, "greater among those born of women is no one."

Matthew has added ἀμήν, "truly," at the beginning of v 11 and substitutes τῇ βασιλείᾳ τῶν οὐρανῶν, "the kingdom of heaven," for Luke's "kingdom of God" (7:28). Vv 12–13, on the other hand, are considerably different from their parallel in Luke 16:16 (Matthew may have moved the logion to this context because of the reference to John the Baptist). The Lukan verse is much shorter: "the law and the prophets were until John. From then the kingdom of God is proclaimed [εὐαγγελίζεται] and everyone forces his or her way into it." εὐαγγελίζεται is almost certainly a Lukan rewriting of Matthew's more original and more difficult βιάζεται. Luke's ἀπὸ τότε, "from then," distinguishes the ministry of John from the kingdom of God much more strongly than does Matthew in the present passage. Luke then lacks Matthew's ἀπὸ δὲ τῶν ἡμερῶν Ἰωάννου τοῦ βαπτιστοῦ ἕως ἄρτι ἡ βασιλεία τῶν οὐρανῶν βιάζεται, "but from the days of John the Baptist until the present, the kingdom of heaven suffers violence" (v 12a). Lacking altogether in Luke (and Mark) are vv 14 and 15. As for the material that is paralleled in Luke, Matthew has πάντες γὰρ οἱ προφῆται καὶ ὁ νόμος ἕως Ἰωάννου ἐπροφήτευσαν, "for all the prophets and the law prophesied until John" (v 13), for Luke's more common ὁ νόμος καὶ οἱ προφῆται μέχρι Ἰωάννου, "the law and the prophets were until John." Finally, Matthew has the difficult βιασταὶ ἁρπάζουσιν αὐτήν, "violent people plunder it" (v 12), for Luke's πᾶς εἰς αὐτὴν βιάζεται, "everyone enters it violently" (RSV). Thus in vv 12–15 we have a further example of Matthew's creative redactional work on the tradition.

C. The passage can be divided into the following subsections: (1) a series of three questions about John and an answer from Scripture (vv 7–10); (2) a two-part saying about the greatness of John and the greatness of those in the kingdom (v 11); (3) the plight of the kingdom (v 12); (4) the identification of John as a salvation-historical turning point and as Elijah (vv 13–14); and (5) a formulaic exhortation to hear the point being made (v 15). The parallelism of the passage is mainly limited to vv 7–9 in the repeated questions and suggested answers also given in the form of questions. A third element is introduced parenthetically in v 8c, the locating of those finely dressed in palaces, and climactically in the description of John as "more than a prophet" (v 9), indeed the forerunner of the Messiah himself, a point stressed by the OT quotation (v 10). The three questions thus exemplify the common pattern of two wrong conclusions followed by the correct one.

D. Justin Martyr quotes vv 12–15 almost verbatim in *Dial.* 51.3, in obvious dependence on Matthew. Vv 7–8 are quoted loosely in *Gos. Thom.* 78, and v 11 is clearly alluded to in *Gos. Thom.* 46.

Comment

7–9 As the disciples of John are leaving to bring their report to John, Jesus addresses the crowds (τοῖς ὄχλοις) concerning the significance of the famous apocalyptic preacher, his role, and his relationship to Jesus' ministry. After John's imprisonment, the meaning of his preaching and baptizing undoubtedly was the subject of much discussion (cf. John 1:19–28; Matt 14:2). Three times Jesus asks the question, "What did you go out to see?" The verb ἐξήλθατε ("go out") is used in all three instances. The phrase εἰς τὴν ἔρημον, "into the wilderness," connotes revelation and messianic salvation (v 7; cf. 3:1, 5) and is assumed in the other two questions. (See *Notes* for the possible alternative translation of these questions.) No difference is intended between the θεάσασθαι, "to see," of the first question and the ἰδεῖν, "to see," of the second and third questions. Each question has a suggested answer posed in the form of a new question. The first of these refers to κάλαμον ὑπὸ ἀνέμου σαλευόμενον, "a reed blown by the wind" (v 7). This metaphor (perhaps suggested by the tall cane grass that grew along the shores of the Jordan) suggests weakness and vacillation, characteristics one does not associate with John. The question implies the conclusion that John was, to the contrary, strong and fixed in his orientation. (This is an indirect compliment, but it also may have put John in danger of rejecting Jesus because of an inability to redefine his concept of messianic fulfillment [see preceding pericope].) Perhaps, on the other hand, an allusion to Herod Antipas is intended since a coin of the time pictures him holding a reed (Theissen). This would also tie the metaphor nicely to the one that follows. The second metaphor, ἄνθρωπον ἐν μαλακοῖς ἠμφιεσμένον, "a man clothed in fine apparel" (v 8), is again just the opposite of John's strong asceticism (cf. 3:4, where John is recorded as wearing "a garment of camel's hair and a leather belt"). Now an additional element points out the obvious: those who are finely dressed, like Herod, are in palaces and not in the wilderness (the Herodian family, however, had a palace in Jericho on the edge of the wilderness, which could indeed emphasize the contrast). On the contrary, John drew attention because of his ascetic demeanor (seemingly patterned after Elijah; cf. 3:4; 2 Kgs 1:8). This leads naturally to the third question and for the first time to an affirmative answer, ναί, "yes" (v 9). The crowds went out to see not a king but a prophet—understandably because one who looked like and sounded like an authentic prophet had not been seen in Israel for generations. So they went out to see "a prophet" (14:5; 21:26), and to an extent this evaluation was correct (cf. Luke 1:76, where John is described as "a prophet of the Most High"). But now Jesus adds that John was περισσότερον προφήτου, "more than a prophet." The meaning of this is spelled out in the next verse.

10 Jesus evaluates John finally by identifying him as the one ("this one," οὗτος) promised by Scriptures to precede the coming of the Messiah and messianic fulfillment. The first line of the quotation is found verbatim in Exod 23:20, but its context, the sending of an angel before the Israelites when they occupy the promised land, does not permit the present application of the words. More likely, Matthew gives again a somewhat free rendition of Mal 3:1, which was the prophetic passage *(hapṭārâ)* read with Exod 23 (the first line of the quotation in Matthew may later have been conformed to the Greek of Exod 23:20): ἰδοὺ ἐγὼ ἐξαποστέλλω [Matthew: ἀποστέλλω, "I send"] τὸν ἄγγελόν μου [Matthew here inserts πρὸ προσώπου σου, "before you"], καὶ ἐπιβλέψεται [Matthew: ὃς κατασκευάσει, "who will prepare"] ὁδὸν [Matthew: τὴν ὁδόν] πρὸ προσώπου μου [Matthew: ἔμπροσθέν σου, "before you"], "Behold, I send out my messenger, and he will look over the way before me." The quotation is found verbatim in the Lukan parallel (7:27), except for the omission of ἐγώ at the very beginning, and in Mark at the beginning of the Gospel (1:2, wrongly attributed to Isaiah), except for the omission of the final ἔμπροσθέν σου, "before you." The shift in the pronouns from μου, "me," to σου, "you," is undoubtedly the result of the application of the passage to Jesus (the μου referred to God, the σου to the coming of God in Jesus). The repeated σου, "your," thus refers here to Jesus. John is accordingly identified as the one who prepares the way, identified later in Mal. 4:5 as Elijah, as also in the present pericope (v 14; cf. 17:12). This indication of the great importance of John as one who is at the turning point of the aeons (vv 12–13) is at the same time, if indirectly, further evidence of the messianic identity of Jesus, whose way (cf. 21:32) had been prepared by John. Matthew pursues this theme further in the verses that follow.

11 ⸍ The point made by this verse depends upon the premise that John is a transitional figure between two separate orders, a point pursued in vv 12–14. John is the climax of the old order: a prophet like those of the past but more than a prophet (cf. v 9). He is the one in whom the OT expectation has finally been distilled into one final, definitive arrow pointing to the presence of the Messiah. Thus from a human point of view no one greater than John has ever been born, i.e., no one of the old order supersedes John in importance. ($\gamma\epsilon\nu\nu\eta\tauο\hat{i}\varsigma$ $\gamma\upsilon\nu\alpha\iota\kappa\hat{\omega}\nu$, "those born of women," is Hebraic idiom [e.g., Job 14:1; 15:14].) That importance (note Matthew's added $\dot{\alpha}\mu\dot{\eta}\nu$, "truly") lies in the position and role of John at salvation-history's turning point. Only this realization makes possible the understanding of the next sentence: $\dot{ο}$ $\delta\dot{\epsilon}$ $\mu\iota\kappa\rho\dotο\tau\epsilonρ\varsigma$ $\dot{\epsilon}\nu$ $\tau\hat{\eta}$ $\beta\alpha\sigma\iota\lambda\epsilon\dot{\iota}\alpha$ $\tau\hat{\omega}\nu$ $ο\dot{\upsilon}ρ\alpha\nu\hat{\omega}\nu$ $\mu\epsilon\dot{\iota}\zeta\omega\nu$ $\alpha\dot{\upsilon}\tauο\hat{\upsilon}$ $\dot{\epsilon}\sigma\tau\iota\nu$, "nevertheless, the least in the kingdom of heaven is greater than he." This greatness cannot refer to intrinsic human merit. John, after all, was "great [$\mu\dot{\epsilon}\gamma\alpha\varsigma$] before the Lord" (Luke 1:15). The intended greatness is the incomparable greatness of the kingdom. The contrast is thus not between individuals but between eras. Nor can John here be thought of as excluded from the kingdom (see 8:11–12; if Abraham, Isaac, and Jacob will be at the messianic feast, so too will John). In effect, so glorious is the new reality dawning through the ministry of Jesus that the greatest of the era preceding him is yet inferior to the least in the new order of the kingdom. The era of present fulfillment (note the present tense $\dot{\epsilon}\sigma\tau\dot{\iota}\nu$, "is") overshadows the era of promise by so much. Again there is an unavoidable christological echo here.

12   An infamous crux in the exegesis of Matthew, this verse has been understood in a variety of ways.

The difficulty arises because of two variables, each of which can be taken positively or negatively (and with further differing nuances): (1) the verb $\beta\iota\dot{\alpha}\zeta\epsilon\tau\alpha\iota$ and (2) the noun $\beta\iota\alpha\sigma\tau\alpha\dot{\iota}$, together with the following words $\dot{\alpha}ρ\pi\dot{\alpha}\zetaο\upsilon\sigma\iota\nu$ $\alpha\dot{\upsilon}\tau\dot{\eta}\nu$. $\beta\iota\dot{\alpha}\zeta\epsilon\tau\alpha\iota$, can be taken as a middle or passive form, the former giving the positive meaning "come forcefully," the latter giving the negative meaning "suffer violence." Similarly it is possible to take $\beta\iota\alpha\sigma\tau\alpha\dot{\iota}$ $\dot{\alpha}ρ\pi\dot{\alpha}\zetaο\upsilon\sigma\iota\nu$ $\alpha\dot{\upsilon}\tau\dot{\eta}\nu$ positively, meaning "forceful people seize it" (thus referring to rigorous discipleship), or negatively, "violent persons plunder it." As a result, four options are possible for the meaning of the verse: both clauses of the verse can be taken (1) positively or (2) negatively, or (3) the first can be taken positively and the second negatively, or (4) the first negatively and the second positively.

The key question for deciding between the first two and the last two possibilities is whether the use of the same root in both clauses ($\beta\iota\dot{\alpha}\zeta\epsilon\tau\alpha\iota$; $\beta\iota\alpha\sigma\tau\alpha\dot{\iota}$) suggests that both have the same meaning, whether positive or negative. Most interpreters argue for the same meaning in both clauses. Those who opt for the positive meaning of the clauses generally do so because: (1) the middle of $\beta\iota\dot{\alpha}\zeta\epsilon\tau\alpha\iota$ is more common than the passive; (2) the parallel in Luke 16:16 ($\epsilon\dot{\upsilon}\alpha\gamma\gamma\epsilon\lambda\dot{\iota}\zeta\epsilon\tau\alpha\iota$, "is preached," and $\pi\hat{\alpha}\varsigma$ $\epsilon\dot{\iota}\varsigma$ $\alpha\dot{\upsilon}\tau\dot{\eta}\nu$ $\beta\iota\dot{\alpha}\zeta\epsilon\tau\alpha\iota$, "everyone presses into it") supports the positive meaning; and (3) the immediately preceding verses in Matthew (vv 2–6) refer to the coming of the kingdom in power and "forcefully." Those who opt for the negative meaning of the clauses do so primarily because (1) there is no evidence available that $\beta\iota\alpha\sigma\tau\alpha\dot{\iota}$, "violent persons," or its cognates were ever used in a positive sense and (2) the verb $\dot{\alpha}ρ\pi\dot{\alpha}\zetaο\upsilon\sigma\iota\nu$, "seize" or "plunder," is almost always used in a negative sense. This strong evidence for the negative meaning of the second clause then encourages the interpretation of $\beta\iota\dot{\alpha}\zeta\epsilon\tau\alpha\iota$ as a passive, with the imprisonment of John the Baptist as a confirming element in the immediate context.

Other interpreters reject the idea that the two words are of the same root and need to be understood the same way; they accordingly opt for whichever interpretation of each clause they find most convincing. The two clauses could be an example of antanclasis, a figure of speech wherein the same word is used with different or contradictory meanings in successive clauses (thus Carson). Those who take both clauses positively (e.g., Zahn; Ladd, *Presence*) thus find here a statement about the forceful coming of the kingdom in the ministry of Jesus and a coordinate description of the hard way of discipleship. Those who take both clauses negatively (e.g., Hill, Fenton, Green, Schweizer, Patte, Gundry, Gaechter, Maier, France, Mounce, Luz, Davies-Allison) understand the verse to refer to the persecution and difficulty faced by those who represent the kingdom. The violent people who plunder the kingdom are regarded variously as the Pharisees, Zealots, evil spirits, or even Herod Antipas. Among those who divide the clauses, the majority favor understanding the first negatively (the kingdom suffers violence) and the second positively (e.g., Dahl, Schlatter, Schniewind). A few argue for the first to be understood positively (the kingdom comes forcefully) and the second negatively (e.g., Carson, Pamment).

It is a mistake exegetically to interpret Matthew's difficult passage through Luke's simpler statement (Luke 16:16), which itself comes from a different context, especially when the logia are formulated so differently. It is furthermore easier to take βιάζεται as a passive, "suffers violence," and thus to understand the rest of the verse in the more natural way, "and violent persons plunder it," rather than understanding the latter as merely a metaphorical reference (and a strange one it would be) to the demands of discipleship. It is possible to take ἁρπάζειν either positively, "seize or claim for oneself," or negatively, "plunder" (see BAGD, 109). But it is particularly difficult to understand βιαστής, "violent person," in a positive sense, since the word or, rather, its close cognates are used only in a bad sense; in the three occurrences of the word in reference to human beings in early Christian literature, βιαστής is used only negatively (see BAGD, 141). The most natural conclusion is that what is in view here is again the reality of persecution and opposition (cf. 10:23; 23:34; and the use of ἁρπάζειν in 13:19; cf. 23:13)— and not necessarily the activity of the Zealots (T. W. Manson, *Teaching*, 124)—which might seem to contradict the greatness of the kingdom. Perhaps behind this opposition lie the forces of evil (cf. Davies-Allison). The reference to John, the last martyr of the old order and the proto-martyr of the new order, probably prompts Matthew to include this saying here. Thus ἀπὸ δὲ τῶν ἡμερῶν Ἰωάννου τοῦ βαπτιστοῦ, "from [and including] the days of John the Baptist," suffering has been the lot of those associated with the kingdom (cf. 10:17–25, 28, 38–39). Thus John is here included with those of the kingdom who suffer (cf. 23:34). The reference to John as "the Baptist," hardly necessary in this context, indicates the logion is independent. The suffering of John comes into view again in 17:12, where Jesus says, "Elijah has already come, and they did not know him, but did to him whatever they pleased." Given the obvious greatness of the kingdom, the present verse is bound to come as a shock. For all its greatness, the kingdom suffers violence and violent men plunder it. The kingdom involves suffering. In the same way, Matthew continues, so must the Son of Man suffer.

13–14 The evaluation of John now comes to its climax. The totality of God's previous revealing activity (note Matthew's added πάντες, "all," the prophets) and the expectation for the future built up in the writings of the OT culminate in John (ἕως Ἰωάννου ἐπροφήτευσαν, "prophesied until John"). πάντες οἱ προφῆται, "all the prophets," is a Matthean emphasis, consistent with the verb ἐπροθήτευσαν, "prophesied," and accounts for the reversal of the usual order "law and prophets" (cf. Luke 16:16). For Matthew, the law and the prophets bear a united witness to Jesus (the law as commandments is not directly in view here). This statement, therefore, cannot be understood to mean that John himself was the goal of the OT, since he has been identified already as the forerunner of someone else (v 9), but that John serves as a transition to the new (contrast Luke 16:16) and as such is here included with the new, which is definitely marked by Jesus. As a transition figure, John can be considered either as part of the old (e.g., v 11; cf. Luke 16:16) or as part of the new (vv 12, 13). The point is that a key turning point has been reached, marking off the old from the new. What has been implied through the quotation of Mal 3:1 in v 10 now comes to exact expression: αὐτός ἐστιν Ἠλίας ὁ μέλλων ἔρχεσθαι, "he himself is Elijah, 'the one about to come.'" What is meant here is not that John is actually Elijah *redivivus* (which is possibly what John denies according to John 1:21) but that he functions in the role that was ascribed to Elijah just preceding the end time. The last phrase, "the one about to come," is a kind of popular description of Elijah based on Mal 4:5 and reflects the widespread sense of the imminence of the eschaton. The expectation of the coming of Elijah prior to the end is found also in Sir 48:10. John is again identified as Elijah in 17:10–13 (cf. Luke 1:17). That those who resisted the truth should do to John "whatever they pleased" (17:12) made it all the more difficult to believe that John, sitting in prison and soon to die, was really the great figure Elijah. Indeed, in the same way they did to Jesus what they pleased and thus made his claim to be the Messiah difficult to accept. For this reason Jesus adds εἰ θέλετε δέξασθαι, "if you are willing to accept it." A degree of faith is required especially where not everything lines up according to one's previous convictions. This apparent allusion to the suffering of John, as well as the reference to it in 17:10–13, confirms the interpretation of v 12 given above.

15   The closing exhortation points to the unusual and difficult character of the preceding section. The formula, or one very similar to it, is often used in contexts where difficult content is present (e.g., 13:9, 43; Mark 4:9, 23; Luke 8:8; 14:35; cf. Rev 2:7, 11, 17, etc.). If John the Baptist sits in prison, can he be the great figure described by Jesus as the messianic forerunner? This exhortation amounts to an invitation to receive in positive response what has been said and is thus an appeal to the will as much as to the intellect (cf. Ezek 3:27). But it connotes also a hearing with understanding; in the last analysis such understanding implies or involves the acceptance of Jesus' own claims.

Explanation

A correct assessment of the significance of John the Baptist can only be made in relation to Jesus and the kingdom he brings. If Jesus brings the era of the fulfillment of the OT promises, then John is by definition at the turning point of the aeons, the last and greatest of the old, announcing and preparing the way for the new kingdom of the messianic king. Thus the attention given to John as the forerunner, fulfilling the role of Elijah, serves at the same time a christological purpose. John cannot be Elijah if Jesus is not the Messiah. So wonderful is the new reality brought by Jesus that the least of its participants is greater even than John. To participate in this reality is to begin to experience all towards which the OT pointed. This is an era of incomparable fulfillment, and those who receive it enjoy an incomparable privilege.

The Dissatisfaction of Israel (11:16–19)

Bibliography

Donahue, J. R. "Tax Collectors and Sinners." *CBQ* 33 (1971) 39–61. **Kloppenborg, J. S.** "Wisdom Christology in Q." *LTP* 34 (1978) 129–47. **Linton, O.** "The Parable of the Children's Game." *NTS* 22 (1976) 159–79. **Ljungman, H.** "En Sifre-text till Matt. 11:18f. par." *SEÅ* 22–23 (1957–58) 238–42. **Lövestam, E.** "The ἡ γενεὰ αὕτη Eschatology in Mk 13.30 parr." In *L'Apocalypse johannique et l'apocalyptique dans le Nouveau Testament*, ed. J. Lambrecht. BETL 53. Gembloux: Duculot, 1980. 403–13. **Mussner, F.** "Der nicht erkannte Kairos (Mt 11,16–19; Lk 7,31–5)." *Bib* 40 (1959) 599–612. **Verseput, D.** *The Rejection of the Humble Messianic King.* Europäische Hochschulschriften 23/291. Frankfurt am Main: P. Lang, 1986. **Völkel, M.** "'Freund der Zöllner und Sünder.'" *ZNW* 69 (1978) 1–10. **Zeller, D.** "Die Bildlogik des Gleichnisses Mt 11,16f./Lk 7,31f." *ZNW* 68 (1977) 252–57.

Translation

[16] *"But to what shall I liken this generation? It is like children who sit in the market-places and who call to others,*[a] [17] *saying:*
We played the flute for you, and you did not dance,
we sang a dirge,[b] *and you did not mourn.*[c]
[18] *For John came*[d] *neither eating nor drinking, and they said: 'He has a demon.'* [19] *The Son of Man came eating and drinking, and they said: 'Look, this man is a glutton and a drunkard, a friend of tax collectors and sinners.' And wisdom is justified by her deeds."*[e]

Notes

[a] C L W Θ *f*[13] TR add αὐτῶν, "of them," making clear that the children cry out to other children, something evident in the context.

[b] C L W Θ *f*[13] TR it sy add ὑμῖν, "to you," in order to parallel exactly the first line of the couplet. See *TCGNT*, 30.

[c] οὐκ ἐκόψασθε, lit. "you did not beat your breasts."

[d] Θ *f*[13] sy[c,h] add πρὸς ὑμᾶς, "to you."

[e] Many MSS, e.g., B[2] C D K L X Δ Θ Π TR read τέκνων, "children," probably by the influence of the Lukan parallel (7:35); some, furthermore, have πάντων, "all," before τῶν τέκνων, "children," for the same reason. See *TCGNT*, 30.

Form/Structure/Setting

A. The preceding discussion of the importance of John and his salvation-historical identity as Elijah leads now to this note about his rejection. Moreover, in their rejection of John this generation has also rejected Jesus. The parallel greatness and fate of John and Jesus are remarkable. The fact that the populace would accept neither John nor Jesus leads to the condemnatory passage that follows.

B. Matthew and Luke (7:31–35) are dependent on Q and agree quite closely in this pericope. Matthew, as usual, shortens the passage by omitting unessential words and phrases. Thus at the beginning, Matthew omits τοὺς ἀνθρώπους, "the people," and the redundant καὶ τίνι εἰσὶν ὅμοιοι, "and to what are they similar?"

(v 16; Luke 7:31). Matthew further omits ὁ βαπτιστής, "the baptist," and the direct objects ἄρτον, "bread," and οἶνον, "wine" (v 18; Luke 7:33), and the πάντων, "all," at the end of the passage (v 19; Luke 7:35). Besides very minor and unimportant changes, there are only two differences that need to be noted: Matthew's ἐκόψασθε, "mourn" (v 17), for Luke's ἐκλαύσατε, "weep" (Luke 7:32), and Matthew's ἔργων, "works" (v 19), for Luke's τέκνων, "children" (Luke 7:35).

C. This pericope is characterized by a carefully constructed parallelism in vv 17–19. V 17 consists of a couplet of almost exactly parallel lines (only the lack of ὑμῖν, "to you," in the second line keeps the parallelism from being exact). Vv 18 and 19 are exactly parallel in structure except for the longer line in v 19 following λέγουσιν and the addition of the concluding sentence. Again the influence of oral tradition is probably evident; the parallel material is easily memorized. The passage has the following structure: (1) the presentation of the simile, consisting of (a) the children (v 16) and (b) their words (v 17); (2) the application of the simile to (a) John (v 18) and (b) the Son of Man (v 19a and b); and (3) a concluding aphorism (v 19c).

Comment

16–17 The generation of John and Jesus (τὴν γενεὰν ταύτην, "this generation") is a generation of unbelief. The phrase "this generation" often connotes unbelief (cf. 12:41–42, 45; the disobedience and unbelief become explicit in 12:39; 16:4; and 17:17; see Lövestam). To throw light on the nature of that unbelief, Jesus likens his generation to the situation of children playing in the marketplaces who taunt their comrades for not joining them in their play. No matter what the one group did—play the flute (as in a wedding) or sing a dirge (as in a funeral)— the other group would not participate. In a similar way, the present generation (i.e., Jesus' contemporaries) will have nothing to do with the messengers sent to them by God. Thus the simile actually likens the unbelief of the present generation to the children who flatly refuse to participate in anything offered to them. This becomes clear in the following verses. The carefully formed couplet in v 17 has a proverbial ring, although it has not been found in any surviving literature (cf. Eccl 3:4). Two of the verbs occur only in Matthew here (αὐλεῖν, "play the flute" [the noun occurs in 9:23]; θρηνεῖν, "sing a dirge"), and ὀρχεῖσθαι, "dance," is found just once again (14:6) and κόπτειν, "mourn," only twice (21:8; 24:30).

18 Those who refused to heed John the Baptist apparently faulted him for his extreme asceticism (cf. 3:4; 9:14; cf. Luke 1:15). His intensity and demeanor made him seem possessed—even demon possessed—by those who were unreceptive; thus they (the subject of λέγουσιν here and in v 19 is the people of that generation; cf. v 16) concluded δαιμόνιον ἔχει, "he has a demon" (the same expression is used of Jesus repeatedly in John: 7:20; 8:48, 52; 10:20; cf. Matt 12:24 and Mark 3:22). John was accordingly rejected (21:32).

19 The Son of Man, here clearly Jesus himself (= "I"; or perhaps [with Luz] "Son of Man" in a titular sense to sharpen the criticism), was faring no better. His opponents found reason to regard him as a "glutton" (φάγος) and a "drunkard" (οἰνοπότης), both words occurring in the NT only here and in the parallel in Luke 7:34 (the same combination is found in Deut 21:20; cf. Prov 23:20). This caricature was perhaps caused by Jesus' frequent attendance at banquets. At the latter in particular he also showed himself to be a friend ($\phi\iota\lambda o\varsigma$) of tax collectors and sinners (cf. 9:10–13; Luke 15:2; 19:7). The concluding sentence, $\kappa\alpha\iota\ \dot{\epsilon}\delta\iota\kappa\alpha\iota\dot{\omega}\theta\eta$ $\dot{\eta}\ \sigma o\phi\iota\alpha\ \dot{\alpha}\pi\dot{o}\ \tau\hat{\omega}\nu\ \dot{\epsilon}\rho\gamma\omega\nu\ \alpha\dot{\upsilon}\tau\hat{\eta}\varsigma$, "and wisdom is justified by her deeds," with its personification of wisdom (cf. Prov 8; Wisd 7–8) appears originally to have been a wisdom saying with its own independent meaning. The aorist tense of the verb is gnomic or timeless. The point is that wisdom does what is right and will finally be vindicated by her deeds (for $\dot{\alpha}\pi\dot{o}$ with the genitive in this sense, see BAGD, s.v., V, 6, "with verbs in passive voice"). In the present context, applied to Jesus the saying means that the deeds of Jesus—including the very ones criticized by the opponents— will ultimately vindicate him. For Jesus, like $\sigma o\phi\iota\alpha$, "Wisdom," can do no wrong. He will ultimately be vindicated in what he does. And thus in Matthew the wisdom saying becomes a piece of wisdom Christology (with Luz contra Hill, Fenton, Carson), wherein the Son of Man is identified with Wisdom. To find Wisdom is to find life (cf. Prov 8:32–36; Sir 24:1–22). This identification is generally thought to be particularly important in the early development of Christology (cf. 1 Cor 1:24). The Christology of Matthew, however, is already much further developed than this, and thus this saying is an element of the primitive tradition (cf. Luke 11:49 and Matt 23:34, where "I" replaces "Wisdom"; cf. too 11:23–30). Schweizer appropriately cites *1 Enoch* 42:2, "Wisdom came to make her dwelling among the children of men and found no dwelling place." Jesus, like Wisdom, is rejected, but Jesus' deeds, like the deeds of Wisdom, are right and good and will ultimately vindicate him.

Explanation

John and Jesus, central figures in the salvation being effected by God, are nevertheless rejected by the populace. The mystery becomes even greater when, as the Gospel proceeds, each is killed. Those who oppose God will always seem to have reasons to resist. At one level the arguments can seem plausible. But at bottom they reflect unreceptive and unbelieving hearts. John is too holy; Jesus is not holy enough. And Jesus in particular does not conform to the accepted standards of righteousness. Can either be what they claimed? The opponents of John and Jesus will in fact accept fulfillment of the promises only on their own terms. Whatever fails to match that preconception, regardless of all other evidence and arguments, is automatically rejected. Yet ultimately John and Jesus, the forerunner and the Messiah, can only be vindicated, for they constitute the turning point and heart of salvation-history.

Oracles of Judgment   (11:20–24)

Bibliography

Childs, B. S. "A Study of the Formula 'Until this Day.'" *JBL* 82 (1963) 272–92. **Comber, J. A.** "The Composition and Literary Characteristics of Matt 11:20–24." *CBQ* 39 (1977) 497–

504. **Mussner, F.** "Gab es eine 'galiläische Krise'?" In *Orientierung an Jesus.* FS J. Schmid, ed. P. Hoffmann et al. Freiburg im Breisgau: Herder, 1973. 238–52. **Verseput, D.** *The Rejection of the Humble Messianic King.* Europäische Hochschulschriften 23.291. Frankfurt am Main: P. Lang, 1986.

Translation

[20] *Then he* [a] *began to reproach the cities in which he had done the majority of his miracles, because they did not repent:* [21] *"Woe to you, Chorazin; woe to you, Bethsaida; because if the miracles that have been done among you had been done in Tyre and Sidon, they would long ago have repented in* [b] *sackcloth and ashes.* [22] *Nevertheless I tell you, it will be more tolerable for Tyre and Sidon on the day of judgment than for you.* [23] *And you, Capernaum: Will you be exalted* [c] *up to heaven?* [d] *You will go down* [e] *to Hades. Because if the miracles that have been done among you had been done in Sodom, it would have remained until this day.* [24] *Nevertheless I tell you that it will be more tolerable for the land of Sodom on the day of judgment than for you."*

Notes

[a] Some MSS (e.g., C K L N W Θ $f^{1,13}$) insert ὁ Ἰησοῦς, "Jesus."

[b] A few MSS (ℵ C 33) insert καθήμενοι, "sitting," by influence of the parallel in Luke 10:13.

[c] The initial μή in the question could allow the translation "You won't be exalted . . . , will you?" Alternatively, without the question mark (an editorial decision, and not in the earliest MSS) the sentence could run "Lest you be exalted to heaven, you will go down to Hades."

[d] f^{13} TR and other MSS have ἡ ("the" or "who") instead of μή after Capernaum, thus making a slight change in the verb necessary and giving the translation "You, Capernaum, who are exalted up to heaven." The μ of μή was lost through haplography because of the μ at the end of Capernaum. See *TCGNT*, 30–31.

[e] A number of MSS (ℵ C L Θ $f^{1,13}$ TR) have καταβιβασθήσῃ, "you will be brought down." See *TCGNT*, 31.

Form/Structure/Setting

A. In this section the focus on the unbelief of Israel becomes sharper. The cities of Galilee are reproached for their failure to receive the message of Jesus. As the Gospel proceeds to chap. 12, unbelief will escalate into outright hostility against Jesus. The rejection Jesus warned his disciples about in the missionary discourse begins already to be the experience of Jesus himself. But the rejection of Jesus will mean a more severe judgment for the people of these cities.

B. The introductory sentence of the passage is unique to Matthew, serving as a transition to the judgment sayings that follow. Vv 21–24, on the other hand, are drawn from Q (cf. the parallel in Luke 10:12–15). Apart from one transposition, the agreement in wording is very close. The transposition involves the placing of the reference to Sodom at the end of the passage (v 24) instead of at the beginning as in Luke (10:12). For the remainder, Matthew has ἐγένοντο for Luke's ἐγενήθησαν (both meaning "had been done"), and Matthew omits Luke's καθήμενοι, "sitting," in the reference to sackcloth and ashes (v 21; Luke. 10:13). Matthew has λέγω ὑμῖν, "I say to you," at the beginning of v 22 (missing in Luke 10:14). Matthew has ἡμέρᾳ κρίσεως, "day of judgment," for Luke's κρίσει, "judgment" (v 22; Luke 10:14), and the same in v 24 for Luke's ἡμέρᾳ ἐκείνῃ, "that day" (Luke 10:12). A few other small changes need not be noted here. The transposition referred to above seems caused by Matthew's preference for having the climax of the passage refer to Sodom. Perhaps more importantly the form of the material in Matthew exhibits a perfect parallelism (see below). Sodom (and Gomorrah) has already been referred to in an almost identical judgment saying in 10:15.

C. As noted above, the first sentence of this pericope serves as a transition, setting the scene for the material that follows. The words of Jesus are yet again presented in a nearly perfect parallel structure. Thus vv 21–22, concerning the unbelief of Chorazin and Bethsaida, correspond closely to vv 23–24, concerning the unbelief of Capernaum. The only significant difference is in the form of the opening words of the indictment. Thus v 21a has the double "woe," whereas v 23a has the exaltation to heaven question and the statement about going to Hades (with parallel verbs and prepositional phrases). But after this difference both parts have similar ὅτι ("because") clauses, but with different content, and practically identical εἰ ("if") clauses (vv 21 and 23). Finally, the statements about judgment being more tolerable for other groups of people are given nearly verbatim (vv 22 and 24). The pericope can be outlined as follows: after the introductory transition statement of v 20, (1) the oracle against Chorazin and Bethsaida, consisting of (a) the ground of the judgment with comparison to Tyre and Sidon and (b) the statement about a less tolerable judgment (vv 21–22); and (2) the oracle against Capernaum, consisting of (a) the ground of the judgment with comparison to Sodom and (b) the reference to the less tolerable judgment (vv 23–24). Again noticeable is the care in the parallel construction of the material and its suitability for oral transmission.

Comment

20 Matthew has given a summary of the Galilean ministry of Jesus in chaps. 5–7 and 8–9. A few signs of unbelief and rejection are given as early as 9:3, 11, and 34 (cf. 10:25; 11:19), but now the extent of the rejection of Jesus comes into full light. With the unbelief of Israel, a turning point in the narrative has been reached (cf. Comber). For the first time we encounter the mysterious fact of the failure of Jesus' mission to Israel. Jesus rebukes the largely unreceptive cities (i.e., villages) of Galilee, particularly since they had been privileged to see the mighty deeds, indeed αἱ πλεῖσται δυνάμεις, "most of the miracles," of Jesus. This word δυνάμεις, "mighty deeds," occurs like a refrain in vv 21 and 23. Although they had witnessed these deeds of power, they did not respond to Jesus' proclamation of the kingdom (cf. John 12:37): they did not "repent" (μετενόησαν). The same verb occurs in v 21 and is implied in v 23. This indicates that Jesus' message about the kingdom (cf. 4:23; 9:35; cf. 10:7) was accompanied, as from the beginning (4:17), by a call to repentance.

21–22 Jesus first laments the unbelief of Chorazin and Bethsaida, cities in the vicinity of the Sea of Galilee. Both are mentioned in Matthew only here. The Gospels provide no record of Jesus' activity in Chorazin, a few kilometers northwest of the lake (the name occurs again elsewhere in the NT only in the Lukan parallel to the present passage [Luke 10:13]). It is probably to be identified with modern Kirbet Keraze about two miles north of Capernaum. Bethsaida, at the north end of the Sea of Galilee, is mentioned in Mark 8:22 as the place where Jesus healed a blind man and in Luke 9:10 as a place where Jesus "spoke to them of the kingdom of God and cured those who had need of healing" (cf. too Mark 6:45). Despite the evidence available to them, the residents of these cities—perhaps meant to be understood as representative of other Galilean cities in which Jesus ministered —did not respond as they should have done, and thus they were culpable. The cities of Tyre and Sidon are mentioned in Matt 15:21 as an area in which Jesus was active (cf. Mark 7:24, 31), but the comparison in the present verse is to the wicked Tyre and Sidon against whom the judgment oracles in Isa 23 are directed (cf. Ezek 26–28; Joel 3:4–8). Even places as bad as pagan Tyre and Sidon would have repented had they witnessed the deeds of Jesus. Thus the day of judgment (ἡμέρα κρίσεως), i.e., the day of eschatological judgment (cf. 12:36; 2 Peter 2:9; 3:7; 1 John 4:17), will be easier for them, despite their wickedness, than it will be for the inhabitants of Chorazin and Bethsaida. And thus Jesus pronounces woes upon these cities. The interjection οὐαί, "woe," used always in Matthew with the dative, expresses painful displeasure (used with special frequency in chap. 23). "Sackcloth and ashes" (ἐν σάκκῳ καὶ σποδῷ), words occurring in the Gospels only here and in the Lukan parallel (Luke 10:13), refer in the OT to the common signs of sorrow for one's sins and the consequent repentance (cf. Dan 9:3; Jonah 3:6; Esth 4:3).

23–24   Capernaum was the headquarters of Jesus' Galilean ministry (4:13; 8:5; 9:1; 17:24; cf. Mark 2:1). It must have been particularly distressing that Capernaum was in the main unreceptive to Jesus' ministry (cf. 13:57). Capernaum was apparently proud and ambitious, as the question "Will you be exalted to heaven?" suggests (cf. Isa 14:13). Yet her fate would prove to be the opposite: she would go down to "Hades" (ᾅδου; Heb. šĕ'ôl), i.e., the unseen realm of the dead (used by Matthew elsewhere only in 16:18). This is an allusion to the LXX of Isa 14:15: εἰς ᾅδου καταβήσῃ (cf. 14:11, which has only a slightly different word order). It is difficult to make the application of the first rhetorical phrase to Capernaum more precise, but it seems to refer to an unwarranted, prideful confidence in an exceptional degree of eschatological blessing. The imagery of v 23 is clearly borrowed from Isa 14:13–15 (for šĕ'ôl, see too Ezek 26:20–21). The comparison with Sodom makes Jesus' indictment of Capernaum all the sharper. Sodom's wickedness and consequent destruction were notorious from the OT record (Gen 18:20–19:29; cf. Isa 1:9; Rom 9:29; 2 Peter 2:6; Jude 7). Had the miracles of Jesus been performed in Sodom, even Sodom would have repented and the city would not have been destroyed: it would have "remained until today" (ἔμεινεν ἂν μέχρι τῆς σήμερον). But in the last judgment, Sodom, like Tyre and Sidon compared to Chorazin and Bethsaida, will fare better than unbelieving Capernaum. The same point was made generally in 10:5 (in reference to "that city," i.e., which does not receive the disciples), but there Gomorrah is added to Sodom (cf. Matthew's γῆ Σοδόμων, "land" of Sodom). Capernaum, so privileged with the frequent presence of Jesus, could expect severe judgment at the end of the present age.

Explanation

This passage vividly illustrates the simple truth that the greater the revelation, the greater the accountability. This is a principle encountered elsewhere in the NT, for example, in Rom 2:12–16. The cities of Galilee were especially privileged. A great light had shone in their midst (cf. 4:15–16), yet they refused to acknowledge that light. They accepted neither the message of the kingdom nor the messenger of the kingdom. They are accordingly more culpable than those who, though very wicked, had less clear evidence of the will of God. The reality of their future judgment points inescapably to the supreme importance of the mission and message of Jesus. This is the true center of the passage. The meaning of the failure of Jesus' mission to Israel will remain unclear until his disciples are forced to grapple with the problem of the failure of *their* mission to Israel (see esp. Rom 11:11–12, 25).

The Mystery of Election and the Central Significance of the Son (11:25–27)

Bibliography

Allison, D. C. "Two Notes on a Key Text: Matt. XI.25–30." *JTS* 39 (1988) 472–80. **Cerfaux, L.** "L'Évangile de Jean et 'le logion johannique' des Synoptiques." In *L'Évangile de Jean,* ed. F.-M. Braun. RechBib 3. Bruges: Desclée de Brouwer, 1958. 147–59. ————. "Les sources scripturaires de Matth. xi. 25–30." *ETL* 30 (1954) 740–46; 31 (1955) 331–42. **Davies, W. D.** "'Knowledge' in the Dead Sea Scrolls and Matthew 11.25–30." In *Christian Origins and Judaism.* Philadelphia: Westminster, 1962. 119–44. **Deutsch, C.** *Hidden Wisdom and the Easy Yoke: Wisdom, Torah and Discipleship in Matthew 11.25–30.* JSNTSup 18. Sheffield: JSOT Press, 1987. **Gibbs, J. M.** "The Son of God as the Torah Incarnate in Matthew's Gospel." *SE* 4 [= TU 102] (1968) 38–46. **Grimm, W.** *Jesus und das Danielbuch: I. Jesu Einspruch gegen das Offenbarungs-system Daniels (Mt 11,25; Lk 17,20–21).* ANTJ 6. Frankfurt am Main: P. Lang, 1984. **Grundmann, W.** "Matth 11,27 und die johanneischen 'der Vater—der Sohn'—Stellen." *NTS* 12 (1965) 42–49. ————. "Die νήπιοι in der urchristlichen Paränese." *NTS* 5 (1959) 188–205. **Hoffmann, P.** "Die Offenbarung des Sohnes: Die apokalyptischen Voraussetzungen und ihre Verarbeitung im Q-Logien Mt 11,27 par Lk 10,22." *Kairos* 12 (1970) 270–88. **Hunter, A. M.** "Crux Criticorum—Matt. 11.25–30." *NTS* 8 (1962) 241–49. **Johnson, M. D.** "Reflections on a Wisdom Approach to Matthew's Christology." *CBQ* 36 (1974) 44–64. **Légasse, S.** "Le logion sur le Fils révélateur." In *La notion biblique de Dieu,* ed. J. Coppens. BETL 41. Gembloux: Duculot, 1976. 245–74. ————. "Le révélation aux NHΠIOI." *RB* 67 (1960) 321–48. **Luck, U.** "Weisheit und Christologie in Mt 11,25–30." *WD* 13 (1975) 35–51. **Marshall, I. H.** "The Divine Sonship of Jesus." *Int* 21 (1967) 89–103. **Norden, E.** *Agnostos Theos.* 1913. Darmstadt: Wissenschaftliche Buchgesellschaft, 1956. 277–308. **Rist, M.** "Is Matt. 11:25–30 a Primitive Baptismal Hymn?" *JR* 15 (1935) 63–77. **Sabbe, M.** "Can Mt 11.25–7 and Lc 10.21–2 Be Called a Johannine Logion?" In *Logia: Les paroles de Jésus.* FS J. Coppens, ed. J. Delobel. BETL 59. Leuven: Peeters/Leuven University, 1982. 363–71. **Steck, K. G.** "Über Matthäus 11,25–30." *EvTh* 15 (1955) 343–49. **Suggs, J.** *Wisdom, Christology and Law in Matthew's Gospel.* Cambridge: Cambridge University, 1970.

Translation

[25] *At that time Jesus, responding to this unbelief,*[a] *said, "I praise you, Father, Lord of heaven and earth, because you have hidden these things from the wise and intelligent*

and have revealed them to the childlike.[b] [26]*Yes, Father, because this was your good pleasure.*[c] [27]*Everything has been given to me by my*[d] *Father, and no one fully knows*[e] *the Son except the Father, nor does anyone fully know*[f] *the Father except the Son and anyone to whom the Son chooses to reveal him.*"

Notes

[a] ἀποκριθεὶς ὁ Ἰησοῦς εἶπεν, lit. "answering, Jesus said." Since no question or dialogue precedes, ἀποκριθείς may be taken as a response to the preceding paragraph.

[b] νηπίοις, "babes," here used metaphorically. See *BAGD*, 537.

[c] οὕτως εὐδοκία ἐγένετο ἔμπροσθέν σου, lit. "thus it was well-pleasing before you."

[d] "My," μου, is omitted in ℵ* sa^ms bo but can be implied even by the definite article before "Father."

[e] "Fully knows" translates the intensive verb ἐπιγινώσκει.

[f] See preceding *Note*.

Form/Structure/Setting

A. The unbelief of the Galilean villages and their rejection of Jesus and his message lead now to a kind of theological assessment of this turn of events. In an extraordinary passage that provides a glimpse of the special relationship between Jesus and his Father and so provides a definitive answer to the question raised by John (v 3), Jesus acknowledges the reality of the mystery of election. The Father remains Lord of heaven and earth despite the Galilean refusal of the Son. To refuse the Son, however, is to refuse the Father (cf. 10:40). And now, astonishingly, the Son is shown to have the prerogative of electing grace on behalf of the Father. This together with vv 28–30 constitutes a climactic passage in Matthew's presentation of Jesus. Davies-Allison say of 11:25–30 that it is "a capsule summary of the message of the entire gospel" (2:29b; prompted by E. P. Blair's statement that the Gospel is "simply a commentary on the crucially important passage 11:27–30" [*Jesus*, 108]; cf. Hunter, 241).

B. Vv 25–27 are here dealt with separately from vv 28–30 only because they constitute a separate part of the larger unity of vv 25–30 and it is convenient to do so. There is no intention in this division to challenge the consensus that vv 25–30 constitute a unity. The larger passage consists of three independent parts: (1) vv 25–26; (2) v 27; and (3) vv 28–30. Norden (277–308) detected here a threefold pattern he found elsewhere in "mystical philosophical" literature: (1) thanksgiving to God; (2) revelation of a mystery; and (3) an appeal (cf. respectively Sir 51:1–12, 13–22, 23–30). Apart from Norden's theory, it is clear that vv 25–26 constitute a prayer of thanksgiving and that the closely related logion of v 27 is an added christological interpretation (cf. Luz's designation of the verse as a *Kommentarwort*). The third part continues in a christological vein, but its invitation gives it a distinctive character that enables it to be treated separately.

For vv 25–27 Matthew depends, with Luke (10:21–22), on Q. Apart from the opening clause, the changes are minor and insignificant. Luke, however, places this pericope after the return of the seventy with joy from their missionary work. Thus in Luke the passage focuses on belief and success, whereas in Matthew it focuses on unbelief and failure. This explains Luke's ἠγαλλιάσατο ἐν τῷ πνεύματι τῷ ἁγίῳ, "he rejoiced in the Holy Spirit," which is lacking in Matthew. Luke also has ἐν αὐτῇ τῇ ὥρα, "in that hour" (of the joy of the seventy), for Matthew's more general ἐν ἐκείνῳ τῷ καιρῷ, "at that time." From this point on, however, Matthew and Luke agree nearly verbatim to the end of the passage. The only differences between the two are the following: Luke's ἀπέκρυψας (Luke 10:21) for Matthew's ἔκρυψας (v 25), both meaning "you have hidden"; Matthew's double ἐπιγνώσκει (v 27) for Luke's single γινώσκει (Luke 10:22), both meaning "know" (Matthew's form is intensive, however); and finally, Luke's τίς ἐστιν ὁ υἱός, "who the Son is," and τίς ἐστιν ὁ πατήρ, "who the Father is" (Luke 10:22), for Matthew's simple τὸν υἱόν, "the Son," and τὸν πατέρα, "the Father" (v 27). Matthew's probable affirmation of Q here has the effect of sharpening this final statement.

C. The present subpericope consists of two distinct parts following the introductory clause (v 25a): (1) Jesus' praise of the Father (vv 25–26) and (2) the unique authority of the Son (v 27). Each of these parts can be further subdivided as follows: for part 1, (a) the thanksgiving (v 25b), (b) the two-fold object of the thanksgiving, (i) the obscuring and (ii) the revealing (v 25c, in close parallelism), and (c) the ground of the preceding (v 26); for part 2, (a) the granting of everything to the Son (v 27a) and (b) the possession of true knowledge (i) of the Son by the Father, (ii) of the Father by the Son (these two in exactly parallel clauses), and (iii) of those to whom the Son reveals it (v 27b–c). Again a degree of parallelism is apparent, and there is evidence of careful crafting of the Q material.

V 27 is quoted by Justin Martyr, *Dial.* 100.1 (cf. *Apol.* 1.63.11).

D. The remarkable character of this passage and its similarity in tone to the Fourth Gospel have caused the passage to be variously described as a meteorite or thunderbolt from the Johannine sky (thus first K. A. von Hase, *Die Geschichte Jesu,* 2nd ed. [Leipzig, 1876] 422, in the nineteenth century). Johannine parallels abound: for the special authority given to Jesus (v 27), compare John 3:35; 13:3; 17:2 (in a prayer of Jesus, similar to the present passage); for the intimate relationship and unique mutual knowledge of the Father and the Son, compare John 7:29; 10:14–15; and 17:25 (again in the prayer of Jesus). It is not unusual to hear the conclusion that this state of affairs, together with the content of the passage itself, calls into question the authenticity of the Synoptic passage (the recent commentaries of Luz and Davies-Allison unhesitatingly conclude that v 27 is a piece of post-resurrection Christology). Can the historical Jesus have possessed such self-consciousness? That Jesus knew himself to be God's unique agent or representative who alone mediated knowledge of the Father need not be regarded as an impossibility. If he referred to God as his Father, there is little reason to deny that he thought of himself as son, even unique Son. This sense of unique sonship is a part of, indeed presupposed by, his messianic consciousness. Even as impressive a statement as v 27d, "and anyone to whom the Son chooses to reveal him," need point to no more than the supreme importance, even indispensability, of the Son in the process of revelation. Of this much Jesus could well have been conscious; it is certain, however, that the early Church soon drew more dramatic christological conclusions from this logion (e.g., Jesus' preexistence and deity), as Matthew may even have meant his church to do. See Marshall for a defense of the authenticity of v 27. It may be, therefore, that this Synoptic passage shows that here, at least, the Johannine material relies on historical tradition paralleling the Synoptic tradition and that this may in turn enhance to a degree the historical character of the Johannine passages. Be that as it may, the present passage constitutes without question one of the highest points of Synoptic Christology. Yet it is not out of keeping with the christological emphasis of the Synoptic tradition generally or of Matthew particularly.

Comment

25–26 ἐν ἐκείνῳ τῷ καιρῷ, "in that time," links the passage with the preceding lament concerning the unbelief of the Galileans. This may possibly explain the ἀποκριθείς, lit. "answered," as pointing to a kind of response to that unbelief (with Sand; contra Davies-Allison). The verb ἐξομολογοῦμαι, "I praise," ordinarily means "confess" (cf. 3:6) or "acknowledge" but, when used in a context such as this, means, as often in LXX (cf. Sir 51:1; Pss 9:2; 135:26), praise or thanksgiving directed to God (see BAGD, 277). The pattern of expression in the opening words is thus Jewish and biblical. Jesus praises here the working out in reality of the sovereign will of God, both in the rejection and in the reception of the message of the kingdom. πάτερ, "Father," probably translates the Aramaic ʾabbāʾ, a term of intimacy (see on 6:9, which in its address to God combines the intimate and transcendent in a way similar to the present passage). The phrase κύριε τοῦ οὐρανοῦ καὶ τῆς γῆς, "Lord of heaven and earth" (cf. Acts 17:24; Tob 7:18), shows clearly that the sovereignty of God is in view. The ground for the thankful praise offered by Jesus is stated in the two contrasting statements of the ὅτι clause in v 25. God's mysterious sovereignty lies behind both belief and unbelief, yet without obviating the culpability of those who fail to believe. That some believed and others did not believe the message of Jesus can be described from this perspective as God either concealing or revealing the truth of that message. (The same notion of God concealing the truth is found at Qumran; cf. 1QS 4:6; 1QH 5:25–26.) In the division that has transpired, God has hidden (ἔκρυψας) and revealed (ἀπεκάλυψας) the truth of ταῦτα, "these things," i.e., presumably the deeds and words of Jesus in his Galilean ministry that disclose the presence of the kingdom. The revelation of truth in this passage has an eschatological ring (it is an "eschatological *gnosis*," but available now in Jesus; thus Davies-Allison) and may be related to such passages as Jer 31:34 and Hab 2:14, which refer to the spread of knowledge prior to the end.

At this point a further and new distinction is made, now between the σοφῶν καὶ συνετῶν, "the wise and intelligent," on the one hand, and the νηπίοις, "the simple," "the childlike," on the other. Paradoxically, the wise and intelligent do not receive the gospel, whereas the childlike welcome it (cf. 21:15–16). There is no arbitrariness in this. Rather, it is simply true that for the most part the wise tend to become proud and self-sufficient in their wisdom and particularly unreceptive regarding the new and the unexpected. It is not hard, for example, to see the majority of scribes and Pharisees as falling into this category (Luz refers to "the entire religious aristocracy"). The blindness of those wise by the world's standards is a motif found elsewhere in the OT (cf. Isa 29:14), Qumran (e.g., 1QS 11:6), and the NT (1 Cor 1:19, 21, 26–29, which may allude to this Synoptic pericope). Contrariwise, the childlike are most often unself-conscious, dependent, and receptive. The word νήπιος is used in the LXX of Pss 18:7; 114:6; 118:30 to refer to "the simple" (where it translates the Heb word פֶּתִי, *petî*, "simple"; cf. the working of wisdom among "infants" in Wis 10:21). Certainly the poor and oppressed are included here (Luz notes the ʿ*ammē ha-ʾāreṣ*). The need to become like a child to receive the kingdom is made clear in 18:1–4 (cf. 5:5). It is the simple, childlike who become the disciples of Jesus. God's will is being worked out in both instances, and in retrospect God's sovereignty can be described in terms of causation: a concealing and a revealing. This same motif will reappear in connection with the parables in 13:11.

V 26 confirms that nothing has happened outside of the good pleasure of God's will (see Sir 39:18 for similar vocabulary). The ναί, "yes," and the additional ὅτι ("because") clause, which must be related to the preceding sentence, have the effect of emphasizing this conclusion. The note of predestination here cannot be missed but is to be held in tension with the culpability of those who refuse to believe (cf. vv 20–24). The noun εὐδοκία, "good pleasure," found in Matthew only here and in Luke only in the parallel passage (Luke 10:21) and in 2:14, refers to God's "gracious elective will" (Schweizer). (For the cognate verb in Matthew, see 3:17; 12:18; 17:5; cf. 1 Cor 1:21, in a context referring to wisdom and faith.)

27 Vv 25–26 focus on the Father's sovereign purpose, worked out in the decisions for and against Jesus and his message. Now the focus shifts to the importance of the Son, Jesus himself. The prayer of vv 25–26 has ended, and now a logion of Jesus is appended to it. The prayer may well have prompted the saying that now follows.

Although this verse is of central importance for Matthew's Christology, its meaning is much disputed. Luz notes that in an attempt to defend the authenticity of this passage and especially this logion some modern scholars (in particular Jeremias, *New Testament Theology*, 56–61) have steadily reduced the meaning of the words. What in particular does the verse say about Jesus? The question must be refined into the following: What would Jesus have meant by the words (assuming, of course, that he said them or something like them)? What did the evangelist mean by them, and what did his community make of them? What might be made of them by later theologians of the Church? To the last-named group, the words may well be taken as pointing to such things as the deity and pre-existence of Christ and to the doctrine of the Trinity, although the text does not of course directly mention these things. Leaving that aside, we may fairly conclude that, as often happens in his narrative, the evangelist means to say more by his text than the historical Jesus may have meant. If in the interpretation of the present passage the self-consciousness of Jesus is used as a criterion, a minimalist reading will be the most plausible. The text of Matthew, however, will first of all reflect the intention of the evangelist. It cannot be doubted that the evangelist has a very high Christology (cf. 1:23; 16:16; 17:5; 18:20; 25:31; 26:64; 28:18–20). The present verse is obviously a high point in which the evangelist points to the uniqueness of Jesus, who alone is to be put with God as the one through whom he reveals himself to humanity. This passage is thus part of a trajectory within the NT that contributes to the conclusions of later theologians who are constrained to draw conclusions that the evangelist himself was not in a position to do.

To begin with, "the Son" (ὁ υἱός) is used absolutely (i.e., without qualification), as it is in only one other place is the Synoptics (24:36 [= Mark 13:32]) and frequently in the Fourth Gospel. This can hardly have originally meant "a son" in relation to "a father" (as Jeremias contends, *New Testament Theology*, 57–58), nor is it a piece of Son of Man Christology (contra Légasse, "Le logion"). "The Son" is to be equated with Matthew's Son of God Christology (cf. esp. 3:17; 14:33; 16:16; 17:5; 27:54). It is the "Son of God" who is uniquely related to his Father. Everything (πάντα) has been granted (παρεδόθη, perhaps a deliberate contrast with rabbinic tradition [παράδοσις]) to the Son by his Father. What is in view in this context is revelation or the granting of knowledge of the truth (cf. the last clause of the present verse). A similar statement is made in 28:18 in connection with the giving of the great commission (πᾶσα ἐξουσία ἐν οὐρανῷ καὶ ἐπὶ [τῆς] γῆς, "all authority in heaven and on earth"; cf. Dan 7:14; John 3:35). Here, however, what has been granted to Jesus is further defined in the final clause of the passage, i.e., knowledge of and hence the ability to reveal the Father. The object of ἀποκαλύψαι must be "the Father," and by implication this is analogous to a knowledge of "these things" (v 25). The point is that Jesus thus has a unique role as the mediator of the knowledge of God to humankind. This role is directly linked with the person of Jesus, his identity as the unique representative of God. The relationship between Jesus and God is accordingly *sui generis*. This is expressed in the statements that only the Father truly knows the Son and only the Son truly knows the Father. The verb ἐπιγινώσκειν with the prepositional prefix ἐπί here probably is deliberately intensive and, if so, would mean to "know exactly, completely, through and through" (BAGD, 291; according to Gundry and Deutsch it means "to recognize"). "Know" here can hardly mean "choose," as it does in other places, since then the symmetrical reciprocity of these statements is nullified. This intimate reciprocal knowledge implies intimate relationship (cf. the ʾabbāʾ probably underlying πάτερ, "Father," in v 25, which is perhaps also to be assumed here). The statement that only the Father knows the Son is christological; i.e., the true identity of Jesus in his relationship to the Father is veiled to his contemporaries and is known only to God (cf. 16:17; Gal 1:15–16). The statement that only the Son knows the Father in this context alludes to the knowledge of God in the sense of his saving purposes, revealed now particularly in the preaching of the kingdom and the ministry of Jesus. Those who know the Father know and receive the good news announced by Jesus and the disciples; those who reject Jesus and his message demonstrate a lack of knowledge of the Father. Behind this mutual or reciprocal knowledge (cf. John 10:14–15) seems to be again wisdom Christology (cf. 11:19). God of course knows Wisdom (cf. Sir 1:6–9); but Wisdom also knows God (Wis 8:4; 9:9–11) and conveys that knowledge to others (Wis 9:17–18).

But perhaps the most astonishing statement in the passage is found in the last clause: καὶ ᾧ ἐὰν βούληται ὁ υἱὸς ἀποκαλύψαι, "and anyone to whom the Son chooses to reveal [him]." Here the same verb used in describing the sovereign revealing activity of the Father in v 25, ἀποκαλύπτειν, "to reveal," is now used in describing the prerogative of Jesus (ᾧ ἐὰν βούληται, "anyone to whom he chooses"). This in principle places Jesus on the side of the Father in contrast to all humanity (cf. too v 27a; contrast the Teacher of Righteousness at Qumran, who despite his importance remains on the side of humanity [1QH 4:27–29]). Jesus is the unique agent of the Father—the one fully known by the Father alone. He is the sole mediator simultaneously of the knowledge of the Father and of his salvation purposes, for the Father and his will are fully known to Jesus. Jesus reveals this knowledge only to those who will receive it. Yet the invitation remains open to "all" (cf. πάντες in v 28).

Davies-Allison have departed significantly from the mainstream interpretation of this passage (i.e., the whole of vv 25–30) by finding its roots not in the wisdom tradition of Sir 51 but in what might be called Moses typology based on Exod 33:12–14. This passage refers to reciprocal knowledge and includes the promise "My presence will go with you, and I will give you rest." Davies-Allison point to the supreme importance of Moses as revealer (they appeal to the similarity with 1 Cor 13:12, the close agreement in the wording concerning rest [LXX: καὶ καταπαύσω σε (for Matthew's κἀγὼ ἀναπαύσω ὑμᾶς)], the fact that both passages are prayers, the agreement of the order of the first two clauses in v 27, and Moses' well-known meekness). They do not deny that Matthew makes use of a wisdom Christology in 11:19 or even that there are wisdom motifs in the present passage (cf. M. D. Johnson's denial altogether that Matthew utilizes a wisdom Christology). They are critical, however, of the hypothesis that vv 25–30 are dependent on Sir 51. While Davies-Allison have made an impressive argument for the possibility that the verses go back instead to Exod 33:12–14, it is unlikely that they will persuade many. Once it is granted that Matthew could think in terms of wisdom Christology, the similarities (if not the precise wording) are so many and so strong that Sir 51 remains the most likely influence: for vv 28–30, note in Sir 51:23–27 the invitation in the first person to come "to me" (πρός με), the reference to needy "persons" (ψυχαί), the call to take the "yoke" (ζυγόν) of instruction, the reference to a light "labor" (κοπιᾶν), as well as the promise of rest that is to be "found" (εὑρίσκειν). The Exod 33 passage lacks the invitation "come to me" (surely of central importance in identifying the source), the reference to the need of the people, the call concerning the yoke (also extremely important), the note about finding, and finally the reference to labor.

Explanation

Confronted by resistance and unbelief, Jesus can yet praise the Father, for his will is being worked out both in those who receive and in those who reject the gospel. Nothing is ever out of the control of God, who is Lord of heaven and earth. Yet God's sovereignty must not be taken to cancel out the free will and responsibility of those to whom the gospel goes. At bottom it is a question of receptivity (cf. the beatitudes, 5:3–12). The wise are often sadly tripped up by their very wisdom; contrariwise, it is the childlike, the unpresumptuous, and the open-handed who most often wait upon God and his provision. The main problem of those who are "wise" centers on Jesus and the apparent nature of the kingdom he announced. That is, everything depends on the ability to perceive the significance of Jesus and the reality of the dawning kingdom. For the "wise," the idea of a Messiah and a kingdom that does not entail an immediate overthrow of the Romans and the establishment of a new, earthly, national-political kingdom in the present era is automatically to be rejected. Thus everything comes down finally to the person of Jesus and the nature of the fulfillment he brings. This Jesus will not be understood if he is restricted to preconceived categories; he will not conform to human conceptual frameworks. He must be understood as God knows him, as the one who on behalf of the Father implements his will, which at the same time can paradoxically be described as the will and work of Jesus. God and his unique agent belong intimately together.

A Renewed Invitation   *(11:28–30)*

Bibliography

Bacchiocchi, S. "Matthew 11.28–30: Jesus' Rest and the Sabbath." *AUSS* 22 (1984) 289–316. **Bauer, J. B.** "Das milde Joch und die Ruhe, Mt 11,28–30." *TZ* 17 (1961) 99–106. **Betz, H. D.** "The Logion of the Easy Yoke and of Rest (Matt 11:28–30)." *JBL* 86 (1967) 10–24. **Maher, M.** "'Take my yoke upon you' (Matt. xi.29)." *NTS* 22 (1975) 97–102. **Motte, A. R.** "La structure du logion de Matthieu 11.28–30." *RB* 88 (1981) 226–33. **Stanton, G. N.** "Matthew 11.28–30: Comfortable Words?" *ExpTim* 94 (1982) 3–9.

Translation

^{28} *"Come to me, all of you^a who are laboring and bearing burdens, and I will give you rest.* ^{29} *Take my yoke upon you and learn from me,^{b} because I am meek and humble in heart, and you will find rest for yourselves.^{c}* ^{30}*For my yoke is kind and my burden is light."*

Notes

a "Of you" added in translation to make sense clear (cf. "you" at end of verse).

b ℵ* and a few other MSS omit ἀπ' ἐμοῦ, "from me," thus making the following ὅτι ("that," instead of "because") introduce the object clause of the verb μάθετε, "learn."

c ταῖς ψυχαῖς ὑμῶν, could mean "for your souls," but here it refers to the personal lives of those who find rest.

Form/Structure/Setting

A. Following the judgment oracles of vv 20–24 and the reference to revealing and concealing in the previous verses, the present passage is both surprising and comforting. Its invitation to discipleship indicates that the door is still open and that all remain invited. Nowhere is the invitation to follow Jesus more personal and tender than here. Again in this passage we find the themes of discipleship, Christology, and eschatology intertwined.

B. The passage is unique to Matthew. Yet much of the vocabulary is uncharacteristic of Matthew and seems to be drawn from earlier oral tradition.

C. The structure of the passage can be analyzed in three parts. The first two parts (vv 28 and 29) are parallel in content, though not so much in form, presenting similar invitations and the same accompanying promise. The third part (v 30) provides further reason to respond to the invitation. Thus the following outline emerges: (1) the invitation to come to Jesus and the promise of rest (v 28); (2) the invitation to follow Jesus in discipleship and the promise of rest (v 29); and (3) the light burden of those who follow Jesus (v 30). Parts 1 and 2 are parallel in form only in having imperative verbs (part 2 has two such verbs) followed by καί, "and," with a promise given in the future tense referring to "rest." Part 2 differs further in having the added ὅτι, "because," clause referring to the humble character of Jesus. Part 3 consists of exactly parallel clauses, Hebraic synonymous parallelism, except for the lack of the verb in the first. Particularly this third part (but even the first two parts to some extent) and the rhythm of the whole seem to have been formed with memorization and transmission in mind.

D. The passage is reflected in *Gos. Thom.* 90, where parallel to "my yoke is kind" is the clause "my rule is gentle." A knowledge of the passage is also reflected in *2 Clem.* 6:7.

E. On the unity of this passage with the preceding verses, see the discussion under *Form/Structure/Setting* §B for the preceding pericope. For a useful discussion of the history of the interpretation of these verses, see Betz.

Comment

28 Jesus has previously given an invitation to discipleship with the words δεῦτε ὀπίσω μου, "come after me" (4:19), but only here in all the NT is the direct invitation δεῦτε πρός με, "come to me," found. Jesus furthermore here continues to call πάντες, "all," thus including Israel, to himself. The invitation "come to me" is spoken by personified Wisdom several times in Sirach (24:19, 51:23). Sir 51:23–27 (cf. too Sir 6:23–31) serves as a particularly promising background for the present passage. Direct dependence, though probable, cannot be proved. (On the alternative theory of Davies-Allison, arguing for dependence on Exod 33:12–14, see the concluding *Comment* on v 27 above.) After the initial invitation "draw near to me," Sirach exhorts his readers to "put your neck under the yoke" (51:26) and notes that after laboring "little" one may find "much rest" (51:27). Jesus thus speaks here in the way that Wisdom was regarded as speaking (rightly Suggs, *Wisdom,* 106–7), and we have here another important element in wisdom Christology (cf. on 11:19b; see too 23:34), where the Christ is identified with the Wisdom that existed with God from the beginning (cf. Prov 8:1–21, 32–36; 9:4–6). The invitation of Jesus is offered in particular to οἱ κοπιῶντες καὶ πεφορτισμένοι, "those who are laboring and bearing burdens." These are not the disciples of Jesus (*pace* Stanton) but those who are not yet his disciples (rightly Deutsch, *Hidden Wisdom;* Davies-Allison). From the context that follows (see v 29) with its reference to "the yoke," the reader naturally assumes that this refers to those who are burdened with the effort to obey the law and in this way to arrive at the goal of righteousness (cf. Sir 6:25). It was, however, not the law itself that was burdensome (the law instead was the delight of the pious Israelite; cf. Ps 119 *passim*) but rather the overwhelming nomism of the Pharisees. The tremendous burden of the minutiae of their oral law fits the description especially well (cf. 23:4: "They bind heavy burdens [φορτία], hard to bear, and lay them on peoples' shoulders; but they themselves will not move them with their finger"). The Pharisees spoke of 613 commandments, and their *hălākôt* ("rulings") involved a complicated casuistry. Jesus appeals particularly to the Pharisaic scribes, the Pharisees and their disciples. Jesus promises to give rest to those who come to him and thus speaks not only as Wisdom does (cf. Sir 6:28; 51:27) but as Yahweh does to Moses in Exod 33:14: "My presence will go with you, and I will give you rest." Astonishingly Jesus calls people in the first instance *to himself* and only subsequently to the yoke of discipleship. It is moreover he, rather than God, who gives rest. Jesus stands not only in the place of Wisdom and truth but even in the place of Yahweh. ἀναπαύσω, "I will give you rest," connotes here a refreshing and a fulfillment, and thus anticipates messianic or eschatological blessing (on the present experience of the eschatological sabbath, cf. Heb 4:1–11; see Bacchiocchi).

29   The meaning of the preceding verse is now made more precise. The invitation to come to Jesus is an invitation to discipleship, that is, to follow him and his teaching. "Yoke" (ζυγόν) is a common metaphor for the law, both in Judaism (*m. ʾAbot* 3:5; *m. Ber.* 2:2; cf. 1QH 6:19) and in the NT (Acts 15:10; Gal 5:1). When Jesus invites people with the words ἄρατε τὸν ζυγόν μου ἐφ᾽ ὑμᾶς, "take my yoke upon you," he invites them to follow his own teaching as the definitive interpretation of the law (see on 5:17–20.). The same point is stressed in the next clause, μάθετε ἀπ᾽ ἐμοῦ, "learn from me." As Wisdom calls to obedience of Torah (cf. Sir 24:23; 6:37), so Jesus similarly calls to a discipleship of obedience to Torah but, as always in Matthew, the Torah as mediated through his teaching—hence, "*my* yoke" (cf. 23:8, 10). The cognate verb μαθητεύειν occurs in 28:19 together with the emphasis on keeping true to the teaching of Jesus. A dimension of personal commitment to Jesus is clearly implied (Maher, 103). The reason people should take Jesus' yoke and learn from him—note again, "from *me*"—is articulated in the ὅτι ("because") clause that follows: ὅτι πραΰς εἰμι καὶ ταπεινὸς τῇ καρδίᾳ, "because I am meek and humble in heart." The words πραΰς, "meek," and ταπεινός, "humble," are found together in Jer 26:6 and Zeph 3:2. Jesus is referred to as "meek" (πραΰς) elsewhere in Matthew (and in the NT) only indirectly in the quotation of Zech 9:9 in 21:5, although the cognate noun "meekness" (πραΰτης) is applied to Jesus in 2 Cor 10:1. Being "meek," Jesus is also similar to Moses (Num 12:3). (Jesus describes his disciples as "the meek" in 5:5.) The word "humble" (ταπεινός) is also applied to Jesus in the NT only here. The word "meek" and the phrase "humble in heart" appear to be essentially synonymous. The contrast here, as in the preceding and following verses, appears to be between Jesus and his primary rivals, the Pharisees. Many of the latter exhibited an extraordinary pride, loving places of honor, special titles, and in general the authority they exercised over others (see 23:5–12). This demeanor had the effect of disqualifying them as true interpreters of Torah. In contrast, despite the overwhelming significance of his person and his mission, Jesus comes meekly and humbly as a servant (cf. the Servant of the Lord in Isa 42:2–3; 53:1–12) and thus shows himself to be more worthy of trust than are the Pharisees. The final clause offering rest is couched in OT language identical in wording to Jer 6:16 (except for Matthew's ἀνάπαυσιν to agree with v 28, where Jeremiah has ἁγνισμόν, "purification"; the MT of Jer 6:16 has מַרְגּוֹעַ, *margôaʿ*, "rest") and close to Sir 6:28 (which, however, lacks ταῖς ψυχαῖς ὑμῶν, "for yourselves"). What Yahweh promised in the Jeremiah passage, Jesus now promises to those who come to him and follow him in discipleship: *he* will give them rest for their souls, i.e., a realization of a deep existential peace, a *shalom*, or sense of ultimate well-being with regard to one's relationship to God and his commandments (cf. the "rest," κατάπαυσις, of Heb 4:3–10). In light of the rejection of Jesus, it is worth noting that following the invitation in Jeremiah are the words: "But they said: 'We will not walk in it.'" This promise of rest relates directly to what is elsewhere in the NT called "salvation." As Betz puts it, "the logion of 11:28–30 is therefore theologically identical with the macarisms of the Sermon on the Mount" (24).

30   As the exposition of the true meaning of the law, Jesus' teaching, *his* ζυγόν, "yoke" (cf. v 28), is χρηστός, "kind." The latter word occurs in Matthew only here (cf. Luke 6:35; and 1 Peter 2:3). The second clause is conjoined to the first in synonymous parallelism and thus can serve as an aid to its exegesis. φορτίον, "burden," occurs again in Matthew only in 23:4, where it refers to the requirements of the tradition of the Pharisees, which are there also described as βαρέα, "heavy." By contrast, the burden of Jesus, his exposition of the law, is ἐλαφρόν, "light" (only here in Matthew). In short, those who follow the way of the Pharisees will of necessity toil and be heavily burdened (v 28); those who follow the way of Jesus, by contrast, will take upon themselves a kind yoke and a light burden. The contrast between Jesus and the Pharisees, though both claim to expound the true meaning of Torah, is remarkable: the Pharisees build a fence around the Torah with their elaborate and complicated exposition of its meaning, while Jesus goes directly to the heart of the Torah (cf. 22:37–40) in faithfulness to it (cf. 5:17–48). This difference exists not simply because Jesus is a better exegete of the law than are the Pharisees (as one rabbi among others) but because Jesus is the messianic king and the kingdom has dawned through his deeds and words. This alone can explain vv 28–30.

Explanation

Because of Jesus' identity and because of the reality he brings, an authoritative path can be cut through the thicket of elaborate human rules and regulations. Jesus invites all to come to him, to enter into relationship with him, and to follow him in discipleship. It is *his* yoke to which he calls; it is *he* who gives rest. That he places himself so much at the center is astonishing and separates him from all other Jewish teachers, who would only call others to obedience to the Torah. Jesus too in a way calls his disciples to righteousness in obedience to Torah. Yet there is a world of difference between the burdensome and tiring way of the Pharisees and the kind yoke and light burden of Jesus. The way of Jesus promises the confident rest and peace that anticipate eschatological blessing. The only explanation for this is the new era brought by Jesus. The fact that Jesus' yoke is kind and his burden is light must not be misunderstood to mean that the discipleship and righteousness to which Jesus calls are easy and undemanding. Discipleship demands nothing less than life commitment and comprehensive self-denial. The righteousness described in the Sermon on the Mount penetrates to the inner world of thought and motive. For Jesus, "the way that is easy" (7:13) leads to destruction, not to rest. In the last analysis it is only because of the dawning of the new era of grace and salvation, in Matthew's language "the kingdom of heaven" of realized eschatology, that the possibility exists of a kind yoke, a light burden, and thus rest for those who have toiled in frustration. In these new circumstances, and here alone, "his commandments are not burdensome" (1 John 5:3).

Plucking Grain on the Sabbath　　(12:1–8)

Bibliography

Aichinger, H. "Quellenkritische Untersuchung der Perikope vom Ährenraufen am Sabbat Mk 2,23–28 par Mt 12,1–8 par Lk 6, 1–5." In *Jesus in der Verkündigung der Kirche,* ed. A. Fuchs. SNTU A.1. Freistadt: Plöchl, 1976. 110–53. **Benoit, P.** "Les épis arrachés (Mt 12,1–8 et par)." *Studii Biblici Franciscani Liber Annuus* 13 (1962–63) 76–92. **Casey, P. M.** "Culture and Historicity: The Plucking of the Grain (Mark 2.23–28)." *NTS* 34 (1988) 1–23. **Cohen, M.** "La controverse de Jésus et des Pharisiens à propos de la cueillette des épis selon l'Évangile de saint Matthieu." *MScRel* 34 (1977) 3–12. **Cohn-Sherbok, D. M.** "An Analysis of Jesus' Arguments concerning the Plucking of Grain on the Sabbath." *JSNT* 2 (1979) 31–41. **Daube, D.** "Responsibilities of Master and Disciples in the Gospels." *NTS* 19 (1972–73) 1–15. **Doyle, B. R.** "A Concern of the Evangelist: Pharisees in Matthew 12." *AusBR* 34 (1986) 17–34. **Hicks, J. M.** "The Sabbath Controversy in Matthew: An Exegesis of Matthew 12:1–14." *ResQ* 27 (1984) 79–91. **Hill, D.** "On the Use and Meaning of Hosea vi.6 in Matthew's Gospel." *NTS* 24 (1977) 113–16. **Leitch, J. W.** "Lord Also of the Sabbath." *SJT* 19 (1966) 426–33. **Levine, E.** "The Sabbath Controversy according to Matthew." *NTS* 22 (1975–76) 480–83. **Lohse, E.** "Jesu Worte über den Sabbat." In *Judentum—Urchristentum—Kirche.* FS J. Jeremias, ed. W. Eltester. BZNW 26. Berlin: Töpelmann, 1960. 79–89. **Riesenfeld, H.** "The Sabbath and the Lord's Day in Judaism, the Preaching of Jesus and Early Christianity." In *The Gospel Tradition.* Philadelphia: Fortress, 1970. 111–38. **Robbins, V.** "Plucking Grains on the Sabbath." In *Patterns of Persuasion,* ed. B. Mack and V. Robbins. Sonoma: Polebridge, 1989. 107–41. **Rordorf, W.** *Sunday.* Philadelphia: Fortress, 1968. 54–79. **Schweizer, E.** "Matthäus 12:1–8: Der Sabbat: Gebot und Geschenk." In *Glaube und Gerechtigkeit.* FS R. Gyllenberg, ed. J. Kilunen et al. Helsinki: Finnisch exegetische Gesellschaft, 1983. 169–79. **Westerholm, S.** *Jesus.* 92–103.

Translation

[1]*About that time*[a] *Jesus went through the grain fields on the sabbath. And his disciples were hungry and they began to pluck some*[b] *ears and to eat.* [2]*But when the Pharisees saw this,*[c] *they said to him: "Look, your disciples are doing what it is not lawful to do on the sabbath."* [3]*But he said to them: "Haven't you read what David did when he and those with him became hungry?* [4]*How he went into the house of God and they*[d] *ate the loaves of the presence, which*[e] *it was not lawful for him to eat, nor for those with him, but for the priests alone?* [5]*Or haven't you read in the law that the priests in the temple on the sabbath desecrate the sabbath and are innocent?* [6]*But I tell you that there is something greater*[f] *here than even the temple.* [7]*But if you had known what this means: 'I desire mercy and not sacrifice,' you would not have condemned the innocent.* [8]*For the Son of Man is Lord of the sabbath."*

Notes

[a] ἐν ἐκείνῳ τῷ καιρῷ, lit. "in that time."

[b] "Some" is not in the Gr. text, which has simply στάχυας, "ears."

[c] C D L Δ Θ *f*[13] it sy[s.c.p] insert αὐτούς, "them," as the object of the participle ἰδόντες, "seeing." In the translation, "this" supplies the understood object.

ᵈ The critical text reads ἔφαγον, "they ate," on the strength of ℵ B 481. The alternate reading ἔφαγεν, "he ate," of P⁷⁰ C D L W Θ *f*¹·¹³ TR lat syr cop is regarded as caused by the parallel in Mark 2:26 and Luke 6:4. See *TCGNT*, 31.

ᵉ The critical text (on the basis of P⁷⁰ B D W *f*¹³) has ὅ, which does not agree in number or gender with its antecedent ἄρτους, "loaves." As the harder reading, it is preferred over the οὕς in ℵ C L Θ *f*¹ TR lat syʰ sa bo.

ᶠ C L Δ *f*¹³ lat have μείζων, "someone greater," rather than the neuter μεῖζον, "something greater."

Form/Structure/Setting

A. The disagreement between Jesus and the Pharisees concerning the way of righteousness implied in the immediately preceding verses now comes to direct and sharp expression. In the present and following pericopes the issue of the sabbath causes direct conflict between the two, ending in the plot of the Pharisees to destroy Jesus (v 14). The tone of increasing hostility dominates chap. 12. The present passage shows Jesus defending his disciples' conduct by means of OT analogies, an OT quotation, and a final logion concerning the authority of the Son of Man over the sabbath. Matthew here returns to the order of events in Mark.

B. Matthew depends on Mark (2:23–28; cf. Luke 6:1–5) for the whole of the passage, except vv 5–7, which are unique to Matthew. In general Mark is followed rather closely. Only the larger and significant differences are noted here.

> Matthew's ἐν ἐκείνῳ τῷ καιρῷ, "in that time," lacking altogether in Mark, ties this passage closely to the preceding material (cf. the same phrase in 11:25). Whereas Mark refers to the disciples plucking the grain in order ὁδὸν ποιεῖν, "to make a path" (Mark 2:23), Matthew and Luke refer to the disciples plucking grain to eat it (ἐσθίειν) and Matthew adds the justification, ἐπείνασαν, "they were hungry" (v 1). Matthew adds the participle ἰδόντες, "seeing," after οἱ φαρισαῖοι, "the Pharisees" (v 2), in order to call attention to their critical observation of Jesus. Matthew changes the question of Mark (and Luke), "Why are they doing on the sabbath what is unlawful?" into a declarative statement with an added ποιεῖν, thus giving it more force. The word order of v 2 is altered so as to put ἐν σαββάτῳ, "on the sabbath," in the emphatic final position. In v 3, Matthew (with Luke) omits Mark's redundant ὅτε χρείαν ἔσχεν, "when he had need" (Mark 2:25), and in v 4 also (again with Luke) the unnecessary and problematic ἐπὶ Ἀβιαθὰρ ἀρχιερέως, "in the time of the high priest Abiathar" (Mark 2:26). Matthew apparently changes Mark's ἔφαγεν, "he ate" (Mark 2:26), to ἔφαγον, "they ate" (v 4). In v 4b Matthew rewrites his Markan source (Mark 2:26b) so as to end the sentence with emphasis on τοῖς ἱερεῦσιν μόνοις, "for the priests alone."

After his special material (vv 5–7), Matthew returns to Mark but picks up only the concluding sentence about the Son of Man being Lord of the sabbath (v 8; Mark 2:28). But this sentence takes on a rather different meaning because of Matthew's omission of the preceding sentence in Mark, a sentence omitted also by Luke (cf. Luke 6:5): "the sabbath was made for humankind and not humankind for the sabbath" (Mark 2:27; cf. too Mark's following ὥστε, "so that"). Matthew presumably found this sentence to be too radical and out of keeping with his purposes. For him there is one issue, a christological one: Jesus as the true interpreter of the sabbath commandment.

C. The pericope, a so-called controversy story ending in an important pronouncement, reveals the following structure: (1) the narrative setting (v 1); (2) the criticizing question of the Pharisees (v 2); (3) the answer of Jesus, consisting of (a) a haggadic illustration (analogy) of David and his men (vv 3–4) and (b) a halachic illustration (precept) of law, commanding priests to work on the sabbath (v 5), followed by three independent logia: (4) the presence of something greater than the temple (v 6); (5) the failure to understand the law (v 7); and (6) the authority of the Son of Man over the sabbath. The sabbath is the unifying concept of the passage, the word (in slightly different forms) occurring in vv 1, 2, 5, and 8. Other key words also tie the different elements together: the verb πεινᾶν, "to be hungry," in vv 1 and 3; ἱερόν, "temple," in vv 5 and 6 (cf. τὸν οἶκον τοῦ θεοῦ, "the house of God," in v 4); ἀναίτιοι, "innocent," in vv 5 and 7; and οἱ μετ᾽αὐτοῦ, "those with him," in vv 3 and 4 (cf. οἱ μαθηταί, "the disciples," in vv 1 and 2). The sayings of Jesus lack the customary parallelism, although the parallel clauses of vv 3 and 5, οὐκ ἀνέγνωτε, "haven't you read," deserve mention.

Comment

1   ἐν ἐκείνῳ τῷ καιρῷ, "in that time," although merely a transition phrase, does have the effect of tying this passage together with the preceding argument concerning the kind yoke and light burden of Jesus' teaching. The evangelist makes the connection by means of the assertion that about the time Jesus had made the previous remarks, these illustrative episodes occurred. Jesus' view of the sabbath in this and the following pericope is seen to be more lenient than that of the Pharisees. Matthew uses the singular verb ἐπορεύθη: Jesus "went" through the grainfields (σπορίμων, probably wheat), focusing attention on Jesus rather than the disciples. The plural τοῖς σάββασιν is to be explained as the plural used of festivals (see BDF §141[3]), although Matthew can use the singular and plural alternately (see vv 2, 5, 8). The careful observance of the sabbath was regarded as of greatest importance in Judaism (cf. Isa 56:4–7). The sabbath was a time of rest (cf. the emphasis on rest in the preceding sentences, 11:28) and rejoicing. Matthew avoids Mark's statement that the disciples plucked the grain "to make a path" (Mark makes no mention of the eating of the grain) probably because this would have been thought to be too much an abuse of the sabbath but also to refer to the disciples' hunger (cf. ἐπείνασαν, "they were hungry") and thus to make the profaning of the sabbath less grievous and the argument of vv 3–4 more directly relevant and convincing. (Luke alone refers to the disciples rubbing the heads of grain in their hands, 6:1.) It is occasionally pointed out that the text says only the disciples and not Jesus himself engaged in the questionable activity. Although this is true, it is also the case that the master and his disciples are mutually responsible for their conduct (see Daube). If Jesus did not himself actually pluck grain, he at least condoned his disciples' doing so and must be prepared to answer for their conduct.

2   To the Pharisees, the conduct of the disciples was a violation of the commandment not to work on the sabbath (cf. Deut 5:14; Exod 20:10). Plucking grain was technically harvesting, a form of work forbidden in the rabbinic interpretation of the commandment: οὐκ ἔξεστιν ποιεῖν ἐν σαββάτῳ, "what it is not lawful to do on the sabbath." Cf. Exod 34:21 and the thirty-nine classes of work prohibited by the discussion in *m. Šabb.* 7:2 (*b. Šabb.* 73b, "reaping"; cf. the rigorous observance of the sabbath at Qumran, CD 10:14–11:8; for a further example, see John 5:10). A relatively late rabbinic text (*b. Šabb.* 128a) allows the picking of

grain with the fingers on the sabbath as long as no tool is used. The Pharisees regarded the conduct of the disciples as an extremely serious matter (cf. v 14). Thus Jesus and the disciples transgress at least the tradition of the Pharisees, and technically, in any event, it is possible to regard their activity as a violation of the Torah commandment itself. No moral problem was seen in the plucking and eating of the grain of another, which was in fact allowed by Deut 23:25. The issue was the violation of the sanctity of the sabbath day.

3–4   When the Pharisees thus called Jesus' attention to the activity of the disciples, they fully expected him to rebuke them. Instead he defends them by citing two different OT analogies. The first of these, referring to David, does not concern the sabbath at all, despite the existence of a rabbinic tradition, possibly known to Jesus, that the event described happened on a sabbath (*b. Menaḥ.* 95b; *Yal.* on 1 Sam 21:5). The argument as it stands in the text, however, is one of straightforward analogy with the story narrated in 1 Sam 21:1–6. The Pharisees would have known the story; the question οὐκ ἀνέγνωτε, "have you not read?" here and in v 5 is rhetorical. David and his men violated a direct commandment of God when on a particular occasion of need they ate the "bread of the presence," which was placed fresh every sabbath in the temple as a thank offering but which only (μόνοις, emphatic by its final position) the priests were allowed to eat (Lev 24:5–9). In this way human need was put before the stipulations of the law. The Pharisees believed David and his men ate the bread to save their lives (thus Zeitlin, cited by Lachs; cf. Cohn-Sherbok), although the text does not say this. It is argued that therefore the violation of the law was justified in contrast to the lesser need of Jesus and his disciples. When David entered the tabernacle (τὸν οἶκον τοῦ θεοῦ, "the house of God"), he also did something only priests were allowed to do in the performance of their duty, but nothing is made of this. The OT law was thus violated in this special instance, and this analogy is at least a tacit admission that in a sense the disciples' activity was not consistent with the sabbath commandment. But the present time is a special time, indeed one without parallel (cf. v 6). If David and his men were allowed to transgress the letter of the law, how much more so was such a transgression allowed in the case of Jesus, the greater Son of David, and his disciples.

5   The second illustration is more directly relevant because it concerns the desecration of the sabbath. The priests in the temple in fact violate the sabbath law by performing their work τοῖς σάββασιν, "on the sabbath" (emphatic at the beginning of the clause), as in the presentation of offerings (cf. Num 29:9–10). "Temple service takes precedence over the Sabbath" (*b. Šabb.* 132b). For other instances of activity of the priests that took precedence over the sabbath law, see *m. ʿErub.* 10.11–5; *m. Pesaḥ.* 6:1–2. Technically the priests desecrate (βεβηλοῦσιν, a particularly strong word) the sabbath commandment, yet they remain ἀναίτιοι, "guiltless" (John 7:23 gives a similar instance). This is yet another special instance. The priests are about the work of God and thus are not bound by the normal regulations concerning the sabbath. So too it is implied by an *a fortiori* argument (or in rabbinic idiom, *qal wāḥômer*) that Jesus and his disciples constitute a special instance and thus are not bound. They preeminently are about the work of God. Although this point is implicit and not explicit, the next saying depends on just such a conclusion.

6   The formula λέγω δὲ ὑμῖν, "but I say to you," draws special attention to the following saying. The initial position of the comparative genitive in the ὅτι ("that") clause, τοῦ ἱεροῦ, "than the temple," makes it emphatic, amounting to something like "than even this temple" (contrast v 41). Given the great importance of the temple, the place of God's presence and the performance of the cultus, this statement is utterly astonishing in its significance. What then is the μεῖζον, "something greater," that is said to be present (ὧδε, "here")? The neuter form of the comparative of μέγα here may be unexpected; had it been μείζων, which is masculine or feminine, one could have thought of Jesus himself or the kingdom, respectively. Although the neuter *can* refer to a person (MHT 3:21; cf. Matt 12:42), here it may refer more generally to the phenomenon of the ministry of Jesus and the disciples and the reality of the dawning kingdom altogether (*pace* Gundry, Davies-Allison). Clearly the μεῖζον has to refer to the wonderful things the Gospel has been describing to this point. This includes the presence of God in the person and work of Jesus (cf. 1:23). Luz identifies what is greater as the mercy of God (cf. v 7). If one extends the thought of the comparison to include the atoning death of Jesus, the appropriateness of the analogy becomes impressive, but this is not in full view just yet. On Jesus and the temple, see also 26:61; 27:40.

7   Again Jesus appeals to Hos 6:6 to describe and defend his conduct. In Matt 9:13 the same quotation (verbatim) served to justify his association with tax collectors and sinners. Now the quotation defends his tolerance of the disciples' plucking and eating grain on the sabbath. The quotation seems more relevant to the pericope that follows, which involves a healing on the sabbath, although mercy can be said to be evident in the feeding of the hungry disciples. The point here, as in 9:13, is that stringency of law observance must give way to the priority of the good news of the kingdom, which is aimed at human need and thus too the need of those who labor on behalf of the kingdom. In the showing of mercy to the needy, the law and the prophets find their fulfillment (cf. the supremely important love commandment in 7:12 and 22:39–40; see too 23:23, where Jesus faults the Pharisees for neglecting the weighty matter of mercy). Had the Pharisees understood (ἐγνώκειτε) the meaning of Hosea, they would not have pronounced judgment upon the innocent (τοὺς ἀναιτίους). For Jesus' disciples are as innocent in their activity on the sabbath as are the priests in their labor on the sabbath (for whom the same word, "innocent," is used). Both fulfill the will of God despite their technical violation of the commandment.

8   The authority underlying this conclusion (cf. γάρ, "for") is that of ὁ υἱὸς τοῦ ἀνθρώπου, "the Son of Man," now described as κύριος . . . τοῦ σαββάτου ("Lord of the sabbath"). "The Son of Man" here probably functions as a title referring to Jesus (perhaps in contrast to the parallel in Mark 2:28, although there too a titular reference to Jesus may be meant). For the title Son of Man, see *Excursus* at 8:18–22. The Son of Man, i.e., Jesus, is said here to be the "Lord of the sabbath" in the sense that he has the sovereign authority to decide what loyalty to the sabbath means (cf. the freedom of a prophet concerning the law in *b. Yebam.* 90b). This is obviously part of the larger fact, to which Matthew has already introduced the reader, that as the promised one, the Messiah, Jesus is the authoritative and definitive interpreter of the Torah. Thus the demands of the sabbath commandment, however they be construed, must give way to the presence and purpose of Jesus, and not vice versa. Matthew ends the pericope on this important christological note. If something greater than the temple is present, then here is also someone greater than the sabbath.

Explanation

The religious restrictions elaborated by human beings into calcified codes of conduct often paradoxically fight the purposes of God. It is particularly grievous when insistence on the letter of the law results in the neglect of genuine human need and thus hinders the expression of love. A commandment-centered system such as that of the Pharisees, however well intentioned, was bound to make this error. The issue in the present passage seems initially to be the question of exegesis of the sabbath commandment, the very sort of thing that the rabbis themselves would debate. But as we move through the passage, we see again that what is being asserted is not that Jesus' exegesis of the commandment is better than the rabbis (although such argumentation is provided) but that something (and someone with that something) dramatically significant is present, forcing the discussion to a completely different level. Jesus makes the astounding assertion that something greater than the temple is present. The Son of Man is with his people as sovereign Lord and messianic king and acts as the final and infallible interpreter of the will of God as expressed in Torah and sabbath commandment. The rest and rejoicing symbolized by the sabbath find fulfillment in the kingdom brought by Jesus.

Healing a Withered Hand on the Sabbath   (12:9–14)

Bibliography

Dietzfelbinger, C. "Vom Sinn der Sabbatheilungen Jesu." *EvT* 38 (1978) 281–98.

See also *Bibliography* on 12:1–8.

Translation

[9]*And he*[a] *went from there and came into their synagogue.* [10]*And look, a man with a withered hand was there.*[b] *And they interrogated him in order to accuse him,*[c] *saying: "Is it lawful to heal on the sabbath?"* [11]*But he said to them, "Who is there among you who, if you had*[d] *one sheep and it fell into a pit on the sabbath, would not grab hold of it and pull it out?* [12]*Therefore, a human being is worth much more than a sheep! So then it is lawful to do good on the sabbath."* [13]*Then he said to the man, "Stretch out your hand." And he stretched it out, and it was restored to health, just like his other hand.*[e] [14]*When the Pharisees came out, they took counsel against him, discussing*[f] *how they could destroy him.*

Notes

[a] C N Σ and other MSS read ὁ Ἰησοῦς, "Jesus."

[b] The best MSS (א B C W l vg) have the shorter and harder reading, which lacks both main verb and adverb. TR and a few other witnesses have ἦν τήν, i.e., the main verb "was" and the definite

article before χεῖρα, "hand." Still another group of MSS (D L [N] Δ Θ $f^{1,13}$ 33) have verb, adverb, and definite article, ἦν ἐκεῖ τήν, all probably by influence of the Markan parallel (3:1).

   c The clause ἵνα κατηγορήσωσιν αὐτοῦ, "in order to accuse him," is found in the Gr. text after the question instead of before it. This awkwardness is caused by Matthew's dependence on Mark, where the clause does not follow a question.

   d The best MSS have future tenses for this and the preceding verb, reflecting the contingency of the question. D has present tense in both places.

   e ὡς ἡ ἄλλη, lit. "as the other," is lacking in א C² 892*, probably by influence of the Synoptic parallels, which also lack the phrase.

   f "Discussing" added to translation.

Form/Structure/Setting

   A. This second sabbath controversy story (related to the first in vv 1–8) centers directly upon the work of healing performed by Jesus on the sabbath. In this instance we have not only the act of Jesus himself but also now something central to the mission and calling of Jesus rather than something incidental to it, as in the preceding passage. In addition, Matthew now describes the Pharisees' eagerness to catch him in the act of violating the sabbath. This event meets that desire, at least to their satisfaction (cf. v 14). To the Pharisees, this healing is a flagrant example of transgression of the Mosaic commandment.

   B. In this triple-tradition passage Matthew depends on Mark (3:1–6; cf. Luke 6:6–11), although with some considerable and important differences. Matthew omits all of Mark 3:3, all of 3:4 but one clause, and half of 3:5, i.e., the reference to putting the man in the center, the question to the Pharisees and their silence, and the reference to Jesus' anger and grief at their hardheartedness. None of this material is vitally important to the basic story, and Matthew does not like emotional language in reference to Jesus. In place of the omitted material, Matthew inserts vv 11–12a, i.e., the analogy of the sheep that is raised from a pit on the sabbath and the comment that human beings are worth more than sheep. This is unique to Matthew but finds a close parallel in Luke 14:5, which, in connection with the same controversy concerning healing on the sabbath, refers to a son (variant reading, "ass") or an ox that has fallen into a well (cf. Luke 13:15). The clause in v 12b, ἔξεστιν τοῖς σάββασιν καλῶς ποιεῖν, "it is lawful to do good on the sabbath," is picked up somewhat freely from Mark 3:4 (where, however, it is part of a question).

   > Among changes in the Markan material that is borrowed by Matthew, the following may be noted: Matthew's addition of μεταβὰς ἐκεῖθεν, "having moved on from there," and αὐτῶν, "their," after "synagogue" (v 9) and omission of Mark's πάλιν, "again" (Mark 3:1); Matthew's addition of ἰδού, "behold" (v 10), and alteration of Mark's syntax into a question resulting in the replacement of παρετήρουν ("they were watching") with ἐπηρώτησαν, "they interrogated him," and the consequent addition of λέγοντες, "saying," and the insertion of ἔξεστιν, "is it lawful?" (v 10). This has the effect of making Mark's question (and its only implicit answer) into a direct statement. Two further departures from Mark must be noted: Matthew's addition of ὡς ἡ ἄλλη, "like the other," which has the effect of confirming the miracle (v 13); and Matthew's omission of Mark's εὐθὺς μετὰ τῶν Ἡρῳδιανῶν, "immediately with the Herodians" (v 14), a piece of historical information of no special interest to Matthew, allowing him to focus on the Pharisees.

   C. This second controversy story finds its core in the question of the Pharisees (v 10b) and the answer of Jesus (vv 11–12). The healing of v 13 becomes of secondary importance in the context, and almost no attention is accorded it. The question of the sabbath is the primary concern. The passage may be outlined as follows: (1) the setting (vv 9–10a); (2) the question of the Pharisees (v 10b); (3) the answer of Jesus, subdivided into (a) the analogy of the sheep (vv 11–12a) and (b) the concluding statement (v 12b); (4) the healing of the withered hand (v 13); and (5) the plot of the Pharisees (v 14). The passage exhibits little structural parallelism (though Luz points out a possible chiastic structure). V 12 is the central and climactic verse, picking up elements from analogy in v 11 and answering the question of the Pharisees in v 10b.

Comment

9–10a μεταβὰς ἐκεῖθεν, "went from there," is another general transitional phrase (cf. 11:1; 15:29) that provides little actual information other than the narrative function of getting Jesus to the synagogue where the interchange and healing take place. Similarly, συναγωγὴν αὐτῶν, "their synagogue," is general in reference (cf. Mark 3:1) and in Matthew regularly means a synagogue of the Jews (cf. *Comment* on 4:23 and the occurrence of the phrase in 4:23; 9:35; 10:17; 13:54; 23:34) in contrast to Matthew's Jewish-Christian community. Here perhaps it was a synagogue specifically of Pharisees (cf. v 14). With Matthew's sign word ἰδού, "look," we are abruptly confronted with a man with a withered hand, i.e., one that was paralyzed and atrophied. No mention is made here or at the end of the narrative of any appeal for healing or Jesus' approach to the man to heal him, of the faith of the man or the power of Jesus. These two brief sentences thus mainly serve the purpose of setting the stage for the dialogue that follows.

10b The subject of the verb ἐπηρώτησαν, "they asked," is understood from the context (vv 2, 14) to be the Pharisees. The purpose of the question, ἵνα κατηγορήσωσιν αὐτοῦ, "in order to accuse him," is connected with the plot mentioned in v 14. The Pharisees were looking for evidence that could be used against Jesus. The question εἰ ἔξεστιν τοῖς σάββασιν θεραπεῦσαι, "Is it lawful to heal on the sabbath?" thus amounts to a kind of challenge (it is not uncommon for a question in Greek to begin with εἰ, "if"). It is quite clear that the Pharisees did not believe it was lawful to heal on the sabbath, except in extreme cases of life or death (see *m. Yoma* 8:6: "Every case where life is in danger supersedes the sabbath"; cf. *Mek. Exod.* 22:2; 23:13). From their point of view, a man who had had a withered hand for some time could surely have waited one day more to be healed.

11–12 Jesus justifies the act of healing on the sabbath by referring to the acceptability of pulling an animal, here a sheep, out of a pit it had fallen into on the sabbath (cf. Luke 14:5, referring to a son or ox falling into a well). In this instance, at least according to some rabbis (cf. the lively discussion in *b. Šabb.* 128b and *b. B. Meṣ.* 32b; the Qumran community, however, disallowed even this activity on the sabbath, CD 11:13–14), the sabbath law gave way to the concern for the welfare of the animal. The reference to "one" sheep (πρόβατον ἕν), which is not necessary to the argument (note its omission in NIV, TEV, Phillips), may be the result of the influence of the story recorded in 18:12–18 or merely a Semitism for "a sheep" (Luz contends the one sheep points to a poor farmer). But if kindness can thus be shown to a sheep on the sabbath, how much more should it be shown to a human being. The *a fortiori* argument depends on the fact that "a human being is worth much more than a sheep" (cf. 6:26; 10:31). From this analogy and argument, the conclusion is drawn that ἔξεστιν τοῖς σάββασιν καλῶς ποιεῖν, "it is lawful on the sabbath to do good," and thus the Pharisees' question in v 10 receives its direct answer. καλῶς ποιεῖν, "to do good," is used because it is broad enough to include delivering a sheep from a pit and performing a healing (cf. Mark 7:37). Again Jesus challenges not the sabbath law itself but the interpretation of that law. And again the criterion of love becomes determinative.

13   The propriety of the deed having been argued, Jesus immediately heals the man's hand. Jesus gives the command to stretch out his hand, and when he does so, it is "restored" (ἀπεκατεστάθη, a verb occurring elsewhere in Matthew only in 17:11), made ὑγιής, "whole" or "healthy" (used again by Matthew only in 15:31 in reference to the "crippled" or "lame"). In the triple tradition, only Matthew has ὡς ἡ ἄλλη, "as the other," thus indicating the success and completeness of the cure (cf. 1 Kgs 13:6).

14   No mention is made of the astonishment of the crowds or the Pharisees at the miracle performed by Jesus, and no christological conclusion is drawn (the same is true of the Markan and Lukan accounts). Instead one reads of the plotting of the Pharisees to do away with Jesus, and thus we are firmly set on the way to the death of Jesus (cf. the same plotting in 22:15; cf. 12:24; 15:2; 21:23; 26:4; John 5:18). The Pharisees were not really interested in Jesus' argument but in finding an excuse to plot against him. Their obsession with the letter of the law apparently made it impossible for them to think of anything else, and so the miracle as a sign of the dawning of the kingdom and of the truth of Jesus' message was lost on them.

Explanation

It is no doubt strange to the modern Christian reader to consider that healing on the sabbath might be thought to be a violation of the sabbath law. An orthodox Jew in the lineage of the Pharisees would explain the sense of strangeness as a failure to appreciate the incomparable importance of the commandments as the express and unchanging will of God for his people. The present passage, like the preceding one, is an attempt to argue with the rabbis on their own ground by raising the legitimate question about the real meaning of the commandment. The irony of human beings treating their animals better than other human beings, not unknown in the modern world, should make its point in connection with the sabbath. Law without love (mercy) may result in the violation of God's will. But the real problem lies on another level, involving the message and the person of Jesus. It is because of who he is and what he announces that his interpretation of the meaning of the commandments is authoritative (cf. v 8). The authority of Jesus thus supplants the authority of the scribal tradition of the Pharisees. But since the debate comes down finally to the person of Jesus, the Pharisees know intuitively that he must be removed if their system is to remain intact. The tragedy is not the failure to accept Jesus' argument but the failure to be receptive to Jesus as the one who brings the kingdom.

The Gentle, Healing Servant   (12:15–21)

Bibliography

Grindel, J. C. M. "Matthew 12:18–21." *CBQ* 29 (1967) 110–15. **Kraft, R.** "*εἰς νῖκος:* Permanently/Successfully: 1 Cor 15:54; Matt 12:20." In *Septuagintal Lexicography*, ed. R. Kraft. Missoula: Scholars, 1975. 153–56. **Neyrey, J.** "The Thematic Use of Isaiah 42:1–4 in Matthew 12." *Bib* 63 (1982) 457–73.

See also the *Bibliography* on 12:1–8.

Translation

[15]*But Jesus, knowing their intent, departed from that region. And many [crowds]*[a] *followed him, and he healed all of them,* [16]*and he warned them*[b] *that they should not make him known,* [17]*in order that*[c] *the word through Isaiah the prophet might be fulfilled, which says:*
[18] *Behold my servant,*[d] *whom*[e] *I have chosen,*
My beloved in whom[f] *I am*[g] *well pleased.*
I will put my spirit upon him,
    and he will proclaim justice to the nations.
[19] *He will not quarrel, nor will he cry out,*
Nor will anyone hear his voice in the public squares.
[20] *A bruised reed*[h] *he will not break,*
And a smoldering wick he will not put out
    until he brings justice[i] *to triumph.*
[21] *And the nations will hope in his name.*

Notes

[a] Although C D L W Θ *f*[1,13] TR sy[p.h] sa[ms] bo have ὄχλοι πολλοί, "many crowds," ℵ B lat have simply πολλοί, "many." The critical Gr. text thus puts ὄχλοι in brackets. Metzger notes that although ὄχλοι could have been accidentally dropped because of homoioteleuton, it is "slightly more probable" that the word was added by scribes in imitation of the phrase in such passages as 4:25; 8:1; 13:2; 15:30; and 19:2.

[b] D it read: πάντας δὲ οὓς ἐθεράπευσεν ἐπέπληξεν, "all whom he healed he reproved." W has the same followed by καὶ ἐπετίμησεν, "and he warned."

[c] Many MSS (L W Θ *f*[13] TR) substitute the nearly synonymous ὅπως, "so that," for ἵνα, "in order that."

[d] παῖς could also be translated "son," but in the Isaiah song it means "servant." See *Comment.*

[e] D adds the ill-fitting εἰς, "in," perhaps by the influence of line 2 of this verse.

[f] For εἰς ὄν some MSS (ℵ* B *ff*[1]) have the simple ὄν, "whom." D *f*[1] 33 have ἐν ᾧ for "in whom" (cf. 3:17).

[g] ἡ ψυχή μου, lit. "my soul [is]."

[h] κάλαμον συντετριμμένον, "a bruised reed," is omitted by D*.

[i] X 28 1424 sy[h] sa mae add αὐτοῦ, "his," modifying κρίσιν, "justice."

Form/Structure/Setting

A. Further healings by Jesus, apparently large in number, are now reported briefly in a summarizing fashion together with a paradoxical warning concerning the spreading of the news of his presence. The "messianic secret" motif is then supported by a long quotation—Matthew's longest—from Isa 42 that indicates how far this Messiah is from the popular expectation. In the present context of hostility and rejection, this passage takes on special significance. The unexpected side of the messianic deliverer as servant is but the fulfillment of the OT promise.

B. Vv 15 and 16 draw on the vocabulary of Mark 3:7–12 (cf. Luke 6:17–19), but Matthew has so greatly abbreviated the Markan passage that the dependence is not significant. Matthew thus takes up Mark's verb ἀνεχώρησεν, "he departed," and the verb ἠκολούθησαν, "they followed" (although the text of Mark is uncertain here); Matthew's reference to ὄχλοι πολλοί, "many crowds," probably reflects Mark's πολὺ πλῆθος, "a large number" (v 15; Mark 3:7). Matthew has altered Mark's πολλοὺς γὰρ ἐθεράπευσεν, "for he healed many," to καὶ ἐθεράπευσεν αὐτοὺς πάντας, "and he healed all of them" (v 15; Mark 3:10), to emphasize the extent of Jesus' healing ministry. Matthew picks up Mark's "he warned them that they should not make him known" (v 16; Mark 3:12), with the major difference that Matthew has the warning addressed to those who were healed, whereas in Mark it is addressed to the unclean spirits who had just confessed "you are the Son of God." Matthew thus widens the application. Vv 17–21, the introductory fulfillment formula and the OT quotation that follows, are unique to Matthew.

C. The passage is structured as follows: (1) the departure of Jesus (v 15a); (2) in parallel clauses the crowds who follow are (a) healed by Jesus (15b) and (b) warned not to make him known (v 16); and (3) the OT quotation with (a) introductory formula (v 17) and (b) text (vv 18–21). The OT quotation (Isa 42:1–4) reflects the poetical structure of the first of Isaiah's Servant Songs. Thus the first two lines of v 18 are parallel in substance (synonymous parallelism) and form (to a lesser degree); parallel verb forms and clauses are found in v 19; parallel and exactly synonymous clauses appear in the first two lines of v 20.

D. Although Isa 42:1 is alluded to several times in the Synoptic tradition (cf. 3:17; 17:5; Luke 3:22; 9:35; 23:35), only here in Matthew do we find this quotation of the opening four verses of the chapter. Although the text of the quotation is in agreement with the LXX at a few points, for the most part it must be described as non-Septuagintal. On the other hand, it does not follow the Hebrew Masoretic Text closely either. Matthew may well have formed the translation from sources available to him (e.g., the Targums) or produced his original translation (so Davies-Allison) in order to suit his own purposes.

Thus in the first verse (v 18), although he does not follow the LXX in identifying the servant as Jacob and Israel, Matthew agrees with the Hebrew text in the word ἰδού, "behold," the simple reference to ὁ παῖς μου, "my servant," and ὁ ἀγαπητός μου, "my beloved" (here LXX's ἐκλεκτός, "chosen," is closer to the Hebrew), the last two nouns each with modifying relative clauses. In the second of these, Matthew's ἡ ψυχή μου, "my soul," agrees with the LXX. In the third line Matthew agrees with the LXX except in his θήσω, "I will put" (closer to the Hebrew than the LXX's ἔδωκα, "I have given"). In the fourth line Matthew again agrees with the LXX except for his verb ἀπαγγελεῖ, "he will proclaim" (cf. the Targum; here LXX's ἐξοίσει, "he will bring," is closer to the Hebrew). In the second verse of the quotation (v 19), Matthew's two verbs in the first line, ἐρίσει, "quarrel," and κραυγάσει, "cry out," differ from the LXX's κεκράξεται, "cry out," and ἀνήσει, "lift up (his voice)." Matthew's second line in v 19 is close to the wording of the LXX, where, however, the sentence is cast in the passive and ἐν ταῖς πλατείαις, "in the public squares," is lacking. The third verse of the quotation (v 20) refers, like the LXX, to a κάλαμον, "reed," and λίνον, "wick," and with the latter uses οὐ σβέσει, "will not quench." Beyond this, the vocabulary of Matthew's quotation differs from the LXX, despite the common form. In the third line of this verse, Matthew's εἰς νῖκος, "to victory," is unique (LXX has εἰς ἀλήθειαν, "to truth") but agrees in thought with both the LXX and Hebrew texts. Matthew (v 21) omits the opening lines of the fourth verse but cites the concluding line in verbatim agreement with the LXX, except for the omission of ἐπί, "upon," before τῷ ὀνόματι αὐτοῦ, "his name."

E. This passage bears a remarkable formal similarity to 8:16–17, where a reference to the healing ministry of Jesus (and where he healed "all") is followed again by a fulfillment formula quotation from Isaiah (53:4). The only element lacking in this parallel passage is the warning not to make him known.

Comment

15 The implication of γνούς, "knowing," is that Jesus knew the thoughts of the Pharisees without anyone telling him (cf. 16:8; 22:18; 26:10). The transition to the present pericope is made simply by the statement that Jesus "departed from there" (ἀνεχώρησεν ἐκεῖθεν), presumably to avoid further encounter with those Pharisees who were conspiring to destroy him (v 14; and cf. Jesus' command to his disciples in 10:23). As commonly in Matthew, wherever Jesus goes, large crowds follow him. Among the crowds are always the sick and needy, and although in his extreme brevity Matthew does not mention them, he writes ἐθεράπευσεν αὐτοὺς πάντας, "he healed all of them" (cf. 19:2).

16–17 The messianic secret motif has already been encountered in Matthew in connection with the miraculous deeds of Jesus (see *Comment* on 8:4; 9:30). The key to the messianic secret is the fact that Jesus has come *not* as the widely expected triumphant Messiah, powerfully transforming the world order then and there, but as a servant Messiah to accomplish the will of his Father. The strange work of this Messiah explains his strange demeanor. Matthew, in common with earliest Christianity, turns to the Servant Songs of Second Isaiah to interpret the paradoxical messiahship of Jesus (cf. too 8:17, where Isa 53:4 is cited as fulfilled by Jesus). In these songs, which culminate in the atoning death of the Servant (chap. 53), the early Church found words that accurately corresponded to the ministry of Jesus. Matthew, through *sensus plenior* (see *Introduction*), finds in Isa 42:1–4 the fulfillment of prophecy and thus introduces the quotation with his special fulfillment formula, ἵνα πληρωθῇ τὸ ῥηθὲν διὰ Ἡσαΐου τοῦ προφήτου, "in order that the word through Isaiah the prophet might be fulfilled" (cf. 4:14). The servant's demeanor in Isa 42:1–4 corresponds closely to the way in which Jesus conducted his ministry, particularly in regard to the messianic secret and the non-triumphalist character of Jesus. For Matthew, the correspondence is divinely intended and we have thus the fulfillment of prophecy in Jesus' command to silence about his deeds of power.

18 For a detailed comparison of Matthew's text with that of the LXX and Hebrew of Isa 42:1–4, see above *Form/Structure/Setting* §D. The words of Isa 42:1 are associated with Jesus at his baptism (3:17) and at the transfiguration (17:5) as a declaration of his special relationship with God. The passage is of central significance to Matthew's servant Christology (contra Luz), developed also elsewhere in the early Church (cf. Acts 3:13, 26; 4:27, 30). Jesus here is ὁ παῖς μου, "my servant," who is specially "chosen" by God. The fact that παῖς (LXX's translation of עֶבֶד, ʿebed, "servant") can be translated as either servant or son makes the application to Jesus even more effective. The quotation of Isa 42:1 cannot fail to remind the reader of the allusion to the same verse in 3:17 (cf. the same in 17:5), where the word υἱός, "son," is used. The second line, in synonymous parallelism with the first, makes the same point, referring to Jesus as ὁ ἀγαπητός μου, "my beloved," in whom God finds special pleasure. The placing of the Holy Spirit upon Jesus again recalls the baptism, where the Spirit descended upon Jesus to equip him for his mission (3:16; cf. Luke 4:18, where Isa 61:1 is cited). A main purpose of the servant Messiah was to be the proclamation of κρίσιν τοῖς ἔθνεσιν, "justice to the nations" (cf. v 20c). That the word κρίσις should be taken in the positive sense of "justice" rather than "judgment" (contra Luz) seems clear from Matthew's inclusion of v 21 (Isa 42:4b). This is to be related to the pervasive universalism of Second Isaiah and the expectation that the good news of eschatological fulfillment would encompass even the Gentiles. And this is an important element in the work of Jesus according to Matthew, foreshadowed at several points in his ministry and announced clearly by the resurrected Jesus in the great commission given to the disciples at the end of the Gospel (28:19). The quotation itself returns to this theme in the last line (v 21).

19–20 Matthew understands these words to refer to the humility and gentleness of Jesus as the servant Messiah (cf. 11:29). The focus here is on what Jesus surprisingly does not do. He does not, for example, "quarrel" with the Pharisees but withdraws from their midst. Despite the significance of Jesus and the importance of his person and mission (cf. v 6; 11:27), he does not come in such a way as to overwhelm or crush those to whom he is sent—not even his enemies. During his earthly ministry, neither Jesus nor his disciples nor those whom he healed acclaim him publicly as Messiah. The mandate to silence is thus directly related to the servant role of the Messiah as announced by Isaiah and fulfilled by Jesus. In a similar way, v 20 confirms that the servant role of Jesus means also the delay of judgment (see especially chap. 13 for this theme; cf. the omission of the clause of Isa 61:2 referring to "the day of God's vengeance," as quoted in Luke 4:18–19). The metaphors of the bruised reed that is not broken and the smoldering wick that is not put out point to the patience of God with the downtrodden in the present era, which yet awaits the reality of eschatological blessing and judgment: ἕως ἂν ἐκβάλῃ εἰς νῖκος τὴν κρίσιν, "until he brings justice to triumph." εἰς νῖκος, "to triumph," which is not from the LXX, probably means "successfully" (see Kraft). But for the present, the Messiah has come as servant and not as judge. And thus he reaches out to the needy, the rejected, and the sinner (cf. 9:13).

21 It is significant that Matthew has included the last line of Isa 42:4 in the quotation, skipping over the first half of the verse to do so. One of Matthew's purposes is to show not only that in Jesus God has been faithful to Israel but that the Gentiles are also to find salvation through him (cf. 8:11–12; 21:43; 24:14; 28:19). This development—that the Gentiles would place their hope in Isaiah's servant figure—was prophesied by Isaiah and finds its fulfillment through the work of Jesus. Almost this same language is also found in the LXX of Isa 11:10 (quoted in Rom 15:12) in a messianic and apocalyptic context. The quotation thus provides from the OT a full picture of the person and mission of Jesus. "The quotation is thus used to express in miniature Matthew's conception of the role of the Christ which is spelt out in the gospel as a whole" (Green, 125).

Explanation

Again we are made aware of the paradoxical character of Jesus' messiahship. Matthew has deliberately portrayed Jesus as powerful in both word and deed. And yet this is not the essence of Jesus' ministry, which is to be found not in power but in servanthood expressed through humility, meekness, and gentleness. Matthew identifies Jesus and the nature of his ministry directly with the servant described in the first of Isaiah's songs. The story of Jesus narrated in Matthew agrees exactly with Isaiah's portrayal of the servant. And thus the unusual, apparently unassertive Messiah, who fails to bring judgment to the enemies of God's people and justice to the earth and who accordingly was unacceptable to his contemporaries, is shown to have been prophesied by the prophet. The one who was uniquely related to God as his chosen and beloved, upon whom the Spirit uniquely rested, came also as a servant who was ultimately to die, in agreement with Isaiah's last Servant Song (52:13–53:12). This strange sequence of events and this paradoxical Messiah are central to the gospel as Matthew relates it.

Can Beelzebul Be against Himself?   (12:22–30)

Bibliography

Duling, D. C. "The Therapeutic Son of David." *NTS* 24 (1978) 392–409. **Fuchs, A.** *Die Entwicklung der Beelzebulkontroverse bei den Synoptikern.* SNTU B.5. Freistadt: Plöchl, 1980. **Hamerton-Kelly, R. G.** "A Note on Matthew 12.28 par. Luke 11.20." *NTS* 11 (1965) 167–69. **Kruse, H.** "Das Reich Satans." *Bib* 58 (1977) 29–61. **Lorenzmeier, T.** "Zum Logion Mt 12.28; Lk 11.20." In *Neues Testament und christliche Existenz,* ed. H. D. Betz and L. Schottroff. Tübingen: Mohr, 1973. 289–304. **Neirynck, F.** "Mt 12,25a/Lc 11,17a et la rédaction des Evangiles." *ETL* 62 (1986) 122–33. **Robbins, V.** "Rhetorical Composition and the Beelzebul Controversy." In *Patterns of Persuasion,* ed. B. Mack and V. Robbins. Sonoma: Polebridge, 1989. 161–93.

Translation

[22]*Then a demon-possessed blind and mute man was brought to him, and he healed him, so that the mute[a] man was able[b] to speak and to see.* [23]*And everyone in the crowds was astonished, and they began[c] to say: "Could this one be the Son of David?"* [24]*But when the Pharisees heard this, they said: "This one casts out demons only through Beelzebul,[d] the ruler of the demons."* [25]*But knowing[e] their thoughts, he[f] said to them: "Every kingdom which is divided against itself suffers ruin, and no city or household which is divided against itself will be able to stand.* [26]*And if Satan casts out Satan, he is divided against himself. How therefore will his kingdom survive?* [27]*If I myself am casting out demons through Beelzebul,[g] by whom do those associated with you[h] cast them*

out? Because of this charge[i] they themselves will be your judges! [28]*But if I myself cast out demons through the Spirit of God, then the kingdom of God has indeed come upon you.* [29]*Furthermore,[j] how is it possible for one to enter the house of a strong man and to steal his goods, except one first bind that strong man? And then he can[k] thoroughly plunder his household.* [30]*The one who is not with me is against me, and the one not gathering with me is in fact scattering."*[l]

Notes

[a] Some MSS (L W Δ Θ $f^{1,13}$ sy[p,h]) add καὶ τυφλόν, "and blind," for agreement with the first part of the verse. Other MSS (TR C q) have both words but in reverse order, τυφλὸν καὶ κωφόν, "blind and mute," for even closer agreement.

[b] "Was able" is added in the translation to complete the meaning.

[c] "Began," reflecting the inceptive impf. tense of the verb.

[d] Important MSS (א B) read βεεζεβούλ, "Beezebul"; others (e.g., c vg sy[s,c,p]) read "Beelzebub." In favor of the text: P^{21} C D (L) W Θ $f^{1,13}$ and TR.

[e] A few MSS (P^{21} א[1] D) have ἰδών, "seeing," for εἰδώς, "knowing."

[f] Many MSS insert ὁ Ἰησοῦς, "Jesus," here in place of the pronoun for the sake of clarity (C L W Θ $f^{1,13}$ TR).

[g] Cf. *Note* d. Here the evidence lines up almost exactly as there.

[h] οἱ υἱοὶ ὑμῶν, lit. "your sons." See *Comment*.

[i] "Charge" added to complete the sense.

[j] ἤ, lit. "or."

[k] "Can" added to complete the sense of the passage.

[l] Some MSS (א 33 sy[hmg]) supply με, "me," as the direct object of the verb σκορπίζει, "scatters," to balance the clause with the preceding. See *TCGNT*, 32.

Form/Structure/Setting

A. The Pharisees again encounter the miraculous power of Jesus in the healing of a blind and mute man (through exorcism, which, however, is not mentioned). When this remarkable healing gives rise to the claim that Jesus may be the Son of David, i.e., the Messiah, the Pharisees are provoked into drawing an opposite conclusion and one that makes no sense at all. But in the attribution of Jesus' healing power to Beelzebul, a name for Satan himself, the escalating opposition and hostility toward Jesus reach a climax. The verdict reached by the Pharisees will continue to impact the narrative until it reaches its bitter end.

B. The Synoptic relationships of the present passage are unusually complex. As a preliminary observation, it is worth noticing that the opening verses (vv 22–24) are quite close in content, though less so in wording, to 9:32–34 (a Q passage; cf. Luke 11:14–15). The latter, however, refers only to a demoniac who is mute and then enabled to speak. We may have here the coalescing of two originally independent stories. The sequence of the two passages is the same: the healing, the crowd's reaction (but in 9:33 it runs, "never has such a thing been seen in Israel"), and the Pharisees' accusation that Jesus casts out demons by the prince of demons (9:34, however, does not mention Beelzebul). There has perhaps been some influence of the passages upon each other, perhaps in the process of oral transmission.

Vv 24–26 are paralleled both in Mark 3:22–26 and in Luke 11:15, 17–18. The agreements with Luke are closer and suggest that Matthew is dependent upon Q. The agreement with Mark is more general, with the only significant similarity being the reference to Satan casting out Satan (v 26; cf. Mark 3:22; lacking in Luke). Mark here quite probably parallels the Q material independently (three major differences from Q: Jesus "has" [ἔχει] Beelzebul [Mark 3:22], speaks to the crowds ἐν παραβολαῖς, "in parables" [Mark 3:23], and refers to the end of Satan's kingdom, ἀλλὰ τέλος ἔχει, "but comes to an end" [Mark 3:26]). The agreements with Luke against Mark (e.g., εἰδώς, "knowing"; πᾶσα βασιλεία, "every kingdom"; ἐρημοῦται, "is ruined" [all the preceding in v 25 and Luke 11:17], and the question πῶς σταθήσεται ἡ βασιλεία αὐτοῦ, "how will his kingdom stand?" [v 26; Luke 11:18]) point to the use of Q. And this conclusion is confirmed by the fact that the following verses (vv 27–28) are not in Mark but are again paralleled in Luke, this time in very nearly verbatim agreement (the only differences are a slight change in word order in v 27b and Matthew's πνεύματι, "Spirit," for Luke's [ànd probably originally Q's, given Luke's favoring of the word "Spirit"] δακτύλῳ, "finger," in v 28 [Luke 11:20]). On the other hand, however, v 29 follows Mark 3:27 almost exactly, except that Matthew casts the sentence into the form of a question beginning with ἢ πῶς ("or how"). In the final verse (v 30), not found in Mark, Matthew reverts yet again to Q, with the wording in verbatim agreement with Luke (11:23). Thus Matthew appears to have alternated in his use of sources, weaving a coherent whole out of material drawn occasionally from Mark 3:22–27 and sometimes from his Q source, witnessed to also by Luke 11:17–23.

C. The form of the passage is complicated because of the different elements Matthew has collected from the tradition to make up the whole. It begins with a healing narrative that serves as the stimulus for opposite evaluations of Jesus and continues with the controversy episode and the appended material that follows. The following outline may be suggested: (1) the healing of the demoniac, further subdivided into (a) bringing of the man (v 22a) and (b) performance of the healing "to speak and to see," a corresponding chiasm with "blind and mute" (v 22b); (2) the response of the crowds (v 23); (3) the opposite response of the Pharisees (v 24); (4) the response of Jesus, in terms of (a) the general principle that a divided kingdom, city, or house cannot stand, with considerable structural parallelism (v 25) and (b) its application to Satan (v 26); (5) the question of the power of Jewish demon exorcism (v 27); (6) the key to and the basis of Jesus' exorcisms, with an opening clause parallel to the opening clause of v 27 (v 28); (7) the separate analogy of plundering a strong man's house (v 29); and (8) an appended saying in nearly symmetrical parallelism about those who do not identify with Jesus (v 30). Apart from the final logion, the passage exhibits little of the symmetry and parallelism usually associated with the sayings of Jesus in Matthew.

D. The Synoptic material about binding the strong man to plunder the house is alluded to in the *Gos. Thom.* 21 and cited in 35, where, however the agreement involves a statement, thus pointing to Mark 3:27, rather than a question, as in Matt 12:29.

Comment

22 A remarkable healing miracle performed by Jesus is reported in the briefest of terms by Matthew in order to focus on the accusation of the Pharisees and Jesus' response. Thus there is no reference to those who brought the man to Jesus and no reference to his request or faith. For the importance of the verb προσηνέχθη, "brought," see *Comment* on 4:24. Matthew has referred to Jesus' healing of the demon possessed generally in 4:24; 8:16, and specifically in 8:28–34; 9:32–34; 15:22–28; and 17:14–18. In this instance demon possession was considered the cause of the man's maladies. (For the connection between physical diseases or handicaps and demon possession, see the *Comment* on 9:32.) Only here in the four Gospels do we find reference to the healing of a man both blind and mute. According to Matthew, Jesus healed the man immediately and directly. λαλεῖν καὶ βλέπειν, "to speak and to see," records very simply but also very powerfully the efficacy of the cure.

23   The crowds were "astonished" (ἐξίσταντο, surprisingly the only occurrence of this verb in Matthew; cf. Mark 2:12; 6:51) and began to wonder whether Jesus might be ὁ υἱὸς Δαυίδ, "the Son of David," i.e., the Messiah (cf. *Pss. Sol.* 17:21), the promised one of the line of David who would alter the present order by bringing eschatological fulfillment. (See *Comment* on 9:27.) Part of that eschatological fulfillment would be the healing of all illness. The healing Servant of God (cf. 8:17; 12:18–21) is thus the Son of David (cf. Ezek 34:23; 37:25). The initial μήτι has the nuance of doubtful wondering ("perhaps"; thus BAGD, 520; cf. 26:22, 25). Such a powerful deed as they had witnessed seemed to point in that direction (cf. 9:33). Their wonder became the solid conviction of the early Church, and Matthew's readers immediately recognized the truth of the conclusion.

24   The Pharisees, however, find such a claim to be impossible. Their mind seems already so prejudiced against Jesus that they are unable to assess correctly the evidence before their eyes. They are already convinced that Jesus is on the side of the enemy and not God. His powerful deeds of exorcism and healing are thus but acts of magic and are attributed to demonic power; consequently a conclusion quite opposite to that pondered by the crowd is drawn: Jesus casts out demons ἐν τῷ βεελζεβούλ, "through Beelzebul," ἄρχοντι τῶν δαιμονίων, "by the ruler of the demons." This charge is in line with that mentioned in 10:25 (cf. 9:34), where Jesus indicates that his enemies referred to him as Beelzebul. It is interesting to note that the same contrast between the Son of David title, on the one hand, and the contrary charge concerning the casting out of demons by the prince of demons, on the other, is found also in 9:27–34. (For the name Beelzebul, see *Comment* on 10:25.) Since the Pharisees cannot deny the powerful deeds of Jesus and since they cannot admit he performs them by the power of God (cf. v 28), their only apparent recourse is to attribute them to the power of the devil, being fully oblivious to the foolishness of such a conclusion. The attribution of Jesus' deeds to the power of Beelzebul amounted to a charge of sorcery, a crime that was punishable by death (cf. *m. Sanh.* 7:4).

25–26   Since Jesus supernaturally knows (εἰδώς) the thoughts of the Pharisees (cf. the same statement in 9:4), we can assume that the charge in v 24 was made only among themselves and not directly to him or to others. The straightforward analogy of a kingdom, city, or (even) house, which being divided against itself cannot stand, shows the absurdity of the Pharisees' logic at this point. ἐρημοῦται, "suffers ruin," and οὐ σταθήσεται, "will not stand," are synonymous expressions (cf. the repeated μερισθεῖσα καθ' ἑαυτῆς, "which is divided against itself"). V 26 then applies the obvious, possibly proverbial, truth articulated in v 25 to the specific instance of Satan's kingdom. Here ὁ Σατανᾶς, "Satan" or "the Adversary" (used elsewhere in Matthew only in 4:10 and 16:23), is clearly an alternate way of referring to Beelzebul. (See *Comment* on 4:10.) The concept of Satan having a "kingdom" (βασιλεία) is found explicitly in the NT only here and in the Synoptic parallel passages (but cf. Rev 2:13). Satan's dominion could clearly survive such internal division no more than earthly kingdoms. It is not only an absurdity but also an impossibility that Satan should oppose his own work by supplying the power to perform exorcisms.

27 To the preceding, a second, supplementary argument is added, substantiating at least that demon exorcism by the power of God was not only possible but was already being experienced by the people of that day (cf. Acts 19:13; Jos. *Ant.* 8.2.5 §45–49; *J.W.* 7.6.3 §185; Justin Martyr, *Dial.* 85). The reference to οἱ υἱοὶ ὑμῶν, "your sons," is not to be understood literally but in the more general sense of "those associated with you" (cf. the expression "sons of the kingdom" in 8:12; and "sons of the bridegroom" in 9:15; BAGD suggest "your followers," 833). The Pharisees were forced to admit that their own exorcists were empowered by God and not by Beelzebul. This at least opens up the possibility that Jesus' exorcisms were also by the power of God. Indeed, as the preceding (main) argument has shown, exorcism by the power of Satan is an impossibility. The only other real option is that Jesus' exorcisms were by the same power as those of the Jewish community. Thus, to condemn Jesus would be to condemn their own exorcists, and accordingly (διὰ τοῦτο) those who knew themselves to be empowered by God in the casting out of demons would rise up to condemn those who attributed their work (and by implication that of Jesus) to the power of Beelzebul. Thus not only were the Pharisees wrong in the assessment of the power by which Jesus exorcized demons, but their accusation made them guilty of opposing the very work of God. For this even their own would become their judges (cf. v 41).

28 The opening of this verse is in exactly the same form as the opening of v 27, except for the earlier placement of the instrumental dative ἐν πνεύματι θεοῦ, "through the Spirit of God," for emphasis. The contrast is an absolute one. Jesus substitutes "through the Spirit of God" for "through Beelzebul" as the true description of his ministry of exorcism. The work of Jesus is accomplished through divine agency. Matthew's deliberate use of "Spirit" here, in place of Q's δακτύλῳ, "finger" (so Luke 11:20), agrees with the reference to the Spirit in v 18 (cf. 3:16). But if there is a similarity between the exorcism of Jewish practitioners and that of Jesus in that both were empowered by God, there is also an all-important difference. The choice of the phrase "Spirit of God" already signals this difference. The exorcisms and healing miracles of Jesus are part of a larger whole and, unlike those of his Jewish contemporaries, are linked inseparably with both his person and the proclamation of the dawning of the kingdom of God. In this case, the powerful deeds of Jesus are considered direct pointers to the reality of that proclamation. These deeds indicate that ἡ βασιλεία τοῦ θεοῦ, "the kingdom of God," is now directly present to the people of Israel (Matthew uses "God" rather than "heaven" elsewhere only in 6:33; 19:24; and 21:31, 43 [cf. 13:43; 26:29]; here it is preferred probably to serve as the direct opposite of the reference to the kingdom of Satan in v 26). The verb ἔφθασεν means "to come upon" and necessitates the conclusion that the kingdom of God has in some sense actually become present (so rightly Davies-Allison)—a clearer statement than that made by ἐγγίζειν, "is near," of 4:17; 10:7. Admittedly this has happened without the fullest effects that one must associate with the kingdom; we thus have fulfillment but fulfillment short of consummation. This problem will again surface in chap. 13, where the presence of the kingdom together with the delay of apocalyptic judgment is addressed (cf. Luke 17:21).

29   The coming of the kingdom of God through the ministry of Jesus entails a fundamental defeat for Satan and his minions (see especially 1 John 3:8). Far from taking place through the power of Satan, demon exorcism can only occur where Satan's power is severely curtailed. Although the details of the parable of this verse should not be allegorized, it is clear from the context that τὸν ἰσχυρόν, "the strong man" (cf. Isa 49:24–25), stands for Beelzebul/Satan, and the plundering of his household (for the "binding of Satan," see *As. Mos.* 10.1; *T. Levi* 18:12; Rev 20:2) refers to demon exorcism (contra Gundry), although it also anticipates the final eschatological victory over evil. But the main point is again christological: Jesus is stronger than the strong one (cf. Isa 53:12) and is hence able to raid his kingdom at will and deliver those who are oppressed in a variety of ways. In this basic sense the ministry of Jesus is the beginning of eschatological deliverance, the turning point of the aeons.

30   Although this verse is an originally independent logion appended to the preceding material, it must be understood within the context. The phrase ὁ μὴ ὢν μετ᾽ ἐμοῦ, "the one who is not with me," alludes probably not to the Pharisees, since then the sentence asserts what is already too obvious, but rather to those associated with the Pharisees who cast out demons (v 27). They seemed to participate in the same enterprise as Jesus and thus in the advance of the kingdom of God; yet they did not accept him or his message. In this they agreed with the Pharisees and thus had finally to be described as κατ᾽ ἐμοῦ, "against me." The gathering and scattering of the second parallel clause are harvest metaphors and point to the eschatological harvest. It is also possible, but less convincing, that gathering and scattering are meant to refer to sheep (cf. *Pss. Sol.* 12:28; John 10:12; Matt 9:36). The point here is a parallel one, namely, that those who labor for good, such as the Jewish exorcists, but who were not among the followers, i.e., disciples, of Jesus, were not at all involved in the bringing of the eschatological kingdom. Nor can they be regarded as neutral, for neutrality is not an option. They instead worked paradoxically against that reality; and thus they in effect were "scattering" (σκορπίζει) rather than "gathering" (συνάγων). The threefold occurrence of the pronoun ἐμοῦ, "me," in relation to which the true character of a person's work is finally evaluated, points again clearly in the direction of Christology. Of the highest importance is the person of Jesus and one's relationship to him. This verse is therefore in effect a "call to decision" (so Luz).

> This observation explains, too, the apparently contradictory statement in Mark 9:40 (cf. Luke 9:50): "He that is not against us is for us," which, interestingly, is also made in a context that refers to demon exorcism by a man who was not a disciple of Jesus. The difference between him and the exorcists of v 27 of our passage is that he used the name of Jesus in his exorcisms and thus at least was not aligned with the Pharisees who opposed Jesus. Thus Jesus concludes, "Do not forbid him, for no one who does a mighty work in my name will be able soon after to speak evil of me." Again, as in our pericope, the focus is christological.

Explanation

There have always been competing assessments of Jesus and his significance. None has been so wrong and so absurd as that of the Pharisees. Confronted with the power of God, they called it the power of Beelzebul. Jesus pointed out the foolishness of their argument. All exorcisms (and all healings) are good exactly because they necessarily counteract the work of Satan. At the same time, the thrust of this pericope is to make the work and person of Jesus the standard for the kingdom. Of Jesus and of him alone can the statement be made "the kingdom of God has come upon you" (v 28). This and this alone is the unique eschatological work of God in history. It is by its very nature definitive, and thus all other good work performed by others must be measured in relation to it and hence ultimately in its relation to Jesus. Only those who are aligned with Jesus can say that the works they perform are part of the eschatological blessing promised in the coming of the kingdom of God. All other good works, though good in themselves, are not a part of the great purpose of God now being realized in Jesus.

The Question of Unforgivable Sin   (12:31–32)

Bibliography

Boring, M. E. "The Unforgivable Sin Logion Mark III 28–29/Matt XII 31–32/Luke XII 10: Formal Analysis and History of the Tradition." *NovT* 18 (1976) 258–79. **Colpe, C.** "Der Spruch von der Lästerung des Geistes." In *Der Ruf Jesu und die Antwort der Gemeinde.* FS J. Jeremias, ed. E. Lohse et al. Göttingen: Vandenhoeck & Ruprecht, 1970. 63–79. **Evans, O. E.** "The Unforgivable Sin." *ExpTim* 68 (1957) 240–44. **Fitzer, G.** "Die Sünde wider den Heiligen Geist." *TZ* 13 (1957) 161–82. **Fridrichsen, A.** "Le péché contre le Saint-Esprit." *RHPR* 3 (1923) 367–72. ————. "Wer nicht mit mir ist, ist wider mich." *ZNW* 13 (1912) 273–80. **Lövestam, E.** *Spiritus Blasphemia: Eine Studie zu Mk 3,28f par Mt 12,31f, Lk 12,10.* Scripta Minora, Regiae Societatis Humaniorum Litterarum Lundensis, 1966, 67:1. Lund: Gleerup, 1968. **O'Neil, J. C.** "The Unforgivable Sin." *JSNT* 19 (1983) 37–42. **Scroggs, R.** "The Exaltation of the Spirit by Some Early Christians." *JBL* 84 (1965) 359–73. **Williams, J. G.** "A Note on the 'Unforgivable Sin' Logion." *NTS* 12 (1965) 75–77.

Translation

31 *"Because of this I tell you, every sin and blasphemy will be forgiven human beings,*[a] *but the blasphemy of the Spirit will not be forgiven.*[b] 32 *And whoever says a word against the Son of Man will be forgiven,*[c] *but whoever says anything against the Holy Spirit will not be forgiven,*[d] *either in this age or in the coming one."*

Notes

[a] A few MSS (B *f*¹) add ὑμῖν, "to you," before τοῖς ἀνθρώποις, "human beings." Metzger describes this as "a scribal inadvertence" (*TCGNT*, 32).

[b] Some MSS (C D L W Θ *f*¹³ TR) add τοῖς ἀνθρώποις, "human beings," to produce a parallelism with the end of the first clause.

[c] ἀφεθήσεται αὐτῷ, lit. "it will be forgiven to him." B* adds οὐκ, "not," before ἀφεθήσεται, "will be forgiven," probably not because of the difficulty of the verse but again because of scribal inadvertence. Cf. *TCGNT*, 32.

[d] οὐκ ἀφεθήσεται αὐτῷ, lit. "it will not be forgiven to him."

Form/Structure/Setting

A. The serious mistake made by the Pharisees in their charge that Jesus performed his exorcisms through the power of the prince of demons gives rise to the present pericope with its concern for the so-called unforgivable sin. The meaning of the present difficult passage can only be derived from an understanding of its immediate context. As in the preceding material, the Pharisees are especially in view in this pericope and in the following one.

B. Matthew draws the present passage from his two main sources, Mark and Q. The one major difference between Matthew and his sources is that he has repeated the basic point found in Mark and Luke (Q) in a second, parallel statement (i.e., v 32 repeats the point of v 31). In the first occurrence of the statement he depends on Mark; in the second on Q. Apart from Matthew's own opening words διὰ τοῦτο, "on account of this," v 31a and v 32b are apparently drawn from Mark 3:28–29. In 31a Matthew omits Mark's ἀμήν, "verily," and the expression τοῖς υἱοῖς τῶν ἀνθρώπων, "the sons of men," as well as Mark's redundant ὅσα ἐὰν βλασφημήσωσιν, "whatsoever they blaspheme" (Mark 3:28). In 32b Matthew substitutes εἴπῃ κατά, "speak against," for Mark's βλασφημήσῃ εἰς, "blaspheme against," and reexpresses Mark's "but is guilty of an eternal sin" (Mark 3:29) in his final words οὔτε ἐν τούτῳ τῷ αἰῶνι οὔτε ἐν τῷ μέλλοντι, "neither in this age nor in the coming one." V 31b, ἡ δὲ τοῦ πνεύματος βλασφημία οὐκ ἀφεθήσεται, "but the blasphemy of the Spirit will not be forgiven," finds no direct parallel in Mark or Luke and has probably been composed by Matthew on the basis of Mark 3:29, used also in v 32b. V 32a, on the other hand, is apparently borrowed from Q (Luke 12:10a). Here Matthew's κατά, "against," sharpens Luke's εἰς, "against," in reference to speaking against the Son of Man. Matthew's fondness for parallelism has thus governed his use of his sources and the alterations he has made to the shape of the material.

C. Vv 31 and 32 are parallel in content, while each verse itself has two parts in rather strict parallelism. The verses can be outlined as follows: after the opening clause, (1) divides into (a) forgiveness of all sin and blasphemy (v 31a) and (b) no forgiveness for blasphemy of the Spirit (v 31b); and (2) divides into (a) forgiveness of those who speak against the Son of Man (v 32a) and (b) no forgiveness for speaking against the Holy Spirit (v 32b). The same verb in the same form (ἀφεθήσεται, "it will be forgiven") occurs as the main verb in each of the four clauses. The parallelism within each verse is striking, especially that of v 32 (exactly parallel except for the time reference in v 32b). Matthew has left his imprint on the material, perhaps in imitation of the parallelism of the logia of Jesus in the oral tradition he specially uses.

D. *Did.* 11:7 alludes to the Synoptic material reflected in this passage, though not necessarily Matthew, apparently understanding by blasphemy of the Spirit the failure to try and discern the spirit of Christian prophets. Matthew (v 32) is however probably reflected in *Gos. Thom.* 44 (cf. the reference to the blasphemy of the Holy Spirit as not being forgiven either "on earth or in heaven").

Comment

31–32   Διὰ τοῦτο, lit. "on account of this," does not link the present short pericope with v 30 but with the entire preceding episode concerning the charge of the Pharisees that Jesus cast out demons by the power of Beelzebul (vv 22–30). That is, these verses are to be read in light of the preceding narrative. It is the Pharisees' charge that raises the question of a form of blasphemy beyond forgiveness. (The rabbis spoke also of unforgivable sins, but these are of a different order than what is spoken of in the present passage [cf. Str-B 1:636].)

Without question, this is a difficult passage that does not exactly encourage optimism in the exegete (Davies–Allison say, "As it stands, Matt 12.32 has no obvious meaning. . . . We remain stumped" [2:348]; cf. Luz, who finds no explanation satisfactory). If the following does not solve the problem, it will at least, we may hope, provide some assistance in understanding it. The initial question to be answered is whether the Pharisees' charge against Jesus falls into the category of πᾶσα ἁμαρτία καὶ βλασφημία, "every sin and blasphemy," against human beings, which are forgivable, or of ἡ τοῦ πνεύματος βλασφημία, "the blasphemy of the Spirit," which is not forgivable. The former of these in v 31a seems clear enough: it refers to sins against and the slandering of other persons. The parallel clause in v 32a, however, refers to the speaking of a word against τοῦ υἱοῦ τοῦ ἀνθρώπου, "the Son of Man." "Son of Man" can mean simply "human being" (see Mark 3:28; cf. Ps 8:4, quoted in Heb 2:6), in which case the parallelism with v 31a is preserved. Matthew's use of the phrase, however, has thus far been consistently in the titular sense, "Son of Man," as it will again be in v 40 (cf. 8:20; 9:6; 10:23; and, though less certainly, 12:8). If we have the titular use here, then we are left with the more difficult statement that a word spoken against the Son of Man, i.e., Jesus, can be forgiven.

We must now turn to the question of key importance in understanding this passage, namely, whether the Pharisees had spoken against Jesus or whether they had blasphemed against the Holy Spirit. It is clear from the context that the latter is the case. Jesus asserts that it was ἐν πνεύματι θεοῦ, "by the Spirit of God," that he cast out demons (v 28). Therefore, to ascribe Jesus' activity to the power of Beelzebul (v 24) was not merely to say a word against the Son of Man but to blaspheme against the Spirit (cf. v 18). To blaspheme against the Spirit was in this case to attribute the work of God's Spirit to Satan and so in the most fundamental way to undercut the very possibility of experiencing the reality of God's salvation. In other words, this blasphemy by its very nature makes forgiveness impossible (in that sense, it is analogous to apostasy; cf. Heb 6:4–6). Even to speak a word against or to slander (εἴπῃ λόγον κατά, "says a word against," is the functional equivalent of βλασφημία, "blasphemy") the Son of Man is at one level forgivable and not as morally culpable as the blasphemy of the Spirit. The Son of Man was, after all, present in veiled form and was thus not unmistakable (Lövestam calls attention to Peter's denial of Jesus and subsequent forgiveness, 75–79). But the blasphemy of the Spirit amounts to final rejection of God's plain salvific activity (see esp. Lövestam on the underlying OT pattern [7–16]; cf. Isa 63:10; Acts 7:51), and thus for this reason it is far more culpable—indeed, something not to be forgiven, οὔτε ἐν τούτῳ τῷ αἰῶνι οὔτε ἐν τῷ μέλλοντι, "either in this age or in the coming one" (this two-age language is common in Judaism and in Matthew; e.g., 13:22, 39, 40; 24:3; see Str-B 4.2:799–976). To put it another way, blasphemy against the Holy Spirit includes the slander of the Son of Man—to oppose the Spirit is to oppose Jesus and his mission—but the blasphemy of the Son of Man need not, although it may, involve something quite so catastrophic as blasphemy of the Spirit. In the case of the Pharisees, the opposition to Jesus had unfortunately ended in the blasphemy of the Spirit.

Explanation

Given Matthew's christological interests and the unique and central position held by Jesus throughout the Gospel, one may understandably be surprised that Matthew has not said the reverse of what stands in the text, i.e., that blasphemy against the Spirit is forgivable but not that against the Son of Man. The gravity of the blasphemy against the Spirit, however, depends upon the Holy Spirit as the fundamental dynamic that stands behind and makes possible the entire messianic ministry of Jesus itself (cf. v 18 and references there). Lesser blasphemies are not beyond forgiveness, including even those against the Son of Man, at least in the humility of his servant role and in his meekness (cf. 11:29). This veiled form delays the powerful expression of his messianic authority, and in it he does not yet exercise the judgment deserved by sinners (cf. v 20) but shows mercy to them (cf. 9:13). The failure to understand Jesus is yet forgivable but not the outright rejection of the saving power of God through the Spirit exhibited in the direct overthrow of the kingdom of Satan. The only unforgivable sin is that of deliberately denying God in a fundamental way, one which goes against plain and obvious evidence. Such hardheartedness is the result of one's own deliberate insensitivity and cuts one off from forgiveness. However, any person who is genuinely worried about having committed the unforgivable sin against God, by virtue of this concern, can hardly be guilty of such blasphemy or denial.

Speaking Good and Evil   (12:33–37)

Bibliography

Dewailly, L.-M. "La parole sans oeuvre (Mt 12,36)." In *Mélanges offerts à M. D. Chenu,* Bibliotèque thomiste 37. Paris: Vrin, 1967. 203–19. **Gerhardsson, B.** "'An ihren Fruchten sollt ihr sie erkennen': Die Legitimitätsfrage in der Matthäischen Christologie." *EvT* 42 (1982) 113–26. **Stauffer, E.** "Von jedem unnützen Wort." In *Gott und die Götter.* FS E. Fascher. Berlin: Evangelische Verlagsanstalt, 1958. 94–102.

Translation

[33] *"Either make the tree good and its fruit will be*[a] *good, or make the tree bad and its fruit will be*[a] *bad. For a tree is proven by its fruit.* [34] *You offspring of vipers, how when you are evil are you able to speak good things? For it is from the abundance of the heart that the mouth speaks.*[b] [35] *The good person brings forth good things*[c] *from the good treasury,*[d] *and the evil person brings forth evil things*[e] *from the evil treasury.* [36] *But I say to you that people will render an account in the day of judgment for every careless word which they speak.* [37] *For from your words you will be justified, and from your words you will be condemned."*

Notes

ᵃ "Will be" added in translation. See *Comment*.

ᵇ D* d add ἀγαθά, "good things," in a misguided attempt to supply the sense of the statement.

ᶜ ℵ C L N Δ *f* ¹ 33 sa^mss insert τά, "the," before ἀγαθά, "good things," perhaps in imitation of Luke 6:45.

ᵈ Some MSS (L *f* ¹ 33 vg^mss) add τῆς καρδίας αὐτοῦ, "of his heart," by the influence of the previous sentence and reflecting the Lukan parallel (Luke 6:45).

ᵉ L N Δ 33 sa^mss insert τά, "the," before πονηρά, "evil things," again reflecting Luke 6:45. Cf. *Note* c.

Form/Structure/Setting

A. This passage about good and bad words follows the preceding pericope with its reference to blasphemy in order to clarify the problem of blasphemy, which is far deeper than the mere words themselves. The problem is one of the basic nature of the speaker; what a person says is inescapably related to what a person is.

B. The passage consists partly of material drawn from Q (vv 33–35; cf. Luke 6:43–45), though reworked, and from Matthew's special source (vv 36–37). V 33 furthermore finds a parallel in substance in 7:16–20, i.e., the reference to the relationship between a good tree and good fruit and a bad tree and bad fruit as well as the conclusion that a tree is known by its fruit (cf. Luke 6:43–44a). The opening question of v 34 is unique to Matthew, but thereafter in vv 34–35, apart from the transposition of clauses, Matthew is in very close agreement with the wording of Luke 6:45 (the main differences are Luke's repeated προφέρει, "bear," for Matthew's ἐκβάλλει, "brings forth," the addition of τῆς καρδίας, "of the heart," after "the good treasury," and the definite articles [singular] before ἀγαθόν and πονηρόν, hence "the good" and "the bad"). Matthew has added his final logion (vv 36–37) from his fund of oral tradition because of the appropriate subject matter.

C. V 33 appears to be a separate logion built from the same traditional materials used in 7:16–20. It serves as an introduction to the material that follows. The pericope can be outlined thus: (1) the tree and the fruit, consisting of (a) the good tree/fruit and (b) the bad tree/fruit, these in perfectly symmetrical parallelism, and (c) the conclusion of knowing by fruit (v 33); (2) the relation between the heart and words of the mouth, consisting of (a) a question directed to the Pharisees and (b) the concluding point (v 34); (3) the speech of good and bad persons, consisting again of two perfectly symmetrical clauses (v 35); (4) the danger of careless words (v 36); and (5) a concluding and summarizing principle, stated in two perfectly symmetrical clauses (v 37). The form of much of the material (so too the grouping of these sayings) thus appears designed for catechetical purposes and oral transmission. The material may to some extent have come to Matthew in this form, but it has also probably been shaped by him for his didactic purposes.

Comment

33 The parallelism ἢ ποιήσατε . . . ἢ ποιήσατε, "either make . . . or make," is a way of stating two principles and could be translated "if you make . . . or if you make." ποιήσατε may also be understood here as meaning "suppose" (see BAGD, 682 [e.β]), i.e., "suppose a tree is good: its fruit will also be good." The point being made here is the same as in 7:17. That is, a good tree produces good fruit and a bad tree produces bad fruit. If you have a good tree, its fruit *will* be good. There is no need to make *both* the tree *and* the fruit good; the one will automatically produce the other. Thus probably the verb "to be," i.e., "will be," is to be supplied in the second part of each of the clauses (thus too NIV and JB). The conclusion is obvious (and stated also in 7:16, 20): a tree is known by the kind of fruit it produces (cf. Sir 27:6). For σαπρόν, see *Comment* on 7:17. Whereas in 7:16–20 the metaphor applies to conduct generally, here it is to be understood in light of the following verses as referring specifically to good and bad speaking.

34–35 From the opening words γεννήματα ἐχιδνῶν, "offspring of vipers," it is clear that the Pharisees are still being addressed (the phrase is used two other times in Matthew, both clearly in reference to the Pharisees: 3:7; 23:33). In view particularly, though perhaps not exclusively, is the accusation of the Pharisees in v 24 (cf. v 31). The Pharisees have earlier been described as πονηροὶ ὄντες, "being evil" (cf. 7:11). It is no surprise therefore that their estimate of Jesus in v 24 is an evil one. A bad tree can produce only bad fruit. They are described therefore as being incapable of speaking ἀγαθά, "good things" (cf. the attack upon their teaching in 15:3, 6; 23:15–33). The point of the metaphor of the tree and its fruit is now made again by the parallel metaphor of heart and mouth: the mouth speaking what comes from the center of a person's being, the heart. The περισσεύματος, "abundance" (in Matthew used only here), of the heart may presumably apply either to good or to evil (cf. ἀγαθά, "good things," and πονηρά, "bad things," in v 35). The key parallel here is found in 15:11 and 19, where what comes out of a person's mouth is equated with what comes out of a person's heart. A person who is at root "evil" (πονηρός) is unable to speak or do good (see Rom 8:6–7 for a similar reference to this inability; cf. John 8:43). The θησαυροῦ, "treasury," is clearly what is contained in the heart (so explicitly in the parallel, Luke 6:45). The expression "to bring forth from one's treasury" (ἐκβάλλει ἐκ τοῦ θησαυροῦ αὐτοῦ) is used in 13:52 in a somewhat different sense, referring to new and old things spoken by the Christian scribe.

36 An apparently separate and different logion concerning the importance of one's speech is now appended by Matthew to the preceding material, and the horizon broadens to include his readers. It points to the great importance of what one speaks, calling attention even to πᾶν ῥῆμα ἀργόν, "every careless word." Here the point is not the danger of bad words but even of useless or worthless words ("a careless word which, because of its worthlessness, had better been left unspoken"; BAGD, 104). ἀργόν would include untrue words (cf. JB: "unfounded") but includes more than that. This logion has the same effect as the teaching of Jesus in the Sermon on the Mount. That is, it sharpens the call to righteousness by noting the danger not only of obviously bad words but even of seemingly neutral words that may, however, imply, presuppose, or in some indirect way aid what is bad even by being themselves merely ineffective and empty. One is thus to speak only what is unequivocally good; for all else one will be held accountable in the day of judgment (cf. Jas 3:1, 6; Jude 15). According to the rabbinic perspective too, a person will be accountable in the judgment for his (or her) words (see Str-B 1:638–9). For ἐν ἡμέρᾳ κρίσεως, "on the day of judgment," see *Comment* on 10:15.

37 This further added statement, which has a proverbial ring (cf. the change from second person plural to second person singular), assumes the preceding view that the words a person speaks reflect her or his inner identity. As a tree is known by its fruit (v 33), so the real nature of a person will be discovered through spoken words (the same could be said of deeds [cf. 7:21–27], but in this pericope the focus is on speech). Thus on the day of judgment one will either be justified (δικαιωθήσῃ, used again in Matthew only in 11:19) or condemned (καταδικασθήσῃ, used again in Matthew only in v 7) by the words one has spoken. Words, like deeds, are indicators of a person's discipleship to Jesus and relationship to the kingdom.

Explanation

As the metaphor of the tree and its fruit was used in 7:16–20 to refer to works, so the same metaphor is used here in relation to words. Both works and words reveal the true nature of a person. The words of the Pharisees revealed their failure to receive the good news of the kingdom proclaimed by Jesus. It is in this sense that they were bad and they spoke bad things; indeed, they blasphemed the Holy Spirit (v 32). This passage calls attention to the importance of all speech; it warns of irresponsible or thoughtless speech as well as bad speech. It reminds the Christian readers of Matthew that on the day of judgment they will be held accountable for all the words they speak as well as the deeds they do. Righteousness consists always of both word and deed (cf. Col 3:17).

The Sign of Jonah   (12:38–42)

Bibliography

Bacon, B. W. "What Was the Sign of Jonah?" *BW* 20 (1902) 99–112. **Edwards, R. A.** *The Sign of Jonah in the Theology of the Evangelists and Q.* SBT 2.18. London: SCM, 1971. **Glombitza, O.** "Das Zeichen des Jona." *NTS* 8 (1962) 359–66. **Howton, J.** "The Sign of Jonah." *SJT* 15 (1962) 288–304. **Landes, G. M.** "Matthew 12.40 as an Interpretation of 'The Sign of Jonah' against Its Biblical Background." In *The World of the Lord Shall Go Forth*, ed. C. L. Meyers and M. O'Connor. Winona Lake, IN: Eisenbrauns, 1983. 665–84. **Linton, O.** "The Demand for a Sign from Heaven." *ST* 19 (1965) 112–29. **Merrill, E. H.** "The Sign of Jonah." *JETS* 23 (1980) 123–29. **Mora, V.** *Le signe de Jonas.* Lire la Bible 63. Paris: Éditions du Cerf, 1983. **Schmitt, G.** "Das Zeichen des Jona." *ZNW* 69 (1978) 123–29. **Scott, R. B. Y.** "The Sign of Jonah." *Int* 19 (1965) 16–25. **Seidelin, P.** "Das Jonaszeichen." *ST* 5 (1951) 119–31. **Swetnam, J.** "No Sign of Jonah." *Bib* 66 (1985) 126–30. ———. "Some Signs of Jonah." *Bib* 68 (1987) 74–79. **Vögtle, A.** "Der Spruch vom Jonaszeichen." In *Das Evangelium und die Evangelien.* Düsseldorf: Patmos, 1971. 103–36.

Translation

³⁸ *Then some of the scribes and Pharisees*[a] *answered him, saying, "Teacher, we want to see a sign from you."* ³⁹ *But he, answering, said to them: "An evil and adulterous generation*

seeks after a sign, and no sign will be given to it except the sign of Jonah the prophet.
[40]For just as Jonah was in the belly of the whale three days and three nights, thus[b] the
Son of Man will be in the heart of the earth three days and three nights. [41]Ninevites[c] will
rise up in the judgment with this generation and will condemn it, because they repented
at the preaching of Jonah, and look, there is something more than Jonah here. [42]The
queen of the south will rise up in the judgment with this generation and will condemn it,
because she came from the ends of the earth to hear the wisdom of Solomon, and look,
there is something more than Solomon here. "

Notes

[a] B and a few other MSS omit καὶ φαρισαίων, "and Pharisees," probably by accident (homoioteleuton).

[b] D L W it sy[c] bo add καί, "also," thus emphasizing the parallel.

[c] ἄνδρες Νινευῖται, lit. "Ninevite men." Cf. LXX of Jonah 3:5.

Form/Structure/Setting

A. The culpability of the Pharisees is now brought into even sharper focus. The request for a sign is only a further indication of their refusal of Jesus and his message. They had witnessed countless miracles pointing to the reality of the kingdom and the truth of Jesus' proclamation and yet would not believe. They had been the recipients of far more evidence than had the Ninevites or the Queen of Sheba. Whereas the latter acted upon what little they knew, the Pharisees not only failed to accept what they saw, but they attributed it to the power of Satan. They are to receive only one sign, a mysterious and overwhelming one involving the death and resurrection of Jesus, but that too will not persuade them to change their view of Jesus. This pericope leads in turn to the next pericope with its grim parabolic characterization of the rejection of Jesus.

B. In two places Matthew records the request of the Pharisees for a sign and Jesus' reference to the sign of Jonah. The present passage thus finds a partial parallel in 16:1–2a, 4 (cf. Mark 8:11–12). V 38 is only similar in content to 16:1 (which has Sadducees in place of the scribes), but v 39 is in verbatim agreement with 16:2a–4, except for the latter's omission of the final two words referring to Jonah as τοῦ προφήτου, "the prophet." So far as Synoptic relationships are concerned, the pericope is mainly dependent on Q, which is more developed than Mark 8:11–12, with some material being drawn from Matthew's special source.

V 38 is probably a rewriting of Mark 8:11 or of the Q source reflected in Luke 11:16 (16:1 is perhaps a little closer to Mark 8:11). V 39, on the other hand, is obviously drawn from Q (cf. especially the description of the generation as πονηρά, "evil," and the verbatim agreement with Luke 11:29, starting with the words καὶ σημεῖον οὐ δοθήσεται, "and a sign will not be given," until the omitted τοῦ προφήτου, "the prophet" [cf. Matt 16:4]). V 40, with its quotation of Jonah 2:1, is unique to Matthew, despite agreement with Luke 11:30 in the phrase οὕτως ἔσται ὁ υἱὸς τοῦ ἀνθρώπου, "thus the Son of Man will be." Although vv 41 and 42 are transposed, compared to Luke 11:31 and 32, they are in exact verbatim agreement except for Matthew's omission of τῶν ἀνδρῶν, "the men" (Luke 11:31), before "this generation," thus producing a more perfect parallelism, and the slight change of the following pronoun. Matthew is responsible for the transposition of vv 41 and 42, which keeps the references to Jonah together rather than separating them. Matthew has thus used Q freely at the beginning of the pericope, introducing his own material in v 40, but has followed Q very closely in the last half of it (vv 41–42).

C. The simple structure of the passage can be seen in the following outline: (1) the request for a sign (v 38); (2) the response of Jesus, subdivided into (a) the refusal to give a sign to this evil generation (v 39) and (b) the sign of Jonah (v 40); (3) the twofold example of (a) Ninevites (v 41) and (b) the queen of the south (v 42). Matthew's unique material (v 40) is given in the comparison of the Son of Man with Jonah, and this is presented in parallel form. The Q material (vv 41–42) consists of symmetrically parallel statements: the rising up in judgment with this generation, the condemning of it, the ὅτι ("because") clauses, and then finally the καὶ ἰδού, "and look," clauses, referring to something greater now being present. This Q material shows clearly the impress of the transmission of the tradition in oral form.

Comment

38 The opening words τότε ἀπεκρίθησαν, "then they answered," relate this passage to the preceding material as a continuation of the exchange between the Pharisees and Jesus begun already at the beginning of chap. 12. "Answered" is used here in this loose sense (cf. BAGD, 93b) rather than meaning the answer to a question. The scribes and Pharisees are commonly linked in Matthew (see 5:20, and esp. chap. 23). Those who have not accepted Jesus most often address him as διδάσκαλε, "teacher," in the Gospel (see on 8:19; cf. 9:11; 17:24; 22:16, 36); it is a term of respect, comparable to "rabbi" (cf. 23:8), but one that in itself suggests a resistance to Jesus and his proclamation and a refusal to follow in discipleship to him. The request to see a σημεῖον, "sign," is not for an "ordinary" miracle but for a legitimating sign that would provide compelling proof to them (cf. the request in 16:1 for a σημεῖον ἐκ τοῦ οὐρανοῦ, "sign from heaven"). Matthew uses the word σημεῖον, "sign," elsewhere in 16:4 (a parallel to the present passage), in 24:3 and 30, where it refers to the sign of the coming of the Son of Man, and finally in 26:48, the "sign" of Judas' kiss. The request of the scribes and Pharisees may seem genuine enough at first glance. As the narrative makes clear, however, the Pharisees had already witnessed numerous miracles of Jesus that had sign-bearing significance (cf. 11:4–5) yet had refused to acknowledge them. Indeed, as we have seen, they went so far as to attribute some of Jesus' works to the power of Beelzebul. Now they ask to see a sign, presumably a miracle performed just for them, something that would amaze them while presenting irrefutable evidence that his claims were true (cf. particularly John 6:30). Yet this is precisely the kind of miracle—a demonstrative display of power for the purpose of impressing—that Jesus would not perform. His miracles were never done for the sake of creating an effect or of overpowering those who witnessed them; they were much more a part of his proclamation and thus designed solely to meet human needs. Even if Jesus had performed some astonishing sign for them, such was their unbelief, it is implied, that they probably would have charged Jesus with sorcery and thus have used it against him.

39 Jesus accordingly faults them for seeking after a sign, describing them as representative of γενεὰ πονηρὰ καὶ μοιχαλίς, "an evil and adulterous generation."

The only other place these two adjectives are used in conjunction in Matthew is in the exact parallel in 16:4. For πονηρός, "evil," as a description of "this genera-tion," see v 45 (cf. v 34; 7:11, and with different vocabulary, 17:17). μοιχαλίς, "adulterous" (cf. Mark 8:38), is metaphorical rather than literal, referring, as com-monly in the OT, to an unfaithfulness in relation to God (for OT language similar to this phrase, see Deut 32:5; cf. Hos 1–3). They had seen miracles already, only to reject them (in the Johannine idiom they had seen "signs" [σημεῖα] and had re-jected them; John 7:31; 11:47–48). The problem was a deeper one (cf. vv 33–35), one within the scribes and Pharisees, and in fact no sign would be adequate to convince their unreceptive hearts. Thus Jesus responds, with a degree of irony, that no sign "will be given" to them (οὐ δοθήσεται, a divine passive, meaning "God will not give"). Yet they would indeed encounter one last sign in the miracle of the resurrection of Jesus from the dead. He means not that they would themselves see the resurrected Jesus but that they would be confronted with the triumphant tes-timony of the Church to the resurrection of Jesus as a final sign given to them. (But even this would fail to convince them; cf. 28:11–15; Luke 16:31.) The sign they would yet experience is described by Jesus as τὸ σημεῖον Ἰωνᾶ τοῦ προφήτου, "the sign of Jonah the prophet," to be explained in the next verse. For an inter-esting parallel sequence of demand for a sign and a reference by Jesus to his death and resurrection (but without the Jonah imagery), see John 2:18–22.

40   The sign of Jonah is now elucidated through the quotation of Jonah 2:1 and the drawing of the specific analogy between Jonah's experience and that which is to befall Jesus. Beginning with ἦν Ἰωνᾶς, "Jonah was," to and including τρεῖς νύκτας, "three nights," the LXX is quoted verbatim. An allusion such as this to Jesus' death, burial, and (implied) resurrection would not have made much sense to the Pharisees (nor even the disciples) at this juncture, but in retrospect the words would have been filled with meaning (cf. 27:63; John 2:21–22). The analogy with Jonah may well have originally concerned only the preaching of Jesus and Jonah (as in Luke 11:30; cf. Luz) and then later have been elaborated by the post-resurrection Church to refer to the burial (and resurrection) of Jesus. The analogy with Jonah as it occurs in Matthew is not quite perfect. Jonah, for one thing, did not die as did the Son of Man. The early Church described Jesus as active during the interim period between his death and resurrection (1 Peter 3:19; cf. Eph 4:9), but in the present passage τῇ καρδίᾳ τῆς γῆς, "heart of the earth" (i.e., Sheol, the realm of the dead), at best only hints at that. Further-more, Jonah was in the whale "three days and three nights," yet Jesus rose from the dead "on the third day" (16:21; 17:23; 20:19; cf., however, 27:63–64). But this kind of minor discrepancy, the obsession of some modern interpreters, was of no concern to Matthew or to any of the evangelists, nor can it be allowed to affect the discussion of the chronology of the passion and resurrection of Jesus.

41–42   Two parallel sayings are now appended that indicate the repentance and receptivity found in those who had much less evidence to depend on than did the contemporaries of Jesus. The Ninevites, on the one hand, who repented at the preaching of Jonah (Jonah 3:5), and the Queen of Sheba (i.e., "the south"), who traveled so far to hear the wisdom of Solomon (1 Kgs 10:1–10; cf. 2 Chr 9:1–9), will "rise up" (ἀναστήσονται) in the resurrection at the final judgment and condemn the present generation. (Cf. the similarity between this argument and that con-cerning Tyre and Sidon and Sodom for whom the day of judgment will be more tolerable than the cities in which Jesus did the majority of his works; 11:21–24.) Note the remarkable fact that the Ninevites and the Queen of Sheba are Gentiles who will rise up to judge Israelites. Again we encounter the Matthean motif of believing Gentiles and unbelieving Jews (cf. 8:10–11; 21:43). Each verse comes to a climax with the assertion καὶ ἰδοὺ πλεῖον Ἰωνᾶ/Σολομῶνος ὧδε, "and look, there is something more than Jonah/Solomon here" (cf. the very similar formula pertaining to the temple in v 6). If Jonah and Solomon were respectively persuasive and thus elicited an appropriate response, Jesus and his message should all the more have elicited a positive response from the scribes and Pharisees. The neuter πλεῖον (cf. μεῖζον in v 6), "more," is understood most naturally as referring to the entire reality of Jesus and his proclamation and the inauguration of the kingdom of God. In the three "greater/more than" sayings we encounter something and someone greater than the temple, and hence a high priest, a prophet, and a king (cf. Jos. *Ant.* 13.10.7 §299). The "wisdom of Solomon" (v 42) is furthermore exceeded by Jesus, who is the incarnation of wisdom (cf. 11:19). That the Pharisees did not respond positively to such conspicuous evidence as Jesus had given them makes them all the more culpable. Jesus and his kingdom far exceeded all else that Israel had witnessed in her history. Ironically, the Gentiles will be able to see what the Pharisees cannot.

Explanation

It is from this episode and others like it that Paul later was able to characterize the Jews as those who "seek signs" (1 Cor 1:22). There is in principle nothing wrong with the desire for a sign from God. The request for a sign only becomes unjustified and intrinsically wrong when one is already surrounded by good and sufficient evidence one chooses not to accept. In that case, unreceptivity and unbelief are the root problem, and it is unlikely that any sign would be sufficient to change such a person's mind. This is not to argue for gullibility or easy belief. The fact is, however, that Jesus' contemporaries had plenty of evidence upon which to act responsibly. In a similar way, evidence of the truth of the gospel exists today both for unbelievers and believers. In these circumstances, to ask for more evidence, more signs, is to reflect a deep-seated unbelief in the reality of God and his grace.

The Parable of the Returning Demons   *(12:43–45)*

Bibliography

Nyberg, H. S. "Zum grammatischen Verständnis von Matthäus 12,44f." *ConNT* 13 (1949) 1–11.

Translation

⁴³ *"Whenever the unclean spirit comes out of a person, it wanders through waterless places seeking a resting place and does not find it.* ⁴⁴ *Then it says: 'I will return to my*

house from which I came out.' And when that spirit comes back, it finds the house[a] *unoccupied,*[b] *swept clean, and put in order.* [45] *Then it goes and brings with it seven other spirits more evil than itself, and they go in and make their dwelling there. And the last condition of that person becomes worse than the former. Thus it will be also for this evil generation."*

Notes

[a] τὸν οἶκον, "the house," is found only in D (sy[hmg]); a few other MSS of lesser importance have αὐτόν, "it." The words are added in the translation for clarity, not in dependence on D.

[b] A few MSS (ℵ C* it) have καί, "and," after σχολάζοντα, "unoccupied."

Form/Structure/Setting

A. The parablelike passage draws an analogy, as its concluding sentence shows, between the person cleansed of demons (cf. vv 22–30, which in Luke [and Q?] immediately precede our passage), but then repossessed by them, and the present "evil generation." Thus this short pericope extends the indictment leveled against the Pharisees through most of this chapter and especially the immediately preceding passage, alluding now not simply to the failure of the Pharisees to accept Jesus and his ministry but also to the miserable future that lies before them.

B. This Q passage is in nearly verbatim agreement with Luke 11:24–26. The only differences apart from a few very minor changes in word order are the following: Matthew's inserted δέ, "but" (though here a simple connective and not in its adversative sense), at the very beginning (v 43); Matthew's ἐπιστρέψω (v 44) for Luke's ὑποστρέψω, both meaning "return"; Matthew's σχολάζοντα, "unoccupied" (v 44), probably an addition to Q; Matthew's μεθ᾽ ἑαυτοῦ, "with it" (v 45), probably omitted by Luke from Q (given Matthew's tendency to abbreviate rather than to add); and finally, Matthew's concluding sentence, "Thus it will be also for this evil generation" (v 45), added to adapt the pericope to its present context and to apply the passage to that generation. Otherwise Matthew has been content to follow Q closely.

C. The parabolic character of this passage is especially evident through the final sentence: "Thus it will be also for this evil generation" (v 45). This sentence could easily have been at the beginning of the passage in the typical form, "This evil generation is like. . . ." The structure of the pericope is as follows: (1) the departure and wandering of an evil spirit (v 43); (2) the return of the spirit to a cleansed house (v 44); (3) the entry of seven other, more evil spirits (v 45ab); and (4) the application (v 45c). The passage is marked by little of the usual parallelism, the most striking being the three participles, σχολάζοντα σεσαρωμένον καὶ κεκοσμημένον, "unoccupied, swept clean, and put in order," at the end of v 44.

Comment

43 It is presupposed that τὸ ἀκάθαρτον πνεῦμα, "the unclean spirit" (this expression occurs also in 10:1; cf. 8:16), is one that has been driven out of the person through exorcism. This demon wanders about (διέρχεται), even through the most inhospitable places, ἀνύδρων τόπων, "waterless places" (demons were associated with the wilderness; cf. Isa 13:21, 34:14), in search of a suitable resting place, but none is found. It seems at least clear that the demon cannot simply enter any person it may choose (cf. 8:31); the circumstances must apparently be right for demon possession. The purpose of the passage, however, is not to provide information about demon possession, and therefore one must be careful in generalizing.

44 The demon decides eventually to return to the person from whom it had been driven out, described by the demon in ironically imperialistic language, τὸν οἰκόν μου, "my house." The demon finds that house, i.e., that person, to be an even more attractive lodging place than before. It would be wrong to allegorize the three participles, σχολάζοντα σεσαρωμένον καὶ κεκοσμημένον, "unoccupied, swept clean, and put in order." Yet it seems clear, especially in the added σχολάζοντα, "unoccupied," that Matthew intends the conclusion that nothing good or positive had taken the place of the evil spirit that had been exorcized. All was arranged in good order since the demon had left, but there was no fundamental difference in the person that would prevent the return of the demon at will.

45 The spirit brings ἑπτὰ ἕτερα πνεύματα, "seven other spirits" (the Greek phrase has a certain euphony; for "seven demons," implying thorough domination, see Luke 8:2), described as πονηρότερα ἑαυτοῦ, "more evil than itself," to lodge in the same person. Again allegorizing is to be avoided. What counts is the punch line of the parable, which concludes that the last state (τὰ ἔσχατα) of the person has become worse than the first state (τῶν πρώτων). (For a similar expression conveying the same principle, see 2 Peter 2:20 and John 5:14; cf. 27:64.) In other words, it would have been better for the person not to have been exorcized at all, since then there would have been possession by only one demon, whereas now there is possession by eight, the additional seven being indeed "more evil" than the first demon. Matthew's added sentence οὕτως ἔσται καὶ τῇ γενεᾷ ταύτῃ τῇ πονηρᾷ, "thus it will be also for this evil generation," applies the parable to the unbelief and resistance Jesus has encountered primarily from the Pharisees. If we draw guidance from the context, the basic analogy is simple. This evil generation (cf. v 39) had experienced the powerful deeds of Jesus, which included demon exorcism, and to that extent had benefited. But there had been no repentance, no acceptance of and commitment to Jesus and his cause, and thus this generation would be as susceptible to the power of evil as ever; indeed, the judgment it would later experience would be far worse than when Jesus began his ministry. In view (contra Davies-Allison) may be the destruction of Jerusalem (cf. 24:2, 15) and not simply eschatological judgment.

Explanation

It is not enough to experience the good things of the kingdom, such as release from the power of evil or healing from physical maladies. In this present age evil is always ready to return, and physical illness is part and parcel of our mortality. Those who are privileged to experience signs of the kingdom must respond in what will truly be a life-transforming and permanent way, namely, in commitment and discipleship to Jesus. Without this, the misery of returning evil and disease will be worse than before the initial experience of deliverance. The burden of this passage is in the implicit call to respond to Jesus. Those who do respond in faith and commitment need not worry about the return of demons, nor need they quaver at future, but temporary, setbacks from disease and even death itself. Those who do not respond in faith and commitment have only worse miseries to expect in the future.

The True Family of Jesus   (12:46–50)

Bibliography

Blinzler, J. *Die Brüder und Schwestern Jesu.* Stuttgart: Katholisches Bibelwerk, 1967.

Translation

[46] *While he was yet speaking to the crowds, look, his mother and brothers stood out-side, seeking to speak to him.* [47] *[And someone*[a] *said to him: "Look, your mother and your brothers are standing outside, seeking to speak to you."]*[b] [48] *But he answered and said to the one who was speaking to him: "Who is my mother, and who are my*[c] *brothers?"* [49] *And he stretched out his hand toward his disciples and said: "Behold, my mother and my brothers.* [50] *For whoever does the will of my Father who is in heaven, that person is my brother and sister and mother."*

Notes

[a] א[1] and a few other witnesses add after τις, τῶν μαθητῶν αὐτοῦ, "(one) of his disciples."

[b] Some very important witnesses (א* B L Γ *ff*[1] k sy[s.c] sa) omit v 47 in its entirety. On the other hand, some MSS (א[(1)2] C [D] W Z Θ *f*[(1)13] TR lat sy[p.h] mae bo) include the verse. Although the verse is lacking in such an impressive array of MSS (thus the brackets), it was probably omitted by homoioteleuton (cf. λαλῆσαι at the end of vv 26 and 27) and thus probably was original. See *TCGNT*, 32. This verse is also obviously redundant after v 46.

[c] B* omits μου, "my," probably accidentally.

Form/Structure/Setting

A. This important section of the Gospel (chaps. 11 and 12) and the lengthy treatment of the unbelief of the Pharisees ends with the present pericope concerning the true family of Jesus. The focus shifts from the negative to the positive: the description of those truly related to Jesus as those who do the will of the Father can be viewed as yet another invitation to the crowds to receive Jesus and his teaching. To be related to Jesus in this way is to become a family member of the kingdom, something far more significant than mere blood relationships.

B. Matthew depends on Mark 3:31–35 for this passage (as does Luke 8:19–21, but with considerably more freedom than Matthew). In typical fashion Matthew abbreviates his source. The differences have to do with the attendant details, and as usual the agreement is close in the discourse and especially in the words of Jesus.

Matthew's opening genitive absolute, ἔτι αὐτοῦ λαλοῦντος τοῖς ὄχλοις, "while he was yet speaking to the crowds" (v 46), is unique and serves as a transition from the preceding material (cf. 9:18). Matthew adds his distinctive ἰδού, "look" (v 46), to introduce a new and interesting occurrence. He alone in the triple tradition has ζητοῦντες αὐτῷ λαλῆσαι, "seeking to speak to him" (v 46, and again in v 47). He alone uses τις, "someone" (v 47), in referring to the message brought to Jesus (Mark has "they"). Matthew omits (as does Luke) Mark's reference to the crowd sitting around Jesus (Mark 3:32, 34). So too Matthew omits Mark's αἱ ἀδελφαί, "the sisters" (Mark 3:32), if it was in Mark's original text. Matthew inserts τίνες εἰσίν, "who are" (v 48; cf. Mark 3:33), thereby emphasizing the question. Matthew substitutes ἐκτείνας τὴν χεῖρα αὐτοῦ, "having stretched out his hand" (v 49), for Mark's περιβλεψάμενος, "looking around" (Mark 3:34), thus intensifying the statement that follows. Matthew substitutes his own favorite language, τοῦ πατρός μου τοῦ ἐν οὐρανοῖς, "my Father who is in heaven" (v 50) for Mark's simple τοῦ θεοῦ, "God" (Mark 3:35). And finally, Matthew has αὐτός, intensive for "he [= that person]" (v 50), in place of Mark's οὗτος, "this one" (Mark 3:35). The agreement with Mark is thus substantial, reflecting Matthew's conservatism especially in conveying the words of Jesus.

C. Jesus turns an ordinary event, the desire of his family to speak to him, into an opportunity to teach yet again about the importance of doing the will of the Father. The structure of the passage is simple: (1) (a) the arrival of Jesus' mother and brothers (v 46) and (b) the report of their arrival in what, because of the parallelism, could be called a mirror statement of the preceding verse (v 47); (2) the teaching of Jesus through (a) a question (v 48) and (b) the answer, again involving some parallelism (v 49); followed finally by (3) a summarizing, climactic conclusion (v 50), with the parallelism broken through the introduction of ἀδελφή, "sister" (as in Mark 3:35).

D. The Matthean version of the pericope, as can be seen from certain distinctives, is found cited or alluded to in *Gos. Eb.* (as in Epiphanius, *Refutation of all the Heresies* 30.14.5), where vv 49–50 are found, in *2 Clem.* 9:11 (v 50), and in *Gos. Thom.* 99 (a brief digest of the whole passage).

Comment

46–47 Matthew, like Mark and Luke, gives no reason why the mother and brothers of Jesus wanted to talk to him. There is no hint in Matthew, as there is in Mark (Mark 3:21), that they were critical of Jesus (cf. John 7:5), yet if this is assumed, the present passage takes on even more forcefulness and links more directly with the preceding material. This is the first mention of the mother of Jesus since chap. 2; the mother, brothers, and sisters of Jesus are mentioned again in 13:55–56. Yet while there could well have been concern, especially over Jesus' sharp confrontation with the Pharisees, this can at most be only part of the assumed background and cannot be made essential for the interpretation of this passage. The fact that no mention of Jesus' father is made implies that he was no longer alive.

48–49 The rhetorical question of v 48 leads directly to the answer of v 49. The key point, emphasized by the gesture, ἐκτείνας τὴν χεῖρα αὐτοῦ ἐπὶ τοὺς μαθητάς, "stretched out his hand toward his disciples," is that the disciples are now the true family of Jesus. The kingdom of God and its demands thus take priority over human relationships, even of the most intimate kind. This reflects a motif already encountered in 10:35–37 (cf. 10:21) in the missionary instructions given to the disciples. As Jesus called his disciples to sacrifice family ties (cf. 4:22; 8:21), so for Jesus too the work of the kingdom, his own teaching ministry, must take precedence over the claims of family. Old loyalties have given way to new ones; everything must now be understood in relation to the dawning kingdom. Jesus and his disciples (i.e., the twelve plus others) shared together in a new and unique relationship as the people of the kingdom. They are now "the mother and brothers" of Jesus (cf. 28:10; 23:8; 25:40). To understand this passage as involving a rejection of the nation of Israel, as dispensationalist interpreters in particular have done, is to go far beyond its meaning.

50 The disciples of Jesus are his true family because they follow his teaching. The essence of discipleship is doing τὸ θέλημα τοῦ πατρός μου τοῦ ἐν οὐρανοῖς, "the will of my Father who is in heaven" (cf. 7:21, for the same phrase practically verbatim). The will of the Father is the righteousness taught by Jesus and is inseparable from the dawning of the kingdom and discipleship to Jesus. For the special "my Father," see too 10:32–33; 11:27; 15:13; 18:10, 19; 20:23; 25:34; 26:29, 39, 42, 53. And thus all who (ὅστις, "whoever") follow Jesus' teaching may be described as his family. For this reason there is a deliberate broadening of the scope of the statement by the inclusion now of ἀδελφή, "sister" (as in Mark), as the counterpart to "brother." This is a particularly important modification by Jesus of the formula "mother and brothers" of the preceding verses. It stands in noticeable tension with the contemporary Jewish perspective, in which women had no equal rights in the study of Torah or in the life of the religious community, and is consonant with the progressiveness of Jesus on the issue of women seen elsewhere in the Gospels. Jesus identifies *all* who follow his teaching, not only the twelve but a much wider circle including women, as his family, his "brother and sister and mother." The Father of Jesus has thus become also their Father (cf. 5:45, 48; 6:1–9, 14–15, 26, 32; 7:11; 10:20, 29; 23:9).

Explanation

The incomparable importance of fulfilling the will of God through the righteousness of the dawning kingdom is seen in the redefining of basic relationships. Jesus here repudiated neither his family (cf. 15:4–5; John 19:27) nor Israel. But he drew attention to the existence of a new family centered on obedience to the will of the Father, ironically the very thing the Pharisees prided themselves on doing. This family, later to be called "the church," represents the new reality of the kingdom on earth and thus takes priority over all else. Those who choose to do so, men *and* women, may become full members of this unique family by following Jesus. The generalized final statement functions also as an indirect invitation from which even the Pharisees are not yet excluded, despite the largely negative tone of chap. 12.

The Third Discourse:
Teaching in Parables   (13:1–58)

General Bibliography

Black, M. "The Parables as Allegory." *BJRL* 42 (1960) 273–87. **Blomberg, C.** *Interpreting the Parables.* Downers Grove, IL: InterVarsity Press, 1990. **Borsch, F. H.** *Many Things in Parables: Extravagant Stories of the New Community.* Philadelphia: Fortress, 1988. **Boucher, M.** *The Mysterious Parable.* Washington, DC: Catholic Biblical Association, 1977. **Brown, R. E.** "Parable and Allegory Reconsidered." *NovT* 5 (1962) 36–45. **Burchard, C.** "Senfkorn, Sauerteig, Schatz und Perle in Matthäus 13." *SNTU* 13 (1989) 5–35. **Cadoux, A. T.** *The Parables of Jesus: Their Art and Use.* London: Clarke, 1930/New York: Macmillan, 1931. **Carlston, C. E.** "Parable and Allegory Revisited: An Interpretive Review." *CBQ* 43 (1981) 228–42. ———. *The Parables of the Triple Tradition.* Philadelphia: Fortress, 1975. **Carson, D. A.** "The ὅμοιος Word-Group as Introduction to Some Matthean Parables." *NTS* 31 (1985) 277–82. **Cave, C. H.** "The Parables and the Scriptures." *NTS* 11 (1965) 374–87. **Crossan, J. D.** *In Parables: The Challenge of the Historical Jesus.* New York: Harper & Row, 1973. **Dahl, N. A.** "The Parables of Growth." *ST* 5 (1952) 132–66. **Dodd, C. H.** *The Parables of the Kingdom.* London: Nisbet, 1935/New York: Scribner's, 1936. **Donahue, J. R.** *The Gospel in Parable.* Philadelphia: Fortress, 1988. **Drury, J.** *The Parables in the Gospels.* London: SPCK/New York: Crossroad, 1985. **Dupont, J.** "Le point de vue de Matthieu dans le chapitre des paraboles." In *L'Évangile*, ed. M. Didier. 221–59. **Funk, R. W.** *Parables and Presence.* Philadelphia: Fortress, 1982. **Gerhardsson, B.** "If We Do Not Cut the Parables Out of Their Frames." *NTS* 37 (1991) 321–35. ———. "Illuminating the Kingdom: Narrative Meshalim in the Synoptic Gospels." In *Jesus and the Oral Gospel Tradition*, ed. H. Wansbrough. JSNTSup 64. Sheffield: Sheffield Academic Press, 1991. 266–309. ———. "The Narrative Meshalim in the Synoptic Gospels: A Comparison with the Narrative Meshalim in the Old Testament." *NTS* 34 (1988) 339–63. ———. "The Seven Parables in Matthew XIII." *NTS* 19 (1972–73) 16–37. **Harnisch, W.** *Die Gleichniserzählungen Jesu.* Göttingen: Vandenhoeck & Ruprecht, 1985. **Hendrickx, H.** *The Parables of Jesus.* San Francisco: Harper and Row, 1986. **Hunter, A. M.** *Interpreting the Parables.* London: SCM/Philadelphia: Westminster, 1960. ———. *The Parables Then and Now.* London: SCM/Philadelphia: Westminster, 1971. **Jeremias, J.** *The Parables of Jesus.* London: SCM/Philadelphia: Westminster, 1972. **Jones, G. V.** *The Art and Truth of the Parables.* London: SPCK, 1964. **Jülicher, A.** *Die Gleichnisreden Jesu.* 2 vols. Freiburg: Mohr, 1899. **Kingsbury, J. D.** *The Parables of Jesus in Matthew 13.* London: SPCK/Richmond, VA: John Knox, 1969. **Kissinger, W. S.** *The Parables of Jesus: A History of Interpretation and Bibliography.* Metuchen, NJ: Scarecrow, 1979. **Kistemaker, S. J.** *The Parables of Jesus.* Grand Rapids: Baker, 1980. **Klauck, H.-J.** *Allegorie und Allegorese in synoptischen Gleichnistexten.* Münster: Aschendorff, 1978. **Ladd, G. E.** "The Sitz im Leben of the Parables of Matthew 13: The Soils." In *SE* 2 [= TU 87] (1964) 203–10. **Lambrecht, J.** *Once More Astonished: The Parables of Jesus.* New York: Crossroad, 1981. ———. "Parables in Mt 13." *TTh* 17 (1977) 25–47. **Linnemann, E.** *Parables of Jesus: Introduction and Exposition.* London: SPCK, 1966. **Little, J. G.** "Parable Research in the Twentieth Century." *ExpTim* 87 (1975–76) 356–60; 88 (1976–77) 40–44, 71–75. **Marin, L.** "Essai d'analyse structurale d'un récit-parabole: Matthieu 13,1–23." *ETR* 46 (1971) 35–74. **Marshall, I. H.** *Eschatology and the Parables.* London: Tyndale, 1963. **Oesterley, W. O. E.** *The Gospel Parables in the Light of Their Jewish Background.* London: SPCK/New York: Macmillan, 1936. **Payne, P. B.** "The Authenticity of the Parables of Jesus." In *Gospel Perspectives*, ed. R. T. France and D. Wenham. Sheffield: JSOT, 1981. 2:329–44. **Phillips, G. A.** "History and Text: The Reader in Context in Matthew's Parables Discourse." *Semeia* 31 (1985) 111–37. **Plessis, J. G. du.**

"Pragmatic Meaning in Matthew 13:1–23." *Neot* 21 (1987) 33–56. **Schweizer, E.** "Zur Sondertradition der Gleichnisse bei Matthäus." In *Matthäus und seine Gemeinde.* Stuttgart: Katholisches Bibelwerk, 1974. 98–105. **Scott, B. B.** *Hear Then the Parable.* Minneapolis: Fortress, 1989. **Sellin, G.** "Allegorie und 'Gleichnis.'" *ZTK* 75 (1978) 281–335. **Sider, J. W.** "Proportional Analogy in the Gospel Parables." *NTS* 31 (1985) 1–23. ————. "Rediscovering the Parables: The Logic of the Jeremias Tradition." *JBL* 102 (1983) 61–83. **Smith, B. T. D.** *The Parables of the Synoptic Gospels.* Cambridge: Cambridge University, 1937. **Stein, R. H.** *An Introduction to the Parables of Jesus.* Philadelphia: Westminster, 1981. **Tinsley, E. J.** "Parable and Allegory: Some Literary Criteria for the Interpretation of the Parables of Christ." *CQ* 3 (1970) 32–39. **Tolbert, M. A.** *Perspectives on the Parables.* Philadelphia: Fortress, 1979. **Via, D. O., Jr.** *The Parables: Their Literary and Existential Dimension.* Philadelphia: Fortress, 1967. **Vorster, W.** "The Structure of Matthew 13." *Neot* 11 (1977) 130–38. **Weder, H.** *Die Gleichnisse Jesu als Metaphern.* 3rd ed. FRLANT 120. Göttingen: Vandenhoeck & Ruprecht, 1984. **Wenham, D.** *The Parables of Jesus: Pictures of Revolution.* The Jesus Library. London: Hodder & Stoughton, 1989. ————. "The Structure of Matthew XIII." *NTS* 25 (1978–79) 516–22. **Wilkens, W.** "Die Redaktion des Gleichniskapitels Mark. 4 durch Matth." *TZ* 20 (1964) 305–27.

Introduction

STRUCTURE OF CHAPTER 13

The structure of the parable discourse, 13:3–52, has been the subject of considerable debate. The contents of the discourse may be listed as follows:

    I.   The Parable of the Soils (13:1–9)
         The Purpose of Parables (13:10–17)
         The Explanation of the Parable of the Soils (13:18–23)
   II.   The Parable of the Wheat and the Weeds (13:24–30)
  III.   The Parable of the Mustard Seed (13:31–32)
  IV.   The Parable of the Leavened Loaves (13:33)
         Further Comment on the Reason for the Parables (13:34–35)
         The Explanation of the Parable of the Wheat and the
            Weeds (13:36–43)
   V.   The Parable of the Hidden Treasure (13:44)
  VI.   The Parable of the Pearl (13:45–46)
 VII.   The Parable of the Dragnet (and explanation) (13:47–50)
         Concluding Comment on the Scribe Trained for the
            Kingdom (13:51–52)

Matthew's discourse is built on the Markan parallel (Mark 4:1–34), from which he has borrowed the first three of the above pericopes as well as the parable of the mustard seed. He omits the parabolic material contained in Mark 4:21–29, supplementing his Markan source with the remainder of the discourse, drawn probably from the oral tradition available to him. Thus an initial problem concerning the structure of the discourse—the apparent digression in the passage on the purpose of the parables (13:10–17)—is explained as something the evangelist decided to accept from his source. Although the initial shape of the discourse starts from Mark, the evangelist is responsible for the shape of the discourse as a whole.

The two most striking structural aspects of Matthew's discourse are the parallelism in the discussion of the purpose of parables followed immediately by a detailed explanation of a parable (both in vv 10–23 and 34–43) and the two groups of three parables each (vv 24–33 and 44–50). In the first, the parallelism is marred by the separation of the parable of the wheat and the weeds and its explanation by two other, albeit brief, parables (mustard seed and leavened loaves). Another structural anomaly is the brief explanation (vv 49–50) of the parable of the dragnet included immediately after the parable itself (with no discussion of the purpose of the parables).

Other features of the text that may have structural significance are the following: the departure of Jesus from the crowds in v 36 (cf. vv 2–3); the parallel references to the disciples coming to Jesus to ask the explanation of a parable (vv 10, 36); the parallel citation of the OT in fulfillment quotations in vv 14–15 and 35; the formulas ἄλλην παραβολὴν παρέθηκεν (ἐλάλησεν) αὐτοῖς, "he presented (spoke) another parable to them" (vv 24, 31, 33), and the introductory ὁμοία ἐστὶν ἡ βασιλεία τῶν οὐρανῶν, "the kingdom of heaven is like" (vv 31, 33, 44, 45, 47); and finally the repeated ὁ ἔχων ὦτα ἀκουέτω, "let the one who has ears hear" (vv 9, 43).

How should the structure of chap. 13 be understood? Among the more creative analyses are those of B. Gerhardsson, D. Wenham, and Davies-Allison. Gerhardsson (*NTS* 19 [1972–73] 16–37) proposes that the six parables following the parable of the sower are further explanations of the latter, in particular of the four kinds of people mentioned. Thus, the parable of the wheat and tares explains the seed that falls by the way; the third and fourth parables (mustard seed and leaven) explain the seed that falls on stony ground; the fifth and sixth (treasure and pearl) the seed among thorns; and the seventh (dragnet) the good seed. While Gerhardsson has pointed out some interesting correspondences, which are no doubt real, not all are equally convincing. As an overall explanation of chap. 13, this analysis leaves many things noted above unexplained and thus lacks credibility. Wenham (*NTS* 25 [1978–79] 516–22), who regards v 52 as an eighth parable, analyzes the discourse as a chiasm with four parables in each half:

parable of the sower: those who hear the word of the kingdom (vv 3–9)
question and answer concerning the purpose of parables and the interpretation of the sower (vv 10–17; 18–23)
parable of the tares: on good and evil (vv 24–30)
parables of the mustard seed and the leaven (vv 31–33)
conclusion of the section concerning crowds and the interpretation of the parable of the tares (vv 34–35; 36–43)
parables of the treasure and the pearl (vv 44–46)
parable of the dragnet: on good and evil (vv 47–50)
(disciples') question and (Jesus') answer concerning the understanding of parables (v 51)
parable of the scribe: the one trained for the kingdom (v 52)

This suggestive analysis is not without problems, however. Even if we allow v 52 to be reckoned as a parable, it is quite different from the parable of the sower both in form and content and is thus hard to regard as a proper inclusio. Furthermore, the interpretations of the parables of the sower (vv 18–23) and the tares (vv 36–43) do not fit at all well into the chiasmus, and the parables of the mustard seed and the leaven, on the one hand, and those of the treasure and the pearl, on the other, do not make the same point. Davies-Allison propose a three-part structure, each part ending with an inclusio: (1) the sower—ending with the interpretation of the sower (vv 1–23); (2) the tares—ending with the interpretation of the tares (vv 24–43); and (3) the treasure—ending with the saying on treasure (vv 44–52). Again the lack of symmetry here, especially in part three but also in the extraneous parables of both parts two and three, makes the analysis less than convincing.

The parable discourse of chap. 13 does not reflect any obvious symmetrical structure. Perhaps we can do little more than to list its contents and note the corresponding elements, as we have done. There is, however, a rather clear transition point in the discourse caused by the narrative insertion at v 36, where Jesus departs from the crowds (contrast vv 2–3) and teaches his disciples in private. This has led several scholars (e.g., Kingsbury, *Parables;* Luz) to speak broadly of two main parts composing the discourse, vv 3–35 and 36–52. No convincing structural analysis can afford to ignore this break, despite the fact that such a division separates the parable of the weeds from its interpretation (the change of scene is indeed due to the purposeful giving of the interpretation in private). This change of audience is a major factor to which all other structural features must be subordinate.

THE INTERPRETATION OF PARABLES

Allegorizing has been the bane of parable interpretation over the centuries. It was largely the work of A. Jülicher, followed by the influential books of C. H. Dodd and J. Jeremias, that turned the tide by emphasizing that parables have a single, main point to make. Dodd and Jeremias further established that this point was to be ascertained from the historical setting of the ministry of Jesus and the early Church. This served as somewhat of an antidote to a vapid moralizing of the parables in the fashion of Aesop's fables by those who overlooked the eschatological drama of the parables. Jeremias showed how the evangelists may have reinterpreted the parables in their own life setting as opposed to their meaning in the life setting of Jesus. These considerable advances have remained intact until relatively recent times in which the parables have again become the subject of intense scrutiny.

The newer literary criticism, new existentialist hermeneutic, recent study of metaphor, structuralist approaches, and reader-response theories have all had a combined effect on the study of the parables, indeed upon virtually every branch of NT study (see Blomberg for a useful introduction). So far as the parables are concerned, the conclusions of Jülicher, Dodd, and Jeremias are increasingly challenged. The single point to be determined by grammatical-historical exegesis has increasingly given way to the recognition of multivalence of meaning and indeed the free construction of meaning of the parable in relation to the personal situation of the reader. While much of the new approach, in its extreme forms at least, is disastrous to the goal of *exegesis* in the traditional meaning of the word, many of the new insights can provide needed correctives. Responsible exegetes (e.g., Blomberg, Boucher, Carlston, Klauck) have for some time now backed away from Jülicher's absolute disqualifying of allegorical elements in the parables. There are allegorical elements in many of the parables, not just those interpreted allegorically by Jesus. Concern over the abuse of allegorizing the parables should not prohibit the interpreter from giving due heed to these allegorical elements. At the same time, this should not be taken to imply the acceptability of all allegorizing. Only those allegorical elements that are relatively clear from the context of the Gospel itself and that may be properly recognized without compromising the single main point of the parable or its historical meaning are acceptable. (On the importance of the context of the Gospel to the interpretation of the parables, see Gerhardsson, *NTS* 37 [1991] 321–35.)

The involvement of the reader in the construal of the meaning of a text, not least the parables, is clearly a valuable insight of the newer scholarship. Every reader brings a totality of background and experience that is bound to affect the interpretation of a text. To recognize this, however, is not necessarily to capitulate to the conclusion that the text has no meaning in itself or that the meaning of a text (and author) is altogether out of reach of a reader. Involvement of the reader in the interpretation of the parables is especially desirable since they were and are meant to be performative (or a "language event") as well as informative. That is, they are intended to have an impact on the reader at the level of his or her existence and not simply to convey information: the parables interpret us as much as we interpret the parables.

Acceptance of valid insights of the newer trends in parable interpretation can be used to supplement and refine the important and valuable work of Jülicher, Dodd, and Jeremias, but need not cancel it out altogether. It is still useful to look for a single main point of a parable, but without necessarily denying supporting allegorical elements. It is still mandatory to understand a parable in its historical contexts (both of Jesus and the evangelists), but without reducing the parable to historical information controlled by the interpreter. As the parables grabbed their initial hearers and readers, so must contemporary readers experience their power, understanding with the heart as well as the head, responding not so much to historical information but to the call of God upon their lives. For further and especially helpful discussion, see the articles of Gerhardsson and the books of Blomberg and Wenham.

The Parable of the Soils   (13:1–9)

Bibliography

Crossan, J. D. "The Seed Parables of Jesus." *JBL* 92 (1973). 244–66. **Didier, M.** "La parabole du semeur." In *Au service de la parole de Dieu*. FS A.-M. Charue. Gembloux: Duculot, 1969. 21–41. **Dietzfelbinger, C.** "Das Gleichnis vom ausgestreuten Samen." In *Der Ruf Jesu und die Antwort der Gemeinde*. FS J. Jeremias, ed. E. Lohse et al. Göttingen: Vandenhoeck & Ruprecht, 1970. 80–93. **Dupont, J.** "La parabole du semeur." In *Études sur les Évangiles synoptiques*. BETL 70. Leuven: Peeters/Leuven University, 1985. 1:236–58. **Evans, C. A.** "On the Isaianic Background of the Sower Parable." *CBQ* 47 (1985) 464–68. **Garnet, P.** "The Parable of the Sower: How the Multitudes Understood It." In *Spirit within Structure*. FS G. Johnston, ed. E. J. Furcha. PTMS n.s. 3. Allison Park, PA: Pickwick, 1983. 39–54. **Gerhardsson, B.** "The Parable of the Sower and Its Interpretation." *NTS* 14 (1967–68) 165–93. **Hahn, F.** "Das Gleichnis von der ausgestreuten Saat und seine Deutung (Mk 4,3–8; 14–20)." In *Text and Interpretation*. FS M. Black, ed. E. Best and R. McL. Wilson. Cambridge:

Cambridge University, 1979. 133–42. **Jeremias, J.** "Palästinakundliches zum Gleichnis vom Sämann." *NTS* 13 (1966–67) 48–53. **Léon-Dufour, X.** "La parabole du semeur." In *Études d'évangile*. Paris: Editions du Seuil, 1965. 256–301. **Lohfink, G.** "Das Gleichnis vom Sämann." *BZ* n.s. 30 (1986) 36–69. **Newman, B. M.** "To Teach or Not to Teach (A Comment on Matthew 13:1–3)." *BT* 34 (1983) 139–43. **Payne, P. B.** "The Authenticity of the Parable of the Sower and Its Interpretation." In *Gospel Perspectives*, ed. R. T. France and D. Wenham. JSOT Press: Sheffield, 1980. 1:163–207. ————. "The Order of Sowing and Ploughing." *NTS* 25 (1978) 123–29. ————. "The Seeming Inconsistency of the Interpretation of the Parable of the Sower." *NTS* 26 (1980) 564–68. **Weeden, T. J.** "Recovering the Parabolic Intent in the Parable of the Sower." *JAAR* 47 (1979) 97–120. **Wenham, D.** "The Interpretation of the Parable of the Sower." *NTS* 20 (1974) 299–318. **White, K. D.** "The Parable of the Sower." *JTS* n.s. 15 (1964) 300–307. **Wilder, A. N.** "The Parable of the Sower: Naiveté and Method in Interpretation." *Semeia* 2 (1974) 134–51.

Translation

[1] *On that day Jesus went out of the house*[a] *and sat down beside the lake.* [2] *And large*[b] *crowds gathered beside him so that he had to*[c] *get into a boat and sit there, and all the multitude stood on the shore.*

[3] *And he told them many things in parables, saying: "Look, the sower went out to sow.* [4] *And as he sowed, some seeds*[d] *fell along the edge of the path, and the birds*[e] *came and ate them.* [5] *And other seeds*[f] *fell on stony ground where there was not much soil, and the seedlings*[g] *immediately sprung up because the soil was not deep.*[h] [6] *But when the sun rose, they were scorched, and because they had no root,*[i] *they withered.* [7] *And some seeds*[j] *fell among the thorn bushes, and the thorn bushes grew up and choked them.* [8] *But some seeds*[k] *fell on good earth, and they kept producing fruit, some a hundredfold, some sixtyfold, and others thirtyfold.* [9] *Let the person who has ears*[l] *hear!"*

Notes

[a] D it sy[a] lack τῆς οἰκίας, "of the house."

[b] πολλοί, lit. "many."

[c] "Had to" is added in the translation to complete the sense of the sentence.

[d] "Seeds" is added in the translation for clarity.

[e] Some MSS (K Θ *f*[13] vg[cl] sy[c,h] sa mae bo[mss]) add τοῦ οὐρανοῦ, "of heaven," by influence of the parallel in Luke 8:15.

[f] See *Note* d.

[g] "Seedlings" is added to complete the sense.

[h] βάθος γῆς, lit. "depth of soil."

[i] Θ *f*[13] and a few other MSS have βάθος ῥίζης, lit. "depth of root," producing a parallelism with the end of v 5.

[j] See *Note* d.

[k] See *Note* d.

[l] Some MSS (‭א‬[2] C D W Z Θ *f*[1,13] TR lat sy[c,p,h] co) insert ἀκούειν, "to hear," probably because of the influence of the parallel in Mark 4:9. See too v 43. Cf. *TCGNT*, 29.

Form/Structure/Setting

A. Jesus teaches the large crowd by the lakeside in this, the third of Matthew's five discourses in which he has collected together seven parables concerning the kingdom. The first of these, concerning the soils, is particularly relevant to the rejection and hostility themes and thus the apparent failure of the kingdom that dominate chap. 12. Those who hear the proclamation of the kingdom respond in a variety of ways; not all seed that is sown is productive. The detailed explanation of this first parable is not given until vv 18–23.

B. In this pericope Matthew depends again on Mark (Mark 4:1–9; cf. Luke 8:4–8). Matthew's transitional opening words (up to παρὰ τὴν θάλασσαν, "beside the lake") are, as usual, his own creation. But after this beginning, Matthew follows Mark very closely, the only differences being minor, many caused by Matthew's characteristic abbreviation of Mark.

Among the minor changes, the following may be noted: Matthew's πολλοί, "many" (v 2), for Mark's πλεῖστος, "large" (Mark 4:1); Matthew's ἐπὶ τὸν αἰγιαλὸν εἱστήκει, "stood on the shore" (v 2), for Mark's ἐπὶ τῆς γῆς ἦσαν, "they were on the land" (Mark 4:1); Matthew's ἐλάλησεν, "he told" (v 3), for Mark's ἐδίδασκεν, "he was teaching" (Mark 4:2); Matthew's addition of τοῦ before σπείρειν (v 3; so too Luke 8:5) to indicate purpose: "[in order] to sow" (cf. Mark 4:3); Matthew's ἐν τῷ σπείρειν αὐτόν, lit. "in his sowing" (v 4; so too Luke 8:5), for Mark's ἐγένετο ἐν τῷ σπείρειν, "it came to pass in the sowing" (Mark 4:4); Matthew's plural ἅ ("which [seeds]") and ἄλλα ("others") throughout (i.e., vv 4, 5, 7, 8) for Mark's singular ὅ and ἄλλο (Mark 4:4, 5, 7; but note the plural ἄλλα in 4:8); and Matthew's transposition of the order, resulting in a listing of the highest yield first: ἑκατόν, ἑξήκοντα, τριάκοντα, "hundredfold, sixtyfold, thirtyfold" (v 8; cf. Mark 4:8). Among Matthew's omissions are the following: ἐν τῇ θαλάσσῃ and πρὸς τὴν θάλασσαν, "in the sea" and "at the sea" (Mark 4:1); καὶ ἔλεγεν αὐτοῖς ἐν τῇ διδαχῇ αὐτοῦ, ἀκούετε, "and he was saying to them in his teaching, 'Listen'" (Mark 4:2–3); καὶ καρπὸν οὐκ ἔδωκεν, "and it brought forth no fruit" (Mark 4:7); ἀναβαίνοντα καὶ αὐξανόμενα καὶ ἔφερεν, "rising up and growing, and it was bearing" (Mark 4:8); and ἀκούειν, "to hear" (Mark 4:9). These changes and omissions do not affect the substance of Mark and amount to improvements of Mark's Greek and an economy of style.

C. The pericope may be simply outlined as follows: (1) the setting (vv 1–2); (2) the parable of the soils, introduced in v 3 and then proceeding through four instances (linked with μέν and subsequent δέ), i.e., the seed that falls (a) along the road (v 4), (b) on rocky ground (vv 5–6), (c) among thorn bushes (v 7), and (d) on good ground (v 8); and finally (3) an exhortation to hear (v 9). Each of these four examples has a secondary element describing what happened. Thus in a birds come and eat the seed (v 4b); in b the sun rises and withers the seedling (v 5b–6); in c thorns choke the seed (v 7b); and in d the seed bears fruit, a hundred-, sixty-, and thirtyfold (parallelism with μέν ... δέ ... δέ, v 8b). Consequently, the parable is beautifully shaped with enough parallel structure to make it striking and easy to memorize.

D. Justin Martyr quotes this parable in the Matthean version in *Dial.* 125.1–2. *1 Clem.* 24:5 is probably dependent on the pre-Synoptic tradition. For further use of the parable in the early Church, see *Gos. Thom.* 9.

Comment

1–2 The introductory words ἐν τῇ ἡμέρᾳ ἐκείνῃ, "on that day," serve as a transition from the preceding passage but have the effect of connecting what follows, especially the early part of chap. 13, with the preceding encounter between Jesus and the Pharisees. That is, the parables have something important to say about the nature of the kingdom and its rejection as well as acceptance. The "house" (τῆς οἰκίας) refers presumably to the place where Jesus was teaching when his mother and brothers sought him (12:46, ἔξω, "outside"; Jesus returns to the same house in v 36, where he teaches his disciples further), probably Peter's house in Capernaum (cf. 8:14). Jesus sat by the edge of the lake, apparently in order to teach (for another reference to teaching by the lake, see Mark 2:13). In that culture, teachers sat (cf. 5:1; 24:3), but because of the press of the crowds Jesus was forced to get into a boat (cf. Mark 3:9; Luke 5:3). Taking advantage of the good acoustics provided by the water, Jesus sat in the boat and spoke to the crowds who stood on the αἰγιαλόν, "shore" (a word that occurs in the Synoptics only here and in v 48). The reference to the large crowds is a favorite Matthean motif in the description of Jesus' ministry (see *Comment* on 4:25).

3 Avoiding Mark's verb "taught" (ἐδίδασκεν), as well as the noun διδαχή, "teaching" (both in Mark 4:2), as perhaps being less appropriate for parables than for the interpretation of the law, Matthew writes that Jesus "told" (ἐλάλησεν) many things (πολλά) to the crowds in parables (cf. v 34: "he said nothing to them without a parable"). Broadly conceived, parable (παραβολή, lit., "cast alongside"; cf. Heb. *māšāl,* an enigmatic saying, based on the meaning of the verb *māšal,* "to liken to") may refer to proverbs, wisdom sayings, or even riddles; it is hence primarily a way to convey truth concerning deep matters by means of an analogy or comparison drawn usually from commonplace things (see Gerhardsson, *NTS* 34 [1988] 339–63). Matthew uses the word for the first time here in introducing the so-called parable discourse (cf. the conclusion in 13:53), where the word occurs repeatedly (ten times; further occurrences of the word are in 15:15; 21:33, 45; 22:1; 24:32). The purpose of teaching in parables will be addressed directly in vv 10–17. Although Jesus speaks to the crowd only until v 10 (v 11 begins a section addressed only to the disciples) and then presumably to the crowd again from vv 24–33, Matthew's seven parables are only representative of many more, thus justifying the πολλά, "many things." The first parable begins with Matthew's favorite ἰδού, "look." The genius of Jesus' parables lay at least partly in his ability to transform the ordinary things of life into vehicles of truth. The sight of the sower (ὁ σπείρων) sowing was a very common one in that agricultural society, and the varied fate of the seeds was well known. For a similar illustration based on the sowing of seed, not all of which sprouts, see 2 Esdr 8:41 (cf. 2 Esdr 9:31–37). The deeper meaning of this parable, which initially may or may not have been clear, was explained to the disciples in vv 18–23. The full exposition of the parable will be given when we examine those verses; here we merely make clear the text as it stands.

4 The first example concerns seed that in the process of scattering ends up παρὰ τὴν ὁδόν, "along the edge of the path" (or possibly "on" the path; cf. BAGD, 611a), on the hardened ground and not in the plowed earth. It remains unclear, however, whether the field would have been plowed before the sowing or *after,* which was apparently done on occasion (see Jeremias; White; Payne [*NTS* 25 (1978) 123–29]; cf. *Jub.* 11:11; *m. Šabb.* 7:2). If the plowing in this instance is understood to have been done afterwards, then the sowing of seed upon the path and upon rocky ground (v 5) becomes perhaps a little easier to understand. The seed on the path becomes easy food for the birds and is thus prevented from producing fruit.

5–6 The second example refers to seed that in the sowing falls ἐπὶ τὰ πετρώδη, "upon stony ground." This seed sprouts quickly because it is in such shallow soil and cannot put down deep roots, without which it cannot trap the moisture of the ground. Hence it burns (ἐκαυματίσθη, "it was scorched") under the hot midday sun (cf. Jas 1:11), withers, and dies.

7 In the third example, the seed falls ἐπὶ τὰς ἀκάνθας, "among thorn bushes." The rapidly growing wild thorn bushes eventually squeeze out and kill the tender seedling (cf. Job 31:40). And thus once again the sower is thwarted and the seed wasted.

8 In the fourth and final example, however, the seed falls ἐπὶ τὴν γῆν τὴν καλήν, "on the good earth." In this instance the seed "kept producing" (ἐδίδου, imperfect tense) fruit in the usual varying amounts; in the best case, some (ὅ, singular, but here to be understood as a distributive plural) a hundredfold, others sixtyfold, and others thirtyfold. Although the yield of a hundredfold is spectacularly good (cf. Gen 26:12; *Sib. Or.* 3.63–64), it is probably not to be regarded as indicating the extravagance of eschatological fulfillment (contra Jeremias; with Gundry; Davies-Allison), which would probably have been expressed with more fantastic numbers than these.

9 With the words "Let the person who has ears hear!" the listener or reader is suddenly alerted to understand that the parable points beyond itself to a greater reality. The phrase "who has ears" refers to a receptivity concerning the underlying truth of the parable. It amounts to an appeal to hear positively and to respond appropriately. The same exhortation is found verbatim in v 43 and 11:15.

Explanation

The focus of the parable is not upon the sower (despite being called "the parable of the sower" in v 18), nor even the seed, but upon the fate of the seed, which is directly dependent upon the kind of soil that received it. This will be seen clearly in the interpretation of the parable given by Jesus in vv 18–23. The parable addresses the failure and success of seed in the goal of fruit bearing. Specifically it describes the environment in which the seed comes to no effect and that in which the seed becomes productive. These circumstances, it will be seen from the following pericope, are not the result of accident, as in the case of sowing, but involve the grace of God and the responsiveness of human beings. The growth of the kingdom is, as the rest of the chapter will show, the work of God.

The Purpose of Parables *(13:10–17)*

Bibliography

Brown, R. E. *The Semitic Background of the Term "Mystery" in the New Testament.* Philadelphia: Fortress, 1968. **Cerfaux, L.** "La connaissance des secrets du royaume d'après Matt. xiii.11 et par." *NTS* 2 (1956) 238–49. **Elderen, B. van.** "The Purpose of the Parables according to Matthew 13:10–17." In *New Dimensions in New Testament Study,* ed. M. J. Tenney and R. E. Longenecker. Grand Rapids: Zondervan, 1974. 180–90. **Evans, C. A.** *To See and Not Perceive:*

Isaiah 6.9–10 in Early Jewish and Christian Interpretation. JSOTSup 64. Sheffield: JSOT, 1989.
Gnilka, J. "Das Verstockungsproblem nach Matthäus 13,13–15." In *Antijudaismus im Neuen Testament?* ed. W. P. Eckert et al. Munich: Kaiser, 1967. 119–28. **Manson, W.** "The Purpose of the Parables: A Re-Examination of St. Mark iv.10–12." *ExpTim* 68 (1957) 132–35. **Siegman, E. F.** "Teaching in Parables (Mk iv.10–12; Lk viii.9–10; Mt xiii.10–15)." *CBQ* 23 (1961) 161–81. **Via, D.** "Matthew on the Understandability of the Parables." *JBL* 84 (1965) 430–32.

Translation

¹⁰*And his disciples came and said to him: "Why do you speak to them in parables?"* ¹¹*He replied to them: "Because to know the mysteries of the kingdom of heaven has been given to you, but to them it has not been given.* ¹²*For whoever has, more will be given to that person and it will abound; but whoever does not have, even what that person has will be taken away.*ᵃ ¹³*For this reason I speak to them in parables, because* ᵇ *although*ᶜ *seeing, they do not see, and although*ᵈ *hearing, they do not hear, nor do they understand;* ¹⁴*and the prophecy of Isaiah is fulfilled in them,*ᵉ *which says:*
With hearing you will hear ᶠ *and not at all understand,*
and seeing you will see and yet not at all perceive.
¹⁵ *For the heart of this people has grown hard,*ᵍ
and with their ears ʰ *they hear poorly,*
and they have shut their eyes,
  lest they should see with their eyes
  and hear with their ears
  and understand with their heart,
  and they repent, and I heal them.
¹⁶*But blessed are your eyes because they see and your ears because they hear.* ¹⁷*For truly I say to you that many prophets and righteous persons desired to see what you are seeing, and they did not see*ⁱ *it, and to hear what you are hearing, and they did not hear it."*

Notes

ᵃ Gr. text includes ἀπ' αὐτοῦ, lit. (away) "from him."

ᵇ Some MSS (D Θ *f*¹·¹³ it syˢ·ᶜ), apparently influenced by the parallel in Mark 4:12, have ἵνα, "in order that," and then have the following finite verbs in the subjunctive mood, down to and including μήποτε ἐπιστρέψωσιν, "lest they should turn." See *TCGNT*, 32≠33.

ᶜ "Although" is added in the translation, taking the participles as concessives. See *Comment*.

ᵈ See preceding *Note*.

ᵉ D it and a few other MSS have τότε πληρωθήσεται ἐπ' αὐτοῖς, "then will be fulfilled in them," apparently in the sense of future judgment.

ᶠ A few MSS (D it mae) begin the quotation with the opening words of Isa 6:9: πορεύθητι καὶ εἶπε τῷ λαῷ τούτῳ, "go and say to this people."

ᵍ ἐπαχύνθη, lit. "grown thick," i.e., insensitive.

ʰ τοῖς ὠσίν can be translated "with their ears" despite the lack of αὐτῶν (the pronoun "their"). ℵ C³³ it vgᵐˢˢ syˢ·ᶜ·ᵖ, however, add αὐτῶν to bring the text of the quotation into verbatim agreement with the LXX.

ⁱ D has ἠδυνήθησαν ἰδεῖν, "they were unable to see (it)."

Form/Structure/Setting

A. When on this occasion Jesus taught the crowds in parables without accompanying explanations, the disciples were understandably prompted to ask Jesus about his strategy in so doing. As it emerges, they were concerned too with their own uncertainty about the meaning of the parables. Jesus provides an answer to the disciples' question that centers on the deep mystery of the reception or rejection of the truth he proclaims. Here, as before, the answer depends on the mysterious working of the sovereign will of God. And again (cf. 11:25–27) in retrospect the free will of human beings to accept or to reject is considered in terms of the experience or non-experience of grace.

B. Matthew uses a variety of sources in the composition of the larger discourse of chap. 13 and also in this particular pericope. Apart from the usual originality in the opening, transitional words, Matthew initially depends on Mark. Vv 10–11 draw upon Mark 4:10–11 (cf. Luke 8:9–10).

After the opening clause, Matthew alone has the question διὰ τί ἐν παραβολαῖς λαλεῖς αὐτοῖς, "why do you speak to them in parables?" In Mark and Luke the implied question concerns the meaning of the parables. Matthew thus focuses more directly on the following material concerning the *reason* for the use of parables. Matthew also alters Mark's οἱ περὶ αὐτὸν σὺν τοῖς δώδεκα, "those around him with the twelve" (Mark 4:10), to simply οἱ μαθηταί, "the disciples" (v 10). In v 11, Matthew alone begins the answer of Jesus with ὅτι "because," again stressing the reason for the parables. Matthew inserts γνῶναι, "to know," after δέδοται, "it has been given" (v 11; so too Luke 8:10), and uses the plural τὰ μυστήρια, "the mysteries" (v 11; so too Luke 8:10), rather than Mark's singular. Matthew sharpens the predestinarian tone of the pericope by ἐκείνοις δὲ οὐ δέδοται, "but to them it has not been given," while Mark and Luke state merely that parables are spoken to them (v 11; Mark 4:11; Luke 8:10). V 12 is also drawn from Mark but from material found later in the chapter (i.e., Mark 4:25; cf. Luke 8:18b). Matthew here alters ὅς, "who," to ὅστις, "whoever," but otherwise follows Mark verbatim except for the addition of καὶ περισσευθήσεται, "and it will abound," unique to Matthew and in keeping with the exceptional bountifulness referred to in the preceding parable (v 8; cf. v 23). V 13 picks up the original Markan sequence again (Mark 4:12) but with the insertion of διὰ τοῦτο ἐν παραβολαῖς αὐτοῖς λαλῶ, "for this reason I speak to them in parables," again emphasizing the purpose of the parables. Matthew, furthermore, changes Mark's ἵνα, "in order that," to ὅτι, "because" (v 13; cf. Mark 4:12; so too Luke 8:10b), which has the effect of softening the statement by calling attention to the responsibility of the hearers but by no means avoids the predestination problem. Matthew departs from Mark by first alluding to Isa 6:9–10 in v 13 (cf. Luke 8:10b) before actually citing the passage under a fulfillment formula of introduction. Matthew's quotation (vv 14–15), furthermore, is much longer than that of Mark 4:12 (where Isa 6:9–10 is greatly abridged). The form of Matthew's quotation is very nearly in verbatim agreement with the LXX text. Matthew rounds out the pericope with a Q passage (vv 16–17, cf. Luke 10:23–24). Here Matthew differs from Luke mainly in the following: in v 16 the omission of ἃ βλέπετε, "what you are seeing," and Matthew's addition to Q (for the sake of parallelism) of the clause καὶ τὰ ὦτα ὑμῶν ὅτι ἀκούουσιν, "and your ears because they hear"; the insertion of ἀμήν, "truly," at the beginning of v 17; and the substitution of δίκαιοι, "righteous persons," for βασιλεῖς, "kings" (v 17; cf. Luke 10:24). Matthew thus reveals considerable freedom in constructing the pericope, although basically he tends to follow Mark.

C. The structure of the pericope is as follows: (1) the question about the purpose of parables (v 10); (2) the answer of Jesus (v 11); (3) the statement of a principle (v 12); (4) (a) the culpability of those who do not receive (v 11), supported by (b) a formula quotation (vv 14–15); (5) the blessedness of Jesus' disciples (v 16); and (6) the reality of present fulfillment (v 17). The pericope is filled with parallelisms: in v 11 the parallel form of the opposition δέδοται ("it has been given")—οὐ δέδοται ("it has not been given"); similarly in v 12, ἔχει ("has")—οὐκ ἔχει ("does not have"); cf. too the parallel verbs in v 12a. The three parallel verbs of v 13 (βλέπουσιν, "see," ἀκούουσιν, "hear," and συνίουσιν, "understand") anticipate the verbs of the following quotation (though not in the same order). In the verbatim quotation from Isa 6:9–10 (verbatim but for a missing αὐτῶν [see above, Note h]), v 14 reveals parallel structures (in tenses and moods of verbs), while v 15 reveals a chiasmus: heart, ears, eyes—eyes, ears, heart. Again these reflect a high degree of parallelism, especially in the four subjunctive verbs following μήποτε, "lest." V 16 contains parallel syntax pertaining to eyes and ears, while v 17, after the introductory formula, consists of almost symmetrically parallel syntax in the infinitive clauses, ἰδεῖν ("to see") and ἀκοῦσαι ("to hear"), as well as in the verbs οὐκ εἶδαν ("they did not see") and οὐκ ἤκουσαν ("they did not hear"). The sayings of Jesus thus again reveal significant parallelism in structure, syntactical form, and verb forms, which gives further evidence of the pre-Matthean transmission of the sayings orally but also of Matthew's impress on the material for catechetical purposes.

Comment

10   The scene changes abruptly, and the evangelist does not relate it to the scene in vv 1–2. The disciples, here presumably the twelve, come to Jesus (προσελθόντες, a favorite of Matthew; see on 4:3)—it is assumed privately (cf. Mark 4:10)—to ask why he is speaking "to them" (αὐτοῖς), i.e., the crowds (v 2) and hence the outsiders, in parables (cf. v 3). Although Jesus had undoubtedly used parables earlier in his teaching (cf. 7:24–27; 9:15–17; 11:16–19), the parables seem now perhaps to have increased in number (cf. πολλά, "many things," in v 3) and to have taken on a character that seemed to make them harder to understand for the crowds certainly but even for the disciples (cf. v 36).

11   The answer of Jesus indicates that understanding the truth he teaches depends on the determining grace of God. The ὅτι is to be understood causally since it introduces the answer to the διὰ τί, "why?" of v 10. The repeated passive verb δέδοται, "it has been given," is a divine passive that assumes God as the acting subject. God has granted the disciples γνῶναι τὰ μυστήρια τῆς βασιλείας τῶν οὐρανῶν, "to know the mysteries of the kingdom of heaven"; to the crowds (ἐκείνοις, "to them") he has not granted this. Matthew's addition of the infinitive "to know" is an important emphasis. The word μυστήρια, "mysteries" (cf. רָז [rāz], e.g., in Dan 2:27–28 and in the literature of Qumran [e.g., 1QH 1:21; 1QS 9:17]; cf. *1 Enoch* 68:5; 103:2; 2 Esdr 10:38; 14:5; Wis 2:22; Sir 22:22; see Brown), refers to "the secret thoughts, plans, and dispensations of God which are hidden from human reason, as well as from all other comprehension below the divine level, and hence must be revealed to those for whom they are intended" (BAGD, 530a). The expression "the mysteries of the kingdom of heaven" refers to the meaning of Jesus' teaching (not of the OT, *pace* van Elderen, 185) about the kingdom, i.e., particularly its reality, yet its veiled existence in the present as well as its future manifestation (cf. "word of the kingdom" in v 19). The need for divine illumination to understand these mysteries, however, does not obviate the culpability of those who are unreceptive to the proclamation of Jesus. This is made clear in the statement that follows.

12   The problem of the apparent injustice of God giving to those who have and taking away from those who have not is alleviated when it is realized that Jesus refers simply to receptivity and unreceptivity. The one who "has" (ἔχει) is the one who has welcomed the message of the kingdom and who has responded in the appropriate commitment, i.e., who has become a disciple of Jesus. It is this person who has the key to further understanding of the purpose and plan of God in the presently dawning kingdom. This one will thus be given more understanding (contra Kingsbury, *Parables,* 46, who argues they will be given more of the gift of the kingdom itself), and that understanding will abound (περισσευθήσεται) in fruitfulness. The one who "does not have" (οὐκ ἔχει) is the person who has not received or responded in commitment to the proclamation of Jesus and the disciples. Of that person it is said that καὶ ὃ ἔχει ἀρθήσεται ἀπ' αὐτοῦ, "even what that person has will be taken away." Having rejected the message of the kingdom from the start, that person is unable to penetrate to the truth of the parables of Jesus. But even what such a person is inclined to fall back on—say, trust in Jewishness and Judaism—that too will be taken away (cf. 8:12; 21:43). The identical saying in nearly verbatim form is given again by Matthew in 25:29, but in a somewhat different connection (cf. too Mark 4:25; Luke 8:18b). For a similar principle in rabbinic Judaism, see *b. Ber.* 40a; *b. Sukk.* 46a; *Qoh. Rab.* 1.7; *Gen. Rab.* 20.5; *t. Soṭa* 4.17–19; *b. Soṭa* 9b.

13   The allusion to Isa 6:9 in this verse and the full quotation that follows presuppose the hardheartedness (cf. Mark 8:17b–18) and culpability of the people being described. If God were arbitrarily hardening the heart of some and concealing the truth from some, could it not be said that his house was divided against itself (cf. 12:25)? The root problem is the unwillingness of the people to receive the message of Jesus (contra Montefiore). This is why he speaks to them in parables. Matthew's ὅτι, "because," which resumes the opening διὰ τοῦτο, "for this reason," makes it quite clear: ὅτι βλέποντες οὐ βλέπουσιν καὶ ἀκούοντες οὐκ ἀκούουσιν οὐδὲ συνίουσιν, "because seeing, they do not see, and hearing, they do not hear, nor do they understand." Here the participles can be understood concessively, "although seeing . . . although hearing" (cf. NIV), but the finite verbs imply a willful closed mindedness: they *will* not see, hear, or understand. This becomes clear from the quotation of Isa 6:9–10 that follows. Similar language is found in Jer 5:21 ("O foolish and senseless people, who have eyes, but see not, who have ears, but hear not") applied to a people who are specifically described as having "a stubborn and rebellious heart; they have turned aside and gone away" (Jer 5:23). On the importance of "understanding" on the part of the disciples in Matthew, see H.-J. Held, in Bornkamm et al., *Tradition,* 106–12.

14–15   Matthew now drives the point home by means of the quotation of Isa 6:9–10 introduced with one of his special fulfillment formulas. This formula is somewhat modified in form: it lacks the typical ἵνα, "in order that," plus the subjunctive and employs instead an indicative verb pointing to a fact: ἀναπληροῦται, "is fulfilled" (the only occurrence of ἀναπληροῦν in Matthew; perhaps ἀνά gives the connotation of "completely fulfilled"). Among the fulfillment quotations only this one is presented not as a comment of the evangelist but as words spoken by Jesus. Nevertheless it, like the others, is to be understood as the evangelist's insertion (here, as in the other cases, the quotation can be removed with no harm to the flow of the passage). The not uncommon view that the quotation was added even later (e.g., Stendahl, *School*, 131–32; Davies-Allison; Kingsbury, *Parables*, 39), i.e., to the completed Gospel, is an unnecessary conjecture. This is a particularly important OT passage in the NT (see Evans), where it is used on several occasions to explain the mystery of the rejection of Jesus by unbelieving Jews (the entire quotation is found again in Acts 28:26–27; part of it is quoted in John 12:39–40; cf. too the partial parallels in Mark 4:12 and Luke 8:10b). Matthew, like the other NT writers, finds in Isaiah's words to his contemporaries about their unbelief and unresponsiveness an analogy to the Jewish rejection of Jesus. The typological correspondence, wherein the former situation foreshadows the latter, is seen to be divinely intended and rests upon the divine inspiration of the Scriptures. It is in this sense that the verb "fulfilled" can be used. In the unwillingness of the majority of Jews to accept Jesus while he was on earth, Matthew sees a deeper fulfillment, indeed one may say an eschatologically tinged fulfillment of Isaiah's words. In retrospect, the Jewish rejection of Jesus is seen mysteriously to have been the working out of the sovereign will of God. The quotation itself is given in verbatim agreement with LXX, except for the omission of αὐτῶν, "their," after ὠσίν, "ears," in v 15 (Matthew's fulfillment quotations usually depart extensively from the LXX). The first two lines of the quotation were already anticipated in v 13. As Isaiah said, they will hear but not at all (οὐ μή, emphatic negative) understand, will see but not at all (same emphatic negative) perceive (ἴδητε). The evidence will have been before their eyes, and they will have seen and heard it, yet without understanding it. Their failure to be receptive of the deeds and words of Jesus in his proclamation of the kingdom will now be paralleled by their failure to understand the meaning of the parables. The syntax of the LXX here and in the following lines is rather different from that of the Hebrew text of Isa 6:9 with its imperatives, "do not understand," "do not perceive." Similarly in the opening lines of v 15, more scope is given to the responsibility of the Jews than is done in the Hebrew text. Thus the LXX avoids the Hebrew imperatives of Isa 6:10: "make the heart of this people fat, and their ears heavy, and shut their eyes." Instead, the LXX describes conditions for which the people are responsible: "the heart of this people has grown thick, with their ears they hear poorly, and they have shut their eyes." It is the unbelieving people who have shut their own eyes. The reference to their heart growing thick indicates their insensitivity and their lack of understanding (cf. 15b). The second half of v 15, beginning with μήποτε, "lest," accordingly also points to the culpability of the people, moving toward a climax in the clause καὶ τῇ καρδίᾳ συνῶσιν, "and understand with their heart," and culminating in ἐπιστρέψωσιν, "(lest) they should repent." It was primarily because they were unwilling to repent that they saw, heard, and understood so poorly. They put upon themselves this fundamental limitation, paradoxically accomplishing the sovereign will of God at the same time (cf. the discussion of 11:27). The LXX version thus suits Matthew's purposes much better than the Hebrew text does. For Matthew, Isaiah's words find close correspondence in the rejection of Jesus noted in chaps. 11 and 12. The future indicative (rather than subjunctive) ἰάσομαι, lit. "I will heal them," follows the LXX exactly. But syntactically it too is almost certainly governed by μήποτε, and the future indicative can function as a subjunctive (see MHT 3:100).

The commentary on the preceding verses tries to hold in tension the sovereignty of God and human responsibility. This seems also to have been a concern of the evangelist, as we can see from his redaction of Mark. Matthew clearly wants to moderate the strong tones of Mark's apparent predestinarianism. Particularly obvious is Matthew's change of Mark's ἵνα, "in order that" (Mark 4:12), to ὅτι, "because" (v 13), when the reason for Jesus' teaching in parables is given. Consequently, whereas for Mark it is the *purpose* of Jesus' parables to accomplish the blindness spoken of in the Isa 6 quotation, for Matthew Jesus speaks in parables *because* of the willful unreceptivity of the blind. It is the fact of blindness/unreceptivity that Matthew explains as the fulfillment of the Isaiah quotation. The introductory formula to the quotation (v 14) in Matthew thus lacks the usual ἵνα (purpose) clause. He writes simply: "And the prophecy of Isaiah is fulfilled [ἀναπληροῦται], which says. . . ." Furthermore, as we have seen, Matthew uses the LXX of Isa 6:9–10—very exceptional in his formula quotations—which enables him to avoid the strong predestinarian imperatives of the Hebrew text: "Make the mind of this people dull, and stop their ears, and shut their eyes." He furthermore avoids the Markan juxtaposition (4:12) of μήποτε and ἐπιστρέψωσιν καὶ ἀφεθῇ αὐτοῖς, which the NRSV translates "so that they may not turn again and be forgiven." Matthew moreover ends on the positive note of the reality of the reception of God's gift of knowledge (vv 16–17). These points have been made by many commentators, sometimes with the implication that Matthew has thereby avoided the unpalatable doctrine of election.

While it is clear that Matthew tempers the severity of the doctrine of election by placing emphasis on the responsibility of the hardhearted and unreceptive, he has not thereby given up the sovereignty of God nor avoided entirely the doctrine of election. Like 11:25–27, the present passage still asserts that the truth has been made known to some and not to others: "to you it has been given . . . to them it has not been given" (v 11). Grace is surely to be seen in the first part of this statement, the fact that it has been given to some to receive the truth (thus rightly Davies-Allison). But the second part—to some it has not been given—is not thereby canceled out; there is a concealing as well as a revelation (rightly Via [*JBL* 84 (1965) 430–31], who points also to v 12). It remains true that Matthew emphasizes the responsibility of those who reject the message. He provides an excellent example of the asymmetrical argument typical of the biblical writers: the understanding of the disciple is due to the grace of God; the failure to understand of the non-disciple is due to that person's rejection of the message. (That still leaves the deep mystery concerning why God does not by his grace make known the truth to all.) See Carson, "Matthew," and van Elderen for excellent discussions. Matthew, it should be remembered, is not discussing the problem of predestination and certainly not engaging in systematic theology here. His immediate concern is the culpable unbelief of Israel, but as a good Jew he can do nothing other than at the same time accept the sovereign action of God behind that unbelief. The asymmetry of his argument ultimately explains Matthew's paradoxical explanation concerning the reason that Jesus taught in parables.

16 The unusual initial ὑμῶν, "you," puts great stress on the contrast between those who have not responded to the message of the gospel, referred to in the immediately preceding quotation, and those who have, namely, the disciples (cf. v 10). Their eyes and ears are described as μακάριοι, "blessed" (the key word of the beatitudes, 5:3–11; used elsewhere in Matthew in 11:6; 16:17; 24:46), because they see and hear in the sense of receiving and understanding. A similar beatitude is spoken in *Pss. Sol.* 18:6 (cf. *Pss. Sol.* 17:44) to those who ἰδεῖν τὰ ἀγαθὰ κυρίου, ἃ ποιήσει γενεᾷ τῇ ἐρχομένῃ, "see the good things of the Lord, which he will do to the coming generation," yet the contrast with the present beatitude is also remarkable; for here it is the present, not a future, generation that is the recipient of eschatological fulfillment. This point is brought home by the statement that follows.

17 With the gravity of the ἀμὴν λέγω ὑμῖν ("truly I tell you") formula, Jesus calls attention to the incomparable privilege of the disciples. They see and hear (cf. 11:4–6) what past generations longed to see and hear, namely, the result of the messianic fulfillment, the dawning of the kingdom of God. πολλοὶ προφῆται καὶ δίκαιοι, "many prophets and righteous persons," deeply longed to experience what the disciples were experiencing in the ministry of Jesus. Matthew appears to have substituted δίκαιοι, "righteous persons," a favorite word of his, for Q's more difficult βασιλεῖς, "kings" (reflected in Luke 10:24), by which he refers to those of the past who were especially deserving and yet who nevertheless did not see or hear (cf. Heb 11:13; 1 Peter 1:10) what the disciples presently see and hear (see 10:41; 23:29; cf. 23:34 for the linking of προφήτης, "prophet," and δίκαιος, "righteous person").

Explanation

Parables function in a dual manner. For those who have responded positively to Jesus' proclamation of the kingdom, the parables convey further insight and knowledge, while for those who have rejected Jesus and his message, the parables have the effect of only darkening the subject further. Thus belief and commitment lead to further knowledge; unbelief leads to further ignorance. The object of knowledge here is called "the mysteries of the kingdom." Central to these mysteries are the concerns of the parables of chap. 13, namely, the affirmation of the certain and real presence of the kingdom in the fulfillment of the OT, beginning with the ministry of Jesus, but also the delay of certain things expected to be part of that kingdom, i.e., the judgment of the wicked and the unmitigated blessing of the righteous. In short, Jesus proclaims that the kingdom has come, yet it has come in a secret or veiled form that does not overwhelm the present order of things. It thus requires faith and commitment to know and experience the kingdom in the strange, interim period of the present. Only people of faith and commitment are given to know the mysteries of the kingdom of God now manifested on earth. Matthew's church cannot have failed to see both itself and the unbelieving Israel of its day in the division reflected in this passage.

The Explanation of the Parable of the Soils   (13:18–23)

Bibliography

See *Bibliography* for 13:1–9.

Translation

[18] *"You, therefore, listen to the parable of the sower.* [19] *In the case of* [a] *every person who hears the word of the kingdom and does not understand it, the evil one comes and seizes*

what was[b] sown in that person's heart. This is what[c] was sown along the edge of the path. [20] But as for [d] what was sown on stony ground, this is the one who, hearing the word, also receives it immediately with joy, [21] but who has no root within[e] and lasts only for a time. But when tribulation or persecution on account of the word occurs, this person immediately falls away. [22] And as far as what [f] was sown among the thorn bushes, this is the one who hears the word, but the anxiety of the world[g] and the seduction of riches choke the word, and it becomes unfruitful. [23] But what is sown on the good soil, this is the person who hears and understands the word, who indeed [h] bears fruit and produces, one a hundredfold, one sixtyfold, and one thirtyfold."

Notes

[a] "In the case of" added for clarity.

[b] D W have τὸ σπειρόμενον, "what is sown."

[c] οὗτός ἐστιν ὁ . . . σπαρείς (masculine), lit. "this one is the one who was sown." See *Comment*.

[d] "As for" added to translation.

[e] ἐν ἑαυτῷ, lit. "in himself."

[f] See *Note* c.

[g] Many MSS (א[1] C L W Θ *f*[1,13] TR lat sy sa[mss] mae bo) add τούτου, i.e., "this world."

[h] D it substitute τότε, "then," for "who indeed"; lat syr[c,p] substitute καί, "and"; k sy[s] substitute both: καὶ τότε, "and then."

Form/Structure/Setting

A. Although the disciples in Matthew ask Jesus not for the meaning of the parable of the sower (as in Luke 8:9; cf. Mark 4:13) but why he is teaching in parables, the explanation of the parable (of vv 3–9) is nevertheless provided. Since in v 36 they ask for the interpretation of the parable of the weeds in the field, however, it is clear that in the present instance the explanation was appreciated. The interpreted parable provides a good example of the truth of vv 11 and 12 so far as the disciples were concerned. Both here and in vv 37–43, details of the parables are allegorized (see too vv 49–50). Allegorical interpretation of parables (or indeed anything else in the Bible) is to be generally avoided as arbitrary and subjective. Only when the original teller of a parable gives an allegorical interpretation is it acceptable, because only in this instance can it be certain that this is the intended rather than an imagined meaning. Although modern scholarship has regarded this interpretation of the parable as stemming from the later Church, it fits the parable so well (like a hand in a glove: so Gerhardsson, *NTS* 14 [1967–68] 192) that there is no compelling reason to deny that Jesus himself provided the interpretation (cf. Davies-Allison's cautious acceptance of its authenticity).

B. For this pericope Matthew depends on Mark 4:13–20 (cf. Luke 8:11–15). In general Matthew follows the Markan text very closely. His opening sentence is his own formulation: ὑμεῖς οὖν ἀκούσατε τὴν παραβολὴν τοῦ σπείραντος, "You, therefore, listen to the parable of the sower." It takes the place of Mark 4:13 with its rebuke of the disciples for their lack of knowledge. After that, the differences are minor. Of particular interest is the fact that whereas in the telling of the parable (vv 3–9; cf. Mark 4:3–9) Matthew refers consistently (except at the very end) to the seed using plural forms and Mark consistently uses singular forms, here in the explanation of the parable the situation is just the opposite, Matthew referring to the seed in the singular, Mark in the plural. This difference is probably due merely to cross-fertilization in the oral transmission of the materials. For a hypothesis concerning the possibility of a pre-Markan text underlying our synoptic Gospels and as an explanation for the differences, see D. Wenham ("The Synoptic Problem Reconsidered: Some Suggestions about the Composition of Mark 4.1–34," *TynBul* 23 [1972] 3–38).

As to other differences, the following may be noted: Matthew puts Mark's initial οὗτοι δέ εἰσιν οἱ παρὰ τὴν ὁδόν, "these are those at the edge of the path" (Mark 4:15), at the end of the explanation of this particular category: οὗτός ἐστιν ὁ παρὰ τὴν ὁδὸν σπαρείς, "this is what was sown along the edge of the path" (v 19c); Matthew alone identifies the word as τῆς βασιλείας, "of the kingdom" (v 19; cf. Mark 4:15); Matthew alone refers in this first instance to those who hear as καὶ μὴ συνιέντος, "and does not understand," this corresponding to the substitution of συνιείς, "who understands," for παραδέχονται, "they receive," in the description of the seed that fell on good soil (v 23; cf. Mark 4:20); further, in v 19 Matthew substitutes ὁ πονηρός, "the evil one" (a favorite term for Matthew), for Mark's ὁ σατανᾶς, "Satan" (Mark 4:15), and the stronger word ἁρπάζει, "seizes," for Mark's αἴρει, "takes"; also in v 19 Matthew adds ἐν τῇ καρδίᾳ αὐτοῦ, "in his heart," in describing what was sown (cf. Mark 4:15). Further on, Matthew abbreviates by omitting Mark's εἶτα, "then" (before γενομένης, v 21; Mark 4:17); substitutes the singular ἡ μέριμνα, "the anxiety," for the plural αἱ μέριμναι (v 22; cf. Mark 4:19); omits Mark's καὶ αἱ περὶ τὰ λοιπὰ ἐπιθυμίαι εἰσπορευόμεναι, "and the lusts concerning the other things enter in" (v 22; Mark 4:19); inserts ποιεῖ, "produces" (v 23; Mark 4:20); and substitutes ὁ μὲν ... ὁ δὲ ... ὁ δέ for Mark's threefold ἕν (v 23; Mark 4:20). These various modifications can be explained as resulting from Matthew's customary abbreviation of Mark, improvement of Mark's Greek style, and alterations in keeping with Matthew's special interests.

C. After the introduction to the explanation (v 18), the passage consists of four main parts referring to each of the four soils in the original telling of the parable: (1) the seed that fell along the edge of the road (v 19; cf. v 4); (2) the seed that fell on rocky soil (vv 20–21; cf. vv 5–6); (3) the seed that fell among thorn bushes (v 22; cf. v 7); and (4) the seed that fell on good soil (v 23; cf. v 8). A major structural difference between the first and the following three explanations results from Matthew's delay of the identifying formula οὗτός ἐστιν ὁ παρὰ τὴν ὁδὸν σπαρείς, "this is what was sown along the edge of the path," until the end of the first explanation (v 19), whereas in each of the other instances he places it at the beginning of the explanation (vv 20, 22, and 23). This modification of Mark's form enables Matthew to put emphasis on ἀκούοντος τὸν λόγον τῆς βασιλείας, "hearing the word of the kingdom" (v 19). This element of hearing is the one element common to all four illustrations (the formula is shortened to "hearing the word" in the last three instances, vv 20, 22, and 23). The form of each of the last three examples is parallel, consisting of: (a) the introductory formula ὁ δὲ ἐπὶ ... σπαρείς, "what was sown on" (vv 20, 22, 23); (b) the description formula οὗτός ἐστιν ὁ τὸν λόγον ἀκούων ..., "this is the one hearing the word ..." (vv 20, 22, 23); (c) further description of the circumstances (vv 21a, 22, 23); and (d) the outcome (vv 21b, 22d; 23c). The first example has elements b (modified), c, d, and a in that order (v 19). There is also a tendency to lesser parallelisms within the individual elements. This explanation, like the parable itself (vv 3–9), thus again gives evidence of careful formulation and parallel structures, making it suitable for catechesis and memorization.

Gerhardsson (*NTS* 14 [1967–68] 176–77) has found a correspondence between this parable and the *Šemaʿ* (Shema) of Deut 6:4–5 that deserves mention here (cf. a similar correspondence in 4:1–11 [see above]). The *Šemaʿ*, which was said twice a day by Jews even in the time of Jesus, contains the confession that "the LORD our God is one LORD," to which is added the call to "love the LORD your God [1] with all your heart, and [2] with all your soul, and [3] with all your might." These elements correspond to the implied call of the parable as follows: (1) the reference to the heart in v 19; (2) the reference to tribulation and persecution in v 21, with the implication of an unwillingness to give one's life (= soul); and (3) the reference to wealth, which would include property, reflecting an unwillingness to give of one's possessions (= might). Given the great importance of the *Šemaʿ* among the Jews, the hypothesis that Jesus may have had it in his mind as he formulated the parable of the sower gains credibility. It fits well, furthermore, the perspective of both Jesus and Matthew in that it sees Jesus' ministry in continuity with the OT, implying as it does a calling back of the people to covenant loyalty and its obligations. Those who follow Jesus are thus faithful to the fundamentally important call of the *Šemaʿ*. Though by its nature a hypothesis of this kind falls short of proof, it is both intriguing and suggestive.

Comment

18   The initial ὑμεῖς, "you," is emphatic and reinforces the privilege of the disciples alone to know "the mysteries of the kingdom" (cf. vv 11, 16). ἀκούσατε here means "listen to (the meaning of)." The title of the parable, τὴν παραβολὴν τοῦ σπείραντος, "the parable of the sower," does not point to the main subject of the parable but is an allusion to the opening words of the parable (the usual way of identifying passages and writings in the ancient world); see v 3.

19   The beginning of the interpretation of the parable identifies what is sown by the sower as τὸν λόγον τῆς βασιλείας, "the word of the kingdom." This phrase is used in the Gospels only here and is the equivalent of Matthew's εὐαγγέλιον τῆς βασιλείας, "gospel of the kingdom," i.e., the essence of Jesus' preaching about the dawning of the kingdom in and through his ministry (4:23; 9:35; 24:14). Thus the sower is probably to be understood as Jesus, implying that ultimately the parable refers to the reception or non-reception of Jesus himself. The problem in the first instance (the interpretation corresponds to v 4) is specified in the words καὶ μὴ συνιέντος, "and does not understand (it)" (cf. the συνιείς, "who understands [it]" in v 23). The problem of failing to understand, however, according to the context, results from the hardheartedness and unreceptive attitude of the hearers (cf. vv 13–15) rather than from any inadequacy in the communication of the message itself (cf. 11:21, 23; 12:28, 41–42). Those who will not receive the message do not understand it. This failure is described further in terms of the coming of ὁ πονηρός, "the evil one" (see on 5:37), who "seizes" (ἁρπάζει) what was sown ἐν τῇ καρδίᾳ αὐτοῦ, "in that person's heart," the interpretive equivalent of the birds eating the seed in v 4 (birds are sometimes associated with the devil in Jewish literature; cf. *Jub.* 11.11–12; *Apoc. Abr.* 13.3–7). The activity of the enemy here works together with, but does not absolve, those who have rejected the message. It is because they have rejected the message that the evil one is enabled to snatch away the seed. The final clause, οὗτός ἐστιν ὁ παρὰ τὴν ὁδὸν σπαρείς, lit.

"this one is the one which was sown along the edge of the path" (see too vv 20, 22, 23), seems to equate the person with the seed (cf. v 38) rather than the soil, although it was the seed that was sown in that person's heart. But despite the slight mixing of images, the point remains clear. (Matthew has thus not avoided the mixed images in Mark 4:14 and 16 [where the seed is equated with the person].) The formulaic clause here at the end of v 19, as at the beginning of vv 20, 22, and 23, "serves as a short-hand reminder of the appropriate scene in the story, rather than being logically integrated into the interpretation" (France, 219). The person is like the particular instance of sowing seed in the described soil.

20–21 In the second instance, that of the rocky soil (cf. vv 5–6), the immediate (εὐθύς, corresponding to εὐθέως in v 5) sprouting of the seed is described as the joyful reception of the word (μετὰ χαρᾶς, "with joy"). Here there is not only the "hearing of the word" (ὁ τὸν λόγον ἀκούων) but also the "receiving" of it (λαμβάνων αὐτόν). The words of v 21, οὐκ ἔχει δὲ ῥίζαν, "but it has no root," reflect the language of v 6, διὰ τὸ μὴ ἔχειν ῥίζαν, "because it has no root." The person (ἐν ἑαυτῷ, "within") is likened to the thin soil, and the response is described as "only for a time" (πρόσκαιρος; in Matthew here only). The interpretive equivalent to the rising sun that burns up the seedling (v 6) is given in the reference to the coming of θλίψεως ἢ διωγμοῦ διὰ τὸν λόγον, "tribulation or persecution on account of the word," i.e., suffering for the message of the kingdom. The expectation of persecution has already been an important theme in Matthew (see esp. 5:11–12; 10:16–25). The follower of Jesus must be prepared for this eventuality and must endure through it to the end (cf. 23:34–36; 24:9–13). In this instance, however, the incipient disciple immediately (εὐθύς) falls away (σκανδαλίζεται) and thereby shows that the initial response was not deep or genuine. For this use of σκανδαλίζειν, "fall away," see also 24:10 (cf. 26:31; 2 Cor 11:29).

22 The third instance again includes a reference to "the one who hears the word" (ὁ τὸν λόγον ἀκούων), while the receiving of the word is left implicit. The thorn bushes which grow up and choke (συμπνίγει) the seedling (v 7) are identified as ἡ μέριμνα τοῦ αἰῶνος καὶ ἡ ἀπάτη τοῦ πλούτου, "the anxiety of the world and the seduction of riches." Both objects, anxiety and wealth, are the subject of Jesus' teaching in the Sermon on the Mount (6:19–34; on riches, cf. 19:23–24). It is easy to see how these areas can become obstacles to genuine discipleship (cf. Luke 12:16–21; 14:18–20; 21:34) and how they can thus thwart response to the message of the kingdom.

23 The seed that fell ἐπὶ τὴν καλὴν γῆν, "on the good soil" (cf. v 8), refers to the circumstance where the word is heard (ὁ τὸν λόγον ἀκούων), as in all the preceding instances, but where in direct contradiction to the first instance (v 19) the word is also understood (συνιείς). "Understanding," the determinative word here as in v 19, implies receptivity (cf. 15:10). Understanding, furthermore, must result in the response of proper conduct. The good soil is that which receives the seed of the word, which nurtures that seed in discipleship, and which bears fruit (καρποφορεῖ; in Matthew only here) in spectacularly abundant measure. Strangely, the explanation of the parable does not further define the fruit or its abundance but merely repeats words similar to those of v 8. The fruit is probably to be understood as the pattern of conduct described in the Sermon on the Mount (chaps. 5–7), i.e., the living out of the kingdom of God here and now (cf. 5:13–16; 21:43). Thus although the parable addresses the problem of unbelief (cf. vv 10–15; and specifically that of Israel), it also contains (contra Davies-Allison) a strong element of parenesis (ethical exhortation), as Luz rightly emphasizes.

Explanation

It is important to understand the explanation of the parable of the soils in its context and with the purpose of the original parable particularly in mind. The key issue is responsiveness or non-responsiveness to the message of the kingdom. It is in this sense that one either understands (v 23) or does not understand (v 19). But there is also the possibility of an initial positive response that proves to be less than adequate. Two instances are given, though it would not be difficult to think of others. In the first we encounter the fair-weather disciple who under the pressure of adverse circumstances immediately abandons faith and commitment. This person has thought only of the blessings of the kingdom, having indeed made a simple equation between the enjoyment of them and being a disciple, and is thus unable to cope with the reality of continuing evil in the world. The shallowness of such discipleship underlines the appropriateness of the metaphor. In the second instance the response of discipleship is cut short by the ordinary cares of this life (cf. 8:21) and the seduction of wealth (cf. 6:24; 1 Tim 6:9–10). The pull of the latter remains, of course, a dominant factor in the modern world with its rampant materialism. We are thus again reminded in this passage of the absolute claim of discipleship. The word of the kingdom when received fully and without reservation results in an unqualified, constant, and abundantly fruitful discipleship (cf. John 15:8, 16; Gal 5:22). The interpretation of the parable thus contains an ongoing challenge to Matthew's church as well as to the Church at the end of the twentieth century.

The Parable of the Wheat and the Weeds   (13:24–30)

Bibliography

Catchpole, D. "John the Baptist, Jesus and the Parable of the Tares." *SJT* 31 (1978) 557–70. **Doty, W. G.** "An Interpretation: Parable of the Weeds and Wheat." *Int* 25 (1971) 185–93. **Luz, U.** "Vom Taumellolch im Weizenfeld." In *Vom Urchristentum zu Jesus.* FS J. Gnilka, ed. H. Frankemölle and K. Kertelge. Freiburg: Herder, 1989. 154–71.

Translation

[24]*He set before them another parable, saying: "The kingdom of heaven is similar to the case of*[a] *a man who sowed*[b] *good seed in his field.* [25]*While his servants*[c] *were sleeping, his enemy came and sowed weeds among the wheat and departed.* [26]*But when the stalks sprouted and produced fruit, then the weeds also*[d] *appeared.* [27]*And the servants of the master came to him and said, 'Sir, you did sow good seed in your field, didn't you? Where, therefore, did the weeds come from?'* [28]*And he said to them, 'Someone who is an*

enemy did this.' And the servants said to him, 'Do you therefore want us to go out and gather the weeds?'[c] [29]*But he said, 'No, lest while gathering the weeds you root out the wheat along with them.* [30]*Let both grow together until the harvest, and in the time of the harvest I will say to the harvesters, "First gather the weeds and bind them into bunches so they can be burned. But gather the wheat together into my barn."'*

Notes

[a] The words "the case of" are added to the translation for clarity. See *Comment.*
[b] Some MSS (C D K L Γ Θ *f*¹) have σπείροντι, "sows."
[c] ἀνθρώπους, lit. "men."
[d] καί, "also," is omitted by D W Θ *f*¹³ it sy^s,c sa mae bo^ms.
[e] αὐτά, lit. "them."

Form/Structure/Setting

A. A second parable in the series of seven is now presented, and like the first it too will later receive an allegorical interpretation (vv 36–43). This parable addresses a major concern of the whole discourse, namely, the delay of judgment—clearly one of the most innovative and difficult aspects of Jesus' doctrine of the kingdom. The immediate, natural reaction of the people to Jesus' proclamation of the presence of the kingdom was to wonder about the continuing presence of evil in the world, as manifested particularly in Roman rule over the people of God. The era of salvation was more or less equated with national-political deliverance. The remaining parables in the discourse deal with one aspect or another of the paradoxical nature of the presently dawning kingdom of God. This parable is put alongside the preceding because of the common agricultural motif and in particular the sowing of seed. Here too is a story of one who sows good seed, the end result of which is mixed.

B. The parable is unique to Matthew and is apparently drawn from the evangelist's special source. Despite some verbal similarities, the parable is too different from that of Mark 4:26–29 to be regarded as dependent on it (contra Gundry, who regards Matthew's parable as a conflation of Mark 4:26–29 and 4:3–9). Matthew has thus replaced the Markan parable with a new one from his own special source. The parallel in *Gos. Thom.* 57 is almost certainly dependent upon Matthew rather than upon a third unknown source.

C. The introductory formula to this parable, ἄλλην παραβολὴν παρέθηκεν αὐτοῖς λέγων, "he set before them another parable, saying," occurs verbatim in v 31, introducing the third parable, and with only minor changes again in v 33, introducing the fourth parable. The parable itself begins with the stylized opening words, distinctive of Matthew, ὡμοιώθη ἡ βασιλεία τῶν οὐρανῶν, "the kingdom of heaven is like" (the five that follow all begin with the similar opening formula ὁμοία ἐστὶν ἡ βασιλεία τῶν οὐρανῶν, "the kingdom of heaven is similar to"). After the introductory formula, the parable may be outlined as follows: (1) the theme of the parable, the man who sowed good seed in his field (v 24); (2) the work of the enemy, (a) the sowing of weeds (v 25) and (b) the growth of wheat and weeds (v 26); (3) dialogue, (a) the servants' question concerning the origin of the weeds (v 27) and (b) Jesus' answer (v 28a); (4) further dialogue, (a) the servants' question about gathering the weeds (v 28b) and (b) Jesus' answer (v 29); and (5) teaching that both wheat and weeds must grow together until the harvest (v 30a) when both (a) judgment (v 30b) and (b) blessing (v 30c) will be experienced. The passage lacks the usual amount of symmetry and parallelism in the teaching of Jesus, perhaps because of the nature of the parable, the first half being narrative (vv 24–26) and the second largely dialogue (vv 27–30). The main parallelisms to be found are in the contrasts made between the wheat and the weeds (cf. vv 26, 27, 29, and especially 30b–c).

Comment

24 In keeping with the statement of v 3 (cf. v 13), further parables are now presented to the crowd. This second parable (παραβολήν; see on v 3) is connected with the first through the common word σπείραντι, "who sowed" (cf. vv 3–4). But beyond this and two other catchwords (ἀγρός, "field"; σπέρμα, "seed"), the two parables have entirely different purposes. As in the case of the first parable, an interpretation is provided to the disciples privately inside the house (vv 36–43), and thus comment here is restricted to the details of the parable as it stands in the present pericope. ὁμοιώθη here (as too, for example, in 22:2) means not simply "is like" but reflects the Aramaic formulaic lĕ, which means "it is the case with . . . as with . . ." (see Kingsbury, *Parables*, 67). The reference to καλὸν σπέρμα, "good seed," is found again in the servants' question (v 27; cf. vv 37–38). For βασιλεία τῶν οὐρανῶν, "kingdom of heaven," see *Comment* on 3:2.

25–26 In its reference to an enemy who comes at night to sow weeds among the wheat, the parable is apparently contrived with the explanation in view (vv 37–39). At the surface level these two verses bear some similarity to the parable of the seed that grows secretly (a parable not found in Matthew) in Mark 4:26–29. There, in a parable that also begins with comparing the kingdom of God to a man who sowed seed on the ground (but Mark's Greek vocabulary is different), one finds reference to sleeping (καθεύδη) and the growth (βλαστᾷ) of the seedlings, as well as a reference to the harvest (θερισμός). But whereas in Mark 4:26–29 the miraculous growth of the seed is in view, here the point is the growing of weeds and wheat together. For ὁ ἐχθρός, "the enemy," see also 22:44 (cf. Luke 10:19; 1 Peter 5:8 [ἀντίδικος, "opponent"]). The word ζιζάνια, "weeds," found in the NT only in Matt 13, refers to a kind of darnel, a common weed (*Lolium temulentum*; thus Jeremias, *Parables*, 224) that plagued grainfields (see BAGD, 339b). With the passing of time, the fruit-bearing wheatstalks appeared, but so too did the weeds.

27–28a The man (ἄνθρωπος) of v 24 is now identified as an οἰκοδεσπότης, "master of the house" (the word is used elsewhere in Matthew in the parables of 20:1–16 and 21:33–44 as well as in 10:25 and 24:43). In this parable the servants address their master as κύριε, which here means "sir" (this address may, however, hint at the identification of the master as Jesus [cf. Jesus as οἰκοδεσπότης in 10:25] and the servants as his disciples). To the servants' query about the source of the abundant weeds—not a real question, but didactically designed—the master responds ἐχθρὸς ἄνθρωπος τοῦτο ἐποίησεν, "someone who is an enemy did this." The use here of ἄνθρωπος, lit. "man," is governed by the world of the parable and thus stands in some tension with the interpretation of the enemy as the devil in v 39. The weeds in this instance are not the result of natural processes but of a deliberate attempt to ruin the work of the master of the house who planted good seed.

28b–29 The servants naturally ask whether they should gather up the weeds. The master responds negatively to their suggestion. The problem lay not in the difficulty of distinguishing the two (see Luz, "Vom Taumellolch," 156; contra Jeremias, *Parables*, 224) but rather in the fact that the weeds would be so closely intermingled with the wheat that some of the latter would inevitably be pulled up with the former and thus be destroyed. The roots of darnel are stronger and deeper than those of wheat, so that the removal of one would often result in the uprooting of the other (so G. Dalman, *Arbeit und Sitte in Palästina* [Gütersloh: Bertelsmann, 1932] 2:250, 325). For a similar use of the verb ἐκριζοῦν, see 15:13.

30 The mandate of the master of the house is to let "both" (ἀμφότερα) weeds and wheat grow together ἕως τοῦ θερισμοῦ, "until the harvest." At that time the two will be gathered and separated, the weeds as fuel for burning, the wheat into the granary (cf. 3:12; 6:26). The key point here, which will be developed further in this chapter, is that it is not yet the time of the harvest (i.e., eschatological judgment) and thus not yet the time for the separating of the weeds from the wheat. The judgment motif of this imagery is clear, being found frequently in Jewish literature, and it will receive considerable elaboration in the interpretation (vv 36–43).

Explanation

If we restrict ourselves here to the self-contained world of the parable, suspending its application until the discussion of vv 36–43, we may at least conclude that the field sown by the man did not turn out as he desired. He had sown good seed, but an enemy had sown weeds in the same field. The result was a mixture of wheat and weeds. The solution, however, was not to be in an immediate separating of the two. Instead, for the time being the two were to be allowed to grow together, so that the field was not an ideal field but one manifesting the contradiction of good and bad. This state of affairs, moreover, was to remain so until the full maturity of the wheat and the time of harvest, when finally the wheat would be separated from the weeds. Then the evil would be brought to its end, and the good alone would remain. The kingdom of God has indeed come, but it has not yet brought the eschatological judgment. For further explanation of the parable, see *Comment* on 13:36–43.

The Parable of the Mustard Seed   (13:31–32)

Bibliography

Dupont, J. "Le couple parabolique du sénevé et du levain." In *Études* 2:609–23. ————. "Les paraboles du sénevé et du levain (Mt 13,31–33; Lc 13,18–21)." In *Études sur les Évangiles synoptiques*. BETL 70. Leuven: Peeters/Leuven University, 1985. 2:592–608. **Kuss, O.** "Zum

Sinngehalt des Doppelgleichnisses vom Senfkorn und Sauerteig." *Bib* 40 (1959) 641–53.
Laufen, R. "*Βασιλεία* und *ἐκκλησία*: Eine traditions- und redaktionsgeschichtliche Untersuchung des Gleichnisses vom Senfkorn." In *Begegnung mit dem Wort.* FS H. Zimmermann, ed. J. Zmijewski and E. Nellessen. BBB 53. Bonn: Hanstein, 1979. 105–40. **McArthur, H. K.** "The Parable of the Mustard Seed." *CBQ* 33 (1971) 198–201. **Schultze, B.** "Die ekklesiologische Bedeutung des Gleichnisses vom Senfkorn." *OCP* 27 (1961) 362–86.

Translation

[31] *He set before*[a] *them another parable, saying: "The kingdom of heaven is like a mustard seed, which someone took and sowed in a field.*[b] [32]*It is the smallest of all the seeds, but when it has grown, it is the greatest of plants and becomes a tree, so that the birds of the sky come and dwell in its branches."*

Notes

[a] D L* N Θ *f*[13] it have *ἐλάλησεν*, "he spoke" (cf. v 33).
[b] *τῷ ἀγρῷ αὐτοῦ*, lit. "his field."

Form/Structure/Setting

A. The third parable of the discourse continues the portrayal of the kingdom of God in connection with the sowing of seed. The vocabulary (catchwords) of "sowing," "seed," and "field" provides continuity. The kingdom again is regarded as a present reality but one that is present in secret form. That is, its presence, though real, can be easily overlooked. The kingdom has come but not in the spectacular, unmistakable fashion in which it was expected. The same point will be made in the following parable (v 33). This is one of the "mysteries of the kingdom" (v 11). This is the first parable in the discourse that will not receive an interpretation. The hearers (and readers) are thus left on their own to interpret it.

B. In this triple-tradition parable, Matthew is dependent on Mark 4:30–32 (cf. Luke 13:18–19; *Gos. Thom.* 20), although the actual agreement in wording is small. The several agreements between Matthew and Luke against Mark, however, suggest the additional possibility of the influence of Q, which may also have contained the parable.

The introductory formula *ἄλλην παραβολὴν παρέθηκεν αὐτοῖς*, "he set before them another parable," is Matthew's own (cf. vv 24, 33). Matthew turns Mark's question (Mark 4:30) into the statement *ὁμοία ἐστὶν ἡ βασιλεία τῶν οὐρανῶν*, "the kingdom of heaven is like" (as also in v 33). "Kingdom of heaven" here replaces *τὴν βασιλείαν τοῦ θεοῦ*, "the kingdom of God," in Mark's question. Matthew omits Mark's initial *ὡς*, "as" (Mark 4:31), and substitutes *ὃν λαβὼν ἄνθρωπος*, "which someone took" (v 31c; thus too Luke 13:19b) and the indicative *ἔσπειρεν*, "sowed," for Mark's *ὃς ὅταν*, "who, whenever," and the subjunctive *σπαρῇ*, "should sow" (Mark 4:31). Matthew's *ἐν τῷ ἀγρῷ αὐτοῦ*, "in his field" (v 31c; cf. v 24), replaces Mark's *ἐπὶ τῆς γῆς*, "on the ground" (Mark 4:31b; cf. Mark 4:26; Luke has *εἰς κῆπον ἑαυτοῦ*, "in his garden," Luke 13:19b). Matthew omits Mark's redundant *τῶν ἐπὶ τῆς γῆς*, "of all those upon the earth" (Mark 4:31c), and substitutes *αὐξηθῇ*, "it has grown" for Mark's *σπαρῇ*, "is sown" (v 32b; Mark 4:32a). Matthew furthermore omits Mark's *ἀναβαίνει καὶ γίνεται*, "comes up and becomes," his *πάντων*, "all," before *τῶν λαχάνων*, "the plants," and his *ποιεῖ κλάδους μεγάλους*, "and produces great branches," for which (with Luke) Matthew writes that the plant becomes a δένδρον, "tree" (v 32; Luke 13:19). Matthew further departs from Mark (as does Luke) in the final words of the pericope by omitting δύνασθαι ὑπὸ τὴν σκιὰν αὐτοῦ, "are able under its shadow" (v 32; Mark 4:32), substituting ἐλθεῖν τὰ πετεινὰ τοῦ οὐρανοῦ καὶ κατασκηνοῦν ἐν τοῖς κλάδοις αὐτοῦ, "the birds of the sky come and dwell in its branches" (v 32; cf. Luke 13:19, where, however, Matthew's ἐλθεῖν and καί are not found). Matthew's use of Mark here thus again reveals his typical abridgment of Mark together with certain stylistic improvements. The similarities between Matthew and Luke against Mark may be due to the influence of the form of the material in oral tradition.

C. This pericope follows the simple pattern of short parables in the discourse. It consists of an introductory formula followed by (1) a basic statement of the analogy (v 31) and (2) an elaboration of the analogy to make its point clear (v 32). In the elaboration, some parallelism is evident in the contrasting μὲν . . . δέ clauses (v 32a), but in this rare instance Matthew's omission of Mark's πάντων, "all" (Mark 4:32), in reference to the bushes lessens the parallelism.

Comment

31 For the opening formula, see its verbatim occurrence in v 24. The actual comparison here is made with the words ὁμοία ἐστίν, "is like," as in vv 33, 44, 45, and 47. The significance of the analogy of the kingdom of heaven and the κόκκῳ σινάπεως, "seed of mustard," is made clear in the following verse. Matthew's insertion of ἄνθρωπος, "someone," is probably ultimately due to the association of this parable with the previous parable, which also uses the word (ἀνθρώπῳ, v 24). The same is to be said for Matthew's ἐν τῷ ἀγρῷ αὐτοῦ, "in his field," found verbatim in v 24, unless Matthew's alteration reflects the rabbinic forbidding of planting a mustard seed in a garden (cf. *m. Kil.* 3:2). These similarities with the second parable also inevitably relate the present parable to the interpretation of the second parable in vv 36–43.

32 In the ancient world and among the rabbis (cf. *m. Nid.* 5.2; *m. Tohar.* 8:8) the mustard seed was known for its smallness (whether it is white or black mustard that is intended makes little difference). It is also referred to as the smallest of all seeds in Antigonus of Carystus 91 and in Diodorus Siculus 1.35.2 (cf. Matt 17:20, where a faith as small as a mustard seed is said to be able to move mountains). From this "smallest" of seeds (it matters not that there are smaller seeds), however, an amazingly large bushlike plant eventually emerges, large enough to accommodate the nests of birds. This fact is so remarkable that it took on a proverbial character. Matthew's final clause, τὰ πετεινὰ τοῦ οὐρανοῦ καὶ κατασκηνοῦν ἐν τοῖς κλάδοις αὐτοῦ, "the birds of the sky [come] and dwell in its branches," agrees verbatim with the Daniel 4:21 Theodotion, except for the word order, Daniel's synonym, ὄρνεα, for Matthew's πετεινά, "birds," and Daniel's κατεσκήνουν, "they were dwelling," for Matthew's κατασκηνοῦν, "to dwell." There is also a close parallel in Ps 103:12 LXX (= ET 104:12), which lacks only "in its branches." The two passages allude respectively to the great tree of Belshazzar's dream (Dan 4:10, 12, 21) and the cedars of Lebanon (Ps 104:16–17, 12; cf. Ezek 31:6). In either case it is the suggestiveness of the imagery that is important and the contrast with the tiny mustard seed. On the large treelike size the mustard plant could attain (eight to ten feet; Fenton), see *b. Ketub.* 111b. More likely, however, the use of the word δένδρον, "tree," indicates that hyperbole and symbolism are involved here, pointing to something beyond agriculture: to a great reality or a kingdom (as often in the OT [cf. Ezek 17:22–24; 31:2–13; Dan 4:20–21]). Although possible, the interpretation (so Gundry; Luz; Davies-Allison) of the birds in the branches as Gentiles (despite OT imagery that can be cited in this regard, e.g., Ezek 17:23; 31:6; Dan 4:9, 18) introduces an allegory alien to the context and unnecessary to a straightforward reading of the text. The miracle of nature symbolized by the mustard seed, which develops from the smallest of beginnings to an astonishing fullness, is similar to the reality of the kingdom. Although this conclusion is not spelled out, it is nevertheless unmistakable. The kingdom has begun inconspicuously, yet *it has begun,* and in the end the greatness of the kingdom in size will provide as amazing a contrast as that between the mustard seed and the tree.

Explanation

The kingdom of God has humble beginnings; it is like a mustard seed, small and unimpressive. It can be overlooked or dismissed as a trifle. Its coming did not overwhelm the world, as had been expected. Yet it is destined to become an impressive entity in radical contrast to its beginnings. It is impossible to rule out an allusion to growth, even if the parable is mainly about contrast rather than growth. This parable serves as an equivalent to the parable of Mark 4:26–29 (omitted by Matthew in his parable discourse), which refers to the miracle of the growth of seed as a metaphor for the growth of the kingdom. The kingdom's mysterious growth is the work of God. If we restrict the analogy to size, then the contrast between Jesus with the twelve and the Church universal has remarkably fulfilled the parable. This is no reason for a triumphalism, however, since the Church remains a people on the way to God's eschatological goal rather than a people who have arrived at it.

The Parable of the Leavened Loaves and a Further Comment on the Reason for the Parables   (13:33–35)

Bibliography

Allis, O. T. "The Parable of the Leaven." *EvQ* 19 (1947) 254–73. **Segbroeck, F. van.** "Le scandale de l'incroyance: La signification de Mt 13,35." *ETL* 41 (1965) 344–72.

See also the *Bibliography* for 13:31–32.

Translation

[33] *He spoke*[a] *another parable to them.*[b] *"The kingdom of heaven is similar to leaven, which a woman took and mixed into*[c] *three measures of wheat flour until the whole was*

leavened." [34] *Jesus spoke all these things in parables to the crowds, and he continued to say nothing*[d] *to them apart from using a parable,* [35] *so that the word spoken through*[e] *the prophet might be fulfilled, which says:*

> *I will open my mouth in parables;*
> *I will utter things hidden from the foundation [of the world].*[f]

Notes

[a] A few MSS (C 1241 sa[mss]) read παρέθηκεν, "set before (them)," by influence of vv 24 and 31.

[b] Some MSS (ℵ C L Θ *f*[13] vg[mss] sa[ms] mae) add λέγων, "saying," on the model of vv 24 and 31.

[c] ἐνέκρυψεν, lit. "hid."

[d] The TR and ℵ[2] D L Θ *f*[1] lat bo read οὐ, "not" (i.e., "he did not speak to them"), by influence of the parallel in Mark 4:34.

[e] Some MSS (ℵ* Θ *f*[1,13]) insert Ἠσαΐου, "Isaiah." This incorrect ascription would ordinarily be favored as the more difficult reading, which others corrected by omitting it. But it is perhaps even more probable that the original text had no name and that Isaiah was inserted (a well-known practice among scribes). A further, but less likely, possibility is that a scribe inserted the name Asaph (but no actual MS evidence supports this), and others changed it to Isaiah. See *TCGNT*, 33.

[f] Some MSS (ℵ[1] B *f*[1] e k [sy[s,c]]) omit κόσμου, "of the world." Others (ℵ[2] C D L W Θ *f*[13] lat sy[p,h] co TR) include it. The shorter reading would ordinarily be favored, with the word κόσμου having been added in imitation of this common phrase (cf. 25:34; κόσμου is found in eight of the remaining nine NT occurrences). But because of the impressive MS evidence in favor of the inclusion of κόσμου, the committee retains the word in brackets. See *TCGNT*, 33–34.

Form/Setting/Structure

A. The fourth parable concludes the public presentation of parallels in this chapter; the three remaining parables are addressed to the disciples (vv 44–50). Again this parable is closely related to the immediately preceding parable, despite the change of imagery. It too speaks of the initial unimpressiveness of the kingdom compared to what it will eventually become. Directly following this short parable is a second statement concerning Jesus' speaking to the crowds only in parables (cf. vv 10–13), together with a scriptural justification of this practice by means of an OT citation introduced with a fulfillment formula (cf. vv 14–15). Following this in turn is the providing of the explanation of the second parable concerning the wheat and the tares (vv 36–43). Thus the sequence here follows that earlier in the chapter (i.e., in vv 10–23).

B. The parable (v 33) is drawn from Q (cf. Luke 13:20–21). Matthew introduces it with his own formula, ἄλλην παραβολὴν ἐλάλησεν αὐτοῖς, "he spoke another parable to them" (cf. almost the same formula in vv 24, 31), which also involves altering the question that was probably in Q to an indicative statement (as also in v 31), ὁμοία ἐστὶν ἡ βασιλεία τῶν οὐρανῶν, "the kingdom of heaven is similar to" (cf. vv 31, 44, 45, and 47). Matthew, as he customarily does, changes "kingdom of God" (thus Luke 13:20 and very probably Q) to "kingdom of heaven." Apart from these initial changes, the agreement in the parable itself with Luke (and thus Q) is verbatim. V 34, on the other hand, seems dependent on Mark 4:33–34, although the wording is not close and Matthew as usual abbreviates Mark, omitting τὸν λόγον, "the word," καθὼς ἠδύναντο ἀκούειν, "as they were able to hear," and finally κατ' ἰδίαν δὲ τοῖς ἰδίοις μαθηταῖς ἐπέλυεν πάντα, "but privately he explained everything to his disciples." Again it may be noted that the tendency to verbatim agreement is much greater in the actual logia of Jesus than in the supporting narrative framework. V 35 is unique to Matthew, being one of the fulfillment quotations with which the evangelist sprinkles his narrative.

C. The pericope, as separated here, consists of three distinct parts after the introductory formula: (1) the parable of the leavened loaves (v 33); (2) a statement about Jesus speaking to the crowds only in parables (v 34); and (3) an OT citation with an introductory fulfillment formula, regarded as pointing to this speaking in parables (v 35). In addition to the similar introductory formula, beginning with ἄλλην παραβολήν, "another parable," and the opening of this parable itself with the words ὁμοία ἐστὶν ἡ βασιλεία τῶν οὐρανῶν, "the kingdom of heaven is similar," parallelism with the preceding parable can also be seen in the form of the following words: ζύμη ἣν λαβοῦσα γυνὴ ἐνέκρυψεν, "leaven, which a woman took and mixed," which are paralleled exactly by κόκκῳ (σινάπεως), ὃν λαβὼν ἄνθρωπος ἔσπειρεν, "a seed (of mustard), which someone took and sowed" (v 31). V 34 exhibits chiastic parallelism in its two main clauses, ταῦτα πάντα ἐλάλησεν . . . ἐν παραβολαῖς, "he spoke all these things in parables," and χωρὶς παραβολῆς οὐδὲν ἐλάλει, "apart from using a parable he continued to say nothing" (τοῖς ὄχλοις, "to the crowds," and αὐτοῖς, "to them," are also parallel). The OT citation of v 35 exhibits synonymous parallelism, although the second line goes beyond the content of the first. The passage cited is Ps 78:2 (LXX 77:2), where the first line of Matthew agrees verbatim with the LXX, while the second, which is closer to the Hebrew text, differs from the LXX entirely in vocabulary, though not in thought: φθέγξομαι προβλήματα ἀπ᾽ ἀρχῆς, "I will utter things foreseen from the beginning." Thus Matthew's editorial creativity is seen throughout the pericope: in the formulaic character of v 33 as a part of the structuring of the entire discourse, in the parallelism of v 34, and in the insertion of the fulfillment formula quotation in v 35.

Comment

33 For Matthew's introductory formula (cf. vv 24, 31) and the opening words of the parable (cf. vv 24, 31, 44, 45, 47), see above. ζύμη, "leaven" or "yeast," was a common and important ingredient in Palestinian households. Its special character of gradual, initially unobservable, fermentation made it a particularly suggestive metaphor for describing similar processes in the moral sphere, giving rise to the proverb, "a little leaven leavens the whole lump" (cf. 1 Cor 5:6; Gal 5:9). Matthew again uses leaven metaphorically in 16:6, 11–12 in referring to the teaching of the Pharisees and Sadducees. Although leaven symbolized the corrupting influence of evil in the OT (though not consistently; cf. Lev 23:17) and was thus to be purged entirely from Israelite households at Passover (Exod 12:15, 19), there is no indication that Matthew here thinks of the leaven as something evil. What he portrays, rather, is the dynamic power of leaven whereby a small amount, which is imperceptible (note the verb ἐνέκρυψεν, "hid") when first mixed in a lump of dough, has an eventual, inevitable, and astonishing effect upon the whole. In this sense, the parable is parallel to the immediately preceding parable of the mustard seed. Both speak of that which appears initially to be insignificant and of no consequence but which in time produces an astonishing and dramatic effect. The kingdom of God is like leaven in this way. Although at the beginning it looks unimpressive, it will have an effect that is out of all proportion with that

beginning. This is the main point of the parable, and while it may again be impossible to exclude altogether the idea of growth from the parable, it is very
unlikely that the work or influence of the disciples is to be seen in the leaven (as,
for example, in the salt and light metaphors of 5:13–14; cf. Allen). Thus there is
no need to allegorize details such as the woman, the three measures, or the whole
lump of dough itself. Nevertheless, it is worth at least noting that an exceptionally large amount of dough is indicated by σάτα τρία, "three measures": one σάτον
= about 13 liters; three = nearly 40 liters, amounting (according to Luz) to about
50 kilograms of bread or enough to feed 150 people. The inflated figures may
suggest eschatological fulfillment (but probably it is going too far to suggest the
messianic banquet, as does Gundry).

34 This statement reaffirms that made in vv 3 and 13 (cf. v 11). It serves to
unify the discourse and to prepare for both the OT citation (v 35) and the interpretation of the second parable concerning the wheat and the weeds (vv 36–43).
Jesus' teaching to the crowds about the kingdom is restricted to parables, a statement made both positively and negatively in this verse. Again it is worth noting
(cf. on vv 10–17) that the parables have the effect of illuminating the subject of
the kingdom for those who are willing to accept the message and of darkening it
for those who reject the message of the present reality of the kingdom.

35 Matthew's addition of an OT citation with the characteristic fulfillment
formula shows that this tactic of Jesus, i.e., teaching in parables, was already anticipated in the OT promise. Although it is said to be the word διὰ τοῦ προφήτου, "through
the prophet," that is being thus fulfilled, the quotation itself is drawn from Ps 78:2.
This suggests either that the supposed author of the psalm is a prophet (David?
the later title ascribes Ps 78 to Asaph, who is said to have "prophesied" in 1 Chr
25:2 and who is dubbed a "seer" according to 2 Chr 29:30) or more probably that
since the words are a prophecy, as so often in the Psalms, they are therefore regarded as the words of a prophet. Since the Psalms were generally regarded by
first-century Jews as having been composed by David, it was easy to apply the words
to David's greater Son, the Messiah. If David spoke such words, how much more
could they be regarded later as appropriate to his son, to whom all Scripture
points and in whom all Scripture is fulfilled. Thus the opening words of Ps 78:1–
2, a prologue to the reciting of OT salvation-history, are seen to have a deeper
meaning that finds its fulfillment in the teaching of Jesus in parables: "Give ear,
O my people, to my teaching: incline your ears to the words of my mouth! I will
open my mouth in a parable [בְּמָשָׁל, bĕmāšāl]: I will utter dark sayings from of
old." The plural παραβολαῖς, "parables," in the LXX makes the passage even more
appropriate to Jesus. The final objective phrase, κεκρυμμένα ἀπὸ καταβολῆς
[κόσμου], "things hidden from the foundation [of the world]," can be coordi-
nated easily with the belief of the evangelist and the early Church that the message
and mission of Jesus were nothing other than the working out of God's plan of
salvation from the beginning. The parables teach "the mysteries of the kingdom
of heaven" (v 11). That is, what Jesus' words were revealing was the design of God
for the final and perfect redemption of his people (cf. 1 Cor 2:7; Col 1:26; Rom
9:23). The teaching of Jesus in parables is accordingly regarded by the evangelist
as the fulfillment of OT prophecy and involves the revealing of the accomplishment of God's salvation in history in a way similar to, but more definitively than,
what Ps 78:1–2 describes.

Explanation

(For comments appropriate also to the parable of the leavened loaves, see the *Explanation* section for the preceding pericope.) Jesus' teaching of the crowds in parables is for the purpose of revealing truth to those who will receive it. The secondary purpose of hindering the understanding of the unreceptive is not mentioned here (cf. vv 11–15). Through his teaching in parables, Jesus fulfills the OT. It is as though he himself were the speaker of Ps 78:2. What he utters in the parables are "the mysteries of the kingdom" (v 11), things hidden from the foundation of the world but now being made known.

The Explanation of the Parable of the Wheat and the Weeds (13:36–43)

Bibliography

Barth, G. "Auseinandersetzung um die Kirchenzucht im Umkreis des Matthäusevangeliums." *ZNW* 69 (1978) 158–77. **Goedt, M. de** "L'explication de la parabole de l'ivraie (Mt 13,36–43)." *RB* 66 (1959) 32–54. **Jeremias, J.** "Die Deutung des Gleichnisses vom Unkraut unter dem Weizen (Mt 13,36–43)." In *Abba.* 261–65. **Marguerat, D.** "L'eglise et le monde en Matthieu 13, 36–43." *RTP* 110 (1978) 111–29. **Smith, C. W. F.** "The Mixed State of the Church in Matthew's Gospel." *JBL* 82 (1963) 149–68.

See also the *Bibliography* on 13:24–30.

Translation

[36] *Then he*[a] *dismissed the crowds and came into the house. And his disciples came to him, saying: "Explain to us the parable of the weeds of the field."* [37] *And he responded:*[b] *"The one sowing the good seed is the Son of Man,* [38] *the field is the world, and the good seed are the children of the kingdom. But the weeds are the children of the evil one,* [39] *and the enemy who sowed them is the Devil; the harvest is the end of the age, and the harvesters are angels.* [40] *Therefore, just as the weeds are gathered up and burned in a fire, thus it will be at the end of the age.*[c] [41] *The Son of Man will send his angels, and they will gather from his kingdom everything that causes stumbling and those who are guilty of lawlessness,*[d] [42] *and they will cast them into the furnace of fire. In that place there will be weeping and the grinding of teeth.* [43] *Then the righteous will glimmer like the sun in the kingdom of their Father.*[e] *Let the person who has ears*[f] *hear!"*

Notes

[a] C L W Θ f^{13} TR read ὁ Ἰησοῦς, "Jesus."

[b] C L W Θ $f^{1,13}$ TR vg^{cl} sy sa^{mss} b^{mss} insert αὐτοῖς, "to them."

[c] τούτου, "this (age)" is added by C L W Θ $f^{1,13}$ TR sy^{p,h} bo. The shorter reading is to be preferred since scribes would have been inclined to add τούτου, thus completing the common expression "this age" (e.g., 12:32; Luke 16:8; 20:34; etc.). See *TCGNT*, 34.

^d τοὺς ποιοῦντας τὴν ἀνομίαν, lit. "those who do iniquity."

^e Θ ƒ¹³ and a few other MSS have τῶν οὐρανῶν, "(kingdom) of heaven," imitating the more common Matthean phrase.

^f Many MSS (ℵ² C D L W ƒ^{1,13} lat sy co TR) add ἀκούειν, "to hear." The situation is exactly the same as in 11:15 (see *Note* there). No apparent reason exists for the dropping out of ἀκούειν in the important MSS where it is not found.

Form/Structure/Setting

A. The second parable, concerning the wheat and the weeds (vv 24–30), is now given its interpretation privately before the disciples. In the construction of the discourse, this explanation of the parable is delayed until this point, exactly because a private setting is required. That this delay can occur suggests the propriety of understanding all the parables as in some sense belonging together and addressing aspects of the same reality, i.e., the mysteries of the kingdom (v 11).

B. Like the parable itself, its explanation is found only in Matthew and is possibly derived from the evangelist's special source, although it could be his own creation. V 43 is cited by Justin Martyr, *Apol.* 1.16.12, but in virtually certain dependence on Matthew (cf. too *Herm. Sim.* 5.5.2).

C. The pericope is structured as follows: (1) the private setting and the request of the disciples (v 36); (2) the explanation, which may be subdivided into (a) identifications of elements, parallel in form and seven in number (vv 37–39), (b) the establishment of the main analogy concerning the end of the age (v 40), and (c) the application of the analogy in two parts, (i) the judgment of the lawless (vv 41–42a), including a parenthesis concerning the torment of Gehenna (v 42b, found again verbatim in v 50b), and (ii) the reward of the righteous (v 43a); and finally (3) a brief concluding exhortation (v 43b). The parallelism in the pericope is mainly limited to the identifications of vv 37–39. The parallelism existing between v 40 and vv 41–42 (with the three major verbs in the future tense) is more in content than in form.

Comment

36 The opening τότε, "then," is a Mattheanism. Jesus' departing from the crowds and entering into the house are Matthew's device for creating the privacy needed for the explanation of the parable (i.e., of vv 24–30). Accordingly, τὴν οἰκίαν, "the house," remains undefined (the last mention of a house was in v 1, and before that in 9:28). The disciples (οἱ μαθηταί) "come to" Jesus (on the significance of προσῆλθον in this connection, see *Comment* on 5:1, where the same formula is found). The verb διασάφησον, "explain," is found in the NT only here and in 18:31. The disciples approach Jesus and ask him for an explanation (cf. 15:15; Mark 4:10; 7:17) of τὴν παραβολὴν τῶν ζιζανίων τοῦ ἀγροῦ, "the parable of the weeds of the field" (in vv 24–30). This is not necessarily to be taken as the title of the parable (cf. also v 18) but indicates a basic point for which the disciples needed clarity if they were to understand the parable as a whole. The parable is not merely about judgment but about the delay of judgment.

37–39 The explanation of the parable begins with the identification of seven key elements: (1) the one sowing the good seed (= the Son of Man); (2) the field (= the world); (3) the good seed (= those who belong to the kingdom); (4) the weeds (= those of the evil one); (5) the enemy who sowed the weeds (= the Devil);

(6) the harvest (= the end of the age); and (7) the harvesters (= angels). Not every element of the parable is given an interpretation (e.g., the sleeping [v 25]; the bearing of fruit [v 26]; the servants [v 27]). If this were to be done, presumably the "master" would be Jesus (i.e., the same as the sower); the δοῦλοι, "servants," would presumably be the disciples; and the bearing of fruit, righteousness. It remains unclear, however, whether the "sleeping" should be regarded as innocent or as reflecting a failure to be watchful, and also what the premature "gathering" and "rooting out" might mean (church discipline? but cf. 18:17, which regulates church discipline). Furthermore, not every element defined here becomes a part of the explanation that follows (thus the world [v 38] and the Devil [v 39] do not appear again in vv 40–43). Not every detail can or should be pressed for meaning, although the extent of the interpretation that is given is remarkable. The sower, ὁ υἱὸς τοῦ ἀνθρώπου, "the Son of Man" (cf. ἄνθρωπος, v 24, and the sower of v 3), refers to Jesus himself (for the title, see *Comment* on 8:20). The field, explicitly identified as ὁ κόσμος, "the world," cannot have been understood as the Church by the evangelist or his readers. This identification of the field as the world does, however, point in itself to the worldwide mission of the Church in the spread of the gospel (cf. 24:14; 28:19). For the phrase οἱ υἱοὶ τῆς βασιλείας, lit. "the sons of the kingdom," but more correctly "those who belong to the kingdom," see *Comment* on 8:12, where it is used in reference to the unbelieving Jews. The parallel οἱ υἱοὶ τοῦ πονηροῦ, lit. "sons of the evil one," is to be understood in a similar sense, i.e., those associated with the evil one (cf. 1 John 3:10; John 8:44). In rabbinic literature, wheat and weeds can refer to Israel and the Gentiles respectively (cf. Luz, 157; Str-B 1:667). ὁ πονηρός, "the evil one," is used elsewhere in Matthew in 5:37, 6:13, and particularly noteworthy is its occurrence in the interpretation of the parable of the sower (v 19), where the evil one, likened to birds, takes away the seed sown by the sower. The enemy (ὁ ἐχθρός) is defined as ὁ διάβολος, "the Devil," a term used by Matthew four times in the narrative of the temptation of Jesus (chap. 4) and once in the apocalyptic discourse (25:41), where, as here, it is also associated with the fire of eschatological judgment. The harvest (cf. Joel 3:13; Jer 51:33; 2 *Apoc. Bar.* 70:2) is an especially common and appropriate metaphor for the judgment that will occur at the end of the present age (cf. 9:37; Rev 14:15). The phrase συντέλεια αἰῶνος, "end of the age," occurs again immediately in v 40 but also in the seventh parable (v 49; cf. 24:3 and 28:20; see too 2 Esdr 7:113). ἄγγελοι, "angels," were commonly believed in Jewish tradition to be administrators of the will of God in the accomplishing of eschatological judgment (see *1 Enoch* 46:5; 63:1).

40 The central point of the parable is now explained. The gathering of the weeds and their burning refer to the eschatological judgment (see the same image in 3:10) that will take place ἐν τῇ συντελείᾳ τοῦ αἰῶνος, "at the end of the age" (cf. vv 39 and 49). The present era of fulfillment announced by Jesus, despite its eschatological character, does not bring with it the final judgment of the end time. That time of future eschatological judgment is described in the verses that follow. Jeremias (*Parables*) refers to vv 40–43 as a "little apocalypse."

41–42 First there is the judgment of the wicked. This is described using the language of apocalyptic: the Son of Man (ὁ υἱὸς τοῦ ἀνθρώπου) will send "his angels" (τοὺς ἀγγέλους αὐτοῦ) to gather the wicked to their punishment. The sower (v 37) is then also the judge. The identical imagery of the Son of Man sending his angels is used in 24:30–31 but in connection with the eschatological gathering of the elect. In 16:27 and especially 25:31–33, the Son of Man comes with his angels to execute the final judgment of the righteous and the wicked. Here the angels gather together πάντα τά σκάνδαλα, "everything that causes stumbling" (cf. Zeph 1:3, MT) and τούς ποιοῦντας τὴν ἀνομίαν, "those who are guilty of lawlessness." The causing of others to stumble is a particularly grievous sin in Matthew (see especially 18:6–7 and the importance of the verb σκανδαλίζειν, "cause to stumble," in the Gospel). Despite the neuter noun, it is undoubtedly persons who cause stumbling that are intended. Lawlessness (ἀνομία), the essence of wickedness for Matthew, is also very important in the Gospel (see 7:23; 23:28; 24:12; cf. 1 John 3:4). ἐκ τῆς βασιλείας αὐτοῦ, "from his kingdom," refers to the kingdom of the Son of Man (for the same concept, see 16:28; cf. 20:21). Here, however, the kingdom is thought of ideally as encompassing the whole world, i.e., the field where the seed has been sown. The wicked are gathered from the kingdom, not in the sense that they actually were a part of the Church (nor does the kingdom exactly equal the field/world) but in the sense that they were in the world, had existed alongside the righteous (cf. v 30), hence were even in the visible church (pace Davies-Allison), and are now finally distinguished and separated from them. V 42 expresses the fate of the lawless, again in vivid apocalyptic terminology. The words βαλοῦσιν αὐτοὺς εἰς τὴν κάμινον τοῦ πυρός, "they will cast them into the furnace of fire," are drawn nearly verbatim from Dan 3:6 (exactly the same quotation is found in v 50). This is to be related to the fire of Gehenna mentioned in 5:22 and 18:8–9 (cf. esp. 2 Esdr 7:36). The formulaic character of this imagery is again apparent in the final clause of v 42, ἐκεῖ ἔσται ὁ κλαυθμὸς καὶ ὁ βρυγμὸς τῶν ὀδόντων, "in that place there will be weeping and the grinding of teeth," which is found verbatim not only in v 50 but also in 8:12; 22:13; 24:51; 25:30 (cf. Luke 13:28).

43 If the lawless are to suffer punishment, then the righteous are to be rewarded. οἱ δίκαιοι, "the righteous," a favorite term of Matthew, occurs in related contexts in v 49 and in 10:41; 25:37, 46. Their blessedness is indicated in the words ἐκλάμψουσιν ὡς ὁ ἥλιος ἐν τῇ βασιλείᾳ τοῦ πατρὸς αὐτῶν, "they will glimmer like the sun in the kingdom of their Father." This language is almost exactly the same as that used in describing the transfiguration of Jesus in 17:2 and suggests the experiencing of the glory of God. It is found occasionally in the rabbinic literature (cf. b. Sanh. 100a; Sipre Deut. 1, 10 §10[67a]; Gen. Rab. 12[9a]). The same imagery is used in Dan 12:3 (they "shall shine like the brightness of the firmament") in describing the eschatological blessing of the righteous (cf. 2 Sam 23:3–4, 1 Enoch 39:7; 104:2). The future eschatological blessing of the righteous will be ἐν τῇ βασιλείᾳ τοῦ πατρὸς αὐτῶν, "in the kingdom of their Father" (contrast v 41, which refers to the kingdom of the Son of Man; cf. 25:34 and 1 Cor 15:24; for the kingdom of the Father, see too 26:29). The kingdom of the Son and the kingdom of the Father refer to the same reality and are essentially interchangeable (contra Luz). The dramatic contrast of the fate of the lawless and the righteous concludes with the brief but pointed exhortation ὁ ἔχων ὦτα ἀκουέτω, "let the person who has ears hear" (the exhortation is found verbatim in v 9 and 11:15).

Explanation

In this world, even after the announcement of Jesus that the eschatological kingdom has already begun, those guilty of lawlessness—the people who belong to the evil one—coexist with the righteous, who are the people of the kingdom. There has not been, nor will there be, a dramatic separation of the lawless from the righteous until the harvest at the end of the age. The present age is thus one in which human society (and thus even the Church) is a mixture of those of the evil one and those of the kingdom. This can result in a confusing situation, especially when the wicked seem to prosper and the righteous suffer (an important motif in Matthew, as we have seen). But the ambiguity of the present situation is a temporary one, and with the end of the age it too will be brought to an end. Then, and only then, will there be a clear demarcation between the two, and each will receive their eschatological due: the lawless a dreadful punishment and the righteous extravagant blessedness. The evil will be shown for what they are, but the righteous too will become conspicuous. To this future expectation Matthew returns again and again, as a warning and encouragement to his readers.

The Parables of the Treasure and the Pearl   (13:44–46)

Bibliography

Crossan, J. D. "Hidden Treasure Parables in Late Antiquity." In *SBL 1976 Seminar Papers*, ed. G. MacRae. Missoula, MT: Scholars, 1976. 359–79. **Dupont, J.** "Les paraboles du trésor et de la perle." *NTS* 14 (1968) 408–18. **Fenton, J. C.** "Expounding the Parables: IV. The Parables of the Treasure and the Pearl." *ExpTim* 77 (1966) 178–80. **Gibbs, J. A.** "Parables of Atonement and Assurance: Matthew 13:44–46." *CTQ* 51 (1987) 19–43. **Glombitza, O.** "Der Perlenkaufmann." *NTS* 7 (1960–61) 153–61. **Schippers, R.** "The Mashal-Character of the Parable of the Pearl." *SE* 2 [= TU 87] (1964) 236–41. **Sider, J. W.** "Interpreting the Hid Treasure." *Christian Scholar's Review* 13 (1984) 360–72.

Translation

[44] *"The[a] kingdom of heaven is like a treasure hidden in the field, which a person found and hid again and out of joy goes and sells everything[b] he or she[c] has and buys that field.* [45] *Again, the kingdom of heaven is like the situation of[d] a merchant[e] who is on the lookout for beautiful pearls.* [46] *And when that person found one[f] precious pearl she or[g] he went and sold everything she or he had and bought it."*

Notes

[a] Some MSS (C L W Θ *f*[1,13] lat sy co TR) begin the verse with πάλιν, "again," on the model of vv 45 and 47.

[b] B bo and a few other MSS omit πάντα, "everything." Despite the possible influence of Luke 18:22, the longer reading is preferred because of a tendency of scribes to omit unnecessary words. See *TCGNT*, 34.

[c] "Or she" is added in the translation.

[d] "The situation of" is added in the translation for clarity.

[e] The critical Gr. text reads ἀνθρώπῳ ἐμπόρῳ, "a person, a merchant," but ℵ* B Γ and a few other MSS omit ἀνθρώπῳ. The translation omits ἀνθρώπῳ merely for convenience in not repeating "person."

^f D Θ sy and a few other witnesses omit ἕνα, "one" (thus "a precious pearl").
^g "She or" is added to the translation twice in this verse.

Form/Structure/Setting

A. The brief fifth and sixth parables have as their focus the glorious character of the kingdom brought by Jesus, which justifies the cost of absolute discipleship. They are linked with the preceding parables, however, by the continuing motif of hiddenness and smallness. Thus the hidden treasure corresponds to the hidden leaven and the smallness of the pearl with that of the mustard seed. These parables, again like those of the mustard seed and the leaven, receive no explanation in the text; this may be because they are spoken to the disciples, who will know their meaning.

B. These two parables are found only in Matthew and are probably drawn from his special source. A highly modified version of the first, and with a rather different point, is found in *Gos. Thom.* 109 and the second is found in *Gos. Thom.* 76, but both are almost certainly dependent on Matthew.

C. In addition to the exactly parallel words ὁμοία ἐστὶν ἡ βασιλεία τῶν οὐρανῶν, "the kingdom of heaven is like," the two parables have the same five elements in the same order: (1) the reference to something very valuable (the treasure; the pearl); (2) finding it (εὑρών); (3) going; (4) selling everything the person has (πάντα ὅσα ἔχει/εἶχεν); and (5) buying it (in the first parable, the field). The first parable has an additional element in the hiding of the treasure in the field and in the mention of the joy (χαρᾶς) at its discovery. The shift to the aorist tenses in the last part of v 46 (εἶχεν for ἔχει; ἠγόρασεν for ἀγοράζει) as well as the substitution of πέπρακεν, "sold," for πωλεῖ, "sells," seems to be without significance. A further small difference between the two parables is that in the first the discovery seems accidental, while in the second the person was in the business of looking for beautiful pearls. Thus although the syntax is not altogether parallel, certainly the content of the parables is quite parallel and probably points to the early linking of the two in the tradition (perhaps even from the beginning).

Comment

44 For the opening formula, see too vv 24, 31, 33, 45, and 47. The kingdom of heaven is likened to θησαυρῷ κεκρυμμένῳ ἐν τῷ ἀγρῷ, "a treasure hidden in the field." It was not at all unusual in the ancient world to hide a treasure in the ground. The background of this phrase, however, is probably to be found in the wisdom literature (cf. Prov 2:4, Sir 20:30), although many secular folk tales also deal with this theme (see Crossan, "Hidden Treasure"). This analogy, like the re-hiding of the treasure by the person who found it, suggests that something of tremendous worth can be present and yet not known to others who may have frequently traversed the same field. Similarly, the kingdom can be present and yet not perceived, because its present form does not overwhelm the world or overcome resistance to it. But the person who does discover the treasure goes with joy (ἀπὸ τῆς χαρᾶς; cf. v 20; elsewhere in Matthew, see 2:10; 28:8; cf. v 16) to sell everything in order to obtain that field and its hidden treasure. The question of the ethical propriety of buying a field with a hidden treasure is not addressed in the parable. The sole point being made is that the kingdom is worth every-thing. (The rabbis debated whether such a treasure would actually belong to the buyer of a field; cf. *m. B. Bat.* 4:8; *y. B. Meṣ.* 2.5, 8c.) Although no explanation of this parable is provided, it is obvious that rigorous, self-denying discipleship is in view (see especially 19:21, 29; cf. Luke 14:33; Phil 3:7). What has been said in the preceding sentences is the basic message of the parable. Other elements, such as the re-hiding of the treasure and the buying of the field, are merely supportive detail and need not be allegorized. This parable, like its following companion, is about the reality of the kingdom and its absolute worth in terms of personal sacrifice.

45–46 The introductory formula (see on v 44) is preceded with πάλιν, "again" (cf. v 47). The parable likens the kingdom to the situation of a pearl merchant (the word for "merchant," ἔμπορος, is also linked with pearls in Rev 18:11–12). This merchant finds one supremely precious pearl (for background, again in the wisdom literature, see Job 28:18; cf. Prov 3:15; 8:11). The pearl is clearly the equiva-lent of the kingdom (μαργαρίτης, "pearl," occurs only here and in 7:6 in the four Gospels). Pearls, it is worth noting, were very highly valued in the ancient world, more so than gold (cf. BAGD, 491b). πολύτιμον, "precious," is found elsewhere in the NT only in John 12:3 in reference to the ointment used by Mary to anoint the feet of Jesus and in 1 Peter 1:7. There is deliberate hyperbole in v 46, in that it is rather unlikely that any merchant would sell everything she or he had to acquire any single pearl. But in the case of the kingdom, wonderful beyond price, the analogous action of the disciple in full and unreserved commitment is more than justified. As in the previous parable, the supportive imagery of "buying" (ἠγόρασεν) is not to be allegorized. Selling and buying together point to the re-sponse of the disciple (cf. Crossan's analysis [*Parables*] of these parables in terms of finding, selling, and buying, which he regards as a paradigm for all Jesus' parables, using the words "advent," "reversal," and "action"). The kingdom is like a small, inconspicuous pearl but one of incalculable value that, once discovered, calls for unrestrained response in the form of absolute discipleship.

Explanation

The kingdom of God is the greatest of treasures. Though its worth is immea-surable by any standard (cf. concerning wisdom, Wis 7:7–9, 14), it is now present only in veiled form and can be possessed by some without the knowledge of those near them. Like a hidden treasure or a pearl that can be held in one's hand, the kingdom is known only to its joyful possessors. Yet those who find the kingdom, i.e., who receive the message and who respond in discipleship, have begun to experience the wonder of the kingdom's presence. They know that the kingdom is a reality that is worth everything. And thus they joyfully make it their one prior-ity in life (cf. 4:18–22; 10:39). They seek first the kingdom, sacrificing all to it, but at the same time paradoxically finding with the kingdom all they need (6:33).

The Parable of the Dragnet   (13:47–50)

Bibliography

Archbald, P. "Interpretation of the Parable of the Dragnet (Matthew 13:47–50)." *VoxRef* 48 (1987) 3–14. **Morrice, W. G.** "The Parable of the Dragnet and the Gospel of Thomas." *ExpTim* 95 (1983–84) 269–73.

Translation

[47] *"Again, the kingdom of heaven is like a dragnet which was cast into the sea and which gathered fish[a] of every kind.* [48] *When it was full, they brought it up upon the shore, and having sat down, they gathered the good[b] fish[c] into a container, but the bad ones they threw away.* [49] *Thus it will be at the end of the age.[d] The angels will come, and they will separate the evil from the midst of the righteous,* [50] *and they will cast them into the furnace of fire. In that place there will be weeping and the grinding of teeth."*

Notes

[a] "Fish" is added in the translation to complete the sense.
[b] D it read κάλλιστα, "the best."
[c] "Fish" is added to complete the sense.
[d] D reads κόσμου, "world."

Form/Structure/Setting

A. The seventh and last parable of the discourse returns to the motif of the eschatological separation of the righteous and the evil, and the judgment of the latter. The parable is reminiscent of the second parable, that of the weeds and the wheat (vv 24–30), and its interpretation (vv 36–43). Indeed, the final verse here (v 50) is the verbatim repetition of v 42. To round out the collection and the discourse, Matthew returns to a favorite theme, the judgment of the unrighteous. Again the stress is on the occurrence of this only "at the end of the age" (v 49).

B. Like the parable of the wheat and the weeds, this parable is found only in Matthew and has probably been formulated by Matthew using material from his special source (perhaps oral tradition). The interpretation in vv 49–50 may well be from the evangelist. A possible distant variant of the parable is found in *Gos. Thom.* 8, which, however, is probably dependent on Matthew, if there is any relationship at all between the two.

C. Formally, the parable has obvious similarities with the preceding parables. The one striking difference is that only this parable has a self-contained interpretation (vv 49–50). After the initial πάλιν, "again," paralleling v 45, and the opening formula beginning with ὁμοία, "like" (cf. v 24, but more closely vv 31, 33, 44, 45), the parable may be outlined as follows: (1) the comparison (v 47), together with other descriptive material (v 48), followed by (2) the interpretation (vv 49–50). The interpretation resembles the interpretation of the second parable: v 49 is similar to v 41, while v 50 is identical with v 42. Some parallelism is again found in the syntax: i.e., in the participles βληθείσῃ, "cast," and συναγαγούσῃ, "gathered" (v 47), and especially in the contrasting and chiastic συνέλεξαν τὰ καλά, "they gathered the good," and τὰ δὲ σαπρὰ ἔξω ἔβαλον, "the bad ones they threw away" (v 48). The similarity between this parable and that of the wheat and weeds and its interpretation may reflect reciprocal influence, perhaps even in the pre-Matthean tradition.

Comment

47–48 The opening words πάλιν ὁμοία ἐστὶν ἡ βασιλεία τῶν οὐρανῶν, "again, the kingdom of heaven is like," occur verbatim in v 45 (cf. v 44, 33, 31, and 24). The appropriateness of this particular parable for the several disciples who had been fishermen is obvious (and could suggest that they had a hand in the ultimate formulation of it). The σαγήνη is a seine-net with floats at the top edge and weights at the bottom that, having been thrown out in the water, encircled the fish and was then dragged up on the shore. The net naturally gathers fish indiscriminately: ἐκ παντὸς γένους, "of every kind." The exaggerated inclusiveness of this phrase may be an intentional reflection of the universality of the invitation to accept the good news of the kingdom (cf. 22:9–10: πονηρούς τε καὶ ἀγαθούς, "both bad and good"). If the parable of the wheat and weeds only implied the mixture of righteous and unrighteous in the Church, the present parable seems to make this point quite clearly. In their proclamation of the kingdom, the disciples have become "fishers of men and women" (ἁλιεῖς ἀνθρώπων; 4:19). Among those who respond are many who will not persevere in their initial commitment (cf. vv 3–8; 18–23); there will be those who do not live up to the standards of the Church (cf. 7:21–23; 18:17). The clause ὅτε ἐπληρώθη, "when it was full," corresponds to ἐν τῇ συντελείᾳ τοῦ αἰῶνος, "at the end of the age" (v 49), and thus hints at eschatological fulfillment (contra Davies-Allison). It would have been very common in Capernaum, for example, to see the fishermen sitting (καθίσαντες) on the beach, going through the day's catch, keeping the good fish and throwing away the bad ones (σαπρά, used also to describe bad trees or fruit in 7:17–18; 12:33). ἔξω ἔβαλον, "threw away," echoes the language of 8:12.

49–50 V 49 is practically the same as v 41, and v 50 repeats v 42 verbatim. The interpretation of the parable begins with οὕτως ἔσται ἐν τῇ συντελείᾳ τοῦ αἰῶνος, "thus it will be at the end of the age," words found verbatim in v 40 (for συντέλεια αἰῶνας, see too *Comment* on v 39; for a similar use of οὕτως, cf. 18:35). As in v 41 the angels are again the agents of eschatological judgment. Here they separate (for ἀφοριοῦσιν, see 25:32) τοὺς πονηρούς, "the evil ones," ἐκ μέσου τῶν δικαίων, "from the midst of the righteous." This last phrase indicates unmistakably the mixture of good and evil in the kingdom, which must point to the Church as presently a *corpus permixtum* (with Gundry; contra Luz and Davies-Allison). The evil, i.e., false disciples, will experience eschatological judgment (cf. Ps 1:5). For v 50, see *Comment* on v 42. After the reference to the separation, the judgment is described in terms of the standardized fire imagery (cf. 25:41), thus departing from the imagery of the parable itself.

Explanation

The final parable focuses again on the reality of an eschatological separation of the evil from the righteous and the judgment of the former at the end of the age.

In the present era, the evil persons are allowed to live together with the righteous—in their midst—even within that manifestation of the kingdom known as the Church. The dragnet of the kingdom thus includes a mixture of both good and evil. That such circumstances could exist in the era of the kingdom itself was nothing less than astonishing—something indeed worth calling one of "the mysteries of the kingdom." That good and evil could be located within the net of the kingdom seemed equally strange, no doubt. Yet at the time of eschatological judgment an unavoidable separation would take place. At that time only the righteous—those who have received the kingdom with appropriate response in the form of discipleship—would survive; the evil would go to their punishment. Focus on judgment within the Church, of course, presupposes the wider context of the judgment of the world. Matthew never tires in warning his readers of the reality of judgment and hence the importance of genuine discipleship. It is a warning that both the world and the Church need.

The Scribe Trained for the Kingdom: The End of the Discourse (13:51–52)

Bibliography

Betz, O. "Neues und Altes im Geschichtshandeln Gottes." In *Jesus: Der Messias Israels.* WUNT 42. Tübingen: Mohr, 1987. 285–300. **Dupont, J.** "Nova et vetera (Mt 13,52)." In *Études sur les Évangiles synoptiques.* BETL 70. Leuven: Peeters/Leuven University, 1985. 2:920–28. **Hoh, J.** "Der christliche γραμματεύς." *BZ* 17 (1926) 256–69. **Kremer, J.** "'Neues und Altes': Jesu Wort über den christlichen Schriftgelehrten (Mt 13,52)." In *Neues und Altes,* ed. J. Kremer, O. Semmelroth, and J. Sudbrack. Freiburg: Herder, 1974. 11–33. **Légasse, S.** "Scribes et disciples de Jésus." *RB* 68 (1961) 321–45, 481–506. **Orton, D. E.** *The Understanding Scribe: Matthew and the Apocalyptic Ideal.* JSNTSup 25. Sheffield: JSOT, 1989. **Schnackenburg, R.** "'Jeder Schriftgelehrte, der ein Jünger des Himmelreichs geworden ist' (Mt 13,52)." In *Wissenschaft und Kirche.* FS E. Lohse, ed. K. Aland and S. Meurer. Texte und Arbeiten zur Bibel 4. Bielefeld: Luther, 1989. 57–69. **Zeller, D.** "Zu einer jüdischen Vorlage von Mt 13.52." *BZ* n.s. 20 (1976) 223–26.

Translation

⁵¹ *"Have* [a] *you understood all these things?" They said to him, "Yes."* [b] ⁵²*And he said to them: "Because of this, every scribe who has been instructed in* [c] *the kingdom of heaven is like the master of a household who brings forth out of the* [d] *storehouse new things and old things."*

Notes

[a] Many MSS (C L W Θ *f*^1.13 TR) begin the sentence with λέγει αὐτοῖς ὁ Ἰησοῦς, "Jesus said to them," an obvious addition.

^b Many MSS (C L W TR it sy^{p,h} co) insert κύριε, "Lord."
^c L Γ Δ and a few other MSS have εἰς τὴν βασιλείαν, "(instructed) into the kingdom."
^d αὐτοῦ, lit. "his."

Form/Structure/Setting

A. The brief ending of the discourse is formed by a question concerning the disciples' understanding and a concluding comment on those who teach this doctrine of the kingdom in the form of yet another parabolic analogy. This concluding analogy throws light on the seven parables of the discourse by focusing on one of the basic tensions maintained in their message: the continuity and discontinuity of old and new.

B. This pericope finds no parallels in the Gospels. The core saying (v 52) is perhaps drawn from Matthew's special source and has been molded into a suitable conclusion to the discourse.

C. The pericope may be outlined as follows: (1) the question of Jesus and the answer of the disciples (v 51), and (2) a summarizing parabolic analogy consisting of (a) the comparison (v 52a) and (b) further information defining the comparison (v 52b, ὅστις . . . , "who . . ."). A key parallelism is found in the contrast of καινά, "new things," and παλαιά, "old things."

Comment

51 Jesus asks the disciples if they have understood ταῦτα πάντα, "all these things," i.e., the preceding parables of the kingdom, and thus the content of the entire discourse as Matthew has constructed it. The reference to understanding the parables recalls the specific discussion of vv 10–17 (the verb συνιέναι, "understand," occurs in v 13 and twice in the Isaiah quotation; cf. too vv 19 and 23). Only if the disciples have understood these things will they be in a position to be fruitful for the kingdom (cf. v 23). Although there is much ahead of them to learn and they will stumble in ignorance on more than one occasion, they are able—at least with regard to the parables — to answer with perhaps a deceptively confident ναί, "yes."

52 The διὰ τοῦτο, "because of this," refers not only to the preceding question and answer but to the content of the preceding parables altogether. That is, given the complicated content of the parables and the note about the understanding of the disciples, a Christian "scribe" may be described in a certain way. The γραμματεύς, "scribe," in Judaism was the Scripture scholar-teacher trained in the interpretation of the Torah (cf. Orton). The scribe is described in Sir 39:2–3 as one who not only "will seek out the wisdom of all the ancients" but also as one who will "penetrate the subtleties of parables" and "be at home with the obscurities of parables." Jesus refers to a new kind of scribe, one instructed (μαθητευθείς, lit. "having been made a disciple") τῇ βασιλείᾳ τῶν οὐρανῶν, "in the kingdom of heaven," i.e., concerning the nature of the kingdom as it has been elucidated through the parables. He thus has in mind the disciples whom he has been teaching (and not specialist theologians, *pace* Luz). The verb μαθητεύειν, "to make a disciple," is used again in 27:57 and 28:19 (Acts 14:21 is the only other NT occurrence). The suggestion of a play on the name Μαθθαῖος,

"Matthew," and μαθητεύειν, "to make a disciple," is far-fetched. Matthew refers again to Christian scribes in 23:34, but there more probably to Christian scholars of the Torah. This new type of scribe, trained in the knowledge of the kingdom, is likened to an οἰκοδεσπότῃ, "master of a household" (cf. 20:1; 21:33), who brings out of his storeroom (θησαυροῦ αὐτοῦ; cf. 12:35) καινὰ καὶ παλαιά, "new things and old things." The key here—indeed the key to the parables themselves—is the combination of new and old. The parables, like Jesus' other teaching about the kingdom, involve old and familiar things but newly juxtaposed with new elements. In view are not merely new hermeneutical applications of the Torah in new situations, with which scribes have always concerned themselves, nor new applications of old sayings of Jesus (*pace* Schlatter; cf. Schnackenburg, "Jeder Schriftgelehrte"), but the relation of the Torah to the genuinely new reality of the kingdom of God (cf. Mark 1:27), the "mysteries" concerning the purposes of God, hidden from the beginning but now being made known (cf. v 35). The Christian scribe, trained in the kingdom and prepared to teach others, must be able to use old and new together to bring clarity and understanding to the message of the kingdom in its application to the present. The old things and the new things of the Christian scribe are both indispensable to the gospel. On the subject of Christian scribes, cf. esp. Orton.

Explanation

The gospel of the kingdom announced by Jesus, believed in by the disciples, and established as the foundation of the Church, is by its very nature a blend of continuity and discontinuity with the old (i.e., the OT as ordinarily understood). At its heart the gospel consists of "new things." But for Matthew these "new things" presuppose and are fundamentally loyal to the "old things" (cf. 5:17–19). The Christian Torah scholar or "scribe" is one trained in the mysteries of the kingdom who is able to maintain a balance between the continuity and discontinuity existing between the era inaugurated by Jesus and that of the past. It is remarkable the extent to which NT theology is characterized by just this tension between the old and the new. And for Matthew, in particular, writing for a Jewish-Christian congregation that probably had its own Christian scribes (the counterpart of the Jewish rabbis), it is no wonder that this is an especially important theme—so much so that some (e.g., von Dobschütz, "Matthew as Rabbi and Catechist") have regarded the description of the scribe in v 52 as a self-description of the evangelist. He certainly would have thought of himself as included among scribes trained in the mysteries of the kingdom. If the Church carries on the work of the disciples, there is a sense in which not only Scripture scholars but every Christian must bring out of his or her storeroom both old things and new things, i.e., must represent a Christianity encompassing both Testaments.

The Unbelief of the People of Nazareth   (13:53–58)

Bibliography

Furfey, P. H. "Christ as Tektōn." *CBQ* 17 (1955) 324–35. **Oberlinner, L.** *Historische Überlieferung und christologische Aussage: Zur Frage der "Brüder Jesu" in der Synopse.* FB 19. Stuttgart: Katholisches Bibelwerk, 1975. **Segbroeck, F. van.** "Jésus rejeté par sa patrie (Mt 13,54–58)." *Bib* 48 (1968) 167–98. **Stauffer, E.** "Jeschua ben Mirjam." In *Neotestamentica et Semitica.* FS M. Black, ed. E. E. Ellis and M. Wilcox. Edinburgh: T. & T. Clark, 1969. 119–28. **Temple, P. J.** "The Rejection at Nazareth." *CBQ* 17 (1955) 229–42.

Translation

[53] *And it came to pass that when Jesus finished speaking[a] these parables, he moved on from there.* [54] *And when he came to his home town, he was teaching them in their synagogue with the result that they were astounded and said: "How did this[b] wisdom and the miraculous deeds come to this man?* [55] *Is not this the carpenter's son? Is not his mother called Mary and his brothers James, Joseph,[c] Simon, and Judas?* [56] *And are not all of his sisters with us? How, therefore, did all of these things come to this man?"* [57] *And they were scandalized by him. But Jesus said to them: "A prophet is not without honor except in his[d] home town and in his own[e] house."* [58] *And he did not do many miracles there because of their unbelief.[f]*

Notes

[a] "Speaking" is added to the translation.

[b] D sy[s] mae and other witnesses insert πᾶσα, "all," before ἡ σοφία αὕτη, "this wisdom."

[c] Some MSS (K L W Δ f[13] k q[c] sa bo[mss]) have Ἰωσῆς, "Joses," which reflects the Galilean pronunciation of "Joseph" and results perhaps from the influence of the parallel in Mark 6:3. Other MSS (אvid D Γ vg[mss]) read Ἰωάννης, "John," but this "scribal inadvertence" is probably due to the frequent mention of James and John together in the Gospels. See *TCGNT*, 34.

[d] א Z f[13] and a few other witnesses add ἰδίᾳ, "own," before πατρίδι, "home town," probably through the influence of John 4:44.

[e] "Own" added to translation.

[f] D K have the pl. τὰς ἀπιστίας, "unbeliefs."

Form/Structure/Setting

A. Following the end of the parable discourse, in characteristic alternation, Matthew places a lengthy narrative section. This particular pericope again picks up the theme of unbelief implied in the preceding discourse (e.g., vv 13–15) but already of particular importance in chaps. 11 and 12. Thus the theme of unbelief not only continues but grows as the Gospel proceeds, here coming to something of a climax in the unbelief of Jesus' own people in Nazareth.

B. After v 53, which is Matthew's own formulaic ending to the preceding discourse and transition to the present pericope, Matthew depends here on Mark 6:1–6a. (Luke 4:16–30, though apparently based on the Markan framework, incorporates much material unique to Luke and is thus quite different.)

In characteristic fashion, Matthew freely abbreviates and rephrases the Markan material. The following omissions are to be noted: not found in v 54 are καὶ ἀκολουθοῦσιν αὐτῷ οἱ μαθηταὶ αὐτοῦ, "and his disciples followed him" (Mark 6:1); καὶ γενομένου σαββάτου ἤρξατο, "and when the sabbath came he began" (Mark 6:2); and in the rephrasing of Mark the omission of πολλοὶ ἀκούοντες, "many hearing"; ταῦτα καὶ τίς, "these things and what"; ἡ δοθεῖσα τούτῳ, "which was given to this one"; and τοιαῦται διὰ τῶν χειρῶν αὐτοῦ γινόμεναι, "such happening through his hand" (Mark 6:2). Matthew may omit Mark's reference to the sabbath because the story does not involve a controversy concerning the observance of the sabbath. In v 55, Matthew alters Mark's ὁ τέκτων, "the carpenter" (Mark 6:3), to ὁ τοῦ τέκτονος υἱός, "the son of the carpenter," as more appropriate to the messianic calling of Jesus. Matthew also avoids Mark's ὁ υἱὸς τῆς Μαρίας, "the son of Mary," perhaps because of Jewish claims concerning Jesus' illegitimate birth. Matthew rephrases the question about Jesus' mother, brothers, and sisters, putting Simon before Judas (for some unknown reason) and adding in v 56 πᾶσαι, "all," in reference to the sisters. Then for rhetorical emphasis, Matthew inserts a repetition of the question concerning the source of ταῦτα πάντα, "all these things" (v 56). In v 57, Matthew follows Mark very closely, though omitting καὶ ἐν τοῖς συγγενεῦσιν αὐτοῦ, "and among his kinsfolk" (Mark 6:4), either because it is redundant or because Jesus' disciples are now thought of as the kinsfolk of Jesus (12:49–50). Finally, Matthew rewords the statement of Mark 6:5, καὶ οὐκ ἐδύνατο ἐκεῖ ποιῆσαι οὐδεμίαν δύναμιν, "and he was unable to do any miracle there," perhaps because it is inconsistent with his Christology, or more probably because Mark contradicts this statement in the next lines, where he refers to the healing of ὀλίγοις ἀρρώστοις, "a few illnesses" (Mark 6:5). Matthew's equivalent is καὶ οὐκ ἐποίησεν ἐκεῖ δυνάμεις πολλάς, "and he did not do many miracles there." As usual, Matthew's changes of his Markan source amount almost entirely to abridgment and stylistic improvements.

C. V 53 forms the conclusion of the parable discourse (note the formula καὶ ἐγένετο ὅτε ἐτέλεσεν ὁ Ἰησοῦς, "and it came to pass when Jesus finished") as well as a transition to the concluding pericope of chap. 13. The passage is thus structured in the following sequence: (1) concluding formula and transition (v 53); (2) the teaching of Jesus in Nazareth (v 54a); (3) the response and questions of the people (v 54b–57a); (4) the response of Jesus in a proverbial logion (v 57b); and (5) comment on the resultant paucity of miracles (v 58). The five successive questions in (3) are particularly notable, especially the parallelism of the first and fifth (πόθεν τούτῳ, lit. "whence to this one"); the three center questions have to do with Jesus' family. Just before the questions is the reference to the crowds being "amazed" (ἐκπλήσσεσθαι); just after is the reference to their being "scandalized" (ἐσκανδαλίζοντο). The references to πατρίς, "home town," in vv 54 and 57 unify the passage. These correspondences thus reflect a chiastic structure.

D. At two points the Johannine tradition parallels Matthew and the Synoptic tradition: in the reference to the father and mother of Jesus (John 6:42) and in the logion about a prophet having no honor in his own country (John 4:44). The latter is also found in Gos. Thom. 31, the second part of which, "no physician works cures on those who know him," seems to reflect v 58 and suggests dependence of the whole on Matthew.

Comment

53 The formula that marks the ending of each of the major discourses (καὶ ἐγένετο ὅτε ἐτέλεσεν ὁ Ἰησοῦς, "and it came to pass when Jesus finished") is found here, but now with the distinctive object τὰς παραβολὰς ταύτας, "these parables" (see further on 13:3). μετῆρεν ἐκεῖθεν, "he moved on from there," is general, functioning as a transition to the following episode in Nazareth, but probably a departure from Capernaum or its environs is meant.

54 Jesus had left Nazareth after the arrest of John the Baptist, moving to Capernaum (cf. 4:13). Although there are indications of a wide ministry (e.g., 9:35; 11:1), the narratives focus on Capernaum and the area around the Sea of Galilee (14:13 assumes his return to this area). At this point in the narrative, however, Jesus returns to his πατρίδα, "home town" (the word can mean "home country" or "home territory," but the context suggests "home town"), and teaches (ἐδίδασκεν, "was teaching," i.e., for some time, or less probably inceptive, "began to teach") "in their synagogue" (ἐν τῇ συναγωγῇ αὐτῶν), probably the very place in which he had worshiped as a young man before embarking on his ministry. Although no attention is given to the emotions of Jesus, this must have been a particularly momentous occasion for him. Here τῇ συναγωγῇ αὐτῶν, "their synagogue," is not, as elsewhere (4:23), the synagogue of the Jews, thus reflecting a break with Judaism (contra Luz), but merely the synagogue of the people of Nazareth. As the result of his teaching, the people there who had known him and his family so well over the years were "utterly amazed" (ἐκπλήσσεσθαι; cf. the same reaction in 7:28; 22:33). Their amazement, however, did not move them to faith but instead provoked skepticism. Their initial question, to be sure, expresses a degree of wonder and, finding no obvious answer, testifies inadvertently to the unique reality and authority represented by Jesus and his message. What indeed is the source of ἡ σοφία αὕτη καὶ αἱ δυνάμεις, "this wisdom and the miraculous deeds"? (The only two other occurrences of σοφία, "wisdom," in Matthew are in 11:19 and 12:42; for the word δυνάμεις, "miraculous deeds," see esp. 11:20–23.) The same question is asked at the end of v 56. The question may imply the possibility of a demonic source for Jesus' wisdom and power (cf. 9:34; 12:24). But the skepticism underlying their question is revealed in the pronoun τούτῳ, "to this one," as also in the questions that follow. "This one" they knew, and thus they judged him by their previous knowledge of him.

55–57a In succession the questions refer to Jesus' father, mother, brothers, and sisters. Each in effect says, "We know this Jesus well." Only here in the Gospels do we discover that Jesus was ὁ τοῦ τέκτονος υἱός, "the son of the carpenter" (and thus Jesus, following the profession of his father, is called "the carpenter" in the parallel in Mark 6:3). τέκτων can mean "builder" as well as "carpenter." The name Joseph is restricted in Matthew to 1:16–20; Joseph probably had died before the public ministry of Jesus. The mother of Jesus, Μαριάμ, lit. "Miriam" (the Semitic form of the name), is mentioned in Matthew (in its alternate form, "Maria") only in 1:16–20 and 2:11. For a parallel allusion to the mother and father of Jesus, see John 6:42. The brothers of Jesus are also mentioned, not by name however, in 12:46, 48. In the remainder of the NT only the names of James (nine references) and Jude (Jude 1) occur again. The people of the synagogue knew Jesus' brothers by name. The sisters (ἀδελφαί) of Jesus are mentioned in the NT only here, in Mark 3:32, and in the parallel to the present passage, Mark 6:3. No names of the sisters are given, but Matthew adds πᾶσαι, "all," for inclusiveness. By far the most natural understanding is the literal one, that these were literally younger (half-) brothers and sisters of Jesus, the children of Mary. Apart from further evidence from the context, it is wrong to press the exceptional Semitic usage on the words (i.e., for "kin"; cf. Gen 13:8; 14:14; Lev 10:4; etc.), thus making these persons "cousins" or relatives of Jesus in order to defend the Roman Catholic doctrine of the perpetual virginity of Mary—an idea found nowhere in the NT. πρὸς ἡμᾶς, "with us," indicates that the sisters still dwell in Nazareth and are accordingly well known to the inhabitants. The point is the same: Jesus and his family are well known. And thus the initial question is repeated: "How did all of these things [ταῦτα πάντα] come to this man?" Although that question remains unanswered, it is clear from the following statement that they found it intolerable that Jesus spoke as he did with the undeniable implication of his own self-importance. Thus, ἐσκανδαλίζοντο ἐν αὐτῷ, "they were scandalized by him" (see *Comment* on 11:6; cf. 13:21, where the same verb is used). The interpretation of this tradition in the Fourth Gospel is revealing: "they said, 'Is not this Jesus, the son of Joseph, whose father and mother we know? How does he now say "I have come down from heaven?"'" (John 6:42; cf. John 7:15).

57b Despite some parallels in thought, the logion of Jesus, "A prophet is not without honor except in his home town and in his house," is not found as such outside the NT (see too Mark 6:4; Luke 4:24; John 4:44). The word προφήτης, "prophet," is appropriate because it was particularly the teaching of Jesus (cf. ἐδίδασκεν, "he was teaching"; v 54) that elicited the wonder of the people. Although it was an inadequate view (cf. 16:14), Jesus was widely held to be a prophet (cf. 21:11, 46). The people in his own home town, however, and even his own household or family (cf. Mark 3:21) were outraged and indignant at the pretensions of one who was to them so familiar and hence thought to be ordinary (for the same point, but with a wider scope, see John 1:11).

58 Although he apparently performed some healings in Nazareth (cf. Mark 6:5), he did not do many (although the people responded to them, or at least the reports that had reached them, v 54). The reason for this was τὴν ἀπιστίαν αὐτῶν, "their unbelief" (the only occurrence of the word in Matthew). This unbelief interprets the sense in which they were scandalized by Jesus (v 57a). Although Matthew avoids referring to inability, clearly Jesus' ministry in their midst was severely restricted by their rejection of his message and his claims. As before (cf. 12:38–39), Jesus will not perform miracles in order to counteract unbelief.

Explanation

The primary mistake of the people of Nazareth was their automatic limitation of Jesus to the familiar framework in which they had previously known him. This made them unable to evaluate Jesus in terms of his message and deeds. It made impossible a fair consideration of who Jesus was and what he had come to offer. Familiarity with Jesus became a liability, since he was thereby forced into a preconceived framework. In this respect outsiders have a distinct advantage. If we widen the scope of this observation, it can be seen again clearly in one of the major transitions of the Gospel: the transition of the kingdom from the Jews to the Gentiles. For it is just this kind of familiarity and set of preconceptions that have been responsible for Jewish unbelief in the gospel, and the lack of the same may have made the Gentiles more objective in their understanding and thus more receptive of the good news of the kingdom. This is a generalization, of course, but it may be true more often than not that familiarity and all that goes with it do not dispose people to see what is really before their eyes. But tragically the central mysteries of the gospel, the Messiah who suffers death on the cross and the centrality of that death to the realization of the kingdom, violated Jewish preconceptions and thus prohibited their reception of the gospel (cf. Rom 9:32–33).